Child Labour's Global Past, 1650–2000

International and Comparative Social History

Issued by the International Institute of Social History
Amsterdam

Child Labour's Global Past, 1650–2000

edited by
Kristoffel Lieten
Elise van Nederveen Meerkerk

PETER LANG
Bern · Berlin · Bruxelles · Frankfurt am Main · New York · Oxford · Wien

Die Deutsche Bibliothek – CIP-Einheitsaufnahme

Bibliographic information published by Die Deutsche Bibliothek
Die Deutsche Bibliothek lists this publication in the Deutsche Nationalbibliografie; detailed bibliographic data is available in the Internet at ‹http://dnb.ddb.de›.

British Library and Library Cataloguing-in-Publication Data:
A catalogue record for this book is available from *The British Library*, Great Britain.

Library of Congress Cataloging-in-Publication Data

Child labour's global past, 1650-2000 / edited by Kristoffel Lieten, Elise van Nederveen Meerkerk.
p. cm. – (International and comparative social history, 1420-5297 ; v. 13)
Includes bibliographical references and index.
ISBN 978-3-0343-0517-4
1. Child labor–History. I. Lieten, Kristoffel. II. Nederveen Meerkerk, Elise van.
HD6231.C459 2011
331.3'109–dc22
2011006114

ISSN 1420-5297
ISBN 978-3-0343-0517-4

Hochfeldstrasse 32, CH-3012 Bern, Switzerland
info@peterlang.com, www.peterlang.com, www.peterlang.net

Printed in Switzerland

Table of Contents

Foreword

Compiling a book on the history of child labour around the world over a considerable period of time is a rewarding task. As editors, we were privileged to get in touch with respected colleagues and were inspired by their enthusiasm for the project. We therefore and foremost should like to thank all authors in this volume, not only for their contribution, but also for their patience during the editing process.

From the beginning of the project, we received encouraging support from various people and institutions. First of all, Angèle Janse of the International Institute of Social History (IISH) assisted us with the organization of the conference *Child Labour's Global Past 1650-2000*, in November 2006 in Amsterdam, organized by the editors together with Marcel van der Linden. Angèle's support then and during the production stage of this volume was literally indispensible. Heike Roschanski was also of great help during the preparations for the conference.

The conference itself, and hence this publication, would not have been possible without the financial support of the Royal Netherlands Academy of Arts and Sciences (KNAW), IISH and the Institute for Research on Working Children (IREWOC).

Jasper Verspaandonk of Leiden University compiled a database with numerous bibliographical data on the history of child labour. Sara Grasman of Vrije Universiteit Amsterdam was of great help at the editing stage, by synchronizing the bibliographical data. Sonja Zweegers of IREWOC corrected most of the English texts written by non-native speakers. Bart Hageraats copy-edited the complete manuscript and compiled the indexes.

Finally, we would like to thank Aad Blok, executive editor, and Marcel van der Linden, series editor of *International and Comparative Social History*, for all their encouragement and support.

Kristoffel Lieten and *Elise van Nederveen Meerkerk*

Acknowledgments

Most of the chapters in this volume are original articles, but some have been reprinted or translated. Our acknowledgments go to the publishers who granted us permission to reproduce the following articles/chapters:

- Oxford University Press:
  Jane Humphries, "Child Labor: Lessons from the Historical Experience of Today's Industrial Economies", *World Bank Economic Review*, 17 (2003), pp. 175-196
- Publications de l'Université de Provence:
  Three chapters from: Roland Caty (ed.), *Enfants au travail: Attitudes des élites en Europe occidentale et méditerranéenne aux XIe et XXe siècles* (2002)
  Roland Caty, "Le travail des enfants au XIXe siècle dans les Bouches-du-Rhône et le Var. Discours et pratiques des élites", pp. 23-40
  Eliane Gubin, "Élites, patronat, travail des enfants et obligation scolaire en Belgique avant 1914", pp. 235-252
  Antonia Pasi, "Les enfants dans l'industrialisation lombarde (1876-1911)", pp. 71-105
- UNICEF Innocenti Research Centre:
  Two chapters from: Hugh Cunningham and Pier Paolo Viazzo (eds), *Child Labour in Historical Perspective, 1800-1985: Case Studies from Europe, Japan and Colombia* (1996)
  René De Herdt, "Child Labour in Belgium 1800-1914", pp. 23-39
  Osamu Saito, "Children's Work, Industrialism, and the Family Economy in Japan, 1872-1926", pp. 73-90
- Biblioteca Luis Ángel Arango del Banco de la República:
  Carlos Edward García Londoño, "Los niños trabajadores de Medellín a principios del siglo XX", *Boletín Cultural y Bibliográfico*, 33 (1996), pp. 21-45
- John Wiley & Sons:
  Nick Van Hear, "Child Labour and the Development of Capitalist Agriculture in Ghana", *Development and Change*, 13 (1982), pp. 499–514
- Boston University African Studies Center:
  Hamilton Sipho Simelane, "Landlords, the State, and Child Labor in Colonial Swaziland, 1914-1947", *The International Journal of African Historical Studies*, 31 (1998), pp. 571-593
- Lynne Rienner Publishers:
  Karen Tranberg Hansen, "Labor Migration and Urban Child Labor during the Colonial Period in Zambia", in: Bruce Fetter (ed.), *Demography from Scanty Evidence: Central Africa in the Colonial Era* (1990), pp. 219-234

CHAPTER I

Child Labour's Global Past, 1650-2000: An Introduction

Kristoffel Lieten and Elise van Nederveen Meerkerk

The history of child labour is also a history of images and stories which have served as bearers of messages of revulsion against the inhuman treatment of children working for extended hours in mine shafts, factories and the street trades. These stories, which have found their way into broad public consciousness, particularly in Europe in the nineteenth and twentieth century, not seldom rested on fiction. English public opinion, and world opinion, had been impressed by the stark examples of child misuse in heavy industries or mining. Children, for example in *Oliver Twist* (by Charles Dickens), became a symbol of the innocent child entering into the adult world of greed and exploitation.[1]

A similar use of images sometimes distorts the perception of the present-day issue of child labour. The images we get are the Dickensian portraits of tender girls working in brothels and infant boys sitting for more than ten hours a day at the carpet frame or the brick kilns. These representations are then blended with aggregate statistics that also include many more children working in much less loathsome circumstances. Statistics frequently serve as "advocacy statistics" as Richard Anker has suggested for present-day accounts,[2] but a similar tendency may have existed in the past once the public campaign for government intervention was launched and official and unofficial commissions started to investigate specific sectors.

It is fair to accept such advocacy statistics as a reflection of dire social reality in the past and in the present, and many contributions in this book will underwrite such a statement, but it is also fair not to generalize and assume that the dramatic misuse of child labourers applied to a majority of the children. In that sense, child labour is a gruesome historical phenomenon but it may have been more prominent in certain sectors and among

1 Kirschner, *Ideological Themes*; Cunningham, *The Invention of Childhood*, pp. 148-160.
2 Anker, "The Economics of Child Labour".

families living in specific socio-economic conditions than in other families who may have been poor indeed but who did not expose their children to a life of labour.

Biases

The overall picture that emerges from nineteenth-century English history is that of child labour as a widespread and ghastly by-product of industrial capitalism. Many testimonies of those days described the factories as "hellish institutions for the destruction of childhood", but Clark Nardinelli has argued that this is a distorted picture. He claims that advocacy reports assumed child labour, especially industrial child labour, to be a more serious problem than it actually was. This distortion has thus left us with the – according to Nardinelli – false image of child labour as an important driving force for the processes of proto-industrialization and early capitalism.[3] Briefly, the argument was that parents and children had always worked and that they actually stopped doing so when, in the wake of technological changes, wages started rising. Industrialization, far from being the source of the enslavement of children, in his view, was the source of their liberation.

There indeed is evidence that the incidence of child labour was less than often assumed and that employers did not always find it easy to recruit child labourers. In agriculture, farmers, apart from engaging their own children for specific activities, had to bring in outside children and had to rely mainly on farmed-out parish pauper children. In nineteenth-century manufacturing industry, demand, it is argued, was concentrated in just a dozen industries and "in some places pauper children may have been about the only labour force available".[4] Many children worked on the land, but the work was not seen as problematic, even when they were hiring out for both farm and domestic work during peak work times or in permanent tasks such as milking and minding livestock. Such work was not seen as taxing. It turned into a problem when the compulsory schooling legislation changed the entire pattern of children's lives.[5] Cunningham, in a

3 Nardinelli, *Child Labor and the Industrial Revolution*, p. 102.

4 Rahikainen, *Centuries of Child Labour*, p. 216; also Rahikainen, "Compulsory Child Labour"; Sjöberg, "Working Rural Children"; Verdon, "The Rural Labour Market"; Taylor, *Sweatshops in the Sun*.

5 See e.g. Murray, "Children's Work in Rural New South Wales".

review of Nardinelli's book, suggests that it continues a trend which had set in during the inter-war years, and which claimed that it was not industrial capitalism as such which had caused child labour. Children had always worked, and conditions were not as gruesome as suggested in some historical accounts. This interpretation became the orthodoxy, and interest in the topic declined: "professional historians in the second half of the twentieth century have rarely highlighted the matter and it has certainly not been at the centre of interpretations of industrialization. A reopening of the issue must therefore be welcomed, for the history of the engagement of children in new forms of labour in the late eighteenth and early nineteenth centuries has received no adequate analysis".[6]

The issue incidentally was reopened. In the recent period indeed quite a number of high-quality books have appeared.[7] Other publications have dealt with the changing perception of childhood.[8] However, our knowledge of what happened in the lower echelons of society, in past times and in present times, is still fragmented, biased by the perspectives of dominant outsiders, and hampered by unbalanced historical source material. This may have led to an overemphasis on the aberrations of factory work, as well as to the stereotyping of child work, with industrializing England as the dominant model.

This is not to deny that child labour in the history of the now developed world often meant a dreadful existence on the margins of society for many children. That was the case with Western Europe and it appears to be even more so the case in the United States. On both continents, in the transition towards capitalism, many phenomena were similar. With the transition to capitalism, working children were taken out of the family trade, the home and the farm and transferred to the factory. Social structures collapsed. That was very much the case in America, where families lacked social moorings to start with. They had all come as immigrants, and the later entrants in particular were sucked into low-paid and grueling

6 Cunningham, "Child Labour", pp. 49–50.

7 Bolin-Hort, *Work, Family and the State*; Weissbach, *Child Labor Reform*; Horn, *Children's Work and Welfare*; Greene et al., *From Forge to Fast Food*; Cunningham and Viazzo, *Child Labour in Historical Perspective*; Coninck-Smith et al., *Industrious Children*; Lavalette, *A Thing of the Past*; Tuttle, *Hard at Work*; Kirby, *Child Labour in Britain*; MacIntosh, *Boys in the Pits*; Hindman, *Child Labour: An American History*; Rahikainen, *Centuries of Child Labour*; Sallee, *The Whiteness of Child Labour Reform*.

8 Wormser, *American Childhoods*; Cunningham, *The Children of the Poor*; Hopkins, *Childhood Transformed*; Heywood, *A History of Childhood*; Heywood, *Childhood in Nineteenth-Century France*; Walvin, *A Child's World*, pp. 61–78.

jobs in mills and mines.[9] "Industrialization's impact on the household was wrenching", writes Hindman, and he uses statistics to show how, around 1900, more than one-fifth of children were economically active: "America's first industrial workers were predominantly women and children".[10]

The industrializing countries in the nineteenth century had a large underclass which was devoid of proper nutrition and health care, of proper education and of social and moral moorings. Similar processes took place in the colonized countries. Nineteenth-century conditions were comparable with present-day conditions in the poorer developing countries, and actually may have been worse. In much of the nineteenth century, in accordance with "capitalist anthropology", as Marx called it sarcastically, childhood ended at age ten or at age eleven at the latest.[11] Thereafter, children were legally allowed to have a normal working day of ten hours and more. Even in the early twentieth century, when child labour legislation had been in place for many decades, children contributed substantially to the family budget. In the Netherlands, for example, detailed budget studies reported that in 1912, children contributed between one per cent in the better-off households to more than thirty per cent in the poorer households; in 1935, the contribution varied between respectively three and 33 per cent.[12] Jane Humphries, later in this volume, argues that, although historical comparisons are problematic, the gap between the level of child labour in nineteenth-century Britain and the developing countries today is large: "The difference may be a source of optimism signaling the spread of technologies that have little use for child labor and values that endorse the preservation and protection of childhood."

This collection of articles aims to overcome the biases in child labour history, first of all by offering a global perspective, by including both national and comparative case studies. Secondly, by focusing on various sectors of the economy, not only industrial work is highlighted, but also the important activities of children in agriculture. Thirdly, it is intended to give a long-term historical perspective, in covering the importance of children's work in pre-industrial and industrial societies, both in colonial and non- or post-colonial settings.

9 Riis, *How the Other Half Dies*; Ireland, *Child Labor as a Relic*; Trattner, *Crusade for the Children*; Hindman, *Child Labor: An American History*.

10 Hindman, *Child Labor: An American History*, p. 33.

11 Marx, *Capital*, p. 266.

12 De Regt, "Children in the Twentieth Century Family Income", p. 374.

Apart from filling gaps in our historical knowledge, there is another important reason why a long-term, global approach to the history of child labour is desirable. Contemporary debates on the reasons for child labour and on the best policies for putting an end to it, may learn from the past. As we will argue, and many have argued before, child labour was, and still is, a social phenomenon, which only makes sense in its historical context. The varying (patterns of) historical experiences over the world can not only enlighten us about specific function of child labour, but also about its causes, and therewith about possible solutions of child labour today. Since around 1990, child labour has again received ample political and academic attention. New commitments have been made to eliminate child labour, but pessimism is still as much prevalent as optimism. Child labour appears to be embedded in obdurate social and economic structures and to be resistant to change. Looking back into history, it may be comforting to realize that changes have never taken place overnight and that the elimination of child labour in the present-day developed countries has been a long-haul process. There are possibly still many lessons to be drawn from history. The meaning of child labour in the past and the present can thus be best understood when studied in a global range over a long period of time.

Child Labour in Historiography

Child labour is a social construct. It denotes work done by children within a specific context and within an historic period. Throughout the history of mankind, most children have worked. In ancient societies, the difference in the daily occupations between adults and children was gradual: children were socialized by learning skills, customs and tricks, so that by the time they passed through the *rite de passage*, they had become fully accomplished adults. Their work was not only a necessary additional labour input in a low production equilibrium (for self-consumption) or in a tributary mode of production, such as feudalism, in which the clan or family had to muster all its resources in order to fulfil its obligations to the landlord or another beneficiary class. Such work even included the delivery of labour services which included all members of the peasant families. It often also implied indebtedness of bonded families who then pledged their children as servants or labourers until such time as the debt has been paid off: "In such circumstances the pressure for children to be integrated into the productive system must surely be considerable".[13] On the other hand, work was also an essential socializing aspect of childhood. It did not keep the child away from education, but it rather constituted much of its education into adulthood. The net return to schooling – if schooling was available anyway – might even be negative because children learned their future skills, essential for their survival, through work in the field or apprenticeship with a master. Children in any case were embedded in a social relationship with reciprocal rights and duties. The colonial administration in many cases, as Hansen argues in this volume, were interested in reinforcing the traditional structures and pre-empt the "proletarianization" of roaming and unattached "free labourers", as had been the case in Western countries after the industrial revolution.

With the onset of industrial capitalism, the nature of the work done by children changed. Whereas some of these informal and unregistered tasks already may have been problematic, this was initially not recognized by contemporaries. Consequently, for most historians, it proved to be difficult to identify the extent of child labour. It was even difficult to establish how many children were working in the factories that came under the purview of official inspection. In all other trades and in the agricultural and domestic sector, such accounting was largely absent. Episodic evidence, particularly when recorded by commissions investigating the worst cases of child labour, has been at the root of the mainstream view that child labour was the weft and warp of early industrialization, in the same way that child labour today is often seen as the backbone of economies in developing countries. That view needs closer investigation. Historians have a difficult job in establishing the extent of child labour in the industrializing as well as in the colonized countries. They are constrained by the available evidence and such evidence usually relates only to what in the specific epoch was considered as child labour and was recorded as such. This was much more the case in the colonized countries where, for various reasons, the administration was not as interested in documenting social relations, including labour relations, as it was increasingly in its home countries.

The difficulty with acquiring an accurate picture also relates to the definition of child labour. Different notions of the meaning of child work and labour,[14] in addition to differences in social perception, thus have made

13 Rodgers and Standing, *The Economic Roles of Children*, p. 15.

14 See also: Lieten, *Child Labour: Burning Questions*; Lieten, "Child Labour in South Asia"; Lieten, "Child Labour: Questions on Magnitude".

assessing its magnitude a complex issue.[15] Historians usually have taken an exclusive view: child labour was placed within exploitative labour relations and denoted the abuse of children for income or profit generation. The inclusive view is a more recent development and is very much related to the gradual emergence of the child rights concept as the cornerstone for judging child-related issues. The inclusive view regards all children who are in productive jobs as well as in non-productive chores (within the household) as child labourers. Whereas the exclusive view focuses on those children who are economically engaged and exploited, the inclusive view takes the right of the child to a proper childhood with education and leisure rather than work as the main ingredients. Rahikainen, for example, is no exception in taking an exclusive view.[16] Boys and girls helping out on the farm and girls helping their mothers in the household are excluded from the purview of her study with the argument, which has some validity, that household chores were a feature of daily family life. Rahikainen argues that extending the concept of child labour to all possible forms of work, including domestic work, would dilute the concept and make it analytically blurred. The sobering conclusion is that not much is known of the various working activities in which children were involved and which may have been as detrimental as industrial child labour.

Disagreement still exists not only on the extent of child labour, but also on its causes and on the causes of its gradual disappearance in the developed countries while remaining a curse in developing countries. The disappearance was due to the interplay, or dialectical relationship, of various mechanisms: ideological changes, political struggle, including the trade union movement, technological changes, increases in productivity and increase in income and social welfare, the need for a skilled labour force, etc.

Traditionally, historians have considered the role of the state as vital for the abolition of child labour in the industrializing countries in the late nineteenth- and early twentieth-century. Indeed, history shows that child labour laws did have some effect in different sectors. In present-day developing countries, a similar impact is not obvious. In these countries, legislation and the introduction of a new normative understanding play a much more important directive role, unlike in the industrialized countries where legislation followed in the wake of productive and technological

15 See for example the discussion between Kirby, "How Many Children", and Cunningham, "Reply"; also Humphries, "Child Labor: Lessons", and Lavalette, *A Thing of the Past?* For a present day world-wide picture, see ILO, *The End of Child Labour.*

16 Rahikainen, *Centuries of Child Labour*; see also Fyfe, *Child Labour.*

changes. The passage of laws in the early industrializing countries, starting with the very moderate first child labour legislation in England in 1833 – which set the minimum age of nine for work in textile mills –, often reflected rather than instigated social change. New legislation symbolized the changing reality. It did not impose a totally new order on that reality, or, "the reform movement lost nearly all the major battles while steadily winning the war".[17]

Legislation was even more difficult in agriculture. In England, the Agricultural Children Act of 1873 was stillborn; it was repealed only three years after its passage.[18] The obvious failings of the act contributed to demands for further and more effective legislation which resulted in the Education Act of 1876, but generally, public intervention against child labour outside the factory system came rather late and was implemented rather hesitantly. Although employers and members of parliament only gradually moved to the side of the reform movement, initially the end of child labour for various reasons actually was a cause to be defended. One reason undoubtedly was that work ethics were considered to be superior to the disorder of backstreet ethics.

The transition from child labour to child education was also a protracted one, in England and in the USA as well as in France and its neighbouring countries. The period marked the transition from the Christian discourse of the *économie charitable* to the modern discourse of an *économie sociale*, the realization that in a modernizing society social order had to be maintained and that education played an important role both as an economic investment and a social investment. Children "were viewed as 'savages' needing rescuing from freedom".[19] The organizations of employers, at least in their public statements, started to see the advantage of keeping children in school, at least up to the age of ten. However, legislation was not necessarily implemented. The labour inspectorate started functioning in the late nineteenth century, but, as a number of articles in this volume illustrate, the official machinery did not always see the need for drastic intervention. As long as certain industries had difficulties switching to a new labour regime and as long as poor families needed additional income, the government machinery was lenient and child labour dragged on. The historical

17 Hindman, *Child Labor: An American History*, p. 64.

18 Horn, "The Agricultural Children Act"; Stewart, "The Political Economy of Agrarian Education"; also Riney-Kehrberg, "The Limits of Policy"; Levine, "'Picannin' Wages and Child Labor".

19 Fyfe, *Child Labour*, p. 33; see also Hendrick, "Constructions and Reconstructions".

record of eliminating child labour thus shows a remarkable analogy with the present record in developing countries: the process is gradual, slow and lenient in its implementation, responding to the economic forces and reflecting the social and political power structure.[20]

As the nineteenth century progressed, it was increasingly realized that education rather than work could play a role in controlling and socializing children. Modern state-building needed full-time and compulsory education. The original position of the contemporary governments was that the state should not interfere with such private matters and should stick to its core business of order and security, and that education was of no use to working-class children. However, by the early twentieth century, it was commonly accepted that education was an excellent instrument for streamlining the working class and building national cohesion, as the article by Éliane Gubin in this volume illustrates.

Whereas in the early industrializing countries legislation had a codifying function, in present-day developing countries it has a normative function. This is one of the reasons why, in the early twenty-first century, many developing countries, despite excellent legislation, have not succeeded in eradicating child labour. Legislation alone, under conditions of poverty, economic stagnation and failing social and educational infrastructure, is not a forcefully enough instrument. Labour legislation helps to codify the newly emerging reality and ideally should go hand in hand with the enforcement of compulsory lower education, but socio-economic reality is adamant.

Historical investigation suggests that legislation and compulsory education only set in when there was already a decline in the number of working children and when a new economic system is emerging. State intervention thus is a necessary precondition to explain the demise of child labour, but its success depends on emerging socio-economic changes. The development of a capitalist labour market, with changes in technology and in the organization of production would have led to the marginalization of children from the labour market, although the introduction of new technologies. Nevertheless, it is far from clear that all attempts to rationalize excluded children. Special machines were, for instance, designed in order to employ children.[21]

20 Weiner, *The Child and the State in India*, argues that culture and religion are the decisive factor in the perpetuation of child labour.

21 See e.g.: Bolin-Hort, *Work, Family and the State*; Tuttle, *Hard at Work*; Rahikainen, *Centuries of Child Labour*; Berg and Hudson, 'Rehabilitating the Industrial Revolution',

On the supply side also, changes must have taken place. A general assumption is that poverty leads families to decide to allocate the labour of children in order to reach a family income up to subsistence level and, later, to withdraw child labour when the income of the family has risen (see Humphries in this volume). Important is also what is happening on the political front. A labour act usually is "the outcome of a political contest, and would not have come into being without the agitation for reform [...] This raises the questions to whether child labour can be combated effectively without a mobilization and articulation of public opinion on a massive scale".[22] But by and large, there is a complex of varying explanations for the decline of child labour in industrialized countries, and historians clearly do not agree on the relative weight of these explanatory factors.

Backgrounds, Contents and Structure of this Volume

The various publications on child labour, which have appeared recently, significantly have augmented the knowledge of child labour and of the socio-cultural context of changing perceptions of childhood. Yet many questions remain. In November 2006, the conference *Child Labour's Global Past (1600-2000)* was organized by the International Institute of Social History and IREWOC,[23] in order to discuss some of these issues. Several of the papers included in this volume were presented at this conference. The papers and discussion focused on the reasons for the decline in child labour, viewed in the perspective of a long-term process of globalization. The central questions behind the conference were:

- Where and why did child labour emerge as a (demand-driven or supply-driven) phenomenon since 1700?
- What was its contribution to the economy and to the household?
- Which were the mechanisms and the developments that helped to solve the child labour problem in some parts of the world and failed to do so, or did so insufficiently, in others?

p. 36; Cunningham, 'The Decline of Child Labour', p. 417; Humphries, 'Child Labor: Lessons', pp. 189-190; Lavalette, *A Thing of the Past?*; Nardinelli, *Child Labor and the Industrial Revolution.*

22 Cunningham, "Combating Child Labour", p. 48.

23 International Institute of Social History, see: www.iisg.nl. IREWOC (International Research on Working Children), see: www.irewoc.nl. Located in Amsterdam and Leiden, the Netherlands. See the report of the conference by Kristoffel Lieten: http://www.iisg.nl/research/childlabour-report.php.

Apart from very lively and substantive debates, the conference resulted in many interesting papers. A number of them have been included in this volume (the contributions by Camps, Cunningham, Goulart and Bedi, Heywood, Hindman, Kassouf and Dos Santos, Kirby, Olsson, Rahikainen, Smit, Tuttle, White). In an attempt to make this publication on the history of child labour indeed more global, other scholars were invited to write on their specific region of interest. We were satisfied to find established historians of child labour who agreed to contribute articles on China (Howard), Australia (Bowden), Eastern Europe (Papathanassiou), Zimbabwe (Grier), Sweden (Engberg) and Russia (Gorshkov). In addition, a number of articles have been translated from French (Pasi, Gubin and Caty) and from Spanish (Garcia Londoňo), or have been reproduced (Chirwa, De Herdt, Hansen, Humphries, Simelane, Saito and Van Hear). All in all, this constitutes a collection of around 30 articles, covering a broad range of geographical, chronological and thematic areas of research on child labour.

The volume begins with three more general articles containing issues of child labour and relevant research questions. Jane Humphries in her article overviews the extent and settings of child labour in Europe and the United States and argues that despite the patchy quantitative record, a fairly solid analysis can be made of the trends. Child labour was particularly extensive in the early-industrialization. Changes in the capitalist labour market, new technologies, family strategies, state policies and cultural norms are examined to shed light on the growth in child labour and the subsequent decline, on its causes and consequences. Since child labour appears to have been more prevalent in the early and late industrializers than it is in developing countries today, Humphries expresses some optimism about the eradication of child labour, but at the same time also argues that the historical record warns that the technological and cultural developments are not independent of underlying economic conditions. These conditions have been dismal in the former colonies and remain so.

In his overview essay, Hugh Cunningham consequently argues that in order to understand the global history of child labour, it is vital to investigate the phenomenon in the context of both capitalism and colonialism. He does, however, acknowledge the restricted value of his generalizations, since his account predominantly concerns the Western "capitalist world", because of a lack of knowledge of non-capitalist countries.

Finally, Carolyn Tuttle offers a comparative perspective of large trends in child labour in the context of industrialization. She argues that child labour was and persistently is primarily a demand-driven phenomenon. For several reasons, most of them relating to (changing) technology and the organization of production, hiring child labour in some phases of the industrializing process was the most profitable strategy for employers. According to Tuttle, this is why child labour was restricted to certain phases and branches. She clearly assesses child labour as a by-product of industrialization in the nineteenth-century Western countries as well as in the present-day developing countries.

Then, more individual case studies follow, covering Europe, the Americas, Asia, Africa, and Australia. These essays all address one or many of the explanations for (changes in) the occurrence of child labour usually given in historiography.

The Importance of State Intervention

In most countries, child labour was already declining substantially before legislation or compulsory education was introduced. On the other hand, after the introduction of legislation and schooling, still many children continued working, especially in the agrarian context. Even in the case of industry, it remains to be seen to what extent it was in fact legislation that caused the decline of working children. Both Heywood and Smit conclude that child labour laws both in France and in the Netherlands heavily borrowed from existing legislation in Great Britain and Prussia and probably therefore were less effective than they otherwise would have been. As Olsson shows in his contribution on Sweden, industrial child labour (especially of children below fourteen) had already drastically declined before industrial legislation was introduced at the end of the nineteenth century, and similar developments can be seen in other countries, for example in Portugal.

The lack of proper legislation for children working in particular sectors, such as domestic service and agriculture, is addressed in several of the articles in this volume. As Hindman notes for the United States, most protective legislation excluded work in agriculture. This exclusion of agriculture from the first child labour laws is in line with the history of many other countries, such as Great Britain, the Netherlands, Sweden, and Central Europe, although in Germany and Austria rural children did appear on the political agenda. Nevertheless, here, the major landowners had a large say in parliamentary debates, and they argued until well into the twentieth century that child labour was indispensable for the rural economy. Also in other parts of the world, under colonial conditions, agricultural labour was explicitly excepted. This was reflected in the ILO Convention of 1919, which typically applied to industrial child labour only.[24] Furthermore, as opposed to its introduction, the *effectiveness* of legislation is of course crucial. The obvious case of successful state intervention is reported in the article by Howard, who argues that child labour in China did not decline until the advent of the Communist State, which began to structurally address the underlying causes of child labour, and promote education in both rural and urban areas. Such legislation was less successful in other developing countries. As Van Hear concludes, legislation in post-colonial Ghana has remained largely ineffective, and the same seems to apply to post-colonial Indonesia, as White states in his conclusion.

The effectiveness of state intervention depended on the relative strength of the social forces who acted as countervailing powers against conservative state politics and the strong control of industrialists over the state structures. Such countervailing powers were organized in political bodies (the emerging socialist parties and later on the communist movement), in the voluntary organizations and, particularly, in trade unions. Usually it was a trade union movement of adult males, but at least three contributions in this book illustrate how children also played a role in the working class movement. One of the reasons to employ children is their assumed docility, but in China, in the 1920s, children were active in the workers' movement, involved in strikes in favour of industrial legislation, as Howard shows. And in Ghana as well, children were active from very young ages in collective workers' actions, albeit, as Van Hear argues, protected by older youth co-workers, who bargained for the younger children and protected them from abuse. Also, children were active in forms of more covert resistance, such as theft. In Russia, at the turn of the twentieth century, the working children got involved in political activities. They were increasingly literate, and their work rendered them a certain degree of autonomy, which stimulated them to resist traditional values and norms, and made them involved in a struggle for greater political freedom and social equality. This would be an interesting line for further historical research. As White notes in his contribution on Indonesia, the history of child labour has all too often been told from the perspective of the adults, tending to see children only as "victims" rather than as "active agents". It may be fruitful to apply both images. In Indonesia, when a foreman from a tobacco plantation refused to pay his child workers, they were so disappointed and angry

24 For the history of child labour legislation and ILO conventions, see Dahlén, *The Negotiable Child*.

that they set a drying-shed on fire. Children occasionally have protested and such protests have not been documented sufficiently.[25]

Legislation usually was restricted to child labour in industry, but even in the case of industry, it remains to be seen to what extent it was in fact legislation that caused the decline of working children. As Olsson shows in his contribution on Sweden, industrial child labour (especially of children below fourteen) had already drastically declined before industrial legislation was introduced at the end of the nineteenth century, and similar developments can be seen in other countries.[26] In some cases, the state in fact instead played an *active* role in stimulating the employment of children in industry. Grier, for instance, notes that the colonial state, especially in African settler colonies, supported the demand for cheap labour by various strategies. By imposing forced labour and taxation upon African men and boys, the state pushed them out of their own subsistence farming and land ownership, which allowed a cheap landless proletariat to come into existence. Furthermore, in periods of labour shortages, such as in the 1920s, legislation was adjusted to the needs of (white) employers, for instance enabling children under fourteen to sign labour contracts, a practice which had been hitherto forbidden. In the case of Zambia, however, colonial authorities were concerned about the presence of child labour in the 1930s and 1940s, albeit not from a genuine concern for the children involved. They were especially afraid of the overrepresentation of poor children in the cities, where many rural children migrated to in order to find work and perhaps schooling, resulting in an "urban proletarianization process", as Hansen defines it.

As with state legislation, the decisive effect of the introduction of compulsory education on the decline of child labour is not straightforward. Kirby claims that child labour in Britain (especially below the age of twelve) had already drastically gone down before compulsory schooling was introduced in 1870. Also Rahikainen, in her analysis of compulsory schooling laws in several European countries, states that it is highly unlikely that this significantly influenced child labour, because in almost every country the decline had already set in. Education had already imposed itself as a norm before legislation made it compulsory for all children, including the then still marginalized child labourers. On the other hand, in many ways child labour persisted well into the twentieth century despite the spread of compulsory education. As Hindman shows for the United States

25 White, "Changing Childhoods".

26 E.g. Van Nederveen Meerkerk, "Child Labor in the Netherlands".

of America, compulsory education did not make such a difference, especially for child workers in rural areas. First of all, there were problems with the enforcement of school attendance in general; secondly, according to US law, migrant children, who were active as farm workers, were by definition prohibited to go to school. Thirdly, many exceptions were made for farm children in periods of seasonal labour shortage, the so-called "apple vacations" or "potato vacations". Such labour employment of children has also been documented in this volume by Engberg (Sweden) and Papathanassiou (Central Europe).

In Japan, a discrepancy between theory and practice in the importance of compulsory education (implemented in 1905) for children's workforce participation is noted as well. Saito shows children who enrolled did not necessarily finish primary education and that many poor children, especially girls, who did not perform paid work, did not go to school either. Probably, they helped their parents out with unpaid household duties, as many girls may have done all over the world before primary education imposed itself as a norm, both for boys and girls. Likewise, Van Hear states that compulsory schooling in Ghana in the 1950s and 1960s did lead to rising school attendance rates, but there were still large numbers of children who were not attending school, and were working on family farms or as agricultural wage labourers. Last but not least, school attendance does not necessarily rule out child labour because both can be combined. For present-day Brazil, for instance, statistics by Kassouf and Dos Santos show that the majority of working children is able to combine school and work. This has also been shown by other studies.

Technology and Labour Demand

Many contributors to this volume, for example Tuttle, argue that, in addition to the role of the state, technological change and, more broadly, changing labour relations, did have a determining impact on the demand for child labour: "The similarities between the past and present places of employment lend support for the [...] argument that child-labor is a demand-driven phenomenon."

Child labour had already been typical in the pre-industrial industries. As Olsson shows for Sweden, children, apart from the obvious work on family farms, took on apprenticeship in crafts, but were also present in the early manufactories and factories. The importance of pre-industrial child labour in the crafts has also stressed been stressed for other countries, such as Great Britain, the Dutch Republic, France and Japan. Children in pre- and proto-industrial production were typically employed in sectors that were not guild-organized, such as glassworks, match & tobacco making, cotton spinning mills. Olsson claims that in these branches, an elaborate division of labour favoured the opportunities to exploit child labour. However, around 1850, a new organization of labour arose, caused by changing managerial strategies aiming at cost-reduction. By mechanizing (parts of) the production process, they increasingly replaced children – who previously had been performing these easy, repetitive tasks – with machinery.

Rahikainen, like Olsson, believes that it was mainly a question of changing demand which led to the decline of child labour in Europe. She links changes in demand to the substantial economic crisis in the 1870s and 1880s, which, according to her, not accidentally coincided with the development of new forms of rationalization of the production process. For the Netherlands, Smit argues as well that in times of crisis, such as during the 1880s, the mass of unskilled (child and female) workers tended to be fired and the more skilled (male) workforce was retained. However, modernization did not necessarily lead to a decline in child labour. Smit argues that after the depression, child labour in the cotton industries again increased and that some of the more modern industries, like the light bulb industry, thrived on employing young (female) workers. Howard, similarly, analyses the demand-related rise and decline of child labour in the Chinese factories. Here, children in the early twentieth century, under semi-colonial Japanese rule, mostly worked in the textile, tobacco and match-making industries, and of course in agriculture and artisanal production. After 1949, China experienced a strong decrease in the demand for children, partly because of the Communist Party's strategy of increasing the importance of heavy industry, which typically did not employ many children. At the same time, technological changes in the textile industry also led to a reduced demand for children in this period.

In most countries, ranging from the United States to Russia and from Sweden to Swaziland, children in rural areas had always worked on the family farm. However, changes in the agricultural system led to alterations in the extent and form of child labour.

Circumstances in different countries were dissimilar. Hindman describes the effects of the advent of commercial agriculture in the United States in the nineteenth century, leading to an increasing demand for labour. In areas where mechanization occurred, child labour usually declined, but when handwork was required, the need for child workers increased. The process of intensification of agricultural child labour due to the introduction of large-scale, capitalist modes of production was also visible in other regions, most notably in the colonies. At the same time, the demand for child labour also continued in more small-scale agricultural production. Often, child labour on these farms was performed in the context of family businesses, not only by farmers' children, but also by "foster children" taken in by agrarian households to fulfill the demand for labour. As Engberg shows in her contribution, this practice of fostering was widespread in rural Sweden. It often concerned children from the age of ten onwards, who were housed and put to work by farmer families with small enterprises, whose own children were still too young to perform farm labour. In Ghana as well, the fostering and pawning of children was common practice. With the onset of mechanization in the cocoa industry in the 1950s, fewer children were required as permanent workers. They became more involved in seasonal labour, not only in cocoa cultivation, but in rice cultivation as well. Such contract labour also existed on a large scale in China, where children were bought and sold in order to fulfill a variety of tasks, such as mill work, but also domestic service and even sex work. This transaction was referred to as "plucking mulberry leaves", a typical child task. It was mostly girls who entered into contract labour, whereas boys' labour traditionally more often took the form of apprenticeships. Grier shows that in Rhodesian mines, boys not only worked in coal and gold mining, but also provided domestic and sexual "services" for adult miners. Both for the mine owners and for the workers, this was cheaper than having to maintain a wife and family. This construction further depressed male mining wages. In Zambia, on the contrary, male miners were encouraged by mine-owners to bring their wives and families in order to profit from their cheap labour as well, as Hansen shows.

A particular development in the demand for child labour relates to the context of colonialism and the increased demand for colonial products in metropolitan countries. In general, this affected labour relations in the agricultural sector most dramatically. Often, colonial rulers actively stimulated the participation of children in agrarian production, albeit in indirect ways. In the Netherlands East Indies, as White describes, the Dutch colonial authorities imposed the so-called "Cultivation System" (*cultuurstelsel*) upon the indigenous people in the 1830s. This system was created in order to derive greater gains from the colonies for the metropolis. As a condition to be allowed to cultivate their own land, the agrarian population was forced to allocate a certain share of their land and labour power for the cultivation of export crops for the colonial rulers. Although hard figures are lacking, White suggests that this intensification of indigenous labour and the increasing poverty will most notably have affected the working lives of women and children, increasing their participation both in domestic chores and in the expanding cultivation of export crops.

In Ghana in the colonial period, the participation of children also increased when the demand for cocoa rose spectacularly. Around 1914, when the cocoa industry boomed, boys and girls worked as carriers and in cocoa cultivation. Initially, they did so out of their traditional unpaid work on the family farm, but later they were also hired as wage labourers. Grier also sees the rising demand for colonial products in the metropolitan countries as a major factor behind the increasing demand for cheap labour (and thus also child labour). Especially in the settler colonies, where land was confiscated by European settlers, children were forcefully recruited into farming, but also into mining, domestic service and commerce. From the 1920s, the demand for tobacco and cotton rose, and children were involved in production. Child labour also expanded in tea cultivation, which had started to become commercially grown in 1930s in Zimbabwe, and in which up to seventy per cent of the workforce consisted of children.

As both Grier and Simelane point out, colonial settlers willingly made use of *pre-colonial* labour relations and forms of subsistence farming in which children were employed. Thus, colonialists in Swaziland, who "owned" black tenants, could also dispose of their families' labour power. The increasing demand for colonial goods in metropolitan countries led to an intensification of cheap (child) labour. In this sense, globalization and entanglement of different regions in the world played a decisive role in determining children's participation in the labour market. The research conducted by Simelane confirms that the influx of white settlers in Swaziland led to a change in the nature of child labour. This did not mean that the colonialists "invented" child labour in Swaziland. Rather, the settlers incorporated pre-colonial forms of child labour (in subsistence farming) into the European-owned large farms. Often, children were employed with their fathers as a family unit, and performed unpaid labour. Later, especially after 1932, a transition to paid wage labour took place, both for adults and children. Still, even in this context, traditional parent-child relations determined the conditions for child labour, because fathers usually were the ones who contracted their own children.

The importance of the tradition of working children in pre-colonial times is stressed in many of the essays, notably by Kassouf and Dos Santos for the case of Brazil. Their central argument is that although the rise of child labour in Brazil rested upon an increased demand by plantation owners and industrial capitalists, these colonists built on a tradition of child labour that had existed in the pre-colonial context. Particularly when slavery was abolished in the nineteenth century, alternative cheap labour was demanded in agriculture, which again led to an increase of child labour in a new form. Later on, industrialization and urbanization led to an increasing involvement of children in industry and in the (informal) urban service sector: peddling, shoe shining, selling newspapers, but also drug trafficking and prostitution.

The Supply Side: Poverty and Family Strategies

Although the demand side is stressed as an important explanatory factor for changes in the development of child labour, most articles in this volume pay some attention to the supply side of child labour. The source material for investigating family strategies is scarcer for the nineteenth century, which is the focus of most of the papers.

It is usually assumed that poverty has been the decisive push force behind child labour. Major unsettling economic, social and political transitions affected the economic positions of families. In the United States, for instance, when slavery was abolished, a system of sharecropping replaced the plantation system, in which farmers – usually former slaves – were contracted to work partly for the landowners and partly for their own subsistence crops. It was customary that the more workers a sharecropper had at his disposal (thus the bigger the offspring), the more acres of land he could cultivate. According to Hindman, this was a clear incentive to raise large families and employ children on the farm.

In the colonies as well, the introduction of capitalist agriculture led to a rising demand for as well as a supply of child labour. Grier argues that land confiscation by European settlers led to impoverishment in rural areas, which brought about a swelling army of landless labourers, at first mostly consisting of men, migrating to the cities in search of jobs, but later also comprising many women and child workers. In colonial Zimbabwe, Africans originally still had access to land where female labour was applied in subsistence farming. In this way, Grier argues, women's and girls' labour subsidized the low wages paid to men and boys in the export sectors. However, in the wake of a new law in 1908, most black families were moved into the indigenous reserves, leading to an abundance of labour supply. Women and girls mostly started to perform wage labour at settler farms, whereas boys and men migrated to look for work in the mines.

Simelane points to a similar downward cycle caused by the advent of capitalist agriculture in Swaziland. Because many Africans were employed in the cultivation of export crops, subsistence crops suffered, eventually resulting in food shortages and increased poverty. In the 1930s, landlords took advantage of the increasing vulnerability and dependency of the indigenous population and directly recruited children. Similarly, in the North of Ghana, poverty in the 1940s and 1950s led to migration of many boys and young men looking for work in the south. They either did so independently, even without the consent of their parents, or more commonly, they were pawned by poor parents, who got paid a little by hiring out their children. There are indications that at least until the 1980s, such illegal employment of very young children on cocoa farms continued.

It was not always the family that hired out children, as for instance Engberg shows in her study of eighteenth- and nineteenth-century Swedish orphans. These children were assigned to their future owners through a public auction. The auction helped to reduce the expenses of the parishes on poverty relief. Similar labour arrangements continued to exist over time, as is shown in Hansen's article on rural children migrating to towns in Zambia, often performing unpaid household duties for the families they are placed with. The receiving households are often direct or distant family, but Hansen prefers to view these contracts as modes of labour extraction rather than as reciprocal arrangement in which the child is offered some form of protection and compensation. The labour of young orphans or otherwise of children transferred to settlers became a normal mode of labour recruitment and provided the employers with a readily controlled and compliant labour force.[27]

In China as well, increasing poverty led many families to rely more heavily on child labour, as Howard shows for the Republican era (1911-1949). And even if parents could have afforded to send their children to school, this alternative was often not even present, since there was one "middle school" for every 300,000 Chinese in the 1930s. Education was just out of reach for most children. Understandably, parents thought that work was a better option than letting them roam the streets. The relevance of education in many areas, also outside China, remained questionable for a long time since it hardly opened up new opportunities for employment or social mobility. The examples from Great Britain, the Balkan, China

27 See for example Australia (Hetherington, "Child Labour in Swan River Colony"), colonial Zimbabwe and South Africa (Grier, *Invisible Hands*; Chirwa, "Child and Youth Labour").

and Indonesia show that parents did not expect general education to be a proper investment in the future of their children. In Portugal in the 1860s, school teachers reported children being beaten by their own mothers if they wanted to attend school instead of helping with the harvesting of grapes. On the other hand, there are also examples of the opposite: poor families, who, in spite of their poverty, chose to send their children to school. This was usually related to the perception of increasing prospects in the labour market. This was the case for example in mountainous Central Greece, where schooling and a future in public service became an ideal for poor people in the 1920s and 1930s.

Culture and Ideology

Dire poverty was not always the reason why children worked, especially not in pre-industrial times. According to Gorshkov, for example, in pre-industrial Russia poverty was not the main determinant of child labour. Rather it was defined as an apprenticeship, and, especially in rural areas, by the common view that in peasant families everybody except the very young and the very old were to participate in the family economy. As such, work was considered to be "the most essential duty in the upbringing and education of children". Indeed, similar reasoning can be found in many of the other historical accounts in this volume. In pre-capitalist societies, there had hardly been a division of labour within a production process and much of the work was within the family or clan structure. Production could only be increased by means of additional labour power, i.e. children, rather than by increases in productivity or longer working hours. Children were anchored in the traditional structure and work was part of the process of socialization. The worst thing for a child to happen was to remain idle, and not to be socialized through work. This found its reflection in the cultural norms and memory systems. It lingered on when the transition to a different economic system – monetized, commercialized, industrialized – took place. The idea that work is wholesome for children, and that it contains many educational and socializing elements, thus has persisted, also in western countries. Thus, in 1925, as Tuttle quotes in her paper, a US senator exclaimed that "[t]he real problem in America is not child labor, but child idleness". And, according to Goulart and Bedi, it was only in the 1980s that Portuguese politicians started to acknowledge the problem of the persistence of child labour in changing times seriously. Especially in agriculture, to which usually legislation does not apply, the notion that child labour is harmless and even healthy, indeed is quite stubborn, as the article on the United States illustrates. Hindman writes: "Ironically, children on the family farm face among the highest occupational fatality rates – substantially higher than that of seasonal and migrant children. Tractor rollovers are a leading cause of death." It has been particularly hard to attack child farm labour because of what he calls the persistence of "agrarian romanticism" in the US.

Agrarian romanticism was not restricted to the US, and many papers in this volume show that the idea that child work on farms is beneficial, exists in many past and present societies and that child labour legislation commonly has not been made applicable to agriculture. For instance, Kassouf and Dos Santos stress the persistent traditional ideology in Brazilian society, which implies that working and contributing to the household economy is good for children. Apart from an idealized image of work in the countryside, agrarian romanticism has been fed by the family-based and private nature of farm work. In the colonies as well, an ideology of work as a contribution to the household economy or as a mode of disciplining and socializing children was prevalent. Grier quotes a Southern Rhodesian colonial report from 1904, in which it is stated that African children should be taught the "love of labour". The same applied to Ghana. According to Van Hear, there was a widespread consensus, not only among colonial authorities, but also among the local population that hard work was not bad for their children. Grier does mention that there were critics opposing child labour, but they did this more in the context of anti-slavery than out of a deeply-rooted principle against child labour as such. They were mainly opposed to the use of coercive methods or the contraction of children without their parents' consent, because exactly these practices resembled slavery.

In the Asian countries, the argument of hard work being beneficial for children seems to have been less prevalent as well. In Japan, on the other hand, it was often reasoned the other way round. Saito points to the specific family values that traditionally determined the low participation of young children, even in the poorest families. Married women and adolescent and grown-up children had a relatively high contribution to the household income and budget a decent upbringing, possibly combined with some education, was considered more important for children under the age of eleven than the meager contribution to the family income. In China, where the exploitation of children in the coastal industries had been a serious problem, calls for the abolition of child labour in the 1930s often went hand in hand with the clarion call of nationalism. Apart from an anticapitalist stance, abolitionists argued that becoming a strong nation with healthy citizens, implied taking good care of the nation's children.

The idea that it was natural for children to work was directly related to the colonial idea of a superior race and the legitimate exploitation of the children of the oppressed nations. The abolition of slavery in both the United States of America and Brazil led to a renewed demand for cheap (child) labour, as Hindman as well as Kassouf and De Santos reveal. More in general, the introduction of agricultural capitalism in many parts of the world and a rising demand for colonial products were systematically supplied by cheap labour, also by children, as for instance Van Hear and White note for Ghana and Indonesia respectively. In Africa, colonial settlers willingly made use of *pre-colonial* labour relations and forms of subsistence farming in which children were employed. Even when wage labour became more prevalent in the 1930s, fathers continued to contract their own sons on the settlers' farms. According to Simelane, although children had been working within the traditional indigenous structures, white capitalists started adapting the existing patriarchal relations. It was the increasing demand for colonial goods in metropolitan countries which led to an intensification of cheap (child) labour. Similarly, Bowden argues that in the dual economic structure of Australia, with its virtual absence of manufacturing and large-scale agriculture, child labour was limited, and mainly present in the "sweated trades". In pastoral areas, white settlers depended on aboriginal labour to fulfill their need of cheap labour, instead of their own children's labour power.

In this sense, globalization and entanglement of different regions in the world played a decisive role in determining children's participation in the labour market. This influence has been persistent, and for a large part structural. Of course, the enduring effects of colonization have usually direct causes, such as the unequal division of property and income between and within countries, leading to widespread poverty. Consequently, also in the post-colonial period, child labour has persisted in many of the countries under investigation, in spite of legislation and education.

A global comparative perspective also reveals clear links between child labour and racist views. In several of the historical accounts in the colonial context, the view of child labour by the colonized was diametrically opposed to views on child labour in the metropolis. White and Van Hear, for instance, show that in colonies such as Indonesia and Ghana, metropolitan colonies did usually not interfere, and showed a remarkable indifference towards indigenous working children, in distinction to the attitudes of the elites in respect of child labour in the motherland. Grier comes to a similar conclusion for Zimbabwe, although she does note that there was some concern and debate, both from the local and the metropolitan side. In China as well, child workers suffered under the double burden of the rise of capitalism and Japanese imperialism with a racist attitude towards the subject populations. Japanese and Western supervisors in the 1920s and 1930s treated Chinese children in the factories exceptionally badly. Of course, Chinese mill owners used child labourers as well, but on a smaller scale, and circumstances in their workshops were less severe.

But outside the imperial setting, racism played a role as well. Hindman, for instance, shows the highly varying experiences of white farmers' children, black children and migrant children working in agriculture. Many child labourers came from sharecropping families (usually black, former plantation workers). Others were children from immigrant workers, who were by law excluded from education. Of course, poverty also played a role, but so did politics and racist attitudes, as Hindman's analysis of the establishment of the Fair Labor Standards Act in 1937 shows. In order to pass his New Deal in Congress, President Roosevelt had to yield to the plantation owners, enabling them to maintain a subjugated black labour force on their "plantations".

To conclude, the articles in this volume confirm that there is a complex of many, social, economic, political and cultural dynamics, to explain the extent, growth and decline of child labour in the past. With this volume we want to do away with oversimplifications. Instead, long-term global historical analysis shows that diversification and comparison of various contexts may help us gain important insights into broad lines of the development of child labour – and its eradication. The articles in this volume cover many regions, many industrial sectors and reflect different approaches. Nevertheless, some sectors have remained underrepresented: in particular, more research into child labour in commerce and trade and a more in-depth analysis of children's work in the informal sector remain important desiderata. We hope that this volume will offer some of the groundwork and a stimulus for new research in this direction. We hope that this collection of articles, covering a wide geographical and temporal scope, will contribute to a better understanding of child labour in the context of a global history of labour and that it will enable us to re-affirm some of the interpretations about the nature of child labour in the past and to question some of the stubborn images often projected by contemporaries as well as by present-day academics and policy makers.

CHAPTER 2

Child Labor: Lessons from the Historical Experience of Today's Industrial Economies

Jane Humphries

Child labor was more prevalent in nineteenth-century industrializers than it is in developing countries today. It was particularly extensive in the earliest industrializers. This pattern may be a source of optimism signaling the spread of technologies that have little use for child labor and of values that endorse the preservation and protection of childhood. Today and historically, orphaned and fatherless children and those in large families are most vulnerable. Efficient interventions to curb child labor involve fiscal transfers to these children and active policies toward street children. Changes in capitalist labor markets (including technology), family strategies, state policies, and cultural norms are examined to shed light on the causes, chronology, and consequences of child labor.

Fifty years ago it might have been assumed that just as child labor had declined in the industrial world in the late nineteenth and early twentieth centuries, so, too, it would eventually disappear elsewhere. But child labor has not faded away.[1] Endemic in today's poor countries, child labor seems to have reemerged in industrial countries as well, raising questions about its importance in national and regional economies and in family economic strategies. What have historians of today's industrial countries learned that may help answer these questions?

The first part of this article overviews the extent and settings of child labor in Western Europe and the United States in the past. Historians must rely on a quantitative record that is patchy and difficult to interpret. As a result, it may not be possible to say with confidence whether the era of proto-industry or the early factories saw the high-water mark of child labor, and the nature and time path of decline remains debated. Nonetheless, broad trends emerge that put the experience of today's poor coun-

1 For estimates of child labor, see International Labour Organization, LABPROJ database; for data on industrial countries, see Lavalette, *A Thing of the Past?*

tries into historical perspective and provide an empirical backdrop for the analysis in the second and third parts of the article, which seek to explain why child labor increased during industrialization and declined thereafter.

Four types of explanation are offered. The first focuses on developments within capitalist labor markets. It examines the effects of technology as well as managerial and trade union strategies on children's work. The second focuses on the parental decision to send children to work. Historical analyses discuss this decision in terms of family strategies and parent-child relations. Economic analyses focus on the possibility of divergent interests within households and the potential for agency problems with implications for underinvestment in children's human capital. Both historians and economists ask whether parents are altruistic or selfish. They seek to determine whether child labor always follows from parental egoism or whether there are conditions in which caring parents would send their children out to work. The third type of explanation relates to the legal and political stance of the state. The fourth focuses on social norms and beliefs about appropriate behavior.

Child Labor during the Industrial Revolution

How extensive was child labor in Western Europe and the United States in the past? Were children concentrated in particular jobs, or did they work in most occupations and sectors? How important were they to the industries in which they worked, and how much did they contribute to economic growth and development?

Investigating the importance of children's work involves difficult conceptual problems of defining work and determining who is a child. Measuring the extent of child labor in the past is particularly difficult because the data are often inadequate. The summary presented here supplements evidence from early censuses and industrial surveys with material from less conventional sources, such as household budgets and the memoirs and diaries of working people.

The earliest censuses in what are now industrial economies began too late to capture the extent of child labor during industrialization. They measured a phenomenon already in decline, and they undercounted child workers, especially outside child-intensive industries, such as textiles. In 1851, when the British census first recorded the occupations of young people, 97 per cent of children age five to nine were without a "specified occupation"; beginning in 1881 the census no longer bothered to count working children in this age group. But by 1851 the Industrial Revolution was already more than seventy years old in Britain, and child labor had been the subject of (albeit imperfect) regulation for almost half a century. Not surprisingly, few very young workers were recorded, although children age ten to fourteen still often worked. The first relevant censuses in France and the United States were not conducted until the very end of the nineteenth century, by which point they, too, recorded few young children at work. For the era of industrialization, then, historians must rely on industrial surveys, household data, and other fragmentary evidence. What do such sources suggest?

Child labor was important in the early phases of industrialization, when large-scale production was a novelty, especially in textiles and mining. It was particularly important to the early starters on the path of industrial progress, notably Britain, Belgium, France, the western parts of Prussia, and the United States. For these early starters the intensive use of child labor in the key sectors of the Industrial Revolution was superimposed on children's employment in protoindustry and occurred in a cultural setting predisposed to "making children useful." The reduced wage costs must have played a role in the competitiveness of the key industries in the Industrial Revolution, although no study has measured the exact contribution of child labor.

A recent survey of the evidence on industry and mining in Britain reveals astonishingly high relative employment levels of children (under age thirteen) and young people (age thirteen to eighteen) in textiles and coal mining in the early nineteenth century.[2] Children and young people made up one- to two-thirds of all workers in many textile mills in 1833, and they regularly represented more than a quarter of the workforce in mines in 1842.

Although Britain was exceptional in the intensity of children's work, the evidence for other early industrializers shows that child labor was not uncommon. A study of French workers in 1839-1843 revealed that children under the age of sixteen made up 12.1 per cent of the labor force.[3] Another, albeit not necessarily comparable, inquiry for Belgium in 1843 counted 10,514 child workers, or 19.5 per cent of the workforce.[4] Goldin and Sokol-

2 Tuttle, *Hard at Work in Factories and Mines*, pp. 96-112, 142-149.
3 Heywood, *Childhood in Nineteenth-Century France*, p. 104.
4 De Herdt, "Child Labor in Belgium", pp. 26-27.

off estimate that in the Northeastern United States, women and children made up about 40 per cent of the manufacturing labor force in 1832.[5]

Household budgets for Britain from the pre-census era provide further evidence that industrialization was associated with a boom in child labor.[6] Though children's contributions were always important, their relative contributions and participation rates were highest in the 1820s and 1830s. According to Horrell and Humphries, more than 10 per cent of five to nine-year old children and more than 75 per cent of ten to fourteen-year olds were in the labor force. These participation rates exceed the rates recorded in the mid-Victorian censuses (which covered all children, not just children in working class families) and those estimated for working-class mothers.

Working-class autobiographies also suggest an increase in child participation rates in Britain during industrialization.[7] Boys age nine to thirteen were more likely to work if born after 1790 than before and even more likely to work if born after 1820. In contrast, only a small proportion of five-, six-, and seven-year-olds worked in the late eighteenth and early nineteenth century. Boys age fourteen and older almost always worked, both early and late in the Industrial Revolution.

Child labor was strategically crucial to the transition to factory production. Domestic industry and mining used large numbers of child workers, but it was factory jobs that witnessed the largest increase in child labor.[8]

U.S. household data for the end of the nineteenth century reveal the relatively high incidence of child labor among children of textile workers.[9] Autobiographical evidence for Britain from the pre-census period also suggests that the children of factory workers started work at relatively young ages and had relatively high participation rates.[10] As population and employment in the factory districts grew in the early stages of the Industrial Revolution, the absolute number of children in work and the aggregate child participation rate rose.

5 Goldin and Sokoloff, "Women, Children, and Industrialization in the Early Republic", p. 743.
6 Computed from Horrell and Humphries, "The Exploitation of Little Children", pp. 496–498.
7 Humphries, *Childhood and Child Labour*, ch. 7.
8 Horrell and Humphries, "The Exploitation of Little Children". See also, Galbi, "Child Labour and the Division of Labour".
9 Goldin and Parsons, "Parental Altruism and Self-Interest".
10 Humphries, "Child Labor in the Industrial Revolution".

Child labor in the early factories in Britain was associated with the apparently large-scale and long-distance movement of pauper apprentices. These wards of the state worked in isolated water-powered mills and endured punishing work and living regimes.[11] The potential for abuse spurred the passing of the Health and Morals of Apprentices Act in 1802, the first legal protection afforded to child workers.[12] Orphaned and abandoned children also figured in the early factory labor force in France[13] and Japan.[14] In the United States in the eighteenth century, the institution of pauper apprenticeship conveyed thousands of destitute and abandoned children into the labor force, although most were destined for agriculture and trades rather than factories.[15]

The importance of child labor in the early mills and mines should not detract from its presence in other sectors, including agriculture, miscellaneous manufacturing, and services, where it was often hidden by the familial and informal nature of employment. Europe and the United States remained primarily rural and agricultural through the nineteenth century, and agriculture provided most children's jobs as it did adult jobs.[16] The most common first job in working-class autobiography was that of farm boy. Bird scarers, shepherds, and ploughboys were also common.[17] Where the family farm predominated, children's work was ubiquitous, though often hidden from census enumerators.[18] Historians have used school attendance registers to reveal the regularity with which the sons and daughters of small farmers were withdrawn from school to help, as well as the wholesale absence of children in agricultural districts at harvest or haymaking time.[19] Such work was tolerated, even approved, because of its family context or seasonal duration, and a blind eye was often turned in its direction even after legal prohibition. Farm service, common across Europe, in which young people aged between twelve and fourteen were sent to live and work away from home, evaded censure because of its family setting and parallels with apprenticeship. But a rosy interpretation is sometimes at odds with

11 Dunlop and Denman, *English Apprenticeship and Child Labour.*
12 Engerman, "History and Political Economy".
13 Chassagne, "La naissance de l'industrie cotonnière en France".
14 Saito, "Children's Work, Industrialism and the Family Economy in Japan".
15 Murray and Herndon, "Markets for Children in Early America".
16 Sjöberg, "Working Rural Children".
17 Humphries, *Childhood and Child Labour*; Maynes, *Taking the Hard Road.*
18 Heywood, *A History of Childhood.*
19 Coombs and Radburn, "Children and Young People".

reported experience.[20] Generally, the larger, more commercial, and more capitalist the setting of children's agricultural work, the less tolerant both contemporaries and historians have been in judging it, with the gang work performed in the eastern counties of England in the mid-nineteenth century representing the nadir.[21]

In industry, too, child labor was entrenched in traditional sectors and small-scale production units as well as factories and mines. A common first job, often taken at a very young age in proto-industrial families, was winding bobbins for hand loom weavers.[22] In miscellaneous manufacturing, children were important in silk, bricks, small-scale metal manufactures, garments, and footwear. In services, boys were employed running errands, delivering messages in offices, and working as monitors in schools. For girls, child-minding and domestic service remained the foremost employment in most European countries in the nineteenth century.[23] It remains unclear whether work in these more traditional jobs was less intense or harsh than work in factories or mines.

Although children's participation was not sustained at the levels characteristic of the crucible of the Industrial Revolution, child labor did not rapidly disappear, as some historians have suggested.[24] Child labor was not a dinosaur, perfectly adapted to early industrial conditions but then driven rapidly to extinction when times changed.

Tuttle notes that in all British textile industries, the proportion of the workforce under age eighteen was close to 50 per cent for the entire period 1835–50, long after the initial phase of factory production, when rural water-driven mills relied on child paupers.[25] Children also worked in most mines from 1800 to 1850, often representing 20 to 50 per cent of workers. Children remained an important part of the workforce in more traditional jobs in agriculture, manufacturing, and services as well. Autobiographical evidence suggests that only the cohort born after 1850 was able to delay entry into work.

The decline of child labor began in Britain and other early starters around 1850. As with the boom in child labor, which affected young but not the youngest children disproportionately, the withdrawal of child workers

20 Humphries, *Childhood and Child Labour.*

21 Kitteringham, "Country Work Girls".

22 Humphries, *Childhood and Child Labour.*

23 Coninck-Smith, Sandin, and Schrumpf, *Industrious Children.*

24 Nardinelli, *Child Labour and the Industrial Revolution.*

25 Tuttle, *Hard at Work in Factories and Mines*, p. 98.

was also age-specific. The youngest child workers, age five to nine, never very common in the labor force, were the first to go, disappearing from the workforce by the time modern census enumeration began. The withdrawal of children age ten to fourteen came later, accelerating after 1870. In 1851, 30 per cent of ten to fourteen-year-olds worked; by 1901 the figure had fallen to just 17 per cent.[26] This withdrawal of children by age represents the first stage in the "adulting" of the labor force, as Cunningham calls it.[27] The systematic undercounting of child workers in the censuses of the mid-nineteenth century means the decline may be underestimated. When the U.S. census finally counted child workers at the end of the nineteenth century, it found only 17 per cent of ten to fourteen-year-olds gainfully employed.[28] The French census of 1896 found only 20 per cent of children this age working.[29] Most of the working children in this age band would have been thirteen or fourteen. The era of extensive child labor was over.

Superimposed on the disappearance of young children from the labor force was a redistribution of older working children. By the late nineteenth century, children in the industrial economies no longer participated in the key industries in which they had been so important.[30] Children also began to withdraw from miscellaneous manufacturing industries.[31] They were not involved in the newer industries developing in the early twentieth century and the interwar years. But the retreat of children from industry did not signal the death knell of child labor. For one thing, the retreat was uneven; for another, children were removed to "a distinct and marginalized children's labor market".[32]

In textiles and mining in the heyday of child labor, although some children did the same work as grown-ups as Tuttle notes, most children held distinct jobs.[33] But they were distinct jobs within key industries. By the early twentieth century, children had been excluded from such industries and were increasingly confined to the service sector and to child-only jobs. Thus by the 1911 census in Britain, more than one-quarter of employed boys under age fifteen worked as messenger boys. As Cunningham notes,

26 Lavalette, *A Thing of the Past?*, p. 124.
27 Cunningham, "Decline of Child Labour", p. 410.
28 Trattner, *Crusade for the Children*, pp. 32-6.
29 Heywood, *Childhood in Nineteenth-Century France*, p. 100.
30 Winstanley, *Working Children*.
31 Schrumpf, "From Full-Time to Part-Time".
32 Cunningham, "Decline of Child Labour", p. 409. See also, Childs, *Labour's Apprentices*; and, Solberg, "Seeing Children's Work".
33 Tuttle, *Hard at work in Factories and Mines*.

these jobs were not only reserved for children but also marginal to the economy.[34]

It is important not to overemphasize this transition. Earlier censuses had also recorded large numbers of boys in industrial service, many of whom were messengers or office boys.[35] Messenger boys were also numerous among autobiographers, representing 7 per cent of an early industrial sample of 506 boys whose first job was known, the second most commonly recorded job.[36] But there is no doubt that this shift represents a distinct and important second stage in the adulting of the labor force and one not confined to the vanguard economies. In Norway, children worked in agriculture, tobacco, and glass manufacture in 1875; by 1912 they worked mainly as newspaper boys.[37] By the twentieth century much of children's work was part-time and thus not incompatible with school attendance. As half-timers in the mills, they clung on in a traditional industrial job, but most part-timers worked in the service sector, working in shops, delivering goods, and running errands.

The history of child labor illustrates the danger involved in drawing simple parallels between the industrializing economies of the nineteenth century and developing economies today. Once considered a paradigm case, the British Industrial Revolution now appears to be shot through with peculiarities.[38] One such peculiarity is the extent and duration of child labor, which was greater in Britain than in any other nineteenth-century industrializer or indeed developing area today. Belgium, another early industrializer whose transition was also heavily based on coal and textiles, ranks a distant second.[39]

Historical comparisons are problematic because of the difficulties of measuring child participation and converting nineteenth-century income levels into 1992 U.S. dollars. Nevertheless, the gap between the level of child labor in nineteenth-century Britain and developing economies today is sufficiently large as to dominate the likely effects of computational errors (see figure 1, which compares historical and present-day experience). The greater use of child labor in the British case complements current reinterpretations of the Industrial Revolution as involving, at least in its early

34 Cunningham, "Decline of Child Labour". See also, Childs, *Labour's Apprentices.*

35 Booth, "On Occupations of the People".

36 Humphries, *Childhood and Child Labour,* ch. 8.

37 Schrumpf, "From Full-Time to Part-Time".

38 Crafts, *British Economic Growth.*

39 De Herdt, "Child Labour in Belgium".

stages, an increase in labor input ("an industrious revolution") rather than an increase in productivity.[40] The apparent restraint shown by today's developing economies in comparison with the first industrial nation affords grounds for guarded optimism.

Figure 2.1. Child Labor and GDP per Capita

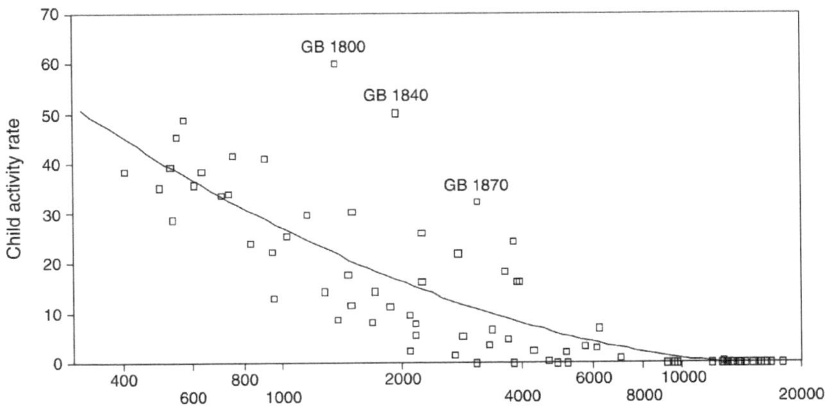

Note: 1870 data are for boys only.
Source: Krueger "International Labor Standards and Trade"; historical observations based on Crafts "British Economic Growth", Horrell and Humphries "The Exploitation of Little Children", and Humphries "Child Labour in the Industrial Revolution".

Explaining the Increase in Child Labor

What explains the importance of child labor during the Industrial Revolution, particularly for early starters? Why was the phenomenon so widespread in Britain, the first industrial economy?

Development of the Capitalist Labor Market

The older literature, with its fixation on the employment of children in mills and mines, emphasized technology. Steam power and machinery allowed women and children to take over work that had previously

40 Crafts, *British Economic Growth*; De Vries, "The Industrial Revolution and the Industrious Revolution".

required the strength and skill of men.[41] Industrial technologies differed in terms of opportunities to employ children.[42] For some of these technologies, child labor appeared essential. Early wooden textile machinery that had to be close to the ground may have dictated child-intensive employment.[43] The narrowness of underground passages in both British and Belgian thin-seam pits hindered the mechanization of transport and so maintained the demand for child drawers, who dragged the coal from the face to the surface.[44] But the child intensity of technology cannot be taken as exogenous. As Bolin-Hort notes, "The relationship between technology and child labor was reciprocal rather than one-sided".[45] Certainly some early machinery was specifically constructed to be used by children to reduce labor costs, as the study of British patents reveals.[46]

The importance of child labor varied significantly across regions, even when the same technology was used.[47] The Waltham system of textile production in New England in the mid-nineteenth century employed young women rather than children, whereas high proportions of children worked in Lancashire. In a sample of 43 Manchester mills, 22.3 per cent of the workforce was under age fourteen and 32.4 per cent under age sixteen; in 29 mills in Glasgow, 35.6 per cent the workforce was under age fourteen and 48.3 per cent under age sixteen.[48] In Alsace in the 1820s, more than a third of mill workers were under age sixteen.[49]

Firms combined the same technology with different compositions of adults and children. In the Ghent cotton industry, the large firm of Voortman recruited women and children.[50] In 1842 just 3.1 per cent of Voortman's labor force was under age fifteen; by 1859 that proportion had risen to ten per cent. But although Voortman's use of child labor was exceptional for Ghent, it was modest in comparison with elsewhere. Technology was only one item in a list of important determinants of the proportion of child workers; the list included the availability of children, industrial organiza-

41 Nardinelli, *Child Labour and the Industrial Revolution.*
42 Horrell and Humphries, "Exploitation of Little Children"; Goldin and Parsons, "Parental Altruism and Self-Intrest".
43 Tuttle, *Hard at Work in Factories and Mines.*
44 Humphries, "Protective Legislation, the Capitalist State and Working Class Men".
45 Bolin-Hort, *Work, Family and the State*, p. 17.
46 MacLeod, *Inventing the Industrial Revolution.*
47 Bolin-Hort, *Work, Family and the State.*
48 *Ibid.*, pp. 36–58.
49 Heywood, *Childhood in Nineteenth-Century France*, p. 100.
50 Scholliers, *Wages, Manufacturers and Workers in the Nineteenth-Century Factory*, pp. 96–97.

tion, the employment strategy of manufacturers, and the strength of labor organizations representing men.

The organization of the labor process had both direct implications for the demand for child labor and indirect implications through its influence over technology, employment strategies, and labor relations. Goldin and Sokoloff argue that in the Northeastern United States, innovations such as a more elaborate division of labor, a more disciplined working environment, and a larger scale may have been just as important as technological change in creating the surge in the demand for female and child labor associated with industrialization.[51] In Britain organizational change promoted the employment of women and children by breaking down customary age and gender divisions in the workplace and undermining the power of labor organizations to defend such customary barriers.[52] The neglect of organizational initiatives in promoting child labor is consistent with researchers' overemphasis on factory production of textiles, for these innovations were particularly important in miscellaneous manufacturing, such as boot, shoe, glass, and paper manufacturing, where children's work has been underestimated.

Far from always following the substitution of machinery for muscle power, children's work was often the consequence of failed or incomplete mechanization. Thus the expansion of child labor in coal mining was the result of increasing output in the absence of changed transport technology. In a swathe of diffused and workshop-based industries outside the celebrated example of textile production, partial mechanization created new jobs for boys and girls. Lathes and presses, along with many simple machines, needed boys to feed them.

Manufacturers' strategies also increased child labor. The older literature documents the turning of British manufacturers to child labor in the context of the labor shortages of the Napoleonic wars.[53] The bellicose background of early industrialization in Europe may have contributed to the intensive use of child labor. In Britain one in ten able-bodied men was in military service in 1794 (one in six by 1809); in France, Russia, and Austria probably about one in fourteen prime-age men was under arms in the early nineteenth century.[54] Military participation on this scale was totally new, and the effect on labor markets must have been substantial.

51 Goldin and Sokoloff, "Women, Children, and Industrialization in the Early Republic".
52 Berg and Hudson, "Rehabilitating the Industrial Revolution".
53 Hammond and Hammond, *Town Labourer.*
54 Cookson, *British Armed Nation*, ch. 4.

Manufacturers fended off government regulation of child labor by appealing to the need to keep labor costs low to compete internationally.[55] Children's work was a necessary evil, essential to the competitive success of the key industries of the Industrial Revolution. Evaluation of the manufacturers' claim awaits counterfactual analysis of competitiveness without child labor.

Employers' strategies to reduce costs affected child employment levels. If employers had market power and children could be substituted for adults, their employment depressed adult wages. At the level of the household economy, this triggered a vicious circle, with lower adult wages increasing the need for children to work to maintain subsistence. The management of Voortmans pursued just such an employment strategy, making it effective even in a densely populated region, without recourse to paternalism.[56]

Labor relations also deserve mention. An older generation of historians emphasized the role that the emasculation of labor organization played in the boom in child labor. The Hammonds' chapter "The War on Trade Unions," which ends with the assertion that "the Combination Laws and the employment of children on a great scale are two aspects of the same system", immediately precedes the chapters on child labor.[57] Recent work has emphasized organized labor's resistance to the introduction of women workers and been less inclined to see trade unions as heroic. Perhaps the strategies of adult male workers should be reexamined in the light of the greater threat posed by competition from children and organized labor's inability to contain the surge in child employment.[58]

Family Strategies

Economic historians have studied the supply of child labor in the context of the household economy, analyzing the decision to send a child to work as part of a "family strategy". A family strategy involves a family acting as a single unit in the interests of all members. How these interests are identified and how possibly heterogeneous preferences are combined remains unclear. If parents do not care enough about the future welfare of their children, agency problems in human capital formation could occur within the household. In particular, selfish parents would prefer that their children work while the parents are alive and able to benefit from their children's

55 Engerman, "History and Political Economy".

56 Scholliers, *Wages, Manufacturers and Workers in the Nineteenth-Century Factory.*

57 Hammond and Hammond, *Town Labourer*, p. 142.

58 See also, Cunningham, "Decline of Child Labour".

labor. Children would overwork, and there would be underinvestment in their health, education, and training. Intervention to influence the household allocation of child labor and lifetime consumption of parents and children would be justified. Options include bans on child labor, compulsory schooling, or educational subsidies that relax the tradeoff between the current consumption of parents and the current education and future consumption of children.

But even altruistic parents may send their children to work. If the payoff to child labor in terms of the return to the physical investment of their earnings exceeds the return to human capital, the optimal strategy would involve child labor. If parents are too poor to meet the necessary expenditures of the household and cannot borrow against the future earnings of their children, dissavings in the form of child labor may be necessary for survival. Even if the family is not so impoverished, borrowing rates that are higher than lending rates shift the tradeoff between the value of schooling and child labor in favor of work, because the family receives the income flows earlier.

Which of these scenarios holds matters, because the optimal policy intervention differs in each case. If the family is so poor that children have to work, legislation would be difficult to enforce and could reduce children's well-being. In contrast, if parents are selfish, the case for intervention must rest on there being greater private than public returns to education, and subsidies to education would be the preferred policy. The same would be true in the third scenario, in which subsidies could offset capital market imperfection.

Economists infer the altruism or selfishness of family members from outcomes in consumer goods markets. If parents are unhappy about children working, then controlling for prices, child labor should be associated with lower parental consumption. The intuition is that parents will equate the marginal utility of consumption to the marginal utility of child leisure, which is higher if children work.

Historians lack the household and consumption data needed for econometric investigation of the relationships between parents and children. A few studies have explored the links between child labor and household poverty, but the construction put on the findings depends on the assumptions. Goldin and Parsons use household data to investigate whether poor parents were altruistic toward their children in the United States in the late nineteenth century.[59] They assume perfect capital markets, allowing resources to move freely across time and generations, and perfect labor markets, allowing families to move freely from one industrial center to another in response to labor and capital market conditions and parental preferences. Altruism (or costlessly enforceable intergenerational contracts) is combined with the capital and labor market assumptions in the rejected model. The negative correlation found between adult and child earnings can then be interpreted as indicating that parents were willing to accept large reductions in their own wages to secure employment in areas having abundant opportunities for child labor. The high savings out of children's earnings are held to be inconsistent with parents using child labor to offset borrowing difficulties alone. Goldin and Parsons conclude that parents did not have strong altruistic concerns for their children:

> The presence of industries with a high demand for child labor reduced the future wealth position of the offspring. Child labor had the obvious, almost definitional, negative effect on schooling attainment. At the same time the family provided little in the way of offsetting physical asset transfers (in the form of gifts and bequests) to compensate children for their lost schooling and future earnings. The increased family income was apparently absorbed in higher current family consumption.[60]

Horrell and Humphries[61] do not explicitly consider the issue of altruism, though their findings are suggestive. They obtained expenditure data for a subset of families in the budget data set. These families were not saving – indeed, some ran deficits, which they financed by pawning or borrowing. Several received poor relief. Spending on food and rent dominated the budgets.[62] These families were closer to subsistence than those in the sample investigated by Goldin and Parsons, and assumptions of perfect capital markets and household mobility are implausible. Thus the finding that fathers' earnings were negatively correlated with the likelihood of participation suggests that poverty was driving child labor. However, the high participation rates of children in the relatively prosperous factory districts

59 Goldin and Parsons, "Parental Altruism and Self-Interest", p. 657.
60 Goldin and Parsons, "Parental Altruism and Self-Interest", p. 657.
61 Horrell and Humphries, "Exploitation of Little Children".
62 Horrell, "Home Demand", pp. 576–582.

suggests that in some situations the desire for consumer goods played a role.[63]

Traditionally, historians have explored parental altruism by examining evidence on the nature of the parent-child relationship. Parents have received bad press in much of the historical literature. "The further back in history one goes, the lower the level of child care, and the more likely children are to be killed, abandoned, beaten, terrorized and sexually abused", according to Lloyd deMause.[64] DeMause may have been extreme in his denunciation of child-rearing in the past, but he was not alone in the 1970s and 1980s, when many historians perceived children as badly treated and parental love as fickle.[65] These historians considered the eighteenth century to have been an important turning point in the way in which children were perceived and treated.

Recently, historians have been less hasty to condemn parents and more careful to distinguish between practices that can be unambiguously condemned and those that are considered cruel or harmful today but were considered appropriate in the past. Pollock uses diaries and autobiographical material on parent-child relations to argue strenuously against any cultural shift or indeed the systematic ill treatment of children in the past.[66] On the basis of working-class evidence given to various public inquiries, she concludes that parents largely did not send children to work for selfish reasons. In her view, poverty lay behind child labor.

In contrast, many observers during industrialization suggested that selfish and greedy parents sent their children to work, often instead of working themselves, using the children's earnings to buy goods such as alcohol and tobacco.[67] Of course, many of these commentators themselves employed children or shared the background and interests of employers who used child labor. In projecting these views, they sought to exculpate themselves and their peers by shifting the blame for what was increasingly seen as a reprehensible practice.

Working-class autobiographies of the period provide rare evidence from the child's perspective. Few children supported the charge of parental

63 Horrell and Humphries, "Exploitation of Little Children", p. 492, pp. 503–504.

64 DeMause, *History of Childhood*, p. 1.

65 Shorter *Making of the Modern Family*; Stone, *Family, Sex, and Marriage*; Badinter, *Myth of Motherhood*.

66 Pollock, *Forgotten Children*.

67 For a summary of such views see Pinchbeck and Hewitt, *Children in English Society*; Pollock, *Forgotten Children*; Nardinelli, *Child Labour and the Industrial Revolution*.

exploitation, instead seeing their parents as kind and caring. What, then, did these children think forced their entry into work?

Custom and practice undoubtedly played a role. Historians have condemned parents for expecting nothing better for their children than they experienced themselves,[68] thereby locking the working class into a low-skill and early work intergenerational equilibrium. But investigation of the autobiographical evidence suggests that the main determinant of children's age at starting work was the family's economic circumstances, with father's earnings crucial.[69] Men in trades and clerical and service occupations constituted an aristocracy of labor, earning more than unskilled workers and enjoying greater regularity of earnings. Predictably, their children were withheld from the labor market longer than those of other workers.[70] Other workers could not always earn enough to ensure their family's subsistence without help from their children. Recent definitive estimates of real earnings show that solid increases did not occur until after 1850,[71] a finding that is consistent with the apparent maintenance of high levels of child participation well into the nineteenth century.

Industrialization involved the rise and fall of sectors, technological change, shifts in the location of work, and an intensification of the business cycle. Even for skilled workers, earnings did not go up without interruption, as Feinstein's data show.[72] Many fathers experienced short-term unemployment and stagnant wages. But it was hard to distinguish a temporary situation from something more permanent and to decide on an accommodation. Responding appropriately to fluctuations was often expensive, involving migration or retraining, and it was hampered by imperfect capital markets and lack of information. A holding strategy involved putting more family members to work, finding jobs for children. When hard times persisted, stopgaps became permanent. Sending children to work became normal and widely adopted by other desperate families. The generation of children sent to work early in response to shifts in the demand for labor had less opportunity to accumulate human capital, therefore becoming less productive and so less able to support its own children. In this way, demand shocks in the labor market echoed through the generations to hold the economy at low levels of productivity and high rates of child

68 See Pinchbeck and Hewitt, *Children in English Society.*
69 Humphries, *Childhood and Child Labour,* ch. 7.
70 Humphries, *Childhood and Child Labour,* ch. 7.
71 Feinstein, "Pessimism Perpetuated".
72 Feinstein, "Pessimism Perpetuated".

labor. Such added-worker effects characterized the prolonged competition between hand trades and factory production, promoting and intensifying child labor.[73]

Mothers were described as caring for their children, though the extent to which their love was manifest in working to help support their children varied across Europe. Child labor may have been more extensive where married women pursued exclusively domestic roles, though children's child care responsibilities surely offset this pattern.[74] Compared with French and German mothers, few British mothers appear to have contributed to family income by participating in the labor market – in contrast to their children.[75] This substitution of children's labor for that of their mothers was embedded in a family strategy that both responded to local economic and demographic conditions and reflected cultural values. Its potential importance in the modern world makes it deserving of more careful study.

Whether or not they worked outside the home, mothers, unlike fathers, were almost never depicted as consuming the fruits of their children's labor. The custom for children to surrender their earnings to their mothers ensured that children's earnings were recycled through the household accounts, to be spent in children's interests. How mothers weighed the claims of older and younger children and of working and dependent children remains unclear.

In a few cases, children did blame parents, in particular fathers, for contributing to their families' poverty and so to early working. Drinking was a cause of misery for many working families, and alcoholic fathers were often associated with children's early working. But children did not always see their fathers' drinking as selfish. Fathers were driven to drink by their inability to provide, the physical demands of their hard jobs, and the grimness of their working lives. Drinking was also a response to bereavement.[76] Alcohol has addictive and stimulant characteristics, which may explain its overpowering of fathers' altruistic intentions. These links between selfishness and drinking are consistent with evidence associating lack of altruism with stimulant and addictive goods consumed mainly by men.

73 Lyons, "Family Response to Economic Decline"; Humphries, "Household Economy".

74 Horrell and Humphries, "Exploitation of Little Children"; Cunningham, "Decline of Child Labour".

75 Horrell and Humphries, "Exploitation of Little Children"; Maynes, *Taking the Hard Road*.

76 Humphries, *Childhood and Child Labour,* ch. 5.

Abandonment destined families for poverty.[77] In contrast to drinking, it was rarely condoned. Being without a father (perhaps even a nonaltruistic father) appears to have had a large and significant effect on the age at which children started working, according to British autobiographies, advancing children's entry into the labor market by more than fifteen months.[78]

Family size also affected family poverty and therefore child labor. Large families increased the need for children to supplement fathers' earnings. In Britain industrialization proceeded against a backdrop of historically rapid population growth and increased average family size. In 1821 children under the age of nine made up 28 per cent of the population, and young people ten to nineteen represented another 21 per cent.[79] This proportion probably increased throughout the nineteenth century. The pressure created by the rising dependency rate has been somewhat neglected by economic historians, but its potential as an explanation of the pattern and extent of child labor in Britain is considerable. Many boys cite the presence of large numbers of dependent siblings as having pushed them into the labor force; their impressions appear borne out in the autobiographical evidence on age at starting work.[80] Britain's unusual demographic experience may well have contributed to the exceptional reliance on child labor.

The Role of the State

The state usually enters the story of child labor only as an agent in its decline. But in Britain the state by both action and inaction facilitated the boom in child labor. This is not to suggest that the state adopted a conscious strategy in support of child labor, although several apocryphal stories repeated in the classic British accounts suggest as much.[81] More likely the boom in child labor was the unintended consequence of policies such as legislation weakening labor organization (the Combination Acts, the repeal of the Statute of Artificers) and the miserly treatment of the wives and children of soldiers. Most important in this context was the operation of poor relief. The Old Poor Law arguably inhibited the indiscriminate growth of child labor by occasionally subsidizing poor families with many children and channeling children into more acceptable forms of work through pau-

77 Humphries, "Female-Headed Households in Early Industrial Britain"; Horrell, Humphries, and Voth, "Destined for Deprivation".

78 Humphries, *Childhood and Child Labour,* ch. 7.

79 Wrigley and Schofield, *Population History of England*, pp. 215-219.

80 Humphries, *Childhood and Child Labour,* ch. 7.

81 Hammond and Hammond, *Town Labourer*; Mantoux, *Industrial Revolution.*

per apprenticeship. It also treated single mothers relatively generously.[82] The retreat of the Old Poor Law in the face of rising expenditures in the late eighteenth century and the transition to the New Poor Law, although not eliminating fiscal transfers, emphasized the conditionality of assistance on children's working with negative implications for human capital formation.[83] In a world in which orphaned and fatherless children are legion, perhaps this is the most pertinent finding from the past.

Cultural Context

The idea of a change in parent-child relations in the eighteenth century is firmly established in the literature, with harshness in the medieval and early modern periods giving way to kinder treatment later on. Such a shift in values has intriguing implications for the historian of child labor. It suggests that countries that industrialized early, before this transition was completed, might be expected to have used child labor more intensively than countries that industrialized later.

Explaining the Decrease in Child Labor

Motivated by the need to discourage child labor in the developing world, economists have looked mainly to the past to understand what caused child labor to decline.

Development of the Capitalist Labor Market

Chief among the usual suspects is technology: the demand for child labor allegedly faded as more advanced industrial technologies replaced the need for unskilled labor of children.[84] As Cunningham observes, "It is assumed that technology has its own in built rationale and that it always acts in favor of adult and in opposition to child labor".[85] But earlier technology had developed to facilitate the substitution of child for adult labor. Why should it suddenly have changed direction unless reversed by a shift in the interests of management or labor? There has to be a motive for its development and introduction.

82 Snell and Millar, "Lone Parent Families and the Welfare State".

83 Horrell, Humphries, and Voth, "Destined for Deprivation".

84 Goldin and Parsons, "Parental Altruism and Self-Interest"; Nardinelli, *Child Labor and The Industrial Revolution*.

85 Cunningham, "Decline of Child Labour", p. 417.

In France in the 1840s and in some industries in Britain in the mid-nineteenth century, employers campaigned for a reduction in child labor.[86] Their motives were both strategic and philanthropic. By promoting protective labor legislation, employers who had already dispensed with child labor or who had technology that obviated the need for child labor sought to gain a competitive advantage over other employers for whom child labor remained essential.[87] Others were convinced that child labor was morally wrong[88] or that it was in the collective interest to develop a healthier and more educated workforce.

But an account of changes in the capitalist labor market, which deals only with employers' strategies, is unbalanced. Managerial strategies may also have shifted toward an intensive labor process in which the strength and power of adults was needed.[89] Moreover, by the mid-nineteenth century male labor had also begun to reorganize defensively within revamped institutions. An extensive literature suggests how strong trade unions, protective labor legislation, and campaigns for family wages led to the rise of the male-breadwinner family. This phenomenon is traditionally presented from a feminist perspective that focuses on the exclusion of female labor. But the timing of women's retreat from the labor market does not coincide with the growing strength of organized labor.[90] Reoriented to provide a political-economic explanation of the decline of child labor, male unionists' campaign for family wages slots neatly into the chronology of adulting.

Family Strategies

Clark Nardinelli's influential book gave family strategies a neoclassical twist.[91] Heavily influenced by the New Household Economics, Nardinelli argued that because working families in the early nineteenth century had the opportunity not to send their children out to work but chose to do so, child labor must have been the best option. Ignoring the possibility of heterogeneous preferences and agency problems by assuming a unitary household, Nardinelli explained the decline of child labor in terms of families' rational responses to changes in relative prices and incomes. Technol-

86 Humphries, "Protective Legislation"; Weissbach, *Child Labour Reform in Nineteenth-Century France*; Dupree, *Family Structure in the Staffordshire Potteries*.

87 Marvel, "Factory Regulation"; Humphries, "Protective Legislation".

88 See Hammond and Hammond, *Town Labourer*, ch. 8.

89 Cunningham, "Decline of Child Labour".

90 Creighton, "Rise of the Male Breadwinner Family".

91 Nardinelli, *Child Labour and the Industrial Revolution*.

ogy rendered child labor unproductive, and economic growth eventually trickled down to raise adult male earnings. Thus the boom in child labor hinged on a fortuitous coincidence of a transient technology and low adult wages. It declined when technology advanced and adult wages rose, allowing children to attend school instead of work.

The policy implications of this hypothesis are profound. According to Nardinelli, low adult wages cause child labor. There is no remedy to the problem, except to wait for economic growth, which, with Chicago School optimism, Nardinelli believes inevitable – provided it is not stymied by well-meaning but inappropriate government intervention.

Nardinelli's analysis of the causes of the decline of child labor is consistent with his chronology of events, which describes a rapid decline in child labor starting before the Factory Acts and coinciding with strong growth in the real earnings of adult males. The decline in child labor, however, is disputed by evidence that children's involvement in productive activities was more extensive and more enduring than Nardinelli suggests. Moreover, Feinstein's definitive series delays sustained growth in real earnings until the mid-nineteenth century, which is out of sync with Nardinelli's account.[92]

A newer view fits neatly with a later and more gradual decline in children's work and with an explanation that draws on the socioeconomic construction of the male-breadwinner family in the second half of the nineteenth century. The growth in adult earnings in the later nineteenth century was not independent of the ongoing struggle – not only in capitalist labor markets but also within Parliament and the press – between opponents and proponents of child labor. This struggle was but one aspect of a campaign to defend the integrity of the working class family.

One variable that emerged as an important determinant of age at starting work that is often forgotten in stories about the decline of child labor is family size. Fertility peaked in Britain in the 1820s, but large families remained standard among some occupational groups and very common among the working class at large.

The Role of the State

An older generation of historians explained the decline of child labor almost solely in terms of the Factory Acts.[93] Neoclassical economics is predisposed to deem intervention unnecessary if not mischievous. Is legisla-

92 Feinstein, "Pessimism Perpetuated".

93 Hutchins and Harrison, *History of Factory Legislation*.

tion possible only when the majority of powerful employers has already dispensed with child labor? Does it harm children by pushing them into more hazardous but less visible work and reducing family incomes?

Moehling uses a "difference-in-differences-in-differences" procedure to isolate the effects of child labor laws on children's participation by state in the United States between 1880 and 1930.[94] Child labor fell precipitously during this period, but the decline was not driven by the legislative success of the child labor movement. The occupation rate of thirteen-year-olds did decline in states that enacted a minimum working age of fourteen, but so did the occupation rates of children not covered by the restrictions.[95] Legal prohibitions emerge as consequences rather than causes of the decline in children's work.

In contrast, other legislation is widely agreed to have had some effect. The classic case is the 1833 Factory Act, whose impact even Nardinelli acknowledges. Cunningham[96] provides a list of child labor laws that historians have deemed effective, including the 1864 act that reduced children's participation in potteries,[97] the 1872 Mines Regulation Act,[98] the 1874 act in France,[99] and the measures taken by the National Recovery Administration in the United States in 1933.[100] Data from the 1960 census suggest that child labor laws and compulsory schooling increased educational attainments of children in the United States between 1915 and 1939.[101]

Chang scrutinized the historical record to establish the time it took for legislation to have an effect.[102] He argues that the child labor standards demanded of the developing world require a swifter eradication of children's work than was achieved by today's industrial countries. Chang takes the industrial countries' stance on child labor as an example of his more general argument that today's wealthy countries industrialized and became rich using policies and institutions that were often the opposite of those they now thrust on developing economies. Industrial countries are attempting to kick away the ladder by which they rose to prosperity, denying poor countries the same route to the top.

94 Moehling, "State Child Labour Laws".
95 Moehling, "State Child Labour Laws", p. 95.
96 Cunningham, "Decline of Child Labour", pp. 415-416.
97 Dupree, *Family Structure in the Staffordshire Potteries*.
98 Church, *History of British Coal Industry*.
99 Weissbach, *Child Labour Reform in Nineteenth-Century France*.
100 Trattner, *Crusade for the Children*.
101 Lleras-Muney, "Were Compulsory Attendance and Child Labor Laws Effective?".
102 Chang, *Kicking away the Ladder*.

Although Chang has a point, his description of historical events should not go unchallenged. First, regulation became comprehensive over a shorter time period than Chang suggests, certainly less than the centuries he cites. Second, wealthy countries industrialized at different times and made different demands on child workers, with implications for legislative progression. Third, the early starters made more extensive use of child labor, suggesting that even among the now rich countries, later entry into the race for prosperity involved different standards of acceptable conduct. Yet this did not kick away the ladder to development for Europe's late industrializers. Fourth, though some of the policies and institutions that rich countries now condemn can be linked to economic development (tariffs, for example, may have helped infant industries develop), the contribution of child workers to economic growth has not been established.

An alternative way of curbing child labor is by requiring school attendance. Unlike child labor laws, compulsory schooling does not encourage a move into unregulated and perhaps less desirable work. Case studies suggest that the desire to limit child labor was sometimes a motive for compulsory schooling.[103] For several European and non-European countries, the decline in child labor appears correlated with the introduction of compulsory education.[104] In Britain, for example, the decline in the participation rate of ten to fourteen-year-olds gathered momentum after the introduction of compulsory schooling in 1870. But the importance of compulsory education has not yet been demonstrated in a study that controls for changes in other possible explanatory variables. Given the important policy implications that ride on the validity of this link, more research is needed.

School subsidies, in principle an attractive option, have not been studied historically. The popularity of charity schools is suggestive, but working-class parents' apparent preference for schools whose curriculum and setting were under their jurisdiction over free state schools implies that they valued the right to control children's schooling.[105] Sunday schools, an enormously important deliverer of nineteenth century education, pose a recurrent dilemma: how to evaluate an educational institution designed to accommodate child labor. Perhaps the considerable achievements of Sunday schools, part-time and seasonal education, reading rooms and mutual improvement societies, ragged schools (free schools for poor children), and

103 Hogan, *Class and Reform*.
104 Weiner, *Child and the State in India*.
105 Gardner, *Lost Elementary Schools of Victorian England*.

apprenticeships have been undervalued because of a distaste for institutions that remained wedded to children's ongoing involvement in productive activities.[106]

Cultural Context

A cultural account of the decline of child labor could be built around the diffusion to the working class of the transition in parent-child relations that historians have documented for the elite.[107] More specifically, the political-economic campaigns of the later nineteenth century for protective labor legislation, the integrity of the family, and the family wage could themselves have influenced values and attitudes. The theory of cognitive dissonance suggests that the routine expression of ideas and beliefs is intolerable unless they are adopted. Victorian working men embraced the schooled child along with a nonworking wife as hallmarks of a desirable and respectable family life that went with (indeed required) higher adult male pay. Their wage demands became inseparable from a package of ideas about proper family structure that went to the heart of contemporary views of enlightened and civilized society. Their claim was eventually supported by groups of men from other ranks of society – employers, politicians, journalists, philanthropists – prepared to sacrifice some immediate self-interest to accommodate the diffusion of a family structure that had powerful appeal.[108]

Conclusions

Countries in which child labor is common today bear a greater resemblance to industrial countries on the eve of industrialization than to those same countries fifty to hundred years later, when child labor began to decline. Among nineteenth-century industrializers, child labor was more prevalent in early starters, and it appears to have been more prevalent in both early and late industrializers than it is in developing economies today. This difference may be a source of optimism signaling the spread of technologies that have little use for child labor and values that endorse the preservation and protection of childhood. But the historical record warns that

106 Silver, "Ideology and the Factory Child"; Snell, "Sunday School Movement in England and Wales".

107 For a dissenting view, see Nardinelli, *Child Labor and the Industrial Revolution.*

108 Creighton, "Rise and Decline".

technological and cultural developments are not independent of underlying economic conditions. Whether such technology and values can survive the impact of the AIDS epidemic, famines, and civil and regional conflicts on family structures and the supply of child labor remains to be seen.

Child labor is hard to document, let alone measure, particularly in the very sectors and jobs in which it is likely to be prevalent, namely: family farms and businesses, the informal sector, and part-time and seasonal work. Historical experience warns against focusing only on public forms of employment and assuming that as children are removed from the visible sectors they will also withdraw from the darker corners of the economy. On the other hand, historians have been too ready to assume that familial or informal employment is intrinsically more benign than work in factories. What are needed are comparative analyses of forms of child labor, which might provide criteria for a normative ranking of jobs for use in a world in which some kind of economic contribution from children is tolerated. The ways in which learning and work were combined in the past are also worth more attention.

Historians' finding that poverty was the main determinant of child labor should not be cause for resignation. Welfare-improving intervention appears possible at low incomes. Moreover, all poor children are not equally at risk. Orphaned and fatherless children and those in large families are the most vulnerable. Efficient interventions to curb child labor involve fiscal transfers to fatherless children and large families and active policies toward street children.

Historians disagree about whether it is possible to regulate the demand for child labor without harming the very children whose protection was intended. Perhaps the lesson here is that interventions must be customized to suit particular circumstances. Compulsory schooling and legislation banning child labor were successful and apparently welfare improving in some times and places, but not others. The discrediting of technological determinism by historians and its replacement with more nuanced accounts of the decline in child labor also suggests the importance of close scrutiny of circumstances and context.

The documentation of the interplay of interests that over time led to the adulting of the labor force has resonance with Basu's theoretical account of a labor market with multiple equilibria, some involving child labor.[109] Policymakers can try to encourage a movement from equilibria that involve

109 Basu, "Child Labor".

child labor to those that do not. The effectiveness of such policies depends on understanding the institutional configuration of the labor market, including how child labor fits into family strategies – that are themselves embedded in historically and culturally determined ideas about mothers' and fathers' roles – and evolving relations among employers, workers, and the state.

CHAPTER 3

Child Labour's Global Past 1650–2000

Hugh Cunningham

Two assumptions underlie this attempt to provide a narrative framework for child labour as a global phenomenon over the last three hundred and fifty years. First, the phrase "child labour" is used, not so much as a description of the work that children do, as a way of signifying that their work has come to be seen as problematic. Second, child labour became a global issue not only when it was found in different parts of the globe, but above all when it became part of a global economy where a development in one part of the globe was reflected in another.

Bearing in mind these assumptions, I want to lay out a narrative framework for child labour from 1650 onwards, with an emphasis both on economic change and on institutional or legal initiatives to control children's work. Of the inadequacies of this grand narrative, I am fully aware, and one needs to be stated at the outset. We know very little about child labour in non-capitalist countries, in the Soviet Union or in China, for example. This, then, is a narrative of child labour in the capitalist world. When I refer to capitalism I am thinking of it rather like Marx did: as innovative, unpredictable, dynamic, revolutionary, the motor of history – and of child labour.

Proto-Industrialism

Proto-industrialism began to be studied and so-named in the 1970s. To some extent it was only a renaming of what had previously been called "cottage industry". Its leading feature was the manufacture (literally, making by hand) of goods for sale in the market, the manufacturers normally being family-based and working from home or small workshops. A master (the capitalist) usually provided the raw materials and negotiated the sale in the market. Child work within a family context was an endemic part of this process, not least because of the advances in productivity achieved by the division of labour: jobs suited to children could be created. As Daniel Defoe described it in the 1720s, in the domestic woollen-weaving districts near Halifax in Yorkshire any child aged over four was likely to be at work.[1]

The date 1650 may in itself have no precise significance, but it is a useful proxy for the development and spread of proto-industrialism in large parts of Northern and Western Europe. There are examples before 1650, for example in northern Italy in the sixteenth century or in cloth-making in Norwich in England in the early seventeenth century,[2] but the main development of proto-industrialism was from the middle of the seventeenth century, and its heyday was in Europe from that time up to the early nineteenth century when it began to be superseded by mechanized production – what we call the Industrial Revolution.

Proto-industrialism not only transformed the industrial and domestic economy in areas, like the West Riding of Yorkshire, where manufacture was concentrated. Another feature of it was that production was frequently for the export market. The textiles that made their way to Spain and the Spanish colonies in America came from proto-industrial Flanders, the nails for the log cabins of North America from workshops in the Black Country, the straw hats made by women and children in Northern Italy were exported to England, France, Germany and across the Atlantic.[3] The work that children did had consequences that were experienced globally.

From the perspective of the history of children's work, the proto-industrial era was not confined to family-based production. It was also remarkable for the employment of children from institutions – from orphanages, workhouses, and so on. In Stockholm in the seventeenth century, the largest industrial establishment, Leijonancker's broadcloth manufactory, took child workers from the pauper's hospice. In Leiden orphans were imported from Aachen and Liege to work in the textile industry – about eight thousand young workers were brought into Leiden between 1638 and 1671.[4] At the turn of the eighteenth and nineteenth centuries in Southern France

1 Quoted in Cunningham, "Employment and Unemployment of Children", p. 121.

2 For a useful survey of the evidence, see Rahikainen, *Centuries of Child Labour*, pp. 70-78.

3 Clarkson, *Proto-Industrialization*, pp. 16-19; Belfanti, "Rural Manufactures and Rural Proto-Industries", pp. 259, 266.

4 Rahikainen, *Centuries of Child Labour*, p. 38; Lis and Soly, *Poverty and Capitalism*, pp. 112-113.

employers could get abandoned children to work for them at no cost up to the age of twenty-five: one manufacturer in Toulouse had five hundred such children from institutions not only in Toulouse, but also from Carcassonne and Montpellier.[5] We have here an early example of something that characterizes child labour throughout its history, a willingness on the part of adults to transport children to the sites where work was available for them. There was a neat symbiosis between the need of manufacturers for cheap labour and the desire of those in control of institutions to find something for their charges to do. Conditions often amounted to gross exploitation. In Potsdam in the early nineteenth century the girls' orphanage contracted with two manufacturers who undertook to train two- to three hundred girls in lace work. The girls were "apprenticed" for seven years, had a nine-hour working day, and received no pay for the first five years, and thereafter one-sixth of the usual wage.[6]

The proto-industrial age was of critical importance in the history of child labour. It accustomed contemporaries to accept that children should work in manufactures – and often laud it. At a time when commentators were acutely aware of the dangers to social order posed by children who were without any structure to their days, work in these industries, whether in the family or via an institution, seemed to provide a solution to a nagging problem. From an institution's point of view, they offered some hope of financial viability, but they could also be justified as preventing idleness and as providing training for the young in the service both of their own futures and that of their nation. The sight of these children at work produced not revulsion but what one writer on the Shrewsbury House of Industry described as "the tear of benevolent sensibility": these children, at work from the age of five, singing "short moral songs" as they worked, reduced grown men to tears at the exquisite appropriateness of what they saw.[7] No one made any pretence of disguising what was happening: there were Schools of Industry in Britain, in Germany Spinnschulen. The children of the poor, said Maria Theresa in 1761, "should grow accustomed to hard work".[8] All over Europe children were doing so, and, as yet, it was seen more as a solution to a problem than a problem itself. Child work had become global in the sense that the products of the work children did were

5 Murat, "Travail des enfants", p. 154.
6 Melton, *Absolutism*, pp. 131-133.
7 Cunningham, *Children of the Poor*, pp. 18-32, quoting p. 26.
8 Quoted in Melton, *Absolutism*, p. 132.

exported all over the globe, but it had not yet become a matter of public concern; it was not perceived or described as "child labour".

It is easy to lose sight of proto-industrialism after the take-off of mechanization. But of course it continued alongside it. In London in the mid-nineteenth century Henry Mayhew had some telling examples of how in unmechanized trades where the possibilities of the division of labour were almost endless, severe competition had put a premium on child labour and a heavy discount on that of adults.[9] Such work was, as Colin Heywood has shown, a major feature of the French industrial scene in the nineteenth century. The "sweated labour" that so worried commentators in the late nineteenth and early twentieth centuries, and made much use of child labour, was in effect a degenerate form of proto-industrialism.

Mechanization

The introduction of water-power and later steam-power to drive machinery represented a step change in production techniques and in an associated division of labour in a competitive world. It facilitated an even more intense use of child labour.

The advantages of using child labour were overwhelmingly obvious, not only in Britain, the pioneer, but elsewhere in Europe. Think of those two British artisans going to France in 1784, arguing that "a child will do, with the aid of a machine, the work of over twelve excellent male or female Spinners in one day". Or of the enterprising citizen of Ghent, Lieven Bauwens, who in 1801 smuggled a mule jenny back from England, and laid the foundation for a textile industry that made extensive use of child workers. Or of the mechanical carding and spinning machines imported from England to Finland in 1800, and using child labour.[10] In short, the advantages of using the new machinery and associated child labour spread rapidly from their British base. Entrepreneurs could see that the new technology reduced labour costs by using cheap child labour and increased productivity.

"Child labour" as a phrase, and as a concept with negative connotations, was a product of the debates that accompanied the use of children to work mills, factories and coal mines during the Industrial Revolution

9 Thompson and Yeo, *Unknown Mayhew*, pp. 477-478.

10 Quoted in Heywood, "Child Labour and Child Labour Reform", this volume, pp. 137-158, 140; Scholliers, "Grown-Ups, Boys and Girls", pp. 202, 208; Rahikainen, "Historical and Present-Day Child Labour", p. 140.

in Britain. It stood in stark contrast to the celebration of child work in the eighteenth century. This idea that child labour was born in the Industrial Revolution in Britain comes up against familiar counter-arguments that the period of intensive use of child labour in (mainly) the textile industry was short-lived, that most children who worked in the industrializing countries worked in agriculture or in service, and that the use of the labour of very young children was in decline even before laws were passed to prevent it.[11] For present purposes, however, that of constructing a global narrative of child labour, they are not really relevant. For in a wider perspective, for good or ill, "child labour" came to have a close association with the industrializing process. As an Italian put it in the 1890s, "it is not only my opinion, but that of almost all the many authors who have written on the topic, that machines are the cause of child labour".[12] Child work in agriculture quite simply was not "child labour". It was seen as "natural", and sanctioned by its prevalence over many centuries.

There was an economic aspect to the debates about child labour as commentators wrestled with the possibility that in a free market there would inevitably be more and more use of child workers, and that economic progress and capital accumulation might be dependent on such use. But the economics were trumped by a sense of moral outrage that a society should be so out of step with "the order of nature" that it put children to work in place of their able-bodied fathers. These debates had a uniquely British tinge to them, as the British wondered whether they were creating "white slavery" at home while they were abolishing black slavery in the colonies, and felt that God might judge harshly a nation whose prosperity was built on child labour. But the issues in the debate could also be cast in universal terms. There emerged a body of feeling that began to look with abhorrence on the very idea of what Michael Sadler in 1831 called "work-children". "How revolting the compound sounds", he wrote. "It is not yet admitted, I think, into our language; I trust it will never be familiarised to our feelings".[13] The history of child labour from that moment is a story of economic pressures to use child workers set against that revul-

11 For recent contributions on this theme, see Horrell and Humphries, "Child Labour and British Industrialization"; Tuttle, *Hard at Work in Factories and Mines*; Kirby, *Child Labour in Britain*; Kirby and Cunningham, "How Many Children were 'Unemployed'?".

12 Quoted in Ipsen, *Italy in the Age of Pinocchio*, p. 87; see also, Heywood, "Child Labour and Child Labour Reform".

13 Cunningham, *Children of the Poor*, pp. 50–96, quoting p. 89.

sion at the thought of children working to which Sadler gave expression. The campaign to end or control child labour that still exercises us in the early twenty-first century, began in the 1830s and it was provoked by what people saw in the cotton mills and coal mines of industrializing countries.

There is, however, one aspect of Britain's experience that has received very little emphasis, and is of particular importance in establishing a global history of child labour. If we think of the cotton industry as not only what went on in Lancashire, but as an industry that had raw materials as well as manufacturing processes, then our assessment of the extent of child labour involved in it will be transformed. Britain's ability to dominate world cotton markets through its exports owed more to cutting the cost of the raw materials than it did to the productivity of new technology in Lancashire. As D.A. Farnie put it: "The decline in [raw] cotton prices made a far larger contribution throughout the whole of the nineteenth century to the reduction in the price of manufactures than either cost-cutting technological innovations or improvements in labour productivity."[14] In short, Lancashire's export success was built on driving down the cost of the raw material, and that meant using cheap and child labour. Children were involved at all stages in cotton's success, from growing the cotton to its transformation into yarn and cloth.

In the middle years of the nineteenth century, as John Bright put it, "what potatoes are to Ireland, cotton is to Lancashire".[15] If the raw cotton supply failed, Lancashire was ruined. Over three-quarters of Lancashire's supply came from the slave society of the Southern United States where the norm was for children at the age of twelve to be put to full-time work in the plantations. The American Civil War, and the interruption of supplies to Lancashire, gave an immense boost to cotton growing elsewhere. Most hope was placed in India, and Manchester merchants placed enormous pressure on British governments to do all they could to increase supply from India. In 1862 three-quarters of Britain's raw cotton imports were from India. Between 1855 and 1872 imports from India rose threefold, with a commensurate increase in the area under production.[16] Egypt's economy became even more geared than India's to cotton production: the area devoted to cotton growing increasing fivefold between 1861 and 1865, and raw cotton production then rose by a factor of six between the late 1860s

14 Farnie, *English Cotton Industry and the World Market*, p. 83.

15 Quoted in Harnetty, *Imperialism and Free Trade*, p. 36.

16 *Ibid.*, esp. pp. 49–57; Silver, *Manchester Men and Indian Cotton*.

and 1913.[17] The economic interests of Egyptian elites gelled with those of Lancashire manufacturers. We know little in detail about labour in the cotton fields in the nineteenth or early twentieth centuries, but in the mid-twentieth century, when figures for Egypt first become available, child labour accounted for at least half the total labour cost of production. There seems no reason to doubt that similar figures would apply for the earlier period. For nearly a century, through to the coming to power of Nasser in the 1950s, the Egyptian economy was geared to the production of highly-valued, long-staple, cotton whose production "depended on the intensive use of illiterate and poorly-paid labor and most particularly on the labor of children".[18] What was true for Egypt was likely to be the case elsewhere: globally, children were employed in weeding, thinning and picking cotton to feed the mills of the industrialized countries.

Our attention has been so focused on Lancashire that we have failed to appreciate the global impact on child labour of the mechanization of textiles. Historians of child labour need to be more global in outlook, looking to see how innovations in the developed world can spark off a demand for child labour thousands of miles away. We need to read between the lines of the histories of empire, between the lines because few historians of empire are at all alert to issues of child labour even though the economic links they demonstrate between metropolis and colony often suggest its prevalence. Most historians have treated with astonishment the naïve view that globalization is a new phenomenon of the late twentieth and early twenty-first centuries: we know that it was evident long before that. But we have not employed that knowledge in our understanding of child labour. We have not seen that the processes so familiar to us today, the use of cheap labour in an undeveloped economy to help reduce the costs of manufacture, date back to the earliest days of industrialization.

Capitalism, Colonies and Law

The passage of laws to control child labour, or the discussion of them, by industrializing countries in the 1830s and 1840s (Britain, France, Prussia, Austria, Russia, Switzerland, Massachusetts) marks the beginning of a process that continues to the present. That process was the creation of a framework of national and later international laws or agreements that would

17 Owen, *Cotton and the Egyptian Economy*, pp. 89, 123, 197.
18 Goldberg, *Trade, Reputation, and Child Labor*, *passim*, esp. p. 65, and quoting p. 2.

attempt to control use of child labour. It was prompted in part by outrage at the exploitation of child labour in certain work situations, especially textile mills and coal mines. Equally powerful was a utilitarian assessment that any benefits of child labour were outweighed by its costs. The children who worked the mills were physically in poor shape and ill-trained for any appropriate adult role. But there were, as has long been recognized, other forces at work. One of them was that leading employers were at precisely this time seeing advantages in an intensive rather than extensive use of labour. They were happy to see shorter hours of labour, provided that productivity increased in the hours that remained: the machines could go faster.[19] In this kind of environment children were more of a hindrance than a help. At the same time leading manufacturers were concerned that their businesses might be undercut by others that used cheap child labour. This operated at both national and international level. Employers, or at least some of them, wanted what came to be called a level playing field. Alongside this, adult male workers were worried that work that they had traditionally done might be simplified, divided up, and become the province of children. For all these reasons there was a momentum behind the movement to control child labour by force of law. Countries that were slow off the mark to legislate began to feel that it reflected badly on them. The Italians discussed at least eight proposals between 1870 and 1886, finally passing a distinctly modest one in 1886 in part because Italy was by then seen to be the only "civilised" nation without a child labour law. Even the Russians had passed a law in 1884.[20]

The Berlin conference of 1890 marks the moment when the bid to control child labour went international. Until the formation of the ILO after the First World War, international organizations could set targets that they hoped signatories might aim at, but they had absolutely no legal backing. The ILO era may be said to have lasted through to the Minimum Age Convention of 1973, which set fifteen as the "normal" minimum age for employment (it was fourteen for developing countries), hoping ultimately to raise it to sixteen. It was a period when it was thought both desirable and possible to "eliminate child labour" through international labour legisla-

19 Hobsbawm, "Custom, Wages and Work-Load"; Marx, *Capital*, ch. XIII, 3c; see also, Heywood, *Childhood in Nineteenth-Century France*, pp. 112-125, 322, and Rahikainen, *Centuries of Child Labour*, pp. 154-157.

20 Ipsen, *Italy in the Age of Pinocchio*, p. 95; Rahikainen, *Centuries of Child Labour*, pp. 142-144.

tion.[21] As we shall see shortly, the ILO's remit extended beyond the metropolitan core, where labour laws originated, to include the colonies.

From the middle of the nineteenth century child labour seemed to be in decline in most metropolitan countries. I don't want to enter into the causes of that – whether labour laws, increasing prosperity, school attendance laws, technological change, new attitudes to children, new managerial strategies or some combination of them. The outcome, however, was not in doubt.[22] By the end of the nineteenth century in the Western imagination child labour became something rather like slavery: there was shame, astonishment perhaps, that previous generations had turned a blind eye to it or defended it, but pride that action had been taken to control it, and a pervading sense that, but for a few pockets of survival, it was a thing of the past.

This was something of a delusion. Child labour in the developed countries continued through the twentieth and into the twenty-first century. By the late nineteenth century it was to be found not mainly in the central industries of the Industrial Revolution, but in a new niche of child jobs in the tertiary sector. The main reason for this was family poverty. Studies of the working-class family economy throughout Europe and North America in the late nineteenth century show convincingly that the contributions made by children were crucial, much more important in cash terms than those of adult women. As an extreme case we might take the poverty of families in the Apennines who apprenticed their children to padrones who put the children to work on the streets of Paris, London, New York, Moscow and anywhere else they might eke out a living performing with animals or musical instruments.[23] Much more mundane was the pressure on children from working-class families to begin earning as soon as they were able, normally while they were still at school, and to contribute their earnings to the family budget.[24]

There was also in the late nineteenth and early twentieth centuries a use of child labour reminiscent of the institutional kind we saw in the proto-industrial period. Children whose poverty or loss of one or both parents (orphanage in fact was relatively rare) resulted in them ending up in institutions, or in danger of so doing, had to be found work. And what was thought the most suitable work was often far away. The Children's Aid

21 Cunningham and Stromquist, "Child Labor and the Rights of Children", p. 73.

22 Cunningham, "Decline of Child Labour".

23 Zucchi, *Little Slaves of the Harp.*

24 Cunningham, "Decline of Child Labour", p. 420.

Society, based in New York, sent out sixty thousand children to work on farms, many of them in the Mid-West.[25] British children, eighty thousand of them in the late nineteenth and early twentieth centuries, were emigrated to Canada to work on the farms as labourers or servants. A Canadian, perhaps imperial, need gelled precisely with a metropolitan one.[26]

The role of colonies was not confined to finding a home for surplus children from the metropolis. In capitalism's imperialist phase colonies were seen also as markets, but more important as sources of raw material. The cheaper the raw materials could be extracted or produced the better, and, far from the metropolitan gaze, children could easily be employed. It is worth stressing how persistently the economies of regions had, almost fortuitously, become linked to imperial and capitalist production. Take, for example, the region between Agrigento and Caltanisetta in Southern Sicily. It happened to be rich in sulphur. For industrializing Britain sulphuric acid was the leading industrial chemical. There was rapid expansion of sulphur mining after the end of the Napoleonic wars, a challenge in the 1840s from an alternative supplier, Spain, and then, in the 1850s, the discovery of a new use for sulphur, to prevent a grape disease, meaning that France joined Britain as an importer. The work of mining was subcontracted to picconiere who employed boys – carusi – mainly to carry the sulphur out of the mines. By the end of the century there were eight thousand under-fifteen year-olds working in the mines, over twenty per cent of the workforce.[27] It is another example of the global reach of capitalism and of its reliance on child labour.

Sicily was not a colony, though the importance of sulphur supplies must have been one of many factors leading the British to place such weight on naval control of the Mediterranean. In real colonies capitalists could extract or cultivate raw materials without much impediment. We have seen how the British looked to colonies or near-colonies for raw cotton production. There are many other examples of child labour in the colonies to produce raw materials, particularly those that fed the consumer boom of the late nineteenth century: cocoa in the Gold Coast, for example, or tobacco and tea in Central Africa. There were attempts in the ILO era to control what was happening, but they were somewhat half-hearted. The ILO 1919 Convention banning the employment of children under fourteen in industrial employment was to be applied in colonies "except where owing to the

25 Hawes, *Children in Urban Society*, pp. 87–111.

26 Parr, *Labouring Children*.

27 Ipsen, *Italy in the Age of Pinocchio*, pp. 91–93.

local conditions its provisions are inapplicable", or "subject to such modifications as may be necessary to adapt its provisions to local conditions". These let-out clauses gave colonial regimes every incentive to drag their feet if legislation was proposed.[28] What would have provoked outrage in the metropolis could pass almost unnoticed in the colony. As late as 1956, the year before independence, it was said that in the Gold Coast, "the time is not yet ripe for progressive legislation to rationalize conditions of service on cocoa farms".[29] In other words, child labour continued unabated.

In 1862 Thomas Bazley, a leading spokesman for Lancashire's cotton industry, declared that "the great interest of India was to be agricultural rather than manufacturing and mechanical".[30] India, however, was to be the most notable example of a colony that failed to conform entirely to its intended role of producer of raw materials. From the 1870s Bombay capitalists rose to the challenge of rivalling the mighty Lancashire in the production of cotton goods. In a highly competitive arena they had one advantage no longer open to Lancashire. As Chandavarkar has noted, "cheap labour remained the chief competitive advantage of Indian industry", and the cheapest labour was child labour.[31] Laws prevented Lancashire from any longer employing children in the younger age ranges, and not surprisingly the demand for a level playing field was heard loud and clear from Manchester. If the metropolis had laws to control child labour, so also should the colonies.

The period between 1830 and 1970 can be seen as one in which there were attempts both in the metropolis and to a lesser extent in the colonies to bring child labour under some degree of control. Or, in other words, to put limits to the use of child labour by capitalists. Many capitalists were quite happy with this, but there were parts of metropolitan economies – for example sweated labour in the home – where the reach of the law was limited, and there were parts of the empires where that was equally the case. But the belief that governments had a right and duty to try to control child labour became deeply entrenched.

Out of this belief, and the success in controlling child labour that seemed to flow from it, there developed a model that assumes that the early stage

28 Cunningham and Stromquist, "Child Labor and the Rights of Children", pp. 72–73; Shivji, "Law and Conditions of Child Labour".

29 Van Hear, "Child Labor and the Development of Capitalist Agriculture", quoting p. 504; Chirwa, "Child and Youth Labour on the Nyasaland Plantations".

30 Quoted in Harnetty, *Imperialism and Free Trade*, p. 6.

31 Chandavarkar, *Origins of Industrial Capitalism in India*, p. 243.

of mechanization or industrialization will be associated with extensive use of child labour, as it was in Europe and North America, that all countries will go through this painful stage, but that all will eventually pass through it to emerge into a sunny upland where there is no child labour. It is what is often called the modernization model that has so dominated thinking since roughly the middle of the twentieth century. I want to suggest a different model: capitalism has an in-built tendency towards inequality. A lot of countries that are hopefully labelled "developing" are doing no such thing. There is no automatic developmental path that all countries will follow. Many countries are likely to remain in a state of dependency on the richer countries. In those countries, unless there are strong countervailing forces, child labour may be endemic rather than a passing phase.[32]

From the 1970s onwards the level of interference with the operations of a free market that had marked the previous century was under challenge. The legitimacy of controls was questioned, the benefits of a free market extolled. A consequence was an increase in the prevalence of child labour. Some analysts now make use of a set of ILO figures that purport to show the opposite, a steady decrease in child labour since the 1950s. These figures need to be handled with extreme caution for there is no reliable base line in the 1950s, and some of the subsequent figures are little more than guesses. Against these figures can be set evidence of a more compelling kind that suggests an increase in child labour in the late twentieth century. For example, the declining trends for the 1980s, in the view of the ILO itself, "can not be because less and less children were economically active". They were due to the fact that more and more countries passed legislation excluding those under fifteen from economic activity, and therefore subsequently did not count anyone under that age in the workforce.[33]

What I have outlined is intended to provide a framework for a history of child labour on a global scale – that is to say, "child labour" as it was first defined in the context of the mechanization of industry. But so far it almost entirely fails to make any reference to the types of work that children have most often and still most often do: work in agriculture and, what is often difficult to separate from it, work in service. It was estimated that in 1990

32 Cunningham and Stromquist, "Child Labor and the Rights of Children".

33 Ashagrie, "Statistics on Child Labour", p. xvi. For increases in the incidence of child labour in Ghana, Peru, the Philippines and Sri Lanka, see also, Cornia, Jolly and Stewart, *Adjustment with a Human Face*, pp. 106-107, 175, 213, 261. For uncritical use of the ILO figures, see, e.g., Basu, "Child Labor: Cause, Consequence, and Cure", pp. 1086-1087.

over three-quarters of all economically active children worked in agriculture, forestry, hunting and fishing. A higher percentage of economically active girls fell into this category than of boys. Is there a quite separate history of children working in agriculture and service, or can it be understood within the framework I have set out?

By and large it fits within the framework. Children's work on the land has rarely provoked the outrage that has become associated with their work in mills or mines. Romantic agrarianism may have been most potent in the United States, but it had a strong hold elsewhere. Many people saw nothing wrong with children working on the land. But, allowing for that, the forces that led children to work in what we think of as industry were the same as those that led them to work on the land: from the supply side, being in the care of the state or of a voluntary organization, poverty and a sense of family obligation, and from the demand side, a desire for cheap labour. Children in care were as likely to be sent to work on farms as in industry. In France, the organizers of orphanages and other such institutions, which were supposed to be places of protection, often came to prefer agricultural work for their charges, but this in no way reduced the level of exploitation the children suffered.[34] For other child workers in agriculture, it didn't make much difference whether the work on the land was for the family farm or peasant holding, on rented land, or on plantations, for in each case there was production for the market, and that had a tendency to create a demand for child labour. In short, agriculture was as much part of the capitalist world as mechanized industry.

Conclusion

I have suggested that the history of child labour globally can be understood only by locating it within the histories of capitalism and colonialism, and of responses to them.

In the first stage, proto-industrialism, the work of children, associated with the division of labour, was a key factor giving Europe its entrance into world markets for its manufactures. This was even more the case in the second stage when mechanization gave the early industrialising countries a more pronounced advantage in world markets. At the same time the raw

34 Guillaume, "Travail des enfants trouvés"; Richard, "Protection et utilisation des enfants"; Guillon, "Enfance assistée, enfance exploitée?"; Murat, "Travail des enfants".

material needs of the industrializing countries meant that in colonies child labour became a feature that endures to this day, of agricultural production for the metropolitan market.

In the third stage, in the later nineteenth and early twentieth centuries, child labour retreated from the mainstream industries of the industrialized countries, and found a new niche in service industries, the dominant reason for this being the necessity that children worked to ease the family poverty of the working classes throughout Europe and North America. The retreat of child labour (though not its elimination) from this service sector was associated with rising incomes and compulsory schooling.

Most analysts in the middle years of the twentieth century assumed that developing countries would follow this path of "modernization", and they sought, through the ILO and national legislation, to prevent these developing countries from suffering the same degree of child labour as, classically, had Britain.

From the 1970s onwards the removal of controls on capitalism resulted in an increase in the incidence of child labour globally. International, national and NGO attempts to re-impose some controls, especially from the second half of the 1990s, have been focused on the worst forms of child labour. The idea that child work as a whole might cease to exist is no longer thought either possible or even desirable.

CHAPTER 4

Why Do Countries Use Children to Industrialize?

Carolyn Tuttle

Most countries have industrialized on the backs of children whether historians examine eighteenth century Britain or development economists examine twenty first century Mexico. Children spun cotton thread in Great Britain, wove linen in Belgium, printed cloth in France and sorted coal in the United States. Their contemporaries cut sisal leaves in Brazil, gather onions in Mexico, sew garments in Guatemala, and pluck tobacco leaves in Honduras. Indeed, "child labour in the age of globalization challenges the idea of progress".[1] Although the use and abuse of child labor was/is invisible to some people and ignored by others, it caught the attention of several famous humanitarians and institutions. Karl Marx, considered an extremist at the time, was entirely accurate in his commentary on the role of child labor in the British Industrial Revolution:

> Children of nine and ten years are dragged from their squalid beds at two, three or four o'clock in the morning and compelled to work for a bare subsistence until ten, eleven, or twelve at night, their limbs wearing away, their frames dwindling, their faces whitening, and their humanity absolutely sinking into a stone-like torpor, utterly horrib*le* to contemplate.[2]

In a letter to Theodore Roosevelt in 1903, Mother Jones wrote:

> [...]We sought to bring attention of the public upon these little ones, so that ultimately sentiment would be aroused and children freed from the workshops and sent to school. I know of no question of to-day that demands graver attention from those who have at heart the perpetuation of this Republic. The child of to-day is the man or woman of to-morrow: the one

1 Rahikainen, *Centuries of Child Labour*, p. 218.

2 Marx, *Capital*, p. 227.

> the citizen and the other the mother of still future citizens. I ask, Mr. President, what kind of citizen will be the child who toils twelve hours a day in an unsanitary atmosphere, stunted mentally and physically, and surrounded with immoral influences?[3]

Eventually the responses to these pleas to eliminate child labor were addressed when the governments in the developed countries passed legislation setting a minimum age for employment. But, despite having passed national laws and having ratified international conventions, many developing countries still make extensive use of child labor. Joint ventures between Mexican and US growers, producing for the US, European, and Japanese markets "are achieving greater competitiveness at the cost of children working in the fields. We're creating a workforce without education, condemned to the lowest wages and to periods of great unemployment," says Gema López Limón, an investigator of child labor in Mexico.[4] In South Delhi raids on embroidery units at Sarai Kale Khan rescued 78 children who "are between eight and four years, used to work fourteen to sixteen hours every day and lived in an unhygienic atmosphere."[5] During the period of industrialization, child labor was used extensively in British, French, Belgian, and American textile mills[6] and British, Scottish, Welsh, American, and Canadian coal mines.[7] Similarly a large portion of the work forces of British, Welsh, Irish, and Belgian metal mines were children.[8] Currently, child labor is used on the tobacco, coffee, and sugar cane plantations of Argentina, Bolivia, Costa Rica, El Salvador, Guatemala, Honduras, and Nicaragua.[9] In addition, children are employed on the surface and underground in Bolivian, Brazilian, Colombian, Guatemalan, Honduran, and Nicaraguan coal and metal mines.[10]

3 http://libraries.cua.edu/achrcua/industrial/document. Last visit 2006.

4 Bacon, *The Children of NAFTA*, p. 31.

5 "78 Child Labourers Rescued", *The Hindu* (New Delhi, 2006), http://www.hindu.com/2006/05/30/stories.

6 Consult the following research by Tuttle, *Hard at Work in Factories and Mines*; Kirby, *Child Labour in Britain*; Heywood, *Childhood in Nineteenth-Century France*; and De Herdt, "Child Labour in Belgium".

7 Consult the following research of Tuttle, *Hard at Work in Factories and Mines*; Pott-Buter, *Facts and Fairy Tales*; and MacIntosh, *Boys in the Pits.*

8 Tuttle, *Hard at Work in Factories and Mines*; Heywood, *Childhood in Nineteenth-Century France*; Pott-Buter, *Facts and Fairy Tales.*

9 US Department of Labor, *By the Sweat & Toil of Children*, 1994, vol. 1.

10 *Ibid.*; US Department of Labor, *2003 Findings on the Worst Forms of Child Labor.*

The use and abuse of child labor in the formal and informal sector of many industrial economies is not a faded memory. Millions of working children are missing out on their childhood and losing the opportunity to become educated. Child labor remains the reality for millions of children born into poor and working-class homes in developing countries within Asia, Africa, and Latin America. Sub-Saharan Africa has the highest rate of children working, 26.4 per cent (1 in 4) while 18.8 per cent (1 in 5) work in Asia and the Pacific and 5.1 per cent (1 in 20) work in Latin America.[11] In 2000, the ILO documented that 7.5 million children between the ages of ten to seventeen work in Brazil, 8 million children under the age of 15 work in Mexico, 1.4 million children between the ages of seven to fourteen are employed in Guatemala, and 241,000 children between the ages of eleven to seventeen work in Honduras.[12]

Child labor is declining worldwide, however, with the greatest progress in the number of children found in hazardous work falling 26 per cent from 170.5 million in 2000 to 126.3 million in 2004.[13] Despite the progress "a staggering number of youths are still victims of abuse; there are over 1 million children annually forced into prostitution, trafficked and sold for sex or pornography each year; more than 300,000 children have been drafted into rebel armies; and nearly 5.8 million children are in some form of forced or bonded labor, working in homes, farms and factories as virtual slaves".[14]

Why is child labor an enduring problem? Initially, reformers and humanitarians asked why it was necessary to employ so many children in the textile mills and coal mines and lamented at the impact of the toil on children's mental and physical development. Today, children's rights organizations, labor unions, and educators are asking similar questions. Why has child labor persisted over time? What is it about industrialization that makes child labor essential? This paper attempts to answer these questions by developing a model which explains the extensive use of child labor in an economy during the early stages of industrialization. The first section describes how the nature of child labor changes when countries develop from an agricultural to an industrial economy. The second section develops a labor market model for children and argues that the increased employment and exploitation of children in industry is demand-driven. In the

11 International Labour Organization, *The End of Child Labour*, p. 8.
12 Schmitz, Traver and Larson, *Child Labor*, pp. 29, 80, 90, 125.
13 International Labour Organization, *The End of Child Labour*, p. 6.
14 Franklin, "Child Labor on Decline Globally", p. 6.

next section, statistical data at the firm and industry level reveal a disproportionate percentage of children employed in certain common "leading" industries in each country. Similarities in the social, economic, and political factors of Great Britain, Belgium, France, the United States, Brazil, Colombia, Guatemala, and Mexico will be incorporated into the model to show the relative importance of demand over supply-side factors. Once the historiography of child labor during the early periods of industrialism is fully understood, policy makers can target reforms at employers who play an integral role in the perpetuation of child labor worldwide.

Child Labor: Household Chores, Farming Duties or Sweatshop Jobs?

Children have worked for centuries in the home, on the farm and in family enterprises. Although most of this would be considered child labor, it is important to distinguish between chores and labor. The term "child labor" refers to children who work to produce goods or services which can be sold for money in the marketplace regardless of whether or not they are paid for their work. The definition used in the Convention on the Rights of a Child in 1989 will be adopted for this discussion in order to present comparable statistical evidence on child labor. The ILO Convention 138 has defined that minimum age for children to work. It should not be less than the age for completing compulsory schooling and in no event less than fifteen, with a concession to developing countries where it should not be less than fourteen years.

In the next pages I shall compare the extent and character of child labor in the early industrializers and in the countries of Latin America that industrialized at a later stage. Both firm and industry data is used in this research to show the importance of child labor in many of the leading industries during the industrialization of first world countries. The data reveals similarities among the labor forces of the past, industrializing Europe, and the present, developing Latin America. For Great Britain the micro-level data on individual factories is found in the *Factory Inspectors Reports* and *Mine Reports* commissioned by the House of Commons while the macro-level data capturing the whole population is contained in the *British Census of Population*. For Belgium, the data comes from the Industrial Census, which gives micro-level data for every occupation – *Statistique de la Belgique, Recensement Général, 1846*. Volume: Industrie. Brussels: Ministère de l'Interieur. The data on child labor for France is taken from Colin Heywood's 1988 book on *Childhood in Nineteenth Century France: Work, health and education among the classes populaires*. The information on child labor in the United States is compiled from Claudia Goldin and Kenneth Sokoloff's 1982 article "Women, Children and Industrialization in the Early Republic: Evidence from the Manufacturing Censuses" and Chapters 4 and 6 of Hugh Hindman's book *Child Labor: An American History* (2002). Documentation on the use of child labor in specific industries in Latin American countries was garnered from the six volumes of the US Department of Labor's series, *The Sweat and Toil of Children*, and the ILO's 1996 book *Child Labour: Targeting the intolerable*. The most recent statistics on the employment of children world wide was obtained from the 2006 ILO report, *The end of child labour: Within reach*. This data is fairly reliable because it is colleted and reported by government officials for most countries since 1980. The employment figures for children in the lower age brackets (ten to fourteen) are most certainly an underestimate of the true number of children working because by law it is illegal to employ a child under the age of fourteen. The fact that there are official reports of children working at this age, instead, presents interesting commentary on the adherence to the laws in that country.

Child Labor Becomes a Social Problem

Before the onset of industrialization, children had worked for centuries on farms, in homes, and in cottage industries. Children worked alongside their parents harvesting crops, tending husbandry, cleaning house, running errands, and spinning cotton. Although children worked all day and often worked six days a week, the tasks were not considered onerous or strenuous. Instead, children talked, sang songs, and even played at points in the day where the work load was light or the parent's attention intermittent. Furthermore, children were allowed to take breaks to eat, to use the bathroom, and to rest. Children's disobedience, moreover, was handled by parents who may have scolded or spanked a child for making a mistake. Whipping or beating children while working was generally unheard of in farming and cottage handicrafts.[15] Because families worked together and children were raised by their parents, society was complacent about this type of child labor.

In fact, many people viewed the employment of children as a positive feature of society. Political officials, wealthy aristocrats, landowners,

15 Nardinelli, "Corporal Punishment and Children's Wages".

and the general populace believed that keeping children busy by working avoided the immorally criminal behavior that they thought accompanied idleness. In 1925 United States Senator Charles S. Thomas argued that "The real problem in America is not child labor, but child idleness. You cannot convince me that it hurts a child either physically or morally to make him work. Where one child, in my experience, has been injured from work, ten thousand have gone to the devil because of lack of occupation[...]".[16] The founder of the Coca Cola Company, Asa G. Caudler, expressed a similar sentiment in 1886 when he said: "The most beautiful sight that we see is the child at labor. As early as he may get at labor the more beautiful, the more useful does his life get to be".[17]

And parents continuing with the family tradition wanted their children to work as they had when they were young. It was customary for children to contribute to the family "purse" while they lived at home. Without the child's contribution, however small, the family would often go without food, heat, clothing or housing. Horrell and Humphries have shown that in both factory and mining families, the child's financial contribution was significant.[18] Falling male wages or household shocks put increasing numbers of families into poverty and "it was supposed that no home could be kept going unless the children of five or six went to the mill".[19]

Finally, loving and caring parents sent their children to work because it was the only way they could learn skills to become self sufficient adults. Poor and working-class families did not view formal education as a way to invest in a child's future. Many parents often viewed education very differently than religious or government authorities. Based on their work experiences, informal education, not formal education, was the best approach for becoming skilled artisans, craftsmen or tradesmen. Working-class parents knew that the jobs available in the fields, textile mills, and coal mines did not require reading and writing. David Mitch confirms this in his research on the rise of literacy in Great Britain. He finds that from 1841-1871 fewer than ten per cent of the male dominated occupations required literacy and fewer than five per cent for female dominated occupations.[20] Sending children to school, moreover, was costly due to lost wages (opportunity costs) and school fees (out-of-pocket costs). Instead, the skills children needed

16 Quoted in Mofford, *Child Labor in America*, p. 44.

17 Mofford, *Child Labor in America*, p. 43.

18 Horrell and Humphries, "The Exploitation of Little Children".

19 Hammond and Hammond, *The Skilled Labourer*, p. 4.

20 Mitch, *The Rise of Popular Literacy*, p. 15.

were acquired while working – learning-by-doing and on-the-job training. Therefore, parents who sent their children to work were providing them the opportunity to become skilled independent adults. The absence of any investment in education makes sense economically because parents believed the private return to schooling was close to zero.

It is when child labor moved from the home (the family farm or family business) to the market (plantations, factories, or mines) that the nature of child labor changed dramatically during the British Industrial Revolution. Child labor became a social problem and people thought of it as a necessary evil of global competition. For children, working with one's parents in the family enterprise was dramatically different than working for a stranger in a capitalist-owned mill, factory or mine. The new industrial regimen demanded complete submission to the relentless automated machines. The factory clock replaced the sun in setting the hours of work and the steam engine replaced the stream which powered the machines and set the pace. Shifts were established with preset fixed hours that allowed only two quick recesses and one longer break for a meal. Children worked an average of twelve hours a day in hot stuffy factories and an average of eight hours in cold, damp coal and metal mines. The long hours, six-day work weeks, short and infrequent breaks and low wages took its toll on the young children.

Along with changes in the routine and the environment for laborers, society's views on the appropriateness of child labor changed. There were still the Optimists (Andrew Ure, a contemporary, and J.H. Clapham and Neil J. Smelser, historians) who believed that hard work was good for children because it taught them a strong work ethic and kept them busy and out of trouble. Andrew Ure, one of the few contemporaries who strongly defended child labor, witnessed the British industrialization unfold and described factory work in the following way:

> They seemed to be always cheerful and alert, taking pleasure in the light play of their muscles, – enjoying the mobility natural to their age. The scene of industry, so far from exciting sad emotions in my mind, was always exhilarating. It was delightful to observe the nimbleness with which they pieced the broken ends, as the mule-carriage began to recede from the fixed roller beam, and to see them at leisure, after a few second's exercise of their tiny fingers, to amuse themselves in any attitude they chose, till the stretch and

> winding-on were once more completed. The work of these lively elves seemed to resemble a sport, in which habit gave them pleasing dexterity.[21]

Clapham argued that factories were not as commonplace during the Industrial Revolution as historian's accounts had documented. He described an economy where a large number of small and medium-sized cottage industries existed alongside the textile factory. Clapham reminded historians that the plight of the child laborer was nothing new:

> How early the child began to help in industries carried on at home, either as handicraft or outwork, or to earn wages from a master is notorious. Whether the factories had lowered the age is doubtful. Factory-owning witnesses before the committee of 1816 had maintained that work began as early, and went as long, in domestic weaving as in the mills, and it was more laborious.[22]

But a group of Pessimists emerged – among them Frederick Engels, Karl Marx, and, at a later stage, S. Webb and B. Webb – who argued that children were being inhumanely exploited in the textile factories and coal mines. They believed that the children were subject to abuses and conditions that were oppressive, even by nineteenth century standards.[23] Philanthropists, enlightened political leaders, reformers, and doctors lamented at the physical, emotional, and intellectual deterioration visible in this new class of young workers. As a factory inspector remarked after examining the children working in a cotton factory:

> The effects of factory labour on children are immediate and remote: the immediate effects are fatigue, sleepiness, and pain, the remote effects, such as least as are usually conceived to result from it, are, deterioration of the physical constitution, deformity, disease, and deficient mental instruction and moral culture.[24]

Samuel Kydd, an outspoken Chartist observed in 1857:

21 Ure, *The Philosophy of Manufactures*, p. 301.

22 Clapham, *An Economic History of Modern Britain*, p. 565.

23 For a detailed discussion of the child labor debate refer to the article by Tuttle, "Revival of the Pessimist View".

24 House of Commons Paper, 1833 (450) xx *Factories, Employment of Children*. R. Com. 1st report, Minutes of evidence (Lord Ashley).

> In stench, in heated rooms, amid the constant whirling of a thousand wheels, little fingers and little feet were kept in ceaseless action, forced into unnatural activity by blows from the heavy hands and feet of the merciless over-looker, and the infliction by the sharpened ingenuity of insatiable selfishness.[25]

The Labor Market Model for Children: Supply and Demand

Why do countries rely on child labor during the early stages of industrialization? The literature has offered many different explanations for the increase in the employment of children during the British Industrial Revolution. Historians have identified poverty, greed, large-scale operations, technological innovation, and cheap labor as leading culprits for the increase in child labor. Some of these explanations assert that the increase in employment of children was supply-induced while others argue it was demand-induced. This paper applies a microeconomic model of the labor market for children to a given industry within a specific country at various points in time. In the labor market model for child labor, the equilibrium of demand and supply will yield a nominal wage rate and employment level for children. This equilibrium will change as various social, economic, and political factors shift either the demand or supply curve. Once these factors are identified, changes in the level of employment of children can be theoretically associated with the demand for labor by employers or the supply of labor by families. Knowing the driving forces behind child labor in the past and present will provide insights into the type of national and international policies that would be most effective in reducing the employment of children.

The main assumption of this model is that the labor market is perfectly competitive. If the labor market is competitive then the market wage paid to children reflects their productivity. In order for the labor market to be competitive, there cannot be a monopoly in the product market or a monopsony in the labor market. The existence of a monopoly in the product market seems unlikely for any country entering the industrial phase of development. Many countries, whether in Europe, Latin America or Asia resemble Britain as they apply the principle of the division of labor to the production processes. Early industrial society in Britain was characterized as one where competition was at its best. Hundreds of small producers in

25 Alfred, *The History of the Factory Movement*, p. 101.

the cottage industry competed alongside many medium-scale manufacturers to produce similar goods. Large-scale factories sprang up in urban centers and competed with one another to produce the cheapest and highest quality of wares. The countryside was littered with numerous stacks from coal and metal mines that were competing to extract the riches underground.[26] During the early stages of industrialization, no single firm had existed long enough to dominate the industry by driving out all of the other competitors.

While this evidence appears to rule out a monopoly in the product market, further discussion is necessary to dismiss the possibility of a monopsony in the labor market. Even in the most developed economies the existence of a single national market for labor is an over simplification. Instead, as in Great Britain, regional labor markets exist that are industry based which results in wage gaps among similar occupations and "pockets" of unemployment and labor shortages. Although limitations of travel in poor developing countries and the segmentation of the economy by skill and gender could potentially lead to local monopsony power, the likelihood of one employer dominating the market is remote. In Britain there were large numbers of textile factories in the manufacturing districts and no counties with only one factory. Similarly, although mining towns often grew around one large mining company, other mines were dug in the vicinity to extract from the same rich bed of coal.[27] Just as British families could move from one mill to another in search of better working conditions, Mexican families can leave one maquila for another located in the same Industrial Park.[28] Labor mobility is still a feature of industrial labor markets in developing countries today. Families are often footloose in search of work, taking along the children on their migratory path and exposing them to work opportunities rather than educational opportunities.

The Supply of Child Labor

The short-run supply of child labor represents the number of children available to work at various market wage rates. In general, the type of activities (work or leisure) a child pursues is determined by its parent's or

26 For a discussion of the competitiveness of the market see Ashton, *The Industrial Revolution*; and Nardinelli, *Child Labor and the Industrial Revolution*.

27 Tuttle, *Hard at Work in Factories and Mines*, App. 1, 2.

28 Fernández-Kelly, *For We Are Sold*; Tiano, *Patriarchy on the Line*.

guardian's preferences. To capture the dependent and submissive nature of children toward their parents, the child's labor supply decision is placed in a household production model. The family is assumed to maximize a common utility function in a specific time period which incorporates the preferences of all the family members in consuming market goods and "home" goods. Becker's unitary model[29] is used here instead of the more advanced collective models[30] because the primary focus is on the demand for child labor, not the supply. The family decides how to allocate each member's time between leisure, time spent in school, and time spent working either in the home or in the market within this maximization problem. The optimal allocation of time is one which maximizes family utility given certain budget constraints and market wage rates. The labor supply curve is upward sloping if higher wages can entice the family to give up some leisure (in this case, the child's leisure) to earn additional income. It can be thought of as the marginal willingness to give up leisure and supply work. Once the market wage exceeds the marginal product of home production, parents will "push" their children into factories and mines because their value in the market exceeds their value in the home. This is pure utility maximizing behavior on the part of parents, not unbridled greed, or family exploitation.

The supply of child labor would also increase for economic (poverty), social (custom), and political (absence of quality schooling) reasons. There appears to be a consensus that in poor families, children must work to help buy the necessities essential for survival. In the industrializing past, poor families, in the absence of social security and protection measures, have no choice but to send their children to work because they are unable to provide for the family on their low wages. Poor and working-class families in Mexico, Brazil, Colombia, and Honduras nowadays are making the same decisions as their historical counterparts in Britain, Belgium, and the United States. María Estela Ríos González of the National Association of Democratic Lawyers commented: "We realize that what drives the children into the fields is that the wages their parents receive (aren't) enough to support the family. We're but dreaming we can end this. But we have to do something".[31] López, a child labor investigator discovered that Lorena

29 Becker, "A Theory of the Allocation of Time".

30 See Bourguignon and Chiappori, "Collective Models of Household Behavior" for a discussion of the advantages of using an efficient household model over the unitary model and the cooperative game theory model.

31 Bacon, *The Children of NAFTA*, p. 35.

had been coming to the fields every year for seven years. "I finished first grade in primary school," she tells López, "but then I left." Her mother adds that she tried to send Lorena back to school, "but what I can earn here by myself isn't enough for us to live on, so she had to come help us."[32] The poverty of parents will increase the supply of children available and consequently increase the employment of children in the economy.

In many developing countries the expectation that children help their family is particularly strong: "In developing countries, children make substantial contributions to household income through child labour and also act as important sources of old-age security".[33] Children understand and accept their familial obligations to help their parents while they live at home and to provide for them in their old age. If the child's earnings are sizeable, custom and tradition will compel parents to send their children to work instead of to school. This increases the supply of child labor in the market which results in a lower market wage and higher level of employment for children.

The Demand for Child Labor

The short-run demand for labor represents the number of children employers would like to hire at various wage rates. Theoretically, in the labor market model, the demand for labor represents the preferences of employers in hiring children to combine with capital in the production of some product or service. The decision made by the employer is based on the value of the child's additional output (productivity). Because we assume that the employer is profit maximizing, the employer hires children up to the point where the additional cost of a child (the wage) equals the additional revenue the employer receives from that child (value of the marginal product). The value of the marginal product depends on the price of the product and the productivity of the child worker. The short-run demand for labor is a derived demand that depends on the existing level of capital services (plant and equipment), the price of the final product or service, and the current state of technology.

The demand for child labor will increase for economic (cheap labor), technological (labor intensive), and political (ineffective child labor laws) reasons. This paper identifies five factors which have been used to explain

32 Bacon, *The Children of NAFTA*, pp. 6, 31.

33 Rammohan, "The Interaction of Child-Labour".

the persistence of child labor in the past and the present. Many have argued that the main reason children are employed is because children are cheap; they can be paid extremely low wages. But this explanation does not tell the whole story. It also occurs that child labor is used in regions and industries where adults lay idle, unemployed. In other words, when adults would be cheap because unemployment is high, employers still hire children. Others, including the ILO and UNICEF have argued that the main cause of child labor is poverty – poverty of the family and poverty of the country. In defining the problem, the ILO claims that "poverty is the most important reason why children work. Poor households need the money which their children can earn, and children commonly contribute around 20-25 per cent of family income".[34] The ILO thus identifies poverty as the key piece in the child labor puzzle: "poverty and economic shocks clearly play an important if not a key role in determining the market for child labour".[35] This is not a complete explanation for the persistence of child labor because researchers have identified the counterfactual. There are several rich developed countries which use child labor – the United States, Australia, and the United Kingdom in the twenty first century. One of the richest countries, the United States, currently employs "more of its children in the workforce than any other developed country".[36] Finally, parents are often found to be acting within a specific cultural norm and within a dominant local custom when they send their children to work to learn skills necessary to become self sufficient. By sending their children to school instead of work, families feel that they would be putting their daily survival at risk. More recently, economists, economic historians and the ILO have argued that the absence of political action in passing child labor and compulsory schooling legislation has allowed the employment of children to go unchecked. This argument is partially misguided because child labor persists in developing countries where schooling legislation has existed for decades. Thus, we must look beyond these common explanations for a more compelling reason that child labor which began during the British Industrial Revolution still exists today in Mexico, Brazil, and Colombia.

34 Ilo/International Labour Office, *Child Labour* (1996), p. 17.
35 Ilo/International Labour Organization, *The End of Child Labour*, p. 24.
36 Levine, *Children for Hire*, p. 3.

Employment of Children in Leading Industries

The fact that children today work in the same industries as children did two centuries ago is not coincidence. These are the same industries that all industrializing societies have specialized in because of natural endowments of certain resources – land, water, minerals, and labor. As documented in table 4.1, the five most common occupations for children in countries as they develop include agricultural laborer, textile (cotton, wool, linen, hemp, lace and silk) worker and miner. Child labor is used in the leading industries of countries as these countries industrialize. The mighty cotton factory dominated the economies of Great Britain and the United States in the same way the textile and electronic maquilas dominate the Guatemalan and Mexican economies today. Rich deposits of coal fuelled the economic growth of Britain and the United States in a similar way that rich deposits of oil, gold, copper, and emeralds boost Brazil's, Chile's, and Colombia's economic development. What do these industries have in common in their early stages and why do they need child workers?

These industries all have the same type of innovations applied to their production processes. During the early stages of industrialization two types of technological change take place. The first involves the way in which production is organized while the second occurs in the machines that are used in the production process. As countries move from a pre-industrial to an industrial economy – production of goods becomes centralized to take advantage of the inanimate source of power. The production of a good is then divided into numerous one-step tasks such that workers become expert at the task. With the division of labor, specialization occurs and unskilled workers replace skilled craftsmen. Braverman identifies the division of labor as the fundamental principle of industrial organization. He argues that applying the division of labor to manufacturing was a salient feature of capitalism which arrived with industrialization.[37] This "dilution of skill" makes it easy for the employer to hire children, who are unskilled. Employers could just as easily hire unskilled adults, however. They prefer to hire children for two reasons – their emotional and physical characteristics. Emotionally, children by nature are submissive and docile and will not give the employer any trouble about the job (boring, repetitive, long hours, etc.). Physically, children have small supple bodies and nimble fingers to perform precise tasks or to maneuver in tight spots.

37 Braverman, *Labor and Monopoly Capital*, pp. 18, 72.

Table 4.1. Most Common Occupations Employing Children in the Past

Country	*Year*	*Industry*
Great Britain	1841	Domestic Service (652,856)
		Agriculture Labourer (210,935)
		Cotton Manufacture (106,964)
		General Labourer (39,897)
		Coal Mining (33,640)
Belgium	1846	Linen, hemp and lace manufacture (24,045)
		Cotton Manufacture (3,999)
		Other textiles (silk, flax) (3,674)
		Paper Manufacture (1,216)
		Coal Mining (10,339)
France	1839-45	Wool Manufacture (26,800)
		Food (6,889)
		Basic Metallurgy (6,340)
		Metalworking (6,315)
		Mines, quarries (6,256)

Numbers in parenthesis represent total number of children in occupation.
Sources: Great Britain – British Parliamentary Papers, *1851 Census of Great Britain – Population: Ages, Civil Conditions, Occupations and Birthplace*, 1851 Vol. *LXXXVIII*, Part *I*, Table 54, pp. cxxvii-cxlix;
Belgium – *Statistique de la Belgique*, Recensement Général 1846;
France – Heywood, *Childhood in nineteenth century France*, Table 4.2, p. 104.

The transition from a pre-industrial to an industrial economy does not occur easily because of the requirements of the new industrial regimen and the newly created separation between the owner of the business and the worker. The owners need to hire workers who will not complain or fight for their rights. Children are the perfect workers for these working conditions; they are easier to supervise and less likely to refuse to work, less likely to organize against employers, and more likely to respond to punishment. Children will work ten to twelve hours a day with only two short breaks, running back and forth without stopping, without complaining, until the whistle blows and it is time to walk home. And employers know they will come back the following day to do the same thing all over again.

They will not disobey the supervisor's commands because they are afraid of being punished. Employers view this submissive/obedient trait as a real asset to exploit. In the gold mines of Madre de Dios in Peru, "Children are very sought-after as workers. They don't complain. They keep their mouths shut. They work hard because they want to be like grown-ups".[38] In the textile factories in Mexico:

> Hundreds of thousands of very young woman have worked in foreign-owned maquiladoras on the Mexican border since the mid-1960s prompting critics to accuse multinationals of engaging in widespread exploitation of the most vulnerable sector of the local labor force. Unquestionably the companies have enjoyed great advantage over the workers, whose acute need for employment makes them ideally suited for assembly-line production. Fearful of losing their jobs, few are in a position to complain.[39]

Secondly, certain innovations which accompany industrialization favor the employment of children over adults in three ways. The first involve labor-intensive technology which increases the demand for children as helpers. The application of the principle of the division of labor to the production processes of making cloth and extracting coal and minerals increases the number of secondary workers. The second type of technological change that increases the demand for child labor is the inventions that make it possible to replace adults with children. The degree of substitutability between children and adults varies considerably by industry and often even within a given industry. For example, it was Roberts' automation of the common mule and Cartwright's automation of the hand-loom that dramatically reduced the effort and strength required to operate these spinning and weaving machines, eliminating the need for strong, skilled operators. Finally, the third type of technological change that favored children were inventions and work situations that had special technical requirements. In this case, the children actually had a comparative advantage in working in some situations and with certain machinery because they either had "nimble fingers" or could maneuver in tight spots. For example, children could maneuver in smaller openings and spaces in underground tunnels of mines which often stood only three feet high.[40] In this instance, children were

38 US Department of Labor, *By the Sweat & Toil of Children*, vol. 2, pp. 17–18.

39 Martinez, *Border People*, p. 186.

40 House of Commons Paper, 1842[380] xv *Children's Employment (mines)*, R. Com 1st rep. (Thomas Took and Southwood Smith), pp. 47–65.

essential because of their size and agility which enabled them to perform work in situations where adults simply could not fit or maneuver. Thus, the innovations which occurred during the early stages of industrialization were biased toward the employment of children such that employers not only *wanted* to hire younger workers but in some cases *needed* to hire children for their plantations, factories and mines.

The similarities between the past and present places of employment lend support for the above argument that child labor is a demand-driven phenomenon. Child labor is concentrated in industries where specialization and the division of labor have been applied to the production method. This pattern emerges from table 4.2. Table 4.2 lists the specific industries where child labor has been documented by researchers, the ILO and the US Department of Labor. In large plantations crops such as tea, coffee, tobacco, strawberries, sisal, and sugar have distinct labor intensive phases in production. In Guatemala and Honduras "children as young as six work with their parents on huge coffee plantations. They usually pick and sort beans, but they can also carry sacks of coffee that weigh up to 150 pounds".[41] In Bogota Colombia, children work in many stages of the cut flower industry, "children who work on the plantations perform virtually all tasks required for the cultivation and processing of cut flowers, with the possible exception of work in the cold rooms".[42] In countries where capital is expensive, the spinning, weaving, and sewing stages of textile products divide production into numerous simple tasks which can be labor intensive and labor substituting. This is obvious in Preito's conclusion on the sentiment of the young female maquila workers, "they feel a certain disdain as they endure the disgrace of being stuck for so many hours in the factory repeating the same boring, painful, and fatiguing movement a thousand and one times".[43] It is also pervasive when children are hired by subcontractors that produce for larger garment maquilas. In the San Pedro de Sacatepequez area of Guatemala, a modern version of the British cottage industry exists – "the area has been renamed 'the cradle' or 'the city of maquila' because in every home there are women and children sewing without any rights or legal protections".[44] In Colombia, "the informal sector – which is more elastic, less protected, more labour-intensive and less capital-intensive than the formal sector – tends to rely on children as a readily available source of

41 Springer, *Listen to Us*, p. 33.
42 US Department of Labor, *By the Sweat & Toil of Children*, vol. 1, p. 51.
43 Prieto, *Beautiful Flowers*, p. 45.
44 US Department of Labor, *US Code of Conduct*, p. 83.

additional labour".[45] Similarly, the production of bricks, pottery, glass, and fireworks has been broken down into numerous steps in order to create an efficient assembly-line production method. The children of Argentina and Guatemala are performing the same tasks their predecessor had in Belgium, Great Britain and the United States.

The final source of technological bias towards children is situational. There are certain types of machines and specific working conditions where children have an obvious comparative advantage. In many fruit and vegetable plantations in Brazil, the US Department of Labor found that "some employers hire children because they are lighter and more able to climb trees without breaking branches."[46] As an electronic maquiladora manger said, "women have natural qualities that make them ideal for these positions. Their delicate hands endow them with finesse and precision. Moreover, the female psyche more easily endures the repetitive work".[47] Mining, one of the few industries that remains labor intensive, keeps costs down and maximizes coal or mineral yield by using workers of small physique. This rings true for most of Colombia's small, informal and marginal mining operations. The US Department of Labor's report found that "it is in these small scale marginal mining operations, which are illegal and generally more dangerous, that children are commonly employed".[48] Child labor is also apparent in Mozambique and South Africa, where Harries found that the "low grade and depths of the mines required narrow slopes in which children could work more efficiently than adults".[49] Although this specific labor demand no longer exists in the industrialized countries, it persists in many developing countries because they do not have the machines to dig deep and large passageways.

45 Vila, "The Working Child in Colombia", p. 97.
46 US Department of Labor, *By the Sweat & Toil of Children*, Vol. 2, p. 67.
47 Prieto, *Beautiful Flowers*, ch. 3.
48 US Department of Labor, *By the Sweat & Toil of Children*, Vol. 1, p. 52.
49 Harries, *Work, Culture, and Identity*, p. 201.

Table 4.2. Percentage of Children Working in Leading Industries in the Past and Present

Country	*Year*	*% of Work Force/ages*	*Specific Industries*
Argentina	2003	0.4% (10-14) 20.4% (15-19)	tea, tobacco, strawberries, flowers, street sales, domestic labor, brick work, trash pickers
Belgium	1846	21% (<16)	beet, oat and flax fields, linen, hemp, lace, cotton, wool, coal mining, quarries, potteries, paper
Brazil	2003	11.5% (10-14) 49.2% (15-19)	oranges, sugar, sisal, tobacco, textile & garments, tin and gold mining, footwear, charcoal, service
Colombia	2003	0.6% (0-11) 22.6% (12-17)	cut flowers, coca picking, coal mining, emerald mining, leather tanning, street vending
France	1839-1845	12.1% (<16)	cotton, wool, linen, hemp, paper, metal-working, pottery, mines
Great Britain	1833	15% (5-13) 40% (13-18)	cotton, wool, flax, silk, lace potteries, coal and metal mining
Guatemala	1999	49.4% (10-14) 52.2% (15-19)	tea, coffee, sugar, macadamia nuts, garment maquilas, fireworks, stone quarries and mines, construction, domestic service
Mexico	2004	7.0% (10-14) 37.8% (15-19)	strawberries, onions, tomatoes, coffee, textile maquiladoras, canning
United States	1820	23% (<16)	strawberries, peas, cranberries, cotton mills, coal mining, paper, glassworks, street vendors

Source: For Latin American countries, the official government statistic for the economically active population is reported from the Population Census for each country on website http://laborstat.ilo.org/cgi-bin/brokerv8.exe. For Great Britain participation rates were calculated based on factory returns published in the House of Common Papers, *1834(167) XIX, Supplementary Report, Part I, pp. 19-39*. For Belgium the participation rates were calculated based on the 1846 Industrial Census, *Statistique de la Belgique, Recensement Général*. For France, the statistics are from Heywood, *Childhood in nineteenth-century France,* Table 4.2 which are based on the 1847-52 French Industrial Census, *Statistique de la France, Industrie*. The figure for the United States is taken from Goldin and Sokoloff, "Women, Children and Industrialization in the Early Republic," *Journal of Economic History*, XLII, no. 4, 741-774.

The contribution and visibility of child labor in these specific industries is quite extensive. Table 4.2 gives the portion of the work forces in the leading industries comprised of children. Since these are official government statistics, the figures may not be very accurate but they anyway provide a broad indication of the high likelihood of children's participation in these industries. Children comprise at least twenty per cent of the work forces of the leading industries. The percentage of children currently working in Argentina and Colombia is almost identical to the percentage of children who worked in nineteenth century United States and Belgium – twenty per cent. In addition, countries where child labor is extensive, employ children in roughly the same proportion as Great Britain did. In Brazil and Mexico children comprise between forty to fifty per cent of the work force in those leading industries. These statistics dispel any myths which claim that child labor's contribution during industrialization is negligible.

Conclusion

Child labor has persisted across time and continents. The extensive use of child labor today in developing countries is undeniable. Sixteen per cent of the world's children work. Child labor is still very common on many continents; 26.4 per cent of children aged five to fourteen work in Sub-Saharan Africa and 18.8 per cent of children aged five to fourteen work in Asia and the Pacific and 5.1 per cent in Latin America and the Caribbean.[50] Children continue, as their predecessors did, to work outside on plantations, inside in textile mills, and underground in mines. Why does it seem that history is repeating itself? Is it because of the poverty in a country that makes it necessary for children to work? If true, this would imply that once a country industrialized and produced wealth, child labor would disappear. Researchers, however, have documented considerable child labor in rich countries such as the United States, Australia, and the United Kingdom. Is it because of global competition and the profit incentives to keep costs down? Undeniably child labor is the cheapest form of labor for employers to hire. If children are hired solely because they are cheap, it would imply that children would always be hired over adults and that child labor would persist in industries forever. The historiography of child labor tells quite a different story. Cheap child labor was only hired by some employers and

50 Ilo/International Labour Organization, *The End of Child Labour*, pp. 8–9.

only during certain stages of their company's production. Child labor was extensive during the nineteenth century in textile, glass, and paper manufacture in Great Britain, Belgium, France, and the United States. There was very little child labor found working in earthenware, woodworking, or leather processing. In the twenty first century child labor is extensive on tea, tobacco, coffee, cotton, orange, sisal, and flower plantations in Latin America. It is rarely seen, however, on rice, beans, or corn plantations.

The only viable explanation which fits with all of the historical and contemporary evidence on child labor is that employers must want to hire children. Child labor is therefore a demand-driven phenomenon, not supply-driven. Tables 4.1 and 4.2 reveal that child labor is concentrated in industries where specialization and the division of labor are applied to the production method. Industrialization brings about changes in the production process which create a new industrial organization among workers, managers and owners. The skilled craftsman who produces a unique finished product is replaced by the unskilled machine operator who performs the same task over and over, never seeing the finished product. The new industrial organization increases the quality and quantity of products produced because the workers become expert at one task. In this new industrial regimen where the division of labor and specialization is applied to the production process, employers need to hire workers with special attributes. Employers want to hire children because children are relatively more productive than adults. Children are more productive because they have the emotional and physical characteristics required by this new industrial organization. Emotionally, children by nature are obedient and docile which makes them easier to manage. Children are much less likely to complain, stop working, or form unions. Industrialists, owners, and managers find getting children to work long hours doing monotonous tasks was much easier than forcing adults into the same rigid demanding schedule. Physically, children are smaller, more flexible, quicker, and able to perform precise tasks and maneuver in tight spots than adults.

Children are especially productive workers given their special attributes and the type of technological change which occurred. Most of the technological change during the Industrial Revolution increased the demand for children over adults in three ways. The first type of innovation applied the principle of the division of labor to the production process. As the number of simple tasks increases, whether it is in spinning cotton or picking tobacco leaves, production becomes labor-intensive and the number of secondary workers increases dramatically. Children, because they are small and unskilled, could easily assist adults on the crowded factory floor or in the highly dense field. The second type of innovation which increases the demand for child labor is labor-substituting. Mechanical inventions which reduce the amount of skill and strength required to perform a task make it easier for children to replace adults as the primary operators. The new machines did most of the work while the worker "tended" over them. Children become spinners, weavers, combers, dyers, and sorters as primary operators of the machinery. Finally, the third type of innovation that favored children was the inventions and work situations that had special technical requirements. Some tasks required speed and fine motor skills while others required smallness and agility, qualities children possess. The "piecer" on the water frame who tied knots quickly or the "breaker boy" who separated the coal from the slate as it rushed below him were jobs that children had a comparative advantage in over adults. Similarly, children were the only workers able to maneuver in the underground coal and metal mines where the seams were thin and the tunnels less than three feet high. Children could also more easily operate machines low to the ground as well as run under moving parts to clean them. Employers realized that the most efficient style of industrial organization and the most productive use of the new technology required child labor. Irregardless of public disapproval, national laws, and international conventions employers needed to hire children to be profitable and competitive.[51]

51 See also United States, Department of Labor, reports: http://www.dol.gov/ilab/media/reports and from the International Labour Organization /Office: http://www.ilo.org/Search3/search.do.

CHAPTER 5

School, Child Labour and Rationalization in Industrializing Europe

Marjatta Rahikainen

The use of industrial child labour decreased and primary-school attendance increased in many parts of Europe during the late nineteenth century. Contemporaries gave the laws on child labour and compulsory education the credit for this development, and eventually their interpretation became a kind of common wisdom. However, contemporary reformers, and in their wake historical writing, may have overrated the power of these laws. The celebrated education laws overshadowed the fact that school attendance also increased in countries that had not introduced compulsory education. Similarly, the spectacular argumentation for and against industrial child labour in nineteenth-century Britain and France dominated contemporary and subsequent perspectives. Not all countries witnessed fervent agitation against it, and yet everywhere at some point of time the trend turned downwards and industrial child labour declined.

My focus in this article is on two issues: the introduction and implementation of compulsory primary education and the late-nineteenth-century decline in the use of industrial child labour. My scanning of standard information on the introduction of compulsory education in encyclopedias, laws, and historical writing revealed that it is far from clear when and under what laws primary education actually was made compulsory in different European countries. This makes it problematic to attribute it to the decline in the use of child labour. The fact that we can follow the development of these two phenomena in nineteenth-century Europe does not enable us to conclude that the one was the cause of the other. Proving any causality would require consistent and long-enough time-series evidence of both – but how many countries can provide that? I suggest that the declining demand for industrial child labour in the late nineteenth century made way for children's school attendance, which by that time was already gaining support among the populations concerned.

Although statistical information is scarce, it seems that the turning point can be traced to the late-nineteenth-century international economic depression. Moreover, the diminishing demand for industrial child labour implies a keener monitoring of productivity and profitability, arguably enforced by increasing international competition. Later on the dissipation of the principles of Taylorism, or scientific management, studies on fatigue and time-motion studies sealed its fate.

By discussing such issues, I also aim to expand the frames in which nineteenth-century child labour is examined from the traditional nation-state approach to a European-wide perspective. Furthermore, it seems to me that the discussion on the history of child labour in Europe is disproportionately coloured by the British case. After all, despite all the economic and cultural integration in eighteenth- and nineteenth-century Europe, the discrepancy between the leading economic power Britain and the largely agricultural European periphery was in many respects striking. The debate between Peter Kirby and Hugh Cunningham on how many children were "unemployed" in eighteenth- and early-nineteenth-century England is a case in point.[1] Not only is the kind of quantitative evidence that they discuss largely non-existent for the period concerned in most of Europe, but even the concept of "child unemployment" appears problematic. Children's "idleness" certainly was an issue in many nineteenth-century European cities, and the coming of industrial child labour may have been welcomed by the poor-relief authorities for offering paid work to children. Nonetheless, in many cases the concept of child unemployment seems out of place – and this is not just a matter of how we define unemployment.

Two Nordic cases exemplify this. First, in early modern Stockholm with its large-scale pauperism, children begging in the streets were subject to many kinds of measures, but the idea of children being "idle" in the sense of unemployed does not seem to have featured in the contemporary discussion. The authorities were concerned more about how pauper children would learn the Catechism than about their lack of work. They strove to limit children's leisure time primarily because "idleness" was considered to constitute a moral danger, and several kinds of pauper schools (*fattigskolor*) were established to keep children off the streets. At the beginning of the nineteenth century Stockholm was a stagnating city with severe

1 Cunningham, "Employment and Unemployment of Children"; Kirby, "How Many Children were 'Unemployed'?"; Cunningham, "How Many Children were 'Unemployed'?: Reply".

unemployment, which was reflected also in the labour market for children. Only now was "idleness" in the sense of child unemployment perceived, even though the concept of unemployment did not yet exist. In order to keep children occupied until they entered the labour market, the 1807 Plan for Poor Relief in Stockholm even suggested compulsory education up to the age of thirteen years. In these inauspicious economic circumstances, parents in the lower social groups seem to have reacted rather rationally. Large numbers of children were set to school (of some kind) for a few years at least, although school attendance was not compulsory. It made sense to parents to send their children to school because they would at least learn the Catechism, which they had to know in any case by the time they were confirmed around the age of fourteen or fifteen. Moreover, even if religion took the bulk of the time in pauper schools, children's school attendance also brought with it material advantages to their families.[2]

Secondly, unlike in Britain, the demand for child labour in early nineteenth-century Finnish towns and cities seems to have been limited, even taking into consideration that, in general, children are seldom visible in the sources. Had urban child labour been really common, however, it would have left more traces. Thus the concept of child unemployment does not appear relevant. One of the few contemporary chroniclers, an old maid running a small school in the commercial seaport town of Oulu (Uleåborg in Swedish) often mentioned various children's activities but never referred to "idleness" and the like. At that time school took little or no time in children's lives, and very few children in Oulu seem to have been occupied by paid work of any kind, save occasionally for boys rowing passengers over the river or driving a cart.[3] It took another half a century for urban children's "idleness" to become a current concept in Finland, by which time practically all urban working-class children were already attending folk school for at least two to four years, though it was not compulsory. What gave the authorities reason to react to "idleness" and to organize unpaid work for school children was these children's activities out of school hours in the streets and public places, for money and amusement, and the transition of primary-school leavers from school to work.[4]

2 Sandin, *Hemmet, gatan, fabriken eller skolan*, pp. 104–126, 202–207, 240–259, *passim*. See also Sandin, "Education, Popular Culture and the Surveillance of the Population in Stockholm".

3 Wackling, *Hundrade minnen från Österbotten*, pp. 230, 236, *passim*.

4 Rahikainen, "'Ingen mat utan arbete'"; Rahikainen, "Children and 'the Right to Factory Work'", pp. 56–59.

Likewise, generalising to the rest of Europe Hugh Cunningham's discussion of children's unemployment in the English countryside is problematic. What makes the history of rural childhood in England often appear so different from its northern European counterparts is the issue of land ownership. Unlike in England, in German-speaking countries, and in Scandinavia and Finland, the elaborate and strict hierarchy among "peasants" (as they are inaccurately called in English) was first and foremost based on land ownership and access to land, on which depended access to other resources, including proper school education. Children's prospects were quite different depending on whether they were born as sons and daughters of the landless or of independent landed farmers. Given the dominance of land in the peasant world view, I would think that in most of Europe the idea of child unemployment may have been rather alien to the peasant reasoning before the profound changes – called for convenience the agricultural, industrial and consumer revolutions – occurred. School attendance made sense to the landless only when learning to read, write and calculate opened up new perspectives. It was only then that parents really had reason to ponder over their children's time use, and rural children's days became organized by the clock.[5]

In the following I first consider the issue of compulsory education and its introduction in different European countries. Then, in the context of the general economic picture I discuss the downward trend in industrial child labour in late nineteenth-century Europe. My aim in the concluding section is to open up new perspectives on historical writing about child labour.

Introduction of Compulsory Education – A Fuzzy Story

In many European countries the introduction of compulsory education was a stepwise process, and it is open to interpretation when it became universal. Exactly which one of many school laws in each country is considered to have given it legal force seems to be a matter of conjecture, since laws rarely had the term "compulsory education" in the name.

Nineteenth-century encyclopedias illustrate this indefiniteness. The *Encyclopædia Britannica* contained little of compulsory education, although it featured in the eighth edition (1858) in the discussion of the role of the state

5 Martinson, *Growing Up in Norway*, pp. 101-114; Rahikainen, *Centuries of Child Labour*, pp. 78-82, 112-118.

in education. Here it was stated that education in the hands of government may be "employed for state purposes", as examples of "any of the more despotic countries of Europe" had proved, the worst being Austria, followed by Prussia – although it was admitted that "the Prussian people [were] really educated throughout the community" and "according to their relative stations in life".[6] At that time primary education was not compulsory in Austria – unless Maria Theresia's edict of 1774 is accepted as its introduction.[7] The Austrian *Reichsvolksschulgezetz* of 1869 is considered to have introduced eight years of compulsory education (*Unterrichtsplicht*), even though the act allowed for an abridged curriculum and exemptions from attendance requirements that were substantially broadened under the law reform of 1883.[8] The *Encyclopædia* entry promoted Holland as a country in which public primary education "may be regarded as fully equal in efficiency to that of Germany, – in some respects, indeed, superior, – and the number of children actually found in the schools shows that although the attendance is not compulsory, yet almost the entire population is really educated". In contrast, primary education in France "has always been, until recent times, in a lamentable defective state". The Guizot law of 1833 was given credit for any recent amelioration and was also presented in great detail.[9]

The German *Brockhaus* encyclopedia did not mention compulsory education in its fifth edition (1822), although it described school systems at length, including public rural schools (*Landschulen*, or *Dorfschulen*). Originally these village schools, established after the Reformation, concentrated on preparing the peasant youth for their first communion, suggesting plenty of Catechism reading. However, according to the *Brockhaus* entry, instruction improved after 1772. The writer of the entry deplored the fact that village schools were still weakly attended. Children stayed away in winter because they lacked clothes and in summer because they were working for their daily bread (*Broterwerb*), and those whose parents were away fulfilling their labour obligations to their landlord frequently missed school. The fifth edition of *Brockhaus*, referred to northern Europe as being far ahead of southern European countries such as France in organising popular educa-

6 *The Encyclopædia Britannica, Eight Edition* (Edinburgh, 1858), vol. 15, entry *National Education*, pp. 813-817; *Ninth Edition* (Edinburgh, 1877), vol. 7, entry *Education*, p. 681.

7 Flora includes it in the column "Compulsory Education" as "1774: Principle of compulsory education, introduced by Joseph II, met with resistance". Flora, *Sate, Economy, and Society*, vol. I, p. 555.

8 Papathanassiou, *Zwischen Arbeit, Spiel und Schule*, p. 235.

9 *The Encyclopædia Britannica, Eight Edition*, p. 818.

tion (*Volksunterricht*), but Germany was not put forward as a forerunner or as superior to Holland, Denmark or Sweden, for instance.[10]

By the seventh edition of the *Brockhaus* (1830), the German standpoint had changed, although the entry writer could not come up with much to boast about, nor did his follower in the eighth edition (1836).[11] The ninth (1847) and tenth editions (1854) then boasted that "[a]mong the countries of Europe, the school institution is the most blossoming in Germany". Interestingly enough, the rhetoric now placed less emphasis on religion and more on the needs of the national economy and on nationalism, "*vaterländische Gemeingeist*". Sachsen was said to have been the model until the Napoleonic Wars, but after 1816 Prussia had led the school reforms and served as a model for all Europe. The countries that had followed the German example (Austria, Holland, Denmark, Sweden and Switzerland) had succeeded in establishing "more regulated school institutions". Now Germany was also a leading country in terms of compulsory education: "In France and England nothing is yet known of compulsory school attendance [*Schulzwange*], which exists all over Germany". However, the *Brockhaus* entries in the ninth and tenth editions did not refer to any particular laws associated with it, nor did the eleventh (1868) and thirteenth editions (1886).[12] They did not appear until in the fourteenth edition (1895), with a reference to the Prussian *Principia regulativa* of 1737 (1736) and *Generallandschulrecht* of 1763.[13] Another German encyclopedia, Meyer's *Conversations-*

10 *Allgemeine deutsche Real-Encyclopädie für gebildeten Stände (Conversations-Lexicon), Fünfte Original-Auflage* (Leipzig, 1822), vol. 5, entry *Landschulen*, pp. 603-605; vol. 8, entry *Schulen*, pp. 836-850.

11 *Allgemeine deutsche Real-Encyclopädie für die gebildeten Stände (Conversations-Lexikon): Siebenter Originalauflage* (Leipzig, 1830), vol. 9, entry *Schulen*, pp. 882-896, 891; *Allgemeine deutsche Real-Encyclopädie für die gebildeten Stände (Conversations-Lexikon): Achte Originalauflage* (Leipzig, 1836), vol. 9, entry *Schulen*, pp. 874-883, and *Schulzucht*, pp. 896-897.

12 *Allgemeine deutsche Real-Encyclopädie für gebildeten Stände: Conversations-Lexikon, Neunte Originalauflage* (Leipzig, 1847), vol. 13, entry *Schulen*, pp. 27-31, quoting pp. 27, 30; *Allgemeine deutsche Real-Encyclopädie für gebildeten Stände: Conversations-Lexikon, Zehnte verbesserte und vermehrte Auflage* (Leipzig, 1854), vol. 13, entry *Schulen*, pp. 651-658, quoting pp. 654, 658; *Allgemeine deutsche Real-Encyklopädie für die gebildeten Stände: Conversations-Lexikon, Elfte, umgearbeitete, verbesserte und vermehrte Auflage* (Leipzig, 1868), vol. 13, entry *Schulen*, pp. 379-383; *Brockhaus' Conversations-Lexikon: Allgemeine deutsche Real-Encyklopädie, Dreizehnte, vollständig umgearbeitete Auflage* (Leipzig, 1886), vol. 14, entry *Schulen*, pp. 512-515.

13 The *Brockhaus* of 1895 dated the first North-German ordinance on compulsory education to the end of the seventeenth century. *Brockhaus' Konversations-Lexikon, Vierzehnte vollständige neubearbeitete Auflage* (Leipzig, 1895), entry *Schulzwang, Schulplicht*, p. 648.

Lexicon, did not mention compulsory education in its first edition (1851),[14] but by the sixth (1907), the Prussian *Principia regulativa* of 1717 had become established as the law that definitely indicated its introduction in Germany.[15] Subsequent generations of German encyclopedia writers managed to find still earlier laws, such as the Weimar *Schulordnung* of 1619, that may have fulfilled this purpose.[16] Nowadays, several major Prussian eighteenth-century school acts feature in this role,[17] while the *Weimar Act* of 1619 appears as just one of several similar post-Reformation acts.[18]

Being among the pioneers does not seem to have been of importance before the mid-nineteenth century. H. Heppe still mentioned the edict of 1717 only in passing in his comprehensive work on the history of the German *Volksschule*, published in 1858, and did not associate it with compulsory education. In fact, he seems to have considered post-Reformatory compulsory education (*Schulpflicht*) as primarily preparing children for their first communion.[19] Soon enough Prussia and Austria were waging a kind of tacit war over which of them led the field in folk-school development. No wonder, then, that in 1910, in his extensive history of Prussian folk schools, Heinrich Lewin proudly described the edict of 1717 as "most important because it introduced compulsory school attendance".[20]

By the 1890s, France was using the introduction of compulsory education as a criterion by which to classify countries. According to the French

14 *Das Grosse Conversations-Lexicon für die gebildeten Stände*, (Hildburgshausen, 1851), vol. 2:8, entry *Schule*, pp. 55-59.

15 *Mayers Großes Konversations-Lexikon: Ein Nachschlagewerk des allgemeinen Wissens, Sechste gänzlich neubearbeitete und vermehrte Auflage*, vol. 18. Leipzig, Bibliographisches Institut 1907, entry *Schulplicht, allgemeine*, p. 69.

16 The Weimar Act of 1619 features in *Der Grosse Brockhaus: Handbuch des Wissens in zwanzig Bände, Fünfzehnte, völlig neubearbeitete Auflage* (Leipzig, 1934), vol. 16, entry *Schulplicht*, pp. 48-49. *Brockhaus* 1956 and 1975 state that the Strassburgian Church Act of 1598 introduced judicial compulsory education. *Der Grosse Brockhaus, Sechzehnte, völlig neubearbeitete Auflage* (Wiesbaden, 1956), vol. 10, p. 503; *Brockhaus Enzyklopädie, Siebzehnte völlig neubearbeitete Auflage dess Grossen Brockhaus* (Wiesbaden, 1975), vol. 17, p. 57.

17 For example the *Principia regulativa* of 1717 and 1736, and the *General-Landschul-Reglement* of 1763. For these laws, see Lewin, *Geschichte der Entwicklung der preußischen Volksschule*, pp. 39-52, 78-91; Raßmann, *Geschichte der preußischen Volksschule*, pp. 14-22; for their implementation, see Füssel and Roeder, "Recht – Erziehung – Staat".

18 For the Weimar law, see e.g. Düsterhaus, *Das ländische Schulwesen im Herzogtum Preussen*, p. 181.

19 Heppe did not even mention the Weimar Act of 1619. Heppe, *Geschichte des deutschen Volksschulwesens*, vol. 1, pp. 30-33; vol. 2, pp. 270; vol. 3, pp. 7-19, 27-35.

20 Lewin, *Geschichte der Entwicklung der preußischen Volksschule*, pp. 42, 345.

La Grande Encyclopédie of the 1890s, the origins of the principle in France went back to 1560, the next stage comprised the legislation passed during the French Revolution, and finally, after a temporary setback in the mid-nineteenth century, it was established under the Ferry law of 1882. The *Encyclopédie* then scanned the Western hemisphere country by country, listing which ones had or had not introduced compulsory education. In England the principle had triumphed (*a triomphé*) in 1870. The Spanish law of 1857 made primary education obligatory, but it was not put into effect (*exécutée*), as was the case with the Greek law of 1834, while Portugal had compulsory education in principle but not in practice, "*en principe mais non en fait*". In Italy the law passed in 1859 was not implemented (*réalisée*) until after that of 1877, and in Luxemburg the obligation was realized (*rendue réelle*) under the law of 1881. In Switzerland the federal constitution of 1874 had established the obligation in "the majority of cantons". The European countries that, according to the *Encyclopédie*, had compulsory primary education – without any reservations – were Germany, Austria-Hungary, Bulgaria, Denmark, Sweden and Norway, Serbia (since 1882) and Turkey (since 1869), and those that did not have it were Belgium, the Netherlands, Romania and Russia. Following this the countries were listed according to whether primary education was free of charge or not – which did not tally with whether or not it was compulsory.[21] The writer of the article seems to have been hesitant in categorising some of the countries.

Furthermore, what is today commemorated as the introduction of compulsory education may not reflect the reality at the time. Norway celebrated its 250th anniversary of universal, compulsory education in 1989. However, the Norwegian and Danish Rural School Acts of 1739 could be said to have paid lip service to universal compulsory education, although they explicitly addressed children of *almuen*, in other words children of the peasantry and lower social groups. The instructions for the implementation of the Norwegian act ordered *klokkerne* (parish clerk-organists) to provide school instruction for at least three months "not only to all the children of the *almuen* but also to their servants", which made it clear that the compulsion was not aimed at middle- or upper-class children. Only two years later, in 1741, a new ordinance watered down the Rural School Act, and it was left to the parishes to decide on instruction covering Christian doctrines and elementary literacy. In cities these *almue* schools developed into

21 *La Grande Encyclopédie: Inventaire raisonné des sciences, des lettres et des arts, Tome quinzième* (Paris, n.d., between 1885 and 1895), vol. 15, entries *École*, pp. 371-372, and *Enseignement*, pp. 1114-1120, 1144-1145.

pauper schools.[22] Subsequent acts in Denmark in 1814 (today credited with introducing compulsory education)[23] and in Norway in 1827, 1848 and 1860 called these schools *almue* schools, and later – as the word *almue* fell out of use – *folk* schools.

The point I wish to make is that the Norwegian and Danish School Acts of 1739 were part of a larger set of school reforms that would discourage *almue* children from undergoing further schooling. The Latin School Acts of 1739 in Denmark and Norway drastically cut down the number of public Latin schools and introduced admittance proof and annual examinations to sort out the boys who should be dismissed. The act explicitly strove to stop poor parents from sending their sons to the remaining public Latin schools – by redefining scholarship regulations – and instructed parents in localities that abolished such schools to arrange private education for their sons if they wanted them to continue to higher education.[24] (A comparable tendency is discernible in Sweden and Finland.)[25] In short, what is celebrated as the early introduction of universal compulsory education in Norway could be seen as the early introduction of the parallel school system.

From a more general perspective, eighteenth-century Danish and Norwegian school laws could be interpreted as local examples of the Europe-wide trend of a growing distance between the high and the low, and of the use of the school system in the exclusion of the popular classes from the "great tradition".[26] In fact, the eighteenth-century Prussian school acts are also open to such an interpretation. The *Principia regulativa* of 1717 was part of a larger set of school laws that had been enacted since 1698, basically to promote Pietism. First, peasant children, pauper children and child beg-

22 Dokka, *Fra almueskole til folkeskole*, pp. 18-20; Martinson, *Growing Up in Norway*, pp. 112-114; *Forordning om skolerne paa landet i Danmark; Forordning, om skolerne paa landet i Norge; Instruction for degne, klokkere og skoleholdere paa landet i Norge; Placat og nærmere anordning angaaende skolerne paa landet i Norge.*

23 E.g., Flora, *State, Economy, and Society*, p. 567.

24 Dokka, *Fra almueskole til folkeskole*, pp. 13-31; *Forordning, angaaende hvoor mange Latinske skoler i Danmark og Norge skall veddblive, samt hvorleded med ungdommens information,ingeniorum prøve, den aarlige examen og stipendiers distribution* [...], *17 Aprilis 1739; Forordning, angaaende fattige børns antagelse i de publique Latinske skoler og forsendelse til academiet, ingeniorum prøve og stpendiorum uddeeling* [...] *23de Julii 1756*. The latter act strove to make it next to impossible for impecunious children to be admitted to Latin schools.

25 Hedenborg, *Det gåtfulla folket*, pp. 98-104, 117-125; Sandin, *Hemmet, gatan, fabriken eller skolan*, pp. 77-87, 94-96, 159-166; Wirilander, *Herrskapsfolk*, pp. 282-318.

26 For European development, see e.g., Ariès, *Centuries of Childhood*, pp. 210-216, 268-291, 307-314, 334-335; Burke, *Popular Culture in Early Modern Europe*, pp. 23-29, 270-281.

gars were compelled to attend school – even this was termed *Schulplicht* in 1914[27] – and later the *Principia regulativa* of 1717 ordained that peasant parents should send their children to school in summer and winter, and pay the school fees, on pain of punishment (the *Principia regulativa* of 1736 stated that every school child aged from five to twelve had to give the school master fifteen *Groschen* a year, irrespectively whether or not the child went to school).[28] Parallel legislation provided for the better-off, and covered Gymnasia and Latin schools (1713) and universities (1718). The latter act regulated the scholarship system and prescribed that incapable (*untüchtigen*) youngsters aged over twenty must not be allowed to stay at school. Several major school acts, including the *General-Landschul-Reglement* of 1763 were enacted after the mid-century during the reign of Friedrich the Great. However, the king himself, like many of his Enlightenment contemporaries, considered religious and moral instruction by village teachers to suffice for peasant children.[29]

Sweden is generally considered to have introduced compulsory education with the School Act of 1842.[30] The section concerned stipulated that "all children of school age must turn up [*inställa sig*] at school, with the exception of only those whose parents or guardians have announced that they will be instructed at home, or at a public grammar school, or at a [...] private school".[31] In mid-nineteenth-century Sweden it was predominantly children of persons of standing and landed farmers who qualified for this list of exceptions – indeed such lists were typical of laws that were directed at lower social groups. Even the name of the new school, *folk* school, suggested to contemporary readers that it was not for the children of persons of standing. Many people associated folk schools with pauper schools, and in the industrial city of Norrköping the authorities deliberately strove to make it into one. Landed farmers at the *Riksdag* (Estates Assembly) neither supported nor were prepared to finance such schools, where their children would mingle with those of the landless poor. The establishment of rural folk schools also became a very long-drawn-out process, watered down by

27 Raßmann, *Geschichte der preußischen Volksschule*, p. 12.

28 *Principia regulative oder General-Schulen-Plan, nach welchem das Land-Schulewesen im Königreich Preussen eingerichtet werden soll. Bestätigt am 1. Aug. 1736*, § 9.

29 Lewin, *Geschichte der Entwicklung der preußischen Volksschule*, pp. 39-44, 114-115; Raßmann, *Geschichte der preußischen Volksschule*, p. 14; Houston, *Literacy in Early Modern Europe*, pp.15-20.

30 Rodhe, "Den svenska folkskolans förhistoria", p. 3.

31 *Kongl. Maj:ts Nådiga Stadga angående Folk-undervisningen i Riket, 18 Juni 1842* (§ 8:3). *Svensk Författnings-Samling 1842*.

the mushrooming of "little schools" that may not have taught anything except mechanical reading skills and Luther's Small Catechism.[32] The public grammar schools mentioned among the exemptions in the School Act of 1842 were a legacy of the Latin schools and were intended for the sons of civil servants, the bourgeoisie and the upper classes. Following a Royal Circular in 1849 and the Grammar School Act of 1856 their classical curriculum was modernized and their status and financing ensured.[33] Thus what is today presented as the introduction of compulsory education in Sweden could just as well be interpreted as the consolidation of a parallel school system.

John Boli very aptly emphasizes "the ritual significance of mass schooling" in nineteenth-century Sweden. Less pertinently he interprets the Swedish School Act of 1842 as an example of the universality of schooling. He reasons that if mass schooling had arisen primarily as an instrument of social control, "we should find that it was directed solely at the lower classes". On this point he seems rather misinformed. Even though the Swedish School Act was not explicitly directed at "the lower social classes", it made this clear in a roundabout way. Boli takes his point further by arguing that, as in other countries the mass schooling was universalistic, and claims that it was characterized in the nineteenth century by "the generalized ethic of equality": "Children of all social strata went to school together".[34] Yet the parallel school system was applied in most of nineteenth-century Europe, Sweden included, and remained the rule well into the twentieth century.

As a legacy of a common history, Finnish popular education shared many features with the Swedish system. The Lutheran Church had basic Christian doctrines drummed into the common people by means of controlled Catechism reading. This kind of mechanical reading ability could be made functional, and could even result in true literacy; many autodidacts achieved that. Yet the whole population became literate only after proper public primary schools became accessible to all children. The first Finnish Folk School Act of 1866 did not introduce compulsory education

32 Aquilonius, *Svenska folkskolans historia,* vol. 2, pp. 279-283, 294-295, 298-300, 329-332, 342, 391, 416-418; Sörensen, *Svenska folkskolans historia* , vol. 3, pp. 74-108; Petterson, *Frihet, jämlighet, egendom och Bentham*, pp. 163-170; *Kongl. Maj:ts Nådiga Kungörelse, angående ytterligare åtgärder till folkundervisningens befrämjande, 23 April 1858. Svensk Författnings-Samling 1858.*

33 *Kongl. Maj:ts Nådiga Stadga för Rikets Allmänna Elementar-läroverk 14 Augusti 1856. Svensk Författnings-Samling 1856.*

34 Boli, *New Citizens for a New Society*, pp. 18-19, 34, 233, 239.

but settled for promoting folk schools. It obliged urban parishes to establish at least one folk school for children who did not receive instruction in any other way. In the countryside – where more than nine out of ten children lived – it was left to the local administration, in practice local landowning farmers, to decide whether or not to establish such a school.[35] The costs largely fell on the local taxpayers; governmental money was sparingly allocated to folk schools, the educational policy favouring general secondary grammar schools (*läroverk*) and university education. As a consequence, much as in Sweden and for similar reasons, less costly slimmed-down versions of folk schools and short-term ambulatory schools were often considered sufficient in the countryside.[36] A compulsory education bill was passed by the Finnish Parliament in 1910, but it never came into force, and in the end the Compulsory Education Act was not introduced until 1921.[37]

The introduction of compulsory education in Catholic Spain seems to have had a somewhat contradictory history, and giving credit to just one law, "the famous Moyano Law of 1857", seems debatable.[38] Likewise in Italy the role of the Casati Law of 1859 is equivocal, since before the unification different principalities and kingdoms had followed rather different kinds of policies in terms of primary education and this did not end with unification. According to Marzio Barbagli, the Casati Law "established for the first time the compulsory and gratuitous nature of primary education", but Giovanni Genovesi puts a damper on such superlatives by arguing that it just aimed at establishing a school for the lower class (*classe subalterna*).[39]

The introduction of compulsory education does not seem to have tallied well with industrialization or economic development, as the cases of the Netherlands and Belgium show. According to René De Herdt, Belgium was Europe's second nation to become industrialized, but among the last to introduce compulsory education. The act was passed in 1914 but was not

35 The Finnish Folk School Act of 1866 did not make instruction in writing mandatory, contrary to what has been claimed by Markusen, "The Development of Writing Ability", p. 40. Cf. *Hans Kejserliga Majestäts Nådiga Förordning, angående organisation af folkskoleväsendet i Storfurstendömet Finland, 11 Maj 1866. Storfurstendömet Finlands Författnings-samling 1866.*

36 Konttinen, "Central Bureaucracy and the Restriction of Education"; Myllyntaus, "Education in the Making of Modern Finland".

37 The act did not stipulate compulsory school attendance. *Lag om läroplikt, 15 april 1921. Finlands Författningssamling 1921.*

38 Guereña, "Infancia y escolarización", pp. 349-373.

39 Barbagli, *Educating for Unemployment*, pp. 5, 50-52, quoting p. 52; Genovesi, *Storia della scuola in Italia*, pp. 69-81.

enforced until after the First World War. Belgium was also a later-comer with regard to the law on child labour, which was not introduced until 1889 – De Herdt suggests that Belgium was the last country in Western Europe to do this.[40] However, Finland was equally late with its first law regulating child labour.[41] As far as compulsory primary education was concerned, Finland even came a few years after Belgium, evidently as a tail-ender in Western Europe. What is the relevance of legislation if Belgium, one of the first industrialized countries in nineteenth-century Europe, and Finland, one of the last industrialized countries, were at one in terms of compulsory education and child-labour laws?

In conclusion, compulsory education appears a rather elusive phenomenon in European history. In many cases it is not clear when compulsory primary education was introduced, and this did not always take place simultaneously in rural and urban areas, or with boys and girls, or with children of all social groups. Likewise, its implementation may have taken so long that it is difficult to tell when it was fully effective. Furthermore, if Serbia and Bulgaria had compulsory education in the late 1890s but Belgium and the Netherlands did not, does that help us to understand child labour? All this casts doubt on the line of argument that gives the enforcement of compulsory education an important role in the decline in the use of child labour. In the following I will consider another approach.

Competition, Rationalization and the Demand for Child Labour

Nineteenth-century French reformers who wrote passionate pamphlets on industrial child labour must have been aware of the fact that from the 1830s on the industrialist in the *Sociéte Industrielle de Mulhouse* lobbied for the stricter regulation of child labour than any reformer had demanded, including a minimum starting age of eight, a ban on night work for children under twelve, a literacy test for industrial employment, and graduated working hours according to age.[42] The French pamphlet writers were quite concerned about the competition between French and foreign industrialists, yet they failed to see that the prominent industrialists in Mulhouse and the banker who raised the issue with the Minister of Commerce were also concerned about competition and needed new rules of the game.

40 De Herdt, "Child Labour in Belgium".

41 Rahikainen, "Children and 'the Right to Factory Work'", pp. 54-55.

42 Heywood, *Childhood in Nineteenth-Century France*, pp. 224-226.

Half a century later the Russian economist Mikhail Tugan-Baranovsky well understood why the owners of the cotton-spinning mills in St Petersburg deemed it profitable to go further than the child-labour law of 1882. He mentioned the high wages in St Petersburg compared with those in Moscow, and the international economic depression, which in 1883 led many cotton mills and other factories to cut back on production and dismiss large numbers of workers. Yielding to the interests of the St Petersburg mill owners, the law of 1885 introduced stricter restrictions on the use of female and child labour. According to Tugan-Baranovsky, it did not encounter great opposition on the part of factory owners as long as the depression lasted. When the economies improved, children aged between ten and eleven were again permitted by law to work in factories.[43]

Despite the sentimental rhetoric in pamphlets on factory children aimed at the general public, nineteenth-century reformers seem to have been quite convinced that what was behind the child-labour laws was international competition. On other platforms shared by professionals efforts to bring about international agreements on child labour, these were very prosaically paralleled with international treaties on postal services, patents and copyrights, and commercial treaties. Adolf Wagner explained in 1871 to churchmen in Berlin why the factory legislation of single states was inadequate, and that "similar regulations must be made to prevail in all industrial states by means of international treaties. [...] If the law forbids or greatly restricts child labour in country A and not in country B, it follows that country B can manufacture a given product more cheaply. Country A will no longer be able to withstand competition." In 1882 German academic socialists debated on international labour legislation, but supporters of industrial child labour opposed such legislation. Their rhetorical tactic was to ask within what limits international labour protection should operate: "[W]hereas international treaties had hitherto negotiated only by civilized states, a labour treaty would have to include China, Japan, and India. Even now, British industry was beginning to suffer from the competition of low-wage Orientals using European machinery".[44] In a way they were proved right. The first Indian Factory Acts of 1881 and 1891 were intended to shield Lancashire's textile industries from "unfair competition" and to restrict child labour in Indian factories.[45] Later on, at the first International

43 Tugan-Baranovsky, *The Russian Factory*, pp. 320-333. See also Rahikainen, *Centuries of Child Labour*, pp. 150-154.

44 Follows, *Antecedents of the ILO*, pp. 66-72, 80-82, 86-91, quoting pp. 80, 89-90.

45 Nieuwenhuys, *Children's Lifeworlds*, p. 184.

Labour Convention of 1919, India was exempted from the fourteen-year minimum-age provision and for Japan it was twelve; like at the ILO convention of 1937 the exceptions to the fifteen-year minimum-age requirement were China, Japan and India, where it was twelve.[46]

The Swiss made their first attempt in 1881, and another one in 1889 to call an international conference on labour legislation and, as Sidney Pollard puts it, "incidentally to ensure that the exports of the more advanced countries were not undercut by unfair labour practices of the others".[47] Only the conference called in Berlin by the German Kaiser in 1890 materialized. The Emperor motivated his act by the "amelioration of the lot of German workers as far as the exigencies of international competition [...] allow". The Berlin Conference of 1890 was not a law-making conference, as the Final Protocol illustrates. For example, in terms of subterranean work in mines, it was "desirable" that the minimum age limit "be gradually raised, as experience will have proven the possibility of it, to fourteen years", and in southern European countries to twelve years. Likewise it was "desirable" that "children of both sexes below a certain age be excluded from labour in industrial establishments", and this age limit be fixed at twelve and in southern countries at ten years.[48]

Sidney Pollard summarizes the Berlin Conference bluntly: "[T]he representatives of fifteen nations subscribed to some desirable principles, though they were nowhere adopted".[49] Karl Heinrich Kaufhold is more nuanced: "In addition the Conference established standards from which the participating countries no longer could step back if they did not want themselves to be disfavoured in the eyes of the world's public." He also points out that it was the first time that different national governments openly discussed issues that had until then been considered national problems.[50] If the Berlin Conference indicated that the leading economic powers now wanted to make sure that each one followed the same rules of the game in terms of child labour, what was it that made them so keen on this? I suggest that it was the economic problems associated with the recent depression and deflation, and the increasing international competition.

46 *Internationales Arbeitsrecht gestaltet durch die Internationale Arbeitskonferenz*, pp. 32–33, 410–411.

47 Pollard, *European Economic Integration*, p. 126.

48 Follows, *Antedecents of the ILO*, pp. 120–125, 132–138, 207–210.

49 Pollard, *European Economic Integration*, p. 126.

50 Kaufhold, "Die Diskussion um die Neugestaltung des Arbeitsrechts", quoting p. 304.

John F. Wilson characterizes the period from 1870 to 1914 as "industrial capitalism under pressure". Under the pressure of the long depression of the 1870s and 1880s (or, if you prefer, the long deflation crisis) it became ever more important to adopt more professional attitudes towards managerial tasks.[51] It is worth emphasising that Frederick W. Taylor began to develop his ideas of scientific management in the wake of the long depression. He had started in the machine-shop in 1878 and later wrote about his first years as follows: "This was close to the end of the long period of depression, following the panic of 1873. [...] For this reason [the writer, Taylor] was obliged to work as a day labourer instead of working as a mechanic".[52]

It seems to me that scientific management with its "scientific selection and development of the workman"[53] represented an essentially similar line of thinking as the psychological, pedagogical and physiological research and experimental testing of child development that mushroomed in Europe and North America at around the same time. In London one medical officer reporting on boys in factory work wrote that "rickets and other type of deformity were much more prevalent among them than among boys just leaving school". In Moscow on the other hand, a professor found that boys and girls aged nine years and over working in Central Russian factories were badly behind in growth in height compared with similar aged school children in Boston, grammar-school boys in Hamburg and English children in general. He concluded that cotton spinning and carding in particular were harmful.[54] Several hundred school children participated in a study on mental fatigue conducted in Virginia in 1913 and 1914, the aim of which was to ascertain "the behaviour of the child mind" during a drill recitation or "during continuous exercise of a single function". In addition, the children's performances were discussed in terms echoing scientific management.[55] With hindsight the whole appears a kind of aptitude test for monotonous assembly-line work. The specialists undertaking such type of investigations seem to have been fascinated by the idea of determining the normal, and thus had something in common with con-

51 E.g., Newcomer, "The Professionalisation of Management", pp. 54-63; Wilson, *British Business History*, pp. 26-31, 102-108.

52 Taylor, *The Principles of Scientific Management*, p. 28.

53 *Ibid.*, p. 60.

54 Erisman, *Untersuchungen über die körperliche Entwicklung*, pp. 14-22, 63-71, 85; Florence, *Economics of Fatigue and Unrest*, p. 381.

55 Garth, *Mental Fatigue*, pp. 1-4, *passim*.

temporary pedagogical reformers who supported eugenics, such as Ellen Key and Édouard Claparède.[56]

Studies on fatigue and efficiency studies in manufacturing occasionally involved young persons. Experimental investigation of their muscular strength confirmed what employers had always been aware of: the pressing force of the hand and the striking force of the arm of fourteen- to seventeen-year-olds were substantially lower than those of adult workers.[57] In his manual covering field research for fatigue studies, Philip Sargant Florence of the US Public Health Services commented on the young labour force as follows:

> The effect of age and sex upon the influence of activity or working capacity acquires importance from the large number of young persons, *i. e.* from 14 to 18 years of age, that are still permitted to pursue industrial occupations in American and European factories, and also from the large influx of women into industry [...].
> Analysis. – The age of workers is obviously enumerable according to years, but the importance of distinguishing between different years lies first in the process of physical and mental growth taking place in the years up to 18 and the comparative weakness of young persons at any rate up to the sixteenth year. Below 13, children are only rarely found in industry. When growing, boys and girls need more sleep and rest to build up tissues and more recreation to develop the character than do adult persons. A length and intensity of activity that will do adults no harm, may permanently stunt the rising generation.[58]

The "girls" featuring in studies on fatigue and efficiency probably were young persons rather than children. "Girls" employed for ten days in "covering chocolates by means of mechanical dipping apparatus" during the Great War were called "women" in the corresponding graph. Correspondingly, "girls" in a munitions factory possibly referred to young women rather than children. Be that as it may, during the experiment the "girls" who were newly "engaged on mouth reamering [of cartridges], an operation involving considerable quickness and dexterity", doubled their hourly

56 Key used the term "Darwinism", Claparède the term "eugenics". Key, *Barnets århundrade*, vol. 1, pp. 29-44, 170-174; Claparède, *Psychologie de l'enfant*, pp. XXIX-XXXIII, 55-56, 309-313, 344-345.

57 Erisman, *Untersuchungen über die körperliche Entwicklung*, pp. 93-96.

58 Florence, *Use of Industrial Statistics in the Investigation of Industrial Fatigue*, p. 142.

output in eight weeks and were on a par with other female operatives by the ninth. Conversely, in an experiment undertaken in a fuse factory, youths "were unable to improve their hourly output sufficiently to make up for the reduction of hours, and their total output showed a distinct fall". The boys themselves were not blamed for this, however, since their jobs ("boring top caps" of fuses) were determined by the machine: about four times a minute they did a task that took about two seconds. "For the rest of the time they stood at their machines doing nothing".[59] They must have offered the time-and-motion man an irresistible opportunity for rationalization.

There is evidence that new management practices travelled from one country to another in the late nineteenth century,[60] while there seems to be no doubt that a convergence of managerial practices took place in Europe after the breakthrough of Taylorism, or scientific management. Industrialists all over Europe eventually learned "the fantastic savings in labour costs which scientific labour utilization would bring", as Eric Hobsbawm put it.[61] After the First World War, the "rationalization movement" was seldom resisted by workers in continental Europe and the Nordic countries[62] and it was even supported by the International Labour Organisation.[63] By the 1920s women in many countries had largely taken the place of children as the low-paid industrial labour force.[64] However, there was much opposition to the principles of Taylorism in England, in particular in the textile industry in which labour-intensive methods and small independent family

59 Florence, *Use of Industrial Statistics in the Investigation of Industrial Fatigue*, pp. 132-133; Vernon, *Industrial Fatigue and Efficiency*, pp. 14-45, quoting pp. 14, 35, 44.

60 E.g. Kaufhold, "Die Diskussion um die Neugestaltung des Arbeitsrechts", p. 292; McCaffray, "Origins of Labor Policy in the Russian Coal and Steel Industry", p. 962; Fellman, "The Professionalisation of Management". For present-day discussion on the dissemination of managerial ideas, see Hedmo, Sahlin-Andersson, and Wedlin, "Fields of Imitation".

61 Hobsbawm, *Labouring Men*, p. 362; Cross, *A Quest for Time*, pp. 104-115, 194-204.

62 Cross, *A Quest for Time*, pp. 205-211; Kocka, "The Rise of the Modern Industrial Enterprise in Germany"; Homburg, "Anfänge des Taylorsystems in Deutschland"; Runeby, "Americanism, Taylorism and Social Integration"; Johansson, *Arbetarrörelsen och taylorismen*, pp. 15-16, 97-103; Christensen, "Rationalisering og arbejderne"; Socialdepartementet, *Rationaliseringsutredningen*; Kettunen, "Taylorismin tulo Suomeen".

63 Devinat, *Scientific Management in Europe*, pp. 9-45, 127-163.

64 Winberg, *Fabriksfolket*, p. 47; Camps, "Transition in Women's and Children's Work Patterns"; Glickman, *Russian Factory Women*, pp. 44-49, 78-81; Cammarosano, "Labouring Women"; Scott, "Women, Other 'Fresh' Workers, and the New Manufacturing Workforce in Interwar Britain".

firms survived.[65] This may have contributed to the fact that child labour also survived in English textile manufacturing for a long time.

Did the converging managerial strategies indicate converging employment strategies in terms of child labour? I am not aware of any analyses of the impact of rationalization or scientific management on the demand for children.[66] I know of one case in which the president of a cartel-type association of Finnish glass industrialists proposed to his fellow-industrialists in an overproduction crisis in 1909 that they should all adopt "the Danish method" in order to rid themselves of boys engaged in carrying bottles to cooling oven.[67] If nothing else, a comparison between manufacturing and agriculture suggests the important role of rationalization in the decline of child labour: indeed, the difference is striking. Undercapitalized family farms had very limited possibilities of introducing the labour-saving rationalization that became standard in manufacturing in twentieth-century Europe. As a consequence, even after the Second World War children of primary-school age comprised a significant part of the labour force in family farms in many parts of Europe, from Italy to Finland.[68]

At the risk of engaging in circular reasoning I suggest that increasing competition and profitability problems during the long depression of the late nineteenth century not only fostered a more professional attitude towards managerial tasks but also made managers more conscious of the relatively low productivity of child labour.[69] This would explain at least in part why industrial child labour evidently declined (as a trend rather than linearly) by and large simultaneously towards the end of the nineteenth century in different parts of Europe. Children were cheap and flexible, and no doubt they had nimble fingers, but they grew tired sooner than adults and despite fines and corporal punishment often proved unfocused as workers. Industrial child labour failed when put to the test of productivity and profitability during the long depression and definitely with the breakthrough of scientific management with its fatigue and efficiency

65 Wilson, *British Business History*, pp. 157-164; Lazonick, "Industrial Organization and Technological Change".

66 A contemporary reference by Drufy to "girls" in connection with scientific management is open to interpretation. Drufy, *Scientific Management*, pp. 22-23.

67 I was not able to find out what exactly "the Danish method" meant. Rahikainen, "Miesten maailma", pp. 139-165, 153.

68 Rahikainen, *Centuries of Child Labour*, pp. 195-203.

69 I have previously briefly discussed this in Rahikainen, *Centuries of Child Labour*, pp. 143-157; and Rahikainen, "First-Generation Factory Children".

studies and assembly lines. Children were the first group of manufacturing workers to be rationalized into extinction.

Concluding Discussion

It is customary to study the history of child labour within the framework of one country. This is, of course, largely due to the fact that most data are organized by and available in nation states, but at the same time it may also be a remnant of the tradition of nationalistic historical writing. Although it may be relevant to study child labour in local, regional and national contexts, there are phenomena that can be grasped only from a more comprehensive perspective. Moreover, a number of received interpretations of child labour and school reforms that appear perfectly valid when applied to one country lose some of their explanatory value in the Europe-wide context. If – as it seems – in most of Europe industrial child labour was declining and school attendance increasing by and large simultaneously in the late nineteenth century, it is difficult to explain this unless we consider Europe as a whole.

Taking the European perspective makes us pose questions that might otherwise not even occur to us. I was surprised to realize that the educational policy of nineteenth-century Finland, in which governmental financing favoured middle-class and elite education at the expense of the elementary schooling of the broad masses, had so many counterparts in Europe: Russia and its Baltic Provinces, Spain, Portugal, and Italy. What else did these apparently quite different countries share that could explain their similarities in terms of governmental educational financing? Moreover, we have examples from various parts of Europe, from Catholic Sicily to Orthodox Russia and Protestant Finland, of common people themselves taking the initiative to acquire literacy and seeing to it that their children became literate. There are also examples of parents struggling for their children's right to instruction in their mother tongue.[70] What unites such apparently separate cases of the quest for literacy and basic education?

70 Barbagli, *Educating for Unemployment*, pp. 40-46; Eklof, *Russian Peasant Schools*, pp. 24-29, 84-91; Krumbholz, *Die Elementarbildung in Russland bis zum Jahre 1864*, pp. 224-234; *Das Bildungs- und Schulwesen Lettlands (Latvijas): kurzer Bericht*, (Riga, 1928), pp. 10-12; Nuñes, "Government Expenditure on Education, Economic Growth and Long Waves"; Kunze, *Sorbisches Schulwesen*, pp. 97-127, 141-156; Reeder, "Women in the Classroom".

The latecomer countries in terms of adequate public primary education – Russia, Spain, Portugal, Italy and Finland – were also latecomers in terms of economic performance. Some of them, at least Russia and Finland, seem to fall nicely into the framework put forward by Jaime Reis in the context of human capital formation. He suggests that human capital, in his example literacy, "may have been causally determined by income", and associates the "expanded willingness to invest in human capital on the part of the poorer layers of society" with the consumer revolution in the eighteenth century. In the very long run, he notes, "this rise in human capital was also very much the result of a spontaneous process, not of one that was exogenously imposed on society by the state or the church". Using estimates of the opportunity costs of child labour in France and England, he maintains that the costs of acquiring literacy were, in fact, rather high.[71] They may not have been equally high in the north European periphery, but this does not reduce the relevance of his line of argument. Taking it one step further implies that in the discussion about the making of "the new childhood" we should perhaps put more emphasis to the role of the common people at the expense of that of the State.

In the heyday of colonialism the European states,[72] whose representatives met at the Berlin Conference in 1890 in order to agree on international rules covering the use of child labour, probably felt that Europe ruled the world. Yet China, India and Japan were already there.[73] So should we not include the rest of the world in the history of child labour in nineteenth- and twentieth-century Europe?

71 Reis, "Economic Growth, Human Capital Formation and Consumption", quoting pp. 195, 203, 212.

72 The German Kaiser sent official invitations to Austria-Hungary, Belgium, France, Great Britain, Switzerland, Denmark, Italy, Sweden, Norway, the Netherlands, and Luxemburg. Follows, *Antecedents of the ILO*, p. 132.

73 Rahikainen, *"At What Cost was Economic Modenization Purchased?"*.

CHAPTER 6

The Transition to Working Life in Eighteenth and Nineteenth-Century England and Wales*

Peter Kirby

A unique feature in the development of all mature economies has been an absolute decline in child employment. This chapter speculates about that unique decline in the context of long-term economic growth in England and Wales. It focuses on the child labour market, the household economy and the life-cycles of children and adolescents and suggests ways in which economic and demographic developments not normally associated with the history of child labour may have contributed to its secular decline. Several discussion points will be considered, including the effects of child dependency, poverty, the age at leaving home, diverse sectoral demand for child workers, industrialisation, state intervention and the structure of the urban labour market.

Traditionally, historians of the British Industrial Revolution have treated the employment of children as a matter of child welfare and, to a greater or lesser extent, have tended to treat working children in isolation from the wider labour market and from more general economic change. In many histories of child labour, children are portrayed as victims of avaricious employers or dissolute parents or as the casualties of the prevailing *laissez-faire* political economy of the period.[1] This was especially the case during the Cold War, when the exploitative nature of early industrial capitalism formed the mainstay of pessimistic accounts of industrialisation. It was almost inevitable that working children (particularly those employed in the industries that epitomised the classic Industrial Revolution) should

* Earlier versions of this paper were given to the Economic and Social Research Council seminar, "The First Modern Labour Market", University of Birmingham, April 2006 and to the conference "Child Labour's Global Past, 1500-2000", International Institute of Social History, University of Amsterdam, November 2006.

1 See for example Thompson, *The Making of the English Working Class*; and Hammond and Hammond, *The Town Labourer*.

be drawn into the polarised debate over the social effects of industrialisation. The Marxist historian E.P. Thompson, for example, described a "mixture of terror and fatalism" among coal-mining children; suggesting that "the exploitation of little children, on this scale and with this intensity, was one of the most shameful events in our history".[2] By contrast, the neo-classical economic historian, Clark Nardinelli, claimed: "Industrialisation, far from being the source of the enslavement of children, was the source of their liberation".[3] The subject has therefore been eclipsed by the moral and ideological inclinations of historians.

The historical debate over child labour has also been affected by more general changes in social perceptions of children. As "childhood" developed as a legal and institutional concept in British society, it was accompanied by a quite reasonable desire on the part of parents, governments and charities to protect children from an increasing number of physical and psychological dangers. Amongst these has been a growing belief that any form of child labour, past or present, is an unnecessary and unacceptable evil. Such beliefs are easy to sustain in societies where children's employment is no longer a widespread strategy for family survival but they contribute little to our understanding of the social dynamics of child labour in the past. The situation is not helped by the fact that much of the historic evidence of child labour as a social problem was collected by contemporary elite observers and campaigners who tended to focus on only a few child employment sectors in which the worst working conditions existed. Qualitative evidence drawn from such sources are therefore frequently beset with problems of interpretation. As a result, the reporting of child labour in the past has leant heavily towards a variety of victim stereotypes such as the ubiquitous chimney sweep, crossing sweeper and mud-lark and bear very little resemblance to the actual structure of the historic child labour market. The emergence of "childhood" as a discrete subject of inquiry has therefore tended to obviate any comprehensive analysis of how child employment was embedded in the wider social and economic environment of eighteenth and nineteenth-century England and Wales. National quantitative labour market data, meanwhile, are sparse before the middle of the nineteenth century and for the eighteenth century are virtually non-existent.[4]

2 Thompson, The *Making of the English Working Class*, pp. 369, 384.
3 Nardinelli, *Child Labor and the Industrial Revolution*, p. 102.
4 See Hutchins and Harrison, *A History of Factory Legislation*, p. 5.

Detailed regional and sectoral studies have, however, disclosed a much wider economic context for child labour and show a much greater diversity of child employment than that encompassed by histories of "exploitation". Research on the early-modern labour market has shown that the spread of proto-industry during the seventeenth and eighteenth centuries provided many more opportunities for children compared with labour-intensive and menial agricultural work.[5] Children played a vital "industrious" role in Britain's long-term economic development. It is now generally understood that the majority of working children were not the victims of parental or employer greed. Most children worked because their households were poor and the marginal incomes available to them often provided the difference between family poverty and subsistence. Child labour existed at the intersection of local labour market demand and the household economy and was valued both by parents and employers. Closer integration of child labour history with mainstream economic and social histories, therefore, should allow a broader understanding of the dynamics of children's employment and its decline.[6]

Some basic facts can be agreed. Almost the entire population of eighteenth- and nineteenth-century England and Wales underwent a transition – predominantly during the second decade of life – from extreme childhood dependency to relative economic independence in early adulthood. This near-universal life-cycle stage was marked by a period of progressively-increasing participation in the world of work (table 6.1).

Understanding how the transition to working life changed through time is crucial to the study of how the child labour market responded to the spread of agrarian and industrial capitalism and, ultimately, to explaining why children's employment declined in developed economies.

5 De Vries, "The Industrial Revolution and the Industrious Revolution"; McKendrick, "Home Demand and Economic Growth".

6 For further discussion of these issues see two new studies: Honeyman, *Child Workers in England, 1780-1820*; and Humphries, *Childhood and Cild Labour*; see also Cunningham, "Decline of Child Labour"; Kirby, *Child Labour in Britain*; Kirby, "A Short Statistical Sketch of the Child Labour Market"; Kirby, "Causes of Short Stature among Coalmining Children"; Kirby, "Short Stature Among Coalmining Children: A Rejoinder"; Kirby, "How Many Children were 'Unemployed'?"; Humphries, "Short Stature among Coalmining Children: A Comment"; Horrell and Humphries, "The Exploitation of Little Children"; Rahikainen, "Historical and Present-Day Child Labour".

Table 6.1. Child Labour Participation Rates, England and Wales (%), 1851

Age group	%
5-9	2
10-14	30
15-19	c. 80

Source: Kirby, *Child labour in Britain*, p. 11

The market for child labour in eighteenth and nineteenth-century England and Wales was strongly affected by demographic structural factors and it can be argued that changing levels of child dependency exerted a powerful influence upon levels of child labour. At least one historian has suggested that under conditions of high demographic structural dependency, the employment of children might be regarded as "normal".[7] During the eighteenth and early nineteenth centuries, the child population in England increased as a proportion of the total population. In 1661, the proportion of the population aged below fifteen stood at around twenty-nine per cent but by 1821 this figure had risen to thirty-nine per cent. By the third decade of the nineteenth century, therefore, half of the English population was aged below twenty and about forty per cent was under fifteen.[8] The steepest rates of increase in child dependency occurred during the classic "Industrial Revolution" (i.e. between c.1760s and 1830s) when children are thought to have entered the labour market in larger numbers. The most substantial increases in dependency, moreover, were felt among the core of the married population.

The supply of child workers in the labour market was also influenced by individual household poverty. Family poverty generally intensified in the half-century to 1830 and poor families living close to a subsistence wage were often forced to draw on a variety of sources of income.[9] Child labour therefore formed an important source of marginal income and fam-

7 Coleman, "Labour in the English Economy", pp. 286-288. This argument has been invoked to explain high levels of child labour in developing economies with high dependency ratios.

8 Mitchell, *British Historical Statistics*, p. 15; Wrigley and Schofield, *Population History*, Table A3.1, pp. 528-29; Anderson, "The Social Implications of Demographic Change", p. 47.

9 Kirby, *Child Labour in Britain*, Ch. 2.

ilies frequently had little choice over whether their children worked. Saito has observed the strong correlation between high wages for male heads of household and low labour force participation among females and children.[10] Humphries has shown that children were also more likely to be working if the head of a household was unskilled or if they lived in a family headed by a lone parent.[11] Levels of child labour in the period 1750-1851 may, therefore, be explained partly in terms of rapid population growth, a more youthful population and greater levels of child dependency.

One of the most important stages in the transition to work was the point at which children and adolescents became wholly independent of parental support. Hence, a child's departure from the parental home marked a fundamentally important life-cycle stage. In traditional rural society, children rarely stayed in the parental home until marriage: the average age at marriage between 1750 and 1799 was twenty-six and a half for men and twenty five for women,[12] whilst a majority of rural children would leave home in their early teenage years to enter farm service on holdings at some distance from the parental home or to take up a "live-in" apprenticeship with a master. Between the seventeenth and nineteenth centuries some two-thirds to three-quarters of the population aged between fifteen and twenty four were engaged in some variety of service in husbandry or apprenticeship.[13] Such periods of "live-in" service often extended well into adulthood and few people married prior to emerging from their period of service or apprenticeship. There were also discernable occupational and social class differences in the ages at leaving home. The children of farmers and proto-industrialists remained at home longest whilst those of poor labourers left home earliest. Evidence taken in 1782 and 1841 suggests that forty-six per cent of the children of skilled tradesmen and craftsmen resided in the parental home at ages above fourteen compared with only thirty-six per cent of the children of proletarians. The greatest variation in ages at leaving home existed within the skilled trades. Children from households in declining trades such as framework knitting, wool-combing and hand-weaving left at ages similar to those of the children of poor labourers.[14]

10 Saito, "Labour Supply Behaviour of the Poor", p. 645.

11 Especially where the head of household was female. Humphries, "Female-Headed Households in Early Industrial Britain".

12 Wrigley and Schofield, *Population History*, table 7.26, p. 255.

13 Kussmaul, *Servants in Husbandry*, p. 3; Wall, "The Age at Leaving Home", p. 182.

14 Snell, *Annals of the Labouring Poor*, p. 330; Wall, "The Age at Leaving Home", Table 5, p. 195; Lyons, "Family Response to Economic Decline", p. 56.

The increasing proletarianization of the rural and semi-rural labour forces almost certainly resulted in children leaving home and starting work at earlier ages – although this pattern was also accompanied by a long-term relative decline in demand for child labour in the agricultural sector.

Variations in sectoral demands for labour brought on by the spread of new production processes were of crucial importance in the changing transition to a life of work. The century to 1851 opened up new opportunities for child workers; however most of the new jobs for children were not concentrated in large centralized manufactories. At the peak of the Industrial Revolution, most child labour existed in a wide range of "traditional" sectors such as agriculture, small-scale rural and semi-rural workshop manufactures and (especially for girls) a wide variety of domestic services (table 6.2).

Table 6.2. Occupations of Working Children Aged 10-14 in England and Wales (%), 1851

	Males	*Females*
Agriculture, animals and fisheries	34.6	21.6
Workshops and handicraft	17.3	23.0
Factory	15.4	24.1
Transport and communications	11.4	1.1
Mines and quarries	8.8	0.8
"Indefinite occupation"	3.9	0.3
Building	3.1	0.0
Retail, foodstuffs and hostelries	2.7	3.5
Domestic service	1.8	25.3
Professional, clerical and local government	0.9	0.4
Armed forces	0.2	n.a.

Source: Kirby, *Child labour in Britain*, table 3.1, p. 52. Figures for agriculture includes estimates for the employed children of farmers. The figures for males must be regarded as more accurate compared with those for females due to enumeration problems. For a discussion of these, see Higgs, "Women, Occupations and Work"; Higgs, *Making Sense of the Census;* and Kirby, *Child labour in Britain*, pp. 9-12.

Explanations of how the growth of the economy affected child participation between 1750 to 1851 should therefore focus predominantly upon changes in the largest child employment sectors. Wrigley has pointed to "the falsity of the belief that manufacturing employment related to distant markets, whether in the home or the factory, was the dominant source of new jobs for the rising generations of young Men" in the early nineteenth century.[15] This is borne out by the fact that by the mid-nineteenth century, agriculture, animals and fisheries accounted for about a third of occupied male children and a quarter of occupied female children. Moreover, the highest concentrations of child labour by occupation tended to exist where workers were required to live-in with farmers and masters. Concentrations of child workers among live-in farm servants, for example, were nearly twice as high as among the agricultural "day-labour" force (table 6.3).

Table 6.3. Concentrations (%) of Children Aged 10-14 in the Main Branches of Agriculture and Fisheries, England and Wales, 1851

	Males	*Females*	*Both sexes*
Agricultural labour (out-door)	8.0	6.0	7.9
Farm Service (in-door)	13.6	16.5	14.3
Working children of farmers	19.8	20.8	20.6

Source: Census of England and Wales, 1851; Kirby, "How many children were 'unemployed'?". Anderson, "Households, Families and Individuals", p. 427. Figures show the concentration of children aged 10-14 as a proportion of the total number of workers in each occupation.

In England and Wales, in 1851, thirteen and a half per cent of male farm servants were aged between ten and fourteen compared with only eight per cent of out-door agricultural labourers. Similarly, sixteen and a half per cent of female farm servants were aged ten to fourteen as against only

15 Wrigley, "Men on the Land and Men in the Countryside", p. 302. By contrast, Cunningham has asserted that "in agriculture children were a 'dubious asset' and that '[i]n most rural areas children were unemployed'." Cunningham, "Employment and Unemployment of Children", pp. 146-147. For the eighteenth century, there is little hope of arriving at a quantitative history of English child labour for, as Hutchins and Harrison observed a century ago, "no materials exist for anything like a statistical or accurate study of child labour in the eighteenth century". By the nineteenth century, however, the available labour market statistics become more accurate and, by the mid-century, allow a qualified understanding of the major child employment groups. Hutchins and Harrison, *A History of Factory Legislation*, p. 5.

six per cent of agricultural labourers.[16] The shift to a greater proportion of outdoor day labour (as agriculture became more intensive and farms grew larger) in the century to 1851, therefore, must have resulted in a decline in the proportion of child workers in the agricultural labour force as increases in the size of agricultural workforces led to severe accommodation problems among farm servants.[17] The largest group of resident, "in-door", workers was the very large group working children of farmers who in 1851 probably accounted for about a third of all agricultural child labour.[18]

Recent research has shown that the greatest diversity in child occupations existed in small workshops and manufactures. Even in the world's first industrial nation, large factories and mines were never the typical location of child labour. The census lists children employed as shoemakers, tailors, hose and stocking manufacturers, blacksmiths, glovers, clog-makers, book-binders, printers, soap-boilers, brush and broom makers, millers, coopers, cabinet makers, rope makers, sailcloth makers and nail manufacturers, lace makers and straw-plaiters. By 1851, the census disclosed that the highest within-county concentrations of child labour existed not in the industrial counties but in rural Bedfordshire (largely accounted for by the widespread cottage-based straw-plaiting industry).[19] Factory child employment was often marginal and ancillary. By the time of the first workable Factory Act of 1833 there was little support among larger employers for the continued employment of young children in the industrial workplace. The exclusionary provisions of the Act (i.e. a prohibition on the employment of children below the age of nine) were actively supported by owners of larger, urban, steam-powered, factories which employed smaller proportions of children. The Act compelled factory owners to provide costly schooling for young children – effectively "taxing" child employment. It has also been suggested that the Act was designed specifically to restrict output, raise prices and place heavier labour costs upon the marginal, technologically-primitive, water-powered, rural manufactories who relied more heavily upon child labour.[20] Such legislation operated in a complex manner but overwhelmingly mirrored changes in the workplace that were

16 Kirby, *Child Labour in Britain*. See also Kussmaul, *Servants in Husbandry*, Table 7.5, p. 134.

17 Knox, "British Apprenticeship", p. 15.

18 Kirby, "How Many Children were 'Unemployed'?".

19 Cunningham, "Employment and Unemployment of Children", Table 1, p. 141; Horn, "Pillow Lace-Making in Victorian England"; Horn, "Child Workers in the Pillow Lace and Straw Plait Trades".

20 Marvel, "Factory Regulation", p. 380.

progressively excluding the already small proportions of young children from an increasingly complex industrial workplace. Rising real industrial incomes for parents contributed further to the decline in child labour as the marginal value of child earnings fell. Technological changes and rising real incomes, therefore, rather than legislation were probably the major causative factors in the decline of child labour in textiles.[21] Research into the coalmining industry has disclosed a similar picture. Marginal collieries using the most primitive technologies employed the largest proportions of child workers, whilst the more highly-capitalized collieries employed fewer children and sought actively to exclude young children through an increasing use of alternative sources of labour power (notably an increase in the use of ponies and horses). Younger children were also regarded increasingly as a dangerous section of the labour force as they were often given jobs that carried great responsibility for underground safety such as the operation of underground ventilation doors. Managers in the largest collieries strongly supported legislative attempts to exclude young children from underground work.[22] Technical advances, coupled with the need to create a safer and more efficient workplace, led within a few decades to the exclusion of most young children from many of the new industries. Child labour in large industries was therefore a transitional phenomenon, proving profitable in some early factories in the later eighteenth and early nineteenth century but never figuring significantly among the wider population of working children.

Arguments ascribing the decline of child labour to the introduction of compulsory education are similarly flawed. One study of modern child labour suggests that "compulsory primary education is the policy instrument by which the state effectively removes children from the labour force".[23] However, the chronology of education laws shows that no such effect occurred historically in England and Wales. Compulsory schooling was only introduced nationally in 1880 and was applicable only to children aged between five and eleven. By that time, the incidence of child labour

21 Nardinelli, "Child Labor and the Factory Acts", pp. 743, 747, 749–50. Serious doubts attend the methods by which individual child workers were recorded by the factory inspectors. For detail see Kirby, *Child Labour in Britain*, pp. 74–5.

22 Hair, "The Social History of the British Coalminers", pp. 166–9; Kirby, "Aspects of the Employment of Children in the British Coalmining Industry", pp. 165–215; Kirby, "The Historic Viability of Child Labour", pp. 101–17.

23 Quote from Weiner, *The Child and the State in India*, p. 3; See also Minge-Kalman, "The Industrial Revolution and the European family", p. 456, for a similar assumption.

in that age group had fallen to extremely low levels. By 1871, for example, the proportion of five to nine year-olds who were recorded with an occupation had fallen to only 0.7 per cent and by 1881, the census had ceased to count occupied children below ten on the grounds that their numbers had become statistically insignificant.[24] Formal and informal educational provision was therefore concentrated chiefly among children aged below eleven who were mostly too young to embark upon any form of remunerative labour.[25] Nor was there any verifiable relationship during the Industrial Revolution between levels of literacy and industrial development.[26] It is clear that between 1750 and 1851, the vast majority of employed children remained beyond the reach of state regulation or education laws. Hence, the state largely failed to enact legislation on behalf of the main body of child workers in agriculture, services and workshops. Indeed, when the state did pass laws to regulate specific forms of child labour or to compel school attendance, those working families affected by such laws were never provided with compensation for the loss of their children's incomes.[27]

It is generally thought that the enlargement of towns and cities exerted a profound influence upon both the levels and quality of child employment but there has been surprisingly little research on child labour in urban society.[28] Many non-industrial towns and major sea ports harboured fundamentally different labour demands compared with the northern English industrial towns. In London, for example, factory employment for children was exceptionally low (at 1.5 and 0.5 per cent of boys and girls respectively in the employed ten to fourteen age group). This was coupled with a much

24 Hair, "Children in Society", p. 47.

25 Rahikainen has argued the same point for Finland. Rahikainen, "Historical and Present-Day Child Labour", p. 143.

26 Mitch, *The Rise of Popular Literacy in Victorian England*; Mitch, "The Role of Human Capital", pp. 115-119.

27 Kirby, *Child Labour in Britain*, p. 98. Middle-class children, too, were probably profoundly affected by the long-term development of capitalism which, as Thane has pointed out, gave rise to more regulated work-patterns and a growing institutionalisation of "childhood" as a medium through which the middle-classes sought "to tighten their control over the next generation, to train them in habits of work-discipline so that carefully acquired wealth was not later dissipated by careless marriages and loose living". Thane, "Childhood in History", p. 10.

28 See Davin, "Working or Helping?"; Davin, *Growing up Poor*; Schwarz, "English Servants and their Employers during the Eighteenth and Nineteenth Centuries"; Schwarz, *London in the age of industrialisation*; Green, *From Artisans to Paupers*; Kirby, "A Short Statistical Sketch of the Child Labour Market".

greater occupational diversity and higher levels of casual work.[29] There was also a substantial increase in the proportion of the population living in towns and cities which increased from 34 per cent in 1801 to 54 per cent in 1851 and 75 per cent by 1891.[30]

The urban child labour market was therefore affected by fundamentally different factors compared with rural or northern industrial regions. Urban children hardly ever migrated to seek work. Parents might migrate to urban districts in order to find work, but child workers were invariably subject to local labour market conditions and casual labour opportunities in districts where their families had settled.[31] Urbanization also reduced the distance between the parental home and the location of first employment. This was a factor of crucial importance in a society in which almost everyone walked to work as it largely removed the need to leave the parental home in order to start work (a practice widespread in rural society). The contrast between the rural labour market (in which children and adolescents were frequently boarded with masters) and the urban setting (in which older, working, children remained resident in the parental home) was statistically striking.[32] According to Wall, in 1861, ninety-eight per cent of urban Preston children in the age-group fifteen to nineteen resided with their parents, compared with only sixty-two per cent in the rural parish of Colyton in 1841.[33] The rise of urban and industrial employment was also accompanied by the emergence of a general custom among the working-class of children of remaining in the parental home until marriage.[34] This demographic shift extended considerably the period during which older children and young adults contributed to household income and relieved parents of the pressure to have the younger dependent children employed outside the household. The increasingly widespread retention of older working children in urban and industrial households marked a fundamental shift in the life cycle experiences of the population and

29 Kirby, "A Short Statistical Sketch of the Child Labour Market", p. 234.

30 Law, "The Growth of Urban Population in England and Wales", p. 130.

31 Rahikainen mentions some instances of child migration but this must be regarded as exceptional. Rahikainen, "Historical and Present-Day Child Labour".

32 In 1851, only ten per cent of Preston children aged fifteen to nineteen lived in lodgings. Anderson, *Family Structure*, p. 53.

33 In modern western societies, the children of more affluent families, almost universally, leave home later than historic populations. Wall, "The Age at Leaving Home", pp. 190, 193, 197.

34 The custom persisted in England and Wales until the later decades of the twentieth century. Burr-Litchfield, "The Family and the Mill", p. 192.

was probably a crucial factor in reducing the supply of young urban child labourers to the labour market.[35] Moreover, whilst higher wages available to urban families may have reduced the household requirement for child labour at early ages, parental perceptions of the declining economic value of child labour – coupled with the rising cost of "childhood" more generally – may have influenced the marked and sustained late nineteenth-century decline in marital fertility. Hence, demographic structural factors, the maturation of the economy and child labour where intimately connected during urbanization. The transition to urban living tied children and adolescents more closely to the household economy compared with traditional rural society in which children and young people had been much more spatially mobile during their early working lives.[36]

The question of whether such changes had any effect upon levels of child employment may be partly tested by comparing the urban labour market with the national picture using available large-scale statistical evidence. The most striking aspect of the metropolitan child labour market in the mid-nineteenth century, for example, was the very small proportion of children who were enumerated with an occupation compared with the rest of England and Wales (table 6.4).[37]

Table 6.4. Proportions (%) Occupied by Sex and Age-Groups: London and England and Wales, 1851

	all ages	*5-9*	*10-14*	*15-19*
Males				
London	64.54	0.32	22.91	82.45
England and Wales (minus London)	65.96	2.59	41.58	90.91
Females				
London	32.52	0.21	11.86	56.49
England and Wales (minus London)	31.42	1.91	24.24	64.50

Source: Census of England and Wales, 1851.

35 Kirby, *Child Labour in Britain*, pp. 32–34.
36 Kussmaul, "Ambiguous Mobility".
37 Kirby, "A Short Statistical Sketch of the Child Labour Market".

Only 0.3 per cent of London boys aged five to nine and twenty-three per cent of boys aged ten to fourteen had a recorded occupation compared with three per cent and forty two per cent in the remainder of England and Wales. Among females, only 0.2 per cent aged five to nine and twelve per cent aged ten to fourteen had a recorded occupation compared with two per cent and twenty-four per cent in the rest of England and Wales. Hence, the proportion of London children between ten and fourteen who were at work was around half the national average. London, therefore, harboured very low relative levels of child employment.

In 1851, general domestic service formed the most popular occupation for London females aged ten to fourteen. In the rest of England and Wales, child domestic servants (i.e. children in the six domestic service categories or charwomen, washerwomen or manglers) formed about twenty-three per cent of all occupied females aged ten to fourteen whilst in London the comparable figure was nearly fifty-nine per cent.[38] Strikingly, however, the age structure of metropolitan servants remained much older: general domestic servants in London aged below twenty formed only thirty-three per cent of the total of female servants compared with forty-two per cent in the rest of England and Wales (table 6.5).

Table 6.5. Domestic Servants Aged Below 20 as a Percentage of All Domestic Servants, 1851

London	33
England and Wales (minus London)	42

Source: Census of England and Wales, 1851.

Errand and message running was by far the largest and most youthful occupation for London males.[39] Despite their overwhelming domination of the London child labour market, however, few *very young* children were

38 In 1851, females in domestic service in England and Wales outnumbered males by about eight to one whereas males in farm service outnumbered females by two to one. Kussmaul, *Servants in Husbandry*, p. 4.

39 Male messengers and porters aged 10-14 in the metropolis were ten times more numerous than then the next largest occupation.

employed as errand runners.[40] This observation is borne out by census statistics, which suggest that only a half per cent of male messengers was aged below ten whilst thirty-two per cent were aged ten to fourteen. In common with the occupational age-structure of female domestic servants, male errand runners in London tended to be older than elsewhere: less than a third of metropolitan male messengers and porters were aged ten to fourteen compared with a half in the rest of England and Wales (table 6.6).[41]

Table 6.6. Messengers and Porters as a Proportion (%) of All Messengers and Porters (males), 1851

	5-9	*10-14*	*15-19*
London	0.5	31.7	27.5
England and Wales (minus London)	3.6	49.5	21.4

Source: Census of England and Wales, 1851.

Table 6.7. Ten to Fourteen Year-Olds as a Proportion (%) of Totals Employed in Selected Occupations, 1851

	London	*England and Wales (minus London)*
Female errand runners	28.6	56.3
Female domestic servant (general)	5.3	8.2
Female domestic servant (nurse)	8.6	22.3
Female domestic servants (aggregate)	3.6	6.2
Male errand runners	31.7	49.5
Male chimney sweeps	4.1	17.5

Source: Census of England and Wales, 1851.

40 One prominent nineteenth-century writer on the metropolitan working class, suggested that children were generally placed as errand boys only after reaching the age of 10. Greenwood, *The Seven Curses of London*, p. 40.

41 Kirby, *Child Labour in Britain*, p. 68. Comparative figures for Northumberland and industrial Lancashire were 63% and 38%. The author is grateful to L.M.W. Shaw-Taylor and E.A. Wrigley for supplying the Northumberland and Lancashire data sheets for males from which these comparative figures were calculated.

Despite the highly casual complexion of the London labour market, therefore, there seems to have been no presumption that children should commence work at ages earlier than ten. Indeed, the participation rate of under-tens was far lower compared with the rest of the nation. There was a consistent trend towards an older age-structure among several prominent metropolitan "child labour" occupations when compared with the rest of the nation (table 6.7).

Overall recorded levels of child employment in the metropolis at ages ten to fourteen were about forty-five per cent lower for males and about fifty per cent lower for females compared with the rest of England and Wales. Less than one per cent of London children aged five to nine and fewer than one in five of those aged ten to fourteen were enumerated with an occupation in 1851.[42] There is little evidence to suggest that London suffered from census under-enumeration of child occupations compared with elsewhere as seasonal factors can largely be discounted. Census statistics collected in Spring tended chiefly to understate seasonal fluctuations in child employment in *agricultural* districts and the child labour gap between London and the rest of England and Wales would therefore have been much greater during summer and harvest time.[43] The availability of child employment in occupations offering longer-term prospects also seems to have been exceptionally low in London (again, reflecting the much higher incidence of casual work in urban areas). If "casual" jobs such as messengers and errand boys are excluded from the metropolitan labour statistics, the overall participation rate for ten-to-fourteen year-old males in London falls dramatically to thirteen per cent of the age-group compared with thirty-six per cent in England and Wales as a whole.[44] It seems clear that the London labour market contained smaller proportions of child labour compared with England and Wales as a whole and from this it might be inferred that it offered few opportunities for the early employment of children. This argument is probably applicable to most other non-industrial conurbations in England and Wales (though the aggregate data to test such a hypothesis for other urban districts is not readily available).

42 Most of the employed 10-14 age group would be concentrated at ages 13 and 14. Kirby, *Child Labour in Britain*, p. 80.

43 The 1851 census was taken on 30th March. In England and Wales (exclusive of London) 37 per cent of occupied males aged 10-14 were engaged in agriculture, animals and fisheries, compared with fewer than 2 per cent in London.

44 Messengers and errand boys made up 43 per cent of the total of employed 10-14 year olds in London but only 10 per cent in the rest of England and Wales.

In conclusion, the empirical fact that all developed economies show a strong relationship between high levels of economic growth and a low incidence of children's employment is easier to describe than explain. The archetypal model of child labour in large factories and mines was never the predominant mode of child labour in England and Wales. Large-scale industrial production was confined to only a small number of regions and could never have been as widespread as previously thought. The vast majority of working children also remained beyond the reach of state regulations which, even by the later nineteenth century, applied only to a very small number of industrial occupations and was rarely enforced. Compulsory elementary schooling, similarly, had no appreciable effect upon overall levels of child employment which, by the time it was introduced, had declined to statistically insignificant levels. Humanitarian campaigns against industrial child labour should be viewed as the product of a convergence of political interests rather than as attempts to improve the welfare of the children of the working class (most of whom where in occupations unaffected by child labour or education laws). Scholars of children's employment therefore need to look further than studies which stress the influence of middle-class campaigners, anti-child-labour legislation and compulsory schooling on the decline of children's employment.[45] Instead, child labour in eighteenth and nineteenth century England and Wales needs to be understood as a complex and diverse relationship with the household economy and the wider labour market. The years between ten and fourteen marked the major transition for children from dependency to paid work. This near-universal transition was crucial for the incomes of households and permitted children to establish an identity within local communities – forming a life-cycle event comparable with the attainment of educational qualifications among children and adolescents today.[46] By comparison, the employment of young children below ten was always a marginal matter and was associated chiefly with the poorest households, lone-parents and orphans. Other profound effects, such as rapid urbanisation and the increasing ability simply to walk to work rather than leaving

45 Rahikainen has argued this point for later nineteenth-century Finland. Rahikainen, "Historical and Present-Day Child Labour", p. 143; Kirby, *Child Labour in Britain*, Ch. 4. One historian has found it "hard to believe that rich philanthropists felt more strongly than parents about the welfare of their children". Hutt, "The Factory System of the Early Nineteenth Century", p. 183.

46 The importance of the relationship between occupations and status in the past is attested by the frequent occurrence of occupation designations as surnames.

home transformed the early home and work experiences of young people. Such factors led to the consolidation of the modern, urban, working-class, family model which prevailed in England and Wales until the later twentieth century.

The development of a fuller history of the dynamics of child labour during urban and industrial growth is crucial to our understanding of modern, globalized, child labour. The complex labour requirements of a developing economy and changes in relative levels of household poverty are central to that understanding. Developed industrial and urban societies seem all to have experienced a secular decline in child employment, shadowed closely by successive increases in school-leaving ages. This transition may reflect a progressive effort by the state to provide education for children or may equally indicate a growing inability of a mature labour market to absorb large numbers of adolescent children (the latter process seems a more obvious explanation). Fundamentally, both industrial and non-industrial urban centres appear to have exhibited much lower levels of child labour compared with rural and semi-rural districts. It is dangerous to generalize, however, since each sector used child labour in different ways and had different demands in terms of labour contracts and the ages at which children were recruited. The processes influencing child labour in discrete regions, amongst differing family forms and in diverse sectors, therefore, require more detailed monographic research. The enormous diversity of the growing nineteenth-century urban child labour force, coupled with the lack of any consistent body of quantitative evidence prior to the second half of the nineteenth century, poses the major challenge to further research in the field. Local labour-market studies and research into the family economy offer the most promising avenues through which to explore further the ways in which the transition to working life changed in the context of an increasingly industrialized and urban society. Ultimately, the problems that exist are chiefly evidential ones: these may require a fundamental conceptual shift towards understanding child labour as part of a series of relative demographic and labour-market transitions rather than as an historically-specific and morally-disputed institution.

CHAPTER 7

Child Labour and Child Labour Reform in Nineteenth-Century France: An International Perspective*

Colin Heywood

The history of child labour often appears as little more than the history of child labour in Britain. Brief outlines for the consumption of social scientists, for example, routinely concentrate on telling the familiar story of the widespread employment of children in British textile mills and coal mines during the early nineteenth century and of the campaigns by factory reformers to curb the practice.[1] The reasons for this narrow perspective are not hard to fathom. Britain mobilized children for work in capital-intensive forms of mining and manufacturing earlier and on a larger scale than other countries. Her parliamentary enquiries, census registers and pamphlet literature provide ample documentation of the phenomenon. Moreover, her case has generated an exceptionally rich historiography – and one obligingly written in the English language.[2] Studies of child labour and reform movements in other countries and even on a global scale are by no means hard to find. In the developed world, studies on such countries as the United States, Belgium, France, Sweden and Italy are illuminating.[3] Yet it might be said that they add little to the overall picture in so far as they follow the same "modernization" model of development as

* The author would like to thank Dr Olena Heywood for comments on earlier drafts, and Prof Ben White for suggestions made as referee of the paper.

1 For examples with a strong British bias, see Nardinelli, *Child Labor and the Industrial Revolution*; Fyfe, *Child Labour*, ch. 2; Lavalette, *Child Employment in the Capitalist Labour Market*, ch. 10.

2 The literature is admirably surveyed in Horn, *Children's Work and Welfare*; and Kirby, *Child Labour in Britain*.

3 For an international perspective, see Hawes and Hiner, *Children in Historical and Comparative Perspective*; Cunningham and Viazzo, *Child Labour in Historical Perspective*; Hobbs, McKechnie and Lavalette, *Child Labor*; Colón and Colón, *A History of Children*; Caty, *Enfants au travail*; and Stearns, *Childhood in World History*.

their British counterparts. According to Hugh Cunningham and Shelton Stromquist, this model locates the origins of the "child labour" issue during the Industrial Revolution in Britain. This was when the harsh conditions for child workers in industry first caused outrage among sections of the population at large. Fortunately, so the story goes, the later nineteenth century brought a long-term decline in child labour, as schools replaced the workplace in the lives of young people. The assumption is that all countries in the world would follow this pattern of industrialization. That is to say, a "dirty" or "savage" phase of industrialization, hostile to child welfare, would sooner or later give way to a later, more benign phase. The young could then flourish with a "proper" childhood, sheltered from the need to earn a living.[4]

French historians during the later twentieth century played their part by focusing on such issues as the impact of mechanization on the division of labour, the links between the poverty of the new industrial workers and the practice of child labour, and the long struggle to bring in effective factory legislation. Edouard Dolléans and Georges Dehove floated a popular theme with the assertion that machinery made possible the substitution of women and children for adult male labour.[5] Pierre Pierrard, another luminary among social historians, wrote of the "dramatic appearance of the children of workers" during the late eighteenth and early nineteenth century, depicting them as victims of insecurity and downright indigence.[6] Any number of authors outlined the pioneering efforts of the Mulhouse Industrial Society to promote child labour legislation, leading to a series of laws in 1841, 1874, 1892 and 1900. Reinforcing the impact of the laws, as elsewhere in the West, it emerges that such changes as technical progress, rising real wages and a growing demand for primary schooling gradually eliminated children (under fourteen) from the workshops.[7] Overall, it is tempting to envisage a pattern of challenge-and-response across Europe and North America, as a series of countries confronted the issue of child labour in the industrial workshops. However, this "silo" mode of thinking has its limitations. In the first place, elites in each country were well aware

4 Cunningham and Stromquist, "Child Labour and the Rights of Children", pp. 55–57.

5 Dolléans and Dehove, *Histoire du travail en France.*

6 Pierrard, *Enfants et jeunes ouvriers en France*, ch. 1.

7 See for e.g. Crubellier, *L'enfance et la jeunesse*, chs 6, 11; Sandrin, *Enfants trouvés*; Braun and Valentin, *Villermé et le travail des enfants*; Chassagne, "Le Travail des enfants"; Rollet, *Les enfants au XIXe siècle.* Among "Anglo-Saxon" authors, one might cite Weissbach, *Child Labor Reform*; and Heywood, *Childhood in Nineteenth-Century France.*

of industrial and legislative developments among their neighbours. As the historian Eliane Gubin noted, the 1830s and 1840s witnessed a flurry of enquiries in Europe on conditions for child labour in countries at varying stages of industrialization. These led to a series of child labour laws aiming to repress abuses.[8] In the second place, child labour did not necessarily fade away in each country as easily as "modernization" models suggest.[9] Following the line of argument of Cunningham and Stromquist, it would be more fruitful to seek out differences in child labour practices and reform campaigns at various periods and in various places. This is particularly important when we think in global terms, in order to highlight the contrasts as well as the well-established similarities between countries.

Accordingly, this paper will reflect on the particular configuration and evolution of the employment of young people in France, to provide a case study for comparative purposes. What stands out in the French case is the persistence of child labour on the land and in so-called "transitional" forms of industrial organization, such as production in small workshops, besides the work on machines that so shocked many contemporaries. The paper will also highlight the peculiar political and cultural context for child labour reform campaigns in France. Here it is the rarefied atmosphere in which these campaigns operated, largely isolated from popular pressure, which stands out for most of the nineteenth century.

The Employment of Children in France

France was one of a small group of countries in Europe that embarked early on the path to industrialization during the eighteenth and nineteenth centuries. Like Britain and Belgium, it experienced relatively slow rates of economic growth, relied on consumer-goods industries such as textiles as engines of growth, and adopted a laissez-faire policy (in the domestic market at least). It follows that there were indeed many similarities in the patterns of child labour on the two sides of the Channel, as the traditional historiography has emphasized.

While Britain dragooned pauper apprentices into her early cotton mills, for example, France took advantage of her *enfants assistés*. Both countries thus resorted to forced labour, drawn from the ranks of disadvantaged

8 Gubin, "Postface"; Cunningham and Stromquist, "Child Labor and the Rights of Children", p. 58.

9 Lavalette, *A Thing of the Past?*; Fyfe, *Child Labour*, ch. 2.

children, to assure a source of cheap and subservient labour for the first generation of industrial entrepreneurs. The French version of this strategy occurred on a large scale during the Revolutionary Wars of the 1790s. Orphaned and abandoned children were threatening at this point to overwhelm the budgets of the Hospices. A convenient solution for the authorities was to allow employers to bid for large numbers of the unfortunate children as tied labour. Traces of the *enfants assistés* linger on throughout the nineteenth century, notably in isolated glassworks and silk-throwing mills, but they were never again marshalled on the same scale.[10]

Child workers were also among the first workers deployed to help operate machinery in the early textile mills in France, as in other industrializing nations such as Britain, Belgium and the United States.[11] Wood and Hill, two "*artistes anglois*" (English artists) attempting to extract a subsidy from the French government for the establishment of a water-powered spinning mill at Louviers, pointed out in 1784 that "a child will do, with the aid of a machine, the work of over twelve excellent male or female spinners in one day".[12] In 1790, nine-tenths of the labour force at a mechanized spinnery run by another Englishman, Foxlow at Orleans, were either children aged five to sixteen, or women too old or infirm to support themselves in any other way.[13] Similarly, a census of factory hands in Alsace during the early 1820s found that, in the mills investigated, over a third were children under sixteen. In the famous Gros-Davillier-Roman mill at Wesserling, for example, 35 per cent of hands in the spinning, weaving and printing workshops were under sixteen years of age.[14] France, like its neighbours, therefore had her cohorts of *rattacheurs* (piecers), *bobineurs* (bobbin boys) and *dévideurs* (winders). It is unlikely that "child labour", in this industrial form, was as widespread as in Britain. Nonetheless, the 143,665 children under sixteen identified by an official enquiry of 1839-45 as working in the

10 Douailler and Vermeren, "Les enfants du capital", pp. 8-12; Chassagne, *Le Coton et ses patrons*, pp. 214-216, 234-242; Murat, "Le Travail des enfants abandonnés".

11 From a huge literature, see for e.g., Scholliers, "Grown-Ups, Boys and Girls"; Herdt, "Child Labour in Belgium"; Bolin-Hort, *Work, Family and the State*; Tuttle, *Hard at Work in Factories and Mines*; and Hindman, *Child Labor.*

12 Archives Nationales, Paris (hereafter AN) F^{12} 1339, Memoir of Wood and Hill, 1784 (these two English workers, James Theakston and John Flint, known as Wood and Hill respectively, were former employees of Arkwright's mill at Cromford).

13 Chassagne, *Le coton et ses patrons*, pp. 193-194.

14 Archives Départementales (hereafter AD) du Haut-Rhin, 9 M 22, Commune de Ranspach, Etat nominatif des ouvriers de fabrique résidant dans cette commune, 9 December 1822.

larger industrial enterprises meant that the scale of the practice was sufficient to provoke "outrage" among a number of influential observers.[15] In the longer term, there is evidence to suggest a decline during the second half of the nineteenth century in the numbers of children employed in *la grande industrie*: the textile mills, ceramics factories, paper mills, glassworks and the like. This is admittedly difficult to measure precisely in the French case, given that the population census did not summarize its data on the distribution of the active population by age groups until 1896, but it seems reasonable to assume that France conformed to the "modernization" model in this respect.

That said, one might suggest that the spectacle of child labour working with machinery in the mills – *l'ouvrier de huit ans* (the eight year-old worker, in the oft-cited words of Jules Simon)[16] – has mesmerized historians as much as it did contemporaries. The rows of machines, the scale of the buildings and the comings-and-goings of large groups of factory hands of all ages naturally attracted the attention of social observers. Towns like Rouen appeared to be the French version of Manchester, provoking speculation on what the future held, for better or for worse, if the country followed the British path to an industrial and urban society. This included the familiar notion that, as the social investigator Eugène Buret put in 1840, mechanization in the cotton mills would pave the way for "feeble beings, imperfect workers, like children and women, fulfilling at lower cost the functions of industry".[17] For the historian, the dramatic story of the rise, and eventual fall, of child labour in the factories can hardly fail to impress.

Yet in the French case it was a rather tame imitation of the British precedent. The French path to industrialization was a far more gradual or "unobtrusive" one, featuring a larger agrarian sector and more of a preference for a small scale of production throughout the nineteenth century.[18] The focus in the French historiography on the phenomenon of "child labour" in the mills therefore appears a case of the tail wagging the dog: a conventional rehash of the story from Britain that distorts the realities on the other side

15 Weissbach, *Child Labor Reform*, ch. 2; Heywood, *Childhood in Nineteenth-Century France*, ch. 8; Chassagne, *Le cotton et ses patrons*, pp. 513–519.

16 Simon, *L'ouvrier de huit ans.*

17 Buret, *De la misère des classes laborieuses*, vol. 2, p. 152. The point was common currency during the mid nineteenth century. See also Villermé, *Discours sur la durée*, p. 61; Dupin, *Du travail des enfants qu'emploient les ateliers,* vol. 2, p. 5; and Simon, *L'ouvrier de huit ans,* pp. 161-162.

18 See for e.g. Asselain, *Histoire économique de la France,* vol. 1, pp. 197-201; and Magraw, "Not Backward but Different".

of the Channel. It leaves open the question of where France might have diverged from its neighbours in its employment of the young. As indicated above, this is a matter of a peculiar configuration of child labour, for it could hardly be claimed that work on a peasant farm, in a small workshop or even in a *couvent-atelier* ("convent-workshop") was unknown elsewhere. What matters for our purposes is the pattern of employment in France compared to other leading European nations during the nineteenth century. Three salient features of the labour market stood out in relation to child workers at this period.

Employment in Small Workshops

First, there was the widespread dispersal of labour in the French manufacturing sector among small workshops. If this was far from being a characteristic unique to France, in the European context it at least stood out from neighbouring countries like Britain and Germany by its greater commitment to and persistence with a small scale of production. As late as 1906, according to the census of population, one third of its labour force was working in establishments with less than ten workers, and the median plant had only 45 workers. It must be admitted that problems of definition make it difficult to compare average plant or firm sizes in different countries. None the less, economic historians generally agree on the French preference for small and medium sized enterprises during the nineteenth century, a few exceptions such as coal mining and metallurgy apart.[19] Certainly French administrators were aware of the peculiar nature of the challenge they faced when attempting to regulate child labour. A report from the Bureau de Manufactures on the subject, summarizing the findings of an enquiry of 1837, noted that whereas in England large workshops were numerous, in France workers were more isolated, being located more often in a domestic workshop or a small unit with two to five looms.[20] The typical organization of production in France was a *fabrique collective* or network of specialized firms in a particular region producing goods by means of an extensive division of labour.[21] This type of activity included such diverse industries as lace making, mechanical engineering and food processing. It

19 The large-scale exceptions are emphasized in Smith, *The Emergence of Modern Business Enterprise*.

20 AN F^{12} 4706, Rapport du Bureau des Manufactures sur les réponses à la circulaire du 31 juillet 1837, preliminary considerations (note that these were omitted from the printed version of the report).

21 Cottereau, "The Distinctiveness of Working-Class Cultures", p. 115.

may have accounted for as much as nine-tenths of production in France during the nineteenth century.

Unfortunately, the small and medium sized workshops involved generally escaped the attention of social investigators. They lacked the novelty of the big factories, and many were buried deep in the countryside or in the "popular" neighbourhoods of the towns. Significantly, the first national enquiry into child labour in France of 1837 appeared to pitch its questions at factories rather than domestic or artisanal forms of production. This encouraged the authorities in many Departments to ignore the questionnaire or claim that the questions did not concern them.[22] The Prefect of the Côtes-du-Nord, for example, claimed that the only industry in his area was cloth weaving, and confined himself to noting that the children all worked with their family. Yet, however elusive, such dispersed industries were substantial employers of child workers. Can one safely assume that the children in question worked under a more benign regime than the "child labour", in the conventional sense, employed in the mills? That is to say, working beside their parents or in the relatively intimate atmosphere of a small workshop, did they avoid the impersonal discipline of the factory system? Or did the personal relationships of the small workshops bring risks of their own? Furthermore, were they spared the relentless rhythm of the machine, or did their hand tool methods require more physical effort from them? It emerges that many contemporaries in nineteenth-century France, like historians since, have doubted the popular perception that children were safe working in the bosom of the family or in a small workshop. The differences between the "formal" sector of industry (large establishments regulated by the law after 1841) and the "informal" one of outworkers, subcontractors and "sweatshops" did not invariably favour the latter.[23]

Take the case of rural industry. "Proto-industrialization" theory asserted that the rise of rural industries in the European countryside during the seventeenth and eighteenth centuries undermined the traditional division of labour by age and sex. Children in the homes of spinners, handloom weavers and knitters were allegedly under considerably more pressure to work than their counterparts in exclusively farming households.[24] The 1837 Enquiry mentioned, among others, children employed in domestic workshops in Lorraine as embroiderers from the age of seven, and in Anjou as

22 AN F^{12} 4705, Enquête sur le travail des enfants, 1837. In the event, 38 out of 86 Departments failed to reply or gave no information.

23 See Grootaert and Kanbar, "Child Labour", p. 195.

24 Medick, "The Proto-Industrial Family Economy".

assistants to hand loom weavers from the age of five.[25] Among the latter, the historian Tessie Liu noted the way parents needed to control children from an early age in the interests of their trade. The weaver depended on the unpaid labour of his family to survive. The result was that the "disciplining of bodies and habits was the first lesson children learnt from weaver parents". A good weaver needed speed and endurance, including patience with a job that tied him to the loom all day, and precision in counting threads, keeping edges square and keeping his cloth taut. Hence, instead of the factory overseer, children had to cope with constant attention from parents attempting to develop these qualities.[26] It was easy for families in these rural industries to become trapped by their routines in an increasingly impoverished existence, as happened to hand loom weavers and framework knitters in various parts of France. Young people in particular moved out of such trades during the second half of the nineteenth century.[27]

The "sweated" trades of the towns also employed large numbers of children in potentially onerous conditions, and persisted longer with them. The silk industry of Lyon provides an outstanding example of French manufacturing industry, successful on the international market but highly dispersed in its structure. In 1837 the local Conseil des Prudhommes did take the trouble to report to the ministry on the extensive resort to child labour by the industry, and the hazards faced by the different trades. It noted that there were no large workshops in the town, only a multitude of small ones, run as their owners saw fit. Among its various branches, the weaving shops employed children from the age of five to assist the weavers, and, according to the Conseil, "this work is only arduous in the constant attention required; it lasts fourteen hours a day, which deprives the children of elementary instruction". Most of these workers were girls. Silk winding shops also employed young children, causing deformities among those who had to turn the wheels. The *tireurs* of the workshops printing silks had to work fourteen hours a day, though intermittently, from the ages of eight to fifteen, while the *lanceurs* of the shawl weaving shops worked similarly long hours, continually returning the shuttle to the weaver.[28] The well-known

25 AN F[12] 4705, Replies from the Sub-Prefect of Lunéville, 14 December 1837 and the Conseil des Prudhommes of Cholet, 15 September 1837.

26 Liu, *The Weaver's Knot*, pp. 224-225.

27 See for e.g. Gullickson, *Spinners and Weavers of Auffay*, ch. 6; and Liu, *The Weaver's Knot, passim*.

28 AN F[12] 4705, Response from the Conseil des Prudhommes de Lyon, 8 December 1837. See also Villermé, *Tableau de l'état physique et moral*, vol. 1, section 3.

working-class autobiography written by Norbert Truquin has helped give small workshops in France a bad name among historians. He was probably far from being a typical child worker in such establishments, given that his father had abandoned him at an early age. Nonetheless, his searing account of working in a wool combing shop in Reims during the 1840s casts a shadow on this sector. His time in the workshop began at the age of seven. While his master straightened the wool with a heated comb, his job was to hold a strand of drawn wool taut between his two hands and pick out any impurities with his teeth. He worked from four in the morning until ten at night, sustained by soup made from vegetables and scraps of meat. His predominant memory was of trying to work through extreme drowsiness: every time he began to fall asleep, his master hit him across the bridge of his nose and set off a nosebleed. He made it clear that he found his next employment, in a wool-spinning mill near Amiens, more tolerable.[29]

During the latter half of the nineteenth century, this supposedly "transitional" form of small workshops in the towns and cities proved remarkably resilient. An enquiry of 1867 prompted the Chamber of Commerce in Paris to report that the number of children to be found in workshops employing fewer than twenty workers, and so not covered by the 1841 child labour law, had increased markedly over the previous few years as apprenticeship contracts had fallen into disuse. It estimated that 360 factories employed 4,500 children under sixteen, while 500 small establishments employing children outside the family accounted for a further 1,500, and an unspecified number with "more or less serious apprenticeships contracts" no less than 24,000. Meanwhile in Lyon the silk industry continued to attract criticism for undermining the health and education of its juvenile workers. The 1867 Enquiry estimated that factories in the Rhône Department occupied 2,650 children, and the smaller workshops a further 5,200.[30]

Even when small workshops began to be regulated, with the 1874 child labour law, inspectors frequently complained that they had little hope of making an impact on the myriads of such establishment scattered around obscure back streets. In 1875, the newly installed inspector for the Seine complained that he had 25,000 children to supervise on his own, and very

29 Truquin, *Mémoires et aventures*, pp. 18–25.

30 AN F^{12} 4722-3, Enquête sur le travail des enfants, 1867: M.E. Pariset, "Travail des enfants dans les manufactures: rapport à la Chambre de Comerce de Lyon", 15 June 1867; Statistics for the Rhône Department, 7 December 1867; Letter from Paris Chamber of Commerce to the Minister of Agriculture, Commerce and Public Works, 30 November 1867; Statistics for the Seine Department, 13 December 1867 and 10 February 1868.

few big industrial establishments. His counterpart in Lyon mentioned struggling to enforce the law in 12,000 small workshops.[31] The Inspector Gauthier reported on the large number of so-called "*apprentis*" in Lyon, for the most part girls, who were employed on the preparatory stages of silk manufacture. Coming in from the countryside, they lodged with families of workers, and earned a small sum each year that was sent back to their families.[32] A peculiar twist to child labour at this period came with the proliferation of charitable workshops undertaking such work as sewing lingerie and shirts for the new department stores. A report of 1882 on orphanages and other similar institutions by Théophile Roussel noted how an *ouvroir* set up to teach young children a trade could easily slide into a money-making operation for a hard-pressed institution. The charities were exempt from the law, leading to complaints of unfair competition from local businesses. In 1883, the Inspector in Paris reported rumours that young girls in an orphanage run by nuns worked through the night when pressed by the Bon Marché store. Others were accused of working the girls for fifteen hours a day.[33]

Work on the Land

A further notable characteristic of French industrialization was the persistence of a large agricultural sector. In 1906, for example, 41.4 per cent of the labour force was still employed in agriculture.[34] No one ever mounted a campaign to regulate or ban child labour on the land. Indeed there was a tendency among the elite to idealize the peasant existence. During the 1830s, for example, the very conservative and very Catholic Villeneuve-Bargemont argued that it was best if young people went into farm work when they left school, on the grounds that its customs were simpler and purer, its wages more secure and its way of life more frugal. At the other end of the political spectrum, and at the end of the century, the novelist Emile Zola could still talk about the city-dwellers "dream about the peasants".[35] Autobiographical accounts written by those brought up in the villages adopted a very different tone, often bringing out the grinding pov-

31 AN F^{12} 4731, Report by Maurice (1st district), 3 November 1875; AN F^{12} 4755, Report by Delattre aîné (15th district), 12 February 1880.

32 AN F^{12} 4755, Report of 23 April 1878.

33 Roussel, *Rapport sur les resultats de l'enquête*, p. XXVII; AN F^{12} 4730, Report by Laporte (1st district), 1883. See also Heywood, "The Catholic Church".

34 Dormois, *The French Economy in the Twentieth Century*, p. 8, table 1.4.

35 Villeneuve-Bargemont, *Économie politique chrétienne*, p. 440; Preface by Emmanuel Le Roy Ladurie to Emile Zola, *La Terre* (Paris, 1980), p. 14.

erty they and their families had faced.[36] Nonetheless, they often appreciated the "apprenticeship" in farming they received within the family and the local community. Ephraïm Grenadou, for example, learned how to plough during the 1900s by watching the men at work in the fields, and having them show him what to do. By the age of fourteen he claimed that he could handle a plough as well as anyone else in the village.[37] In France, the scandal of agricultural gangs exploiting women and children never arose.[38] The small family farms pervasive in a number of regions provided various tasks suitable for children, such as shepherding or looking after younger brothers and sisters.[39]

The main drawback for children leading this peasant existence, particularly in the more isolated areas, was its incompatibility with schooling. During the 1830s, for example, the Prefect of the Ardennes reported that education was far more advanced in the industrial areas of his department than the agricultural ones. In the latter:

> As soon as the children of most farmers have reached the age of eight to ten years they follow the livestock into the fields, and lead the plough horses. Their physique develops better and their health is better assured than among industrial workers, but their instruction is non-existent. Living in isolation, in the middle of the fields, having no opportunity to exchange their thoughts, or exercise their intelligence, they forget over the summer the little they have managed to learn attending school during the winter.[40]

Doubtless the growing demand for schooling throughout the nineteenth century, even before it was made free and compulsory during the 1880s, affected the villagers, encouraging many to seek careers in the towns. All the same, there was a tendency for peasants to remain suspicious of the school well into the twentieth century. For them, there was no substitute

36 See for e.g. Sylvère, *Toinou*; Emilie Carles, as told to Robert Destanque, *A Wild Herb Soup: The Life of a French Countrywoman*, transl. Avriel H. Goldberger (London, 1992); Pitaud, *Le pain de la terre*; Déguignet, *Mémoires d'un paysan Bas-Breton*. See also Heywood, *Growing Up in France*, chs 8, 10.

37 Grenadou and Prévost, *Grenadou*, pp. 25-32.

38 See for e.g. Kitteringham, "Country Work Girls", pp. 98-112; Cammarosano, "Labouring Women", p. 171.

39 See Heywood, *Childhood in Nineteenth-Centurt France*, ch. 2.

40 AN F[12] 4705, Reply of Prefect of the Ardennes to the 1837 Enquiry on Child Labour, 15 November 1837.

for learning to farm on-the-job. As a village lad from a family of tenant farmers in the Vaucluse put it during the 1950s:

> My great-grandparents were farmers. My grandparents were farmers. My parents are farmers. My father decided to be a farmer because he liked it and because he didn't know how to do anything else. He learned to farm by working in the fields with his father. I shall be a farmer, too, because I like it. I am learning to be a farmer by helping my father in the fields.[41]

The Mix of Industries

Finally, the industries in the "formal" sector of the economy that caused the most problems for child labour inspectors were not necessarily the same in France as elsewhere. Coal mining did not loom as large in French reform campaigns as it did in those of some of its neighbours. This was partly a matter of the relatively small size of the French industry. On the eve of the First World War, France was producing forty million tonnes of coal, well behind the 275 millions extracted in Britain, and the 248 millions in Germany. There was also a decree of 1813 that banned boys under ten from work in the mines, admittedly not always observed, and a general policy of employing women and girls on sorting at the pit head only. Mining areas such as the Nord and the Loire made only passing references to children working in the mines when responding to the 1837 enquiry on child labour.[42] This might be compared to the widespread employment of women and children in coal mines in Britain and Belgium at the same period.[43] By the time child labour inspectors were active at the end of the nineteenth century, starting ages for underground workers were around the ages of thirteen or fifteen. Half-time working for children was also a practice that found little favour in French industry, so that there was no equivalent to the notorious attachment of Lancashire cotton spinners to child labour in this form towards the end of the nineteenth century.[44] Conversely a very substantial industry in southern France (and northern Italy) that plagued the existence of child labour inspectors was silk throwing. The mills were difficult to reach in their remote, hilly areas, and determined to hold on to the girls employed in them when they experienced

41 Wylie, *Village in the Vaucluse*, p. 99.

42 AN F[12] 4705, Letters to the Minister of Commerce from the Prefect of the Loire, 20 March 1837, and the Conseil des Prudhommes de Valenciennes, 31 December 1837.

43 For e.g. see Hilden, *Women, Work, and Politics*, ch. 4.

44 Bolin-Hort, *Work, Family and the State*, ch. 10.

difficulties on the international market during the 1880s. The isolation of the *moulinages* meant that most of the girls boarded in *internats* during the week, often under the supervision of nuns from Catholic orders specializing in this line. According to one estimate, there were around 40,000 girls working in the "silk convents" and other silk mills during the 1860s.[45] Glassworks were another bastion of child labour, again quietly defying child legislation in their obscure rural locations. As late as the 1890s, glass manufacturers were still proving reluctant to exclude children under thirteen from their workshops.[46]

Conclusion

A small sample from the 1851census registers of selected communes in France suggested that at least a third of children in the age-group ten to fourteen were working – probably a similar level to that observed in Britain during the same year.[47] By 1896, the population census revealed a participation rate that only around twenty per cent for this same age group. Given that primary education was by then compulsory, most of these were probably aged thirteen or fourteen.[48] The decline of child labour, especially of those under twelve years of age, was by then nearly complete in the mines, ironworks, textile mills and factories of *la grande industrie*, in France as elsewhere in the West. However, in the French case in particular, children continued to work around their school hours in the villages, absenteeism from school remained a persistent problem in the countryside until the 1930s, and large numbers of "apprentices" in urban workshops risked exploitation as child labour. Inevitably such work in the "informal" sector of the economy is hard to measure, making it easy to be lulled into a feeling that child labour was a thing of the past by the time of the First World War. The evidence of "sweated" labour in small workshops in contemporary Europe makes one wary of such a reassuring assumption.[49]

45 Reybaud, *Etudes sur le regime des manufactures*, *passim*; Monnier, *De l'organisation du travail manuel des jeunes*, pp. 49-55; Benoit, "Les Couvents ateliers", pp. 23-26.

46 Ministère du Commerce, *Rapports sur l'application pendant l'anneé 1894 des lois règlementant le travail* (Paris, 1895), p. xiii.

47 See Heywood, *Childhood in Nineteenth-Century France*, p. 99, Table 4.1; and Cunningham, "Employment and Unemployment of Children". The participation rates in the French sample, for both sexes combined, range from 34 to 51 per cent, but they do focus on a few manufacturing centres.

48 Calculated from Toutain, *La population de la France*, pp. 112-116.

49 Fyfe, *Child labour*, ch. 2.

Child Labour Reform: French Style

Histories of child labour reform have a long and honourable tradition. Yet they might be accused of a certain insularity, ignoring the comparisons possible with other case studies. Here we will seek to identify the particular characteristics of the French campaigns with this in mind. Three features stand out, partially related to the nature of child labour outlined above: firstly, the derivative nature of the campaigns, as the French self-consciously borrowed from their neighbours; secondly, the leading role taken by members of the elite, in the absence of any pressure from below; and finally, the prominence of statistical rather than literary material in the propaganda.

Foreign Models

From the start, during the 1820s and 1830s, French campaigners borrowed heavily from foreign experience of child labour legislation. If the British reform movement necessarily welled up from within, the French one had the precedents of British laws from 1802 onwards to follow, and later Prussian and Austrian examples also. Just as French commentators on the "social question" invariably looked across the Channel to see what the future might hold with an urban-industrial society, so their counterparts in the area of child labour almost always referred to the British experience of factory legislation. The famous speech to the Société Industrielle de Mulhouse by the young industrialist Jean-Jacques Bourcart, usually taken as the starting point for child labour reform in France in 1827, appealed to the British precedent as evidence that legislation in this sphere was workable. Bourcart ended by exhorting the Society to petition the government for a factory law "as in England".[50] The first official enquiry into child labour in 1837 began with a circular to the Prefects from the Minister of Commerce drawing attention to British experience. It even included a résumé of the 1833 Factory Act. Hence many of the replies pondered the usefulness of the British experience. Jean-Scipion Mourges, Prefect of the Hautes-Alpes and a former cotton spinner, went further than most. His many visits to Manchester brought a detailed knowledge of British conditions, down to the recollection that from early in the morning in the spinning mills steam from the engine served to make tea for the workers.[51] In 1840 the

50 Bourcart, "Proposition sur la nécessité de fixer l'âge", pp. 325-328.

51 AN F[12] 4704, Circular from Martin du Nord, Minister of Commerce to the Prefects, 31 July 1837; AN F[12] 4705, Letter from Jean-Scipion Mourges, Prefect of the Hautes-

Deputy Hippolyte Carnot briefed the Minister on the details of the Prussian regulations of March 1839.[52] After the passing of the first French law in 1841, preparations for a new one included sending a M. Pinède, lawyer to the Royal Court and to the Ministry of Commerce, on an "economic mission" to England, partly to investigate child labour legislation. Charles Dupin, reporting in 1847 to the Chamber of Peers on the draft legislation that eventually emerged, began with a very full description of the British Acts, and gave a systematic comparison of the main provisions of the 1841 law and the 1833 Act.[53]

All this inevitably led to questions on the appropriateness of foreign legislation to local conditions – a continuing theme today as countries face pressure to conform to international conventions on child labour generated in the West. French reformers saw the British factory acts as useful models, providing a framework for their own *projets de loi* with the now-familiar list that included restrictions on very young children entering the mills, limits on working hours and provision for some schooling. Their opponents took the line that conditions for working children in France were perfectly acceptable, so that interference by the state in the running of industry was unnecessary. French employers, in other words, were in no way comparable to their rather grim neighbours to the north. Even Martin du Nord, the Minister of Commerce who launched the 1837 Enquiry on Child Labour, asserted that there was no evidence to suggest that the abuses the English needed to remedy were to be found in France. Some of his respondents in the provinces followed suit. The Prefect-Jean Scipion Mourges agreed on the need to avoid the danger of imitating the English without "reflecting on the differences in the climates, the customs, the routines and the needs of the two populations". The Chamber of Commerce at Avignon (Vaucluse) presented a pleasing image of children in the silk industry working on a variety of tasks in the warm southern climate. In similar vein, the Chambre Consultative of Sommières, in the Gard, asserted that the division of land and political events had made French workers very inde-

Alpes, to Minister of Commerce, 9 September 1837. See also the very full account of the campaign during the 1820s and 1830s in Weissbach, *Child Labor Reform*, chs 2–3.

52 AN F[12] 4704, Hyppolyte Carnot, *Lettre à Monsieur le Ministre de l'Agriculture et du Commerce sur la legislation qui règle, dans quelques états de l'Allemagne, les conditions du travail des jeunes ouvriers* (Paris, 1840).

53 AN F[12] 4707, Mission économique en Angleterre de M. Pinède, avocat du Ministère, 1845; Chambre des Pairs, session of 29 June 1847, Rapport fait à la Chambre par M. le baron Dupin.

pendent in their way of life.[54] Others, such as the Chambre Consultative of Yvetot (Seine-Inférieure), picked up on the theme of French children being very different from their British counterparts in that they generally worked at home with their families. There was also the assertion that the law in Britain was a dead letter in the big manufacturing towns. The Chambre Consultative of Louviers (Eure) used this as an argument for rejecting restrictions on working hours for children in its woollen mills.[55]

In the event, enforcement of the 1841 law proved difficult, and efforts to extend it dragged on for decades. It took another type of foreign influence, the shock of defeat at the hands of the Prussians in 1871, to secure further legislation. The 1870s and 1880s brought a series of measures to improve the quality of future French citizens, affecting such areas as wet-nursing and education as well as child labour. The 1874 law extended coverage to all "factories, mills, works, mines, yards, and shops", and finally followed the British in establishing a corps of inspectors. It in its turn met with more success in coping with some areas than others, struggling above all with the dispersed industries of the big cities or the more remote rural areas.[56] One might therefore argue retrospectively that legislation to curb abuses of child labour in the factories and workshops was likely to prove difficult to enforce in a nation so heavily committed to agriculture and small-scale industry. This did not stop the process of governments borrowing from one another, including countries such as Belgium and Italy that were even later in coming to child labour legislation than France. Indeed, French as well as British laws acted as a model for Italian welfare legislation during the late nineteenth century.[57]

Reform from Above

French child labour reformers during the nineteenth century, certainly in comparison to some of their British counterparts, were notable for their "bourgeois" origins. The Baron de Gérando, a leading Social Catholic, countered the argument that a law would harm French industry in no uncertain terms before the Chamber of Peers in 1840:

54 The Chambre Consultative des Arts et Manufactures of the smaller industrial centres played a similar role to the Chamber of Commerce in the larger ones.

55 See the dossiers in AN F[12] 4705 for all of these responses.

56 Weissbach, *Child Labor Reform*, chs 10–11, Appendix C; Heywood, *Childhood in Nineteenth-Century France*, chs 10–11.

57 Ipsen, *Italy in the Age of Pinocchio*, ch. 3.

> Who prompted this law? Who called for it insistently? A meeting of industrialists.
> Where? In one of the most important manufacturing centres in France.
> And who are these industrialists? Industrialists running precisely the kind of industry affected by this law. It is petitions addressed to the Chambers that have begun this great and fine pursuit of a law.
> Who has been consulted on the utility and the opportunity for this law? The elite of industrialists all over France, the Chambres Consultatives des Arts et Métiers, the Conseils de Prudhommes, the Chambers of Commerce.
> What have they replied? Their replies are unanimous on the need for protective measures.[58]

Gérando was certainly right to argue that it was textile manufacturers from Alsace who first pushed for a law, and that the Government confined its consultations to official representatives of business. Besides the manufacturing interest, a diverse group of social reformers like Gérando himself supported the campaign. The most prominent were all from elite institutions of the July Monarchy regime, notably Dr Louis Villermé from the Académie des Sciences Morales et Politiques, and the Baron Charles Dupin from the Chamber of Peers.[59] Governments under the Second Empire and the Third Republic followed similar procedures during the flurry of reform activity in the 1860s and 1870s, once again relying on their network of official representative bodies.[60]

While successive French governments consistently refrained from asking workers on the shop floor what they thought of the proposed laws, leaders of the labour movement also remained conspicuously absent from the scene during the 1830s and 1840s, and again at the end of the century. Child labour might appear an obvious issue for socialists and trade unionists at these periods. However, the political climate in France proved hostile. The early socialists were more revolutionary than reformist in their approach, perhaps not surprisingly with the Revolutions of 1789, 1830 and 1848 in the background. The Utopian Socialist Charles Fourier cheerfully included child labour in his scheme of things. The trade unions were also much weakened during key periods for child labour reform, notably during the clamp-down on all forms of popular dissent after 1834, and dur-

58 AN F^{12} 4706, *Le Moniteur*, 11 March 1840.
59 On Villermé, see Braun and Valentin, *Villermé et le travail des enfants*, ch. 4.
60 AN F^{12} 4722-3, Enquête sur le travail des enfants, 1867, and F^{12} 4727, Préparation de la loi du 19 mai 1874 et règlements d'administration publique.

ing the ruthless repression that followed the Paris Commune of 1871. The Churches were also largely silent on the issue. It is true that the Alsatian textile magnates stood out by their largely Protestant backgrounds, and leading Catholics like Villeneuve-Bargemont and Gérando were bitterly opposed to what they saw as the crass materialism of English-style capitalism. Nonetheless, the Catholic hierarchy, one must assume, was reluctant to challenge authority, even that of industrial employers.[61]

The Rhetoric of Child Labour Reform in France

It follows that the arguments deployed for and against child labour in France reflected these same "bourgeois" concerns. In France, as in Britain and Belgium, there was a strong disposition in favour of laissez-faire policies among the elite.[62] Intervention from the state in relations between employers and employees, so the argument went, risked cooking the goose that had generated so much wealth during the eighteenth and nineteenth centuries. The scientist Gay-Lussac argued in 1840 that the industrialist operated outside the public domain: "his establishment is a refuge for work; it is a sanctuary that should be as sacred as the paternal house". The economist Pellegrino Rossi suggested that the eight bills on child labour introduced by the British over the previous forty years revealed the difficulty of legislating in this area.[63] Yet there was a gradual shift to a consensus that employing children in industry was wrong. Besides changes in the law, various lines of argument emerged in the propaganda campaign that might have encouraged people to change their view. Again, although most of these were found elsewhere, there was a peculiarly French flavour to the campaign.

The first to be deployed, and the one that was the most influential throughout the nineteenth century, took the form of what we would now call the "human capital" argument.[64] Groups of industrialists such as those in Alsace had no objection to children working in the mills, but they were concerned that abuses were undermining the quality of their labour force. Hence, looking into the long term, they proposed various measures to

61 See Weissbach, *Child Labor Reform*, pp. 56-57, 147-148. On relations between the Catholic Church and business, see Heywood, "The Catholic Church".

62 For e.g. see, Devleeshouwer, "Logique sociale et legislation du travail".

63 AN F[12] 4706, *Journal des débats*, 7 March 1840; and *Le Moniteur*, 6 March 1840.

64 In this and the following paragraphs, we refer to three of the four social constructions of "child labour" identified by Judith Ennew *et al.* in "Defining Child Labour as if Human Rights Really Matter", pp. 28-31.

improve the health and education of their employees. These included the exclusion of the very youngest children from the mills: those under eight in 1841, and, with some exceptions, those under twelve in 1874. Thus the Chamber of Commerce of Mulhouse proclaimed in 1837 that "one cannot hide the fact that employment in the mills is a benefit for young workers, inspiring early on habits of work and order, at the same time as it becomes a relief for their family and a boost for the growth of the population". Yet they accepted the need for a law on a minimum working age, restrictions on hours in the workshops and a ban on night work for the under-twelves.[65] Their vision revolved around a well-organized factory system that would maximize productivity by creating a healthy, well-educated and disciplined labour force. Similar concerns arose once again during the 1860s and 1870s, as French industry came under more intense foreign competition with the passing of free trade treaties, and as military defeat at the hands of the Prussians raised painful questions on such issues as "depopulation" and education. The upshot was a ban on night work for women and a tightening of the schooling requirements.

A potentially more radical argument was that children had no place in the workshops at all. In the French case one can trace this back to the economist Simonde de Sismondi (1773-1842). He began as a faithful disciple of Adam Smith, but the economic crises that followed the Napoleonic Wars, and the sufferings of workers around him, changed his mind. He accused economic liberals of paying too much attention to the creation of wealth, and not enough to its distribution. As he put it, wealth is only desirable in society when it spreads affluence to all classes. He drew attention to the costs as well as the benefits of free competition, notably in terms of the burdens it was placing on women and child workers. His *Nouveaux principes d'économie politique* from 1819 suffered from a poor prose style, and from a reform programme that fell far short of meeting his aims, but it did as least counter the widespread assumption that restricting child labour would reduce the already precarious family incomes of the poor. In an oft-cited passage, Sismondi reasoned that:

> If the children did not work at all, their fathers would have to earn enough to support them, until their strength developed. Without this, the children would die young, and labour would soon cease. But since children have been earning a part of their living, it has been possible to reduce the wages of the

65 AN F12 4705, Chambre de Commerce de Mulhouse, 6 September 1837. See also Tyl, "L'Enfant rebelle ou le patronat dépassé?".

> fathers. Their activity has not produced any improvement in the incomes of the poor. All that has occurred is an increase in the amount of work performed but it has been paid the same amount as before.

The notion that a ban on child labour would lead to a rise in adult wages intrigued Karl Marx and any number of economists since. In the short term it appealed to social observers in France who shared Sismondi's nostalgia for an agrarian society, notably Eugène Buret and Alban de Villeneuve Bargemont.[66]

A third line of attack was to assert that the employment of children in industry victimized some of the weakest and most vulnerable members of society. Dr Louis Villermé applauded the rise of modern industry, and as a reformer demanded no more than a grading of hours according to the age of child workers in the mills. Yet there was a contradiction between the timidity of this approach and the forcefulness of the case he made against child labour. His enquiry into the conditions for workers in the textile industry during the 1830s, supported by the authority of the Académie des Sciences Morales et Politiques, left a number of searing images for posterity.[67] This fed the indignation of reformers working towards the 1841 law, a law of "high morality" according to its supporters. Villermé asserted that children in the textile manufacturing centres were already victims of the "debauchery and thriftlessness" of their parents. On top of that, the mills were ruining their health. He contrasted the signs of poverty, suffering and despondency borne by the factory children of Alsace with the liveliness of their country cousins. He famously described the sixteen to eighteen hours they spent on their feet each day, cooped up inside and watching over a machine for at least thirteen of them, as "not work but torture, and it is inflicted on children aged to six to eight, badly fed, badly clothed, obliged to walk at five o'clock in the morning the long distance which separates them from the workplace".[68] Otherwise, Villermé concentrated on the mass of statistical evidence that he had amassed during the 1820s and 1830s on such indicators of child welfare as mortality rates, heights and rates of rejection for military service.

66 Simonde de Sismondi, *Nouveaux principes d'économie politique*, pp. 353 and 358. See also Gide and Rist, *A History of Economic Thought*, pp. 170–97; and Goetz-Girey, *Croissance et progress*, pp. 295–312.

67 Villermé, *Tableau de l'état*.

68 Villermé, *Discours sur la durée*, *passim*.

The early debates on child labour in France revolved heavily around this type of material. In particular, the institution of military conscription generated a mass of statistical information on all young men aged twenty that proved a happy hunting ground for social investigators. Villermé led the way by calculating that over the five-year period 1824-1828 the Department of the Haut-Rhin, centre for the Alsatian textile industry, had a higher percentage of its men rejected as unfit for military service on medical grounds than its neighbours. Similarly Charles Dupin asserted that in ten highly industrialized Departments, for every 10,000 men declared fit for service, 9,930 were too weak or deformed to be accepted, while in the ten most agricultural Departments, the equivalent figure was only 4,029.[69] The statistical methods used to produce these results will not stand up to close scrutiny today, but they made persuasive propaganda at the time. What was missing from the debate was any effort to discover what child workers and their families had to say. Nor was there any sign of a literary movement to stir the passions on this issue. Romantic poets like Victor Hugo may have written moving works on the subject of childhood, but it was a highly personalized view far removed from the shop floor.[70] The first novel in French literature with a child as its central character did not appear until 1876, in the form of *Jack*, by Alphonse Daudet. Jack had a background on the fringe between the *demi-monde* and the upper bourgeoisie. His story was one of struggle to make his way in a highly stratified, and even malignant society. This included a spell during his early teens as an apprentice in an ironworks. Daudet likened the foundry to a temple dedicated to a wild and demanding idol: a 30,000 kilogramme steam-hammer. Jack lacks the strength and stamina to wield his hammer, and struggles with the din all around him. Yet the whole point of this episode is to show how the intelligent and sensitive Jack stands out from the rough-and-ready types around him, rather than to elicit sympathy for child labour.[71] There was the image of the "eight-year-old worker" from Jules Simon, but in general the 1874 law originated in the midst of concerns about the future of French society rather than emotions generated by the plight of children themselves.

69 Villermé, *Tableau de l'état*, II, p. 245; Dupin, *Du travail des enfants*, p. XLVII.

70 See Lloyd, *The Land of Lost Content*, ch. 2.

71 Alphonse Daudet, *Jack* (Paris, 1973 [1876]), pp. 266-315.

Conclusion

Child labour reform was very much "in the air" during the 1830s, as the British hoped that other countries would follow their example, while their neighbours pondered being left behind in the march towards a new industrial world. There were enthusiastic supporters of British-style factory legislation in France. The Alsatian industrialist Jean-Jacques Bourcart played the role admirably. He associated the child labour problem with mechanized industry where young and old worked side-by-side, notably in his own spinning industry, and proposed only minor variations on the British acts for France. This type of strategy prevailed in 1841, but in the event those who doubted its appropriateness for French conditions were partly proved right. Although France had much in common with other industrial nations in Western Europe, the process of eliminating or much reducing child labour in the workshops there was a protracted one in its own way. The large number of family farms and family workshops led many to conclude that, as a present-day economist put it, "for a child to work was not the worst thing that could happen".[72] The assumption that employment under these conditions was both a useful support for the family and a practical way of learning on-the-job died hard. The more malignant forms in small workshops and remote factories also proved difficult to combat with legislation. The lengthy wrangles over a replacement for the 1841 law, not settled until 1874, suggest that the decline was only partially attributable from this quarter. Instead one might point to the growing appetite for primary education among large sections of the population, supported by government initiatives, and a growing disillusionment with child labour in large-scale industry. The French experience suggests that governments that borrow foreign models of social legislation without negotiating them with the population concerned, risk a long struggle.

72 Basu, "Child Labor", p. 1093.

CHAPTER 8

Nineteenth-Century Child Labour in the Departments of Bouches-du-Rhône and Var

Roland Caty

Elites are not a homogeneous entity. In their diversity, and their greater or lesser involvement in the world of childhood and labour, they were led to take varied positions on this question. Besides the administrative authorities whose attitudes are analysed elsewhere,[1] certain elites such as doctors, representatives of the church, and engineers, though not directly affected by legislative texts, found themselves faced with the application of these. Others, such as the employers in general, were directly concerned. The application of the laws on child labour in the departments of Bouches-du-Rhône and Var, between 1841 and 1892, offers an occasion to study the reactions of these regional elites, note their characteristic discourses and take a look at their practices.

Although not considered as very industrialized departments, Bouches-du-Rhône and Var nonetheless saw the widespread use of child labour. This could be found in several sectors of activity, though to a variable degree. Children were numerous in handicrafts and small firms, which made up the great majority of establishments in this region. Statistics for workshops, factories and industrial plants in Bouches-du-Rhône in 1867 show 1,261 young people between eight and sixteen years of age, of whom 920, i.e. nearly three-quarters, worked in handicrafts or small firms. On the other hand, very few could be found in the large traditional industries of Marseilles, such as the oil and soap works and sugar refineries. The main centres of child labour in the mid-nineteenth century were the Toulon Arsenal, the naval dockyards of La Ciotat and La Seyne, the mining basin of Gardanne, Aix-en-Provence with its spinning works and calico-

1 See on this subject Kharaba, "Élites économiques et administratives du Var". I am in debt to Ivan Kharaba for a large part of our documentation on the Var.

printing, and – in Marseilles and its suburbs – in glass and spinning works, mechanical construction and tile-making.[2]

Doctors' and Churchmen's Attitudes to Child Labour

The health professions were very quickly faced with this question, by way of their presence on the supervisory and local inspection commissions that were established. In the Var, for example, the Toulon commission appointed in 1854 included a doctor and two pharmacists, that for Brignoles established the same year had two doctors, whilst those of Draguignan, Collobrières and Cotignac each included one doctor at this time. The local commissions appointed in December 1874 also had representatives of the medical profession in Toulon and Draguignan.[3] In Bouches-du-Rhône, certain doctors took their role to heart, for example Dr Chapplain, appointed to the Marseilles commission in 1855, or Dr Gibert, appointed to the same commission in 1875. Moreover, by prefectoral decree of 20 April 1849, the inspection of child labour in Bouches-du-Rhône was entrusted to a number of councils for health and hygiene, who performed this function until 1855. On the Aix council, for example, the ten members included two veterinary surgeons, two pharmacists and three doctors, including Dr Goyrand who was well known for his scientific work and his social action.[4] One could thus say that this health personnel, who were not employed in the enterprises inspected, occupied an appreciable place in the newly established system.

Rather like the national investigations conducted by certain doctors of the time, the reports drawn up by these representatives are valuable evidence on the conditions of children's work. They provide first of all information on the kind of activities to which children were subjected. Dr Chapplain, for example, distinguished three categories of employment after inspecting some sixty factories and workshops in five districts of Marseilles. In the first of these categories, children who were often very young

2 Caty, "Travail des enfants"; Guiral, "Brèves observations". More generally on the history of children at work in France, see "Les Enfants et les jeunes au travail. Études et documents pour l'histoire de l'administration du travail" (Cahier du comité d'histoire, Ministère de l'emploi et de la solidarité, supplément avril 2001).

3 Archives départmentales du Var (hereafter AV),16 M 6/1 and 16 M 7/1.

4 Archives départmentales des Bouches-du-Rhône (hereafter ABdR), 14 M 21/2 and 14 M 21/3.

acted simply as helpers and did not perform actual labour; the second category was that of apprentices learning a trade; while the third comprised young people used as unskilled labourers, in repetitive tasks that did not lead to acquiring any kind of skill.[5]

Moreover, these reports also give an insight into the context in which unskilled child labour was performed: the silk-spinning plants of Cotignac were judged "intolerably filthy",[6] the cotton-spinning plant of the Pastré brothers in Aix-en-Provence was situated "in a very large workshop. The machines are generally established in two lines. On entering these workshops, one is deafened by the noise".[7] The writer describes the children's movements and their bodily positions. At the Silvy wallpaper factory in Aix, girls between six and ten sat on high stools to reach the machine, passing the brush five or six times a minute.[8] In the lignite basin of Fuveau, young porters had to descend into the mine on foot by a slippery staircase of 700 steps, negotiate 1,200 to 1,400 metres of tunnels, then climb fifty to sixty metres in galleries less than a metre high, in order to reach the cutting face and fill their bucket with coal which they carried on their back on the return route, through tunnels, galleries and even stairways, in the absence of steam-powered skips.[9]

Above all, these reports focus on the children's health, noting the repercussions of this work on their general condition, and signalling the diseases that they suffered. If the young people in the Aix textile industries appeared "happy, strong and in good shape", the children of the mining basin, who sometimes started work before the age of eight, and even worked at night, presented alterations to the lung, chronic bronchitis, asthma and scrofulas that did not heal in adolescence;[10] the reports insist on the risk that only "rachitic men, with no strength for the natural function of reproducing the species", would be left.[11] The health and hygiene council of Aix was aware of the important issue involved: it believed that it had to "trace this rather sad but accurate picture of the diseases and infirmities of the young miners who work the lignite deposits in our vicinity, in order to make clear how

5 Report of inspector Chapplain, Marseilles, 17 July 1856, ABdR, 14 M 21/2.
6 Report of the inspection commission of 25 February 1856, AV, 16 M 7/1.
7 Report of the health and hygiene council, Aix-en-Provence, 20 July 1851, ABdR, 14 M 21/2.
8 Report of the health and hygiene council, 20 July 1851.
9 Report of the health and hygiene council, 20 July 1851.
10 Report of the health and hygiene council, 20 July 1851.
11 Official report of the supervisory commission on children in manufacturing, with the participation of Dr Gibert, session of 30 November 1876, ABdR, 14 M 21/3.

important it is to strictly apply in this industry the laws bearing on child labour".[12]

The attitude of representatives of the church was more qualified. Some ecclesiastics were completely involved themselves, directing workshops and orphanages that used child labour. They were thus linked with the milieu of the employers that we shall come on to discuss. Other members of the clergy were concerned by way of education, especially in the religious schools that were a source of tension following the establishment of the Republic. In the coalfields, for example, churchmen were accused of connivance with the directors. Analysing the ministerial inquiry of 1880, Gérard Pio notes that "the church is the main support of the mining companies, which do it a good turn by favouring its undertakings and financing the installation of denominational schools". In Gréasque, young people were only taken on at the mine on presentation of a note from the priest; in many companies, the miners had to send their children to the denominational school established by the company if they wanted to keep their jobs.[13]

But it is important not to generalize. Some members of the clergy were not prisoners of the system and reacted against practices of the employers that they deemed excessive. An example of this is given by Abbé Pin, vicar of La Viste in the Marseilles suburbs, who denounced the abuses that he witnessed. In a letter addressed to the prefect in 1872, he noted that, in the tile-works of L'Estaque:

> A throng of children aged between nine years of age and twelve or thirteen are put to work [...] and these young children are condemned to work from five in the morning to seven in the evening [i.e. fourteen hours a day]. They do the work of a good labourer, exhausting their health and deprived of the benefit of an instruction that is still necessary for them [...] acquiring habits of vice and ending up being very bad individuals, and all this to earn twenty to thirty sous a day. Their parents and the employers benefit, but the children are sacrificed morally and physically. This is nothing less than murder.[14]

An inquiry was immediately demanded from the mining engineer in charge of this sector.

12 Report of the health and hygiene council, Aix-en-Provence, 20 July 1851, ABdR, 14 M 21/2.

13 Pio, *Mines et mineurs de Provence*, p. 57. See also Galliard, "Vie ouvrière", pp. 430, 923.

14 Abbé Pin to the prefect of Bouches-du-Rhône, La Visite, 4 October 1872, ABdR, 14 M 21/3.

The Position of the Engineers

Mining engineers were faced with the problem of child labour from two sides. First of all in the coalfields, where they exercised their usual supervisory function, and secondly as having sole responsibility for the inspection of child labour in manufactures between 1869 and 1874, under the terms of the Imperial decree of 7 December 1868.

For the Marseilles mineralogical district,[15] this post was occupied by Ernest Villot, an engineer then thirty-eight years of age, who spent the greater part of his career in the Midi.[16] Aimé Olivier de Sanderval, who visited the coal districts of the Ebro region of Spain together with Villot, described his colleague in his *Mémoires* as "a large and intelligent young man, who graduated in seventh place at the Polytechnique, the son of a road contractor in an eastern department, if I am not mistaken".[17]

The stand taken by this engineer is recorded in two reports that have been preserved. The first of these precisely concerns the tile-works denounced by Abbé Pin. In his conclusions, Villot first asks why the vicar of La Viste has got involved with this, given that the children in question came from other parishes than his own. Two-thirds of the youngsters, moreover, were foreigners, Italians in particular, which in his eyes significantly attenuated the seriousness of the charge. He certainly recognized that in the case of seventy children under twelve years of age, there was a contravention of

15 At this time this covered the three departments of Bouches-du-Rhône, Vaucluse and Var.

16 Born at Dijon into a very modest family, Ernest Villot entered the École Polytechnique in 1853 and joined the mining corps in 1855. Appointed engineer at Avignon in 1858, he was soon after posted to Marseilles, where he particularly supervised the mining basin of Gardanne until 1880. In 1886 he was called to Paris, joined the Conseil générale des mines, and died in 1897 with the rank of inspector-general. Villot was the author of several articles published in the *Annales des Mines* and the bulletin of the Société scientifique de Marseille, a company that he headed from 1878 to 1880. He was appointed *chevalier* of the Légion d'honneur in 1873, and promoted to *officier* in 1896. On his career and writings, see the speeches given on his death by the inspector-general of mines, Haton de la Goupillière, and the inspector of roads and bridges, Gouin, *Annales des Mines 1897*, pp. 637-643. On the mining engineers in general: Thépot, *Ingénieurs des mines*, p. 511 ff.

17 Sanderval added: "He had the useful faculty of sleeping whenever he wished, if only for five minutes, no matter where, and deeply, i.e. usefully. On board [i.e. in the horse-carriage used], when conversation flagged, I often saw him say with a smile: 'Let's have a sleep, then!' After five minutes he would wake up and take part in life again, ready with a smile to recommence without a break, as if nothing had occurred to keep him away ". (Sanderval, *Mémoires d'Aimé Olivier comte de Sanderval,* p. 91).

the law of 1841 that limited their working time to eight hours a day. But, he immediately adds, "this contravention exists, thank God, more in the details than in the spirit". For in his view:

> The work of these children is not hard; for the youngest of them, it consists in carrying in each hand a small board with a tile just out of the mould, and going to place this on a conveyor belt where these tiles are put out to dry. This does not involve any awkward position that is damaging for the development of bodily organs, nor an unhealthy atmosphere, nor a burden that it hard to bear. It is rather for these children, I do not hesitate to say, a useful physical exercise [...] that cannot be seriously detrimental to their health.[18]

A rather hasty judgement, given that an uncut tile weighed around four kilos. Inspector Blaise, more vigilant than Villot, analysed some twenty years later the amount of work required of the little porters at the brickfields of Bernay, in the department of Eure, whose work was comparable to that of the Marseilles tile-works. He calculated that in a fourteen-hour day, a child carried 5,000 bricks, two by two, for a distance of between twenty and twenty-five metres, making a total distance of fifty kilometres with a load of some ten kilos, not counting the effort of bending twice on each journey. By comparison, a soldier on campaign might cover a distance of thirty kilometres with a load of twenty kilos, without being subject to the constant bending that was an additional source of fatigue.[19]

Engineer Villot did indeed note that at the Estaque tile-works these young people had to work half the night, and that no heed was paid to their education, but, he remarked, this was the case with other establishments in Bouches-du-Rhône, and probably in the entire territory of France. In conclusion, wrote this engineer, "there is no demonstrated need, and above all no urgency, to take any coercive measure. I have confined myself to advising the industrialists verbally."[20]

The second report dates from June 1876, and bears on two infractions of the law of 1874 in the mining basin of Fuveau-Gardanne: night work by

18 Mining engineer Villot to the head of mines, Marseilles, 11 November 1872, ABdR, 14 M 21/3.

19 Quoted by Viet, *Voltigeurs de la République*, p. 96. On the new body of inspectors established by the laws of 19 May 1874 and 2 November 1892, see also Guérard, *1892-1913. L'inspection du travail*.

20 Mining engineer Villot to the head of mines, Marseilles, 11 November 1872, ABdR, 14 M 21/3.

children, and their having to carry quite excessive weights on their backs. On the first point, Villot defended the existing situation, rejected possible changes, and concluded: "There are all kinds of good reason why the mine-owners demand that children should be tolerated in the mines until midnight." As far as carrying loads on the back was concerned, the engineer accepted that the infringement was blatant, and advised that the use of children under sixteen for this work, which was contrary to the law, should be gradually discontinued:

> It is good and useful, from every point of view, that of health not excluded, that these children, who will grow up to be miners themselves, have experience of the mines before the age of sixteen. I do not approve of the absolute exclusion of those under sixteen [...] and I fear that the companies that impose this obligation on themselves may later have to regret it.[21]

We can only conclude that Villot accepted the arguments of the employers as beyond criticism. The 1880 inquiry into the coalfields had good reason for accusing him of supporting the employers' policies,[22] an accusation all the more well-founded in that he was connected by schooling and friendship with Ernest Biver, a civil engineer who managed the Société des charbonnages des Bouches-du-Rhône, the largest mining company in Fuveau-Gardanne.[23]

A difference in approach is thus perceptible between the two groups of doctors and engineers. The engineer tended to view the child as an agent of production, whose output was essential; the doctor was sensitive to the context, to problems of health, and – after the defeat of 1870 – to the long-term consequences for the future of the population. For the one, children were producers; for the other, they were future reproducers.

Contrasting Attitudes among the Employers

Along with these two professions concerned to a greater or lesser extent with child labour, there was a further elite category affected by laws and

21 Report from mining engineer Villot, Marseilles, 13 June 1876, ABdR, 14 M 21/2.

22 Galliard, "Vie ouvrière", pp. 915-916.

23 Both men had worked in particular on the project for a 'tunnel to the sea', an underground route of fourteen kilometres designed to dry out the basin and transport lignite to the port of Marseilles. Cf. the article by Villot, "Étude sur le basin de Fuveau".

regulations, that of the employers themselves. In Provence as elsewhere these were very diverse – in their sector of activity, the size of their business, and their attitude towards the legislation. Beside exemplary employers who observed the regulations to the letter, there were factory and workshop owners whose abuses were still reported at the end of the century.

The Toulon Arsenal offered exceptional conditions for the time. It was the leading industrial establishment in the Var, and directly controlled by the state through the naval ministry. The Arsenal did not take on apprentices younger than twelve, children did not work more than ten hours a day on an annual average, when the legislation still allowed twelve, and they never worked at night. They all had Sundays and public holidays off. If they had not received any basic instruction before their recruitment, they attended classes at a special school, with the ministry bearing the costs. In 1846, the maritime prefect of Toulon emphasized to the minister that "these conditions are very lenient in comparison with how they might be if the advantage was taken of the latitude left to the head of the industrial establishment under the law of 22 March 1841".[24] And indeed, the Arsenal attracted to its workshops the great majority of those children from the Toulon region who undertook an apprenticeship. Few boys worked in the private sector, forcing industrialists to offer them conditions equivalent to those of the Arsenal, if not better.[25]

The naval dockyards of La Ciotat were just as remarkable. From 1852 they belonged to the Messageries impériales, renamed in 1870 the Messageries maritimes. This major armaments firm based in Paris was headed from 1860 to 1891 by Armand Behic, an individual of national status who was for several years minister of agriculture, commerce and public works under Napoleon III.[26] The dockyards of La Ciotat constructed and repaired a large part of the Marseilles commercial fleet. They were at the cutting edge of naval technique, and practised an advanced social policy towards their personnel. In 1855, out of a complement of 1,410 workers, they employed only 130 children; in 1856, eighty were used in boiler-making, scaffolding, adjustment, fitting, forging, etc. On 18 October 1853, i.e. a few months after the dockyards came under the ownership of the Messageries,

24 The maritime prefect to the Ministre de la Marine, Toulon 21 February 1846, Arch. du Port de Toulon, 2 A 3/139.

25 Kharaba, "Élites économiques et administratives du Var".

26 On the role of Armand Behic, cf. Caty, Échinard and Richard, *Patrons du Second Empire*, pp. 69-72.

an elementary school was established; these classes were extended in 1855.[27] In 1862, a school was established for apprentices between twelve and fifteen, operating along the same lines as factory schools at Schneider and Le Creusot. Instruction was given in the factory itself, with workshop tasks performed under the guidance of a foreman. Those children who worked at the Messageries were held to be privileged. Inspector Collard wrote to the prefect in July 1859: "I am happy to give you a guarantee that the company takes a genuinely maternal care of these children. It keeps constant watch over their wellbeing, both moral and physical, making ample provision for their instruction and encouraging them through prizes."[28]

At the opposite end of the scale, many employers placed themselves outside the limits of legality, either by compromising with the regulations, or purely and simply ignoring them. This was more common in the middle of the century than at the end; it was particularly noticeable in the very many small workshops where inspection was rare and ignorance was as current as abuse.[29] This was abundantly reported. In Var, the divisional inspector Lagard, who undertook a tour in 1885, noted that at La Garde-Freinet the cork manufacturers took not the slightest notice of the law of 19 May 1874, and still violated this with impunity ten years after it came into force.[30] In Bouches-du-Rhône, 78 per cent of workshops visited in 1884 completely failed to observe this law.[31] The reports of the inspectorate and gendarmerie drawn up between 1876 and 1881 make clear the nature of the most frequent infringements: absence of the compulsory workbook (*livret*) in 61 per cent of establishments inspected, lack of school attendance (58 per cent), and dangerous work leading to more or less serious accidents (50 per cent).[32]

The tendency of certain religious foundations, to which the 1874 legislation did not apply, should also be noted. To finance their philanthropic action, these functioned as mixed structures: from associations of charity and good deeds, they tended to become commercial enterprises using a free and unprotected source of labour. The inspection commission for

27 "État des ouvriers, femmes et enfants employés dans les ateliers des Messageries impériales à La Ciotat", 22 February 1855, ABdR, 14 M 21/2; report of inspector Collard, La Ciotat, 21 July 1856, ABdR, 14 M 21/2.

28 Report of inspector Collard, La Ciotat, 21 July 1859, ABdR, 14 M 21/2.

29 See for example the letter from divisional inspector Tavernier to the prefect of Var, 10 July 1883, AV, 16 M 7/1.

30 Divisional inspector Lagard to the prefect of Var, 17 December 1885, AV, 16 M 7/1.

31 Report of inspector Lagard, Marseilles, 29 June 1885, ABdR, 14 M 21/4.

32 Caty, "Travail des enfants", p. 140.

Arles cites the example of two workshops, supposedly orphanages, that employed young girls between nine and fifteen years of age in heavy sewing work that was beyond their strength.[33] Inspector Largard, for his part, drew attention to religious orphanages for which the training of children had become "an object of profit and speculation":

> We have been able to establish that [...] work here was organized with a view to large-scale production. In the lingerie workshops, for example, the custom was to give the same worker always the same task. This way of proceeding is contrary to all principles of the professional instruction of children [...]. Following observations on this form of work that we presented to some managers of these establishments, these agreed to let children take part in the variety of tasks that the production of a particular object requires. In this way, children can gradually learn the different elements of a trade.[34]

This was also the case with the Petite-Oeuvre, a workshop run by nuns and patronized by many leading Marseilles families, established to train young girls from the popular classes. The proclaimed purpose was "to learn a position, become good workers, and prepare a temporary future under the aegis of religion". To this end, the trades of linen maid, milliner and florist were taught. But the establishment was openly accused of having become "a religious-capitalist factory" that exerted unfair competition with the city's artisans.[35] The law of 2 November 1892 settled controversies of this kind.

When the employers were asked to conform with the legislation, they responded in terms that are sometimes recorded. For example, in the Silvy wallpaper factory at Aix-en-Provence, children were recruited at the age of six or seven (instead of the legal minimum of eight), they worked twelve to fourteen hours a day in summer (instead of eight hours), and had no chance of school attendance. An initial inspection in 1851 led to a warning. A further visit in 1856 saw the employers still infringing the legal regulations, but this time they justified themselves at length. They declared that "there were countless advantages for these children working for them and for society." Were they too young? In actual fact, coming as they did from a poor background, they had a great need to find a place that could ben-

33 Official report of the session of 19 August 1876, ABdR, 14 M 21/3.

34 Report of divisional inspector Lagard, in "Rapport au Président de la République de la Commission supérieur du travail des enfants", Paris, 12 July 1888, p. 76, ABdR, 14 M 21/4.

35 Gaillard, "Vie ouvrière", p. 436.

efit from their weak strength. Was the summer working day too long? The winter day was only six and a half hours, which made an annual average in conformity with the legislation. And if schooling was compromised for a part of the year, it was possible in winter, and "that should suffice in our view to fulfil the legal requirements". In short, the proprietors declared:

> Significant damage would be done to these children by depriving them of the means of existence that they find in our workshops, all the more so as they would not attend primary school for any greater length of time; besides, while unoccupied in this way, they would not be surveyed by their parents and could as a consequence fall into blameworthy activities.[36]

These assertions were tendentious, to say the least, but they did not challenge the facts of the matter. They aimed rather to justify these, using more or less specious arguments.

Words and Deeds of Certain Employer Elites

In the case of other employers, words and deeds failed to coincide; we can even note a gap between their public stance and the actual practices observed in their businesses. This ambiguity can be perceived from the reports drawn up in the wake of reported infringements. Some of these place the blame on individuals well known in economic and social circles. We can mention here the cases of three Marseilles industrialists.

The first of these, Louis Régis, was the brother of Victor Régis, one of the richest shipping magnates in the city, and vice-president of the chamber of commerce. Louis Régis also owned a candle factory in a Marseilles suburb, and was also a large landowner, a municipal councillor under the Second Empire, and above all, administrator for fifteen years of the powerful Société de bienfaisance et de charité, of which he became president in 1872. This body, which covered the entire city, had the object of rescuing

36 Report of the council for health and hygiene, Aix-en-Provence, 20 July 1851; report of the police commissioner for the district of Aix to the sub-prefect, Aix, 25 June 1856; letter from the sub-prefect of Aix to the prefect of Bouches-du-Rhône, Aix, 28 June 1856, ABdR, 14 M 21/2.

various categories of people in need, and helping the working class by the formation of friendly societies for mutual support.[37]

Louis Régis's factory was inspected for the first time in December 1874, and once again on 7 March 1875. The inspector reported the absence of two under-age girls, and noted: "According to the statements of their fellow-workers, they were employed on night work and rested during the day", which was absolutely against the law. A third inspection took place two days later, in the presence of M. Régis himself. The report states: "The two girls, then present, acknowledged that they had spend the night working", and the inspector goes on to say: "Already, on our first visit to the factory, in the absence of M. Régis, we left verbal and written instructions for the law to be observed, but he failed to take account of these." The president of the Société de bienfaisance et de charité, and defender of the unfortunate, was prosecuted for repeated infraction of article 4, paragraphs 2 and 3, of the law on the labour of children and under-age girls.[38]

A second example is that of Édouard Jullien, the son of a shoemaker whose career showed a spectacular rise. Starting from nothing, he found himself thirty years later at the head of a tannery that occupied a site of 14,000 square metres and was believed to be one of the largest in France. He received three gold medals for the excellence of his products at the Paris Exposition universelle of 1878. More than simply a prominent businessman, Jullien was also a municipal councillor and deputy mayor under the Second Empire, member of the chamber of commerce under the Third Republic, involved with a number of charitable institutions as well as the savings bank, of which he was administrator in 1869 and director in 1890.[39] The studies of Laurence Américi on the directorate of this body have reported the stand taken by Édouard Jullien: an energetic social concern, a pronounced sensitivity to the difficulties that working people experienced, in short, an expert on working-class life, whom Eugène Rostand took as a reference.[40]

The information that comes to light about Jullien's establishments, however, stood in striking contrast to this glowing picture. Already in his study

37 On Victor Régis and his brother Louis, see in particular Caty and Richard, "Un négociant dans la ville". On Victor Régis's career, cf. Caty, Richard and Échinard, *Patrons du Second Empire*, pp. 237-240.

38 Official report of divisional inspector Livarès, Marseilles, 9 March 1876, ABdR, 14 M 21/3.

39 On the exceptional career of Édouard Jullien, cf. Caty, Richard and Échinard, *Patrons du Second Empire*, pp. 189-191.

40 Information kindly provided by Laurence Américi. See also his doctoral thesis, "La Caisse d'épargne des Bouches-du-Rhône au XIXe siècle".

on working-class life in Marseilles under the Second Empire, Lucien Gaillard depicted this industrialist as one of the few employers who was genuinely hated by his workforce for his brutality.[41] We can add that he took no trouble to let the children he employed enjoy their legal rights. On 16 April 1883, the divisional inspector Tavernier visited the Jullien tanneries, and reported the case of five boys aged between eleven and fourteen who were working completely illegally: one of them was below the authorized minimum age, all worked for too long hours, and none of them attended school. On top of this, the lack of workbooks was noted, along with the absence of employment records and a display of the law and regulations. This contravened articles 2, 8, 9, 10 and 11 of the law of 19 May 1874.[42]

A no less marked discrepancy between word and deed is shown by the case of Amedée Armand, a big industrialist who headed one of the largest mining enterprises in the coalfield of Fuveau-Gardanne – Michel, Armand & Cie. He was an enterprising businessman, founder of the Forges de La Capelette, and director, vice-president or president of several banks, insurance and armaments companies. He was a member of the chamber of commerce for twenty years, being its vice-president on four occasions, and its president from 1866 to 1872. A royalist and legitimist in his politics, Armand was a devoted Catholic who initiated a number of works of charity. His proclaimed motto was: "To live in justice, piety and sobriety, in expectation of the glory to come".[43]

As president of the chamber of commerce, Amedée Armand approved and signed the official positions of this body towards child labour. He demanded in this capacity that the working age should be raised to ten years, the working day reduced to eight hours, and the law of 1841 extended to all industrial establishments, going so far as to declare that "it is of the greatest importance that society should monitor that children are not exposed to premature physical exhaustion by over-hasty use of their strength and too early recruitment to the workshop".[44]

41 Gaillard, "Vie ouvrière", p. 491.

42 Official report of divisional inspector Tavernier, Marseilles, 16 April 1883, ABdR, 14 M 21/3.

43 On this individual, cf. Guiral and Reynaud (eds), *Marseillais dans l'histoire*, p. 34; Caty, Richard and Échinard, *Patrons du Second Empire*, pp. 48–50.

44 Reply to the circular from the minister of agriculture and commerce on child labour in manufacturing, the chamber of commerce to the prefect of Bouches-du-Rhône, Marseilless, 12 April 1870 ABdR, 14 M 21/2. In his capacity as president of the chamber, Amédée Armand was the first to place his signature at the foot of the text.

Here again, there was a large gap between public words and reported practice. Already in 1851, the health and hygiene council of Aix reported several infractions committed by the Michel-Armand company in the lignite field of Fuveau. Among the three hundred children whom it employed, some had been taken on at the age of eight, despite the regulation that forbade employment under ten, all were compelled to do night work, and the combination of their working hours and the distance from school deprived them of any education. The council insisted that the legislation should be rigorously observed,[45] but this was in vain, since in July 1859 inspector Collard still reported that "in the mining district [...] the benefits of the law [on child labour] are almost entirely unknown".[46]

The company was again challenged by the mining engineer Villot, whom we mentioned above, in his report of June 1876. Villot stressed that, out of the three companies active in the Fuveau coalfield, Michel-Armand was the hardest to bring into line with the legal requirements, since it was the one most at variance with these. Out of the ninety-eight children employed at this time, all worked nights, and more than seventy-five carried loads of twenty to twenty-five kilos on their backs, instead of the ten to fifteen that the regulations permitted.[47]

These facts led to action on the part of the local commission for child welfare, established by the prefect of Bouches-du-Rhône in 1875. Its members included five representatives of the Marseilles elite: Dr Gibert from the medical professions, and four company directors: the banker Félix Abram who was a committed republican, and three shipowners, including Louis Fraissenet, director of one of the leading Marseilles shipping companies, and whose brother Adolphe, also a shipowner, was at the time a centre-left republican deputy in the National Assembly. This commission was thus a collection of very prominent individuals with a left-wing orientation, experience of public affairs and a sense of the responsibilities that went with this.

The commission took a stand against the practices of the mining companies, in particular Michel-Armand.[48] It actually decided to send two of

45 Report of the council for health and hygiene of Aix-en-Provence, 20 July 1851, ABdR, 14 M 21/2.

46 Inspector Collard to the prefect of Bouches-du-Rhône, La Ciotat, 21 July 1859, ABdR, 14 M 21/2.

47 Report of mining engineer Villot, Marseilles, 13 June 1876, ABdR, 14 M 21/2.

48 'The commission holds that Messrs Michel and Armand could reduce the number of children carrying loads on their backs. It brings this situation to the attention of all concerned, despite the drawback that this restrictive measure on the work of children

its members on location to conduct an inquiry: Dr Gibert and the banker Abram visited the mines of Valdonne. Their report was devastating. All the information they received confirmed that the law of 1874 was not being applied. The two observers reported that:

> If some of these [the children employed by the Michel-Armand company] seem to enjoy good health, the great majority are thin, pale and anaemic, short of breath, and their faces show a precocious sadness denoting a general fatigue that is very pronounced. Such evident sadness [...] proves that these children are unable to accustom themselves to, nor perform without fatigue, a work that is excessive for their age and to which they have not been gradually trained.[49]

The supervisory commission held that "children should not be exhausted at an early age, at risk of preventing normal growth and development". After deliberation, it adopted the formal opinion that such infractions of the law of 19 May 1874 should not be overlooked in the way that engineer Villot tended to advise. It therefore requested the divisional inspector and the mining inspectors to draw up a case for prosecution.[50] Yet it was only slowly that the legislation was enforced. Six years later, the divisional inspector Tavernier visited "by chance" the workings of the same Michel-Armand company, and noted at the bottom of the mine five children who "were occupied in carrying baskets of coal on their backs. These baskets, which they picked up and carried to the surface to be weighed, had an acknowledged average weight of eighteen kilos." The infraction was blatant, and deemed to be all the more serious, in that "the weight carried is too heavy not to crush such young and fragile children, even if they were working upright, in the open air, and on a horizontal level." The company was accordingly prosecuted for contravention of the law.[51]

is bound to provoke discontent on the part of the parents of children working in the mines, but the duty of the commission is to invite the mine-owners to suppress within a short time the work of such porterage by children under sixteen', in Official report of the session of 18 October 1876, ABdR, 14 M 21/3.

49 Report by Dr Gibert and Félix Abram, cited by Pio, *Mines et mineurs*, p. 61; and minutes of the local commission for supervision of children, session of 30 December 1876, ABdR, 14 M 21/3.

50 Minutes of the local commission for supervision of children, session of 30 December 1876, ABdR, 14 M 21/3.

51 Official report of divisional inspector Tavernier, Marseilles, 27 September 1882, ABdR, 14 M 21/3.

Finally, we can draw a few conclusions from this rapid survey. The application of the legislation on child labour confirms that elites took up different positions according to their training and profession. In the examples given above, it is clear that the typical perspective of doctors, external to business and sensitive to the problems of health and reproduction, was opposed on all points to the attitudes of engineers or the practices of industrialists, for whom what counted above all was the performance of a workforce that was numerous, pliable, and cheap.

This study also brings to light certain of the fractures that divided the world of the economic elites, fractures that were a function of the individuals concerned, their sectors of activity and their political choices. The duty of respecting legislative texts in the case of state-owned establishments, an eminent national position combined with a sensitivity to social questions on the part of the minister Armand Behic, made these responsible employers concerned for the future of the children who worked for them. This was not the case with the industrialist Amédée Armand: the criticisms made of him by the local supervisory commission show the tensions that could exist among the economic elites of Marseilles. If the banker Félix Abram and the ship-owner Louis Fraissenet, members of this commission, opposed the practices of one of the leading enterprises in the coalfield, we might see this as a divergence of character, with political antagonisms also involved – it is likely that the fervent republican Abram was far from unhappy to put the legitimist Armand on the spot –, but it also indicates a difference of attitude in their relations to the workforce. A banker at the head of big investments, or a ship-owner having little to do with child labour (apart from a few cabin boys) did not react in the same way as a mine-owner employing a large number of young people.

Finally, we can note the discrepancies between the words and practice of some of these same elites. The official positions taken by Amédée Armand as president of the chamber of commerce, like those of the savings-bank director Édouard Jullien and the charitable actions of the president of the Société de bienfaisance Louis Régie, all show a noticeable gap from the real position in their respective businesses. These contradictions accentuate the diversity and complexity of the relations that these elites maintained with the world of child labour.

CHAPTER 9

Child Labour in Belgium 1800-1914

René De Herdt

Industrialization, Poverty and Child Labour

Child labour in the nineteenth and early twentieth centuries in Belgium was associated both with industrialization and with poverty. The first manifestations of the Industrial Revolution in Belgium had become obvious in about 1800. The steam engine was introduced, the first textile companies were established in Verviers and Ghent, and textile labour was gradually mechanized. Both the mining and steel industries expanded. In 1817, John Cockerill built a coke blast furnace, and it was in Belgium that the first steamboat on the European continent was built. Amidst the cheering of numerous interested spectators, the first train on the continent steamed from Mechelen to Brussels in 1835, the coal for it having been mined in the provinces of Liege and Hainaut.[1] By 1840 Belgium possessed the infrastructure necessary to become Europe's second industrial nation.

These industrial developments put immense pressure on traditional crafts and home industries.[2] Home workers had to produce against ever-lower prices in order to be able to compete, and this meant longer hours of work and increased participation in work by all family members, including children.[3] Even so, many families were in acute poverty. In the late 1820s, one person in seven was estimated to be in need; by the later 1840s, this had increased to one in six. In 1850 in the industrial city of Ghent, one third of the population was supported by the authorities. Inevitably in such circum-

1 Lebrun *et al.*, "Essai sur la révolution industrielle"; Dhondt, *Machten en mensen*; Brabander *et al.*, *De industrie in België.*

2 Veraghtert, "Ambacht en nijverheid in de Zuidelijke Nederlanden".

3 Chlepner, *Cent ans d'histoire sociale*; De Herdt and De Graeve, *Kinderarbeid*; Vander Meersch, *De l'état de la mandicité*; Van den Eeckhout and Hannes, "Sociale verhoudingen en structuren"; Ducpétiaux, *Mémoire sur le paupérisme.*

stances, children were more likely to be sent to work in factories than to school; a boy's wage might be one third that of his father, a crucial addition to the family income.[4]

In the second half of the nineteenth century, labourers' wages gradually increased, aided by a drop in prices in the last quarter of the century; there was more money available for food, and its quality improved. But, significantly, the first measures to restrict child labour in Belgium were passed as late as 1889, by which date the importance of children's contributions to the most basic needs of the family budget had diminished.[5]

Children in the Labour Process

Children were to be found at work in virtually every sector of the Belgian economy in the nineteenth century. Agriculture was one of the most important employers of children, much of it seasonal work which resulted in school absenteeism, particularly in the summer months. Many young boys worked as cattle herders or stableboys. In the polders and the "Land van Waas" region, children were engaged in the so-called weeding groups, which were formed by a number of adults from the village who were called weeding bosses. They recruited between thirty and forty children eight to fourteen years of age, who were put at the disposal of the local farmers to pull out the weeds in the beet, oat and flax fields. These groups rose at five a.m., often walked for an hour to reach the fields, and remained there until seven p.m. Other children sold milk before school started.

Children played an important role in rural and craft industries such as rope making, metalworking, domestic weaving, processing skins or weaving baskets. In rope making, for example, young children worked throughout the day, turning the rope wheel or moistening the ropes before they were twined. Children as young as six or seven worked in the widespread straw-plaiting industries, making baskets, hats and chairs. Industries of this

4 For a discussion of wages in industry, see Dhondt, "Opkomst van de burgerij als politieke macht".

5 De Weerdt, "Arbeiderstoestanden"; De Herdt and De Graeve, *Kinderarbeid*, pp. 21-29. In about 1840, the purchasing power of a large number of workers was fairly high, but declined sharply thereafter. By 1850, for instance, a 25 per cent decline over 1840 levels could already be observed in the purchasing power of cotton workers. This rate would fluctuate considerably in the following years, reaching, by the end of the century, only slightly higher levels than it had been in 1840. The situation for mineworkers, however, was much more favourable. See Gaus, *Politieke en sociale evolutie*, p. 156.

kind were particularly affected by mechanization. In order to compete with the machine, cottage industry workers had to work longer hours for a smaller return and make increasing use of the assistance of wives and children. A typical example of this process could be seen after the creation of the first mechanized flax mills in Ghent and Brussels in the late 1830s. The 220,000 Flemish women who spun flax, assisted by their children, were gradually forced to abandon this work.[6]

Some of the worst conditions of child labour were in the coal mines of Wallonia, where in 1846 there were as many as ten thousand children between ten and twelve years of age. During the Napoleonic regime, in 1813, child labour in the mines had been prohibited for children under ten years of age. Thereafter, officially at least, child coal miners had to be ten years old before accompanying their fathers or mothers to the mine where they were registered to haul ("traineur") or to push ("hiercheur") the mining carts.[7] Up to 1840, children hauled the carts by means of chains. From about 1840, there was a new transport system which required children to push the small rectangular carts on iron rails. Since many mining shafts were barely four feet high, children had to work with bent backs. Young miners only rarely saw daylight in the summer, and never in winter. Many, indeed, having worked during the day, joined the night shift, remaining underground for 36 hours without any "proper rest".[8] Most children were allowed to keep the supplementary income they thus earned, whereas they generally gave their entire wages to their parents.

In the brickyards, children brought up the clay and carried the moulded bricks to the drying sheds. At night they slept in open sheds where they were exposed to wind and rain. It was often difficult to wake the young children in the morning even after a dousing with cold water thrown at their faces; sometimes they were dressed while they slept, and carried to their place of work by their father or a neighbour.[9]

A number of surveys enable us to gain some indication of the proportion of the total labour force made up of children in different industries. From the beginning of the nineteenth century, both child and women's work was especially widespread in the mechanizing textile industries. Lieven Bauwens, who introduced the first mechanical spinning mule in Ghent in

6 Coppejans-Desmedt and Van Schoenbeek, "Van passiviteit tot sociale beweging"; Veraghtert, "Ambacht en nijverheid", p. 287.

7 Ministère de I'Interieur, *Enquête sur la condition des classes ouvrières*, pp. 225-304.

8 De Weerdt, "Zwetende arbeidsters".

9 Van de Velde and Vinck, *Geschiedenis van de socialistische arbeidersbeweging*, pp. 17, 35.

about 1800, mentions in one of his letters that 75 per cent of the workforce in spinning mills in Ghent – the "Manchester of the Continent" – was made up of women and children.[10]

Table 9.1. Child Labour in Some Ghent Factories, 1817

Kind of factory	*Number of factories*	*Number of labourers*	*Number of children under 17 years*	*%*
Spinning mill	12	1,093	277	25
Weaving mill	5	148	24	16
Textile printing mill	7	360	45	12
Sugar factory	4	71	3	4
Paper mill	3	123	32	26
Tobacco factory	2	18	6	33
Yards	3	131	2	1
Joineries	2	24		
Hatters	2	25	4	16
Cooperage	1	7	–	–
Roof slating	1	8	1	12
Total	42	2,008	394	20

Source: Stadsarchief Ghent, Reeks K15, 1817.
Note: Only some of the documents mentioned the age of the labourers.

Table 9.1, covering a sample of the Ghent workforce, shows that children below the age of seventeen years constituted on average 20 per cent of the workforce in a selection of Ghent industries. Especially high proportions of children were to be found in the spinning mills (25 per cent), paper mills (26 per cent) and tobacco factories (33 per cent). The spinning mills provided by far the largest amount of child employment.

An additional indication of the overall participation of children in the economy comes from a government-sponsored enquiry into child labour set up in 1843, and reporting in 1848.[11] In a survey of 54,181 workers in a

10 Balthazar, "Groei tot een industriële grootstad", p. 158.
11 Ministère de l'Interieur, *Enquête sur la condition des classes ouvrières.*

range of industries, the enquiry found that 1.3 per cent were under nine and 19.5 per cent were under sixteen years of age (table 9.2).

Table 9.2. Child Labour in Factories in Various Belgian Provinces, by Age and Gender, 1843

Age	*Male*	*Percentage of total workers*	*Female*	*Percentage of total workers*	*Total*	*%*
Under 9 years	532	1	164	0.3	696	1.3
9-11 years	1,615	3	684	1.3	2,299	4.3
12-15 years	5,638	10.4	1,881	3.5	7,519	13.9
16-20 years	5,768	10.6	3,377	6.2	9,145	16.8
21 and over	29,520	54.5	5,002	9.2	34,522	63.7
Total	43,073	79.5	11,108	20.5	54,181	100

Source: Ministère de I'Interieur, *Enquête sur la condition des classes ouvrières*.

In 1845, the failure of the potato harvest, the collapse of traditional linen and cottage industries (which were no longer competitive with the less expensive machine-made linen from England), and a series of epidemics, focused the government's attention on social questions. A general census was carried out in 1846 under the leadership of a great Belgian statistician and astronomer, Adolphe Quetelet, who is regarded as the father of the quantitative method in sociology.[12] The census, the first carried out in Belgium on a genuinely scientific basis, provided detailed information on the Belgian workforce (see table 9.3).

It showed that children featured prominently in the workforce, not only in textiles, but also in coal mining, brickworks, potteries, the food industry, leatherwork, metalwork and woodwork. Altogether children made up 21 per cent of the labourers, the proportion being higher in craft and home-based work than in mechanized industry. Child labour in the mining sector was a constant throughout the nineteenth century, and, according to one source, the number of children under sixteen employed underground in coal mines increased significantly between 1843 and 1864.[13]

12 Vander Mensbrugghe, "Quételet", pp. 468-477.

13 Puissant, "Un lent et difficile processus de démocratisation", p. 162.

Table 9.3. Child Labour in Some Important Belgian Crafts and Industries

Type of company	*Number of companies*	*Number of labourers by gender and age*				
		Male	*Female*	*> 16*	*< 16*	*Total*
Coal mines and coke works	202	39,120	7,066	35,847	10,339	46,186
Craft metal treatment	12,028	15,853	158	13,583	2,428	16,011
Industrial metal treatment	2,419	24,345	1,933	23,674	2,604	26,278
Craft brickyards and potteries	6,786	11,624	165	10,843	946	11,789
Industrial brickyards and potteries	1,613	18,231	1,745	16,367	3,609	19,976
Craft flax and hemp	18,732	13,920	28,874	22,387	20,407	42,794
Industrial flax and hemp	2,401	8,497	8,732	13,591	3,638	17,229
Wool	768	12,210	5,943	14,820	3,333	18,153
Craft cotton processing	43	4	358	101	261	362
Industrial cotton processing	350	10,042	4,276	10,580	3,738	14,318
Silk	27	588	87	438	237	675
Clothing	10,036	7,169	3,888	8,458	2,599	11,057
Craft food processing	7,928	6,979	478	6,725	732	7,457
Industrial food processing	8,434	19,780	2,624	20,508	1,896	22,404
Craft woodwork	20,636	19,020	215	17,129	2,106	19,235
Industrial woodwork	1,032	1,659	63	1,577	145	1,722
Craft leatherwork	11,841	10,189	270	8,257	2,202	10,459
Industrial leatherwork	968	2,449	243	2,472	220	2,692
Craft paper factories and printing works	611	2,666	39	2,054	651	2,705
Industrial paper factories and printing offices	142	1,582	1,089	2,106	565	2,671

Source: Statistique de la Belgique. Industrie. Recensement general (15 octobre 1846) (Brussels, 1851), pp. x–xi.

Some employers, perhaps most prominently the Ghent cotton firm Voortman, seem deliberately to have employed large numbers of women and young children in order to keep down their labour costs. Low wages and high female and child employment went hand in hand in Voortman's mill, and in the Ghent textile trade as a whole. The figures in Table 9.4 give some indication of the effects of this employer strategy on the structure of the workforce, though they considerably understate the number of young children by omitting the spinners' helpers. As Peter Scholliers has put it,

> women were forced to do wage labour as long as their children were too young to contribute to total family income. So the *cercle vicieux* – profitable to the employer and unbreakable to the labour movement – was established: cotton wages were low due to the many women and young people in the factories, and women and youngsters were obliged to do wage labour because of low textile wages. In general this led to low purchasing power, harsh working conditions and a low standard of living.[14]

Table 9.4. Textile Workers in the Voortman Cotton Mill in Ghent, in %

	1842		*1859*		*1879*		*1902*	
Age	Male	Female	Male	Female	Male	Female	Male	Female
5-9	0	0.6	0	0	0	0	0	0
10-14	0	3.1	2.6	7.4	1.0	7.0	0	3.8
15-19	4.4	9.5	11.2	9.5	2.0	22.0	6.6	22.8
20-24	7.6	13.4	11.1	13.7	5.0	12.0	7.6	14.6
25-29	3.2	14.5	7.9	5.4	6.0	10.0	4.8	6.6
30-34	8.2	3.9	5.4	3.1	4.0	4.0	3.8	4.3
35-39	5.1	3.1	2.6	0	2.0	3.0	5.5	1.6
40-44	7.6	1.3	5.9	3.1	5.0	3.0	3.8	2.3
45+	9.5	5.0	9.5	1.6	8.0	6.0	10,4	1.5

Source: Scholliers, "Grown-Ups, Boys and Girls".

In the Ghent cotton industry as a whole in the 1870s, about one fifth of the workers were children aged between ten and sixteen years. By 1896, seven years after the passing of the first law controlling child labour and

14 Scholliers, "Grown-ups, boys and girls", p. 218.

after a rise in the standard of living, there had been a significant decrease in the number of working children under twelve, but still one tenth of the 842,000 industrial workers in Belgium were children under sixteen, the largest numbers being in textile factories (11,863), coal mines (10,167), clothing (9,674), and glass factories (4,429).[15] The youngest children were in the ceramics, glass, tobacco and matchbox industries. Children continued to remain active in agriculture, domestic work, and even in heavy industry. In 1914, when compulsory education prohibited children from working under the age of fourteen, there were still 1,500 children under that age at work in the coal mine of Mons (Bergen, province of Hainaut), 406 of them working underground.[16] In rural Flanders, 5.2 per cent of the male workers and 3.9 per cent of the female workers were between the ages of twelve and fourteen years.[17]

Working Hours and Health

Working hours for children varied by industry, but as a general rule they were the same as those for adults, between ten and sixteen hours a day. Hours were often longer in summer than in winter, particularly in industries where good light was essential.

A typical example was Aalst (East Flanders) where in 1843 working hours were from 6 to 8 a.m., and then, after a half-hour break, until noon. There was a one-hour break for lunch, but then a non-stop working schedule until 8 p.m. In Ghent cotton mills in 1845, children had an extra half-hour break at breakfast and at supper, but otherwise worked the same hours as adults, from dawn to 10 p.m. in winter, and from 5 or 5.30 a.m. until 8 p.m. in summer.[18] Since many children did not live in the immediate vicinity of the factories, they might have travelling time of between one and three hours, both morning and evening, to add to their long working hours.[19]

There is evidence, however, as table 9.5 shows, that as the century progressed working hours were reduced.[20]

15 Recensement general des industries et des metiers (31 octobre 1896), XVIII: *Expose general des methodes et des resultats* (1902), Brussels, p. 135; Kruithof, "De grootte van het Belgisch proletariat", p. 199.

16 Puissant, "Un lent et difficile processus de démocratisation", p. 162.

17 Vandenbroeke, *Sociale geschiedenis*, p. 146.

18 Mareska and Heyman, *Enquête sur le travail*.

19 De Weerdt, *Gentse textielbewerkers*.

20 See also Gaus, *Politieke en sociale evolutie*, p. 150.

Tabel 9.5. Working Hours in Ghent Industries, 1840-1914

Year	*Hours/day*	*Hours/week*
1840	13	78
1847	13	78
1859	12	72
1869	12	72
1871	12	72
1892	12	72
1897	11	66
1900	11	66
1904	11	66
1914	11	66

Source: De Neve, "Kinderarbeid te Gent", p. 17.

The long working hours, sometimes during the night, inevitably affected the health of the children. The monotonous and repetitive work they had to do was further detrimental to their well-being. And there were, moreover, conditions specific to each industry which could be extremely damaging to health. To give some examples:

– In both cotton and flax mills, children's health was seriously impaired by dust. In addition, the steam of the boiling water was so dense that girls standing only two or three metres apart could scarcely see each other. The condensation from the factory ceiling fell onto their bare necks, and hot water splashed upon their already drenched clothes. They worked barefoot in mud, with an ambient temperature of between 39° and 49° C. Consequently, hands and feet were quickly affected by gangrene. Moreover, since the girls went home in their wet clothes, even when there was heavy rainfall or freezing conditions, lung disease was a frequent occurrence.[21] There were no proper measures to protect workers against moving parts until an Act of 1903; girls and boys risked

21 Gilbert, *Filatures de lin*; De Weerdt, "Arbeiderstoestanden"; and Samyn, *Uit het martelaarsleven van de kinderen der vlasfabriek*, pp. 8-24. See http://cageweb.be/cageweb-view?q=%22Gezinsinkomen%22&start=7&filter=&sort= (last accessed 28 March 2010).

having their arms and fingers crushed, or their clothes or hair caught and being dragged along by the transmission belts and driving wheels.
- In the matchstick factories, which were set up in the second half of the nineteenth century, mainly near Lessines (in the province of Hainaut), Ninove and Geraardsbergen [Gramont] (in the province of East Flanders), conditions were even more appalling. Children as young as five had to fill matchboxes or dip matchsticks in a phosphoric mixture that contained thirty per cent white phosphorous, a substance that rapidly affected the bones. There was no proper system of ventilation.[22]
- Lace schools economized on heating costs in winter by squeezing as many apprentices as possible in a small room. For example, in the lace school of Mrs. Sabien in Turnhout (province of Antwerp), 51 lacemakers, including two teachers, were packed into a room 75 square metres. Lace workers also suffered from curvature of the spine.[23]
- Children in the tobacco workshops of Antwerp had serious chest complaints, caused by tobacco dust.
- Girls working in the sewing workshops, stitching collar buttons, often suffered from tuberculosis and anaemia.[24]
- In the processing of skins and fluffing of hair, boys and girls used large scissors to cut the skins which had previously been prepared with mercury.[25]
- In coal mining, dust and coal grit affected the lungs of the child workers.

It is hardly surprising that the weakest among those who worked in these industries died from exhaustion after a few years or were marked for life. It could not be claimed, moreover, that these were conditions of which contemporaries were simply unaware. In 1844, a medical commission had given the following description of working children:

> They are skinny, shrivelled, uncured-for, they suffer from chlorosis, scrofulous tumors and rachitis. Their lean, pale faces show signs of suffering. Their muscles are hardly developed, their bellies are swollen, they suffer from troublesome digestive systems coinciding with acid indigestion. The

22 De Winne, "A travers les Flandres".
23 Ministère de l'Interieur, *Enquête sur la condition des classes ouvrières.*
24 Ministère de l'Interieur, *Enquête sur la condition des classes ouvrières.*
25 De Winne, "A travers les Flandres".

children complain of headache, diarrhoea and intestinal colics, they grow slowly and irregularly and their stature is below average.[26]

Tabel 9.6. Height and Weight of Children Working in the Ghent Cotton Industry, by Age and Gender and Compared with Normal Values, 1843

	Boys				*Girls*			
	Height (meters)		*Weight (kg)*		*Height (meters)*		*Weight (kg)*	
Age	*Normal*	*Working*	*Normal*	*Working*	*Normal*	*Working*	*Normal*	*Working*
10	1.275	1.210	24,52	23.40	1.248	1.204	23.52	22.96
11	1.330	1.300	27.10	26.62	1.299	1.240	25.65	23.80
12	1.385	1.310	29.82	28.47	1.353	1.339	29.82	27.14
13	1.439	1.368	34.38	29.45	1.403	1.372	32.94	29.57
14	1.493	1.367	38.67	31.69	1.453	1.388	36.70	31.23
15	1.546	1.480	43.62	38.49	1.499	1.415	40.37	34.61

Source: De Neve, "Kinderarbeid te Gent". Figures for working children are derived from Mareska and Heyman, *Enquête sur le travail*, pp. 134 and 136. Normal values are the ones estimated by Quetelet in his *Sur l'homme et le developpement de ses faculties ou Essai de statistique sociale*, a work that marks the beginning of modern anthropometrics.

Height and weight are one way in which historians measure the well-being of populations in the past, and they are often taken as an effective indicator of an overall standard of living.[27] Some figures for Ghent working children in table 9.6 show that their heights and weights were considerably below the norm. Not all of this deficiency can be ascribed to working conditions, which were only one element alongside poor living conditions, a low-calorie diet and lack of sleep. The figures do nonetheless indicate that young Belgian workers were subject to a process of physical deterioration.

Children's Earnings

Table 9.7 shows the extent to which children's wages rose in the second half of the century. In 1880, children in the Ghent cotton industry earned twice

26 Vandenbroeke, *Sociale Geschiedenis*, p. 245.
27 Floud, Wachter and Gregory, *Height, Health and History*.

to three times what was paid in 1846.[28] The lowest wages were paid in the textile industry, particularly in flax. Part of the reason for this may lie in the way children were taken into employment. In the Ghent cotton industry, for example, there was a system of subcontracting whereby children were paid by the spinners rather than by the factory owner. The spinners tried to keep the wages of their helpers as low as possible, and on holidays (saints' days as well as a few days at Carnival and the Ghent festival) they were not paid at all. Children's wages varied not only according to the sector of the economy in which they were employed, but also, as can be seen in table 9.8, by gender. Girls earned less than boys. The differences in earning by sector of the economy are also apparent.

Table 9.7. Average Wages (per day) Paid to Children Under 16 Years of Age, 1846 and 1880

Sector	*1846 Belgian Francs*	*1880 Belgian Francs*
Ceramics industry	1.28	1.64
Glassworks	0.81	1.69
Mining industry	0.72	1.82
Steel industry	0.48	1.76
Cotton industry	0.47	1.36
Flax and hemp	0.33	1.20

Source: De Weerdt, "Arbeiderstoestanden".

A survey of Ghent workers in 1845 carried out by Mareska and Heyman gives some indication of the contribution children made to the family economy. An adult male cotton worker could earn about 656 francs a year, an adult female about 383 francs. A factory child under twelve could earn 114 francs, while one between twelve and fifteen years could earn up to 241 francs. The annual expenditure of a family consisting of parents and four small children was about 742 francs. The older child's earnings would be enough to meet the family's expenditure on the staple food, bread, and

28 Varlez, *Salaires dans l'industrie Gantoise*, I, pp. 207-211; *Ibid.*, II, pp. cxxxvii-cal.

the younger child's would nearly pay for the family's potatoes. These were levels of contribution which no family could afford to do without.[29]

Table 9.8. Daily Wages of Ghent Children Under 16 Years of Age, in Cotton, Flax and Steel Industries, before 1896

Wage group	*Cotton*		*Flax*		*Steel*
Belgian Francs:	*% Boys*	*% Girls*	*% Boys*	*% Girls*	*% Boys*
-0.5	3.19	1.51		5.42	22.53
0.50-0.99	16.23	38.49	23.07	37.12	45.79
1.0-1.49	54.52	60.00	72.37	57.46	23.76
1.5	26.06	–	4.56	–	7.92
Total	100	100	100	100	100

Source: De Neve, "Kinderarbeid te Gent".

School or Work?

In 1830, Belgium broke away from the Netherlands and proclaimed itself a sovereign state. In the absence of specific legislation, the number of schools quickly soared, increasing from one school for every 1,007 inhabitants in 1830 to one for every 785 inhabitants by 1840. This trend was mainly the result of a proliferation of private schools, which working-class families could not afford.[30] The first organic law relating to primary education was passed in 1842. It required each community to support at least one primary school providing free education to poor children.[31] Parents were not obliged to send their children to school, and, because of the difficulty in meeting their primary needs and the importance of their children's contribution to the family economy, there were strong pressures on parents to put their children to work at as early an age as possible.

In rural areas, some children did not go to school at all; particularly keen learners might attend Sunday school. In urban areas, the schooling situation was better, although it was still common for very young children to be at work.

29 Mareska and Heyman, *Enquête sur le travail.*
30 De Vroede, "Van oud naar nieuw".
31 Luykx, *Politieke geschiedenis in België.*

To counteract high illiteracy rates, the city council of Ghent, in 1853, set up a school for adult factory workers, offering evening classes in literacy. However, because of their long working hours, workers were unable to take full advantage of this opportunity. Consequently, the city council decided in 1861 to open a Sunday school for approximately 350 students. Enrolment was nearly double capacity, leading to the creation of a second Sunday school servicing an industrial area. Because many pupils left primary education at the age of eleven, the city council set eleven as the minimum age for entry to the Sunday school rather than fourteen years as suggested in government guidelines. The lower age limit facilitated the link between day classes and adult education and was clearly favourable in terms of educational efficiency. In 1865, a letter was sent to every factory in Ghent informing them of the adult education available and requesting them to encourage their workers to take it up. Sunday education was especially successful. During the 1865-1866 school year, more than 1,100 men and women factory workers followed adult education courses (44 per cent of the numbers in adult education). One industrial company, the flax spinner La Lys (from where 275 students came) even offered cash incentives to workers who excelled in these courses.[32]

Some children's schooling amounted in effect to a participation in the labour process. In the hundreds of lace schools in Flanders, girls primarily, but also boys, served an apprenticeship from the age of five or six. In theory they were first given a general education before gradually acquiring qualifications in lacemaking. By the age of twelve, they were considered fully skilled lacemakers, and they were kept at the schools until they were eighteen. Their work contribution covered the costs of their schooling and maintenance. Sometimes they were paid a supplement, but it was very small. Even their contemporaries were very much aware of this form of exploitation.[33]

Second-chance schools were established in the 1840s to re-educate girls who had become unemployed due to the decline of the Flemish linen industry. Girls were trained in handwork (lace and linen), but received only scant general instruction, usually religious. In 1845, there were 611 of these private institutions, servicing 35,996 students. By 1857, their numbers had shot up to 962, but then declined rapidly, reaching, for example, 430

32 Steels, *Geschiedenis van het stedelijk onderwijs*, pp. 143-144.

33 Ministère de l'Interieur, *Enquête sur la condition des classes ouvrières*.

schools attended by 22,810 girls in 1875.[34] According to an 1896 commission, these schools were

> [...]only small, dirty workshops where a woman with a financial interest makes these girls work beyond their capacities, apparently with the agreement of their parents. There is no other aim than to make as much profit as possible from these poor creatures' drudgery and they thereby remain deprived of any education or proper upbringing. [...] They occupy themselves exclusively with making bobbin lace and remain sitting on their chairs for 12 of the 13 or 14 hours of the working day, their bodies permanently bent and their eyes focused on the lace pillow.[35]

Throughout the second half of the nineteenth century, manufacturers firmly opposed making education compulsory, claiming that many industries would be forced to close if they had to do without child labour; that factory work was an easy way for children to learn a trade; and that there was a close connection between knowledge, virtue and work. The manufacturers also voiced a widespread fear that social unrest and even social revolution would ensue if the lower social classes received too much education.[36]

Nevertheless, despite the lack of legal obligation, the number of children receiving an education increased. Factors contributing to this trend included demographic developments, governmental efforts and, generally, a greater awareness of the advantages of education. In 1845, according to one source,[37] 33.7 per cent of seven to fourteen-year-olds were not educated at all, whereas by 1875 this figure had fallen to about 27 per cent. According to another source,[38] the percentage of children aged five to fourteen enrolled in school rose from 48 per cent in 1846 to 60 per cent in the mid-1860s, where it would remain up until 1914. Incomplete schooling was a major concern. In 1877-1878, 80.4 per cent of the non-paying pupils left school before completing the primary cycle, compared with 62.9 per cent of the paying pupils.[39] This situation improved after the passage of the 1889

34 De Weerdt, *En de vrouwen?*; De Nauw, "Geraardsbergse kantnijverheid", pp. 8-10.

35 De Vroede, "Onderwijs 1840-1870", p. 120.

36 *Ibid.*

37 Ministère de l'Interieur, *Enquête sur la condition des classes ouvrières.*

38 Mitchell, *European Historical Statistics*, pp. 40, 786, 789; see also Flora, *State, Economy and Society*, pp. 561-566.

39 De Vroede, "Onderwijs 1840-1870", pp. 118-119.

law limiting child labour. In 1897, drop-out was 9 per cent, whereas by 1910, of a total of 929,347 pupils, drop-out was only 4 per cent.[40] Table 9.9 shows broad trends in literacy in Belgium from 1866 to 1910.

Table 9.9. Literacy in Belgium, by Gender, 1866-1910

Date	*Male population x 1000*	*Number literate x 1000*	*% literate*	*Female population x 1000*	*Number literate x 1000*	*% literate*
1866	2,420	1,209	50	2,408	1,070	44
1880	2,758	1,661	60	2,762	1,527	55
1890	3,027	1,948	64	3,042	1,838	60
1900	3,325	2,309	69	3,369	2,247	67
1910	3,681	2,781	76	3,743	2,765	74

Source: Mitchell, *European Historical Statistics*, p. 29 (all figures rounded).

Child Labour Legislation

Although Belgium in the nineteenth century was one of the most industrialized countries in Western Europe, it was the last one to introduce a law on child labour. This was not for lack of awareness of the extent and conditions of child labour. In 1841, partly as a consequence of similar enquiries in England, the government's attention was drawn to the miserable physical and moral conditions under which children had to work in Belgian industry.[41] In his speech of 8 November 1842, King Leopold announced a bill for the protection of children working in the manufacturing industry. In 1843, a special commission was appointed to enquire into the working and living conditions of the working class and at the same time to study child labour. The commission gathered information from 164 industrialists, 14 Chambers of Commerce, 8 mining engineers and 19 medical associations.[42] This led in 1848 to the introduction of a rather progressive bill which, had it been passed, would have prohibited child labour under the age of 10, and restricted the working day for ten to forteen-year-olds to 6.5 hours. Indus-

40 De Clerck *et al.*, *Dag meester*, p. 35.

41 De Herdt and De Graeve, *Kinderarbeid*, p. 22.

42 Thijs, "Overleveringen", pp. 42-43; De Weerdt, *Gentse textielbewerkers*, pp. 17-20.

trialists, however, were the dominant force in Belgian politics, and they successfully argued that the bill's restrictions on their economic freedom would make Belgian industry uncompetitive; it did not become law.[43]

Although industrialists remained hostile to government intervention, in the 1860s a number of them in the Ghent textile industry began to impose restrictions on themselves, employing children only when they reached the age of twelve, rather than, as previously, when they were seven or eight. In other industries, however, there were no such self-imposed restrictions: an investigation in 1869 showed that there were still significant numbers of children under the age of eight employed in the cigar industry in Antwerp; in lace work-shops in Bruges, Ypres and Courtrai; and in sewing workshops in Aalst. Night work for children remained common practice, especially in paper factories, sugar refineries and rolling mills. In the coal industry there were still 1,700 children working underground, and a law passed in 1884 prohibiting boys and girls under twelve from working in the mines had little practical consequence.

In 1886, there was a severe economic recession, accompanied by major strikes and serious unrest. This prompted yet another investigation into working conditions, one that led to the passage of a law in 1889 that made it illegal for a child under the age of twelve to be employed in industry at all, and for boys aged twelve to sixteen and for girls aged twelve to twenty-one to work more than six days a week or more than twelve hours a day. Night work was prohibited for boys under sixteen and for girls under twenty-one. From 1892 onwards, girls under twenty-one were prohibited from working underground in mines. The law of 1889, however, applied only to industry, and not to domestic labour or farming. Moreover, in the handicraft industries, to which it did apply, it was often circumvented by registering the boys and girls as apprentices. Although other child labour laws were passed subsequent to 1889, the next decisive legislative act was the introduction of compulsory schooling for children under fourteen in 1914, an act only enforced after the First World War.

In both child labour and compulsory schooling legislation, Belgium lagged behind comparable countries in Europe, a fact best explained by the dominance of bourgeois liberalism throughout the nineteenth century. It was only the severe unrest of 1886 that eventually pushed the government into legislation which was still less restrictive of child labour than in other countries.

43 Kuypers, *Bergop*, pp. 60–62.

Some Conclusions

Belgium made extensive use of child labour in virtually every sector of the economy; it was an essential element both in agriculture and in industrial processes. Belgium lagged behind comparable countries in its failure to take any steps to control child labour by means of legislation until the late nineteenth century (in the case of child labour laws) or the early twentieth century (in the case of compulsory schooling laws). There is evidence that a consequence of this was a lower level of schooling and a higher level of child labour than existed in other countries at a similar stage of economic development. It is easier to state this than to explain it, but it is likely that it is connected to a balance of political forces which effectively gave power to the industrial bourgeoisie who themselves had espoused an ideology hostile to any state intervention. Although most Belgian children almost certainly received some schooling prior to the Act of 1914 which made it compulsory up to the age of fourteen, that voluntary school attendance was compatible with an extensive engagement by children in a wide variety of forms of child labour.

CHAPTER 10

Elites, Employers, Child Labour and Compulsory Education in Belgium before 1914

Éliane Gubin

Bourgeois elites played a fundamental role in the extension of popular education in nineteenth-century Belgium. They undertook major efforts to establish networks of adult teaching and training,[1] efforts that contrasted strikingly with the opposition that the same elites displayed towards compulsory education. It was only on 19 May 1914 that the Belgian parliament decided on compulsory education for all children from age six to fourteen.

This delay appears all the more incomprehensible given that the country was receptive to the new pedagogic tendencies and itself produced such noted educationalists as Pierre Tempels and Ovide Decroly. The Liberal party consistently showed a definite interest in problems of education, and the Ligue de l'enseignement established in 1864 was the direct inspiration of its French counterpart. The influence of neighbouring countries was also felt: France imposed compulsory education in 1882, Luxembourg in 1881, England between 1870 and 1880, and the Netherlands in 1900.

Persistent Illiteracy

The objection could be made that the general development of instruction in Belgium did not make legal regulation necessary. This was the view widely proclaimed by the opponents of compulsory education, but it does not resist factual analysis. The first investigation of industrial conditions, carried out in 1843,[2] showed that only two per cent of the 14,313 workers questioned were able to read and write. Until the end of the century, subsequent inquiries showed a similarly desolate situation;[3] in the 1870s, 24

1 See Belgium Ministère de l'intérieur, *L'Enseignement populaire en Belgique au* XIX*e siècle.*
2 Ministère de l'intérieur, *Enquête sur la condition des classes ouvrières et le travail des enfants.*
3 Depaepe, "Kwantitatieve analyse", p. 49.

per cent of conscripts called up for military service were totally illiterate.[4] As for girls, more than a quarter of those born between 1850 and 1860 and married between 1876 and 1880 were unable even to sign their marriage certificate.[5]

The Indispensable Work of Children...

This situation was a direct result of children being sent out to work at an early age. Among the labouring classes, childhood was in no way a privileged period that warranted "special protection and concern"; it represented on the contrary an immense reservoir of cheap unskilled labour that industrial employers could draw on according to the economic conjuncture. The young worker of nine years old was a social reality that placed the question of education at the very heart of economic life. The reports of provincial inspectors of primary education are filled with complaints about the unequal struggle between school and factory: "the childhood of the poor is sacrificed to industry".[6] Work triumphed over schooling on all sides.[7]

The fact is that child labour was inherent to the success of industrial capitalism, and indeed represented the cornerstone of this system. A little over one-fifth of the total labour-force (21 per cent of all workers) in 1846 were under sixteen years of age. Large variations were notable, however, according to gender and industrial sector: out of 497 establishments covered, the 1843 investigation counted 18 per cent of male workers under sixteen, against 24 per cent of female workers.[8] In the collieries, the average figure was 22 per cent, and as high as 48 per cent in linen manufacture.

This recourse to abundant and very cheap labour, which could be dismissed without scruple in times of recession, made it possible not only to achieve considerable gains in the price of products, but also to maintain throughout the century a downward pressure on wages in general, including those of adults. Even at the beginning of the twentieth century, Bel-

4 This was still the case in the 1880s, see Lory, *Libéralisme et instruction primaire*, pp. 82-85.

5 Lory, "L'enseignement libre", p. 232.

6 Ministère de l'intérieur, *Rapport triennal sur la situation de l'enseignement primaire en Belgique*, 1852-1854, p. clxiii; *ibid.* for 1858-1860, p. cxx; for 1862-1864, p. civ; for 1870-1872, p. xcvll, etc.

7 Ministère de l'intérieur, *Rapport triennal*, 1852-54, p. clxiii.

8 "Réponses des chefs d'industrie", *Enquête sur la condition des classes ouvrières* (1843), vol. 1, p. vi.

gium was a country of very low wages, this being a determining element in the competitiveness of its products on the world market. To restrict the labour of children in order to let them attend school thus appeared as principally a question of economics, and this argument was recurrent in the mouths of industrialists: "To seek to remove children from exploitation in the workshops would mean spoiling *for everyone* the fertile source of labour, making us unable to contain the struggle and antagonism of similar manufactures from abroad".[9] Any restriction on child labour would provoke, according to the spokesmen of this time, increased unemployment and the generalized impoverishment of working-class families.

It is understandable, therefore, why the industrial employers paid particular attention to proposals for compulsory education, which in their eyes were still more dangerous than the regulation of certain sectors of industry, and why child labour formed the backdrop to debates on such proposals. No parliamentary discussion on compulsory education failed to refer to its economic consequences; and conversely, no debate on the condition of the workers overlooked the lack of instruction, at a time when this appeared as the principal reason for the misery of the working classes, their immorality, drunkenness, and lack of foresight. All the major social investigations of the nineteenth century closely linked the physical state of the labouring classes with their moral state, and devoted a major section to the educational situation.

In all these aspects, the question of compulsory education reveals very well the attitude of the bourgeoisie towards the children of the poor, yet it also reveals profound tensions within the governing classes. The question mobilized such varied groups of notables as doctors, engineers, economists, educationalists, philanthropists, industrialists, and later on also lawyers; it claimed the attention of Chambers of commerce, of the Conseil supérieur de l'industrie, the Académie de médecine, associations for public health, the Société d'économie politique and the Ligue de l'enseignement. It constantly arose at gatherings with a social purpose such as congresses of hygiene or welfare. In the face of diverse interests, and drawn between conflicting values, these notables were forced to reconcile philanthropic and moralizing practices with industrial and political interests. These tensions were particularly marked in the Belgian parliament, where employers' representatives and lawyers close to economic milieus were prominent. Until the end of the nineteenth century, a regular "symbiotic relationship"

9 *Avis de la Chambre de Commerce de Liège sur le projet de loi relatif à la condition des classes ouvrières et du travail des enfants* (Liège, 1849), p. 15.

between the state and such economic elites was the rule, placing parliament in a "very clear and personal subjection to the private interests of a few".[10]

The present chapter aims to make clear certain facets of a question that was highly complex, in particular by viewing it from a political, economic and social angle.

The Political Aspect

It is certainly the political aspect of compulsory schooling that has been most studied, in a society where control of primary education had become a major issue between the parties alternating in power. Before 1914, the struggle in education constantly not only set Catholics against Liberals, but also divided the Liberals themselves. It would be reductive, however, to see this only as an opposition between progressives and conservatives; as well as ideological options, positions were taken up according to a dividing line determined by two preoccupations: the sphere of state intervention and the recognized purpose of popular education.

Until the mid-nineteenth century, the Belgian bourgeoisie had broadly accepted the notion of a liberal state in which the area of state intervention was strictly limited to the functions of policing and security (the gendarme state). The very idea of state intervention in private or industrial relations was rejected with such vigour that it kept any regulation of working conditions at bay until 1889.[11] In this context of total liberty, compulsory education, which meant a radical ban on child labour, immediately appeared a monstrosity. Form actually obscured content on this question, and a by no means negligible fraction of Liberals, though won to the virtues of education, refused to commit themselves to a path of legal regulation, fearing where this might lead. Théodore Verhaegen, for example, a well-known Liberal and co-founder of the University of Brussels, called compulsory education a "dangerous and illiberal theory", which would lead "straight to communism and socialism".[12]

Divided between a doctrinaire wing that was powerful in the economic field, consisting of industrialist and bankers, and a progressive wing made

10 Van Themsche, *Paradoxes de l'État*, pp. 46-47.

11 The first social legislation, voted after the revolts of 1886, remained governed by the idea of the superiority of individual initiative over regulation, see Nandrin, "Genèse du droit du travail".

12 Desmed, "À propos du mémoire de la Loge", p. 394.

up of an urban and intellectual citizenry, Liberals warred with each other over this question, while the Catholics, equally (if not still more) champions than the Liberals of a non-interventionist state, presented a united front of rejection.

This first dividing line was overlaid by a second one, concerning the purpose of popular education. For a long time, primary education was seen as a way of maintaining social order.[13] It represented, in the words of Destriveaux, rector of the University of Liège in 1824, "a guarantee against political conflagrations".[14] This notion persisted, with certain variations, until the end of the century. Despite speeches glorifying the struggle against ignorance, the chief mission of primary schooling was seen as integrating the working classes into the political system, rather than instilling them with basic knowledge: it aimed above all at teaching children to respect established values, making them into workers "subject to the duties of their condition". In this perspective, the church was viewed as an indispensable auxiliary, and the first organic law on primary education, voted in 1842, inscribed Catholic religion in the curriculum of compulsory subjects:[15] "In order to be useful", wrote the *Journal Historique et Littéraire*, "instruction must be essentially religious".[16] The Liberals of the time very broadly shared this idea, which the Mons Chamber of commerce summed up very well in a report of 1842: it was indispensable to extend religious instruction in the mining districts, "to preserve the subordination so necessary to the preservation of order among the numerous populations of the Borinage".[17] This notion explains why the coal masters, in their majority Liberals, subsidized the schools of the Frères de la Doctrine chrétienne through to the 1860s.

But the appearance of an anti-religious fraction within Belgian liberalism suddenly broke this consensus in the middle of the century. The "young" Liberals, as they were called, now aimed to instruct the people, denouncing religion as a moral poison that maintained them in superstition and under the thrall of the clergy. They demanded an extension of literacy teaching as a means for improving conditions of life and guaranteeing social peace. Like a peaceful revolution, instruction would strengthen cohesion between social classes by attenuating the differences between them "in

13 See on this aspect, Gubin and Lefebvre, "Obligation scolaire et société", p. 340 ff.

14 Destriveaux, *Discours sur l'instruction publique*, p. 185.

15 *Journal Historique et Littéraire*, 1836-1837, p. 177.

16 *Journal Historique et Littéraire*, 1834-1835, p. 37.

17 Archives de l'État à Mons, Mons Chamber of commerce, bundle 615.

terms of intelligence". In parallel with this, they saw education as offering further advances, such as secularization.[18] By combining compulsory education with the demand for a wider suffrage, they hoped to democratize an electoral system based until then exclusively on property qualifications and defended by both Catholics and doctrinaire Liberals.

The freemasons, or at least certain of their more advanced lodges,[19] supported compulsory education – in diametrical opposition to the Catholics. Equated with a "masonic conspiracy" to take pupils out of confessional schools to the benefit of the state schools,[20] compulsory education was vigorously opposed at three general assemblies of the Catholic party, in 1864, 1864 and 1867. It was considered contrary to individual liberty and the rights of the family, and an attack on paternal authority;[21] in short, nothing less than the start of a dangerous tendency towards the suppression of other liberties that would limit the power of the church.[22]

Against this clear unanimity in Catholic ranks, Liberals presented a spectacle of raging discord. They were divided on everything, even their programme. Though certainly anti-clerical, the "*doctrinaires*" persisted in the view that the presence of the clergy in primary schools was necessary, seeing religion as indispensable if the people were to accept their condition without revolt. The old formula that "one village priest did more to preserve public order than a hundred gendarmes" seemed to them still justified. Many of their number equated compulsory education with a "socialist" reform, an "attack on the rights of man and the authority of the father in the family, which weakens the mainspring of liberty by confiscating a part of the free decision, initiative and will of the individual." These were the words of Charles de Brouckère[23] (1796-1860), a well-known economist and the Liberal *bourgmestre* of Brussels. De Brouckère was also the administrator of the paternalistic association La Vielle Montagne, and

18 Funck, *L'Enseignement primaire*, pp. 17-18. Jean-Michel Funck (1822-1877) was a lawyer, liberal municipal councillor in Brussels, and in charge of public education from 1862 to 1870.

19 See on this subject Desmed, "Franc-maçonnerie belge"; Lory, *Libéralisme et instruction primaire*, vol. 1, pp. 277-291.

20 The Belgian bishops had "excommunicated" freemasons en bloc in 1837, and from this date there was a total incompatibility between freemasonry and the Catholic church.

21 *Assemblée générale des catholiques 1863*, vol. 1, pp. 122 and 126-128.

22 *Assemblée générale des catholiques 1864*, vol. 2, pp. 98-107; *Assemblée générale des catholiques 1867*, vol. 1, p. 327.

23 *Annales Parlementaires*, 24 January 1859, p. 380.

admitted that, as an employer, he did not want "the people en masse to go to school when they could find a useful occupation".[24]

The education of children from the popular classes was discussed sporadically in parliament, which particularly focused on it on three occasions, in 1862, 1869 and 1878, but without significant changes being notable in the positions of the respective parties.

A few moderate Liberals sometimes proposed certain limited initiatives, such as taking children out of the workshop for a few hours to give them classes. Others retorted that this was a false problem, as since nothing prevented children from being taught after working hours! "I do not see the difficulty of giving them lessons after this time [7 pm] in writing, mathematics, and even physics and mechanics," the Liberal deputy for Ghent, Édouard Jaequemyns, declared in 1862.[25]

But this idea of classes after working hours was quickly abandoned. Certain mining engineers, whose voices were heard in the coalfields, stressed its utopian character: "It is absolutely impossible for a young worker, who leaves home between two and five o'clock in the morning, and returns exhausted around five in the afternoon, to then attend school to receive lessons in reading and writing".[26] Mining engineers thus clearly posed the alternative as early as 1843: if the idea was to educate children, they must be prevented from working. The majority of them clearly came out in favour of compulsory education, except for engineers in the Liège coalfield, who stressed in 1843 the danger of instruction (strikes were always led by "educated" workers) and the risk of seeing miners' children refusing to become miners themselves, once they had been to school.[27]

Compulsory Education as an Economic Question

Compulsory education as a political question was dominated by its economic implications. This is why it arose in all debates about labour conditions and the "social question" in general, leading to reactions not only on

24 Devleeshouwer, "Logique sociale et legislation", p. 509.

25 *Annales Parlementaires*, 5 December 1862, p. 69. Jaeqemyns was also a company director. This solution had already been proposed by the Ghent chamber of commerce in 1843.

26 Gonot, mining engineer in the Mons coalfield, *Enquête sur la condition des classes ouvrières*, vol. 2, p. 228.

27 *Enquête sur la condition des classes ouvrières*, vol. 2, pp. 307, 332, 341.

the part of employers, but also of doctors and engineers who were in touch with the world of work.

Industrial milieus

A first attempt to regulate child labour was made in the wake of the 1843 inquiry. This proposed prohibiting children under ten from working, and limiting the working day of those under fourteen to six and a half hours – measures that would make it possible to organize a half-time educational system. This proposal was successfully defeated by economic circles, as it "did not take account of the necessities of industrial work",[28] and would therefore plunge working families into destitution.

The argument over children's wages as indispensable to working-class families was certainly the greatest handicap for the champions of compulsory education. Its self-evidence could not be denied: only the combined income of each member of the family made survival possible.

The opponents of compulsory education had a fine time stressing this paradox: if child labour were forbidden, it would be necessary to "return to the poor what you have taken away. If the wages of their children are indispensable, you will have to indemnify the father for this loss. But take care, this principle will lead you further, you will necessarily and irresistibly create a right to assistance [...]. The fatal and inflexible result of the right to assistance is the right to work [...]. And there you are, with complete socialism."[29] The economic argument mingled with the doctrinal creed of non-intervention by the state. The difficulty was real, and certain people tried to circumvent it by proposing palliative measures, such as the distribution of free soup at school.[30] But many recognized that these advantages would not be sufficient, and that it would be necessary to waive the educational obligation for the most deprived.[31]

The employers were all the more eager to emphasize this aspect as it was a sensitive point in the working class itself. In democratic circles, compulsory education was not seen as a priority, the problems of poverty having priority over those of instruction. "If you want instruction to have a place

28 *Documents relatifs au travail des femmes dans les manufactures et les mines* (Bruxelles, 1871), p. 13.

29 De Groux, *Congrès de l'Association pour le Progrès*, p. 263.

30 Altmeyer, *Quelques mots sur l'enseignement*, p. 68.

31 *Ibid.*; opinion of the Liège lodge (p. 71) and that of Verviers (pp. 178-179), two lodges established in industrial regions where child labour was particularly developed.

in the proletarian family, then start by getting rid of hunger",[32] since "the needs of the stomach are more immediate than those of intelligence".[33]

This is why part-time instruction (preferably half-time, on the English model) seemed to some people the lesser evil, an acceptable solution that would respect at the same time the interest of the child, that of the family, and the needs of industry. A few attempts were made in this direction, notable in Ghent, where the municipality "established part-time courses in its schools [...] along with classroom workshops that provided girls with a small wage".[34] Though supported by cultural associations and the Ligue de l'enseignement, these attempts still met with opposition from the factory-owners, since – in their opinion – two teams of children working alternately for six hours risked disorganizing the work of adults.

But the industrialists did not restrict themselves simply to economic arguments, they combined these with moral considerations. They denounced compulsory schooling as a slight on the leaders of industry that implied that these "abused" their child workers, and they also boasted of the philanthropic work and achievements of "socially inclined" employers. The bosses even presented themselves as defenders of their workers, who were doubly attacked in their dignity as fathers: the law would encroach on paternal power, as well as implying that fathers sought to exploit their children. Financial prejudice to working-class families would be coupled with moral prejudice: "A law on child labour", exclaimed Walthère Frère-Orban, the leader of doctrinaire Liberalism, in 1869, "is a law proclaiming that within working families the fathers are heartless and the mothers unfeeling!"[35]

But such language on the part of the employers was not always coherent, and several industrialists did not hesitate to attribute total responsibility for the precocious employment of their children to the workers themselves. To hear them, it would seem that employers only engaged young children when compelled to do so, in order to avoid their being placed in still worse conditions, small workshops or decentralized factories.

The final leaf in their argument was the need for training "on the job". Precocious labour was presented as indispensable for learning a trade, and above all acquiring the habits of order and work at the earliest age, these being the source of all virtue. Children would accustom themselves all the

32 *Le Prolétaire*, 28 March 1858.

33 *Le Prolétaire*, 23 May 1858.

34 *Revue de Belgique*, vol. 22, 15 January 1876, pp. 42-44.

35 *Annales Parlementaires*, 19 January 1869.

better to work if they were forced into this at an early age, and thus overcome the laziness that was a current vice among the popular classes: "Children can be used for work at the most tender age, especially with the aim of rooting out idleness."[36]

Champions of compulsory education replied by recalling on the contrary the moral dangers of the factory for young people, the corruption of the workshop and its sexual promiscuity. Against the paternal power that the defenders of liberty maintained, they championed a general interest. The Ligue de l'enseignement, for its part, evoked the rights of the child – a completely new idea that would yield its fruits at the end of the century. In its view, the debate should not be restricted to the rights of just three parties – the state, employers, and the family – but had also to include the duties of society towards children. Taking a stand against the common opinion of the time, the Ligue maintained that "it is not up to children to cover their own needs, nor to help support the family, nor to take part in the industrial work of the nation".[37] But as the Ligue could not avoid the question of the inadequate wages of working-class families, it confined itself to demanding, in the immediate future, support for families in terms of food and clothing, to make up for the lost wages of children attending school.[38]

As for the Chambers of commerce, these were initially unanimous in stressing the necessity of child labour, even if they recognized as early as 1843 that most young workers were completely illiterate. They declared nonetheless that they were ready to envisage forms of compulsory teaching – on condition that lessons were given after working hours and did not disturb the proper operation of industry.[39]

Beyond this, however, their opinions varied, according to the individuals in question and whether the industries they were connected with did or did not employ child labour. They took up an extremely broad range of positions, from total support for compulsory education to total rejection. The Brussels chamber of commerce, for example, which was favourable to compulsory education, justified this position by the technological devel-

36 "Rapport de la Chambre de Commerce de Termonde", p. 62.

37 *Bulletin de la Ligue de l'Enseignement*, 1868-1869, p. 34. The same ideas are found on pp. 41 and 90.

38 *Bulletin de la Ligue de l'Enseignement*, 1865-66, pp. 226, 396.

39 In the *Enquête* of 1843: Brussels Chamber of commerce (vol. 2, p. 31), also those of Termonde (vol. 2, p. 81), Charleroi (vol. 2, p. 127), Antwerp (vol. 1, p. 9), Ghent (vol. 1, p. 45), Tournai (vol. 2, p. 135) and Mons (vol. 2, p. 120).

opment of industry, which would soon require increasingly skilled workers capable of adapting themselves to new forms of labour. At the opposite end of the scale, the chambers of commerce of the mining districts, and that of Liège in particular, persisted in a total rejection, as likewise did the chambers of Verviers and Tournai, areas where the textile industry was dominant.

Other prominent figures also took part in the debate, including doctors, economists, and a few social commentators. Since the start of the nineteenth century, it was undoubtedly doctors who were privileged observers of the working class. They were the first to systematically associate themselves with the study of social problems, as experts qualified to describe the conditions of labour and existence of the working population, and the results of these.[40]

Though little represented in parliament, doctors nevertheless exerted a strategic weight on a number of bodies such as provincial medical committees, and commissions of public health and hygiene. They were regularly called upon by the public authorities on questions of the conditions of life of the lower classes. The Académie royale de médecine, shortly after its foundation in 1840, was charged by the government to report on child labour in industrial establishments.[41] In the inquiry published in 1843, medical contributions are legion, and doctors were the first to emphasize the physical and moral damage that industrial work wreaked on children: "Examine the factory child [...]. He is stunted and sickly, presenting every sign of physical degradation".[42] It was also children, having to be on the alert at all times, who were most exposed to accidents: out of 395 accidents recorded by the Ghent medical commission in 1843, 270 (i.e. 68 per cent) involved workers under twenty years of age.[43] The Académie de médecine, headed by Dr Vleminckx,[44] also took a clear stand in support of compulsory education, which it saw as a measure needed to preserve the physical integrity of future generations of workers. The same phenomenon can be seen in other industrialized countries. In France, Villermé and Parent-Duchâtelet explored the diseases of the working classes, and an intimate

40 Morelli, "Les médecins parliamentaires".

41 De Burggraeve, "Rapport sur l'état physique et moral".

42 "Rapport de l'Académie Royale de Médecine", vol. 2, p. 335.

43 "Rapport de la Commission médicale de Gand", *Enquête* of 1843, p. 445.

44 Jean-François Vleminckx (1800-1876), medical doctor and inspector-general of the army health service (1830-1864), liberal deputy for Brussels (1864-1876), member of various health commissions and president of the Royal Academy of Medicine.

knowledge of conditions of life enabled them to appear as social experts.[45] Their reports are filled with information on the health, diet, housing and hygiene of the popular classes, and laid the foundations for a social science that was still in its infancy.

Within the medical profession, however, opinions diverged as to the remedies recommended, since doctors, like the bourgeoisie as a whole, were divided between clerical and anti-clerical, progressive and conservative. They sometimes represented interest groups, and the alignment of views between doctors in the coalfields and the mine-owners was a particularly manifest example. The Académie de médecine, despite its internal tensions, adopted in the main a "social" point of view, undertaking on its own behalf in 1867 an investigation on the work of women and children in the coalfields, to the great chagrin of the coal lobby. This investigation concluded, after lively debate, by condemning child labour underground and demanding regulatory measures, including in the field of education.

The coal lobby immediately mobilized, challenging the legitimacy of the Académie members outside a purely medical role. For almost a year, a very harsh confrontation took place between these doctors and the mine-owners, even though both sides professed liberal views.

In a society that was detaching itself from the grip of the church, which could no longer be recognized as a moral authority among the popular classes, the question was to decide who would now fulfil this function; in other words, who could say what limits should be set to human exploitation, and decree the rights and duties of a state which, even though liberal, could not risk compromising future generations. Doctors sought to have their competence recognized in this field, arguing on the basis of the ability to determine not only the medical consequences of work, but also their economic and moral implications. On this basis, they sought to exert an effect on the government and on legislative initiative.

The coal lobby was not wrong about the important issue at stake here, and this is what led it to mobilize: in this quite astonishing joust, in which prominent individuals struggled for the control of human resources, it was the medical profession that came out weakened.[46] Though it had previously been closely associated with all investigations into working conditions, it was from now on left aside, as witness its absence from the Commission du travail of 1886. As a general rule, doctors were excluded from labour leg-

45 Cited in Perrot, *Enquêtes sur la condition ouvrière*, p. 28.

46 See on this aspect, Gubin, "Femmes, travail, protection".

islation as well as the social sciences, to the benefit of a new rising class of experts, the lawyers.

Economists

One might have expected that industrial circles should find support from theorists of economic liberalism; paradoxically, this was not the case. It was precisely within the strictest Manchester School, grouped round Gustave de Molinari,[47] that compulsory education was championed most vigorously. Certain historians have been surprised by this. In reality, however, this position followed with implacable logic. For the economic liberals, the state should be reduced to "a simple apparatus for producing security: nothing more and nothing less".[48] It was above all the close link that these economists saw between ignorance and criminality that led them to class compulsory education among the state's policing prerogatives. This notion found support in the danger that ignorance posed for the social order, but the economists also emphasized the brake it represented on industrial progress and national prosperity: on both counts, to instruct the working classes was a duty of the state.[49]

This new dimension did not leave industrialists indifferent, and some of these even established schools within their businesses, above all with the aim of forestalling any intervention by the government. One industrialist made this point clearly before the Commission du travail in 1886: "We are not among those who believe that the government should intervene in these questions. It is on the contrary the business leaders who should recognize the advantage there is for them in having workers with a certain instruction, so that at the required age, which in our view is fourteen, we shall have in production a robust and intelligent personnel, enabling us to struggle against foreign markets in favourable conditions."[50]

47 Member of the Institut de France, Molinari taught in Belgium during the 1860s before returning to France, where from 1891 to 1901 he edited the *Journal des Économistes*. In Belgium he inspired *L'Économiste belge*, which became a prominent periodical.

48 *L'Économiste belge*, 19 November 1859.

49 *L'Économiste belge*, 20 January and 1 March 1858, 10 July 1868.

50 *Commission du travail*, vol. 4, pp. 39–50.

Compulsory Education as a Social Question

The development of criminal statistics also led to investigation of the means to struggle against ignorance and the possibility of promoting compulsory education as a corollary of this. The first statistical works on criminality stressed right from the start its relationship with illiteracy, and led certain reformers of the penal system, quite logically, to include education among the means of correction. These writers also displayed an almost complete range of the arguments signalled above, ranging from the wellbeing of the child, through considerations on delinquency and public order, to the preservation of future productive forces. But, as opposed to politicians and industrialists, these social commentators focused their attention on individual revolt expressed in crimes and offences, rather than collective movements. "To deny society the right to make instruction compulsory would mean more or less refusing it the right to repress those offences that are simply the consequences of ignorance or defective morality."[51]

This is the reason why Édouard Ducpétiaux,[52] administrator-general of Belgian prisons, and concerned equally by crime, poverty, and the social consequences of industrial capitalism, was an ardent defender of compulsory education. In the same perspective, prisons for young people applied a system of part-time schooling: children worked for eight hours, then attended class for two hours. The paradox of such a situation was frequently emphasized: children placed under state authority as the result of crime, judgement and condemnation were the only ones to benefit from a certain compulsory instruction. The results were certainly slight, given the very poor educational resources available to these institutions, but for all that, eighty per cent of children leaving prison had acquired elements of instruction that many young workers lacked.[53] This led Ducpétiaux to plead that "innocent children should be granted something that would not be refused them if they were guilty".[54]

As a regular laboratory for the observation of childhood, in which doctors, teachers and chaplains were all involved, the prison reform movement gradually extracted children from prison and put them into charitable reform schools. From the 1880s, this movement formed part of a broad international current for the (re)moralization of society on the one hand,

51 Ducpétiaux, *Quelques mots sur l'état actuel*, p. 14.

52 Dupont-Bouchat, "L'ère Ducpétiaux".

53 Dupont-Bouchat, "Travail des enfants dans les pénitenciers", pp. 19, 21.

54 *Ibid.*, p. 19.

and the protection of childhood on the other, in which the doctors were partly replaced by charitable ladies and lawyers.

New elites were mobilized in this crusade for the protection of childhood, and contributed to imposing a new model: education rather than repression, i.e. instruction as a preventive remedy to delinquency. This movement steadily spread the idea that the state could – and even should – intervene in the interest of the child, and that this intervention was not limited to the public sphere, it could and should reach into the intimacy of the family.[55] The state's mission to replace deficient parents was all the greater when the drastic fall in births at the end of the century transformed children into "a capital to be protected".[56] This is why an association such as the Société des Enfants martyrs, founded in Brussels in 1892, called for compulsory education and equated the lack of schooling to mistreatment and an abuse of paternal power. The movement thus took over the concerns already advanced by the Ligue de l'enseignement, when this stressed the rights of the child as superior to respect for paternal power.

This brief survey of elite attitudes towards childhood in the popular classes brings out the complexity of a question that is simple in appearance, that of the instruction of children from the working classes in a society that now very broadly recognized the values of education. It brings out the apparent contradictions between the philanthropic activity of these elites, who were prepared to spend freely to create a genuine network of popular education, and the bitter opposition of a majority of their number to any compulsory teaching, which they perceived as dangerous for the economic system, and above all, as a breach in the principle of state non-intervention.

This study also brings to light the weight of economic and social motivations in the question of education. It was, among other things, "the needs of industry" that led to initial positions being either reinforced or corrected. The political struggle for extension of the suffrage gave this process a particular resonance.

Paradoxically, while Catholics had fought compulsory education throughout the nineteenth century, it was eventually voted by a Catholic majority, under a Catholic government in power for thirty years. The political issue at stake was then dominant, and led the parties of the left, both liberal and socialist, to oppose it, fearing that the Catholics would

55 Dupont-Bouchat, *De la prison à l'école*, pp. 78-81.

56 Huart, "La Société protectrice des Enfants martyrs de Bruxelles"; and Dupont-Bouchat, *De la prison à l'école*, pp. 85-88.

turn the supposed benefits of compulsory education to their advantage, and privilege their own "free" schools to the detriment of the public schools.[57]

For a long while, the idea of compulsion being "impossible" pervaded the champions of generalized education, paralysed as they were by the meagreness of working-class budgets and the inability to compensate for children's wages. This led to clumsy proposals such as half-time education or compensation in kind for workers' families. The end of the century saw the formation of a range of associations with the object of distributing food or clothing at school: the Assiette de Soupe, the Oeuvre de la Soupe, the Bouchée de Pain, the Vestiaire Scolaire, etc. But by organizing in this way a broad voluntary movement designed to promote the education of the popular classes, the bourgeoisie contributed to maintain a regime of liberty even in educational matters, a state that was as little interventionist as possible; this system would survive until the eve of the First World War.

Finally, the manifold implications of the issue of compulsory education illustrate the internal conflicts among notables, and the lines of fracture and unity within the bourgeoisie, which did not necessarily correspond to their ideological division. If Catholics long remained opposed to compulsory education, Liberals on the other hand very soon dispersed into opposing camps, which made a major contribution to the weakening of their party.

Finally, the attitude of the ruling classes towards popular education also casts light on the real issues hidden beneath certain philanthropic initiatives, as well as the struggles among members of the elite for the control of society.

57 The public authorities, in fact, as well as the municipalities and provinces, were able to grant subsidies to the independent establishments already existing (adopted schools), which dispensed them from establishing and maintaining an official school.

CHAPTER II

Children in Lombard Industrialization, 1876–1911*

Antonia Pasi

Italy was one of the slowest European countries to industrialize. It was still an agricultural country at the time of national unification in 1861: agriculture then made up 46.1 per cent of Gross National Product, while the share of industry was only 18.4 per cent.[1] Certain regions, however, such as Piedmont, Liguria and above all Lombardy, already possessed in the mid-nineteenth century the manufacturing basis that enabled them to stand at the head of the process of Italian industrialization. It is an interesting question to what extent child labour made a contribution to this development, and what costs it involved. We shall seek to answer this question by studying the case of Lombardy, which was the most industrialized region of Italy and remains so till this day.

Though the figures available relate to the work of "minors", we should make clear that this term is not used in its legal sense, but rather as a synonym for "children". Childhood was customarily seen as the period of life between seven and fourteen years of age, in the wake of Roman law that distinguished three phases of minority. It was only with the Code Zanardelli of 1889 that this concept appeared in Italian legislation, in relation to the legal responsibility of minors, with a division that defined four phases of responsibility according to age. The second age was precisely that between the ninth and fourteenth birthdays, which was also the age limit that the law of 1886 defined for child labour. Even in statistics regarding the workforce employed in manufacturing industry that date from after Italian unification, "minors" still means workers under the age of fourteen. Above this age, they formed part of the adult workforce. Up till the promulgation of this law, there was no lower age limit for entry into the world

* This research was conducted with the help of a grant from MURST 'Famiglia e sistemi demografici in Italia in età moderna e contemporanea' (1996).

1 Zamagni, *Dalla periferia al centro*, p. 54.

of work, whether in manufacturing or agriculture; this was solely a function of the physical strength of the individual boy or girl. It is clear, then, that in the absence of legislation regulating child labour, these statistics can hide a mass of young people of indefinite age; whereas, to the degree that the legislation regulating child labour was respected, these figures referred to a workforce of a clearly defined age.

Statistical Sources

It is fairly hard to obtain an overall quantitative view of the phenomenon of child employment in Lombard industry between the time of unification and the First World War, i.e. the crucial period of industrial take-off, for want of full and reliable figures, even though starting from 1861 the new Italian state created an official structure able to produce demographic, economic and social statistics. The initial difficulties were several, and the criteria adopted did not always rest on scientific requirements. For example, the Italian population census did not make it possible to estimate the number of children employed in manufacture. The census of 1861, which distinguished workers under sixteen from adults, provided figures that are open to question. It showed for Lombardy a total of 459,044 workers in manufacturing industry, whereas fifteen years later the total number of industrial workers for the country as a whole was given as only a little above 382,000. As for the subsequent censuses, those of 1881 and 1901, these simply counted the active population as those over the age of nine, while that of 1911 counted those of "exactly ten years and over". It is thus impossible to separate adult workers from minors.

Even the "industrial inquiry"[2] launched in 1870 by the ministry of agriculture, industry and commerce (MAIC) does not bring much help on this point. This did not produce industrial statistics, it was rather a cognitive and descriptive investigation, conducted on the basis of a questionnaire provided for industrialists, who were not obliged to respond to all questions, and could be more or less precise. The inquiry was concerned only

2 Ministry of Agriculture, Industry and Commerce [MAIC], *Atti del Comitato dell'inchiesta industriale*; *Idem.*, *Atti del Comitato dell'inchiesta industriale. Relazioni delle Camere*. A detailed examination of the contents of this document in relation to Lombard industry is given by Soresina, "Fonti per la storia". On the Italian state's first industrial statistics, cf. Lungonelli, "Tra industria e burocrazia"; Marucco, *L'amministrazione della statistica*.

marginally with the number of workers, their wages and conditions of work. The first available data on these elements, therefore, are those supplied by the statistics that MAIC compiled in 1876,[3] supplemented shortly after by a new census begun in 1883 but stretching over several years. As far as Lombardy was concerned, the results initially led to a series of departmental monographs produced between 1887 and 1894,[4] but only published in 1890[5] and 1905[6] after being vaguely brought up to date.

The final statistical information that can be used to quantitatively establish the extent of child labour in Lombard industry in the period before the First World War is the *Censimento degli opifici e delle imprese industriali al 10 guigno*,[7] which may be considered the first genuine investigation of Italian industry on a statistical basis.

On the whole, therefore, though there are a number of sources, their use raises certain problems of interpretation. The data they provide is not homogeneous, and it is impossible to compare one set of figures with another, given the changes introduced into the criteria used. For instance, one of the difficulties arises from the ongoing disparity with which those working at home were treated. If they were employed by a company, they were sometimes considered as factory workers, yet self-employed workers were never included. It is not unusual, therefore, even in a brief lapse of time, to find differences between the various figures on workers and on factories.

We can conclude therefore that the results obtained by the 1876 inquiry are only an approximation to reality. Vittorio Ellena, commenting on these figures, notes a margin of error due to lack of exactness in the collection of data, but also and mainly to imprecision in the replies, whether this was deliberate or not. In effect, the fear that information provided could be used for taxation purposes led the industrialists to be very vague and insincere in their responses, as well as avoiding, in the specific case of minors, "awkward discussions of a humanitarian nature".[8] None the less, by tightening the field of questions and excluding "anything that might resemble a tax investigation", the 1876 inquiry did succeed in defining "a quite faithful

3 MAIC, *Notizie statistiche*. The results were re-published two years later with a commentary by Vittorio Ellena, a MAIC official involved with the conduct of the inquiry and its original publication in 1878. Cf. Ellena, "Statistica di alcune industrie".

4 In *Annali di statistica*, series 4.

5 MAIC, Direzione generala di statistica [Dirstat], *Statistica industriale Lombardia.*

6 MAIC, *Statistica industriale per il Regno.*

7 Published in five volumes by the good offices of MAIC.

8 Romano, *Industria cotoniera*, p. 285.

picture of the forces of production".[9] It should not be forgotten, however, that this information was drawn from different and heterogeneous sources – Chambers of commerce, independent observers, industrialists – which explains its lack of homogeneity and objectivity. The same limits affected the results of subsequent inquiries, so much so that in that of 1903, the ministry believed that the number of factories and workers counted was very likely less than their real number. As far as children were concerned, we can assume that these figures excluded all cases that did not respect legal obligations, starting with the minimum age. It was very useful for these figures to be kept secret.

But if a large part of the data are no more than an approximation to reality, they do offer orders of magnitude that are acceptable for the purpose of assessing the significance of child labour in the Lombard economy, and giving a picture of its development over time in this region.

The Relative Scale of Child Labour

The 1876 figures[10] counted 382,131 workers in the whole country, of whom 161,320 worked in Lombardy: 24,438 men, 78,743 women, and 58,139 children[11] – these being defined as "workers of fourteen years and less". The inquiry did not divide these by sex, but in the case of these minors, too, girls was clearly predominant; it would be more accurate in this case to speak of girl children, girls, and young women. Over time, the number of minors occupied in the industrial sector recorded a slight fall of 2,400 (-4.1 per cent) between 1876 and 1903, before undergoing a sharp and consistent rise of 49 per cent in the eight following years.

9 MAIC, *Notizie statistiche*, p. vi.

10 According to the criteria set out by MAIC, the responses should refer to the date of 1 July 1876, but it took time to complete the first Italian industrial statistics, due to the problems that arose from the temporary suppression of MAIC. It is highly likely that the data collected refer to different and imprecise periods. Here we attribute all the data to 1876, even if this may seem somewhat arbitrary.

11 Ellena, "Statistica di alcune industrie", p. 35.

Table 11.1. Young People in Lombard Industry

Year	*Boys*	*Girls*	*Total*
1876			58,139
1903	16,458	39,272	55,730
1911	29,788	53,246	83,034

Source: For 1876, Ellena, *La statistica*, pp. 45, 48, 50, 60, 78, 79; for 1903, MAIC, Dirstat, *Statistica industriale*, 1900, *passim*, and *Idem*, *Statistica industriale per il Regno*, 1905–06, vol. 2, *passim*; for 1911, MAIC, Dirstat, *Censimento degli opifici*, vol. 4, p. 397.

If the statistical data of this inquiry do not contain the errors that might have led to an overestimation of the number of children in 1876, and we make the assumptions that these young workers were not below seven years of age[12] and that the Lombard population was still more or less the same as in the census of 1881,[13] then about seven per cent of children would have been employed in manufacturing. The figure is quite substantial, but we should bear in mind that the majority of these would have been employed in a family circuit of home production. At the end of the period under discussion here, i.e. in 1911, not only had this proportion risen, to over eleven per cent,[14] but the nature of child labour had changed, with the creation of the factory system in the textile sector, imposing as it did a working day of eleven hours throughout the year, in an impersonal environment in which the rhythm and pace of work were enforced by the machines.

The process of Lombard industrialization was not homogeneous throughout the region. It was more marked in some provinces (Bergamo, Brescia, Como and Milan) than in others, and this was still the case at the end of the period considered here. There was a pronounced contrast between the agricultural south and the piedmont north. Factory work was thus not the shared reality of all Lombard children. The figures in Table 11.2, on the relationship between the number of children at work and the population of working-age minors in 1911, depict a major difference between the textile provinces (Milan, Como, Bergamo) and the others.

12 It could indeed be the case that even children of five and six worked.

13 The 1881 census counted 824,280 individuals between seven and fourteen years inclusive (MAIC, *Censimento 1881*).

14 The 1911 Census gave the Lombard population between ten and fourteen years old as 504,010 (Cf. MAIC, *Censimento 1911*).

Table 11.2. Population and Workers in the Age Class Ten to Fourteen in 1911 (distribution by province)

Province	*Population*		*Workers*		*Workers / Population per cent*	
even	*Boys*	*Girls*	*Boys*	*Girls*	*Boys*	*Girls*
Bergamo	28,945	28,607	2,744	8,761	9.5	30.6
Brescia	30,868	30,690	2,174	3,843	7.0	12.5
Como	32,573	34,311	4,126	11,166	12.7	32.5
Cremona	18,464	17,891	1,064	2060	5.8	11.5
Mantua	18,600	18,052	799	417	4.3	2.3
Milan	88,965	87,535	17,008	24,309	19.1	27.8
Pavia	23,965	27,083	1,752	2,421	7.3	8.9
Sondrio	6,689	6,653	121	269	1.8	4.0

Sources: MAIC, Dirstat, *Censimento degli opifici, passim*; Dirstat, *Censimento della popolazione*, 1911, *passim*.

There was also a strong disparity between boys and girls, the latter being preferred for work in the textile factories, especially the silk sector. This is shown by the figures for the province of Como, where, out of a total of 11,166 girls at work, 10,247 or 91.8 per cent were employed in textiles, of which 7,966 or 77.8 per cent in the silk sector. There were several reasons why industrialists preferred girls: they accepted the lowest wages in absolute terms, without creating problems of discipline, while their physical disposition made them particularly adept at tying threads, winding the yarn onto the spindles, and working on mechanical looms.

In a situation of general development of the region's industrial structure, it is necessary to compare the development of the factory work of minors with that of other types of labour (cf. table 11.3). Between 1876 and 1903, the total number of adult workers rose considerably. The final decades of the century seeing Lombardy win a predominant position in Italian industry by way of a steady and clear transformation of its productive structure. The number of children employed, however, declined, before rising again in the following decade by 49 per cent, while the total number of working women rose by "only" 35 per cent, and that of male workers by 90.5 per cent.

These changes had the effect of shifting the relative weight of these three components of the work force, with a steady reduction in the number of children in relation to the total of industrial workers: from 36 per cent in 1876, down to 15.8 per cent at the start of the new century, falling again by a further per cent in less than a decade.

Table 11.3. Workforce Employed in the Industrial Sector in Lombardy

Year	*Absolute numbers*			*Per cent*		
	Adults		*Minors*	*Adults*		*Minors*
	Men	*Women*	*Boys and Girls*	*Men*	*Women*	*Boys and Girls*
1876	24,438	78,743	58,139	15.1	48.8	36.0
1903	139,657	156,420	55,730	39.7	44.5	15.8
1911	266,092	211,234	83,034	47.5	37.7	14.8

Source: as Table 11.1.

The Respective Weight of Boys and Girls in the Lombard Textile Industry

There were a number of reasons for these changes. The criteria used in the investigation may have been modified, excluding in 1903 a section of young people who had previously been included; it could be that the new laws on child labour played a part; but above all, account must be taken of the transformations under way in the structure of the Lombard industrial apparatus during the period concerned.

Until at least the end of the 1880s, the strong point of this was the textile industry,[15] with a pronounced specialization in silk, which sought to exploit the advantages offered by women and girls as a cheap and docile workforce. In the years leading up to 1911, the structure of Lombard industry completely changed. This was the time of industrial take-off, which took place by way of the rise of new sectors such as steel, engineering, chemistry and hydro-electricity – all of these attracting in the main a male workforce, as we remarked above. Though even the textile sector "enjoyed a clear expansionary tendency until 1907",[16] its importance in relation to

15 Zamagni, *Dalla periferia al centro*, p. 115.
16 Carreras, "Ritratto quantitative", p. 244.

other sectors significantly declined. In other words, these sectors were in the process of recording an expansion due to modern industrial development, whereas the textile sector definitively lost its historical supremacy,[17] especially following the decline of silk production. If we make a more precise analysis by comparing this sector with the rest of industry, we find that despite the evident increase in the number of children at work between 1903 and 1911 (cf. table 11.4), their proportion of the total workforce declined from 11.7 per cent to 9.8 per cent. The textile sector, however, displays the opposite tendency, with a rise from 18.2 per cent of the workforce in 1903 to 19.5 per cent eight years later (cf. table 11.5).

Table 11.4. Workforce Employed in Textiles and Other Industries

Year	*Textile industry*			*Other industries*		
	Adults		*Minors*	*Adults*		*Minors*
	Men	*Women*	*Boys & Girls*	*Men*	*Women*	*Boys & Girls*
1876	18,235	74,804	56,945	5,872	3,180	1,194
1903	45,761	139,408	41,094	93,896	17,012	14,636
1911	50,945	176,933	55,219	215,147	34,301	27,185

Source: as Table 11.1.

Table 11.5. Workforce Employed in Textiles and Other Industries (Per cent)

Year	*Textile industry*			*Other industries*			*Minors in textiles/ Total minors employed*
	Adults		*Minors*	*Adults*		*Minors*	
	Men	*Women*	*Boys & Girls*	*Men*	*Women*	*Boys & Girls*	
1876	12.2	49,9	38.0	57.3	31.0	11.7	98
1903	20.2	61.6	18.2	74.8	13.6	11.7	74
1911	18.0	62.5	19.5	77.8	12.4	9.8	67

17 Zaninelli, "Aspetti economico-produttivi", p. 9.

It is easy to conclude, therefore, that the textile industry played a central role in the employment of minors, particularly in the early stages of industrialization. In 1876, it counted for 98 per cent of the total number of minors working in industry, before falling to 74 per cent in 1903 and 67 per cent in 1911. This workforce, moreover, took part in the development of other sectors when these became more important in the regional economy.

The two main activities in the textile sector need to be distinguished, i.e. silk and cotton production, in order to understand the reasons for the varying number of children employed, and the relative distribution of individuals making up the Lombard workforce. A different development of the sectors as a whole resulted from two contradictory tendencies: a contraction or stability in the number children employed in the production of silk, and an expansion of child labour involved in cotton production.

The Silk Sector

The Lombard silk industry had a long tradition going back to the seventeenth century. It consisted in the cultivation of mulberry trees, the rearing of silkworms, and the production of silk as a semi-prepared raw material. It became the backbone of the Lombard industrial system when the region was irreversibly launched on the path of industrialization.[18] Yet this was technologically the least advanced among the developing industries, even if certain modernizations took place, leading to a radical transformation of the first two stages of silk manufacture, as well as an expansion in weaving that began in the 1880s and had major effects on employment.

In the long term, of the three stages constituting the production process – drawing, twisting and weaving – it was the first two that made up the main weight of this sector. Even before national unity, northern Italy had become the leading supplier of semi-worked silk to the European market. And at the end of the 1870s, Italian production – which meant in the greater part Lombard – maintained this position, being overtaken only by China, whilst in Europe it had no competitors "either as far as quality was concerned, or in terms of economy of labour".[19] In cloth production, however, Lombardy lagged far behind not only France, but also Switzerland and Germany.[20] All this was expressed in the distribution of the workforce

18 Federico, "Per una storia dell'industria serica"; Federico, *Il filo d'oro*.
19 Ellena, "Statistica di alcune industrie", p. 35.
20 Ellena, "Statistica di alcune industrie", pp. 35–36.

between the three stages of production: from the "extraction" of the raw material through to the finished product – i.e. cloth.

Table 11.6. Workforce Employed in the Silk Industry in 1876

Operations	*Men*	*Women*	*Adults*	*Minors*	*Children per 100 adults*
Drawing	2,039	36,425	38,464	16,841	43.8
Twisting	4,016	21,814	25,830	33,051	128.0
Weaving	4,492	5,882	10,374	2,196	21.2
Total	10,547	64,121	74,668	52,088	69.8

Source: Ellena, *La Statistica*, pp. 45, 48, 50.

As the figures in this table show, children were a major presence at all stages of the manufacturing process, and even predominant in twisting. To understand the reasons for such a large use of child labour, which at this time was still not subject to any regulation, we have to take account of the state of the silk industry at the time of the *Statistica industriale*. The production of raw silk had been affected by the silkworm disease that appeared in 1854 and damaged harvests for a number of years. The crisis due to prebine (a silk-worm illness) posed a further challenge, to which Lombard industry responded by importing eggs of unaffected silkworms, modernizing the drawing equipment, and importing raw silk from Asia to supply the twisting shops.[21] When the worst was over, by the early 1870s, the Lombard silk industry displayed a sharply modified structure, since the small and less efficient producers had been largely eliminated in favour of those better equipped, which modernized at substantial cost. Drawing was, in the process of losing its former character of a seasonal activity, conducted on the farm. If the industrial inquiry of 1870-1874 showed a heterogeneous picture, the responses given by the Lombard silk producers show that old and new methods coexisted at this time, though the new ones were in the course of gaining the upper hand.

There now existed more modern spinning workshops, where steam was used for motive power and the heating of vats, and either steam or in many

21 Ellena, "Statistica di alcune industrie", p. 64.

cases hydraulic power for mechanically turning the reels. Those workshops that combined steam heating with manually turned reels, however, still remained numerous, and they employed "many girls in relation to the number of woman spinners".[22] Finally, certain "traditional" plants, i.e. those with direct heating and manual movement of the reels, still managed to survive. The quality of the product yielded by the more backward technology was inferior, whilst the quantity of labour needed was greater. As far as the consequences of these transformations on the workforce were concerned, we should note that the small spinning workshops with direct heating were established in open-air plants that operated only in summer, while the steam-heated workshops functioned for about eight months of the year, and the most modern ones practically the whole year round, so as best to profit from the investments made. Above all, a notable increase in raw silk production took place in the 1870s, needing an increased workforce.[23]

On the whole, however, while drawing remained on the whole labour-intensive, and the spinning plants were still located in the main production zones of silkworms, cheap labour was abundant. The competitiveness of the Italian silk industry on the international market was totally dependent on a labour cost about 15 to 20 per cent below that in other countries.[24] And it obtained, thanks to both lower average wages and the massive employment of young girls, without any legal regulation and governed solely by the necessities dictated by the different stages of production. It was possible, in fact, to make girls of eight to ten years old work for twelve or thirteen hours on knotting threads and carrying out preliminary operations, at a pay of thirty to forty centimes per day, i.e. between a third and a half the wage of an adult woman. Older girls received a daily wage of fifty to seventy centimes, and it was only the adult spinners, women from the age of about twenty, who received between eighty centimes and 1.10 lire per day.[25]

The phase in which the presence of children was most important, however, remained that of twisting. This had for a long while been more mechanized than the preceding phase, so that its location was tied more to the availability of hydraulic power than to the supply of labour. But certain operations that helped prepare the silk for the actual twisting had not

22 *Atti dell'Inchiesta industriale*, cat. 6, para. 1, p. 10.
23 Zamagni, *Dalla periferia al centro*, p. 116.
24 Zamagni, *Dalla periferia al centro*, p. 48.
25 Zamagni, *Dalla periferia al centro, passim.*

yet always been mechanized, such as the winding of the yarn on the reels, unless the same factory combined the two operations of twisting and drawing. At this time, however, there were few large-scale enterprises able to do this, even in the provinces of Bergamo and Como; as a general rule, twisting remained separate from drawing. In this case, the winding required a great deal of labour and little motive power, so that it was advantageous to locate it where labour was most plentiful and its costs accordingly lowest: at home, where the labour-power available within the peasant family could be used. Or else in secondary workshops, located in zones that were "rich in population" even if far from the main factory.[26] In both cases, it was more profitable to employ "girls or often even boys",[27] whose small stature, among other qualities, made them more adept for the work of winding than older girls, who bridled at sitting bent over the machines for the whole day. But the true reason why young girls were preferred was again the difference in pay: the daily wage of a girl under ten was at most half that of a girl between ten and fourteen, and could be as low as a third. It was only with the "spin winding" system, which was still little adopted at the time, that there was no longer "a need for girls under the age of ten".[28]

In the final decades of the nineteenth century, the silk industry underwent profound changes, with the spread of steam power and a series of technical advances:[29] the stifling of cocoons was now done in ovens that used hot-air systems instead of steam:[30] "mechanical trimmers" were deployed along with "skilled female workers"; a whole series of measures were adopted to facilitate the gradual mechanization of the drawing and twisting of silk. A greater use of steam power was probably the key to the transformation of this sector, with major consequences for the organization of work. In the twisting phase, in particular, a better use of power by the use of a single motor for the whole factory in place of several small motors[31] made possible a reduction in the number of workers[32] at the same time as an increase in the number of spindles.

Mechanization also affected the preliminary operations such as winding, which in the earlier system of production were carried out by a large

26 *Atti del Comitato della Inchiesta industriale.* Deposizioni scritte, cat. 6, para. 2, p. 20.
27 *Ibid.,* "Note sulla torcitura".
28 *Ibid.*, p. 14.
29 Federico, *Il filo d'oro*, p. 193.
30 Caizzi, *Storia dell'industria italiana*, p. 332.
31 "L'industria della seta in Italia", *Annali di statistica*, XXXVII (1980), p. 18.
32 MAIC, Dirstat, *Statistica industriale. Lombardia*, pp. 191, 401.

number of children working at home, or in small workshops that operated for only part of the year. The increase in fixed costs imposed a minimum threshold below which it was not profitable to operate, along with an extension of work by several hours a day and over the entire year. Under the new conditions, the same operations could be performed by a relatively smaller number of children, and with a greater output. The Milan Chamber of commerce observed on this subject that, if the 1876 figures had counted such a high number of minors in the province's silk industry, it was because it had still included those carrying out "the preparatory operations [...] in small workshops of a temporary and unstable character".[33]

It is thus no surprise to see a dramatic reduction, of the order of some fifty per cent, in the number of minors employed in the silk industry between 1876 and 1891, as shown by table 11.7. This involved in particular the twisting process (including the winding of the yarn) as well as that of drawing to a lesser extent.

This was thus one of the areas in which the employment of minors reached a peak in the proto-industrial era, rather than in the crucial phase of industrialization, even if in the course of the latter, child labour became a major factor in economic development in general.[34]

Mechanization, on the other hand, had a contrary effect on weaving, by making this operation easier and less exhausting, and thus bringing it within the reach of both adult women and younger girls. This happened just at the time when Lombardy was in the process of asserting itself as a cloth-producing region, and particularly of silk cloth, thanks to the use of mechanical looms. These only begun to be introduced in the 1870s, but their adoption spread very rapidly. The province of Como, for example, counted 250 in 1880, rising to 686 by 1890 and 976 two years after that; in the province of Milan they spread still faster, rising from 112 in 1876 to 1,725 in 1896.[35] The final decades of the century saw a complete transformation of weaving, with the almost complete abandonment of manual looms, which were now used exclusively for the production of difficult and complicated cloths. Mechanization brought an expansion of cloth production, which in turn attracted a greater number of workers, but this was at the expense of the male workforce that had traditionally worked on manual looms. One hundred mechanical looms required an average of 215 woman workers, either adults or girls, whereas hundred manual looms required

33 *Note sulla trattura*, p. 10; "Statistica industriale. Milano", p. 257.
34 Horn, *Children's Work and Welfare*, p. 7.
35 MAIC, Dirstat, *Statistica industriale. Lombardia*, pp. 201, 404.

hundred weavers, whether women or men, plus seventy unskilled workers[36] – even if it is not easy to make comparisons, given the differences in productivity between manual and mechanical weaving. In this phase of the development of weaving, the number of minors rose from 3,373 in 1891 to 3,555 in 1903.

Between 1903 and 1911, weaving recorded a reduction in the number of girls employed, as likewise did drawing and twisting (cf. table 11.7). It is possible that the law of 1902 on the protection of child labour was beginning to have an effect, fixing as this did a minimum age of twelve years for factory employment; but other factors were probably also at work. Though the greater part of innovations in the silk sector had already been realized, the first decade of the new century saw other improvements that made it possible to economize on labour-power at the stage of stifling and drying the cocoons. And especially in weaving, whereas the relatively weak process remained that of drawing, where labour remained the key element in relation to the machine, despite significant innovations.[37] All this took place while the silk industry in Lombardy was faced with difficulties that particularly made themselves felt from 1907 among the less efficient producers.

Table 11.7. Minors Employed in the Three Major Phases of Silk Fabrication

Year	*Drawing*	*Twisting*	*Weaving*	*Total*
1876	16,841	33,051	2,196	52,088
1891	14,742	8,107	3,373	26,222
1903	13,542	7,257	3,555	24,354
1911	20,907		2,797	23,704

Sources: for the years 1876, 1903, 1911, as Table 11.1; for 1891, "L'industria della seta".

We should note all the same that this reduction was more marked for adult workers than for minors, as shown by a slight rise in the proportion of children employed in the silk sector; from around 25 per cent in 1903, this rose to nearly 27 per cent eight years later.

36 *Ibid.*, p. 201.
37 Zaninelli, "Aspetti economico-produttivi", pp. 48-50.

Table 11.8. Workforce Employed in the Silk Sector

Year		*Minors*		*Adults*	*Minors per 100 adults*
	Boys	*Girls*	*Boys & girls*	*Men & women*	
1876			52,088	74,668	69.8
1891	1,991	24,321	26,312	86,095	30.6
1903	1,232	23,498	24,730	98,381	25.1
1911	634	23,069	23,707	87,900	27.0

The annual totals in this table are different from those in the previous table, as they also include minors employed in the sericulture factories or in other operations than the three basic ones, such as work on residue material.
Source: as Table 11.7.

The Cotton Industry

The cotton industry was marked by very different characteristics. First of all, cotton was not a traditional activity in Lombardy, and despite the production of mixed linen and cotton fustians, not one of the major textile industries was established before the end of the eighteenth century.[38] The production of cotton cloth was only introduced in the mid century, and was still at this stage a "novelty".[39] It experienced a certain development under French rule,[40] but in the 1830s and 40s was still a "small and feeble sector".[41] On the eve of Italian unification, despite the improvements introduced, it was only spinning that used sophisticated machinery brought in from abroad, while the greater part of weaving was manual and performed at home. During the following decades, this sector grew more dynamic, thanks to the protectionist measures of 1878. The number of both spindles and mechanical looms rose considerably, and a system of large-scale industrial production began to take shape, even if domestic weaving continued to exist. From 1893, Lombardy was the leading region for cotton production in Italy, and between 1904 and 1908 this position was consolidated with an exceptional development of its productive apparatus.

38 Moioli, "Assetti manifatturieri nella Lombardia", pp. 10-24.
39 Moioli, "Assetti manifatturieri nella Lombardia".
40 Cova, "Tradizione e innovazione", p. 125.
41 Romano, *Modernizzazione periferica*, p. 68 ff.

The development of employment was linked less than proportionately with the expansion of the sector: while the number of spindles rose around tenfold between 1876 and 1911, and that of mechanical looms by sixteen times, actual employment rose "only" by less than a factor of four.[42] Yet within this figure, strikingly different tendencies are displayed according to age and sex.

Table 11.9. Workforce Employed in the Cotton Sector

Year	*Adults*			*Minors*			*Boys per 100 men*	*Girls per 100 women*	*Minors per 100 adults*
	Men	*Women*	*Men & women*	*Boys*	*Girls*	*Boys & girls*			
1876	5,467	7,653	13,120			3,110			23,7
1891	10,948	21,895	32,843	1,650	5,318	6,968	15.1	24.3	21.2
1903	14,897	34,262	49,159	1,621	7,686	9,307	10.9	22.4	18.9
1911	13,136	35,838	48,974	2,271	10,129	12,400	17.3	28.3	25.3

Source: as Table 11.1, and R. Romano, *L'industria cotoniera*, pp. 287-288.

The development of the cotton sector between 1891 and 1903, as shown by the data in the above table, absorbed a large share of the female workforce, especially adults (+ 56 per cent) but also girls (+ 45 per cent). Adult male workers also showed an increase, but this was less great (+ 36 per cent); only the employment of under-age boys did not rise. The situation in the following years was totally different: the number of adult workers remained practically stable, and this industry now seemed to prefer child labour, which rose by around 33 per cent.

Table 11.10. Rate of Variation of the Workforce in the Cotton Sector

Period	*Adults*			*Minors*		
	Men	*Women*	*Men & Women*	*Boys*	*Girls*	*Boys & Girls*
1896-1903	0.36	0.56	0.50	-0.02	0.45	0.34
1903-1911	-0.12	0.05	0.00	0.40	0.32	0.33

42 Romano, *L'industria cotoniera*, p. 286.

This difference in the development of employment between minor and adult workers shifted the balance within the workforce, and very sharply so its sexual balance. In the female workforce, this varied from 1 to 4 in 1891, to 1 to 4.5 in 1903, and 1 to 3.5 in 1911. In cotton as in silk, therefore, the employment of children seems to have been relatively greater after 1903. This result is surprising, as one would have assumed the contrary, following the law of 1902 that increased the minimum age for factory employment from nine to twelve; even if, as a transitional measure, children of ten who were already working when the law came into force in June 1903 were permitted to keep their jobs. At all events, the active population of minors was reduced by the age group between nine and twelve, or even more so, since the law of 1886 had been little respected, and it was not unusual for girls even younger than nine to be employed in manufacturing. On the other hand, even before this law was passed, children between ten and twelve could only have made up a very small percentage, as following checks made in a number of industrial plants during 1900, it was revealed that "out of 6,231 children employed, 15.2 per cent were under the age of twelve, whereas in 1888 the figure had been 33.76 per cent".[43]

This same law of 1902 strictly limited the use of minors on night work, as well as the length of the working day, and established a weekly rest day. It is likely that it became necessary to employ more minors than in the past in order to perform the same amount of work. In fact, if the discussion on the proposed law mainly met with the strongest disagreement and most lively hostility on the part of industrialists in the silk sector, the cotton-spinning employers also protested against the reduction in working hours, the abolition of night work for minors and women, and the compulsory rest day.[44] Once this law was approved, they were forced to resort to shifts, rather than change the organization of production, at least while the phase of expansion of equipment and production continued, this reaching its peak in the years 1905–1907.

All the same, it cannot be ruled out that a certain role was also played by the difference in wages between adult workers and children. As R. Romano has observed: "among the different hypotheses that can be made to explain the 1911 figures [...], there is also that of the crisis affecting this sector, with industrialists being that much the more keen to resort to workers who cost them significantly less".[45] Of course, minimization of

43 *Il lavoro delle donne*, p. 53.

44 MAIC, Ufficio del lavoro, *L'ispezione del lavoro*, p. 18.

45 Romano, *L'industria cotoniera*, p. 293, n. 2.

costs has always determined entrepreneurial choices, but it may well have become all the more pressing from 1908, in parallel with the period of difficulties marked by overproduction. Besides, we have to note that the cost of labour, even if it remained under control in relation to other costs, probably recorded an upward tendency. It is estimated that in the spinning shops, excluding the price of raw materials, its proportion rose from 33 per cent in 1891 to 42 per cent in 1914. The figures for weaving are less clear, but they allow us to assume that labour costs fluctuated between 10 and 25 per cent of total costs, excluding the price of yarn, and were around 25 per cent in 1911.[46]

As well as low wages, the youngest workers also offered the advantage of being less involved in the strikes in the textile sector that intensified with the new century, in the cotton industry in particular.[47] Their aim was to obtain improvements in the organization of production, as well as in conditions of work.[48]

There was also a further reason why the employers preferred young female workers. The law of 1902, which we have already mentioned, as well as regulating the work of minors, tried for the first time to set rules relating to maternity, by imposing a period of one month's stoppage of work before childbirth. Thus discouraging industrialists affected by the new legal dispositions from employing women more exposed to the risk of pregnancy. According to the national figures on the distribution of women textile workers by age, more than half of these were between twelve and twenty-one.[49] We can expect these figures to be fairly representative of the Lombard situation, since "a few years before the First World War, the cotton sector was [...] chiefly a Lombard industry".[50]

46 Romano, *L'industria cotoniera,* pp. 336-339.

47 The cotton sector saw 39 strikes in 1905, with 7,173 strikers, rising to 45 strikes with 11,734 strikers in the following year; the figures for the silk sector in the same period were respectively 20 strikes with 1,910 strikers and 25 strikes with 3,840 strikers. At the same time, the number enrolled in the trade-union organization for this sector (the Italian Federation of Textile Workers) rose until 1909, before experiencing a period of crisis, from which the organization rapidly re-emerged with new strength. Cf. Cristofoli and Pozzobon, *I tessili milanesi*, pp. 112-118.

48 Romano, *L'industria cotoniera*, pp. 324-326.

49 *Il lavoro delle donne*, p. 62.

50 Romano, *L'industria cotoniera*, p. 40.

Debates on the Regulation of Child Labour

The figures recorded above show how important in general terms was the contribution of under-age workers to the industrial development of Lombardy. But this contribution had its costs, and Italian society had to confront the problem of child labour in the factories in the same manner as other industrialized countries. Even if with a certain delay given that industrialization here was that much later. In Lombardy, because of the diffuse proto-industrialization characteristic of this region, the employment of children had begun to present itself as a real social problem already in the 1840s. It attracted the interest of journalists and philanthropists, who denounced the negative consequences of work on the physical and moral development of children.[51] The public administration also applied itself to this problem, being concerned on the one hand by the very low level of school attendance – due in its opinion to the conflict between the emergence of factory work and the fulfilment of compulsory schooling – and on the other hand by the deterioration in the physical condition of boys recruited by the army, as well as the rise in accidents at work. The Austrian government of Lombardy finally issued a decree in 1843 that fixed the minimum age for starting work at nine years old, imposed flexible working hours depending on age, banned night work and prohibited corporal punishment.

With the unification of Italy, these measures – which were incomplete to start with and had never been respected – were completely abandoned. The need to regulate child labour was not debated again until the 1870s. Then it had become unavoidable, both because child employment was changing with the move into the factories, and because legislation of this kind had already been introduced, even if with difficulty, into those countries that were most advanced economically and socially.

The debate in Italy started from a more retrograde position, as it was even questioned whether a law on child labour would not damage the economic freedom of the industrialists. It is true that this was never a majority position. The greater part of commentators emphasized the true interests of society, which, for want of regulation, paid a high cost for precocious and overtaxing child labour that led to poor soldiers, a weak and uninstructed workforce, and serious risks to the race.

51 Zaninelli, "Il lavoro dei fanciulli".

There was also a section of society, however small, that was more sensitive to the needs of the less favoured classes, and demanded state intervention in order to prevent the abuse of minors perpetuated by the industrialists. Or even by their own families, "both interested in present gain and drawing the greatest profit, without heed to the well-being and future of the child".[52] And finally, there were a few individuals that deemed it against the law of nature that children of an early age should contribute to the economic support of their families, in a kind of reversal of the normal roles.[53] Seen in this light, child labour seemed improper to the eyes of those rare philanthropists and politicians bothered by the exploitation and endangering of childhood.[54] This fitted into a wider debate under way on the protection of children in general. The regulation and protection of child labour, whether in the factory or within the family, was now seen as a duty of the state. This was not an interference into private life, since "the factories are not a private dwelling." And even the family could not be considered as an "inviolable asylum" in which the father could inflict on his children treatment that outside the family would be not only blamed but also punished.[55]

There were thus a number of views in the debate on the regulation of child labour, running between two extremes: not to submit this to any restriction, or to prohibit it completely. This latter position, in fact, was not widely shared, since the preoccupation of politicians and even philanthropists was not simply child labour as such, but rather the conditions in which this was performed in the factories and mines. The children employed in agriculture, not always in good conditions, were not a source of concern, and no more were those in domestic industry. Child labour at home took place in small productive units, where children helped an artisan, often a family member, who was free to set their hours of work. In the factories, on the other hand, work was under the direct control of the employer, for twelve to fourteen hours a day, even at night, and for around 290 days a year[56] in both the silk and cotton factories,[57] even 360 days in the largest plants.

52 Bonomi, "Sul lavoro dei fanciulli", p. 13.
53 Amar, "Sullo stato attuale delle leggi", p. 217.
54 Becchi, "L'Ottocento", p. 188.
55 Bonomi, "Sul lavoro dei fanciulli", pp. 17-18.
56 *Annali di statistica*, p. 88.
57 Zaninelli, "Aspetti economico-produttivi", pp. 138-139.

Yet the attempt was made to represent factory work as easy, on the grounds that machines, thanks to their technological innovations, required no more than agility and attention, rather than physical strength. For example, work at the loom in the silk industry around Como was described as very easy because women and young girls only had to "assist" the loom.[58] In other words, it was the loom that actually did the work!

It is true that the mechanical loom had transformed weavers from skilled workers into guardians of the machine.[59] But the reality was not that agreeable: young girls remained on their feet for twelve or fourteen hours, stuck in front of the machine without the least interruption, always on the same spot. "This is equivalent to torture," denounced Serafino Bonomi,[60] a Como doctor who was very familiar with working conditions in the region's silk industry.

The 1879 Inquiry

In short, the attitudes towards child labour varied widely. It is not surprising therefore that in the 1870s a number of legislative proposals were presented to the Italian parliament.[61] Each proposing a more or less drastic solution to the key problems of child labour: a minimum age, a maximum working day, a ban on night work and a weekly rest day. A number of subjects were raised, each being the focus of antagonistic interests. Thus in 1879, the MAIC deemed it necessary to familiarize itself with the opinions of industrialists and institutions on the new legislative proposal to be discussed in parliament. This was submitted for the views of local authorities (prefects, mayors, provincial health councils), economic associations (chambers of commerce, mutual benefit societies), and the industrialists themselves. The inquiry was conducted on a national scale by way of a form comprising fifteen questions. Certain of these aiming to gather information on the conditions in which children's work was being performed (degree of instruction, working hours, minimum age, rest, wages, etc.); other questions sought to assess the consequences of work that was too early or too strenuous, as well as the possible "damage" that the law might

58 Bonomi, "Sul lavoro dei fanciulli", p. 3.
59 Mokyr, *Lever of Riches*.
60 Bonomi, "Sul lavoro dei fanciulli", p. 12.
61 Rizzo, *Legislazione sociale*, p. 256 ff.

cause industrialists and families.[62] Finally, the persons questioned had to give their views on the proposed legislation.

Almost nine hundred responses were obtained, though these were not always completely clear. All the same, the results provided precise information on the extent of child labour in the factories, and the conditions in which this was performed. They also gave an idea of the way in which those asked to respond to the inquiry saw the need for the law and its scope: 790 were favourable to it, either unconditionally or with modifications; sixty rejected it completely; thirty were neither for nor against.[63] It seems from these results that almost everyone who responded accepted the need for this legislation, but at the same time many emphasized that it was necessary only for cases of abuse, i.e. if work was unsuitable for children of a particular age. It was on this point that positions diverged. The Bergamo chamber of commerce, for example, thought that it was not excessive to make children between eight and ten years old work, since – apart from some "rare exceptions" – their tasks were "little tiring, or not at all", and they "never worked more than twelve hours".

It goes without saying that the industrialists and Chambers of commerce, organizations that were naturally close to the industrialists themselves, generally wanted a law less restrictive than that proposed, whereas the provincial health councils and mutual benefit societies demanded firmer intervention on the part of the state. We should also stress that not a single worker was consulted, so that the verdict of the working class is totally absent.

The industrialists also rejected responsibility for injuries to children caused by their work in the factory. It was accepted that in the spinning shops, young girls of six and seven were employed. But this was hastily followed up by the remark that this was scarcely tiring, and that they were simply assisting their mothers. In the same sense, it was accepted that older girls worked fifteen hours a day, but this was "only in summer", and "the average real working time was between eleven and twelve hours a day".

In these responses from the industrialists, it is possible to see certain glaring contradictions. For example, they accepted that children received no instruction, but the cause of this was not the early age of work nor the lack of time to attend school: it should rather be sought in the parents' lack of attention to their children.

62 *Archivio di statistica*, vol. 2, p. 93. Cf. also Bretoni Jovine, *L'alienazione dell'infanzia*, pp. 60–63.

63 *Archivio di statistica*, vol. 5, p. 355.

To respect the law that had just made education compulsory up to the age of nine,[64] the industrialists proposed the establishment of evening or Sunday classes. Clearly, a proposal like this could not be taken seriously, yet there were few respondents who noted that children were too tired in the evening and needed to rest.

The condition of hygiene in the factories was also investigated. It goes without saying that the responses from the factory-owners were rather optimistic, despite a few discordant voices. It seems hard to believe that factory work was performed in the healthy and appropriate environment that was claimed, since the factories of this time were located in whatever buildings were already to hand. And only from the 1870s did these begin to be replaced by workshops that were deliberately planned for their purpose.

As for the economic consequences of the law, opinions were still more diverse. Almost all the factory-owners saw the law as damaging for both industry and families, with no benefit in exchange. Some of them deemed the law dangerous only for families, and – under cover of a hypocritical concern for children – were really protecting their own interests.

The health councils, mayors, and a few chambers of commerce took an opposite position. They agreed that the law would mean an economic loss for firms and families, but thought that this loss would be compensated by an improvement in education. Finally, very few of those questioned were completely in favour of the law, though they did think it would generate benefits for society and even for businessmen. Since individuals whose health was affected by precocious work would no longer be a burden for society, while the workforce would become stronger and better trained, with great advantage to the industrialists themselves.

Children in the Industrial Production Process

Despite everything, we have to note that the responses given by these industrialists had a kernel of truth. The cost of labour, for example, was indeed a fundamental point for the embryonic Lombard industry. This was a time at which foreign firms already had to accept restrictive norms on the employment of women and children, but their capital was far more productive than that in Italy. They used more modern machines, and so each worker was that much more productive. It was just in the course of

64 The "Coppino law" of 15 July 1877.

the years when the debate on the new legal proposals took place, that the statistical inquiry on the condition of certain Italian industries mentioned above[65] showed the difference existing between the Italian (including Lombard) situation, and that in countries that were already industrialized or in the course of industrialization. The fact that the inquiry counted 1,800 silk manufacturers should not give us the wrong idea, since by taking note of other parameters provided by the same inquiry it is clear that this silk industry was backward. It was not organized in large factories, but still haphazardly dispersed over a large area, in farms and whatever buildings were available, wherever vats and spindles could be set up, even on a very small scale, and for a limited time. As far as the cotton industry was concerned, it is true that this already included large plants. But the same statistical study of 1876 counted only 159 factories where the number of workers per spindle was higher than that in other countries, so much so that "in our country cotton is still in its infancy".[66] There were two different reasons for this. Above all, the lack of specialization in the cotton industry itself. For instance, while "the English spinning works always spin the same numbers", the yarn produced in Lombardy varied on average from number six to number thirty.[67] The same workshop often produced both simple yarn and twist, and sometimes even dyed its own products, a task that needed additional workers. And whatever the dimension and number of spindles, an almost similar set of equipment was required. On top of this, account had to be taken of the general lack of specialization that characterized Italian industry, and cotton producers, as well as others. They were forced to make their own arrangements for repair and maintenance of their machines, given the lack of suitable repair workshops nearby.

Certainly, if the early decades are ignored – when the gap between Italy and the countries already industrialized was very hard to make up – the terms of the problem would seem to be reversed in the following period. And one might object that Lombard industry long remained labour-intensive precisely because, instead of modernizing, it preferred to continue exploiting the two resources it had in abundance, unskilled labour and hydraulic power. Yet we should not forget that the weak ability to use more advanced techniques, as well as the lack of experience on the part of entrepreneurs[68] and the cost of coal (which was about 30 per cent more

65 MAIC, *Notizie statistiche.*
66 Ellena, *Statistica,* pp. 55–56.
67 Ellena, *Statistica,* pp. 63–64.
68 Zamagni, *Dalla periferia al centro*, pp. 117–119.

expensive than abroad), also discouraged the adoption of steam[69] and more complex machine-tools, all these being factors in the country's industrial backwardness.

Despite everything, both the silk industry and especially the cotton industry did embark on innovations. But the availability of a workforce whose "price" was the lowest possible long remained the structural advantage of Lombard industry, and Italian in general.[70] The objection may be made that mechanization itself pushed for a reduction in the use of minors in the textile industry, except in the transition phase from the proto-industrial form of organization to that of the factory. As we have seen above, even if a strategy of cost reduction cannot be excluded, as the response of industrialists in the textile sector to the difficulties that appeared after 1907, the relative importance of children seems to have actually increased in the first decade of the twentieth century, in parallel with the modernization of productive structures in the textile sector. At the start of the century, large investments were made in the cotton sector, productivity per worker increased, and the growth in the workforce was proportionally less than the growth in equipment.[71] Yet the industrialists in this sector continued to prefer minors to adult workers.

In other words, the abundant and therefore cheap supply of labour with little or no training, such as adolescent and younger girls from peasant families, rather constituted an advantage for mechanization,[72] thanks to which certain phases in the manufacture of cotton and silk became easier and less tiring.

The concern of industrialists not to deprive families of the meagre wages of their children, even if this was clearly to their own advantage, had a real foundation, as the direct consequence of the geographical situation of the textile plants. From the beginning of Lombard proto-industrialization, these plants were in search of two factors: a supply of cheap labour and the availability of motive power for machinery, which could be provided by rivers, at least before the large-scale use of steam. These two factors were combined in a particular region of Lombardy, especially the Olona basin, the Brembana and Seriana valleys, the shores of Lago Maggiore, the Monza zone and Adda valley. From the end of the eighteenth century, throughout this hilly region, the replacement of share-cropping

69 Bardini, *Senza carbone nell'età del vapore*, p. 62.

70 Romano, *La Modernizzatione Periferica*, p. 19.

71 Romano, *La Modernizzatione Periferica*, pp. 212-216.

72 Federico, *Il filo d'oro*, pp. 55-56.

contracts by new mixed contracts (known as *fitto misto a grano*) produced considerable changes in the region's agriculture, leading to a sharp decline in the standard of living of share-cropping families.

To supplement their poor agricultural incomes, these populations embarked on various extra-agricultural activities, such as the rearing of silkworms and the production of yarn.[73] In the early nineteenth century, the silk sector had become a village activity, and it was commonplace to find women and girls working on silk as a form of domestic industry. The work of twisting and winding was considered an integral part of the rearing of silkworms, and it was so important for girls that the equipment used for these operations often formed part of their dowry.[74] When in the course of the nineteenth century the steady mechanization of the spinning process led to the gradual disappearance of domestic industry, women and girls "embarked on the struggle to find employment in the factories".[75] The mechanization of weaving did the rest, even if this was somewhat later, along with the development of the cotton industry.

The transition from agriculture to industry thus did not mean the immediate elimination of field work. For a long while, industrial work remained complementary to agriculture, and the worker-peasant hybrid seems to have lasted longer here than elsewhere.[76] The majority of families had "a few women or children who gained a wage by working in industry, while living with the rest of the agricultural family".[77] The typical individual of the textile industry in the *alto Milanese* and the province of Como was thus a woman or girl worker from a rural family. Their wages were a meagre addition to their income, but enabled them to advance from the characteristic indigence of families completely dependent on agriculture to somewhat better conditions of life. Families possessing the same extent of land could thus show a wide differential of income, so that the agricultural researcher Jacini did not manage to determine the average income of the agricultural families in this zone, "factory or industrial wages almost always being involved, to a lesser or greater extent".[78] It was not unusual for parents to themselves demand employment for their daughters in a spin-

73 Corner, *Contadini e industrializzazione*, pp. 35-36; Dewerpe, *L'Industrie aux champs*, pp. 221-239.

74 Merzario, 'Città-campagna', p. 127.

75 Corner, *Contadini e industrializzazione*, p. 56.

76 Consonni and Tonon, "Alle origini della metropolis".

77 *Atti della Giunta*, vol. 6, pp. 55-56. The quotation is taken from Rodolico (ed.), *Storia del Parlamento italiano*, vol. 17, p. 203.

78 *Ibid.*, p. 204.

ning-works or factory, or else boast that these worked there for twelve or fourteen hours a day for a wretched wage.[79]

The fact that agriculture remained an extremely important resource for the population – without the family household being able to survive from it – enabled the industrialists to maintain wages at a very low level, especially in the case of children, which is also why "the backwardness of the countryside was almost artificially maintained".[80]

The Legislation of 1886, 1902 and 1907

After a great deal of debate,[81] a law was eventually promulgated on 11 February 1886 that banned children under nine from work in the factories and mines. The age-limit of nine was the result of a compromise that pressure from the industrialists forced on the reforming zeal of the Italian state. In the textile plants, especially the silk-works, children had started their training between six and eight.[82] The law then eliminated, at least in theory, a section of the youngest workers who made up nearly 10 per cent of the total in Lombardy. Yet the Lombard firms in this region still kept a certain advantage in relation to those of other European nations who had already passed stricter legislation. The minimum age in other European countries varied from ten – in England, Spain, Hungary and Denmark – to fourteen in Switzerland. Except in Hungary, however, this early age of recruitment was counterbalanced by a shorter working day than in Italy. In England, for example, the age limit of ten was combined with a maximum working day of six hours until the age of fourteen. Under the Italian legislation of 1886, the working day was set at eight hours until twelve years of age. As for night work, this was abolished for children under twelve, and a maximum of six hours allowed for those between twelve and fifteen.

Children under fifteen also had to supply a medical certificate from the "Consiglio circondariale da sanità"[83] before obtaining employment, while the employer of these young people provided a workbook giving their

79 Nejrotti, "Aspetti della condizione femminile", p. 204.

80 Romano, *La Modernizzazione Periferica*, p. 18.

81 On the various legislative proposals, the previous regulatory measures, and law no. 3657 of 11 February 1886, cf. Merli, *Proletariato di fabbrica*, p. 337 ff.; Monteleone, "Legislazione sociale"; Ballestrero, "Tre proposte ottocentesche"; and Rizzo, *Legislazione sociale*, pp. 255–262.

82 Bonomi, "Sul lavoro dei fanciulli", p. 9.

83 District health council.

civil status, vaccination record, and level of education. This law completely failed to allow for a rest day.

According to the executive regulations, the legislation applied to industrial workshops, i.e. businesses "where manual work of an industrial character is performed with the aid of a mechanical motor or permanent fire", whatever the number of workers employed, as well as to workshops with at least ten permanent workers.[84] Responsibility for the application of the law was delegated to the existing inspectors and mining engineers.

The legislation as a whole had serious gaps and was not very rigorous: it seemed to pay more heed to the demands of industry than to the protection of child workers. Perhaps this is an example of the "transformism" characteristic of the Italian parliamentary regime and government programmes after the elections of 1882, which favoured a certain kind of clientelism. On the other hand, this same transformist coalition consolidated the power of the various bourgeois groupings. It promoted the industrialists and landed proprietors of both North and South – a very limited section of the population – while ignoring the demands and agitation from the mass of the people. And thus interrupted the already weak reforming action embarked on by the previous government.

The most serious gaps, however, became clear when the law came into force. Doubts about this had already been raised in the course of the parliamentary debate, with the fear that the law would not be able to change the state of things if the poverty of those it was intended to protect was not eliminated.[85] In point of fact, the indigent families of these young workers had no interest in respecting the law, having too great a need for a wage, however small.

A few years after the passage of this law, there was no doubt that the protection of child labour was still in need of a solution. It could be that the law was not respected, especially in southern Italy, whereas in the North, where there were large factories, it was less easy to evade it – we have seen from the statistics that it did have some effect in the case of Lombardy.

The backwardness of Italian legislation relative to that of other European countries, in both its content and application, was made strikingly clear at the International Labour Conference held in Berlin in 1890, in the course of which the intent was expressed that children under twelve should no longer be employed in factories. Yet the question was raised again over a decade later, especially after the progressive government of Giovanni Gio-

84 Rizzo, *Legislazione sociale*, p. 266.
85 Rizzo, *Legislazione sociale*, p. 263.

litti (1901-13), which showed greater sensitivity towards labour problems and sought to reconcile the demands of workers with the claims of capital. The most important area of intervention was that of the protection of women's and children's labour, and a new law was passed in July 1902. The minimum age for factory work was now raised to twelve, with an eleven-hour working day for those under fifteen. For the first time, a weekly rest day was also legally defined.

These measures were certainly not on the same level as those of countries whose social legislation was more developed. For example, there were other countries where the minimum age was the same as that now in Italy, but with a working day no more than six hours. And when the working day was set at eleven hours, as for example in Holland and Switzerland, this was until the age of sixteen. Once again, the Italian choice was a compromise between social requirements and the strong resistance opposed by employers' interests. A resistance that continued to weigh on the vigour of the law and the circulars of application. Even before the law came into force in July 1903, the ministry received many requests from industrialists to obtain derogations or exemptions, regarding age limit, working hours, or daily and weekly rest. Justifying all these in terms of economic needs or production difficulties, or by reference to tradition. At all events, the complaints presented by the industrialists were sufficient to convince the ministry that the law was too severe. And it was necessary to show, even if in an exceptional and transitional fashion, "a reasonable tolerance towards the applicants, in view of the severe damage that a rapid application of the law might create".[86]

Yet if we examine the responses supplied by the "Ufficio del lavoro",[87] the organ of the ministry in charge of assessing these industrialists' requests,[88] we do find that the line of conduct adopted sought to respect the underlying principles, though granting temporary derogations and a certain time for adaptation.

The effects of the law, of course, cannot be assessed by its formal scope; what counted was how it was respected in reality. Once again, it becomes clear that the supervisory bodies were poorly adapted, likewise that fines were derisory, and levied for formal violations more commonly than material ones. It was easier, for example, to note the absence of an under-age

86 MAIC, Ufficio del lavoro, 'Relazione sull'applicazione', p. 7.

87 The "labour bureau" was established in 1902 within the ministry of agriculture, industry and commerce.

88 MAIC, Ufficio del lavoro, 'Relazione sull'applicazione', *passim*.

worker's workbook than to discover the employment of young girls who were carefully concealed in the attic when the inspectors made their round.

The law of 7 July 1907 sought to make up for the inadequacies of the 1902 law, yet this still permitted similar derogations. As in the case of night work, which could be "exceptionally" reduced to ten hours "in industries with particular manufacturing processes" – this referring once again to the silk industry. Despite this, it was the industrialists in this very sector, as well as a certain number of cotton-masters, who raised "bitter challenges and several attempts at resistance".[89]

Taking into account the gradual introduction of the 1902 law – the exceptions granted and infringements more or less tolerated – it is not surprising that the employment of children in Lombard industry increased by 49 per cent between 1903 and 1911, attracted above all by the expansion of new industries.

Simplifying the causes for the spread of child labour, we can say that the most important were on the one hand the desire of industrialists to gain a maximum profit and on the other the economic necessity of the families concerned. Even so, it would be wrong to neglect other explanations that are less immediate at first sight. In pre-industrial societies and those at the beginnings of industrialization, the share of the population aged less than fifteen represents at least a third of the total, and some 90 per cent of what we today call the "inactive" population.[90] To raise this large number of children with a limited life expectancy was always one of the most difficult and constraining problems, given the low productivity of labour. It was only the high productivity of industry that made it possible to gradually increase the age of compulsory school attendance up to the present level. In the underdeveloped societies of the time, children began work as soon as possible, while the old continued to work until they lost their strength, performing tasks that were gradually less strenuous. Lombard society in the second half of the nineteenth century, and until the First World War, does not seem to have escaped this situation, which was rather aggravated by a reduction in infant mortality combined with continuing high rates of fertility.

If, "in the years that followed Italian unification, one new-born infant in four died before reaching its first birthday",[91] by 1881-82 the infant mortality rate had fallen to 196.5 per thousand, and twenty years later to 154.8.

89 Cabrini, *Legislazione sociale*, pp. 154-157.
90 Cipolla, *Storia economica*, pp. 72-76.
91 Ge Rondi, "Dinamica demografica", p. 78.

This led to an increase in population, especially in the age group zero to fifteen which made up 32.8 per cent of the population in the census of 1881, and 37.1 per cent in that of 1911.[92]

Moreover, the location of the Lombard textile industry facilitated the use of children in the factories. It was originally concentrated above all in regions with a very poor agricultural economy, thus able to rely on an abundant and low-cost workforce composed mainly of women and children, and on cheap hydraulic energy. The increase in family size (six on average),[93] and the reduction in peasant families' income in the wake of changes in the share-cropping contract and the mechanization of old rural industries,[94] compromised still more the already precarious balance between population and resources; peasants found that the work of their children in the factories was a good opportunity to improve the livelihood of the whole family. On the other hand, there were no moral restrictions, since children had always worked in agriculture or domestic industry, in conditions that were often worse than those of the nineteenth-century factories. For example, one alternative to spinning was for girls to take part in agricultural work. They would cut hay and wheat, look after the garden, dig the fields, and above all carry weights on their shoulders in the form of large sheaves, wood, manure or mulberry leaves. In May and June also rearing silkworms, an exhausting and disgusting process.[95] In a certain sense the employers were right in claiming that, after all, children were better off in the factory than outside. And that, apart from the prosperity of their businesses, it was necessary above all to help young people support their families when they found themselves forced to replace parents who had died as the result of accident, occupational disease, or at an early age. It was easy to explain why factory work was preferable to work in the fields, which was sometimes still harder and even less well paid, let alone the hunger associated with unemployment, vagabondage, or charity.

There was not even any kind of economic limit, as the employment of children in the rural economy had always been in the nature of a complement or support for the activity of adult workers. It is true that the employment of children in the new industrial activities drew some of its strength from agricultural work, but this continued to rely without a problem on the remaining family members, adult men and partly women. There was

92 Ge Rondi, "Dinamica demografica", pp. 78-83.

93 Romano, *La Modernizzazione Periferica*, p. 198.

94 Corner, *Contadini e industrializzazione*, p. 56.

95 Nejrotti, *Aspetti della condizione femminile*, p. 205.

thus a division of tasks by age and sex: the head of the family worked in the farm, possibly aided by a son, while the girls worked in the silk and cotton industries.[96]

Towards the end of the century, certain factors intervened to modify the structure of the workforce: the development of heavy industry, which traditionally employed fewer children; the steady modernization of industry, which made possible a rise in labour productivity; crises of over-production, as for example in the cotton industry, which imposed a gradual reorganization more oriented to specialization; and finally an improvement of income per capita. These were the necessary preconditions for a definitive solution to the problem of child labour.

96 Romano, *Modernizzazione*, p. 198.

CHAPTER 12

The Rise and Decline of Children's Labour Participation Levels During the Early Stages of Industrialization: Catalonia 1850–1925*

Enriqueta Camps

Introduction

The study of child labour in the past not only has historical ramifications, but also has a bearing on the study of labour markets in developing countries today. The analysis of the early stages of industrialisation in certain European countries and regions sheds light on various aspects of the early stages of economic development: the extensive use of child labour, extremely rapid urbanisation, rural-urban migration and overseas emigration, among others.

In addition – to the extent that generalisation can be valid – household life shows a variety of differentiating characteristics in comparison with developed societies. We aim to show that during the initial period of industrialisation and during the interwar period, families made highly flexible use of their human resources, including their boys and girls.[1] And that the strategies applied by families to deal with the prevailing economic and demographic circumstances were logically adaptive.

In any analysis of labour markets focussing on a specific sector of the population, such as boys and girls, the first question that must be asked is whether the behaviour of those markets is determined primarily by factors of supply rather than demand. The first aspect of supply that we

* The first version of this article was published in Spanish in Camps, "Trabajo infantil y estrategias familiares". The author would like to express her gratitude to José M. Borrás-Llop and Xavier Sala-i-Martín for their advice and suggestions which helped to improve the final draft of this paper. Most of the empirical basis for the analysis set out here can be found in Camps, "Family Strategies and Children's Work Patterns". See also Camps, "Transitions in Women's and Children's Work Patterns".

1 See Hareven, *Family Time and Industrial Time*; Horrell and Humphries, "Child Labour in British Industrialization"; Wall, "Work, Welfare and the Family"; and Reher and Camps, "Las economías familiares".

will attempt to explain is schooling or the lack of schooling. This is normally seen as the basic factor for explaining why children go from being employed to not being employed. A lack of family income or infrastructure for the schooling of children is also seen as one of the main causes of child labour. Literature on the formation of human capital states that the lack of schooling has medium and long-term effects, since it leads to slower future growth of per capita income. Therefore, the presence of boys and girls at school or in agricultural labour or factories appears, at first glance, to have consequences for later economic development.

In dealing with factors of demand, we must also differentiate between boys and girls, as they belong to different employment groups. Nevertheless, in general the most commonly recognised factors of demand are the low cost, obedience and dexterity of boys and girls in comparison with adult males. In the early stages of development, the availability of cheap labour appears to be a crucial factor in determining the demand for labour by enterprises. It is well known that cheap labour also includes women and we will attempt to show that from the standpoint of the family, women and children's contribution to income was largely interchangeable.

Besides the determining factors related to the market, child labour has given rise to other controversies since the publication of the first studies linking its rationale to the logic of family strategies. According to this view, which we share, family demography and kinship, along with the wages of family members, provide abundant evidence as to the reasons for a greater or lesser intensity of child labour and its subsequent elimination. The strategies and demographic characteristics of families, the child labour market and technological change would appear, as we will see, to be the three basic factors for the analysis of patterns of occupation by boys and girls. In addition,[2] school truancy and the disregard for laws on the employment of women and children were often the most usual response to government regulation when families required the income of family members. Likewise, Spain's Social Reform Commission proved ineffective in its efforts to inspect the employment of women and children, particularly in the Barcelona area.[3] Of course, we are not trying to justify child labour, as Catalan employers would in their references to the insufficiency of wages of the heads of families to cover the household needs. Nevertheless, it should be stressed that the employment decisions of children must be placed in the context of the nature of the labour market in the Catalan

2 Borras Llop, "El trabajo infantil en el mundo rural español".

3 Borras Llop, "El trabajo infantil en la industria barcelonesa".

textiles industry of the nineteenth century.[4] The textile industry in Catalonia ran a labour market with highly elastic labour supplies and therefore low wages. In this context, the main objective of this manuscript is to show how family economies adapted in terms of mobilisation of their own resources to the situation of economic hardship.

Below, we will attempt to outline the logic of child labour in the nineteenth century on the basis of the characteristics of the labour market of that time, family strategies and demographics, and the technologies in use. The third part of this study will analyse the initial decline of child labour in the period between the wars, by means of the aforementioned analytical framework.

Child Labour and Family Economy during the Initial Stage of Industrialisation

The data available on the age at which children began work in the first Catalan factories varies widely, depending on the documentary sources consulted. The censuses of workers from the middle of the nineteenth century (1858-1863) in Catalan municipal archives generally give an age of approximately ten for commencement of employment in factories. On the other hand, in the context of the city of Barcelona in 1856, Ildefons Cerdà gives eight as the age at which children entered active employment.[5] Felipe Monlau and Joaquim Salarich state that in inland Catalonia, employment began at the age of six.[6] In other words, children started working between the age of six and ten. Based on the large number of censuses on workers that establish ten as being the age at which children started work in factories, we will use this hypothetical minimum age to calculate the family income of factory workers. In spite of the government's recommendation for children between the ages of six and nine to go to school, there is evidence that proves that in Sabadell, boys and girls received only one and a half years of schooling, often between the ages of five and six.[7] We can assume, then, that before starting work at the factory at the age of ten, children would have been helping their parents with auxiliary piecework or other tasks, in small family enterprises that do not figure in the censuses of

4 Camps, *La formación del mercado de trabajo industrial*, pp. 233-249.

5 Cerdà, "Monografía estadística de la clase obrera".

6 Monlau and Salarich, "Higiene pública".

7 See Borras Llop, "Mercado laboral, escolarización y empleo infantil".

workers,[8] or with work carried out in teams for which the company payrolls only name the supervising adult. Nevertheless, the fact that children left school at such an early age shows the unquestionable need on the part of families for supplementary income to support them by mobilising their very young offspring.

According to the same censuses of workers, the duration of the active working life in factories was from the age of ten to sixty for men and ten to thirty for women. In other words, men remained in paid employment throughout their lives, while women did so as children, adolescents and young mothers.

On the basis of the definition of age to which we refer as child labour, the second question that we must ask is the quantitative importance of child labour in the textile industry. Most of the quantitative information used in this article concerns the town of Sabadell.[9] This is not merely coincidental. Sabadell is a representative example in Spain of a town with a higher, sustained population growth throughout the nineteenth and twentieth centuries, due to immigration. The labour census for 1858 shows that children made up approximately 21 per cent of the workforce in the wool and cotton industries. To this end, let us recall our earlier mention of the fact that censuses of workers do not record auxiliary work done by children and therefore underestimate labour by children aged six to nine. We believe that the occupation rate for children must have been higher, since the local rates for adults in the textile industry were 31 per cent for men and 28 per cent for women. In any event, it is impossible at present to accurately specify the rate of child labour in the textile industry, which must have been in the region of 25 per cent. Nonetheless, the rates of child labour participation in 1858 compared to those in 1849-1850 suggest that during these years the industrial sector began to make increasing use of children's labour.[10] Since in this period Sabadell's industry witnessed a quick process of mechanisation we could infer that this was the cause of the

8 In spite of the rapid shift to factories in the textiles industry, many other trades maintained their handicraft status until the end of the century, including tinsmithing, boilermaking, ironworking, carpentry, sewing and tailoring, etc. The workers census of 1858 only records factory employees and not those of small businesses. We believe that a part of child occupation between the ages of 6 and 9 must have been in this sector and in auxiliary work for their parents. For the underestimation of child labour in domestic production, see Camps, "Family Strategies and Children's Work Patterns".

9 Our results on family strategies apply in fact to the general framework held by Hugh Cunningham in Cunningham, "Decline of Child Labour".

10 See Camps, "Family Strategies and Children's Work Patterns".

intensive use of children's labour. Previous handicraft technologies usually conceive children's work as a byemployment and this is the reason why it was rarely registered. Nonetheless, and in the absence of statistical evidence in the manual era, we can only guess that the intensity of children's labour increased with the initial technological change leading to industrialisation.

On a different level, it is interesting to note that, during the initial stage of industrialisation in Catalonia, the work of mothers and children was interchangeable, at a time when the demographic transition was still at its earliest stages.[11] On the one hand, it is important to stress that the number of children born and living with their parents was high and therefore constituted a substantial contribution to the amount of work that the family could do. Mothers could therefore not dedicate themselves exclusively to paid employment. In fact, as already mentioned, women worked in factories in the nineteenth century up until they were 30–35. This appears to be a universal pattern in female labour as seen in Catalonia in 1858, in England and Wales in 1851, in Japan in 1879 and in the US at the end of the nineteenth century.[12] There is abundant evidence that this did not mean the underuse of women's potential for work. In the context of large families and given the technologies in use at the time in domestic tasks, social and demographic reproduction required huge amounts of work. Thus, some approaches suggest that domestic tasks led women to work more hours than men in the lower strata of society where families had no domestic help or wet nurses.[13] The work requirements stemming from demographic patterns and the remunerated and unremunerated economic needs of families would both appear to be crucial factors in explaining the greater intensity of work by women.

Having many children did not only mean an increase in mothers' workloads. In fact, children constituted an important source of income for families. Taking ten as the hypothetical minimum age at which children began receiving an individual wage, they became the financial basis of the family economy when the head of the family reached the age of fifty, prior to commencement of their inactivity. The precariousness of levels of welfare in the Catalan context provides a convincing explanation as to why families would prefer remunerated work for their children rather than their schooling. The lack of supplementary income, mothers' devotion to the

11 See Cabré, *El sistema català de reproducció*; Nicolau, "Trajectoires regionales".

12 Goldin, *Understanding the Gender Gap;* Hareven, *Family Time and Industrial Time.*

13 Wall, "La contribución de las mujeres casadas". This view is further detailed in Borderías, "Suponiendo que este trabajo lo hace la mujer".

demographic reproduction of families and its high cost are all factors that explain the motivation of working families in their choice of child labour over schooling.

But other reasons must also have existed. The other main reason was that nineteenth-century factories, before the advent of white-collar jobs, did not demand formal education.[14] In fact, one of the conditions imposed by employers when taking on new workers was that they had completed formal manual apprenticeship in trade workshops or in factories.[15] To a large extent, then, the demands for human capital by employers in the nineteenth century were limited to learning how to use the equipment and subsequent continuance with the job, with workers adapting to technological change through the accumulation of knowledge from day-to-day experience of trial and error. In other words, if working families wished to ensure that their children had a future as employees in the textile industry, they had to start at the factories at an early age.

This all helps to shed light on the imminence of child labour in the context of industrialised societies in the nineteenth century, regardless of whether we approach it in terms of labour supply or demand. In turn, the results clarify the validity of the use that has been made of such indicators as schooling to measure the formation of human capital in this context.[16] The labour required by emerging industries is manual labour and hardly requires schooling. This would appear to indicate that both families and industrial employers were greatly interested in child labour. This is why literacy levels in Catalonia were mediocre and very possibly limited to the middle and upper classes. Given the living conditions of workers, learning must have been a very low priority for them.

In addition, we can show that families assigned their human resources rationally, including children. We have seen that children started working in factories at the age of ten and mothers left remunerated employment at the age of 30-35, coinciding roughly with the time when their oldest child was able to begin contributing very supplementary income. Furthermore, the growth of income with age was stagnant for women throughout their working life. In addition, from the outset of their employment in factories, the income of boys and male adolescents was higher than their mothers' and grew steadily throughout their working life.[17] From these different

14 Goldin, *Understanding the Gender Gap;* Hareven, *Family Time and Industrial Time.*

15 Camps, *La formación del mercado de trabajo industrial.*

16 Nuñez, *La fuente de la riqueza.*

17 Camps, *La formación del mercado de trabajo industrial*, p. 166.

wage paths on the basis of gender, it may be deduced that it was logical for families to replace women in employment with children. It was not only logical, but also absolutely necessary. The domestic responsibilities of mothers gradually reduced their availability for remunerated work. On the other hand, children's work offered, in the medium term, higher income for families than mothers' work. The highly pronounced segmentation of the labour market according to gender and the demands of demographic and social reproduction, referred to earlier, would appear to explain the logic of these dynamics. Furthermore, if we look at the nature of family economies towards the end of the century, in 1890, it can be seen that in such a demographic and family situation, no family member could afford the luxury of inactivity, not even for going to school, since the family's capacity for saving was fragile even at the best of times, when none of its members were idle. In fact, in that context, children's financial contribution to the household was indispensable, since it represented over half of the family income after the head of the family reached the age of fifty, and its full income when the head of the family reached the age of sixty and became inactive.[18] In this context, where the contribution by children and adolescents to the family economy could be critical, it is easy to understand why families disregarded official regulations (while not enforced) on schooling.

By way of conclusion to this section, we should stress that the demographic aspects of the family itself and its impact on women's work, the low standards of living and the working careers that had to start at an early age, all together, would appear to have led manufacturing industry to make intensive use of child labour. To this end, and due to the consequences of child labour on schooling, it is important to note that, at first glance, the causal relationship between schooling and economic growth must be approached cautiously at the initial stages of industrialisation.[19] We have attempted to show how informal and formal manual apprenticeship of trades was crucial for access to employment, while schooling played a secondary role. We do not mean to insinuate that apprenticeship did not involve the training of human capital. Nevertheless, this type of human capital is far removed from the indicators used by conventional historiography, based solely on literacy rates. We have calculated that for the company España Industrial, S.A. between 1847 and 1887, apprenticeship lasted

18 Camps, "Family Strategies and Children's Work Patterns", p. 65.

19 Núñez, *La fuente de la riqueza*.

three years.[20] In the working life of an industrial worker, the alternative of schooling during those three years was an enormous opportunity cost, consisting mainly of the need to look to a different area of occupation with lower growth potential than industry. In reality, to discern the effects of education on economic growth, we must wait until the twentieth century, particularly after World War II, and the technologies and business management methods of that time.

Initial Transition from Child Labour during the First Third of the Twentieth Century

In spite of mediocre rates of schooling in the nineteenth century, in the first third of the twentieth century, Catalonia was one of the regions of Spain that underwent the fastest economic growth. It is well known that this coincided with the second energy transition, the birth of the first major firms and labour reforms. With regard to this last factor, it is worth noting that after World War I a substantial portion of the largest Catalan enterprises introduced standardised labour processes.

Another phenomenon associated with these decades is the rapid decline in population growth among the Catalan population. In 1930, Josep Vandellós wrote *Catalunya Poble Decadent* (Catalonia, A People in Decline) to express his concern for the very low fertility rate among Catalans. Anna Cabré calculates that at that time (1920-1930) not all woman of childbearing age succeeded in reproducing a female to take her place and men only barely succeeded in producing a male successor.[21] If we look at the number of dependant minors in Sabadell in 1925, the results show that the average number was below two.[22] In other words, in the context of Catalonia, we can say that fertility dropped drastically, and was cause for alarm at the time. In addition, it would appear that one of the consequences of the serious decline in demographic reproduction was that the logic of families when deciding on alternative uses of children's time also underwent modification. It was undoubtedly a different situation for the family economy to have only one or two children at home, as was the case in 1925, in comparison with the moderately large families of the second half of the nineteenth century. During a substantial portion of the family cycle,

20 Camps, *La formación del mercado de trabajo industrial*, p. 204.

21 Cabré, *El sistema català de reproducció*, pp. 157-176.

22 Camps, "Transitions in Women's and Children's Work Patterns", p. 147.

one or two dependant minors did not represent an economic asset for the family compared with the number of children at the end of the nineteenth century.

If we follow the evidence provided by the case of Sabadell in 1925, another new consequence is the high degree of schooling of both boys and girls. The rate of schooling for children under the age of fifteen was around seventy per cent. The age at which children entered employment in factories receiving individual wages rose from 10 in nineteenth century to fifteen. A number of the factors mentioned so far must have contributed to parents deciding to prolong their children's schooling.[23]

On the one hand, we have already pointed out that contraception and the drastic decrease in the size of families meant that children's contribution to the family economy lost its traditional importance as a source of supplementary income. On the other hand, children's contributions did not become less important for supporting ageing parents during their critical situation in later life. As had been the case in the nineteenth century, in 1925 the children provided the largest portion of family income after their father reached the age of fifty.[24] In spite of its small size, the family emerging through the demographic transition was flexible in the use of its economic resources. Thus, the absence of income resulting from the prolonged schooling of children was mitigated, as we will see, by remunerated work on the part of their mother and immigrant collateral relatives. Altogether, schooling up until the age of fifteen is proof of the new concept implicit in procreation during this new phase and of the willingness of families to invest in the education of their children through the greater income obtained from the work of mothers and relatives.[25]

Although it has not been conclusively shown, it would appear plausible that at this new stage, during the second technological revolution, industry in Sabadell demanded education. The view of local historians stresses, however, that during the first third of the twentieth century the town's wool industry did not undergo much modernisation.[26] The extraordinary profits brought about by World War I were not reinvested in the manufacturing industry. Nevertheless, the structure of occupation in Sabadell during the 1920s suggests that the industrial framework was in fact transformed: new industries appeared, such as gas and electricity, and oth-

23 Camps, "Transitions in Women's and Children's Work Patterns".
24 Camps, "Transitions in Women's and Children's Work Patterns".
25 Camps, "Transitions in Women's and Children's Work Patterns", p. 145.
26 Deu, *La indústria tèxtil llanera de Sabadell.*

ers, including metallurgy and metalworking, grew. From the standpoint of labour markets, there are other results that allow us to clarify the view that industry did not modernise. Although we have not followed up the business sources that would allow for linear tracking, a cross section of ages and income on the basis of occupation does provide evidence to the effect that company labour structures changed in comparison with the nineteenth century, even in the textile industry (see tables 12.1 and 12.2).[27]

On the one hand, adult labour supply increased notably with the incorporation of more married women and immigrants from the rest of Spain. With regard to women, a consequence of the demographic transition in Catalonia was that it freed them of a part of their domestic workload and prolonged their working life from the age of thirty to the age of forty. Mothers' increased availability also meant they were able to increase their income as they progressed in their active life, although that income was still considerably lower than men's. To a certain extent this was also due to factors of demand. Table 12.1, which gives a selection of significant occupations, shows the hypothetical movement of women by sequences of promotion within textile enterprises. Women and girls would commence their employment with training and then be promoted to trades with the corresponding wage increases. It should also be noted that of all the occupations shown in table 12.1, the best paid is that of *knotter*, a job which started at the age of sixteen on average. In fact, this occupation required a high degree of precision, concentration, dexterity and energy, and it seems logical that it should be carried out by younger women, while other tasks such as seamstress or launderer would be embarked upon towards the end of their working lives when their strength diminished. At the same average age as knotters, we find a new female occupation, that of typist, which required studies and was certainly still in its early stages. Note that, in spite of the fact that it was a non-manual job, wages were lower than for that of knotter, which, as we have mentioned, was highly complex. In fact, until the more widespread advance of technology, many manual occupations continued to be more complex and better paid than non-manual ones.

27 *Tables 12.1 and 12.2*, found in the annexes, do not show all occupations in the textiles industry. The documentary source for the information given here is the Municipal Register of Inhabitants for 1925, which, in addition to all demographic variables, gives the income of all family members. In the first place, we worked with a random sample of 6,500 inhabitants and almost 2,000 families, whose occupations are the only ones at our disposal. To draw up the tables, we took only those who were born in the town. It is our opinion that for immigrants, the average age for entering an occupation was not representative of their active working life.

Tables 12.1 and 12.2 also show that in 1925, the town's industry was still in its transitional state between tradition and innovation, as seen in the still pronounced predominance in the textile industry of manual over non-manual trades. Nevertheless, the change in the pattern of the evolution of women's income in comparison with the nineteenth century is clear both in the succession of occupation and in wages spanning their working life. In other words, the labour market had become less segmented in so far as gender was concerned.

It can be said that the patterns of employment for women show that the labour market in enterprises was somewhat modernised, giving rise to new sequences of internal promotion in enterprises. Therefore, it also appears logical that the modernisation of labour and employment associated with the new technologies and management systems required formally educated employees, as in the rest of the industrialised world. So families wanted schooling for their children not only due to greater physical and financial availability, but also because it was an investment for the future in the industrial environment. However, youth education (ages fifteen to nineteen) still only reached levels of under ten per cent in 1925.[28] In addition, although our source (the Municipal Register) is not overly reliable as to the extent of education, our results show only three secondary school graduates and no university studies among the juvenile population. Note that at the age of fifteen, when adolescents entered employment in 1925, they had normally completed lower secondary education, and this was the principal improvement on the nineteenth century. Very few young people continued their education to the upper secondary school level, which was the prerequisite for entering university. In fact, the case of Sabadell presents the paradox that its active population included a large number of workers from neighbouring cities, including Barcelona, which we suppose was the source of people filling the top positions in industry.

By way of conclusion to this section, we can once again state that factors of both supply of and demand for manpower contributed to the decline of child labour in the context of Catalonia during the first third of the twentieth century. On the supply side and in a context of a rapid decrease in population growth, child labour ceased to be indispensable for family economies except for supporting the elderly. However, in this case, we must speak of juvenile rather than child labour. The new availability of mothers for remunerated employment and the economic support of col-

28 Camps, "Transitions in Women's and Children's Work Patterns", p. 143.

lateral relatives brought income to families that had previously been provided by child labour. In addition, we have seen that families were smaller, with only one or two dependant minors and with an average size of less than four individuals. In turn, the growth of mothers' incomes over the course of their working life and the support of income earned by collateral relatives provided the economic basis needed to pay for children's schooling. All of these factors indicate, in fact, that in the short space of these decades, the very notion of childhood and reproduction was radically transformed, at least in Catalonia. It would appear that, in view of this evidence, an indispensable point of reference is the work of Eduard Masjoan,[29] whose central working hypothesis is that the deep-rooted anarchist movement among the Catalan workers and thinkers of the time, and with it the dissemination of neo-Malthusian reproductive practices, are factors that explain the aforementioned process of transformation of working families.

Conclusions: Child Labour, Economic Development and Adaptive Strategies by Families

In the preceding pages we have attempted to show the rationality of the economic players involved, i.e. the members of working families, in the assignment of children's time to schooling and employment. The general conclusions that we can draw deal with issues of education and economic development, as well as the logic of adaptive family strategies in historical populations.

It should be stressed that the judgement of the use of children's time in the past is highly restrictive with regards to the understanding of time dedicated to instruction; the economic literature on the formation of human capital is not restricted to schooling. Even the instruction that is expected to produce greater economic returns, the specific formation of human capital, is basically carried out on the job.[30] This is relevant for the clarification of the paradoxes observed in the case of Catalonia and the low levels of literacy in the region. We have attempted to show how, during the nineteenth century, factors of both supply and demand encouraged child labour rather than schooling. However, this does not lead to the conclusion that there was little investment in human capital in Catalonia. The human capital required by industry during the age of nascent capitalism

29 Masjoan, *Neomalthusianismo y anarquismo ibérico.*
30 Becker, *Human Capital.*

was not schooling, but rather informal manual training during childhood and formal manual training during adolescence. It is to be supposed that employers had their reasons for preferring manual training and subsequent specific training in human capital, rather than formal education. In other words, it would appear that industrialisation in Catalonia during the nineteenth century did not need a greater formation of human capital.[31] Perhaps results in the area of schooling were mediocre, but the endogenous factors acquired on the job show how children adapted to the demands of industry.

Furthermore, we see that families actively adapt to changes in the child labour market and cover their economic needs through the rational use of their human resources.[32] During the initial phase of industrialisation, in the nineteenth century, the intensive use of child labour appears logical, owing both to the uncertainty of subsistence and to the limited availability of mothers for remunerated employment. In addition, we have stressed that the work of women and children was interchangeable for the family economy, depending on their respective availability. During the first third of the twentieth century, the first changes in the concept of childhood itself were assimilated by the Catalan population. Firstly, couples drastically reduced their levels of reproduction. This would indicate that for the first time couples were having only the children that they wanted to, particularly among workers who adopted libertarian ideology.[33] Secondly, this gave mothers greater availability on the labour market, which freed a part of the family's economic resources to pay for prolonged education for their children. All of this came about in the context of the second technological revolution, which demanded schooling.

Simplifying the situation greatly, in order to analyse the logic behind the use of both manual and intellectual potential child labour, we must not limit our search to only schools and factories. Family economies and all the factors conditioning them shed light upon the rationality of their decisions concerning work. This is an important factor for the evaluation of the results of campaigns in favour of schooling for children in developing countries at present. It would appear that one lesson to be learned from history is that in the absence of changes in the demographic and economic conditions of the families involved, they will continue to take the

31 Rosés, "Early Phase of Catalan Industrialisation".

32 In this connection, the recent synthetic article by Hugh Cunningham demonstrates the universal nature of our postulates. See Cunningham, "Decline of Child Labour".

33 Masjoan, *Neomalthusianismo y anarquismo ibérico*.

same decisions on the assignment of their human resources and particularly children, in spite of government regulations. In our case study no government would have had the chance to undertake effective measures to abolish children's labour since it represented an important source of income for the household. Technological change, demographic transition and the impact of modernised labour markets resulting in less segmentation of the labour market according to gender would appear to be the main causes of decreased use of child labour in our case.

Table 12.1. Formal Education and Wage-Earning Occupations in the Textile Industry for Non-Immigrant Women, According to Age and Average Income, Sabadell 1925

Women's occupations	*Average age*	*Average wage (Ptas/day)*
School	8	
Apprentice	13	1.00
Apprentice seamstress, piecework	13	
Apprentice darner	14	3.88
Apprentice weaver	14	1.50
Looper	14	3.50
Apprentice spinner	15	3.67
Typist	16	3.50
Knotter	16	7.50
Student	17	
Stitch looper	17	5.00
Stitcher	19	4.71
Warper	23	4.86
Slubber	23	5.00
Weft winder	24	5.50
Weaving preliminary tasks	25	4.50
Spinning preliminary tasks	26	4.19
Weaver	28	5.50
Darner	30	4.88
Spinner	31	6.00
Finishing weaving	32	4.17
Day labourer	33	5.63
Seamstress	44	6.00
Launderer	45	2.40

Table 12.2. Formal Education and Wage-Earning Occupations in the Textile Industry for Non-Immigrant Men, According to Age and Average Income, Sabadell 1925

Men's occupations	*Average age*	*Average wage (Ptas/day)*
School	8	
Apprentice finisher	11	3.25
Apprentice weaver	14	2.00
Worsted spinner	16	6.00
Finishing weaving	17	4.00
Student	17	
Presser	17	5.00
Loader	18	6.00
Theorist	19	8.00
Dyes and colourings	24	7.50
Office boy	25	8.00
Dyer	25	8.00
Wool washer	26	7.00
Factory day labourer	27	7.50
Finisher	29	8.09
Spinning day labourer	29	9.00
Spinner	30	9.20
Weaver	35	8.79
Weaving day labourer	35	7.74
Wool grader	44	9.00
Spinning preparation day labourer	49	9.50

Sources table 12.1 and 12.2: Municipal Register of Inhabitants for 1925; see further note 27.

CHAPTER 13

A History of Child Labour in Portugal

Pedro Goulart and Arjun S. Bedi*

Introduction

Children in Portugal have provided labour contributions for many centuries, and while there has been a temporal decline in child labour during the twentieth century, it still persists in some parts of the country. The progressive decline and yet the persistence of child labour reflect the dual social and economic structures that characterize modern-day Portugal. Child labour in Portugal appears to be rooted in the partial backwardness of the country and is a shadow from the past.

This paper is motivated by the progress made on child labour in a developed country setting, but also by its enduring nature. Based on an analysis of data drawn from various sources this paper puts together a picture of the evolution of child labour in Portugal. It analyses the intergenerational pattern of child labour and identifies policies that may be used to reduce its incidence in Portugal and in developing countries.

The article is organized as follows. Based on two industrial surveys conducted in the latter half of the nineteenth century the next section of the paper provides an account of child labour in Portugal before 1926. Section III covers the period of the dictatorship (1926-1974), distinguishing between the inward-looking period (until 1950) and a latter more open period. Section IV examines child labour in the post-1974 period drawing a distinction between child labour until the mid-1990s and the present day situation. Based on this material, the final section presents some policy suggestions.

* The authors thank Hugh Hindman, Hugh Cunningham, Colin Heywood and other participants at the Child Labour's Global Past (1500-2000) Conference and João Guimarães and Lúcia Grilo for helpful comments. The authors would specially like to express gratitude to Catarina Grilo for assistance, to Tiago Mata for comments at an earlier phase and Kristoffel Lieten at a later stage.

Early Accounts and Early Legislation

After being one of the richest countries in Europe through the seventeenth century, by the beginning of the twentieth century Portugal had become one of the poorest.[1] It had a late industrial take-off and for the nineteenth and most of the twentieth century made limited economic progress (see table 13.1).[2] In terms of literacy the situation did not differ much. In 1850, Portugal had a 15 per cent literacy rate which rose to 25 per cent by 1900. These literacy rates were comparable with Russia and the Balkans, but lagged behind most other European countries.[3]

In a country where the Inquisition had had a long history,[4] the fall of the Absolute Monarchy and the rise of the Constitutional Monarchy (1820-1910) led to periods of more intellectual openness, but it took decades to consolidate.[5] Accordingly, modern legislation approved at the beginning of the 1800's was poorly enforced. In the context of education, in spite of timely diagnoses of the need for teachers and schools, the state lacked the will and capacity to fulfil the requirements.[6] The republican period between 1910 and 1926 would see the creation of a Ministry of Public Instruction and of other important educational measures. However, insta-

1 Candeias *et al.*, *Alfabetização e escola*, p. 36.

2 Alternatively, some authors suggest a gradual slow growth also through the twentieth century, opposed to a strong surge implied by "take-off". See Manuel Lisboa, in: Valério, *Estatísticas Históricas*, p. 262.

3 The front runners were the Nordic countries, Germany, Scotland, The Netherlands and Switzerland followed by England and Wales, France, Belgium, Ireland, Austria and Hungary, Spain, Italy and Poland. Details are available in Candeias *et al.*, *Alfabetização e escola*, p. 36.

4 Up to 1770, books by authors such as Hobbes, Diderot, Rousseau, Voltaire, La Fontaine, Espinosa and others were still burnt in Lisbon due to alleged heretic thought. Carvalho, *História do ensino em Portugal*, p. 468.

5 Mónica, *Educação e sociedade no Portugal de Salazar*, p. 4.

6 Reis estimates that in the period 1864-1910, the necessary increase in expenditure to catch up with leading European countries in terms of literacy standards would have been negligible. It would have amounted to 0.5 to 0.75 per cent of the State's expenditure (0.1 per cent of GNP) in the 1864-90 period and 2.8 per cent (0.5 per cent of GNP) in the 1890-1910. This author further cites Maria Eugénia Mata that in both periods the State's expenditure in education varied between 3 to 5 per cent of the budget while defence and repayment of the debt absorbed 15 to 19 and 29 to 54 per cent, respectively. The small amount needed suggests that criteria other than affordability prevailed. Reis, "O analfabetismo", p. 238.

bility in the government (45 changes) compromised major changes in policy enforcement.[7]

Table 13.1. Per Capita GDP Evolution, 1990 Purchasing Power Parity (International Geary-Khamis) Dollars

Per capita GDP						
Year	*1820*	*1870*	*1913*	*1950*	*1973*	*2001*
Portugal	923	975	1250	2086	7063	14229
Spain	1008	1207	2056	2189	7661	15659
Greece	641	880	1592	1915	7655	12511
Rate of growth of per capita GDP						
Year	*1500-1820*	*1820-1870*	*1870-1913*	*1913-1950*	*1950-1973*	*1973-2001*
Portugal	0.13	0.11	0.58	1.39	5.45	2.53
Spain	0.13	0.36	1.25	0.17	5.60	2.59
Greece	0.12	0.64	1.39	0.50	6.21	1.77
Rate of growth of GDP						
Year	*1500-1820*	*1820-1870*	*1870-1913*	*1913-1950*	*1950-1973*	*1973-2001*
Portugal	0.51	0.66	1.34	2.35	5.73	2.95
Spain	0.32	0.93	1.77	1.06	6.60	3.10
Greece	0.39	1.56	2.32	1.41	6.98	2.40

Source: Maddison, *The World Economy*: pp. 260, 262 and 263 for Portugal and Spain. Figures for Greece are based on pages 54–57 and 66–69.
Note: Rates of growth are annual average compound growth rates (in percentages).

After rejecting a proposal on containing child labour in 1881, modern legislation designed to prevent child labour in industry was adopted only in 1891, much later compared to other European countries.[8] After centuries of

7 The Ministry of Public Instruction had 49 ministers in fourteen years and as a consequence zigzag reforms were quite common.

8 For instance, England introduced legislation in 1802, which was followed by more important and effective legislation in 1833. Pinto, "A Universidade e o trabalho infantil". France introduced legislation in 1841 and Spain, Denmark and The Netherlands in the 1870's. Williams, *Child Workers in Portugal*, p. 39.

'natural' work contribution by children, the need to regulate child labour in Portugal stemmed from rising social unrest.[9] Proximate causes included a workers revolt in Porto, demanding better working conditions. With a view to pacifying workers and demonstrating support for their needs, the decree passed in 1891 included phrases such as, "the legislative care in favour of workers continues"[10], and the decree intends to protect both women and children "as society has an obligation to protect the weak [...]".[11] As a result of this legislation, the minimum working age for industrial employment was set at twelve years old (agriculture was excluded), with an exception of ten years with completed primary education for metallurgists.

Child labour prior to 1926

As may be expected, systematic detailed accounts of the existence and practice of child labour for the pre-1926 period are scarce. The earliest mention of children working comes from ship logs that report children being an important part of vessels' crews during the sixteenth century.[12] The most reliable quantitative accounts of the extent of child labour are provided by two industrial surveys conducted in 1852 and 1881, a time of a rather incipient industry.[13] The 1852 industrial survey reported that 3,147 children below the age of sixteen, corresponding to about 25 per cent of the surveyed workers, were working in an industrial enterprise. In 1881, the absolute number of working children rose to 5,998 while children as a percentage of surveyed workers fell to seven per cent. In terms of their distribution, data from both the surveys shows that about 50-55 per cent of the minors worked in the textile and weaving industry (cotton, wool and silk). Other important sectors employing minors were metallurgy (13 per cent) and carpentry (10 per cent) – see table 13.2. The dangerous pyrotechnics

9 Campinho, *Regime jurídico do contrato*, p. 22.

10 IEFP, "Regulamento de 1891", p. 38.

11 IGT, "Centenário de uma lei histórica", p.14.

12 Ana Lúcia Kassouf and Marcelo Justus dos Santos, "Child Labor in Brazil: More than 500 Years of National Shame", *Child Labour's Global Past (1500-2000) Conference*, (Amsterdam, 15-17 Nov. 2006).

13 While it is likely that both surveys underestimate the use of child labour they are the best sources available. The 1852 survey was an indirect survey (questionnaires were sent to firms) and included factories with 10 or more workers. The 1881 survey used a direct and indirect approach and included factories regardless of the number of workers. While the 1881 survey was an improvement over the 1852 survey, some firms did not respond to the queries while others provided responses without always distinguishing between minors and adults or minors and women.

industry was the most "minor intensive" with minors representing almost 63 per cent of its labour force. Most of the reported child workers were concentrated in the Porto district, indicating its early industrial development. In addition to Porto, districts specializing in specific products, such as Guarda (Covilhã) in wool weaving, Portalegre in cork, Leiria (Marinha Grande) in glass and Santarém in paper, relied heavily on children (see table 13.2). In terms of working conditions, minors received considerably less pay than other male workers. In public works, in 1883-1884, the salary ratio between male adults and children was around two to one, while minors' salary was similar to that of women.[14]

Table 13.2. Children Age 16 and below Working in Industry, 1881

Industry	*Minors in workforce*		*Predominant district*		
	Number	*Share of total workers (%)*	*District*	*Number*	*District's share in total number of child workers (%)*
Carpentry	512	10	Porto	473	92.4
Ceramics	180	8.8	Porto	82	45.6
Stone works	207	3.1	Porto	207	100.0
Cork	168	10.4	Portalegre	120	71.4
Metallurgy	680	13	Porto	559	82.2
Paper	105	7.7	Santarém	36	34.3
Pyrotechnics	129	62.6	Porto	128	99.2
Tobacco	354	8.8	Porto	275	77.7
Cotton weaving	1991	5	Porto	667	33.5
Wool weaving	905	10.1	Guarda	479	52.9
Silk weaving	91	10.7	Porto	91	100.0
Typography	106	17.9	Porto	104	98.1
Clothing	264	5	Porto	236	89.4
Glass	83	9.2	Leiria	38	45.8
Other	223	2.6	Porto	144	64.6
Total	5998	7			

Besides these industrial surveys, reports by labour inspectors and lawyers are additional sources of information on the work contribution of children in industry. A participant at a national congress of jurists in 1898, Sebastião

14 *Anuário Estatístico*, Lisbon, 1884, p. 415.

Centeno, denounced child labour in the industrial centres, especially faraway from Lisbon. He pointed out that male and female children as young as seven worked for nine or ten hours per day, or three or four hours per night.[15] To illustrate the widespread use of child labour Campinho[16] cites a labour inspector from 1904:

> It is enough to enter, by surprise, any factory, even humble (and maybe even more in small industrial establishments) to recognise the falseness of the reports; (...) in some of the employment registers of each of the establishments, appear minors who are less than 10 years and in one registry there was even the naïve observation: 'In addition to the registered individuals, when there is need of work some women and minors are temporarily called'.

Data on children working in agriculture and services is not readily available. However, several reports suggest the widespread use of children in these sectors. Henriques Carneiro[17] presents insightful reports from educational inspectors, which help to further characterize child labour in the mid nineteenth century. According to António Carvalho, a school inspector in the Centro region, low school attendance is "related to the students' parents poverty and in part to their negligence, very often they see the need of occupying their children in services, either domestic, or rural."

In 1863, school inspector Manuel Barradas, on an inspection in Alentejo, was surprised to find zero enrolment:

> The teacher assured me that after the harvest [of grapes] is finished, maybe some students will apply to come to school [...]; before that it would be impossible, because their own mothers would beat them up if they want to attend school.

Francisco Dinis, inspector in a county in Centro also noted changes in the school timetable as "the children had the need to walk the cattle".

The limited educational enrolment of children may be attributed to child work as well as to the quality of schooling. The latter was often said to be very poor and its usefulness doubtful, both motives to skip school. The literature offers several reasons for this aspect of schooling in Portugal, including poor qualifications of teachers (the primary criteria of selection

15 Cardoso, "O Caso Português", p. 171.
16 Campinho, *Regime jurídico do contrato*, p. 27.
17 Henriques Carneiro, *Evolução e controlo*, pp. 455, 458, 465.

was moral integrity), low remuneration (several teachers performed additional activities) and lack of infrastructure.

The Period of the Dictatorship, 1926-1974

A military coup in 1926 led to an extremely conservative dictatorship that kept the country under tight control until 1974. The regime idolised a rural and modest life style, and feared economic development. The conservative philosophy was summed up in the motto "God, Fatherland and Family". Accordingly, the Portuguese economy tended to be one of subsistence and closed to external markets.[18] Rural lobbies were strengthened and industrialisation slowed down.[19] The industry that did develop was characterised by unsophisticated consumer goods. The mode of production was predominantly artisanal with reduced use of physical capital and intensive use of low-skilled labour.[20]

On the education front there were several changes. In the first instance, education was perceived as a threat to social unity and coherence and therefore reduced to a minimum. In 1926, schools that trained secondary school teachers were closed and in 1929, compulsory education was reduced from five to three years, and co-educational schools were forbidden. The opinions expressed by some supporters of the regime were even more enlightening than the laws. João Ameal, writer and historian wrote: "Portugal does not need schools".[21] Another writer, Virgínia de Castro e Almeida, referring to the rural inhabitants, wrote in 1927:

> The more beautiful, stronger and healthier part of the Portuguese soul resides in the 75 per cent of the illiterate. [...] What advantages did they get in school? None. Nothing won. Everything lost.[22]

> [...] knowing how to read and write they create ambitions: they want to go to the cities, apprentice store clerk, sales clerk, gentlemen; they want to

18 At that time, the internal market also included Portugal's colonial territories.

19 Mónica, *Educação e sociedade no Portugal de Salazar*. In a famous movie song of that time a "typical" Portuguese sang: "[I am] poor but honoured/owing to Providence the grace of being born poor".

20 Aguiar and Martins, "A indústria", p. 215.

21 Carvalho, *História do ensino em Portugal*, p. 726.

22 Carvalho, *História do ensino em Portugal*.

> go to Brazil. They learned to read! What do they read? Criminal relationships; wrong notions of politics; bad books; leaflets of subversive propaganda. They leave the hoe, become uninterested in the land and only have an ambition: to become civil servants.[23]

However, soon after this downsizing of the educational system, and coinciding with the rise of António Salazar to Prime Minister, additional measures were introduced to use the school system as a way of controlling the population.[24] In 1935, the regime "purified" the public system from oppositionists and especially communists. A parliamentary discussion of education laws in 1938 provides compelling information on how mass education was feared and despised by the ruling elite and how work and family values were praised.[25] On education, for example:

> Is compulsory schooling commendable to support, in principle? Observe the case of USA, where all know how to read and write, but there are also so many crimes [...]; Looking over our history for the three most brilliant periods of our past, when our nationalist cause rose the highest: the [Christian] reconquering [of Iberia peninsula], the [overseas] discoveries and of restoration [of independence]. The mass of men that was then mobilised was composed by literate or illiterate? Did the companions of [Vasco da] Gama know how to read and write? [...] I have a certain fear of this alphabet's fetishism [...]. (Querubim Guimarães, participant in a parliamentary discussion).[26]

> I would try to reproduce today the environment I met fifty years ago in the rural school of my village. (Fernando Borges, participant in a parliamentary discussion).[27]

Thus during the period 1926 to 1950, education was reserved for a minority, which included urban and rural elites and an increasing urban middle class.

23 Mónica, *Educação e sociedade no Portugal de Salazar*, p. 120.

24 Salazar, a well-known professor of economics at Coimbra University, was finance minister between 1928 and 1932 and was given sweeping powers to manage and transform the Portuguese economy. In 1932 he became prime minister, a position that he held for 36 years.

25 Mónica, *Educação e sociedade no Portugal de Salazar*; Carvalho, *História do ensino em Portugal*; Henriques Carneiro, *Evolução e controlo*.

26 Carvalho, *História do ensino em Portugal*, p. 765.

27 Carvalho, *História do ensino em Portugal*, p. 766.

Mónica[28] suggests that, for the poor population, the opportunity cost of education was high while the perceived future benefits of schooling were low. The impoverished families could not afford to spare children's work or salary and since there was no room for upward mobility in the regime's rigid social structure, investment in education did not make sense: "[i]n an illiterate society, ignorance does not constitute [...] a disadvantage; and it is also not a stigma because illiteracy is the rule, not the exception".[29]

In terms of figures, by 1950, literacy had reached 55 per cent. Despite this increase, by this time, Portugal lagged even further behind other European countries which – with the exception of Greece and Yugoslavia (75 per cent), Italy, Spain and Poland (80 per cent) and Bulgaria and Romania (85 per cent) – had literacy rates above 90 per cent.[30] Given the prevailing attitude towards education, it is no surprise that new legislation on child labour, introduced in 1934 and 1936 simply confirmed the 1891 law, with the minimum permissible working age for industrial employment set at twelve years, (excluding agricultural work) and allowances for some cases, *e.g.* ten years for metallurgists with fourth grade education.[31]

Child labour between 1926 and 1950

During this period, information on the labour force participation of minors is available from the 1940 and 1950 census.[32] In industry, official labour force participation amongst children in the age group ten to fourteen, which was about two per cent in 1940, rose to five per cent in 1950. Similarly, the participation rate for minors in the age range fifteen to nineteen rose from 9.1 in 1940 to 14.5 per cent in 1950. Despite the rise in child labour force participation, their actual share in the industrial labour force may have fallen. Although direct comparisons are hindered by the different age ranges, as mentioned earlier, in 1881 minors accounted for about seven per cent of the industrial labour force, and in 1950, twelve to fourteen year olds accounted for about three per cent of the labour force. In terms of their industrial concentration, by 1950 about 70-75 per cent of the minors were involved in the manufacturing of shoes and clothes, textiles, furniture, construction

28 Mónica, *Educação e sociedade no Portugal de Salazar*, p. 253.

29 Mónica, *Educação e sociedade no Portugal de Salazar*, p. 255.

30 Candeias, *Alfabetização e escola*, p. 34.

31 Campinho, *Regime jurídico do contrato*, p. 30.

32 The 1940 and the 1950 census were conducted by INE, the National Statistics Institute which had been set up in 1935.

and metals and machines. During this period their presence in hazardous industries like chemicals was relatively small.

In terms of payment, earnings of minors' remained lower than adults and the difference may have even widened. The poor working conditions of children were highlighted by newspaper articles in *Diário de Notícias* on cases of "children of 10/12 years that earned 11 escudos per week, underfed, and working excessively long hours".[33] Specific details are available for the glass industry where the salary ratio between adults and children was three to one. The adult to child ratios of salary per day are slightly higher than the salary per hour, suggesting that minors may have worked more days than adults.[34] Furthermore, accident rates in the glass industry suggest that minors were almost three times more likely to get hurt at work compared to adults and about two to three times more likely to be incapacitated.

Further information on the conditions faced by children working in industry comes from Soeiro Pereira Gomes' 1941 book *Esteiros*, which he dedicated to the "children of men who had never been children".[35] The novel describes the harsh life of a group of boys and the physical and psychological difficulties faced by doing a "man's" work from an early age. These factories operated only during the hotter, non-rainy months and relied heavily on children. Children as young as seven worked in the industry and were engaged in heavy and dangerous tasks. First, digging out the mud from the *esteiro*, then moulding it and taking it to the kiln. Finally, the bricks, often too hot, had to be transported to the boats. Accidents were common and the pay was low: "The coins did not cover the bottom of the pockets; but the projects filled their young brains."[36]

Turning to agriculture and domestic services – given the regime's rural bent and the lack of attention devoted to spreading education – it is no surprise that during this period children remained an important part of the rural labour force. In 1940, labour force participation among children aged ten to fourteen was about 10 per cent while in 1950 it was 16 per cent amongst children aged twelve to fourteen. While the labour participation ratio of children in agriculture was three times as much as in industry, twice as many children worked as domestics, where the pay was very often in meals. Thus, in 1950, the participation of children in the age group

33 Mónica, *Educação e sociedade no Portugal de Salazar*, p. 250.

34 *Anuário Estatístico*, Lisbon, 1941, pp. 456–457.

35 The book title refers to the small water canals supplied by the river Tagus and from which tile/brick factories obtained necessary mud.

36 Gomes, *Esteiros*, p. 14.

twelve to fourteen was at least 60 per cent, with agriculture accounting for 16.1 per cent, domestic services for 38.1 per cent, and industry for 5.1 per cent.

While working conditions in agriculture may not have been as poor as they were in industry, they were probably not harmless. Real life stories of men and women who lived in Alentejo from 1920 to 1974 and had migrated to Setúbal, a town in the coastal area, provide a dynamic picture of what rural child labour meant. According to these life histories, children did not stay long in school and girls were worse off because of prejudice and of their usefulness for other tasks. Most children started working when they reached nine years, sometimes sooner. The ones who did not go to school used to work full time while those who did attend school worked after school hours. Girls worked in domestic services for the big landowners, or would go to the nearest village, city or even Lisbon. Often there was no remuneration and the work only assured their meals. Boys started by taking care of cattle, chicken and pigs and by twelve or thirteen they could try to work in the fields. The tasks were plucking olives and harvesting wheat, and children were always included in large groups of workers, but earned less. The money would go to the family or more likely to the father. Children would usually get up at five o'clock in the morning, eat something before work and then walk many miles to the fields. The work finished at sunset and they reached home at nine, ten o'clock in the evening. Girls could still have to take care of domestic chores.[37]

While children provided agricultural labour throughout the country, there were regional differences. The Northern region was characterised by ownership of small plots of land, land inheritance from parents to children and high emigration. Typically, such farms drew on labour from their own family or from children in nearby farms. In the South, where farm plots were larger, children were less hierarchically dependent on their household as they rarely worked under parental supervision and also did not expect to inherit land in the future. As a consequence, in 1940, the Northern districts of Bragança, Braga, Vila Real and Viseu had a high incidence of child labour, while Lisbon had the lowest incidence.[38]

37 Colectivo 9° ano da Escola Secundária D. João II *De Sol a Sol. O Alentejo dos Nossos Avós* (Setúbal, 2006).

38 Mónica, *Educação e sociedade no Portugal de Salazar*, p. 247.

Background and legislation, 1950-1974

In 1950, the regime finally began promoting economic and social reforms. After an initial rejection of the Marshall Plan, the regime formalised a development plan for the 1949-1951 period.[39] Key aspects of this plan included internationalisation and industrial development through upgrading of production technology. Industrial development was promoted and low agricultural wages and low cereal prices were used to transfer surpluses from agriculture to industry.[40]

According to Afonso and Aguiar,[41] this period was characterised by increases in international trade, the inflow of foreign direct investment, a massive outflow of labour and increased reliance of the economy on remittances. Portugal joined the European Free Trade Agreement (EFTA) in 1960 and signed bilateral labour supply agreements with France and The Netherlands in 1963 and the German Federal Republic in 1964.[42] Estimates set emigration figures, between 1950 and 1974, at more than 1.7 million, or about 18-20 per cent of the Portuguese population.[43]

Whereas the increase in exports to European countries led to industrial specialisation, the import of investment goods and the adoption of more advanced technologies led to more child-free production methods. For example, the textile industry, a key employer of children, began to modernize and become more capital intensive after the 1960's.[44] The requirements of the modernization strategy led to an increase in educational expenditure. The focus was on increasing investments in primary schooling and the training of technicians.[45] In 1956 and 1960, compulsory education was increased from 3 to 4 years of schooling, first for boys and later for girls. In 1964 it was raised to six years. In 1969, the minimum legal working age was raised to fourteen years.[46]

39 Garoupa and Rossi, "Instituições e quadro legal", p. 443.

40 Confraria, "Política económica", p. 402.

41 Afonso and Aguiar, "A internacionalização da economia", p. 305.

42 Veiga, "A transição demográfica", p. 58.

43 Valério, *Estatísticas históricas*, p. 84. This mass migration that led people from the countryside to urban areas or from Portugal to the exterior was mainly to escape from starvation and in search of a better life. Some also had political motives (opposition to the regime) or wanted to escape army conscription that from 1961 on would lead them to fight the colonial war. The destination of emigrants was mainly Europe. While in 1957 more than 10 per cent of the legal immigrants went there, by 1963 it had increased to 59 per cent. Most emigration was illegal.

44 Mateus, "Tecnologia".

45 Carvalho, *História do ensino em Portugal*, p. 808.

46 Williams, *Child Workers in Portugal*, p. 40.

Driven by these reforms, Portugal recorded rapid economic growth (see table 13.1). Although agriculture stagnated,[47] industry prospered and annual industrial growth rates were between 7 to 9 per cent in the 1950s and 1960s. Income, however, was extremely unevenly distributed and was concentrated in a few families which were allowed to build powerful economic groups. By 1971, 0.4 per cent of companies retained 53 per cent of the capital.[48]

Despite this growth, the regime did not last. Costly colonial wars that were internationally deplored and domestically unpopular exhausted the country and marked the dusk of the regime. In 1968 the dictator Salazar literally fell from his chair, and soon after the period of dictatorship came to an end.

Child labour between 1950 and 1974

To examine the evolution of child labour in this period we rely on a household survey which was conducted by the Portuguese Government in co-operation with the International Labour Organization in 2001. This survey provides credible and comprehensive information for 26,429 youngsters aged six to fifteen years old and their families. In addition to enquiring about the work practices of children the survey gathers information on the labour market experience of children's parents and their age of entry into the labour market. Using information on these adults and their working patterns while they were children we are able to sketch a picture of the patterns of child labour during the second half of the twentieth century.

Figure 13.1 depicts children's activity rate in specific age groups.[49] As shown in the figure, children below nine had low rates of labour force participation (below 6 per cent) which declined throughout this period and reached zero by about 1964-66. In 1960, the participation rate of children aged ten to twelve was still about 22 per cent, but by 1974, it had fallen to about 10 per cent. During this period the share of overall workers in agriculture began to decline, probably driven by increased mechanisation, and made possible by the greater access to machines and technology which

47 See F.B. Soares for an analysis of the misallocation of resources within different agricultural sectors and other agricultural problems as the small average land ownership and low land use for grazing. Soares, "A agricultura".

48 Williams, *Child Workers in Portugal*, p. 9.

49 Activity rate was calculated using the reported age at which an individual started working and assuming that the child continued to work until he/she was 16. The chosen threshold ages correspond to the age at which children should be in different school levels.

accompanied the new policy environment. The reduction was accompanied by a decline in the participation rate of ten to twelve year old children. In addition, increases in the minimum years of compulsory schooling (six years in 1964) and increases in the minimum working age laws (fourteen years in 1969) probably provided additional impetus to reduce the labour contribution of children in this age group ten to twelve.

Figure 13.1. Child Labour Incidence Rate

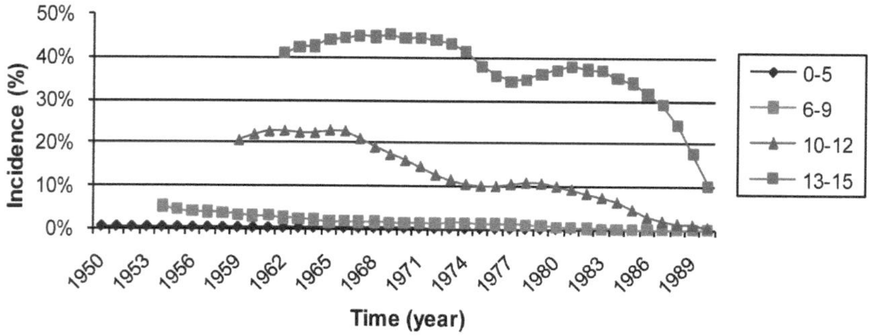

Source: GIASE, Education Ministry.

In contrast, however, for youngsters in the age group thirteen to fifteen, the increasing labour force participation of the 1950's continued well into the 1960's, to around 43-46 per cent in the period 1965 to 1973. Several factors are likely to have caused this increase. First, while increasing compulsory schooling and raising the minimum working age are likely to have reduced the participation rate of children aged ten to twelve, these policies may have led to a corresponding increase in labour participation of thirteen to fifteen year old children. Second, the availability of official secondary schools' only in district capitals may have prolonged the labour contribution of thirteen to fifteen year olds. Third, labour shortages due to emigration and army conscription to fight colonial wars (from 1962 onwards) are likely to have raised demand for children in this age group. While young men were drafted and sent to fight colonial wars in Africa, migrant workers contributed to the post-war European boom and children were forced into the Portuguese labour market.

The Post-Dictatorship Period

The end of the dictatorship led to political and economic changes. A trade agreement with the EEC signed in 1972[50] and a sliding devaluation experienced by the Portuguese currency from 1977[51] made Portuguese exports and subcontracting from European companies more attractive. Accordingly, the early years of the post-dictatorship were marked by a resurgence of specialisation in labour intensive and low-skilled sectors. For example, exports of products like textiles, clothes and shoes increased from 2.9 per cent in 1970-1980, to 7.3 per cent in 1980-1990. During 1988-1992, their 25 per cent share in exports was as large as the share of Port wine in the previous century.[52]

In 1986, after nine years of negotiations, Portugal joined the European Economic Community (EEC). The country received substantial flows of European funds which supported a restructuring of the economy (investment in machines, technology and training) and allowed increases in public expenditure.

During this period the importance attributed to education increased and in 1976 the educational budget finally surpassed the military budget. School conditions improved and accessibility at all levels of the education system was enhanced, while a school milk programme became a powerful weapon against absenteeism and hunger.[53] Compliance with EEC norms led to an increase in compulsory education from six to nine years of schooling in 1986.

Consistent with these educational requirements, currently, minors are only allowed to work under three conditions – at least sixteen years old, completion of nine years of schooling and a medical confirmation of their physical and psychological capabilities for that job. There are some exceptions: at fourteen and fifteen "light work" is allowed, some additional activities are permitted when the child is sixteen and seventeen years old and at eighteen all types of work are allowed.

The sharp increase in educational attainment due to these changes is evident in figure 13.2. In spite of the progress, however, Portugal still lags behind most of its European counterparts. For instance, while at 47 per

50 Lains, "Catching-up to the European core", p. 380.

51 Aguiar and Martins, "A indústria", p. 220. See also Afonso and Aguiar, "A internacionalização da economia".

52 Silva, *A pobreza infantil em Portugal*, p. 17.

53 Silva, *A pobreza infantil em Portugal*, p. 17.

cent the school completion rate for youth aged twenty to twenty-four is higher than the previous generations, it is still quite low compared to the EU average (75 per cent). The level of early school leavers aged eighteen to twenty-four with less than upper secondary education is 41.1 per cent in Portugal. This is much higher than the EU average of 18.1 per cent.

Figure 13.2. Real School Enrolment 1977-2005

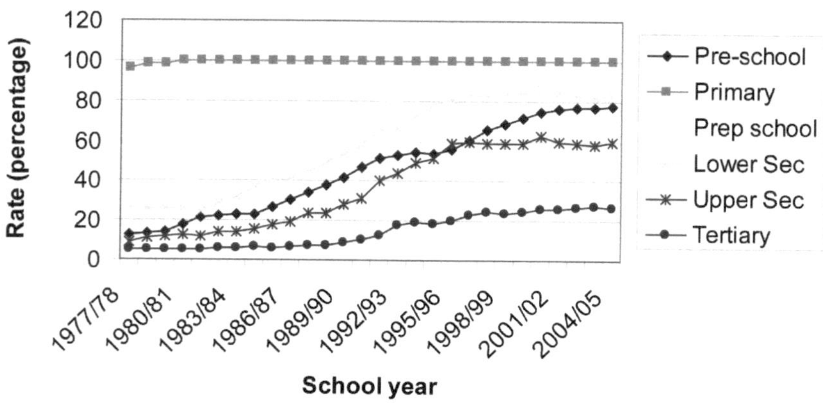

Source: GIASE, Education Ministry.
Note: Pre-school, three years prior to official schooling (3-5 years old); primary school, the first four schooling years (6-9 years old); preparatory school, the fifth and sixth grade (10-11 years old); lower secondary, the seventh to ninth grade (12-14 years old); upper secondary, the tenth to twefth grade (15-17 years old); tertiary education (18 and above).

Continuing with the analysis of figure 13.1, we see that the labour participation rate of children in the age group ten to twelve, which had begun to decline in 1965-1966, maintains a downward trend. By 1986, the year of EEC accession, the labour force participation of this age group was almost negligible. In contrast, between 1977 and 1981, the participation rate of children in the age group thirteen to fifteen increased from 35 to 40 per cent. As mentioned above, this increase is consistent with the increase in demand for Portugal's traditional labour intensive products and child labour demanding industries (textiles, clothes and shoes).[54]

54 Eaton and Pereira da Silva, "Portuguese Child Labour", p. 331.

While demand for child labour increased during this period, supply factors also played a role. Silva[55] suggests that the second oil crisis and the government's restructuring policies, which were coordinated with the IMF, increased child poverty and labour around 1980. The share of social expenditures that had more than tripled since 1974, and had its peak in 1979, declined thereafter until 1982. Even the school milk scheme was considerably reduced. However, after this interruption, child labour fell sharply. This trend is most likely to have been driven by EEC accession. The extension of compulsory schooling from six to nine years is likely to have prompted a decline in child labour. At the same time increasing returns to education probably provided a strong incentive to acquire education.[56] Maybe more importantly, during the 1980s and 1990s, closer contact with the international discourse brought a sharper consciousness about child labour into the country. Unions and catholic organisations highlighted and disparaged child labour. In marked contrast to the views expressed by parliamentarians in 1938, in 1989, the Portuguese President referred to child labour as a "true scourge".[57] The cascading effects of these changes in attitudes, and in the demand and supply factors, led to rapid decline in the labour force participation, to around eight to ten per cent in the thirteen to fifteen age group by 1991 (see figure 13.1). Based on a narrower concept of work that includes only children working for an employer, we obtain employment rates of about three per cent in 1992 and 1.5 per cent in 1993 for children aged twelve to fifteen.[58]

Notwithstanding the sharp declines in child labour since 1986 and the low employment rates reported in 1992 and 1993, several reports in the popular press continued to highlight the plight of working children. A 1992 report by Anti-Slavery International estimated that there were 200,000 working children in Portugal employed mainly in the export-oriented shoe, garment, ceramics and stone-breaking industries in the Northern districts of Oporto and Braga.[59] Under increasing national and international scrutiny the government undertook several measures, including increased labour inspections and the collection of information to place the child labour debate on an informed footing. In co-operation with the ILO, two household surveys especially designed to gather information on work-

55 Silva, *A pobreza infantil em Portugal*, pp. 45, 48.
56 Santos, "Education and Earnings Differentials"; Pereira and Martins, "Portugal".
57 Williams, *Child Workers in Portugal*, p. 3.
58 Extrapolated from Roque Antunes, *Algumas características da população jovem*, p. 96.
59 Williams, *Child Workers in Portugal*, p. 18.

ing children were conducted in 1998 and 2001. Based on these household surveys, table 13.3 provides the most recent figures on child labour in Portugal. For both years, about four per cent or between 43,000 and 49,000 children in the age group six to fifteen were involved in some form of economic work.[60]

Table 13.3. Incidence of Child Work in Portugal (% and absolute number of working children)

	1998	*2001*
Age group[a]		
6 to 12 years old	2.2 (14,656)	2.6 (20,258)
13 to 15 years old	7.0 (28,421)	6.9 (28,655)
(12 to 15 years old)	6.3 (32,432)	6.3 (34,480)
Type of boss[b]		
Working for a family member	2.9 (31,590)	3.3 (39,508)
Working for another person	1.1 (11,487)	0.8 (9,626)
Total	4.0 (43,077)	4.1 (49,134)

a Incidence is defined as the percentage of children in the respective age group who report working at least one hour per week.
b Refers to the 6 to 15 age group. Work refers to paid or unpaid activities performed on the family farm/enterprise or for an employer. Estimates of the absolute number of working children are based on weighting the sample data to obtain population figures.

The table also provides figures on the incidence of work for different age groups. While these figures are not directly comparable with the figures for 1992-1993, they show that between 1992 and 1998, the number of children working for an employer declined and that in 1998 and 2001 most working children worked for family members. It is of course possible that through subcontracting or even sub-subcontracting, part of the illegal labour may have been transferred from factories to families.[61] This substi-

60 In 2001, the average economically active child in Portugal was male, between 12 and 13 years old and worked 14 hours per week. For more details on present child labour see: Chagas Lopes and Goulart, *Educação e trabalho infantil*; and Goulart and Bedi, "Child Labour and Educational Success".

61 For example, in 2006 the weekly newspaper *Expresso* reported children sewing shoes for Zara, a Spanish multinational. Eaton, "Child Labor in Portuguese Textiles".

tution pattern is consistent with the information available in table 13.3 and with figures obtained from the labour inspectorate. Between 1996 and 2000 labour inspections of firms increased and after an initial increase in the number of working children detected in these companies, there has been a rapid decline. Since the labour inspectorate confines its visits to firms, the increased scrutiny may have prompted the transfer of work to households.[62]

Table 13.4. Working Children According to Parents' Labour Status when Children (%)

Type of labour	*Father child labourer*		*Mother child labourer*	
	Yes	*No*	*Yes*	*No*
Domestic	5.3	3.7	6.8	3.8
Economic	7.4	2.8	8.6	3.1
Both	0.7	0.4	1.3	0.3
Total	13.4	6.9	16.7	7.2

Source: Own calculations based on DETEFP/SIETI 2001 Survey.

While the main story during this period is the rapid decline since mid-1980's, the latest available data inform us that there are still about 40,000 working children. Thus, despite economic growth, child labour continues to persist in some areas of the country. As late as 2001, the incidence of child labour in the Southern areas of the country (Lisbon, Alentejo, Algarve) was around 2.8 per cent or less, while in the North and the Centre, it was still as high as 4.8 and 5.8 per cent, respectively. These are areas of small farms and small firms which have proved difficult to modernize, psychically and physically.[63] Sarmento *et al.*[64] suggest that in these areas the opportunities for subcontracting are merely an extension of small-land ownership, often in the surroundings where the urban and the rural meet. Within certain families in these regions work is considered natural and there are strong intergenerational patterns.[65] Children of former child workers are at least three times more likely to work compared to children

62 Source: Labour Inspectorate.

63 In the North, the traditional sector prevails under different forms and the informal economy has more weight. Technology is low and production units (farms, industries or other companies) have often failed to upgrade the process and the product. The population is also more dispersed which makes enforcement difficult. In contrast, in the South the population is more concentrated in villages and towns.

64 Sarmento, Bandeira and Dores, *Trabalho domiciliário infantil*.

65 IAC/CNASTI, *O Trabalho Infantil*, p. 43.

whose parents did not work (see table 13.4). As recently as 2001, at a conference *against* child labour, Barroso, a representative of CAP, the farmers' association connected mostly to large and medium land owners, said that working would "avoid the [children] wandering having nothing to do, or better spending the money they don't have, gaining addictions, some of them very serious, [...] on which the State spends millions in prevention (that prevents few or none) and in treatment (with very doubtful results)".[66]

Synthesis and Discussion

Looking back over the course of the last 150 years there are several points about the Portuguese experience with child labour that should be highlighted. As the data presented in the paper shows there has been a decline in the incidence of overall child labour since 1850. However, this decline was by no means monotonic and should not be viewed as an inevitable outcome of economic growth. There were periods after 1850 where child participation in the labour market increased and periods where it declined. As summarized in table 13.5, although compulsory schooling laws and minimum working age laws were passed in 1891, between 1891 and 1950 the involvement of children in the labour force continued unabated. It was only in the 1950s and 1960s, after a long period of limited economic growth (see table 13.1) and the desire to modernize and industrialize the economy that the demand for child labour began to subside (see table 13.5). At the same time the need for more educated workers to support industrialization prompted additional educational expenditure, and led to increases in minimum years of schooling in 1956, 1960 and 1964, and increases in the minimum working age to fourteen. After an increase in labour force participation among thirteen to fifteen year olds in the 1970s, the involvement of children in the labour force has displayed a sharp, perhaps permanent decline since 1986.

As a recently developed country, Portugal offers some lessons for developing countries facing child labour. Setting the changes in patterns of child labour between 1850 and the present against the backdrop of the structure of economic growth, educational legislation and quality, labour legislation and the prevailing norms and attitudes towards working children, shows that child labour is amenable to policy. However, the patterns also suggest

66 Barroso, "O papel dos parceiros sociais e da sociedade civil", p. 239.

that, similar to other social issues, no single legislation or policy is likely to be effective unless the various pieces come together.

Table 13.5. A Summary of Laws, Economic Changes and Child Labour Force Participation

Period	*Compulsory schooling in years*	*Minimum working age in years*	*Employment in agriculture (%)*	*Employment in industry (%)*	*Labour Force Participation Rate*	
					10-12	*13-15*
1890s	5	1891:12	60.7	17.7	–	–
1900s	5	12	61.4	18.5	–	–
1910s	1911:3	12	56.7	21.5	–	–
	1919:5	12				
1920s	1929:3	12				
1930s	3	12	49.2	18.6	–	–
1940s	3	12	51.3	20.4	43.9‡	72.8†
1950s	1956:4 (boys)	12	47.6	23.7	59.3‡	77†
1960s	1960:4 (girls)	12	42.2	28.1	22.0	37.4
	1964:6	1969:14				
1970s	6	14	31.6	33.0	16.0	44.6
1980s	1986:9	14	18.3	38.5	10.1	37.2
1990s	9	1991:16	10.1	37.5	0.4	10.4

Notes The child labour force participation rate for 1940 and 1950 are for the age groups 10–14 (‡) and 15–19 (†).

As the post-1986 Portuguese experience shows, when the various pieces are in sync, the pace of reduction in the incidence of child labour may be viewed as nothing short of astounding. The cascading effects of changing norms – which in turn may have been driven by national and international pressure and the need to be seen as a modern European nation as well as the needs of the country's economy – changes in the economic structure which demanded a more educated workforce, changes in educational and labour legislation which promoted education and increases in educational quality coupled with labour inspections all contributed to the rapid reduction in child labour.

While it is difficult to discern a clear policy sequence from the Portuguese story, our interpretation of the pattern of change in child labour set against the various other economic and social changes suggests that the long-run evolution of child labour is determined mainly by the needs of the economic structure of the country and the consequent pattern of labour demand. While the passage of minimum working age laws, compulsory schooling laws and monitoring efforts do provide additional impetus, they are unlikely to be implemented and to yield sustained reductions in child labour in economies that continue to rely on low-skill and low-wage labour to generate economic value.

CHAPTER 14

Child Labour and Industry in the Netherlands, 1600–1910

Cor Smit

In 1874, when industrialization in the Netherlands was just taking off, the Van Houten Act banned the employment of children younger than twelve years of age. Although some pockets of more modern industry were present, the country was still predominantly agricultural, with trade, finance and the colonies as important additional sources of wealth and modest economic growth. By the end of the nineteenth century, when industry had grown considerably and was entering a new phase of modernization, new legislation was introduced concerning the labour of women and children (1889), as well as compulsory schooling (1901).

The question that will be treated here is how industrial child labour actually developed in the transition from a pre-industrial society to industrial capitalism. Can we find any relationship between the growth and decline of child labour and modernization of industry? Modernization refers to the introduction of capitalist wage relations, the concentration of labour, and the introduction of new technology and non-human power sources, such as steam engines. Child labour in this paper will be restricted to market orientated production performed by boys and girls younger than sixteen years. Two important sectors where child labour occurred on a large scale will be ignored in this study: agriculture and household services. Both were explicitly excluded from the 1874 child labour act.

The article will trace the long term development of industrial child labour in the Netherlands from the seventeenth to the beginning of the twentieth century and will try to find the relation with modernization, with changing attitudes and the effects of legislation. The general historical account of child labour in the Netherlands will be illustrated on the basis of the textile industry, particularly in Leiden.

Child Labour and Industrialization

There are different views on the relationship between the modernization of industry and the use of child labour, and even more opinions on the reasons for its decline. Many modern historians have stressed that mass child labour was mainly a thing of the early stages of industrialization. According to Fyfe, industrial capitalism is associated with a long term decline in child employment.[1] According to Nardinelli, demand was declining because of technological change, the disappearance of the special situation of (rural) isolation and labour-shortage associated with early industrialization and, most notably, because the supply of child labour was declining due to rising incomes.[2] More recently Rahikainen has argued that the decline of child labour was caused neither by restrictions on labour nor by compulsory education. It was rather "better managerial competencies and keener monitoring of profitability and productivity" that produced this decline; productivity proved more important than cheap labour, as industrialists found out during the depression of the 1870s en 1880s.[3]

The mitigating effects of the modernization of production techniques have been highlighted by Dutch historians as well, most notably by Brugmans and Vleggeert. They have argued that, unlike in early industrializing countries such as England and Belgium, where child labour and exploitation grew in the early stages of industrialization, the worst forms of exploitation in the Netherlands disappeared when steam-powered machinery was introduced, implying that child labour had more to do with the old, pre-industrial production techniques.[4]

Proto-Industry and Early Capitalism

Traditionally, the prosperity of Holland in the seventeenth century has been attributed to the country's commercial activities. The importance of agriculture and industry has been somewhat overlooked. In fact industry (e.g. textiles, ship building, pipe making) was growing fast. By the mid-

1 Fyfe, *Child labour*, p. 4.
2 Nardinelli, *Child Labor and the Industrial Revolution*, pp. 111-122.
3 Rahikainen, *Centuries of Child Labour*, p. 156.
4 Brugmans, *Arbeidende klasse in Nederland*, pp. 92-108; Vleggeert, *Kinderarbeid in Nederland*, p. 56. See also de Jong, *Industrialisatie in Nederland*, p. 106; and Schenkeveld, *Kinderwetje*, pp. 27-34, 75-76.

dle of the seventeenth century, the town of Leiden was the most important centre of production of woollen fabrics in Europe, exporting all over Europe, the Levant and the Far East. Export industries required large numbers of cheap labourers and in Leiden and many other Dutch towns children were recruited to supply this demand. Thousands of children could be found in towns all over the Dutch Republic, working in textiles, button making, pin making, and so on.[5]

Manufacturers could make deals with orphanages to hire orphans. Orphanages from other towns would send their pupils to Leiden or Amsterdam to get work and learn a trade. In general these deals involved some arrangements concerning training and payment. Hundreds of orphans were 'imported' by Leiden from places as far away as Aachen and Liège.[6] Many other, usually poor children, were also employed, not only in Leiden. Exact numbers are hard to obtain, and it has not been possible to compute the relative importance of child labour for the branches of industry they worked in. In the case of Leiden for instance, we only have records of apprentices in the *laken* (cloth) industry, one of the seven different branches of wool production in this town. This branch of textiles alone took in about 330 apprentices a year in the period of 1639 to 1659, when the Leiden wool industry reached its zenith. Certainly, not all children actually working in this branch, were recorded. About seventy per cent of these children – most of them boys – were hired for spinning.[7]

Labour relations in most towns, especially in the Leiden textiles and other large scale industries, can be characterized as early-capitalistic. The cottage economy associated with pre-industrial production, in which the family worked as one unit, had gradually given way to wage labour, which was dominant in the Leiden wool industry.[8] Although work also continued to be carried out in the homes of the workers, there was a growing number of (small) workshops owned by the *fabriqueurs*. Many children may have been engaged in helping their father or mother working at home or in a workshop, but most of them seem to have been wage earners, employed directly.

5 Van Nederveen Meerkerk, "Child Labor in the Netherlands", p. 626.

6 Vleggeert, *Kinderarbeid in Nederland*, p. 10.

7 Van Nederveen Meerkerk, *Draad in eigen handen*, pp. 132-141. Computation of average by Cor Smit, based on table 4.6, p. 135. Children were taken in as an apprentice for a period of two or three years, but probably most of them kept on spinning much longer, p. 134.

8 See Kloek, *Wie hij zij, man of wijf*; Smit, "Arbeidersvrouwen", pp. 130-134.

The municipal authorities apparently felt uneasy about the exploitation of the children. Regulations were issued to maintain the formative character of the apprenticeship period. The manufacturers were told that children – boys and girls – should have the opportunity to learn to read and write and sometimes maximum working hours were set. When it turned out children were made to work exceedingly hard, often being beaten in the process, the Leiden municipality tried to counter this by employing supervisors to verify that children could go to school, had a reasonable payment and were not mistreated by their employers.[9]

Whereas the local authorities tried to uphold apprenticeship, most children in the new early capitalist proto-industry were primarily used as cheap labourers. Real apprenticeship was the practice in the more traditional crafts, but started at a later age (twelve to fourteen) and only a few children of the lower classes could gain access to this.[10]

Dealing with Crisis and Pauperism

After the bounty of the golden seventeenth century, the Dutch Republic in the eighteenth century fell into a deep economic crisis. Industry, especially the export industry, was hit hard. In the old industrial towns of Holland, formerly the most prosperous part of the Republic, unemployment and poverty were rampant.

The Leiden *fabriqueurs* tried to secure their businesses by putting out work to the cheap labour districts of the Netherlands, especially in the rural South-East of Brabant. Some of them moved their complete companies, but many transferred only the labour intensive parts of production (like spinning) and kept the profitable finishing activities (that involved specialised craftsmen) in Leiden.[11] In this way the Brabant wool industry (especially in Tilburg) started as a kind of annex of the Holland industry (especially that of Leiden). In the nineteenth century Tilburg would surpass Leiden as the most important wool production centre of the Netherlands. The Brabant

9 However, it is not clear how effective these measures were. See Vleggeert, *Kinderarbeid in Nederland*, pp. 10-14; see also van Nederveen Meerkerk and Schmidt, "Tussen arbeid en beroep".

10 Van Nederveen Meerkerk and Schmidt, "Tussen arbeid en beroep", pp. 46-50.

11 The reason for this move was that wages in the rural East and South were about thirty per cent lower than in the towns of coastal Holland. See Smit, *Ondernemers en geleerden*, p. 59.

textile industry was rural, not urban. Labour was predominantly recruited from the small farmers. The household, including the children, still functioned as the unit of production. Children constituted about 16 per cent of the labour population.[12] Industrial child labour moved from the towns of the West to the rural areas outside Holland, to the cottage-industry of Tilburg and Helmond and to places like Veenendaal and Amersfoort in the province of Utrecht.

In the second half of the eighteenth century, unemployment in the towns of Holland led to deep poverty and to the disintegration of working class family life. The call for education became stronger and was related to the need for re-establishing the moral and social order. Universal education was deemed to help to counter poverty, to strengthen civil life and morality and ultimately to benefit the industry.[13] During the Batavian Republic and the French domination (1795-1813), the national reform of education (1806) had as a side-effect that it led to the emergence of a group of professional teachers, who in the later decades would keep on stressing that education was important to all children.

However, the virtue of work continued to be stressed. Paupers (and their children) were put to work instead of simply giving them poor relief. This policy, at first related to beggars, started at the end of the sixteenth century, creating the first workhouses. In the eighteenth century the number of both state controlled and private work institutions grew. While in the seventeenth century protection and maintaining the standards of the apprenticeship institution were important aspects of policy regarding child labour, now child labour as such became ideologically sanctified as beneficial for the working classes. Attention to protection was lost. Factories which claimed they provided some education to the children they employed, were uncritically praised.[14] This dominant line of thought on child labour would continue into the 1840s. The importance of such work institutions, however, should not be exaggerated. For instance, the private Poor Factory in Leiden around 1800 employed only a few dozen children,

12 De Jong, "Enige sociale aspecten van de arbeid", pp. 168-171.

13 See Damsma, *Familieband*, pp. 80-110.

14 Vleggeert, *Kinderarbeid in Nederland*, pp. 1-3 and pp. 16-25; Schenkeveld, *Kinderwetje*, pp. 12-13.

only a small portion of the thousands of children from the households that depended on poor relief.[15]

The importance of providing employment to fight the disruption caused by pauperism is also seen in the industrial policy in the first decades of the nineteenth century. King William I had established the *Nederlandsche Handel-Maatschappij* (Dutch Trading Company, NHM) to stimulate the lingering industry. The NHM placed orders in the old industrial centres of Holland (Haarlem, Leiden), especially with cotton factories that had been moved from the rebellious south of the Kingdom, where Belgium had declared its independence in 1830s.[16] The emphasis in NHM policy, however, was on providing work to as many people as possible. As a consequence, once modern and mechanized factories shifted back to manual work, their steam engines rusting away.[17] In the two Leiden cotton factories in 1841, both depending on NHM orders, only the minority of workers were adults and 38.5 per cent was younger than thirteen years, of which most were girls.[18]

The NHM also played an important role in turning Twente (Overijssel, near the German border) into the dominating area of cotton industry in the Netherlands. Since the creation of employment was an important objective and the low wages made it attractive to compete without introducing steam powered machinery, manual work remained predominant into the 1840s and 1850s. Several thousands of children, about one third of all workers involved, worked in these *manufacturen* (and probably at home, too).[19] The NHM-based industry- and employment policy was creating a new proto-industry with considerable child labour.

15 "Journaal der Reize van den agent van nationale oeconomie der Bataafsche Republiek (Ao 1800)" *Tijdschrift voor Staathuishoudkunde en Statistiek,* 19 (1860), p. 137. This Poor Factory did not last long.

16 In 1815 the former Dutch Republic had been united with the former Austrian Southern Netherlands into one Kingdom. In 1830-1839 the South separated itself from the North, creating the independent state of Belgium.

17 See Schoevaars and Lubben, "Ondernemen in gebondenheid en vrijheid". This unpublished paper (masters, university of Utrecht, 1987) can be found in the Regional Archives of Leiden (hereafter RAL).

18 Report by city council, 28 september 1841. RAL, Stadsarchief 1816-1929, inv. nr. 378, Missivenboek 3L, app. 477.

19 Fischer, *Fabriquers en fabrikanten*, pp. 59-77.

Industrialization and Child Labour

Before the 1850s, industrialization in the Netherlands was very limited. By 1836 only 72 steam engines were in use, steamships included, and by 1853 there still were only 364 industrially used steam engines.[20] Because of many different reasons it was hard for industrialization to take off in the Netherlands. In many industries it was even economically inefficient to introduce full-scale mechanization until the 1860s.[21] However, Amsterdam and Rotterdam had some important metal industries (machinery, shipbuilding). Maastricht (Limburg) had metal and earthenware factories after the 1830s. By 1850 the majority of workers (both wool and cotton) in the Leiden textile industry were working in steam powered factories and by 1860 outwork, including weaving, had disappeared completely. In Tilburg and Twente the first steam factories also appeared in the 1820s and 1830s, but here cottage-industry (Tilburg) and manual work concentrated in *manufacturen* (Twente) were still dominant in the 1850s and 1860s.

In the 1860s the first phase of industrialization started. In this phase, especially the production of consumer goods, including textiles, was modernized. By 1880, the Twente cotton industry was thoroughly modernized and mechanized. In Tilburg the pace of industrialization accelerated, though cottage-industry would still be of importance even in the beginning of the twentieth century, especially in weaving. Overall, in the period 1895-1914 the Netherlands witnessed a second phase of modernization, broadening the industrial structure and characterized by a growth of the metal and chemical industries. The changes are clearly reflected in the occupational structure. While agriculture was the largest sector of employment in 1849, by 1899 it was surpassed by industry, which by then employed over one third of the registered professional population (agriculture just under thirty per cent).[22]

When comparing the censuses of 1849 and 1899, it turns out that child labour in general (including in agriculture, household services, trade, etc.) in the Netherlands had declined. But the decrease was not very signifi-

20 De Jonge, *Industrialisatie*, p. 27.

21 Smits, "Economische ontwikkeling", p. 18. For more elaborate accounts on Dutch industrialization: De Jonge, *Industrialisatie*; and van Zanden and van Riel, *Nederland 1780-1914*.

22 All censuses on CD ROM, CBS/NIWI, *Publicaties Volkstellingen 1795- 1971* (1999); database containing census of 1899 also on separate CD ROM, CBS/NIWI, *Data en publicatie Volkstelling 1899* (1999). Censuses also to be found on http://www.volkstellingen.nl/nl/.

cant. In 1849, about seven per cent of all children under sixteen were registered in one occupation or the other. By 1899 this had decreased slightly to around six per cent. Whereas registered child labour of children under twelve had dropped dramatically (from 15.6 per cent to 1.5 per cent of working children), the incidence of children of twelve to sixteen years who worked, had grown considerably. In 1899 almost 16 per cent of all children of twelve and thirteen years had a (registered) job and over 40 per cent of the Dutch fourteen and fifteen years-olds. Legislation cannot fully explain the disappearance of the labour of under-12-year-olds, because its effects were limited to industry and crafts. Access to school, rising living standards, changing attitudes and demographic changes must have had their effects too.[23]

Contrary to this general decline, child labour in industry had increased. In 1849 children under sixteen years constituted about 5.9 per cent of the industrial labour force. By 1899 it has grown significantly to 8.8 per cent. About one third of these belonged to the twelve to thirteen year old category. The majority of the twelve and thirteen year olds who worked, were actually employed by industry (53.3 per cent), the older children to a lesser degree (46.3 per cent). Again the number of under twelves had fallen, both absolutely and relatively. Here we can expect the influence of the legislation, especially since 1889, when the Labour Act provided for an enforcement agency, the Labour Inspectorate.

The census figures have to be used with some reservation. They only registered what people considered to be an occupation. In general, labour of children and women is underestimated, especially when it was done at home or had a seasonal or out-of-school character. But both proto-industrial and industrial child labour appear to be underestimated and the 1849 census left out less child labour than many of the later ones.[24] Bearing these caveats in mind, the overall conclusion remains that industrial child labour

23 Van Nederveen Meerkerk, "Child Labor in the Netherlands", p. 627.

24 See van Zanden, *Economische ontwikkeling van de Nederlandse landbouw*, p. 76. Research in Leiden and Tilburg shows even factory child labour is underestimated in the 1899 census. In Leiden the number of labour cards in use by children and women (reported in the *Gemeenteverslag*, the Leiden council report, 1899) was seventeen per cent higher than the numbers of these groups according to the census, most of the difference caused by under 16 year old girls. According to G.F.A. de Jong in 1899 1643 boys and 421 girls were employed in Tilburg industry: de Jong, "Enige sociale aspecten", pp. 194-196. The occupational census of the same year only gives 860 boys and 169 girls. The 1859 census proves to be the most unreliable on children and women labour.

had increased with industrialization. On the other hand, child labour in the under twelve category disappeared almost completely.

To get more insight in what was happening and to be able to say more about the relationship between child labour and industrial modernization, it will be necessary to look deeper into its branches and different localities. Research into the Leiden textile mills has produced a meaningful series of figures relating to child labour from the 1840s into the 1910s. These will be presented below. Also, we will try to get a closer look on what was happening during the second phase of modernization. But first, we shall present an overview of the legislation on child labour and the reform movement behind it.

The Road to Legislation

In the 1830s, the first critical notes on child labour were heard. Some local authorities (most prominently from Twente), teachers, Roman Catholic priests and academics expressed their concerns. They worried about education, morality – boys and girls were working together and shared the same public space – and about the quality of future working class housewives. They pointed to England, where unbridled industrialization had led to great abuses. In response, the Dutch government started an investigation in 1840/1841, in answer to which some regional governors advised them to introduce the 1839 Prussian legislation. But nothing in that direction actually happened. When in 1848 the Dutch monarchy was reformed, the orthodox Liberal position on the role of state institutions prevailed too. Social legislation was out of the question.

In the 1850s concerns about child labour were expressed again with even more vehemence. Schoolteachers were among the first to raise the alarm. Conservative philanthropists were worried too, because of falling school attendance rates, morality and the physical condition of the nation. Professional physicians, most importantly S. Sr. Coronel, started to point at the effects of modern industry on health, especially that of women and children. In the end, even some industrialists started to question whether child labour was in the interest of industry in the long run; the Leiden manufacturer S. Le Poole was their main spokesman. Among the reformers were Liberals, Conservatives, orthodox-protestant Antirevolutionaries (Le Poole) and the catholic clergy. They found each other in a proposal to introduce the English part time system, not abolishing child labour altogether, but providing for six hours of work a day and six hours of school.

Education was important to all reformers, even when they differed much as to the content or how education should be organized. It was increasingly seen as the most important remedy against pauperism.

The government in 1861, responding to growing public pressure, decided to launch a second investigation. Again nothing was done with the results and recommendations. Public agitation mounted and various petitions by organizations of teachers, physicians, philanthropists and even industrialists were submitted. In 1863 the Liberal leader of government J.L. Thorbecke – one of the greatest statesmen of the Netherlands and responsible for the 1848 Dutch constitution, but unwilling to interfere with industry – had to install a special State Committee. Even though this was headed by A.A.C. de Vries Robbé, a fierce supporter of state intervention who had been in charge of the 1861 investigation, Thorbecke provided for a majority on the Committee of his own Liberal supporters, all of them originating from Leiden. The Committee submitted its report after six (!) years, the majority proposing compulsory education, only De Vries Robbé pleading for labour legislation. However, a parliamentary majority to compulsory education was impossible. Many Liberals and all Conservatives and Antirevolutionaries saw such legislation as an infringement on the authority of the father of the household. Antirevolutionaries and Roman Catholics also feared that compulsory education would lead to non-religious, state dominated schools. Again, legislation was abandoned.

At the same time, concerns were growing about the Social Question in general. Young Liberals were conferring with (Liberal) trade unionists, looking for ways to defuse the growing class tension. Child labour would be the first issue tackled. To growing numbers of Liberals, protective legislation for children (and women) was acceptable, because children (and women) were considered as weak partners who could not look after their own interests and, unlike male adult workers, needed state protection. In 1873 the young Liberal Samuel van Houten brought his own bill to parliament. This included a ban on all child labour under ten, a part time system for ten to twelve year olds and compulsory education to the age of thirteen.

Many reformers wanted to stretch protection to fifteen or even sixteen years. This included the liberal trade union, which organized the first big Dutch working class demonstration when the bill was discussed in parliament. But conservative members of parliament (also inside the Liberal movement), religious politicians, the agricultural lobby and many industrialists opposed the bill in parts or in its entirety. An overwhelming majority dismissed all legislation on compulsory education. Agriculture and household and personal services, which were said to be harmless and even salutary, were excluded from the provisions of the amputated bill, which was passed in 1874.

The law did not include any means of enforcement, leaving this to the local police. Moreover, the formulation of the law left room for different interpretations. No wonder that as early as 1876 the first proposals for a more elaborate law were formulated, but only in 1889, was a new Labour Law introduced.[25] This law confirmed the minimum age of twelve years for industrial work, but added protective measures regarding working hours and dangerous situations for children up to sixteen. Protection and restrictions were extended to working women. An enforcement agency was established, the *Arbeidsinspectie* (Labour Inspectorate). Children up to sixteen (and all women) also had to apply for labour cards before entering a job in industry. Compulsory education for a period of six years was introduced in 1901.

The Example of Leiden

Many diverse examples of exploitative child labour were highlighted during the 1830s to 1860s, ranging from the old fashioned industries to quite modern industries. One of the most famous cases was the rope-walks of Moordrecht, an industry which had hardly changed since the seventeenth century. Brick yards also involved much child labour as part of a family contract system. The modern earthenware factories of Regout in Maastricht were another famous example of exploitation and misery, as were the mechanized and steam powered textile factories of Leiden. In Tilburg, the Roman Catholic clergy prevented children younger than twelve being admitted to the factories, but they were very much involved in cottage-industry.[26] The modern sugar refineries also made ample use of child labour.

Dutch historians like Brugmans noted a rise of child labour between 1819 and 1871, before the take off of Dutch industrialization. At the same time they concluded that the introduction of steam power resulted in a sharp decline of child labour, especially of the youngest children, for example, during the industrialization of the textile mills in Twente in the 1860s to 1880s. Comparing the 1849 en 1859 censuses he concluded that the process

25 See Postma, *Mislukte pogingen*.

26 In the Dutch South, including Tilburg, most people were Roman Catholics, while in the North Calvinism was dominant.

of withdrawing the youngest children from the labour force had already started nationwide in the 1850s. However, especially the 1859 census omitted many women and children from its enumeration.[27] The case of the Leiden textile industry may shed some more light on what really happened.[28]

The old textile industry of Leiden had to deal with competition from the upcoming industries of Tilburg and Twente. The wage differences (in the late nineteenth century still about twenty per cent) made this difficult. In Leiden, as in other towns in the coastal areas of Holland, wages could not be lowered without causing starvation and hunger riots.[29] The solution was to be found in modernization. Already in the eighteenth century, Leiden entrepreneurs had sought to modernize production, introducing machines and horse and wind power. In 1816 the first steam engine was introduced. Especially in the 1830s, many steam engines were installed and new factories were built. By 1852, only 15 of the 77 wool processing firms used steam power, but they employed around three quarters of the labour force. Several types of Spinning Jenny were already in use in the early 1800s, self-actors were introduced in the 1850s at the latest. Mechanical looms were introduced from the 1830s onwards. Labour was concentrated in factory buildings. By 1860 outwork had disappeared almost completely from the textile industry. The period of 1830 to 1860 can be seen as the first phase of modernization of the Leiden textiles.

From 1860 to 1890 modernization continued, but at a somewhat slower pace. In the 1860s the last big and medium wool firms switched to steam power and the old-fashioned small companies disappeared altogether. In the early 1870s the specialized spinning factories, which had been established in the 1830s to 1850, closed down, and spinning was integrated in the wool factories.

During the 1880s the Leiden textile industry was hit by the international depression. This was followed by a new wave of modernization in the period 1890-1914; many new factories were built, new machinery (for

27 Other Dutch historians like Vleggeert and Schenkeveld are mainly relying on Brugmans. See Smit, "Fabriekskinderen". The problems with the 1859 census were observed for agriculture before, for instance de Jonge, *Industrialisatie*, pp. 9, 365; and van Zanden, *Economische ontwikkeling van de Nederlandse landbouw*, p. 76.

28 For an account of modernization of the Leiden textile industry up to the early 1860s, see Smit, "De asem van Beëlzebub". On child labour in Leiden textiles, see Smit, "Fabriekskinderen". New research was added and will be presented here.

29 Leiden wages were higher, but prices were too, because of local taxes. Moreover, Brabant and Twente workers often had a kitchen garden, a goat etc., which could be used for feeding the family.

instance ring-spin machines) was introduced, as well as new power sources (gas, electricity). At the same time, the number of employees rose again after the dismissals during the depression.

During the period 1854-1863, the exploitation of child labour in Leiden came under the public's gaze. Leiden was an example of the abuse of children. At the same time a number of Leiden philanthropists and industrialists made important contributions to the discussion on legislation, with prominent supporters (Le Poole) as well as opponents (Van Heukelom, Eigeman). Some opponents of legislation maintained that modern factories had no use for child labour, like Jan van Heukelom did in 1855; other opponents, like A.H. Eigeman (in 1863), emphasized children were better suited than adults to handle modern, steam powered machinery.[30]

Figure 14.1. Age at First Employment of Leiden Textile Factory Workers

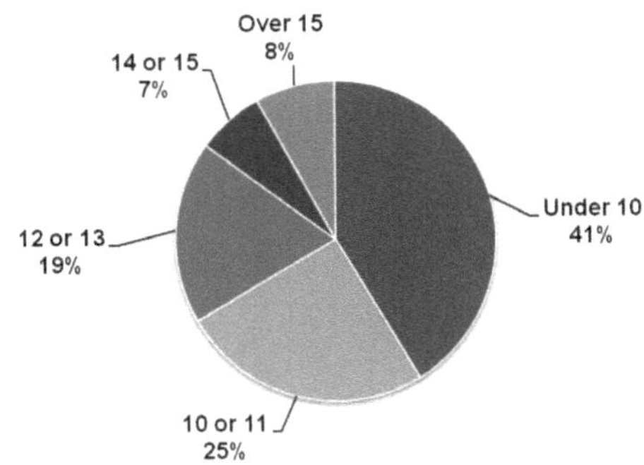

Source: *Rapport van de Staatscommissie betreffende de arbeid van kinderen in fabrieken* (Den Haag 1869) p. 749.

As a consequence of the discussions in and around Leiden, several surveys, trying to chart the volume and character of child labour, were undertaken in the years 1859-1864.[31] Of specific importance was the 1864 survey by the

30 The statement of Van Heukelom in 1855 was signed by two other industrialists, including the important camlet manufacturer C. Leembruggen, see Smit, "Actie of onderzoek", p. 55; Eigeman, "Philantropie en nijverheid", p. 5. This was originally published in a Leiden newspaper in 1863. Both Van Heukelom and Eigeman (chairman of the *Vereeniging van en voor Nederlandsche Industrieelen,* Association of Dutch Industrialists) owned a modern spinning factory.

31 The deaconries, religious organisations for poor relief, started an investigation in 1859. The findings were used by a committee of the *Nederlandsche Maatschappij tbv Nijverheid* (NMN) in 1860. These Leiden figures were used in the 1861 rapport by De Vries Robbé.

State Committee on Industrial Child Labour. The Committee asked 1644 workers in the wool and cotton industries (approximately three quarters of all textile workers) in which year they had started working and at what age. Much to the discomfort of the majority of the Committee, it turned out that about 41 per cent of them had been first employed below the age of ten and another 25 per cent at the age of ten or eleven (see figure 14.1). In the 1840s and 1850s approximately half of the new textile workers were children younger than ten years; about three quarters of the newly employed in those years had been younger than twelve years.

With these figures it is possible to estimate the age groups in the labour population. The younger age groups were increasing sharply from the middle of the 1840s, stabilizing in the 1850s, when 7 per cent of the work force was under ten, around 15 per cent was younger than twelve and over 25 per cent was under fourteen.[32]

Figure 14.2. Changes in Age at First Employment of Leiden Textile Factory Workers 1850-1864

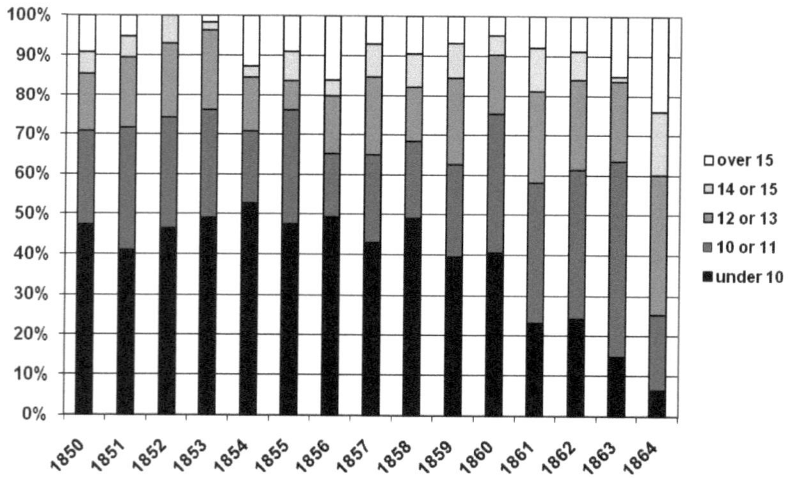

Source: *Rapport van de Staatscommissie betreffende de arbeid van kinderen in fabrieken* (Den Haag 1869), p. 783.

Also, the Leiden council collected information for his national survey. In 1863/1864 the physician Coronel investigated the Leiden wool industry. In 1864 the State Committee on Industrial Child Labour made its Leiden enquiries.

32 *Rapport van de Staatscommissie betreffende de arbeid van kinderen in fabrieken* (Den Haag 1869), pp. 747-749.

Table 14.1. Children and Women in the Leiden Textiles, Percentages of All Personnel, 1850s-1909

	1850s	*1864*	*1874*	*1890*	*1899*	*1909*
Under 12	ca. 16.5	4.5	7.3	0	0	0
Under 16	30-35	28.2	28.2	22.1	ca. 25.5	ca. 28.5
Women		40.1	40.2	42.2	ca. 50	ca. 53
Women + under 16		ca. 55	53.6	52.2	ca. 58	ca. 63

Source: 1850s: Report State Committee; 1864: State Committee and Coronel; 1874: municipal report and report Chamber of Commerce; 1890: H.W.E. Struve, A.A. Bekaar, *Nijverheidsstatistiek 1887-1889*, (n.p., z.d.), census and Chamber of Commerce; 1899 and 1909: census and municipal reports (labour cards).

While the age of first employment had been pretty steady in the 1850s, suddenly, from 1860 onwards, the numbers of newly recruited young workers sharply declined (see figure 14.2). By 1864 (the year the survey was done), the situation had changed perceptibly. Less than one per cent of the factory population was younger than ten years, 4.5 per cent was under twelve and 15.5 per cent under fourteen. The number of workers younger than sixteen years had declined from 30-35 per cent in the 1850s to 28 per cent in 1864 (see table 14.1).

These trends agree with the figures on school attendance. School attendance had declined in the 1850s, stabilized by 1860 and began to increase again after 1863. Something odd was going on in 1863; this was also indicated by Coronel, the well-known social physician and reformer, who was doing his own Leiden investigation at the same time. He noted that many children in the seven to twelve age category, whom he personally had observed in the factories in 1863, apparently had disappeared from the lists which the employers sent to him some months later.[33]

The increase of child labour in the 1840s and 1850s followed the modernization of the Leiden textile industry. But what happened in the early 1860s? Some have concluded there was "a trend" that entrepreneurs preferred to work with "somewhat more mature" workers in technically advanced textiles factories.[34] However, the important technological and managerial

33 Coronel, "Leidsche wolfabrieken", p. 1.
34 Schenkeveld, *Kinderwetje*, p. 34.

changes had already taken place in the earlier period and no trend is visible, only a sudden change. Since no significant changes in industrial structure occurred between the late 1850s and 1864, the sudden reduction in child labour must have been a reaction to specific circumstances. The most likely candidate in this respect is the public discussion about child labour itself.

The debates on child labour were worrying Leiden industrialists from the start. When Van Heukelom made his statement about the uselessness of children in factories in 1855, he did so, as chairman of the local branch of the *Vereeniging voor Fabrieks- en Handwerk Nijverheid* (Association for Factory and Handicraft Industry, VFHN), because his aim was to prevent public discussion. When in 1860 a Leiden committee of the *Nederlandsche Maatschappij ter bevordering van de Nijverheid* (Dutch Society for the Advancement of Industry, NMN) pleaded for legislation, the Leiden branch of the VFHN reacted by calling for calm and research, instead of any action, whatsoever.[35] The debate, and the focus on Leiden, was troubling the local industrialists.

When the Van Houten Law was implemented in 1874, the municipality made an inventory of all working children, which the law would apply to. The use of children under ten turned out to have decreased further, but the incidence of the under-twelve-year-olds had increased to 7 per cent, considerably more than in 1864, although not as high as in the 1850s (see table 14.1). The percentage of under-sixteens was exactly the same as in 1864. The employers may have decided to forego the labour force of the youngest children, but they still found it attractive to employ ten and eleven-year-olds, even when modernization had continued. Only legislation could put an end to this.

There apparently was no immediate mitigating effect of the introduction of steam power and modern equipment, at least not under conditions of competition with textile companies elsewhere, which could rely on lower adult wages. Raising productivity by mechanization etc. was one answer to this competition, but continuing to use the cheapest labour possible and available, child labour, was another option. The Leiden textile industrialists combined both options.

From 1874 onwards, factory work was forbidden to children below the age of twelve. It is not clear whether this provision was violated in Leiden

35 Contrary to the VFHN (*Vereeniging voor Fabrieks- en Handwerk Nijverheid*), most active members of the NMN were not industrialists, apart from B.F. Krantz, who was a member of the 1860 committee. Krantz changed position regarding legislation at the same time when he changed his political affiliations from the Conservative to the Liberal movement. Smit, "Actie of onderzoek", p. 90.

as much as it was in other places (probably not), but in any case, school attendance was steadily rising. The main problem was that many working class kids left school immediately after turning twelve.[36] By 1890, the incidence of children below the age of sixteen in the textile factories had dropped considerably, but it rose again quite rapidly at the end of the century. In 1909, the proportion of children under sixteen years in the workforce was even slightly higher than in the 1860s and 1870s (see table 14.1). At the same time there was a further feminization of the textile industry and by 1909 this industry for the first time counted more female factory workers than male. Almost all female textile workers were younger than 23 years: they left the job as soon as their first child was born. By then, twice as many girls as boys found a job in the textile factories. Most of the boys, who left school and went to work, were employed in small artisan workshops and in the building trade.[37]

School attendance fell again after 1895. The introduction of compulsory education in 1901 seemed to turn this trend but this proved to be largely temporary, at least till the First World War.

So again a rise in child labour – this time of children from twelve to sixteen years old – must be associated with a period of modernization of the Leiden textile industry. Child labour had decreased in the period before, a difficult one for some industries that brought along redundancies. To a high degree the reduction of child labour in Leiden during the crisis of the 1880s, can be explained by the recurrence of an old pattern in personnel management: in hard times the mass of unskilled workers (children and women) was fired, but not the schooled and skilled workers (mostly male). Employers did not want to reduce knowledge and experience of the workforce for when times would get better; you could hire and fire unskilled labour whenever you needed, without a problem.

Comparing Leiden, Twente and Tilburg

The pace and character of industrialization in Leiden was very different from Twente and Tilburg, the other two textile centres that would push Leiden to a secondary position. The effects on child labour were different as well.

36 Smit, "Leidse kinderen tussen fabriek en school", pp. 84-86.
37 Smit, "Arbeidersvrouwen", pp. 114-115.

When Twente started modernizing in the late 1850s, the *manufacturen* where manual work had dominated and child labour was abundant, started disappearing. The workers in the new factories were predominantly male, adult workers. Somewhat optimistically Brugmans described the work of the children as of secondary importance, 'doing errands'.[38] But, as Van Zanden and Van Riel have pointed out, to get the new factories productive, it was not enough to take all kind of measures to discipline the adult workers and keep them on the machines continuously. Children were needed to do all kinds of other jobs.[39] Despite the decline of the 1860s-1880s, child labour in Twente was of more importance in keeping the factories running than has been suggested.

The situation in Tilburg was different. Industrialization went ahead at a slower pace. Even many companies that had built a modern factory, kept on using the putting-out system for some time. In the late 1880s, there were still hundreds of hand-weavers working at their own homes. Mechanization in weaving got a major impulse only after the crisis of the 1880s.[40] Child labour at home must have been declining along, but at the same time the numbers of children working in the factories were rising, especially after 1894.[41] Unfortunately, it is impossible to make a balance of child labour in cottage and factory based industry at this moment, but evidently, at the end of the nineteenth century, with industrialization and modernization well on the way and entering its second phase, child labour in the textile mills of Tilburg was rising again.

Table 14.2. Child Labour (under sixteen) in Textile Industry, Percentage of the Workforce, 1889-1909

	1889	*1899*	*1909*
Netherlands	13,6%	15.7%	17.6%
Overijssel	17%	17.7%	28.7%
Noord Brabant	8.9%	9.6%	14.7%

Source: national censuses of 1889, 1899 and 1909.

38 Brugmans, *Arbeidende klasse*, p. 102.
39 Van Zanden en van Riel, *Nederland 1780-1914*, pp. 292-296.
40 Keune, "Industriële ontwikkeling", pp. 53-54.
41 De Jong, "Enige sociale aspecten", pp. 194-196.

This rise was not confined to Tilburg and, as we have seen, Leiden textile industries. Table 14.2 indicates that child labour in textiles in the Netherlands was rising between 1889 and 1909 rather than declining. In 1899 over 42 per cent of these children were younger than fourteen years, much higher than in industry in general.

Since specific figures for Tilburg or Twente cannot easily be inferred from the census reports, the provincial figures are used as approximations; Overijssel, including the Twente cotton industry, and Noord Brabant including Tilburg and other wool producing places in its vicinity, such as Helmond.[42] The trends are the same everywhere: an increase of children under sixteen years. Particularly striking is the rise in the incidence of child labour in Overijssel during this period, from almost 18 per cent to over 28 per cent of the work force, the same level as in Leiden in 1909. The child labour incidence in Brabant was very low, especially in 1889 and 1899, but these figures probably reflect the persistence of cottage-industry, where working children working were apparently not registered as such. On the other hand, the rise in the first decade of the twentieth century was impressive again. In both Overijssel and Brabant the importance of women working was growing too, but men still exceeded women by far, in Overijssel by two to one, in Brabant by four to one.

The conclusion apparently is that there was no decline in child labour in the wake of modernization in the Dutch textile industry and that cheap and unskilled labour of both children and (young) women was actually rising at the turn of the century. There had been an initial decline in the early stage of industrialization in Twente, but at a later stage, the incidence of child labour again approached the high proto-industrial levels. The Tilburg case is less clear, because it is hard to estimate the importance of children working in cottage-industry,[43] but in the Tilburg factories child labour was rising too.

When the Leiden industrialization started, child labour, even of very young children, was more widely accepted, praised as a contribution to fight poverty and even pressed on the working class by poor relief.[44] To

42 The development of the wool industry in these localities was very much the same as in Tilburg.

43 Besides sheer numbers it would be important to know more about the working hours. Did children in the cottage-industry work 12 to 13 hours a day, six days a week like the children did in the factories of Leiden, Twente and Tilburg or the *manufacturen* of Twente? Was it to some extent out-of-school work?

44 In 1840 Leiden manufacturers were looking for means to discipline the workers and agreed with the deaconries to oblige everyone on benefits to work in the factories,

Leiden industrialists improving productivity by mechanization and the extensive use of child labour were complementary and necessary strategies to face the competition by the low wages districts of Tilburg and Twente. Only when they were facing the consequences of changing attitudes, expressed in the debates of the 1850s and 1860s, did industrialists feel obliged to adjust their labour recruitment policies. But the option was for recruiting the slightly older children, from the age of twelve onwards, who had similar skills and equally low wages, and recruiting young women, another source of cheap, unskilled labour.

To explain this, we must realize modernization in the textile industry did not lead to an overall increase in necessary skills or requirements of higher education. The skills needed in spinning, weaving etc., were actually less than what they had been in pre-industrial days. Skilled labour to maintain the machines and supervise production involved only a minority of the personnel. Labour discipline, agility, and some elementary education, were all that was required of an average worker. The use of cheap, unskilled labour would always remain of great importance to this industry.[45]

Other Branches of Industry

So far we have concentrated on the textile industry; but what about other branches of industry? Children were used in other industries before industrialization really took off, particularly in the earth ware and brick making industries, sugar refineries and cigar making, as well as in all kinds of crafts. Though some figures are available for 1819 and 1871, it is not possible at this moment to make reliable series of estimates for the nineteenth century differentiating between branches or between crafts and more modern industry. Data that can be used to compare branches are available for the later period, the 1890s and the first decade of the twentieth century.[46] Table 14.3 gives an overview of child labour in all branches of industry.

including their children "any age whatsoever." RAL, Archief NMN, Notulen 1841, apps. 40, 50, 51, 57, 58, 59.

45 The lure of low wages countries in the 1970s meant the end of Dutch textile industry.

46 Some caution is necessary, because the 1889 census possibly underestimated the incidence of children more than the censuses of 1899 and 1909 did.

Table 14.3. Child Labour in Different Branches of Industry, Percentage of Workforce, 1889-1909

	1889	*1899*	*1909*	*Characterization*
Textiles	13.6%	15.7%	17.6%	Industrial
Paper	16.7%	16.9%	15.4%	From mixed to more industrial
Printing and publishing	17.3%	16%	14.3%	From mixed to more industrial
Metal (smiths, forges, foundries)	10%	12.7%	10.5%	From crafts to mixed
Leather	9.3%	8.2%	10.4%	Crafts dominating
Earth ware, bricks etc.	8.4%	9.1%	9.7%	Industrial
Applied art	8.4%	9.5%	8.7%	Crafts dominating
Food and luxuries (incl. cigars)	8.3%	9.2%	8.7%	Crafts dominating
Wood processing	8%	9.8%	8.4%	Crafts dominating
Clothing and cleaning	6.4%	7.2%	8%	Crafts dominating
Chemical industry	6%	7.7%	7.4%	Mixed
Shipyards, carriages	6.7%	8%	7.2%	Mixed
Instruments, tools, machinery	6.7%	7.9%	5%	From crafts to mixed
Building	4.2%	6.2%	4%	Crafts dominating
Mining, ore processing, peat	3.5%	4.2%	3.8%	Industrial
Diamond	16.9%	2.9%	2%	Industrial
Gas and electricity	0.7%	1.2%	0.4%	Industrial

Source: national censuses of 1889, 1899 and 1909.

The textile industry had the highest incidence of industrial child labour in 1909. But this was not so in 1889, when printing and publishing, paper producing and diamond cutting exceeded textiles. The first two mentioned still made extensive use of child labour in 1909. Both industries were characterized in 1889 by a mixture of crafts and industry and acquired a more industrial character in the following decades.

It is not clear whether the (relatively modest) decline in the graphic industry was related to modernization. The example of the important Leiden printing and publishing industry, suggests otherwise. Here, child labour rose from about 10 per cent in 1876 to 20 per cent in 1899 and to about 25 per cent in 1909.[47] Most children were actually working in modern factories such as that of Sijthoff, which was one of the most important publishers/printers of the Netherlands. Sijthoff was an advanced company, both in technology and market policy. Modernization here actually meant an increase in child labour, rather than a decline.

Regarding the (small) diamond industry in Amsterdam, which had already been industrialized in the 1840s,[48] it is not clear whether the sharp drop in child labour should be connected to technological changes or for instance to the fact that workers in this industry were highly organized in a modern socialist trade union, which opposed child labour.

In most branches child labour was higher in 1909 than it had been in 1889, but in most cases the differences are too small to make conclusions. In general, however, modernization does not appear to have brought about a decrease of child labour in its wake, while in some industries – textiles, leather, earthenware and bricks – child labour was even rising in the first decade of the twentieth century. At the same time it is interesting to observe that the branches that were dominated by the old crafts did not necessarily make more use of child labour than those dominated by modern factories.

While on average in 1899 about one third of the children employed were twelve or thirteen years old, three branches are notable for a much higher use of this age group. In paper production, textiles and the chemical industry the percentages of those younger children reached over 40 per cent. The diamond, and gas and electricity trades did not only use just a few children, about 85 per cent of them were fourteen or fifteen years old.

Differences within branches were quite significant. Smithies, forges and foundries, for example, scored quite high in terms of child labour. This industry was still dominated by crafts and made ample use of apprentices. This branch also included a large and modern crude iron producer and foundry like the Leiden *Grofsmederij*, which only had a child labour inci-

47 Based on RAL, *Gemeenteverslagen Leiden* (annual municipal reports) 1851-1914, annual reports of Chamber of Commerce and reports concerning the Labour Law, including use of labour cards; censuses of 1849, 1859, 1889, 1899 and 1909, local results. These sources are also used for all Leiden figures presented in this paragraph.

48 Brugmans, *Arbeidende klasse*, p. 50.

dence of 6 per cent, lower than the average, a percentage that had not changed since the 1860s. In the production of instruments and tools, child labour was of much less importance. This branch, however, also included the very modern light bulb industry, where a third of the labour force consisted of children and most of the other workers were young women.

In the very diverse food and luxury branch differences were large too. Though on average, they used the nationwide mean incidence of industrial child labour, this branch also contained industries that made extensive use of children, both old fashioned ones and modern. The cigar industry used many children, as in the past. This industry was not mechanized yet, but working for wages had remained dominant since long past and concentration of labour was ongoing. The food branch also included some new and modern industries like the biscuit and tin can factories. In the two Leiden biscuit factories, extensive use, up to 50 per cent, was made of young girls. In the expanding Leiden tin can industry (which had been set up in the 1870s), most personnel inside the factories were adults and almost no children worked there, but at the same time, outsourcing involved five hundred households that prepared the vegetables at home. In this way possibly thousand to two thousand young children were participating in out-of-school work.[49]

This short survey of the different branches of industry confirms the conclusion that modernization did not necessarily lead to a decrease in child labour. On the contrary, some modernized industries even involved large numbers of children.

Conclusion

Large scale child labour was characteristic for early modern industry in the Netherlands, notably in the export industry. Because of the prolonged depression of the eighteenth century, a large, impoverished proletariat was created, from which the factory children of nineteenth century Leiden were recruited.

In Leiden, the employment of young children increased substantially after the introduction of steam power and modern machinery. In the face of high adult wages industrialists tried to resist the competition from the low wages areas of Brabant and Twente by employing child labour and

49 This kind of work was not registered at all.

modernizing the production at the same time. The decline in the use of the youngest children in the early 1860s was most likely a response to changing attitudes and public opinion. In Twente and Brabant, textile proto-industries were organized quite differently, but in both cases child labour was extensive as well. Here, modernization from the 1860s onwards probably led to a decline in child labour in the textile industry at first. However, the incidence of child labour in the Dutch textile industry (including Tilburg and Twente) was rising again after the depression of the 1880s. Industrialization and further modernization did not lead to a decline of child labour in textiles, due to the continuing importance of cheap, unskilled labour.

Overall, although child labour seems to have been declining in the Netherlands during the age of industrialization, in industry itself, the incidence of child labour was on the increase. An overall relation between modernization and the incidence of child labour is hard to establish, but several modern industries made extensive use of children (and cheap labour in general), directly or indirectly.

It is clear, however, that industrial child labour under the age of twelve did disappear almost completely. The Van Houten Act of 1874, introduced at a time when industrialization in the Netherlands was just taking off, must have been an impediment for factory-owners to resort to the use of young children in the 1880s and 1890s, especially when enforcement was effected by the 1889 Labour Law. Thus, the character of industrial child labour changed, the youngest children disappearing from the labour force, but the number of children in the twelve to sixteen years category growing, at least to 1910.

The changing character of child labour cannot be explained sufficiently by looking for managerial strategies related to the modernization of production. Industrialization and modernization demanded a new approach for social policies, an urge not only felt by industrialists, but by the bourgeoisie in general. Fear for the dangers of pauperism, the threat of the poor (including their children) and of class war, the urge to discipline working class family life, all had their effects on the way child labour (and the child in general) was approached. Changing attitudes towards the usefulness of education by the working class, the gradual rising of incomes and the rise of the labour movement, must probably be taken into account as well.

CHAPTER 15

Industrial Capitalism and Child Labour in Sweden, 1800-1930

Lars Olsson

Introduction

At the industrial take-off in Sweden in the 1870s, child labour was intensively discussed both in parliament and in the public debate. In the liberal newspaper *Göteborgs Handels- och Sjöfartstidning* and in the poem "Den nya Grottesången" (1891), the poet and professor Victor Rydberg criticised the extreme exploitation of mankind through industrialism and worship of money by singling out industrial child labour in particular.[1] The poem and the public debate illustrate that in Sweden too, the factory system, as British historian Christopher Hill said, "shocked philanthropists by bringing it into the public view, and making brutally clear the dependence of the capitalist profit on such labour".[2]

In 1875, the Swedish parliament initiated a state investigation on industrial child labour – the first ever state investigation on industrial work in Sweden – and in 1881 a state decree was issued that regulated child labour much more distinctly than earlier regulations had done. No child was permitted to be employed for industrial work before the age of twelve, and children of the ages twelve and thirteen were permitted to work for six hours a day, while those who had passed their fourteenth birthday could be hired for ten hours a day. After the age of eighteen there were no limitations. The regulation also said that every child had to have fulfilled the minimum educational level of schooling. Local authorities were supposed to check that the regulations were observed, and offenders prosecuted.

1 "Grotte" was a magic mill that according the Icelandic mythology was owned by the Danish king Frode, whose wealth was based on slavery. The Grottesången was sung in protest by the slave workers. *Nationalencyklopedin*, 20 dl. (Höganäs, 1989-2000), VIII, p. 93.

2 Hill, *Reformation to Industrial Revolution*, p. 263.

Both employers and parents of children who worked in contravention of the regulation were to be fined.[3]

Table 15.1. All Workers and Child Labour in Selected Industries in Sweden in 1875

*Production**	*All workers*		*Children under 14*		*Child*
	Men	*Women*	*Boys*	*Girls*	*labour, %*
Glass	1,675	67	335	22	20.5
Matches	2,160	1,885	374	280	16.2
Tobacco	1,695	1,561	248	142	12.0
Cotton and linen spinning	2,736	6,013	382	417	9.1
Paper (pulp)	2,628	989	118	86	5.6
Brick and porcelain	2,785	488	155	22	5.4
Sawmill work	9,000	665	375	110	5.0
Cloth making	2,054	1,942	145	54	5.0
Stone cutting	1,465	13	70	1	4.8
Ironworks	14,533	298	374	44	2.8
Carpentry shops	1,708	8	46	2	2.8
Iron mines	3,218	147	49	13	1.8
Engineering shops	10,491	15	132	–	1.3
Breweries	878	128	4	–	0.4
All sectors	64,566	15,726	3,113	1,293	5.5

Source: *Betänkande angående minderårigas antagande och användande i fabrik, handtverk och annan handtering* (Stockholm, 1877), table 3, pp. 143–149.
* Sectors are in descending order of the percentage of child labour.

In the middle of the 1870s, about 4,400 children below the age of fourteen worked in industrial plants in Sweden (table 15.1).[4] They made up about 5.5 per cent of all workers. The majority of the children were boys, but nearly

3 *Svensk Författningssamling* (Swedish Statutes), 1881: 64. Stockholm.
4 If additional but uncontrolled children's work in the workers' homes is also included, the number of child workers will be considerably larger.

one third of them (1,300) were girls. There was significant variety between the different sectors of industry. Most children worked in textile mills, but many worked in sawmills, match and tobacco factories, ironworks, and glassworks. In terms of the proportion of all workers, which indicates the importance of child labour for the employers, child labour was of greatest importance in glass making and in the production of matches and tobacco. Quite astonishingly, children were less important in textile production; only 9 per cent of the workers in cotton and linen spinning were children, and they accounted for just 5 per cent of cloth workers. Girls outnumbered boys only in cotton and linen spinning, but quite a lot of girls also worked in match and tobacco production and in sawmills.

Referring to the state investigation of child labour, one of the most prominent scholars of an older tradition in Sweden, Torsten Gårdlund, argued that child labour was of little importance for Swedish industrial capitalists.[5] The figures in table 15.1 give some support to the statement, and indeed, children were of significant importance for capitalists only in limited parts of Swedish industry at that time. Gårdlund hints at some decline in child labour, which might have been caused by technological changes. But most of all, he says, any decline was due to the development of liberal ideas:

> Large employers *probably* were so enlightened and so familiar with the ideas of those days that they could over-exploit child labour only by hardening their hearts. Influenced by these ideas, several large employers diminished their use of child labour even when the legislation was not efficiently observed (my emphasis).[6]

Other researchers hold a similar position, while still others say that the legislation of 1881 and the introduction of factory inspections in 1890 caused the decline in industrial child labour.[7] There is, however, no empirical evidence for any idealistic type of historical explanation. Nor can the actual legislation explain the decline in child labour, *if* that decline started before the legislation was introduced. Instead of speculating about social change in labour history, we have to take a closer look at what happened in the daily life of individual industrial sectors and workplaces.

5 Gårdlund, *Industrialismens samhälle*.
6 Gårdlund, *Industrialismens samhälle*, p. 324.
7 Sellberg, *Staten och arbetarskyddet*; Nygren, "Barnarbete och arbetsavtalets frihet", p. 198; Nestor, "Varför minskade barnarbetet?".

In this article, I will discuss industrial child labour in Sweden in a broader perspective as well as the social background of some child workers. I will argue that child labour was part of the early phase of the factory system and that it decreased when work organisation changed during the industrial take-off. I will also argue that liberal and philanthropic ideas and work legislation were of less importance for the decline of industrial child labour. As I see it, child labour was part of the extensive exploitation of labour in early industrial capitalism but decreased as more intensive forms of exploitation were introduced. This process varied in time and intensity between different industries. My perspective does not deny the influence of ideas on societal transformations. For most of the time on which I focus in this study, the idea that young children of poor families should work for industrial capitalists definitively was important! Ideas, however, do not float freely in space, but are related to (the interests of) social groups and classes, and the influences of ideas are related to power relations between those groups and classes.

Origins of Child Labour

Child labour was not introduced by industrial capitalism but was common in pre-industrial and pre-capitalist traditional peasant societies. At very young ages, both boys and girls had to help their father and mother with simple tasks on the farm. With increasing ages they gradually became more and more qualified to work in agriculture, cattle breeding, dairy farming, and cloth making. Peasant children were cheap labour for the family farm economy, and often they had to do hard work. The more help they could provide, the fewer hired hands were needed on the farm. But child labour in peasant society also had a gendered socialising character. Boys were supposed to be trained in all tasks that were expected of a future peasant, and girls were trained to run a household, to do dairy farming,[8] and to become a peasant wife. Children were trained to do skilled work, and they were also in the long run expected to be able to manage a farm in every respect and to become parts of a peasant society.

In pre-capitalist and pre-industrial societies, children also worked for craftsmen, starting at much higher ages than in the case of work on farms. According to the Swedish guild legislation from 1720, boys could not be

8 Dairy farming was organised very much like craft work; see Olsson, "Den vita piskan".

accepted as apprentices before the age of fourteen; girls were very seldom accepted for guilded craft training in pre-capitalist society. This age regulation refutes all declarations that children had to start working at very young ages in order to become skilled workers, which was an argument that was used at the end of the nineteenth century by some employers who wanted to employ very young children. Still, the main aim of apprenticeship was to train workers as journeymen, who later on expected, and were expected, to end up as masters themselves.[9] In many respects, there were great similarities between the peasant society and the craft system: children had to start with simple tasks and work hard. In the end, they were supposed to end up as skilled workers, able to do all kinds of work and to organise work themselves. Children's work in both systems was gendered. Apart from the need to work hard, most industrial child labour differed quite a lot from that in peasant society and in the craft system.

Industrial Capitalism and Division of Labour

Industrial capitalism was developed in three ways. First, a craft shop could be expanded to large-scale production, based on a greater division of labour. In Sweden, that kind of work organisation was already called a factory in the eighteenth century. Second, a capitalist could assemble several craft shops into one factory, and third, a capitalist could assemble household work into a factory. These processes could also be combined.[10] Gradually, most factories were organised on the basis of a division of labour, but still as late as the early nineteenth century most of them were industries. In Sweden, the glass industry and most tobacco shops developed according to the first method as a totally male activity, while the early textile factories and some tobacco factories were organised according to the second model. Tobacco making was a male job, while the early textile factories were often organised on the basis of family work. The skilled father was the head of a team, and the rest of his family supported him with semi-skilled and unskilled work. The match industry was established in the middle of the nineteenth century as large-scale manual production with a distinct division of labour. A few skilled men supervised the work of many children and women.[11]

9 Edgren, *Lärling – Gesäll – Mästare.*
10 Nyström, *Stadsindustriens arbetare.*
11 Olsson, *Då barn var lönsamma*; Göransson, *Från familj till fabrik.*

None of these forms of production were regulated by the guild system. Anyone with capital could start a factory, and from 1739 onwards the owner – the capitalist – could employ whomever he wanted from the ages of "10 to 12".[12] In 1846, the age limit was fixed at twelve years of age.[13] Female workers could also be employed, and women turned out to be of great importance in several industries.[14] Even the masters were employees, although managers faced great and long lasting difficulties in subordinating them into industrial workers.

Division of labour, i.e. splitting a full job into separate operations, was one of the most distinctive indications of a capitalist mode of production. As Adam Smith noticed in his *Wealth of Nations* (1776), capitalists could profit from division of labour in at least three ways. Workers could be more skilled by just doing a few things instead of doing a lot of different tasks, they could save time by not changing too often from one operation to another, and, thirdly, routine work could be mechanised. Smith noticed that many managers not only divided a work operation into pieces but also distributed single work operations to individual workers. Skilled work, the most expensive type, was reserved for skilled workers, semi-skilled work for semi-skilled workers, and unskilled work, the cheapest kind, for unskilled workers. Heavy work was designed for adult male workers and easy work for women, old people, and children.

Smith's ideas about work organisation were already known and discussed in Sweden at the end of the eighteenth century.[15] In 1839, the professor and MP Erik Gustaf Geijer announced the potential of using women and children at work by practising these ideas:

> By a division of labour [...] even weakness can be exploited. Even a child can be strong by using a machine, so, even if the exaggerations of child labour in most English factories have revealed terrible views of misery, we have to admit that the possibility to use children at work, if done with care and tenderness, is a great favour for a poor household.[16]

12 *Barnarbetskommitténs betänkande* (Parliamentary report on child labour), Stockholm, 1877, p. 59f.

13 *Svensk Författningssamling* (Swedish Legislations), 1846: 39.

14 Montgomery, *Industrialismens genombrott*. Later on it happened that also women owned factories, see Göransson, "Gender and property rights".

15 For instance, he was discussed in *Läsning i blandade ämnen* (1797–1801).

16 Geijer, *Samlade skrifter*. Vol. III, p. 135.

There are two important statements in the quotation to be observed. First, the possibilities for a capitalist to exploit children were dependent on the character of the specific work in his factory, especially how far he and his manager(s) could design simple work operations for the division of labour. Second, especially poor families were the main source of (cheap) labour. It might be an understatement that also capitalists could profit from child labour.

Industrial Capitalism and Child Labour

Since the eighteenth century the Swedish board of trade (Kommerskollegium) collected information about industrial work at individual workplaces. The information is only available as primary sources at the National Archives of Sweden (Riksarkivet), so it is very labour-intensive to analyse it. For that reason, I limited my study of child labour in the early factory system to those four industries that were the most child-labour-intensive in 1875: the glassworks, the match and the tobacco factories, and the cotton spinning mills. The main focus is on the tobacco industry.

Table 15.2. Number of Mills and Workers in Glass Making, Tobacco, Cotton Spinning, and Match Making, Sweden 1830-1890

	Glass		*Tobacco*		*Cotton*		*Matches*	
	Mills	*Workers*	*Mills*	*Workers*	*Mills*	*Workers*	*Mills*	*Workers*
1830	13	590	77	695	9*	721	–	–
1840	14	644	84	836	8	899	–	–
1850	16	795	86	1,129	13	2,221	6	287
1860	21	1,156	103	1,780	20	4,021	14	1,167
1870	26	1,270	97	2,590	20	3,282	24	2,790
1880	33	1,903	104	3,217	24	4,206	31	3,956
1890	36	2,904	85	3,147	24	4,613	26	5,227

Sources: Kommerskollegii arkiv. Årsberättelser. Fabriker 1830, 1840, 1850 and 1860 (The National Archives in Stockholm); BISOS. Fabriker och handtverk (Statistics Sweden. Industries) 1870, 1880 and 1890. Stockholm.

* The figures for cotton spinning in 1830 cover the year 1835.

Table 15.2 shows that the number of glassworks was rather stable until the middle of the nineteenth century, but thereafter there was a significant increase from sixteen in 1850 to thirty-six in 1890. The average number of workers at every mill was fairly stable and remained around fifty until the 1880s, but in 1890 there were on average as many as eighty workers at every glassworks. The structure of tobacco production was quite different. There were many more workplaces, and the number of them did not change very much but varied between eighty and a hundred. The average number of workers in the tobacco mills was lower than in glassworks, although it rose from a dozen to close to forty during the century. Cotton spinning and match making had the largest-scale production of the studied industries. It started with around fifty workers at each factory in the middle of the century, a number that doubled within two decades, and in 1890 there were on average two hundred workers in each mill.

Table 15.3. Number of Child Workers and Percentage of Child Labour in Glassworks, Tobacco Factories, Cotton Spinning Mills, and Match Factories in Sweden, 1830-1891

	Glass		*Tobacco*		*Cotton*		*Matches*	
1830	151	25.6%	164	23.6%				
1835	172	33.5%	249	35.8%	(231)	41.4%		
1840	137	28.1%	260	31.1%	569	63.3%		
1845	169	30.9%	387	39.1%	507	46.1%	99	84.6%
1850	273	34.3%	404	35.8%	733	33.0%	133	46.3%
1855	317	31.2%	570	32.6%	(608)	28.6%	177	37.0%
1860	304	28.1%	478	25.4%	(1,026)	26.6%	461	43.9%
1875		32.2%		15.5%	(317)	19.4%		17.7%
1891	375	20.8%	178	3.1%	(384)	12.3%	556	12.0%

Sources: Kommerskollegii arkiv. Årsberättelser 1830, 1835, 1840, 1845, 1850, 1855, 1860. Fabriker (The National Archives, Stockholm); 1875 års barnarbetskommittés arkiv (The National Archives, Stockholm); 1891 års revisionskommittés arkiv (The National Archives, Stockholm).

The board of trade also collected information about child labour. Until 1862, it registered the employment of children under fifteen years of age, but thereafter the board changed the age limit to eighteen. A changed view on the limit between children and adult workers was established, indicating a changed concept of childhood. Since information on child labour at individual factories is occasionally lacking, including the state investigation in 1875, the numbers of child workers can be considered to have been at a minimum for some years. The relative figures are more certain, because they have been calculated based on workplaces where child labour has also been registered, so they seem to be useful for long-term analyses. Since another state investigation on child labour was conducted in 1891, noting on children under 15, we can study the exploitation of children under the age of fifteen in different industries for the period 1830–1862 and for 1891. For 1875 we have information about children of the ages below twelve, and twelve to fourteen (see table 15.3).

There was a significant growth in the number of children who worked in the four industries; at least until, but also beyond, 1860. But also the percentage of child workers in glass making and tobacco manufacturing increased significantly until mid-century. Match making, on the other hand, was initially more or less based on child labour.

One of the basic ideas of industrial capitalism was that work could be divided into several operations in several large-scale industrial production units and that some of these sub-divided operations were unskilled and easy to perform. In the late 1740s, none other than Carl Linnaeus – the world-famous botanist – observed the existence of a far-reaching division of labour at a large tobacco spinning mill in Norrköping, the industrial centre of Sweden in those days:

> We visited the tobacco spinning workshop in the afternoon [...] Some (workers) were quid makers putting on a table slender strips of tobacco, which had absorbed a special tobacco juice [...] others spread out the tobacco leaves, others turned leaves around the quid and made them into pupps, others cut the stems out of the leaves, others spun leaves around the pupps into a kind of cordage, others made rolls of tobacco, others pressed the tobacco, and others chipped cartouche tobacco (*my translation*).[17]

Linnaeus noticed the existence of many child workers but he does not say how many there were or what kind of work they performed. His observation, however, gives support to my thesis that a far-reaching division of labour was favourable for the possibilities to exploit children at work. It is

17 Von Linné, *Den öländska och gotländska resan*, p. 24.

also worth noticing that division of labour had been practised in Sweden for quite a time, when Adam Smith formulated his theory on the topic.

The Frans Suell Tobacco Factory in Malmö in the Early Nineteenth Century

In the 1740s, the German immigrant Frans Suell settled in Malmö in southern Sweden to establish himself as a tradesman. He was successful, and half a century later his grandson and namesake was one of leading tradesmen and capitalists in the city. Around 1800, Frans Suell's Tobacco Factory was one of the largest tobacco factories in Sweden.[18]

Like all other employers Frans Suell had to give annual reports to the city administration on those who worked in his tobacco factory in the autumn of each year.[19] For two years, 1807 and 1812, his bookkeeper for some reason not only noted the names of the workers but also their ages. The names reveal that only men and boys worked in the factory. Tobacco manufacturing in Sweden in those days generally had a distinct gender character, being a male job.

Table 15.4. The Ages of the Workers in Frans Suell's Tobacco Factory in Malmö, November 1807 and 1812

Ages	*<14*	*15-19*	*20-29*	*30-39*	*40-49*	*50-59*	*60-69*	*70<*
1807	42	13	4	6	23	19	8	2
1812	26	6	3	3	10	17	17	2

Source: Hall-och manufakturrättens arkiv. Inneliggande handlingar till protokoll (Malmö City Archive).

Most of the workers were young or past mid-life (table 15.4). One third of them were boys under the age of fifteen, less than 10 per cent were men between twenty and forty, and half of them were older than forty. The profits of Frans Suell were based on the exploitation of children and older workers (who, in those days, also included people of an age that is now

18 The Suell family emigrated in the 1740s from Schleswig-Holstein in Germany to Malmö, where they settled as trade capitalists and later became deeply involved in both industrial and agrarian capitalism and politics.

19 Malmö Stadsarkiv (hereafter MSA), *Hall- och manufakturrättens arkiv,* Inneliggande handlingar till protokoll. Unfortunately, those lists are in general seldom preserved.

considered young).[20] Probably, many sisters – and probably some mothers – of the boys worked in or for the two cloth factories in the city.

Unfortunately, the annual reports have no information about the operations that individual workers performed. The bookkeeper called most of the adult workers "workman", a title that indicates semi-skilled or unskilled work. However, we can get a little more information on the work operations from a hand-written manuscript from the late 1880s by a man who started to work in the factory as a child in 1830, when the factory was run by Suell's nephew Frans Henrik Kockum. "Perhaps the reader of this story might be interested in how the factory was organised in 1830," he says.[21] Indeed, we are! And there is no reason to believe that it was much different from a decade or two earlier, except from the fact that cigar making started around 1830.

In *tobacco spinning* (making of chewing tobacco) a master spinner, a spinner and ten boys were involved in the work. It is obvious that many more children were employed than could be expected if tobacco spinning was pure craft production. In *snuff* making, there was one snuff grinder, three cutters, two rollers, and two boys. In the making of *cartouche tobacco* – tobacco for smoking – there were two young draughtsmen, a smearer, a roll presser and a boy, two pressers, and one man who handled a drying machine. Two carpenters made boxes. Six other men were involved in different operations, and another six boys were helping hands.[22] It is quite obvious that most child labour was involved in tobacco spinning, which still was the dominant part of tobacco production at the beginning of the 19th century.[23]

Fortunately, there is still another highly valuable source for this study: two wage books from Mr Suell's factory, covering the full period 1806–1824.[24] There is no information on the workers' ages or work operations in the books, but every single worker's monthly payment is registered. Thus, we are able to analyse the wage structure. *First*, we can conclude that wages

20 In another study, I have shown how typographers in Sweden around 1900 talked about "our older fellow workers, the veterans of the trade, those who were older than 35"! The average death age in that trade then was 37, and indirectly the bad air conditions in printing houses caused their death. See Olsson, "We Stand Here".

21 Winqvist, "Andreas Winqvists Minnen och Anteckningar".

22 Winqvist, "Andreas Winqvists Minnen och Anteckningar", p. 123.

23 *Undersökning af tobaksindustrien i Sverige*, Arbetsstatistik II. Stockholm 1899, p. 36.

24 MSA, *Suellska arkivet*, Avlöningsböcker, 1806–1824.

were fixed; they only changed four times during the period 1806–1824.[25] Thus, there was no totally free labour market yet and some state regulations still remained. *Second*, there was a great variety in wages, most probably reflecting the status of different work operations and thus the hierarchy at work. It is reasonable to state that skilled workers had individual wages, while all semi-skilled and/or unskilled men – we do not know their exact positions – were paid the same amount of money every month, which in 1806 was 5 Riksdaler and 24 Shillings.[26] The child workers were paid between 36 Shillings and 3 Riksdaler a month, and their wages varied quite distinctly with their ages. The wage system, however, does not say anything about individual careers.

About two hundred boys worked in his tobacco factory between 1806 and 1824. I succeeded in identifying 104 of them in the registers for the three parishes in Malmö,[27] and out of these 104, I was able to trace 72 in the wage books for their full employment time at Mr Suell's factory.[28] In table 15.5 a–c, we can see the ages at both the start and the termination of employment of the children and, thus, the duration of their work for Suell.

First, we can conclude that Mr Suell violated the state regulations by employing children younger than ten to twelve years of age (see above, note 12). Four children started to work at the age of seven, eight at the age of eight, and another nineteen were employed at the age of nine. The average age at which Suell employed children was ten. One conclusion is that 43 per cent of the child workers were hired illegally by Mr Suell, who besides being one of the largest capitalists of the city was also a leading politician. There is no evidence that he was ever charged with infringement of the labour legislation. In contrary, he was honoured as a symbol of the economic breakthrough of Malmö by having a statue of him erected at the

25 The wage raises were certainly due to the rise in living costs due to the Napoleonic wars.

26 48 Shillings made up 1 Riksdaler.

27 Since 1686, every individual person in Sweden and Finland was registered in the church records. Even if some of the material is destroyed, we have excellent abilities – although it is an extremely labour-intensive task – to shape life trajectories of individuals. For the three parishes of Malmö the records, unfortunately, are only partly preserved. Even when we have the records, it is virtually impossible to find persons whose family names are patronymics if there is no additional information apart from the name.

28 I counted those who started to work no earlier than February 1806 and left no later than November 1824.

city harbour. And after the Second World War, a day care centre for children in Malmö was named after him!

Table 15.5. Child Workers at Frans Suell's Tobacco Factory in Malmö, 1806-1824

a) Age at employment

Age	*7*	*8*	*9*	*10*	*11*	*12*	*13*	*14*
Numbers	4	8	19	15	13	8	5	–

b) Age at termination of employment

Age	*8*	*9*	*10*	*11*	*12*	*13*	*14*	*15*	*16*	*17*	*18*	*19*	*20*	*21–*
Numbers	1	–	1	2	5	11	11	16	14	6	2	1	1	1

c) Numbers of years at work

Number of years	*1*	*2*	*3*	*4*	*5*	*6*	*7*	*8*	*9*	*10*
Numbers of children	7	12	8	10	12	6	8	5	3	1

Sources: Suellska arkivet. Löneböcker 1806–1824 (Malmö City Archive); Kyrkoböcker (Church registers) för Caroli och Petri församling and Garnisonsförsamlingen (Malmö City Archive).

Another conclusion is that most children stopped working for Mr Suell between the ages of fourteen to sixteen, irrespective of what age they joined the factory. Only one boy stayed beyond his twentieth birthday. Since church records normally say nothing about the occupation of youngsters, we do not know what other work they left for. As there was no other tobacco factory in Malmö at that time, we know that they did not become trained tobacco workers. Instead they left the trade.

The same system was practised at a cotton spinning mill in the 1830s, where "very few stayed until adulthood".[29] Indeed, Andreas Winqvist was representative of child workers in the early nineteenth-century tobacco industry in Malmö. He started to work in the factory at the age of ten, and

29 Göransson, *Från familj till fabrik*, p. 253.

he stayed for four years and eight months, when he left to train as a baker. But after five years of apprenticeship he had not graduated as a journeyman, so, instead, in 1840 he returned to the tobacco factory as a "workman".[30]

We also realise that those children who left the factory were replaced by younger ones. As also Karl Marx noticed, this systematic labour turnover caused some problems in society.[31] Other children might not as easily get a new job as Andreas did after working as a child. In the 1840s, the managers of a school in Malmö complained that many youngsters were insufficiently educated due to working at a too early age. They worried especially because those circumstances might cause problems both for the youngsters themselves and for the community, "when they had to leave their routine work at factories and were replaced by younger children of their own sort".[32]

So far, we can conclude that child labour was of major importance for a capitalist like Frans Suell in Malmö. Children were employed because they could be made to do simple and easy operations, especially at tobacco spinning, which Suell did not want to pay adult workmen to do. And the wages really were low. In a letter to the Poor Relief Committee in Malmö in 1808, Mr Suell even admitted that child workers could not survive on them. He testified himself:

> Pehr Andersson is a boy who has worked for me in the tobacco factory for four years, and he has always behaved decently and faithfully to me. Since he is very poor and *the wage I reasonably can pay him* is far from enough to cover his living costs, I very deeply recommend him for support from the Poor Relief Committee (my translation and emphasis).[33]

Obviously, the idea that employers should be subsidised by the community for parts of their labour costs has a long history! Mr Suell confirmed that the costs of living of the young part of the work force at his factory were not covered by the wage he "reasonably" could pay. Indeed, the low wages for the many children is one very important reason why Mr Suell, according to established reference books in Sweden, could advance from being "an assistant in his father's shop" to "the position as the most successful

30 Winqvist, "Andreas Winqvists Minnen och Anteckningar", p. 120. For the proletarianisation of married journeymen, see Edgren, *Lärling – Gesäll – Mästare*, pp. 187ff.

31 Marx, *Kapital*, 1, ch. 13.

32 Tunander, *Fattigskola – Medborgarskola*.

33 MSA, *Fattigvårdsdirektionens handlingar* år *1808*, p. 452.

merchant in the city".[34] His friend, Mayor J. Kjellander, who also was the chairman of the board of the Poor Relief Committee, confirmed the connections after Mr Suell's death in 1817:

> Always thinking of the increase of his own capital, [he] founded a lot of industries, where old and young women and children were employed, and where all of them, from their work ability, could either fully earn their living costs or, at least, partly contribute to them by a smaller income... After his death the tobacco factory especially declined, where hundreds of children had a small but daily earning, so that they were prevented from begging but instead were used to do hard work.[35]

It is quite clear that the accumulation of capital in Mr Suell's hands was of great significance for him, and child labour was of the utmost importance for that process. The company, soon in the hands of Mr F.H. Kockum, quickly recovered from the decline of the tobacco factory after Mr Suell's death, and the process of accumulation of capital within the tobacco industry in Malmö was re-established. Child labour increased again, and it culminated in the middle of the century, when the profits of the tobacco factory helped Mr Kockum to start the Kockum Mechanical Workshop in 1840. That company later included the Kockum Shipyard – one of the flagships of the industrial take-off in Sweden. So, for sure, child labour was of importance for its industrialisation!

As indicated by Mr Kjellander, child labour was not only a base of capital accumulation but also prevented poor children from begging. For, as Jürgen Kuczynski pointed out, with capitalism the people in power were no longer willing to let poor children find their living by, for instance, begging.[36] A few decades later, the English foreman at a Swedish cotton spinning mill pointed out to an American visitor at the mill "child after child who had been beggars on the highway, and were now industrious workers in the establishment".[37] In capitalism, proletarian children were to contribute to the subsistence of their poor families only by selling their labour, and their work was part of the capital accumulation in Sweden.

Poor underclass children also had to learn to respect the social order by attending schools. Mr Suell organised an evening school for the boys who

34 *Nordisk Familjebok* and *Svenska män och kvinnor*, s.v. Suell, Frans.
35 Quotation from Bjurling, *Stadens fattiga*, p. 55.
36 Kuczynski, *Die Geschichte der Kinderarbeit*, 1, p. 32.
37 Brace, *The Norse-Folk*, p. 147.

worked for him, which they attended after work – between 7 and 9 p.m.[38] Basically, the children had to learn the idea of hard work for capitalists, a problem that Swedish capitalists and managers dealt with at least until the 1850s. The American visitor to the cotton mill was also told about those problems, especially with women:

> They were never accustomed to such close work. Always at 'ome, they've been in the 'abit of talkin' and chattin', you know, as they work, and I find it very 'ard to keep 'em attentive and consideratesome. And they are so tricky. Why can't possibly two Swedish women meet without a little dance, just together, which won't do you know here, sir. But they'll learn. It's a young nation, sir; very young… It will take time – time, sir, before they do as the English and Americans.[39]

Certainly, it was easier to socialise children than adults to the capitalist conception of time and the work discipline of capitalism that E. P. Thompson described for the factory system. Workers were expected by capitalists and managers to do nothing but work the whole working day.[40] After that conclusion, it is time to focus on the children at work.

The Child Workers in Malmö

As said in the introduction, debaters of the time stressed that not only capitalists could profit from child labour but that it also could do "a great favour for a poor household". Thus, it would be no surprise to say that industrial child workers were children of poor families. They were. But more than this can be said about the social background of the children who worked for Mr Suell.

Andreas Winqvist tells us a little about his family. His father had "left" his mother, when Andreas was born. The mother had to provide for herself as a wet nurse for another newborn child – a child of the bourgeoisie in Malmö.[41] Little Andreas became "a workhouse child", most of the

38 Tunander, *Fattigskola – Medborgarskola*, p. 315; Sandin, *Hemmet, gatan, fabriken eller skolan*, pp. 219-226.

39 Brace, *The Norse-Folk*, p. 147.

40 Thompson, "Time, Work-discipline and Industrial Capitalism".

41 It was quite common at that time that bourgeois families hired proletarian wet nurses for their new born children, See Mattsson, "Ammor och barnafödande", pp. 173-198.

time until he was ten, supporting himself by begging. On 2 January 1830, when Andreas was eleven, "a distinguished gentleman" came to the workhouse looking for another child to work for him, and the caretaker selected Andreas to work in Mr Kockum's tobacco factory. He started work the next day. As Andreas was crying quite a lot because his grandmother had recently died, Mr Kockum gave him "some extra money", mostly "to satisfy" his new foster parents![42]

Andreas Winqvist's tragic story was not unique. In May 1811, the nine-year-old Bengt Olin got a new baby sister. Since his father, a journeyman, had severe pulmonary consumption, the new baby might have been more of a burden to the family than a joy. However, a month later the six-year-old sister Elna died, and her death, of course, caused a lot of sorrow – but maybe it also eased the economic burden for the poor family.[43] Another month later, the father died too, and Bengt's mother was left alone with him and his two-month-old sister. At that time Bengt started to work for Mr Suell in the tobacco factory. Bengt, however, did not stay working there for more than one and a half years, until January 1813, because Bengt's mother died – from pining (sic!), and Bengt Olin was moved to a foster family.[44]

As Pehr Andersson (see above p. 316) was also an orphan, there might be some reason to believe that a lot of those children who were put to work for capitalists like Mr Suell came from very poor circumstances. In order to obtain more knowledge about the social background of the child workers, I searched for as many of them as possible in the church registers, i.e. a "family reconstruction" method was used. The 104 identified child workers belonged to 67 families.

Most fathers represented three occupations: 27 of them were soldiers, 13 were titled journeymen and 11 were tobacco workers, while three were said to be artisans. Some of the fathers were already dead, so their children lived with widowed mothers. There were also six unmarried mothers, who worked as maids. The soldiers in Malmö have been characterised as the real underclass of those days, and married journeymen had already given

42 Winqvist, "Andreas Winqvists Minnen och Anteckningar", p. 20.

43 In those days it was sometimes said that very young children in peasant Sweden were a heavy burden for families in times of epidemics. See Winberg, *Folkökning och proletarisering*, p. 58.

44 MSA, *Suellska arkivet*, Avlöningsböcker, 1806–1824; MSA, *Church books* on Births and Deaths and Minutes of parish catechetical meetings for the parishes of Garnisonen and Caroli.

up their ambitions to become masters, so they were part of the developing working class of the city.[45] There is a bias in the findings of fathers in the church registers, because soldiers and to some degree also journeymen, had odd family names instead of patronymics, which otherwise was the rule for peasants and underclass people in Sweden in those days. Thus, soldiers and journeymen were easier to find than others, and they are over-represented in the survey. Tobacco workers might also be over-represented, although they had patronymics as family names, because they were grouped together with one or several sons in the wage books. The combination of a father and his son(s) could be identified in church registers with high degree of certainty. In addition to poverty, sons of tobacco workers also might have gone to work in the factory out of tradition and as part of a family strategy.

It is sometimes said that poverty increased in working-class families as more children were born, and families with many children sent the oldest ones to work as soon as someone employed them.[46] In a contemporary study of social conditions in Stockholm in the 1890s it was said that the most severe deprivations of working-class families were not gone until the children had grown up so much that they could contribute to the subsistence of their family.[47] So, did the children who worked for Mr Suell come from large families?

Table 15.6. Number of Children in Families at the Time When the Oldest Son Started to Work in Mr Suell's Tobacco Factory. Families with One or Two Parents Living with the Children

Number of children	*1*	*2*	*3*	*4*	*5*	*6*	*7*	*8*
Two parents	3	4	3	9	5	3	1	1
One parent	4	7	8	6	1	–	–	–

Sources: see the text.

Table 15.6 shows us that the number of children in families, of which at least one son worked in Mr Suell's tobacco factory, varied from one to eight. Only eleven families had more than four children. We cannot say that the

45 Bjurling, *Stadens fattiga*, p. 56; Edgren, *Lärling – Gesäll – Mästare*, ch. 6.

46 See for instance Lorimer, "Economics of family formation", II; Bull, "Barnarbeid i norsk industri".

47 Geijerstam, *Arbetareförhållanden*.

families in general were very large. The main reason was that nearly half of all families consisted of only one parent, mostly single mothers and widows, the poorest part of the working class. In the two-parent families the numbers of children were significantly higher than in one-parent families, so it is correct to say that child workers partly came from large families.[48]

Some families sent more than one son to work for Mr Suell. Indeed, it looks as if families who sent the oldest son also sent his younger brother(s). Two-parent families sent no fewer than 61 out of their 73 sons who had reached the age of eight. In corresponding one-parent families more or less every younger brother also worked in the tobacco factory. Three conclusions can be drawn.

First, the boys who worked for Mr Suell came from a limited group of families, consisting of large or one-parent families from the lower classes in Malmö; some were orphans. A systematic analysis of the registers of the orphanage of Malmö County and the lists of conscription of the poor people in Malmö 1806-1824 underlines the impression that most of these families were very poor. Close to all one-parent families and half of the two-parent families received poor aid for at least one of the investigated years. In those days, poor aid was paid only to individuals or families, "who lived under subsistence level in the sense that they would die if they did not get any support".[49]

Second, the eldest brother of those families – and in some cases the father (a tobacco worker) – might have found employment for his younger brother(s), helping Mr Suell to get cheap labour and simultaneously helping their families to survive.

Third, since Mr Suell himself voluntarily gave large sums of money to the Poor Relief Committee of the city, he cannot be accused of neglecting the situation of its poor people. Why, then, did he not raise the very low wages he paid his (child) workers? Even if the theory of "the low wage economy" was the ruling idea among economists of those days,[50] nothing prevented Mr Suell from raising the wages for those who worked for him. Instead, he supported poor families via the local administration, over which he had some control himself. One reason might be that the board

48 It is worth noting that several two-parent families were still fertile at the time when the oldest son started to work, so they might have had more children later on.

49 Bjurling, *Stadens fattiga*, p. 12.

50 Anders Berch (1711-1774), the first professor of economics in Sweden, held the idea that poor people were an important part of the wealth of a nation. Only poor people would work for others. See Strindberg, *Arbetare och radikaler*, p. 30.

of the Poor Relief Committee could put a pressure on the poor families which they supported, to send their children to work for those who asked for cheap labour.

After those conclusions it might be time to return to the long-term development of industrial child labour in Sweden.

Declining Child Labour, Intensification of Work, and a New Gender Division of Labour

As was already shown in table 15.3, child labour was still of great importance in the middle of the nineteenth century. The exploitation of child labour, however, fell significantly in several industries after that. In the tobacco industry the number of employed children peaked in 1855, and the percentage of all workers fell from 39 per cent in 1845 to 25 per cent in 1860. In cotton spinning the number of child workers peaked in 1860, and their proportion of all workers fell from 63 per cent in 1840 to 33 per cent in 1850 and 27 per cent in 1860. In match factories, however, the number of exploited children did not peak until the turn of the century, while child labour fell from 44 per cent (<15) in 1860 to 18 per cent (<14) in 1875. Thus, there was a dominant tendency of significantly decreasing child labour in Swedish industrial capitalism in the second half of the nineteenth century, even if child labour was still of great importance in parts of glass making into the twentieth century.

Table 15.7. The Average Age at Employment of Youngsters (<18) in the Tobacco Industry, 1850-1898

	Before 1860	*1860–1864*	*1865–1869*	*1870–1874*	*1875–1879*	*1880–1884*	*1885–1889*	*1890–1894*	*1895–1898*
Ages	11.5	12.3	12.7	13.3	13.6	14.2	14.1	14.7	14.7
Numbers	161	115	140	272	192	210	369	609	987

Source: Calculated from *Undersökning af tobaksindustrien i Sverige*, pp. 244–247.

At the same time as child labour became less important for industrial capitalists, the average age of employment for youngsters (<18) who started to work in the tobacco factories and in match making rose significantly from 1860 to 1875 and beyond. Those who started to work in the tobacco industry before 1860 were under twelve when they were employed. In the

1860s they were 12.5 years old, in the 1870s another year older, in the 1880s the children had passed their fourteenth birthday at their employment, and during the 1890s they came closer and closer to the age of fifteen (table 15.7) and, thus, could legally work for ten hours a day.

An investigation of wage lists of Jönköpings Tändsticksfabriks AB (JTAB)[51] reveals that also the world-leading Swedish match-making company ceased to employ very young children. Before 1868 children were employed at an average age of 13.1 years, between 1868 and 1873 at 13.6, and between 1874 and 1881 they were 14.3 years old – far beyond the twelve-year limit of the legislation. Consequently, the head manager Mr Hay at JTAB in 1877 stated to the state investigation into child labour that they did not use children at his factory any more. Out of about one thousand workers in 1875 only two were younger than fourteen, and they employed "not many" aged between fourteen and eighteen either.[52]

How, then, to explain the decline in child labour and the rising age at the moment of employment? Why did employers cease to exploit children, especially very young children? The new legislation cannot be the main reason, because the decline started long before the legislation came into force and the decline had different trajectories within single industrial branches. Besides, the legislation did not forbid industrial child labour but regulated it for children who had passed the age of twelve. The legislation possibly increased the speed of the process by making it more difficult for employers who still sought the labour of very young children. Mr Hay at JTAB explained the circumstances: "Indeed, it would be in our interest to have legislation, because a law would put hard pressure on our competitors, who still use child labour".

The legislation might, after all, have had some hastening effects on the abolition of the industrial child labour. As was shown in table 15.3, the percentage of child workers in the tobacco industry fell from 15 per cent to 3 per cent between 1875 (<14) and 1891 (<15), in cotton spinning from 19 per cent to 12 per cent, in matchmaking from 18 per cent to 12 per cent, and from 32 per cent to 21 per cent in glass making. On the other hand, apart from glass making, the falling figures might primarily indicate an ongoing process that started before 1881 and was only marginally influenced by the legislation. Besides, the legislation was, at least now and then, violated. A glass blower tells us how they "put away the young boys when [the glass-

51 Vadstena Landsarkiv (Regional Archive in Vadstena).

52 Riksarkivet, Stockholm (The National Archives, Stockholm), *Civildepartementets arkiv*, Konseljakter 18.11 1881.

works] Kosta was inspected and put them to work again when the inspector had left".[53] But what about the liberal and philanthropic ideas, that one scholar said had influenced several large employers of the time? Liberal employers did not have to wait for new legislation to stop exploiting children. So, let us return to one of them, Frans Henrik Kockum, a man who has been said to be guided by the motto "love of mankind",[54] and his tobacco factory in Malmö.

Table 15.8. Child Workers and Skilled Workers at Kockum's Tobacco Factory, 1858 and 1898

	Cigar making					*Tobacco spinning*				
	All workers	*Children*		*Cigarmakers*		*All workers*	*Children*		*Spinners*	
1858	121	46	38%	40	33%	93	34	37%	11	12%
1898	84	5	6%	57	68%	124	42	34%	14	11%

Sources: F. H. Kockums Tobaksfabriks arkiv. Handlingar efter ämne 1835–1907 (Malmö City Archive); Church registers for three parishes in Malmö (Malmö City Archive); Kommerskollegii arkiv. Arbetsstatistiska undersökningar II. Tobaksindustrien (The National Archives, Stockholm).

In 1858, children made up a little less than 40 per cent in both the tobacco spinning and the cigar making at Kockum's. Forty years later, Mr Kockum's managers still hired a considerable number of children for tobacco spinning, while cigars were made more or less without the help of children. Like other capitalists, and in accordance with the legislation, Mr Kockum's managers employed double half-day teams of children, who could work for six hours each in the mornings or in the afternoons. Perhaps the local trade union, which was founded in 1884, made them regulate the remaining child labour according to the labour legislation? But, why did Mr Kockum and his managers abolish child labour in the cigar making, but maintained, or even increased, the number of children employed in tobacco spinning? Was the work more dangerous in cigar making than in tobacco spinning? Let us have a look at the work environment in the factory.

All tobacco work was, according to another state investigation, very unhealthy work and the workers risked attacks on their respiratory organs due to the polluted air in the factories. The handling of dry tobacco leaves

53 "Glasarbetarminnen från Surte", *Arbetarrörelsens Årsbok* 1974, p. 12.

54 Isberg, *Malmö Stads 600-årsjubileum*, p. 463.

caused the pollution, and the dust polluted the air of all the workrooms.[55] If Mr Kockum was guided by the idea that children should not work, especially not in unhealthy factories, he and his managers should have abolished child labour in both the tobacco spinning and the cigar making, not just one of them. So, to understand the differences in child labour between the two types of production, we have to take a closer look at the organisation of work in them.

In the 1830s, Professor Geijer (above) said that both children and women could be put to work in factories due to the division of labour. As we have seen, Mr Suell only employed boys to help skilled workers in his tobacco factory in Malmö at the beginning of the nineteenth century. When cigar making was started at that factory around 1830, it also was done by skilled men and boy assistants. Andreas Winqvist, who came back to the factory in 1834, told us that Mr Kockum employed a German cigar maker and had him teach Swedish boys how to make simple cigars. Gradually, more and more (German) cigar makers were employed, and these skilled men had a great influence on their own work situation. In a contract with Mr Kockum in 1847, the cigar makers collectively allowed the manager to allocate the young helpers of a cigar maker to other kinds of work, *if* the cigar maker did not show up for work on Mondays![56]

In 1858 men still upheld the privilege of doing the skilled work in the factory. In the tobacco spinning, eleven men, i.e. 12 per cent of all workers, were skilled spinners, so the relation between skilled and semi-skilled/unskilled work remained the same as half a century earlier. In cigar making 40 out of 46 men were registered as cigar makers, so the cigar making was well organised on the basis of skilled men and helpers.

In the middle of the century, however, a new work organisation was established and there was a significant shift in the gender composition of the tobacco workers (table 15.9). Both girls and women were employed in addition to the men and the boys. In the tobacco spinning 20 per cent of the workers were women, and some girls were added to the boys. In the cigar making most of the females were girls, who accounted for one third of the child workers.

55 *Arbetareförsäkringskomiténs betänkande* III: 7. Stockholm, 1888, p. 101.

56 MSA, *F.H. Kockums Tobaksfabriks arkiv*, Handlingar efter ämne 1835-1907. The Blue Monday was a craft tradition saying that master-workers did not work on Mondays, because they had to recover from the Sunday party. See Edgren, *Lärling – Gesäll – Mästare*, pp. 259-264.

Table 15.9. The Gender Composition of the Work Force at Kockum's Tobacco Factory in 1858

	All workers	*Men*		*Women*		*Boys*		*Girls*	
Tobacco spinning	93	18	19%	19	20%	49	53%	7	8%
Cigar making	121	46	38%	12	10%	42	35%	21	17%

Source: F. H. Kockums Tobaksfabriks arkiv. Handlingar efter ämne 1835–1907 (Malmö City Archive).
Note: A few of those whom the management of the factory called boys and girls were older than 15.

Since both the tobacco spinning and the cigar making (still) were manual jobs, the new gender division of labour cannot be explained by, for instance, the introduction of new technology. Unfortunately, I have found no sources to help explain why Mr Kockum and his managers added girls to the boys working in the tobacco industry in the middle of the nineteenth century. We can merely conclude that girls and women were employed at industrial work that previously had been totally male-coded. This loosening of the male-coded work had vast consequences for the future of the work organisation at the tobacco factory in Malmö.

To sum up: tobacco spinning had its traditions in Sweden back in the seventeenth century. As a manufacture it remained a manual job throughout the nineteenth century with a limited number of male skilled workers and a large number of semi-skilled and/or unskilled workers. One third of the unskilled workers were children, but the gender composition of the workforce changed so that women and girls gradually were added to the boys to do unskilled work. In the cigar making, on the other hand, dramatic changes happened. It started as a totally male-dominated work by teams of skilled men and assisting boys, but soon both women and girls were involved in the work. At the end of the century child labour was rather uncommon. The decline was part of a wider process, in which skilled men partly were replaced by women as cigar makers. The female cigar makers, however, were not skilled manual workers but semi-skilled machine operators.

Mechanisation of cigar making started in the middle of the nineteenth century. In Kockum's archive there is a description from 1857 of an American cigar-making machine, with the help of which two men could make seven to eight cigars a minute, at least according to the propaganda of the machine making company. These cigars were said to look as if the most skilful cigar maker had made them. Mr Kockum was convinced that mechanisation of cigar making could be most profitable, so several machines were brought to the factory. In 1870, they reported to the national board of trade that forty cigar-making machines were installed in the factory.[57] As we have seen, Mr Kockum and his managers gradually employed women to operate these machines. So too did other capitalists and managers of the tobacco industry in Sweden. Altogether, 43 per cent of the workers in the tobacco industry in 1875 were women, a percentage that rose to 56 per cent in 1891 and to 58 per cent in 1898.[58] A lot of these women replaced teams of skilled men and their assisting children of both sexes. Children were no longer required for the production of cigars. They had to make their living, and spend their days, in other ways.

Mechanisation of work and its influence on child labour is even more evident in matchmaking in Sweden. At JTAB, Mr Hay hired the engineer Alexander Lagerman to construct machines for the company. Already in the 1860s, Mr Lagerman had the idea of constructing a complete matchmaking machine, which was expected to do all the work operations without any interruption at all. The managers, however, were more pragmatic and made him focus on individual work operations such as box making and box filling, and in the 1870s all the individual work operations were mechanised individually. Finally, Mr Lagerman's all-in-one matchmaking machine was installed at the factory in 1892. As we have seen, child labour was abolished, and so too was the making of matchboxes as an unhealthy household job.[59] Now we can see why Mr Hay did not employ children any more. In a city like Jönköping, where matchmaking dominated industrial work, children of poor families had problems finding jobs. Thus, to local working-class families Mr Lagerman was "the man who took the bread out of the mouths of poor people".[60]

There are indications that child labour also declined in the textile industry due to mechanisation, most of all the introduction of more complicated and high-speeded spinning machines in the 1850s and 1860s.[61] Even in parts of the glass industry, mechanisation meant less demand for child labour, for

57 Riksarkivet, Stockholm, *Kommerskollegii arkiv*. Årsberättelser, 1863-1870.

58 Calculated from *Barnarbetskommitténs betänkande*, table 3; *Revisionskommitténs betänkande*, table 1; and *Undersökning af tobaksindustrien i Sverige*, table 7.

59 Riksarkivet, Stockholm, *Kommerskollegii arkiv*. Årsberättelser, 1860–1900; Lundström, *Tändsticksindustrien*, pp. 32-37.

60 Vadstena Landsarkiv, Andersson and J. Hjelmberg, "Några minnesanteckningar".

61 Göransson, *Från familj till fabrik*, p. 135.

instance at bottle making and transportation. As one glass maker recalled: "It was jolly good when the bottles were transported on mechanical assembly lines into the storage rooms to be cooled down, because then we did not use boys to do the transportation any more".[62]

In this article, I claim that there was not only a statistical connection but also a causality between mechanisation and declining child labour in important Swedish industries in the second half of the nineteenth century. Employers introduced new machines for work that many children had performed before. The logic says that children had been used to do simple work operations that had been established when complicated work had been divided into several individual work operations. The logic also says that simple work operations were easier to mechanise than more complicated ones, so it was easier to mechanise work operations that children had performed.[63] Most often detailed calculations of the gains were made before new machines were bought to replace human labour. Poor children of increasing ages faced increasing problems in being employed for factory work. Instead of labour, children of poor families faced the risk of child unemployment.

The process accelerated at the beginning of the twentieth century, when the number of youngsters under the age of eighteen dropped dramatically both in the tobacco industry, from 1,071 in 1900 to 85 in 1935, and in matchmaking, from 1,965 in 1900 to 51 in 1935.[64] The percentage of youngsters fell from 24 to 4 in the tobacco industry and from 32 to 2 per cent in matchmaking. The development was caused by the introduction of all-in-one machines in both industries. The driving force, however, was a dramatic monopolisation of the two industries into a state monopoly of the tobacco industry (by then mostly the making of cigarettes) and into a private monopoly in matchmaking, controlled by one of the most well-known Swedish capitalists – Ivar Krueger. The changes made it close to impossible for working-class youngsters to get a job in the two industries. The social problem of child labour was about to be replaced by its opposite – child and youth unemployment.

62 "Glasarbetarminnen från Surte", *Arbetarrörelsens Årsbok*, 1974, p. 42.

63 Some skilled work was also mechanised, often resulting in what was considered to be less valuable products.

64 *BiSOS*, Serie D, 1900-1911; *SOS: Industri*, 1912-1935 (Statistics of Sweden, Industries).

Industrial Capitalism and Child Labour

A lot of children were put to work long before industrial capitalism, but industrial child labour differed quite a lot from children's work in pre-capitalist and pre-industrial societies. Most of industrial child labour was not an introductory phase of vocational training for skilled work as it had been in peasant societies and in the guild system. Instead, most industrial child labour – although not all of it – was part of a new capitalist view of labour as a production cost that capitalists and managers had to minimise as much as possible. That is the main reason why children and women were of interest to industrial capitalists and their managers. Another reason was that children were more easily subordinated than adult workers were to the work discipline that managers tried to introduce in factories. Local authorities, widely controlled by the bourgeoisie, helped capitalists to get poor children to work for them in the factories by not permitting begging and by pressing poor parents to send their children into factory work. In that political economy employers could, without taking any greater risks, even break the legislation by employing children at a younger age than was permitted.

Division of labour was another characteristic of industrial capitalism that promoted the exploitation of children. Since they could only perform easy and simple operations, the number of children that could be employed depended on the possibilities to develop such operations. In Sweden, those possibilities were most considerable in glass making, tobacco manufacturing, cotton spinning, and matchmaking, and children were employed in those industries more widely than in others. Poor large families or one-parent families provided the capitalists with child labourers, although a few of them were orphans.

Child labour, however, peaked in cotton spinning, matchmaking and tobacco manufacturing in the middle of the nineteenth century and it decreased significantly thereafter. Since the industrial take-off in Sweden is said to have started in the 1870s, child labour does not seem to have too much to do with the deepening of industrial capitalism. On the contrary, child labour was part of the early phase of industrial capitalism, in which a lot of work was done manually and workers were exploited in extensive ways, i.e. even at very young and very old ages, during long working days and so on. In contrast to what capitalists, managers, and some bourgeois ideologists hoped, child labour in general – although not always – decreased as work was mechanised and employers replaced the extensive ways of exploitation with intensive ways, i.e. efficient work in limited working days. Indeed, the ambitions to facilitate the exploitation of children at mechanised work failed. Child labour remained where work was not mechanised, and the exploitation of child labourers in those industries probably intensified as managers of low-mechanised workshops competed with those who ran more mechanised mills. The social problem of child labour was replaced with its opposite – child unemployment that later turned into youth unemployment. Consequently, in 1863 Statistics Sweden replaced the category "children" up to fifteen years of age with "youngsters" up to eighteen, when registering workers. Today, the age limit for the registration of youth unemployment in Sweden is 24!

So, why did employers mechanise work? First of all, mechanised work was most often more profitable than manual work; managers made careful calculations before buying new machines. The managers at JTAB , for instance, calculated in the late 1860s in detail before mechanising the manual work done by children.[65] Another important reason for managers to mechanise work was to minimise their dependence on skilled workers. Due to their control over the means of production, several employers succeeded in replacing skilled workers with semi-skilled machine handlers. Sometimes, as in cigar making, the change included a new gender division of labour, since women were trained to handle the cigar machines. Unintentionally, child labour was abolished as part of that process.

When it was efficient, labour legislation only speeded up the introduction of new machines and a new work organisation. Whether the legislation is efficient or not depends basically on the power relations in society. The educational system and the welfare policy of any society likewise depend on its power relations, and they might encourage poor families to send their children to school instead of selling their labour.

65 Vadstena Landsarkiv, *JTAB:s arkiv*, Kalkylbok.

CHAPTER 16

Useful and Industrious: Fostering and Rural Child Labour in Nineteenth-Century Sweden

Elisabeth Engberg

Throughout the last three generations, attitudes towards child labour, in Sweden as well as in other European countries, have undergone a radical change. Underage children are no longer expected to contribute to the household economy with their work or their salary, and fostering for manual labour is no longer a crucial aspect of a child's upbringing and education. For children of the welfare state, their grandparents' or great grandparents' memories of hard work at an early age easily sound like unrealistic tales from a distant past. Yet child labour was an inherent part of the rural society long into the twentieth century, although its importance gradually declined.[1]

This chapter discusses norms and practices of child labour in nineteenth-century Sweden, with emphasis on the situation of poor children in a rural context. In historical research, industrial child labour has generally attracted more interest than the working conditions for children in rural settings.[2] The same situation prevailed in the past. In comparison to labouring children in industry, the working conditions of rural children were not a subject of debate. There was no protective legislation regulating their working hours, and their participation in work could not be followed in official statistics.[3] The simple explanation is that rural child labour to a

1 Sjöberg, "En källa till välmåga", pp. 50-52; Rahikainen, *Centuries of Child Labour.*

2 For Sweden see for example Olsson, *Då barn var lönsamma*; Hedvall, "Debatten om barnarbete"; Bjurman and Olsson, *Barnarbete och arbetarbarn*; Sandin, "In the Large Factory Towns".

3 In Sweden, industrial child labour was widely debated already in the late 1850s, but it was not regulated in law until 1881, with a lower age limit of 12 years for industrial work. For 12-14 year olds, working hours in factories were restricted to 6 hours a day and for 14-18 year olds to 10 hours a day. Working children were also obliged to attend school. The iron, mining and sawmill industries, at that time the most important industrial branches in Sweden, were, however, exempt from the legislation. In a new

large extent was family based and existed within the framework of parental responsibilities and socialization. By Swedish law, parents had an almost unlimited right of disposition of their children's labour.[4] Participating in domestic and agricultural work was a part of the fostering, and unlike industrial work, its nature and limits were not regulated by any legislation.[5] Poor laws and local policies are, however, more outspoken about what was expected of a child and usually tell us more about the attitudes towards child labour on the household level than other normative contemporary sources. When the parental duties were taken over by society, the private became public, and norms and expectations regarding child labour thus became more visible.

Shaping Useful Citizens

In the Swedish poor laws, children have for a long time had a privileged position. This special attention was largely motivated by the fact that underage children were not to blame for their poverty and should thus always be entitled to support. Besides alleviating material needs, there were also other motives for society's interest in the children of the poor. With the right fostering, it was argued in the *Act regarding Hospitals and Orphanages* from 1763, there was always hope that poor and underprivileged boys and girls could be raised into useful citizens, able to support themselves.[6] At that time, Sweden was deeply influenced by mercantilist ideas, and better care of neglected children was proposed as one effective measure to increase the population and improve society.[7] Since institutions intended for childcare were uncommon in rural areas, foster care was usually the

act, issued in 1900, working hours were increased for certain age groups: for 13 year olds from 6 to 10 hours, and for 14 years from 10 to 11 hours, 6 days a week. The lower age limit for industrial work was still 12 years, with exception for children working in ironworks and sawmills, where children were allowed to perform lighter work from the age of 11. A comprehensive overview of Swedish research regarding industrial child labour legislation can be found in Sandin, "In the Large, Factory Towns", pp. 18-21. See also Bjurman and Olsson, *Barnarbete och arbetarbarn*, pp. 27-33.

4 Kongl Maj:ts förnyade nådiga Lego-Stadga för husbönder och tjenstehjon, Svensk Författningssamling [hereafter, SFS] 1833:43, 18-20§§; Sjöberg, *Att säkra framtidens skördar*, p. 94.

5 Sjöberg, "En källa till välmåga", pp. 42ff.

6 *Kongl. Förordning, angående Hospitals och Barnhus Inrättningarne i Riket*, 11 April 1763, 1:1.

7 Johansson, "Fattigvård i Sverige", p. 272.

favoured kind of welfare.[8] The assumption was that children would be better off in families, where they could escape pauperism and be brought up to be responsible citizens in a healthy environment. In the foster home they could further be raised and educated in the "first and most essential industry in the state", that is, agriculture.[9]

Preparing poor children for adult life by specific training was an early objective of Swedish welfare legislation. In the seventeenth century, an appeal was made to artisans and skippers to take in poor boys, with the explicit intention that they would learn a trade, and in Swedish towns, workhouse children were engaged in the manufacturing industry. Boys learned various crafts, while girls were educated in female chores such as sewing, weaving, and spinning.[10] Taken together, the seventeenth- and eighteenth-century poor laws express very clearly that labour was regarded as an inherent and essential part of poor children's fostering. The measures of relief were not only intended to alleviate material needs, but also to educate impoverished children into useful citizens, able to support themselves in the future. By good and beneficial labour they would escape pauperism, wickedness, and beggary.

In contrast to their predecessors, the nineteenth-century poor laws are not very explicit about the role of labour in fostering, but bear witness to several demands imposed upon poor-relief authorities and foster parents in the past. Each parish was supposed to care for their own poor, and great emphasis was laid upon society's responsibility to provide poor children with food, shelter, education, and a Christian upbringing. Children supported by public welfare were supposed to have a permanent residence where their education could be supervised, and the poor relief board was also assigned the responsibility to support and facilitate poor children's attendance at school. Begging was explicitly and unconditionally banned.[11] Besides these basic requirements, no details were given of what was supposed to be included in the measures for relief. This absence of detailed instructions and measures was in fact for a long time a particular trait of the Swedish poor laws. The social practice of poor relief was a local mat-

8 Engberg, "Boarded out by auction", pp. 432-433.

9 *Kongl. Förordning, angående Hospitals och Barnhus Inrättningarne i Riket*, 11 April 1763, 4:2; Lönnroth, "Översikt över fattigvårdens utveckling", p. 96.

10 Lönnroth, "Översikt över fattigvårdens utveckling", pp. 89-91.

11 *Kongl. Maj:ts Nådiga Förordning angående Fattigwården i Riket*, SFS 1847:23, 6:2, 20 §§; *Kongl. Maj:ts Nådiga Förordning angående Fattigwården i Riket*, SFS 1853:39, 6:2, 20 §§; *Kongl. Maj:ts nådiga Förordning angående Fattigwården*, SFS 1871:33, 1, 4-5 §§; Sjöberg, *Att säkra framtidens skördar*, p. 44.

ter, and the precise measures were not specified in national legislation.[12] To find out more about nineteenth-century attitudes towards child labour it is thus necessary to change perspectives and turn from national legislation to local poor relief policies and regulations.

Beneficial Labour

In Skellefteå, a large rural parish in northern Sweden, the local regulations of poor relief from the nineteenth century bear witness to an attitude towards child labour that is very similar to the one found in the eighteenth-century Swedish poor laws. Learning to work was a crucial part of children's fostering, and labour in itself was an indispensable measure to educate them into good, useful, and self-supporting citizens. In Lutheran Sweden, labour was highly valued. Man's labour was the foundation of every society, and as a God-given vocation it had to be taken seriously.[13] The local poor relief policy obliged foster parents to "accustom the child to industriousness by providing it with suitable work, suited to its age and ability".[14] Taking in a foster child, the foster parent was expected to fully shoulder parental rights and responsibilities towards its fosterling, including benefiting from its contributions to the household economy.[15] The local regulations in Skellefteå also reflect the fact that, regarding children, relief had a more long-term aim than to merely fulfil immediate material needs. Food and shelter, fostering, beneficial labour, adequate schooling, and a Christian upbringing were supposed to protect the children from pauperism and beggary and turn them into good labourers serving society and providing for themselves.[16]

What kind of labour was expected from a child in the rural household economy in the nineteenth century? In several studies, Swedish historian Mats Sjöberg has discussed the character of child labour in rural households before and after the turn of the century in 1900. One of Sjöberg's impor-

12 Engberg, *I fattiga omständigheter*, pp. 57-64. In this respect, the detailed, politically influenced Orphanage Act of 1763 is very much a divergence from an otherwise distinct Swedish pattern.

13 Midré, *Bot, bedring eller brød*, p. 27. A detailed discussion of the Lutheran ideas about work and vocation can be found in Grenholm, *Arbetets mening*, p. 168.

14 Skellefteå Municipal Archive (hereafter SMA), Local Poor Relief Policy 1846, 27 §. C.f. SMA, local policies also from 1862 and 1868.

15 SFS 1833:43, 19 §.

16 SMA, Local Poor Relief Policy 1846, 1 §; 1862, 1 §; 1868, 1 §.

tant conclusions is that children were gradually socialized into work.[17] The first step was to watch, the next to help and assist. The third and final step was to be assigned individual responsibility of specific chores in the household economy. Initially, children mostly followed their parents in their daily work, but around the age of seven, they were expected to take a more active part in the household work. At the beginning this often meant carrying firewood and water, feeding cattle or helping out with the small children. With increasing age, the responsibilities increased, as well as the gendered division of labour, and it was generally considered that a twelve year old was capable of performing more or less the same work as an adult. Boys accompanied the men in their outdoor work, while the girls were introduced to female domestic duties. Both boys and girls worked with herding and in the fields, especially during the intense period of haymaking and harvest, which frequently engaged the entire household.[18]

A similar picture is provided by historian Britt Liljewall, who has studied childhood narratives from boys in peasant families, born in the late eighteenth and the early nineteenth century. Around the age of six, the time of play and leisure was over, and the child entered a new phase in life characterized by increasing demands and participation in the household's labour force. Initially, both boys and girls were supposed to assist with domestic duties within the female sphere of the household. By the age of ten to eleven, however, a gendered division of labour started to occur. The boys were socialized into the male labour force and were successively introduced into the male fields of responsibility in order to actually function as farmhands on the family holdings in their early teens.[19] Liljewall's sources also point out that for a farmer's son childhood ended around the age of fifteen, in Sweden usually coinciding with the age of protestant confirmation, an important rite of passage into adulthood. After that age, a boy was expected to perform the work of an adult on the family farm or as a hired farmhand. In Sweden, the system of life-cycle servitude was well established, and it was very common that young people from all social

17 Sjöberg, "En källa till välmåga", pp. 19-20; Sjöberg, *Att säkra framtidens skördar*, pp. 116, 140.

18 Children's work with herding in rural settings is explicitly discussed in Sjöberg, "Working Rural Children". See also Jablonka, "Paths towards autonomy", p. 412. Jablonka describes a similar pattern for rural France in the early 20th century, where teenagers were considered essential to the labour force of a small-scale family holding.

19 Liljewall, "Minnen av barnarbete", pp. 65-68.

classes, including sons and daughters of farmers, spent some years as maids and farmhands in other households before marriage.[20]

As Swedish ethnologist Marianne Liliequist points out, child labour also had a disciplining effect. Learning to obey authorities and follow advice from those more experienced was also a part of fostering. Step by step, these children were socialized into rural life and fostered to industriousness and independence-desirable virtues for farmers as well as for the lower strata of the rural society.[21] Although rural child labour could be hard and strenuous, Liliequist demonstrates that from the children's perspective it could also give a sense of pride and satisfaction as they learned more advanced skills and thus took further steps towards adulthood.[22] However, it is important to bear in mind that the gradual and adaptive introduction into labour was largely a privilege for children of smallholders and farmers. As Sjöberg remarks, children who belonged to the landless classes in rural society usually had to enter the open labour market earlier, something that most likely also implied greater demands and harder working conditions.[23]

An even more vulnerable position, however, was that of the underage children and paupers boarded out for fostering that actually could be used as indentured servants by their foster-parents.[24] Yet the local poor relief policy suggests that there existed certain norms and limitations regarding how the almost unlimited parental right was to be exercised towards these children. In Skellefteå, foster parents were explicitly exhorted to not use corporal punishment carelessly. Like all parents, they had the right to chastise their children when necessary, "but not when it is possible to correct the child without it," it was stated in the local policy.[25] Further, schooling was important. A foster parent that neglected a fosterling's elementary education could risk getting the annual allowance from the parish reduced.[26] It is, however, a well-known fact that in rural Sweden compulsory school attendance at times caused several conflicts between local authorities and parents who were less interested in school education than keeping their

20 *Ibid.*, p. 69; Lundh, *Life Cycle Servants*, p. 9; Gaunt, *Familjeliv i Norden*.
21 Liliequist, *Nybyggarbarn*, p. 107.
22 Liliequist, *Nybyggarbarn*, pp. 112ff.
23 Sjöberg, "En källa till välmåga", pp. 19ff.
24 Cf. Rahikainen, "Compulsory Child Labour", p. 164; Gunnlaugsson, "Everyone's Been Good to Me", p. 344; Gunnlaugsson, *Ómagar og utangarðsfólk*, p. 178. See also Guttormsson, and *Bernska, ungdómur og uppeldi á einveldisöld*, pp. 133–185.
25 SMA, Local Poor Relief Policy 1846, 27 §; 1862, 23 §; 1868, 14 §.
26 SMA, Local Poor Relief Policy 1846, 28 §; 1862, 24 §.

children in the labour force.[27] In case of maltreatment, the authorities were allowed to remove a child from an unsuitable foster home. The extent to which these protective rules were observed and put into practice is, however, unclear.[28] On the national level in Sweden, specific legislation protecting children in foster care was not issued until 1902.[29]

Fosterlings and Labourers

Attitudes, norms, and expectations of children's participation in the labour force also become visible in the practice of boarding out poor children, when the parental duties were taken over by society and were assigned to foster parents. A study that involves 495 children that were boarded out in Skellefteå parish during three periods in the nineteenth century, 1830–1837, 1868–1871 and 1891–1895, gives further evidence of the importance of child labour in a rural pre-industrial context.[30]

Fostering in a Rural Context

In Skellefteå, as in most rural parishes in the northern Sweden, there were no institutions intended for childcare, and fostering on the household level was the usual solution to provide care for needy children. Following a traditional practice found all over Scandinavia, the children were boarded out by public auction in which the prospective foster parents bid openly against each other to find the least costly fostering arrangement for each child. The one who demanded the lowest compensation to take in the child won the bid.[31] In rural areas, this was a common way to stipulate the price of goods and services, in many ways similar to the municipal practice of public procurement used today.[32] The public auctions usually took place during the major holidays and were open to anyone who wanted to attend. Before the bidding started, the children were presented individually before the assembled audience of potential foster parents. This method of contracting foster homes was a risky, but rational, way for a parish

27 Sjöberg, "Working Rural Children", pp. 106, 123-125.
28 Engberg, "Boarded out", p. 436.
29 Lag om fosterbarns vård, SFS 1902:63.
30 These data are discussed in detail in Engberg, "Boarded out".
31 Jørgensen, *Studier over det offentlige*, pp. 253-257; Rahikainen, "Compulsory Child Labour", p. 170; Gunnlaugsson, *Ómagar*, p. 178. The auction practice is described in Engberg, "Boarded out", pp. 433-437.
32 Lundberg, *Going Once, Going Twice*, p. 1.

with a weak economy to provide children in need of relief with the barest essentials. The competition between the bidders without doubt helped the poor relief authorities to keep the costs at a reasonable level, with the disadvantage that it was almost impossible to perform any advance control of the suitability of the prospective foster parents.[33] Certainly, poor laws and the local poor relief policy spelled out the foster parents' obligations towards their fosterling, but there was no guarantee that this always protected the children from maltreatment and exploitation.

Most children that were put into the awkward situation of being boarded out in a public auction were already socially vulnerable boys and girls from families in various kinds of crises. Several came from poor households with a large number of dependents, where placing one or several children with foster parents was intended to improve the poor parents' chances to provide for themselves and their offspring. Others had lost one or both parents and were in need of guardianship and support. More than 50 per cent of the children that were boarded out in Skellefteå during these three periods actually came from families in which at least one parent was dead. For others, social problems in the family, such as heavy drinking, neglect or abuse, was the main reason why they were taken into custody by society.[34]

The Useful Child

The results indicate that when there was a choice, it was most likely not entirely up to the parents to decide which child had to leave the family. In addition, the prospects of boarding the child out at a reasonable cost had to be considered, and in this respect, the children's ability to work seems to have been of crucial importance. In rural Skellefteå, where agriculture entirely dominated the economy, primarily children who had reached an age at which they could begin to be useful in the household were boarded out. Throughout all three of these periods in the nineteenth century, there was a particular predominance of the age group ten to fifteen, closely followed by five to nine year olds, while infants and toddlers were in the minority. Children below the age of five were clearly underrepresented

33 The auction method was criticized by contemporaries for being hazardous and allowing unsuitable foster parents to exploit children for economic reasons. Engberg, "Boarded out", pp. 435ff. See also Jørgensen, *Studier over det offentlige*, pp. 255-257.

34 Demographic Data Base (hereafter DDB), Umeå University, Parish Records, Skellefteå; SMA, Poor Relief Records and Boarding Registers 1830-1895. A detailed discussion of the familial background of the children that were boarded out is found in Engberg, "Boarded out", pp. 443-451.

in comparison to the number of children at risk in the same age group in the population.[35] This pattern is also recognized in other Nordic contexts and can, according to Icelandic historian Gísli Ágúst Gunnlaugsson, be explained in at least two possible ways. Either poor parents were more reluctant to give up small children, or foster parents were more willing to take care of children who could be useful in the household.[36] In this case, the latter hypothesis seems to be the more reasonable. Swedish economist Sofia Lundberg shows with historical data and economic models that nineteenth-century farmers and smallholders in northern Sweden, in comparison to foster parents in the lower strata in society, seemed to favour older, more productive and useful foster children, preferably boys. The municipality's payment to the foster parents decreased proportionately with the age of the child, but this was readily compensated for by a child that was more useful in the household economy. Unhealthy children were, according to Lundberg's study, significantly less attractive.[37]

A Need for Child Labour

A closer look at the households that took in foster children during the first of the three studied periods, 1830–1837, gives further evidence for the importance of the child's usefulness. The large majority of the foster parents in rural Skellefteå were independent farmers with a household structure that suggests that they could have had use for child labour in the household. More than 60 per cent were in the normal childbearing period of life, most of them in the early stages of family formation with children that were too small to participate in the household economy. These growing households might not have needed another mouth to feed, but they nevertheless needed help with domestic duties. A lucid illustration is the nine-year-old Carolina who in 1835 was boarded out to the 28-year-old farmer Hans Olof Degerman and his wife Maglena. When Carolina was taken in for fostering, the spouses already had three small children to support: four-year-old Olof, two-year-old Per and the infant Anna. Two years later the next child was born.[38] Most young farmers, who like this household had their hands full providing for a growing family and had children

35 DDB, Umeå University, Parish Records, Skellefteå; SMA, Poor Relief Records and Boarding Registers 1830-1895; Engberg, "Boarded out", pp. 439-441.

36 Gunnlaugsson, "Everyone's Been Good to Me", p. 353.

37 Lundberg, "Child auctions".

38 Härnösand Regional Archives (hereafter HRA), Parish Assembly Records Skellefteå, 25 Dec 1831; DDB, Umeå University, Parish Records Skellefteå.

that were not yet old enough to help their parents, seem to have preferred foster children like Carolina. Two out of three young households took in foster children that were 10 years old or older, with a certain overrepresentation of girls. It is not difficult to assume that for these young families the foster children fulfilled a role that could not yet be taken on by their biological offspring, assisting with childcare and domestic duties.[39]

Among the foster parents in the later stages of family formation as well, the need for child labour seems to have been a motive for taking in foster children. Most of these families had quite large holdings, something that could suggest a greater need for a useful child, and in addition, in comparison to weaker farmers and landless people with the same household size, also better resources to feed an extra child. During almost a decade, 1828–1837, the parish was hit by a severe subsistence crisis with a general food shortage and economic hardship that affected all strata in the population and brought even previously self-supporting households to destitution.[40] What, then, made these households willing to take an extra child into their homes at a time when large parts of the population struggled to support themselves and were reluctant to share their meagre resources with others? In the sources, it is difficult to find reliable support for the idea that they were solely motivated by true altruism towards poor and unfortunate children. The only reasonable reward a foster child in rural Skellefteå between 1830 and 1837 could have had to offer its guardian, besides the compensation paid for the fostering and companionship, was its usefulness and capacity for work.

Yet when it comes to the ages of the foster children taken in by these slightly older foster parents, the image of large households primarily interested in useful children suitable for work becomes less distinct. Instead of the expected predominance of somewhat older children, useful as maids and farmhands, the results show that more than half of the fosterlings in these families were eight years old or younger.[41] This observation does not contradict the suggestion that the child's usefulness was important, but nevertheless indicates that, besides the need for labour, other motives also

39 DDB, Umeå University, Parish Records, Skellefteå; SMA, Poor Relief Records and Boarding Registers 1830-1837. See also Sköld, *Fosterbarnsindustri eller människokärlek*, pp. 359-362.

40 Engberg, *I fattiga omständigheter*, pp. 75ff, 88-92.

41 DDB, Umeå University, Parish Records, Skellefteå; SMA, Poor Relief Records and Boarding Registers 1830-1837.

operated when poor children were boarded out to foster parents in rural nineteenth-century Sweden.[42]

Although it evidently existed, the nineteenth-century poor relief records in Skellefteå do not say anything about the occurrence of exploitation and abuse of foster children.[43] In 1863, however, one case of neglect was brought to public attention. It was the local newspaper that reported about a boy that had been mistreated by his foster parents. Despite several warnings, the situation had not improved and the child was finally removed from the foster home, which had failed to give him "the proper care and upbringing". Not one single word is said about the presence of exploitation and hard work. The editor pays tribute to the intervention of the authorities and notes that unfortunately, some foster parents seemed to be more conscious about their own profit than about their fosterlings' welfare.[44] Even in a case such as this, in which it is reasonable to assume that a child had been exploited over the limits, rural child labour is dressed in terms of care, upbringing and parental duties towards the child.

Conclusions

Rural child labour is in many ways an elusive phenomenon. Although for a long time it was as frequent as it was widespread, it is usually embedded in a fostering context and is shaped by family relations as well as by unspoken norms and attitudes towards socialization, education, and childrearing. This study of norms and practices regarding the fostering of poor children in a rural nineteenth-century setting allows us to get a glimpse of the norms, expectations, and attitudes towards children's work within a sphere that otherwise remains very private.

From a normative perspective, child labour is unanimously described as useful and beneficial. In national legislation as well as in local polices, good labour stands out as the antipode to pauperism, vice, and beggary.

42 In previous research, four main motives stand out as important for fostering in a historical context: a need for labour, a need for an additional income in the family, kinship responsibilities and to some extent childlessness. All available evidence suggests that these motives operated in early nineteenth-century northern Sweden as well. See further Eliosabeth Engberg, "Master or substitute parent. Household structure and motives for fostering in a 19th century Scandinavian context", Sixth ESSHC (European Social Science History Conference), Amsterdam 22-25 march 2006.

43 Engberg, "Boarded out", p. 450.

44 *Skellefteå Nya Tidning*, 15 April 1863.

In the endeavour to educate useful and self-supporting citizens, labour in itself was a prerequisite as well as an important instrument. Yet it is evident that the great importance of child labour in rural settings did not solely rest upon ideas and notions about what best promoted a child's upbringing. There was also a need for child labour in society, and many smallholders depended upon children's participation in the household economy. Thus the ideological foundation and society's demands legitimatized and underpinned each other and shaped the attitudes towards rural child labour long into the twentieth century.

The practice of boarding out poor children gives additional evidence of the same norms and attitudes that were expressed in national law and local policy. A foster parent fully shouldered the parental rights and responsibilities and was thus supposed to provide the fosterling with useful and nurturing work. In most cases, there was also an apparent demand for child labour among the foster parents, and a child's potential usefulness and capacity for work were in fact of great importance for the prospects of boarding it out. Hence, also in social practice, norms, attitudes and society's demands reinforced and legitimatized each other. As the American sociologist Viviana Zelizer argues, fostering can under favourable circumstances be understood as a process of exchange, where the foster child provided the household with productive labour, and got board, clothing, education and, in this case, fostering to labour and industriousness in return.[45] However, these circumstances were delicately balanced and could easily be turned into a situation of abuse and exploitation.

It can no more be taken for granted that biological bonds at all times vouched for the absence of maltreatment and abuse than it can be assumed that farmers always wanted to profit from their foster children. Letting the child take part in the daily work in the household does not exclude parental care and affection, neither from foster parents nor from biological parents. The nature of the labour, the working conditions and the working hours may have been shaped by norms, attitudes, and expectations, but were ultimately settled within the personal relationships between parents and children. For this reason, rural child labour remains a multifaceted phenomenon with many manifestations that can be illuminated to some extent, but probably never fully captured.

45 Zelizer, *Pricing the Priceless Child*, pp. 170ff.

CHAPTER 17

Child Labor in Imperial Russia

Boris B. Gorshkov

"Approaching the factory building, an enormous 1,613-yards-long beast, one cannot even imagine that the mouth of this creature absorbs a huge mass of children", wrote a late nineteenth-century observer about one of thousands textile mills in Russia. This histrionic image illustrates all too well the pervasiveness of child labor and children's role in Russia's industrialization in the late nineteenth century. Children made up about fifteen per cent of factory workers, ranging from zero to forty per cent in single enterprises. These proportions involved hundreds of thousands of child laborers, about two-thirds of whom worked in textiles. Children performed various, usually unskilled chores, and sometimes were assigned adult responsibilities. In textile production they ran errands: carried bobbins and spindles, cleaned equipment and floors, and so on. At times, they worked as spinners, weavers or dyers. In mining, children sorted ore, fueled lamps and carried tools inside the mines. Their workday lasted for twelve or more hours and remuneration of their labor was one-third of the lowest adult wage rate. Most factory children came from the country, while a few were lower class urban dwellers or siblings of orphanages and foundling homes.

Origins of Child Labor

Child labor in Russia was hardly a novelty of nineteenth century industrialization. Children's involvement in productive labor was as a traditional practice and existed well before mechanized factories began to appear on Russia's landscape. From ancient times, children had worked in the countryside in agriculture, cottage industry and all other types of domestic manufacturing. In addition, Russian children worked in manorial and state factories and mines. The principal goal of having children engaged in productive labor during earlier times was less economic than educational. Child labor commonly functioned as the means of training children and preparing them for adult life. Lower social strata families in Russia viewed the early commencement of children into productive work suitable to their age and ability as a form of education.

Besides its vital educational aspect, the child labor in the countryside signified the extent to which most families of rural Russia depended for their livelihood on labor contributions from all family members. The commonly held view that the economic hardship of peasant families was the foremost cause of child labor in the countryside is inaccurate. Not poverty, but rather the origins and evolution of the local peasant economy within the context of the family influenced the use of children in production. Obviously, the economic conditions of the individual family might affect the degree of children's participation in productive labor. They were, however, hardly its major cause. Because the family was the basic production unit of the rural economy, the nature of the peasant household economy and the conditions of its maintenance entailed the labor participation of all family members, with the exception of very small children and elderly people. The rearing and education of children went side by side with the actual productive economic activity of the peasant household. Even so, apprenticeship, rather than possible contribution to family income was the central factor of child labor in the countryside.

In peasant families, teaching household activities and agricultural occupations was considered the most essential duty in the upbringing and education of children. Sources suggest that in those cases, when foster-parents reported to the village commune about fulfillment of their parental duties, they usually emphasized their efforts to teach the children they adopted all common household and agricultural occupations. Peasants believed that if a child has not begun learning peasant labor from an early age, it would hardly develop the aptitude for work in the future. The wide popular acceptance of child productive work in the countryside was reflected in an old Russian custom of calling juveniles by names according to the labor task they performed. Boys engaged in helping to plow or harrow were called variously plowboys or harrow boys; those who helped to pasture animals were called herds-boys. Girls were called variously nanny-girl, mentor girl, or *kazachikha* (maids who worked as domestic servants in other families) and so on, all names that reflected occupational activities. "Our plowboy," "our herds boy," or "our nanny girls" were habitual terms parents used to address their children.

Russian-language anthropologists suggest that peasants, in general, distinguished three major stages of the life cycle, which included childhood, adulthood, and old age, with a complexity of subdivisions, stages, and phases within each stage. These divisions not only rested upon popular notions about human biology but were also entrenched in a broad range of cultural assumptions and social roles. The divisions also corresponded with the individual's capability to work and clearly reflected peasant customs of distributing labor duties among family members. In the village the criteria for transitions from childhood to adulthood and to old age were relative and depended on the individual's physiological condition and readiness to undertake one or another duty. Labor duties in peasant families were carefully delineated according to the age, sex, and physical abilities of family members. Very small children, under the age of five or six, and people over sixty-five usually did not work. In impoverished families, or in families in which one of the adults was absent or deceased, children fulfilled all adult responsibilities at an earlier age.

In the countryside, the types of labor tasks children performed differed according to age, sex, and strength, and depended on the local economy. Introduction into productive work for both boys and girls usually started from the age of six or seven. To engage very young children into labor activity, parents developed various treats and rewards, or assigned simple tasks in the form of play. Many children's and juveniles' games and recreational activities imitated adult work-related and social activities.

Boys engaged in work traditionally fulfilled by male peasants – helping to sow, thresh, and spread manure. As boys grew older and gained more physical strength and ability, parents gave them greater responsibilities and assigned them more complicated tasks. At the age of seven, eight, or nine, boys began to help adult peasants with land cultivation. Their work involved leading horses during plowing and harrowing. From the age of nine or ten, boys began to carry out various other activities: accompanying the cows to water, feeding animals, carting manure, harrowing, helping adults in plowing and harvesting, and carrying provisions for adult males who worked away from the village (in local forests or on nearby rivers, ponds, and so on). From the age of thirteen to fourteen, the male peasant was supposed to work with the scythe, sickle, thresher, and axe, and began to learn how to work with the plough.

Girls' activities involved helping mothers in maintaining the household, caring for the younger children, and carrying out all agricultural responsibilities of adult female peasants, which included raking, strewing, reaping, binding sheaves, gleaning, and so on. Depending on the province, girls also learned various crafts and cottage industries, which in Russia were predominantly female endeavors. Girls' occupations were usually within the household or the local community, whereas boys' activities were inside as well as outside the village. Nevertheless, the occupational roles of boys and girls were sometimes interchangeable. In families without male children, girls helped with agricultural tasks normally performed by boys and, vice-versa, in families with no female children boys helped with female work. Depending on province, boys and girls also learned various crafts and worked in cottage industries. By the age of eighteen, children were regarded as "full workers" and assigned full labor obligation.

The state views coincided with the popular perceptions about child labor as a form of education and preparation for adult life. During the eighteenth century, with the goal of making children "learn a craft" or "gain a professional skill," the state authorized sending ten-year-old urban and rural children, including inmates of orphanages and foundling homes as apprentices to state and manorial factories. We should note at this point that the state also followed popular notions about the age to begin apprenticeship. Nevertheless, this "learning a craft" sometimes took abusive forms. Alongside apprenticeship, or even instead of it, state and manorial factories on occasion employed children as auxiliary workers. During the first half of the nineteenth century, the state undertook some timid measures to restrict child labor. An 1845 decree prohibited night work for children under the age of twelve, though without any significant provision for enforcement. The decree was almost totally ignored.

Was there abuse of child labor in the rural society before the Industrial Revolution? This question provokes exceedingly conflicting responses from historians of child labor. One may assume clearly that the extent of exploitation depended on the specific time and place in which they lived. In small nuclear families and in families with no adult males, child labor might prove to be more economically significant and the labor burden placed upon children therefore heavier than in extended families. Furthermore, when the rural economy in Russia became increasingly market-oriented labor burden on children in some families increased.

Nevertheless, the purpose and meaning of children's involvement in productive activities in the Russian countryside were not about profit or the value of children's labor. Historians of child labor suggest that children's output in agriculture was usually low and greatly lagged behind their consumption until children attained the age of thirteen or fifteen. The same was true for the non-agricultural sector of the rural economy. Most evidence suggests, therefore, that parents in the countryside occupied their children in productive work primarily for the purpose of teaching and apprenticing. Moreover, children were given labor tasks according to their gender, physical strength, and abilities, and they worked under the supervision of their parents or other adult members of the family. Thus, the ultimate goal of child productive activities in the countryside was to prepare children for adult life, to help them become full functioning members of the family and community. Perhaps the term "child labor" is inappropriate for young children's involvement in production in the countryside. Instead, it was for peasant families a form of schooling, education, or apprenticeship. Children were taught what they would be expected to do when they became adults. Children's involvement in productive activities in the countryside as an educational rather than economic fact is what constitutes one of the principal differences between child labor in traditional and early industrial economies.

Child Labor and Industrialization

During the second half of the nineteenth century, Russian industrialization entered a remarkable period of development. The speeding pace and intensification of the industrial economy during this period, coupled with mechanization and technological innovation, created a massive demand for industrial labor. These developments went together with rapid population growth and changes in the rural economy after the 1861 reform that led millions of rural residents, adults and children, to seek industrial employment. According to the economic historian A. G. Rashin, the number of industrial workers grew from 706,000 in 1865 to 1,432,000 in 1890. These figures cover only workers reported by the factory inspectors and do not include millions of workers in thousands of enterprises of all sizes and types that factory inspectors, by nature of their restricted legal mandate, did not scrutinize. During 1879-1885 about 33 per cent of Moscow province's factory workers began their employment under the age of twelve and 31 per cent between the ages of twelve and fourteen.

The factory inspectors statistics on industrial labor suggest that in the early 1880s, 49,581 (9.2 per cent) of 540,794 factory workers in some 2,792 surveyed factories were children of fifteen years of age and under. The overwhelming majority of child workers (30,171 or 60.9 per cent) engaged in textile production and, particularly, in the cotton industry (18,826 or 38 per cent). Many children also worked in mines and metallurgical plants (7,667 or 16 per cent) and in food processing industry (6,458 or 13 per cent).

Children also worked in food and organic materials (animal skins and bones) processing mills.

The number of girls of ages fifteen and below was significantly lower than the number of boys of the same ages. In Moscow's factories, for instance, out of 1,756 children of age fifteen and under, 1,451 (82.6 per cent) were boys and only 305 (17.4 per cent) girls. For children sixteen years and older, the proportions between boys and girls were closer. In Vladimir province, men comprised 63.7 and women 36.3 per cent of the province's workers, proportions that applied to underaged workers as well. Most girls remained in the countryside. Others left to work in various domestic services. Many of those who remained in villages worked in cottage industries in addition to their numerous household and agricultural activities.[1] For all its personal, social, and economic significance, none of this latter type of labor appeared in contemporary statistics.

Why did so many children enter the factory labor force during industrialization? Why did industries employ children? What changes did industrialization bring to the traditional practice of engaging children in production? As we have seen, before industrialization, children's productive activities had been broadly accepted as a means of preparing children for adult life and such factors were crucial in influencing children's factory employment during early industrialization. But industrialization itself produced new economic and social realities that spurred industrial child labor. On the one hand, dramatic economic and social changes in the countryside during the second half of the nineteenth century, including acceleration of the market economy, decline of traditional domestic manufacturing, rapid growth of rural population, and decline of traditional extended families, created a ready supply of labor. On the other hand, rapidly growing industries, along with mechanization and technological innovation, created massive demand for semi-skilled and unskilled industrial workers. The wide popular acceptance of child productive labor and the absence of any efficient child labor regulations in private factories made children an easily available and often desirable source of labor for late nineteenth century industrialization. In addition, as industrialization deepened, production switched from the household to mechanized factories along with certain rural work practices such as child and family labor. All these factors stirred the employment of children in industries during early industrialization.

1 Rashin, *Formirovanie rabochego klassa Rossii.*

Most late-nineteenth-century commentators about factory labor put forward a multitude of economic, technological, and social factors as the causes of widespread children's factory employment. Those who emphasized technological factors argued that mechanized factories often favored the employment of children because work on the new machines often did not require specific skills or great physical strength, unlike in traditional crafts; mechanized production involved tasks that could be performed without special training or skill. If possible, they preferred to use child labor for such tasks. In addition, contemporaries noted that manufacturers regarded children as more adaptable than adults to the new factory regime, better able to learn to work with the new machinery and technology, and often better fitted physically to perform certain tasks. Some manufacturers even maintained that without children's participation many manufacturing tasks could not be accomplished by adult workers alone. One contemporary, who observed children working as doffers in a spinning factory, wrote that doffing is not hard and the bobbins are located so low, fitted only to children's height. Mature workers could hardly carry out this task. In this contemporary view, the new industrial technology and the growing number of mechanized factories created a huge demand for child laborers.

Other observers emphasized economic factors as the chief ones in the increased use of child labor. They maintained that mechanized factories were extremely interested in child workers because they remunerated children's labor less than the work of adult workers. One commentator wrote that manufacturers drive out adult workers and replace them with children. By keeping low labor rates, the mill owner tried to gain as much profit as possible. This observation was supported my factory inspectors. They maintained that the labor of children in industries was caused mainly by economic reasons, i.e., by its cheapness; they felt that most of the tasks children performed could easily be accomplished by adult workers.

Nineteenth century observers also noted that child labor resulted from the economic and social strategies of peasant families. Driven by economic and social goals, parents were frequently willing to put their children to work in factories. A Finance Ministry commission maintained in 1860 that the custom of putting children to work became widespread among peasant-migrant workers. According one of its officials, "the enormous proportion of children employed in the factory … suggests the strong need of the population; [parents] … have decided to take the opportunity to turn into profit the physical feebleness of their children … Children's employment provides these families with a valuable financial contribution".[2] In 1878 the Vladimir provincial governor noted that some parents were "tempted by the small profits" they could gain by sending their children to factories.[3] Likewise, some manufacturers claimed that they employed children upon their parents' requests. One factory owner claimed that he "employed children only as a favor and deigned to concede to their mothers' humble requests. … As for me, I do not need them at all".[4] Whether this industrialist's assertion of his humanitarian motivation was sincere or not, his remark about the parents' desires seems credible. Industrialists' motives and their debasing comments about parents' supposed greed aside, children's factory employment usually reflected the desires, needs, aspirations, and decisions of their families and parents. At this point, one should note that child productive labor began to receive more economic significance, whereas the educational features were disappearing.

Both local government officials and late imperial scholars explored the economic conditions of lower social strata families and estimated how these economic conditions affected children's employment. Gathered by the St. Petersburg government, data on some of the city's working families during the early 1880s indicates that in most instances, children's factory employment seemed to be determined by the economic needs of the families. In his study on factory labor, the historian M. Balabanov cited an example of a peasant family that had migrated to St. Petersburg in the late nineteenth century. The family consisted of six members, including mother, who did not work, father, and four children. The father worked in a calico factory and earned twenty rubles a month. According to the historian, the family could not sustain itself for a month on twenty rubles in St. Petersburg, where living was costly, and the parents sent their older daughter to the factory. She earned seven to eight rubles a month, an amount that provided a significant contribution to the family budget.[5] Other observers described similar cases of peasant families, which, after their migration to cities, sent their elder children to factories. In most cases these children could no longer continue their schooling which they had begun before the move to the city.

Doubtlessly, not all families who put their children to factory work were needy. In some recorded cases, children from relatively well off working

2 Rashin, *Formirovanie rabochego klassa Rossi*, p. 251.
3 Gessen, *Trud detei i podrostkov v Rossii*, p. 49.
4 Kirov, *Na zare iunosheskogo dvizheniia v Rossii*, p. 40.
5 Balabonov, *Ocherki po istorii rabochego klassa v Rossii*, p. 125.

families worked in factories as well. For example, a St. Petersburg government inspector described a family of three members, two parents and an eleven-year-old daughter. All three worked in a mill and earned a total of 46 rubles a month, including six rubles received by the daughter. This family spent about 35 rubles a month on its living, whereas the rest was accumulated as savings. In addition, the family had a land allotment in the countryside that had been leased to one of their relatives, who in return paid all local and communal dues and taxes for the family. The government inspector pointed out that this family had no serious economic need for sending their daughter to a factory but did it solely out of a longing for more income.[6] Obviously, for some families children's employment and wages reflected aspirations for a better life in the present or in the future.

Regardless of the desire for a little extra income and the longing for a better future life noted by some contemporaries, economic need and poverty were the lashing force behind most parents' decisions to send their children to factories. Contemporary scholars estimated that, in order to survive in St. Petersburg, a family of two adults with two or three children needed earnings of at least 25-30 rubles a month. The monthly cost of basic food provisions in a large city in Russia during the late decades of the nineteenth century was on average four to six rubles per adult person. In addition, an individual family made outlays on housing and other necessary items, such as soap, kerosene, candles, and so on. The cheapest living space in St. Petersburg at the time cost about one silver ruble a month, whereas an average space could cost three to four rubles. Consequently, factory employment was crucial for older children of most families with small dependent children. One factory inspector recorded in his report that a family with "many dependent mouths who could not work was happy to gain every little kopeck" earned by an older child.[7]

Clearly, the economic importance of child factory employment was greater in nuclear families than in traditional, extended ones. Anthropologists and historians of the family have noted the general decline of the traditional multigenerational household and the growth of nuclear families during the late nineteenth-century decades. Scholarly studies have shown that nuclear families of two adults with children were not rare in rural Russia and, after the 1861-1864 reforms as capitalism accelerated in the countryside during the second half of the nineteenth century, their

6 Andreev, *Rabota maloletnikh v Possii i zapadnoi Evrope*, pp. 168-169.

7 Rashin, *Formirovanie rabochego klassa Rossii*, p. 260.

number grew rapidly.[8] Some late nineteenth-century observers suggested there were better personal opportunities for people to realize their essential expectations for independent living and for working exclusively for their own immediate families' well being in a small nuclear family than in the traditional multigenerational household.[9] This desire to live autonomously as well increased the economic pressures on individual members. As noted above, even before industrialization, the labor burden on children in nuclear families usually exceeded that in extended families. During industrialization, factory employment of children often made possible the survival of nuclear families, when, repelled by harsh economic conditions on the land, they moved from the countryside to industrial areas. Thus, the decline of the extended household and the rise of the nuclear ones seem to have affected the increase of children's factory employment.

Likewise, the rapid growth of the rural population of the Russian empire during the second half of the nineteenth century affected the economic conditions of many peasant families. In 1858 the rural population of Imperial Russia (without the Kingdom of Poland and the Duchy of Finland) was 68 million and by 1897 it had increased to 116 million. In 1913 the population of rural Russia reached 163 million. According to demographic historians, in European Russia this growth occurred because of a decline in mortality rates and the simultaneous rapid increase in birth rates. Demographers suggest general overpopulation in the countryside along with an increase of the proportion of children in the general population. This resulted in a sharp rise of the number of families with small dependent children. Historians of child labor in industrializing Europe and America have noted that the presence of small children in a nuclear family increased the pressure on older children to engage in wage labor.[10]

The speedy rural population growth spurred peasant migration to industrial centers, which were growing significantly by the late nineteenth century. Agrarian historians find that about 12.5 million peasants, including many children, annually migrated to industrial areas during 1900-1910. This figure, however, is based on the number of documents given to peasants for leave and therefore may not represent the actual number of peasant migrants. Usually, peasants migrated without these documents. In order to find employment outside the village, peasants moved individually or in work units known in Russia as *arteli*, which typically included from four

8 Milogolova, "Semeinye razdely v russkoi poreformennoi derevne", p. 37.

9 Milogolova, "Semeinye razdely v russkoi poreformennoi derevne", p. 37.

10 Kirby, *Child Labour in Britain*, p. 30.

to twelve people, both male and female adults and children. Sometimes, however, they consisted of only one sex or only of children. Rural children frequently migrated with their families, fathers, or other adults. In other cases they joined *arteli* led by older children.

Many peasants worked in industries located in the countryside and did not have to leave their villages for factory employment. In Vladimir province, for example, most factories were situated in the local rural districts or villages rather than in cities. The largest province's city Vladimir had no factories and only a few artisan workshops. The city's nearest factory, the Nikitin's Cotton Mill, was located in a village about sixteen kilometers from the city. This trend probably finds its most excellent expression in V. I. Lenin's words, when he noted that "if the peasant does not go to the factory, the factory does go to the peasant".[11] In summary, as a consequence, the rapid growth of the rural population and the evolution of the peasant household created increased economic and social pressure on children to seek factory employment.

Additionally, the factors that influenced the entrance of children into wage labor during industrialization were complemented by the lack of labor regulation laws. Child labor in private businesses remained largely unrestricted by law and in practice the employment of children was as easy as the employment of adults. During industrialization children continued to be employed in factories much as they had long before. Employment contracts were often informal and oral. In many instances, children were hired not by the business administration but by factory foremen who worked under the administration. An appropriate conclusion is that child labor during industrialization resulted from a multiplicity of economic, social, and cultural factors. These included the broad popular acceptance of child labor as a form of education, the economic and technological interests of entrepreneurs, the growth of the child population, family economic pressures, and the absence of labor protection laws. All these factors worked together to make children an important part of the labor force during industrialization. During industrialization, however, child labor became more economic than educational in nature.

Children's employment in industries and the type of work they performed seemed to have been determined by many factors, including the size and character of the business, its location, and various local and individual enterprise arrangements. By no means did industrialization bring

11 Tiukavkin, *Velikorusskoe krest'ianstvo (i Stolypinskaia agrarnaia reforma)*, p. 55.

about an immediate break with all the old customs of employment and work. Many traditional practices of children's employment and family labor continued. During the late nineteenth century, some industries in Russia still used manual labor. They were traditionally organized, relied on family labor, and operated on a seasonal basis, working only six or eight months a year. Although the number of such enterprises was declining sharply to the advantage of new mechanized ones, the proportion of children to the total number of workers in these traditional enterprises was quite high, reaching sometimes 40-50 per cent.

Evidence suggests that many children were in fact hired not by manufacturers, the factory administration where they worked, or even by foremen but by individual workers whom they assisted. According to factory inspectors' reports, factory administrations sometime did not even know how many children were employed because the latter were recruited by foremen as individual workers, who hired their own children or the children of their relatives. This practice persisted in traditionally organized mills and to a lesser degree in mechanized factories. Children worked for their own fathers or other relatives (uncles or older brothers) or assisted non-related adult workers. In spinning mills, for instance, some children often helped their own fathers who worked as spinners. Thus, although a pre-industrial tradition of family employment was in decline, it still persisted in some enterprises during the late nineteenth and early twentieth century. It needs to be emphasized that under this type of labor organization children usually worked under the supervision of their parents or other family members. Especially as regards small artisan-type enterprises, industrialization brought only slow change to practices of family labor as traditionally practiced in the countryside.

Regardless, most employed children worked in mechanized businesses, where the majority of wage workers worked. The cotton industry, for instance, was far and away the most mechanized of the various textile industries and, at one and the same time, employed the largest number of child laborers. In 1874, about 22 per cent of the cotton industry labor force consisted of child and juvenile laborers from six to eighteen years of age. The figures for 1883 suggest that about 61 per cent of children employed in industries and reported by factory inspectors worked in textile factories. Children of fifteen years old and under accounted for about 12 per cent of the industry's workforce. As mentioned, mechanized production included many operations that did not require special skills or strength and could be performed by persons with little or no training. As industrialization extended, the demand for those types of workers increased. Most children who worked in factories engaged in ancillary activities including errands. The workday for working children was the same as for adult workers and lasted for twelve hours in two six-hour shifts. The working week consisted of 5.5 days.[12]

Many children worked in the cotton industry because the cotton production process included many operations and tasks that required unskilled or semi-skilled labor, as well as ancillary activities. Most of these children performed auxiliary operations including setting up bobbins, sorting, and other secondary tasks such as cleaning machines and floors and so on. Some children were assigned to piece together broken threads, which ordinarily would be a regular task for a worker on a spinning machine. The new mechanized process of spinning associated with the introduction of the self-acting mule created a demand for semi-skilled and unskilled workers to assist spinners. Most spinners, however, were male adult workers because the operation of the self-actor required strength. In weaving shops, adolescents between the ages twelve and fifteen also worked as weavers and younger children – as secondary workers. Children were also employed in printing and dyeing shops; they performed auxiliary tasks, such as grinding dye, cleaning equipment, and carrying things.

Contemporaries noted that men in cotton mills usually performed jobs that required greater strength, whereas women and children performed "lighter" tasks, which nevertheless were often dirtier and more dangerous. According to factory inspectors, many children employed in cotton spinning mills worked in preparatory facilities on carding and scutching machines. In weaving rooms, children usually worked as helpers. Their job consisted of putting warp through the openings of reeds. The helping boy passed the thread through reeds and the boy who assisted him took it. Many children also worked on spooling and winding machines. Children who worked as weavers usually had their own looms and performed all the tasks of adult workers. In the dyeing and printing departments, most children worked on drying and starching drums. There they usually watched that the cloth did not jam when it went onto the drum. Many children served as assistants of workers who operated dyeing and washing equipment. They also carried calico and engaged in final tasks of cloth finishing. In all these shops, children also cleaned machines and equipment, carried products, wiped floors, and did all other errands. While helping adult workers, children learned to work with machines on which in a few years

12 Gorshkov, *Russia's Factory Children*, see esp. ch. 2.

they could replace adult workers. When they learned all the operations required for spinners, they began to work as spinners themselves.

Working and Health Conditions of Factory Children

The new industrial environment had a very harmful impact on the physical condition of working children. Unlike work in traditional agriculture and cottage industry, work in the new mechanized factories subjected children to the fast speed of machines and exposed them to moving belts, shifting parts, intense heat, high noise levels, and perilous conditions associated with dust and chemicals. In addition to numerous illnesses, factory children were more prone to work-related injuries than adult workers. According to some 1881–1882 data from cotton mills, about 53 per cent of work-related accidents occurred among working children, whereas children accounted for only about eleven-twelve per cent of factory workers. About 16 per cent of the employed children experienced accidents, as opposed to less than 3 per cent of adult workers. Most accidents involved cuts, wounds, broken limbs, and fractures of arms, fingers and legs. The most frequent accidents happened among children who pieced thread and set up bobbins. About 37 per cent of accidents in spinning shops were associated with setting up bobbins.[13]

Various state and local governments' commissions also reported that the highest number of work-related injuries occurred among child workers. Medical and police reports, for instance, illustrate that the most common work-related accidents involved hand and limb injuries to children. According to government officials, a similar pattern of child injuries existed in Moscow and its province, confirming that children were more vulnerable to injuries than adult workers. A St. Petersburg government factory commission set up in 1859 also reported that the highest number of work related accidents occurred to children. The commission found that in one given period, there were 148 accidents with "serious consequences" that required a physician's attention. Children aged fourteen and under incurred 48 of these accidents, and children fifteen and sixteen incurred 28 accidents, for a total of 76. This compares to only 72 accidents among adults, even though the number of adult workers greatly exceeded the number of employed children. Work-related accidents sometimes resulted

13 Gorshkov, *Russia's Factory Children*, ch. 2.

in deaths. For example, according to police records, in the Guk factory in St. Petersburg, two to four children died annually.[14]

Most contemporaries attributed the ill health among factory children to their physical immaturity and to hazardous conditions in factories. They suggested that labor in mechanized factories and the high pace of new machines required greater energy from working children than they actually possessed. Overall, rates of work-related accidents were highest in textile (cotton spinning) factories and in metallurgical plants, both industries with high levels of mechanization.

What underlay the frequent industrial injuries among children? Recent medical studies shed significant light on differences between adults and children as regards physical condition and mental abilities. For example, one study finds that eye movements of children differ from the eye movements of adults, a factor that limits children's ability to acquire adequate visual information.[15] One may imagine the significant impact this factor would have had, especially when children were working with high-speed mechanized equipment. Alongside the impact of incomplete physical development, another explanation for high rates of work-related accidents among children can be found in recent research about neurology and developmental psychology. This research emphasizes stages of development of the human brain, which in turn produce different patterns of behavior and responses to environment. Children cannot think in abstract terms.[16] Thus, children's behavior and responses to the factory environment and machines were dissimilar to those of adult workers. Below a certain age, children and young adults fail to project the consequences of their actions. Medical research suggests that humans reach complete cerebral maturity only by the age of 21. In turn, conditions of brain immaturity and low ability to coordinate attention would have increased the incidence of work-related injuries among working children.

Child Labor Protection Laws

The decline of working children's health and physical condition produced concern among many statesmen and public figures about its potential con-

14 Gorshkov, *Russia's Factory Children*, ch. 2.

15 Kowler and Martins, "Eye Movements".

16 Sugarman, *Piaget's Construction*; Hetherington *et al.*, *Child Development*; Paterson *et al.*, "Development of Structure and Function in the Infant Brain".

sequences for the security and well-being of the empire. At this point the state began to take the issue of children's engagement in productive labor seriously and generated an important discussion of industrial labor among state officials, industrialists, lawyers, and academicians. During the 1860s and 1870s, the government organized commissions to inspect labor conditions in factories and review existing labor legislation. These commissions produced legislative proposals concerning employment, welfare and health of working children, which were subsequently discussed in local councils and industrialists' associations.

Most state and local level bureaucrats supported state involvement and legislative measures to restrict children's factory employment. They were the first ones to observe and mediate worker's complaints. As members of the ruling class, they believed it was their paternalistic and humanitarian duty to protect working children. In contrast, most employers opposed the proposed restrictions. They argued that without the input of children, factory work could not be conducted successfully. Some contemporaries associated children's factory employment with the poor economic conditions of working families and emphasized the material benefits that children's wage labor brought these families. Legislative initiatives and the debates about child labor laws continued during the 1870s.

From the 1870s on, various periodicals began to publish regular articles on the working and living conditions of working children. These publications exposed to public view child labor and conditions among children in industry. Educated society had previously been largely unaware of these matters. Many publications now devoted whole issues to child rearing, upbringing, and children's health and education. Most of these articles portrayed child labor as an evil practice that must be outlawed. Childhood had always been a subject of Russian literature, but during the second half of the nineteenth century, themes of childhood and children were especially prominent in literary publications. Many authors exposed and, in effect, denounced abuses against children employed in factories, workshops, and domestic service. The public discussion of the whole issue of childhood produced an environment and an important foundation for the introduction and enforcement of child labor laws in the late imperial period.

In 1882, the State Council abolished employment of children under the age of twelve, and limited the workday for juveniles from twelve to fifteen years of age to eight hours (no more than four consecutive hours). The law also banned night and Sunday work, and employment in "harmful industries," and introduced the factory inspectorate to supervise implementation of the regulations. An 1884 law called for mandatory schooling for all children employed in industries, requiring children to complete a one-year curriculum at a public school or its equivalent. Additional laws in 1885 and 1886 prohibited night work for children under the age of seventeen, and for women in the cotton, linen, and wool industries, and in mills that processed mixed fibers considered harmful to workers.

How did the child labor law affect labor conditions for children working in industries? To be sure, the laws of 1882, 1884, and 1885 initially regulated child labor only in private businesses, and only those that used certain kinds of technology and employed at least sixteen workers. Furthermore, the laws applied only to European Russia. Although they affected hundreds of thousands of children, the laws did not address labor in agriculture, domestic services, and small artisan workshops where many children also worked. The labor of children working in agriculture, where work was usually supervised by adult family members, and in domestic services, still remained entirely unregulated and unprotected. Furthermore, after the introduction of the 1882 law which restricted their industrial employment, many children under the age of twelve from poor families in all likelihood shifted to agriculture, domestic services, or other unregulated tasks out of sheer necessity.

Factory Children Education, Socialization and Involvement in Political Life

Compulsory education of children employed in factories was another significant aspect of late imperial labor law. Before the reforms of the 1860s, elementary education for children of all social estates was provided in district schools, elementary schools for peasant children, elementary schools of the mining industry, and in orphanages. However the vast majority of children in Russia, especially serf children, remained outside these schools. Peasant schools were usually limited to state and royal family villages and were almost nonexistent in serf communes. Only a few serf children received an elementary education privately with priests, retired soldiers, or village communal scribes. Some working children of peasant origin could receive an education at factory schools. The history of factory schools in Russia seems to date back to the early nineteenth century. During the first half of the nineteenth century, the growth of new mechanized industries with their elaborate technologies created a new demand for educated workers. Deeply concerned about qualified workers at a time when the government restricted education for lower social estates to elementary schooling, some entrepreneurs, on their own private initiative, began to establish factory schools, technical schools, Sunday schools, and schools for teenage workers.

The laws of 1882 and especially of 1884 constituted a significant turn in the question of education of employed children. The laws prioritized the education of working children. The law obliged children employed in factories to attend an at least one year program of elementary schooling and receive a diploma. Those children without the required education had to receive it either before entering factory employment or during it. In addition, the reduction of the workday for children to six and eight hours further opened an opportunity for children to attend factory or local boarding schools. The number of factory schools, however, still remained low, despite the effort of factory inspectors to motivate employers to build factory schools. According to some sources, there were only 163 private factory schools in 1885. In 1899 their number increased to 446, at which point about 44,400 working children were attending these schools. Although the number of factory schools remained low and could not accommodate all employed children who needed an elementary education, during the late nineteenth century many employers did undertake a significant effort to promote literacy among their workers.

Late nineteenth and early twentieth century sources offer abundant evidence of employers' support for the education of their workers. According to one set of 1914 data, 76.8 per cent were literate, 3.2 per cent semiliterate, and 12.7 per cent illiterate with the balance (7.3 per cent) unknown. Overall, literacy rates among employed children grew significantly during the late imperial decades. According to the 1918 census, the general literacy rate among workers was 64 per cent, or 44.2 per cent among working women and 79.2 among working men. Literacy prevailed among young workers. Among workers between the ages of fifteen and nineteen, 93.6 per cent were literate and among those between twenty and twenty-five – 88.6 per cent.[17]

In addition to the new opportunity for working children to receive an education, factory labor also seemed to facilitate their rapid involvement in social and political life. In some instances, the factory environment proved to have a corrupting influence on young individuals. Factory children worked side by side with adult workers and often resided in the same crowded quarters with unrelated adult people, where, as one historian of Russian labor put it, "people cooked, smoked, argued, chatted, and tried

17 Gorshkov, *Russia's Factory Children*.

to rest [and] children dashed around." A description of workers' lives in an Eastern Siberian gold mine noted that "your twelve-year-old boy at the mines already smokes tobacco ... swigs down a jigger of vodka in one gulp ... and neatly washes a tray of gold".[18]

From a different viewpoint, many working children became involved in political life, a factor that signified the development of a new culture among the younger generation. This generation, increasingly literate and autonomous, felt itself to be emancipated and yearned for ever greater liberties and opportunities. Its culture emphasized protest of and resistance to official values and norms, as well as political freedoms and social equality. Contemporaries noted the increasing generational conflict occurring during the late imperial decades. They observed that youth felt with more strength the impassability of the gap between parents and children. Because they were young, children's and youths' hopes were high. They desired a better life than that of their parents. Despite the efforts of the government to ameliorate labor conditions and promote welfare and education among workers, the cultural conflict between the expectations of a rapidly changing society and the state's stagnant political structures grew exponentially. Most citizens found themselves dissatisfied with a tsarist political system that proved itself quite incapable of dealing with the hardships caused by World War I. When the war broke out and the tsarist government showed the first signs of weakness, factory children and youth actively plunged into the revolutionary movement that ended the old regime in Russia.

18 Melancon, *Lena Goldfields Massacre*, pp. 59, 87.

CHAPTER 18

Child Work and Its Meanings in Rural Europe: Comparisons between Central Europe and the Balkans During the Late Nineteenth and the First Decades of the Twentieth Century*

Maria Papathanassiou

Introduction

In early and mid-nineteenth century Europe opponents of child labour were interested in child work in industry and factory children, rather than in child work in agriculture and in rural regions generally. Later, as the number of children employed in factories diminished and compulsory schooling expanded, child work in rural areas was recognized as part of the general issue of child labour in many European states.

This essay compares child labour in rural regions of two neighbouring and to some extent overlapping parts of Europe: Central Europe and the Balkans, during the late nineteenth and the early twentieth century. It should be made clear that there are limits to this comparative approach. Mainly, a systematic comparison is made between two rural mountain regions on which I have conducted research: the eastern part of the Austrian Alps, which principally shaped the mountainous Austrian landscape in geographical, social and economic terms (Eastern Tyrol, Carinthia, Styria, Salzburg)[1], and villages in mountainous Central Greece (district of

* This essay draws extensively on a previous article comparing rural childhoods in Austria and Greece: Maria Papathanassiou, "Rural Childhood(s) in Mountain Regions". There are, however, significant differences in terms of perspective between the two papers; while in the former I compare various aspects of children's lives in an Austrian and a Greek mountain region, in this paper I concentrate on child labour and make a comparison between these two mountain regions within broader geographical contexts, utilizing evidence on (old and new) Austria and on other Balkan countries.
My warmest thanks go to Professor Kristina Popova, Professor Maria Efthymiou as well as Mr. Dimitris Kontogiorgis, Ph.D. candidate in History, for their advice and essential help with literature.

1 Papathanassiou, *Zwischen Arbeit, Spiel und Schule*, pp. 86-106; Papathanassiou, "Aspekte der bergbäuerlichen Lebenswelt in Österreich".

Dorida).[2] It also draws on evidence regarding broader geographical areas, namely the so-called Austrian lands of the Habsburg Empire (Old Austria – *Altes Österreich*) and interwar Austria,[3] as well as Balkan states other than Greece (notably Bulgaria and Yugoslavia).[4] The cases of the eastern Austrian Alps and mountainous Central Greece are thus linked to other examples, and certain aspects of child labour are placed within broader geographical, social, economic and cultural contexts.

The chapter comprises two parts. The first part investigates what rural child labour in Central Europe and in the Balkans had in common, drawing comparisons in regard to its extent, its place within public/official debate, as well as its forms, gender and age-specific characteristics. The second part examines divergences, comparing the socio-economic meanings and functions of child labour within specific regional contexts. Such differences show up clearly in the role of gender and in attitudes toward schooling; these topics are thus commented upon separately.

2 The study I conducted is based largely on interviews and concentrates on children's history in the village of Krokylio (Papathanassiou, *Megalonontas ston oreino choro*); however, I also draw comparisons with ethnographic information on neighbouring villages, from which a common pattern emerges in regard to children's lives and prospects in the region. We should note that in Greek historiography there are barely any historical studies on the history of children's, especially rural children's, everyday lives and experiences.
Foreign social anthropologists, such as Campbell, du Boulay, Adman conducted fundamental research on mountain or semi-mountain populations in the 1950s, 1960s and 1970s; their work includes some valuable information on childhood and child labour: Campbell, *Honour, Family and Patronage*, pp. 154-172; Du Boulay, *Portrait of a Greek Mountain Village*, pp. 100, 106, 107, 123; Adman, *Via kai Poniria*, pp. 182-211.

3 Papathanassiou, *Zwischen Arbeit, Spiel und Schule.* For the purposes of this paper I also draw on published autobiographical accounts by persons who grew up in rural (old and new) Austria (series: "Damit es nicht verlorengeht...", edited by Michael Mitterauer and Peter Paul Kloß at the Böhlau Verlag). Most of these accounts are kept in their original form in the Documentation of Life History Records (*Dokumentation lebensgeschichtlicher Aufzeichnungen*) at the University of Vienna. Extracts cited in this essay come from published and thus more easily accessible accounts.

4 Historical studies on child labour in the various Balkan states are generally lacking. I make use, *inter alia*, of autobiographical accounts by persons who grew up in Bulgaria and former Yugoslavia, which have been translated in German and published in the series "Damit es nicht verlorengeht...". Accounts from Bulgaria were collected by the Bulgarian historian Kristina Popova in the late 1980s. Accounts from former Yugoslavia were collected by the American anthropologist Joel Halpern in the 1950s and 1960s, and come from the Halpern Collection at the University of Graz: Popova, *Ein roter und ein weißer Zwirn*; Grandits and Kaser, *Birnbaum der Tränen*.

The chapter argues that child labour was a common, fundamental experience for the societies under consideration, that almost all rural children worked, undertaking very similar tasks, that child labour had certain gender- and age-specific characteristics common to all rural societies of Central as well as Southeast Europe, but that, at the same time, child labour had certain distinctive features in each case; it functioned in different ways and took different meanings within different social and economic contexts.

Convergences

We may reasonably assume that most people and indeed most scholars expect to find two entirely different societies when comparing continental Balkan societies with Central or more precisely West Central European ones. After all, research in family history and, especially, Hajnal's "European marriage pattern" – dividing nineteenth-century Europe by a line running from St Petersburg to Trieste – point out deep differences. It may be for this reason that similarities, when found, dominate the picture on the first level.

There was an obvious gap in regard to industrialization and urbanization processes between Central Europe and the Balkans; yet some common features may account for the significant numbers of rural children at work in both regions and the general similarities in the tasks these undertook.

In the course of the nineteenth and during the first decades of the twentieth century rural life retained its economic and social importance in the vast regions of Central Europe that belonged to the Habsburg Empire. After the end of the First World War and the dissolution of the Habsburg Empire, the rural economy remained important in interwar Austria, although the percentage of the population living in the countryside and employed in agriculture was steadily declining (in 1900 almost two-thirds of the population in the Austrian half of the empire and almost 45 per cent of the population living in the territories of the future Austrian State were employed in agriculture; a percentage that fell to little more than 37 by 1934).[5]

For their part, Balkan economies and societies were predominantly rural. At the end of the nineteenth century in most Balkan states more than 80 per cent of the population lived in the countryside and worked

5 Sandgruber, *Ökonomie und Politik*, p. 255.

in agriculture (in Bulgaria almost 81 per cent, in Serbia 87 per cent, in Greece 70 per cent).[6] In the 1930s more than 75 per cent of the Bulgarian and Yugoslavian,[7] and at least 50 per cent of the Greek population were still employed in farming.[8]

In both Central Europe and the Balkans, despite differences, agriculture was not yet commercialized to the extent that the rural world would be absorbed into the urban one.[9] In Austria, and in particular in the Austrian Alps, rural societies retained, to a considerable extent, some distinctive features that brought them closer to Balkan rural societies, notably subsistence economy, parallel to the development of animal husbandry and its commercialization.[10] In the Balkan states too, the rural populations consumed the goods they produced, although commercial crops were being cultivated in some places (tobacco in the Rhodopi Mountains of Southeast Bulgaria and, after the end of the Balkan Wars, in northern Greece, or raisins in southern Greece) and in the past (during the eighteenth and nineteenth centuries) domestic industry (in particular textile industry) had flourished in rural parts of the Ottoman Balkans.[11]

Child labour was indispensable to rural economies during the entire period considered here, up to the outbreak of the Second World War. For both Central and Southeast Europe the first four decades of the twentieth century were an economically turbulent time, favouring subsistence economies and impeding, at least to some extent, rural migration to urban centres.[12] Mountain-dwelling peasants faced particular difficulties when cultivating steep and less fertile slopes, without being able to apply modern agricultural techniques.[13]

6 Stojanović, "Children in Villages", p. 9.

7 Berend and Rànki, "Polen, Ungarn, Rumänien, Bulgarien und Albanien", p. 777.

8 Papathanassiou, *Megalonontas ston oreino choro*, p. 39.

9 Sandgruber, *Ökonomie und Politik*, pp. 252, 253, 368, 369.

10 Sandgruber, *Ökonomie und Politik*, pp. 253, 370.

11 Brunnbauer, *Gebirgsgesellschaften auf dem Balkan*, pp. 154ff., 187, 188, 219-237; Mazower, *The Balkans*, p. 34.

12 On Greek agricultural economy and its deficiencies see Petmezas, "Agrotiki Oikonomia"; on the effects of the 1930s crisis on Austrian agriculture see Sandgruber, *Ökonomie und Politik*, pp. 369, 370; on the effects of the First World War and the world crisis of the 1930s on mountain peasants in Tyrol, in connection with subsistence economy see Wopfner, *Bergbauernbuch. Siedlungs- und Bevölkerungsgeschichte*, pp. 707-709; on the extent to which the settling of Asia Minor refugees in urban centres in the early 1920s impeded rural exodus in Greece see Foundanopoulos, "Misthoti Ergassia", pp. 88-94.

13 See Kallivretakis, *I dinamiki tou agrotikou eksynchronismou*, p. 264; Wopfner, *Bergbauernbuch. Wirtschaftliches Leben*, pp. 159, 162-164.

Extent of Child Labour

Due to a unique, large-scale survey conducted by the Habsburg State in cooperation with school authorities, in 1908, we have a rather elaborate quantitative picture of child work in the countryside of the Habsburg Empire's so called Austrian lands. According to this survey, 34.8 per cent of Austrian schoolchildren were working; most of them lived in rural communities (44.1 per cent) or small towns (38.3 per cent), considerably fewer (22.3 per cent) in urban centres.[14] Furthermore, the great majority (62.4 per cent) worked in agriculture, very often in combination with housework (particularly girls, which brings the gender issue to the fore) or domestic industry, or both.[15]

However, we should note that questionnaires had been sent to only a part of the schools (3,497) and regarded a part of the Austrian schoolchildren (751,830) – around 18 per cent.[16] In addition, many reports had been considered unreliable and their data were not been taken into account; statistics were finally drawn upon data concerning one-tenth of Austrian schoolchildren (418,391). According to contemporary scholars and state officials themselves, child work in the countryside had been under-recorded. They noted particularly that, despite instructions, many school reports had omitted references to unpaid child work in the parental home.[17] Personalities such as the Austrian writer, university professor and landowner Michael Hainisch, or the German researcher Helene Simon, believed that neither the Austrian survey on child labour, nor similar ones conducted in neighbouring Switzerland (1909) and Germany (1904, 1922), recorded the real percentages of working rural children.[18] In Michael Hainisch's words, "[...] in the Austrian alpine lands almost every child of medium- or small-landholders works in agriculture".[19]

Statistical sources on child labour in Greece and in the Balkans generally are scarce. In these barely-industrialized regions of Europe, there is some statistical information on children working in industrial settings – though the history of industrial child labour, which has actually opened histori-

14 k.k. Arbeitsstatistisches Amt im Handelsministerium, *Erhebung über die Kinderarbeit in Österreich im Jahre 1908* [hereafter *Erhebung*], Issue 1, p. 20ff.; Issue 2, pp. 10, 13.

15 *Erhebung*, Issue 1, p. 20ff.

16 *Erhebung*, Issue 1, p. XIV.

17 Simon, *Landwirtschaftliche Kinderarbeit*, p. 37.

18 Hainisch, *Vorschläge zur Regelung der Kinderarbeit*, pp. 620, 576; Simon, *Landwirtschaftliche Kinderarbeit*, p. 37.

19 Hainisch, *Vorschläge zur Regelung der Kinderarbeit*, p. 576.

cal research on child labour in most countries, has yet to be written.[20] For example, we know that in 1874 girls between twelve and fourteen years of age accounted for approximately 60 per cent of the workforce in silk mills in Greece, or that in 1910 at least 5 per cent of industrial workers were under fourteen years old in Serbia.[21] But we have no (or very little) quantitative information on children working in rural settings. Yet, autobiographical accounts as well as ethnographic material show clearly that most, if not all, rural children worked; work turns up in these accounts in an effortless way, spontaneously, as a self-evident childhood experience. Moreover, since the dominant majority of the population lived and worked in the countryside, the vast majority of Balkan children worked in rural settings.

Child Labour as a Social Problem

Following a general European pattern, child labour in rural areas actually remained beyond the reach of laws in Central and in Southeast Europe until after the First and the Second World War respectively.[22]

By the late nineteenth century, in Germany as well as the Austrian part of the Habsburg Empire, rural children appeared on the agenda of child-labour opponents, of (mainly social democrat) school teachers, journalists and politicians. During the last decades of the nineteenth century, in parliamentary debates, major landowners defended child work in the countryside (and on their estates). In the early twentieth century landowners, politicians and local officials participated in public debates on children's protection, noting that children were indispensable to the Austrian rural economy, although they condemned overworking and exploitation.[23]

Relevant debate seems to have been less vigorous in the still primarily rural Balkans. State officials and intellectuals in that area were concerned more with children's work in industry and less with children's work in agriculture. At least this is the impression given by official sources on child labour, such as labour statistics or factory inspectors' reports, as well as by the lack of such comprehensive surveys on child labour as those published

20 Industrial child labour in Greece has been studied by Riginos, *Morfes paidikis ergassias*. On his work see also in French Riginos, "Formes du travail".

21 Ristović, "Children and Work", p. 78.

22 Ristović, "Children and Work", p. 79.

23 For a presentation and analysis of the child labour debate in old and new Austria as well of the relevant discourse see Papathanassiou, "Protected from Work?", pp. 144–153.

in Austria during the late 1890s and the early twentieth century – above all, the large-scale "Survey on Child Labour in Austria" carried out in 1908.[24]

This does not mean that there was no movement to protect children and childhood, including rural children and rural childhood, in the Balkans, though this seems to have developed later and on a more restricted scale than in German-speaking Europe. We know, for example, that in Bulgaria a Union for Child Protection was established in 1925, supporting children's rights as proclaimed by the Geneva Declaration. The Union was very active in various respects during the 1920s and 1930s. It was concerned *inter alia* with village children and their poor living conditions, noting (in the magazine it published) that legislation did not protect them from exploitation (though the Bulgarian State had undertaken various steps towards child protection since 1934).[25]

In 1918 – after the proclamation of the republican new Austrian State – an all-encompassing child labour law was passed, strictly prohibiting child work under twelve years of age.[26] But laws can be, or become, very flexible and in 1936 the representatives of the by then authoritarian, anti-parliamentarian Austrian State, refused to abide by the International Labour Office's decision and raise the minimum age of children's employment in agriculture, claiming that "people would strongly resist it, since conditions in the rural economy are different from conditions in industry".[27]

Children's Tasks

In Central Europe and the Balkans children played an important part in the rural domestic economy; turning households into highly flexible production units and thus contributing to their families' survival. In both regions children assumed similar, if not identical, tasks within the context of the rural household economy from a very early age. At first these were simple tasks: four, five, six-year-old children, and older ones too, fetched water and wood or ran errands.[28]

24 Papathanassiou, "Protected from Work?", p. 145.

25 Kristina Popova, "Impure Person has No Success", pp. 154-156; Angelova, "Student Summer Camps", pp. 163, 169-170.

26 Ernst Bruckmüller, *Sozialgeschichte Österreichs*, pp. 367, 368.

27 Österreichisches Staatsarchiv, *Archiv der Republik, Bundesministerium für Soziale Verwaltung, Sozialpolitik*, Karton 480, Sammelakten 16/XIX, 57324 5/36.

28 Stojanović, "Children in Villages and in Towns", p.10. In the late 1980s J.R. McNeill noted that peasants who kept sheep or goats in the eastern Mediterranean mountain regions, "grazed their animals around their villages, *usually charging children with the task*": J.R. McNeill, *The Mountains of the Mediterranean World*, p. 112.

From an early age children herded livestock – according to what has been recorded for many other parts of Europe, such as early modern and/or nineteenth-century Spain, France, England, Italy or Sweden, although driving animals to pasture was by no means undertaken exclusively by children, they were crucial to large-scale animal husbandry.[29] In the Balkans, the children of transhumant pastoralists were assisting adult shepherds, and in the Alps, rural servants (male or female) spent the summer in high-altitude pastures, assisted by child herders.[30]

American anthropologist Irwin Sanders, who conducted his pioneering fieldwork in Dragalevtsy, a Bulgarian village near Sofia, in the 1930s, notes that "caring for animals in the pasture" was a job undertaken by children.[31] In autobiographical accounts from Central as well as Southeast Europe (either written or recorded oral ones), herding recurs constantly and is depicted as typical child work – a time-consuming task that did not demand special skills and was thus regularly and preferably assigned to boys and girls, usually between eight and twelve years old. Selina N., who was born in 1915 in Bosnia Herzegovina (at the time still under Austrian rule) and grew up in Yugoslavia – created, under a different name, in the aftermath of the First World War – told the American anthropologists who interviewed her in the 1960s: "I have spent my childhood, herding cows and sheep and romping on the pastures together with the other children, who also drove animals into pasture".[32] And Johann Birnbauer, born in 1921 in Lower Austria, wrote in his autobiographical account: "In summer, that is from spring until late autumn, we had to herd the goats, when we came back from school. While herding, we played with everything possible, for example we tied a lash around a stone, so that we could throw it far away".[33] In all the societies considered here, herding was associated with fun, communication between children, singing, playing, building up friendships or enmities, watching the animals and thus learning about sexual behaviour. It was also associated with the weather or other practical difficulties (for example, children were faced with the problem of keeping

29 Rahikainen, *Centuries of Child Labour,* pp. 57-59; on Sweden see Mats Sjöberg, "Working Rural Children".

30 Brunnbauer, *Gebirgsgesellschaften auf dem Balkan*, pp. 250-251; Barbara Waß, *"Für sie gab es immer nur die Alm…"*, pp. 98-103.

31 Sanders, *Balkan Village*, p. 54.

32 Grandits and Kaser, *Birnbaum der Tränen*, p. 52. See also *ibid.*, pp. 65, 86, 87, 95, 107, 190, 208 (evidence from six different individuals). On rural child labour in early twentieth century and interwar Bulgaria (Pirin mountains) see Popova, "Einleitung", pp. 35-38.

33 Weber, *Häuslerkindheit*, p. 209.

animals away from growing crops, which was not at all simple and played an important part in regard to their socialization, since they learnt a lot about the structure of land ownership and their obligation to respect it).[34]

In Central European as well as in Balkan societies young boys and girls undertook household tasks, but boys tended to undertake those tasks that took place outside the house (they fetched water and went shopping).[35] And though both boys and girls would herd animals, because herding meant that children would spend their time unattended, away from their house it was in principle "a boy's work". Balkan shepherds and Austrian rural servants taking care of cattle, were assisted by boys rather than girls, though girls did drive animals to pasture as well. When in Austrian texts the term *Hüterbub,* which means "boy herder", refers to children of both sexes driving animals to pasture, this points to herding being in principle (but only *in principle*) a boy's work.[36] There was then some gender division of labour, albeit a loose one – at least as far as boys and girls up to twelve or thirteen years of age were concerned.

Children also helped adults in the fields, with ploughing, harvesting and threshing. They helped in all sectors of the agricultural economy. For example, in Austria they would help sow potatoes and then dig them out. In the Rhodopi Mountains, in Bulgaria, five-year-old children would unravel harvested tobacco leaves.[37] A greater variety of agricultural tasks appears in the Austrian records, corresponding, as will be shown later, to a higher level of economic organization, but in both cases work was an integral part of a child's socialization process. It was assigned by adults and functioned, consciously or subconsciously, as a means of disciplining children.

Divergences

Although on a first level of human experience Balkan and Austrian rural childhoods ran parallel to one another, at the same time they constituted

34 On Austria and Greece see Papathanassiou, *Zwischen Arbeit, Spiel und Schule*, pp. 61–72, 74–78; Papathanassiou, *Megalonontas ston oreino choro*, pp. 95–97; on Bulgaria see Popova, "Einleitung", p. 38.

35 Irwin Sanders notes that in Dragalevtsy, the Bulgarian village he studied in the 1930s, "getting the water" and "buying necessities in the village" were jobs undertaken by "children and unmarried daughters" and "the women and children" respectively: Sanders, *Balkan Village*, pp. 53, 54.

36 Papathanassiou, *Zwischen Arbeit, Spiel und Schule*, pp. 68–70.

37 Brunnbauer, *Gebirgsgesellschaften auf dem Balkan*, p. 410.

two clearly separate worlds. This is not to underestimate similarities, which certainly caution against oversimplifying generalizations on "rural" and consequently "primitive" or even "exotic" Balkan childhood(s). But differences should not be underestimated either. Within different socio-economic and cultural contexts child labour had different meanings; it functioned in different ways and served different purposes.

On the whole, the post-Ottoman Balkan societies were, in Mark Mazower's words, "'peasant democracies' [...] a fundamentally different form of society from that found almost everywhere in Europe".[38] Balkan rural societies differed from Central European ones in crucial respects. For one thing, as shown above, the number of people employed in agricultural activities may have been *considerable* in Austria (old and new), but was *dominant* in the Balkans. This general difference is certainly indicative of different levels of industrial and urban development. It must have meant that rural residents in Central Europe could look for alternative occupations in urban centres or industrial areas within the Empire and the interwar Austrian State to a much greater extent than rural residents in Southeast Europe.

However, it is beyond this general level, when we look into particular regions within the two parts of Europe dealt with here, that differences between socio-economic contexts and, thus, labour systems and the meanings of child labour become more obvious. At the same time, as comparisons bring the internal diversity of rural Austria or Balkans to the fore, the distance between Central and Southeast European childhoods becomes, once again, smaller.

For example, child labour in the eastern part of the Austrian Alps had deeply different functions and meanings than child labour in mountainous Greece or the Balkans generally, whereas this appears to be less true in regard to child labour in Western Tyrol and Vorarlberg in the western part of the Austrian Alps. Available evidence permits a closer comparison of the eastern part of the Austrian Alps with the Greek case but we can certainly draw analogies with other Balkan examples and comment on the case of Western Tyrol and Vorarlberg.

Two Research Examples in Comparison

Social, economic and cultural structures in mountainous Greece differed fundamentally from those in the eastern part of the Austrian Alps. Moun-

38 Mazower, *The Balkans*, pp. 28, 29.

tain regions in Greece were particularly poor.[39] People could by no means survive (let alone "live") on agriculture alone. Land was fragmented, landholdings were tiny and barren, only a few hens and small milk-producing animals (goats and sheep) could be kept, whereas it was considered a privilege for villagers to have their own mule and their own draught animal (an ox). Even the size of the flocks of most shepherds was small; in the village I studied, an average flock ranged between 150 and 200 animals.[40] Besides, most villagers did not live on animal husbandry. If people could not survive on agriculture, then other resources were needed, of which migrant remittances, mostly from the USA, were the most important one. Half a million Greeks emigrated overseas between 1890 and 1920, and there was at least one migrant in almost every household in the village I studied (which in this and most respects was no exception among mountain villages in the interwar years, at least in central and southern Greece). Greek mountain rural societies were egalitarian societies, in the sense that differences in living patterns were not striking at first sight. Nevertheless, income differences did exist and could account for a family not spending cash to buy its grain for the whole year or not being able to send its children to high school. Remittances contributed to higher living standards (much was actually being spent on rebuilding village houses), but cash remained scarce and children whose fathers owned a small shop, a coffee shop or received a small salary or pension were in fact privileged.

Greek mountain villagers still attributed a high value to land and livestock, since they did not abandon subsistence farming, although this was rather due to limited employment prospects offered by inland urban centres. Urban living patterns penetrated rural space by means of monetary incomes (above all remittances) and people wavered between their old world and a new one. If children incarnate a society's future, then obvi-

39 There is no general analytical account of mountain rural economy, nonetheless all locally focused accounts agree on its constituting "a subzone, based on a subsistence family economy, resisting monetarization and commercialization of production", see: Tsoukalas, *Koinoniki anaptyxi kai kratos*, p. 194, though such a general statement may somewhat underestimate the importance of transatlantic remittances. See especially the essays of a contemporary, Alexandros Krikos, who conducted an analysis of a mountain village economy on the eve of the First World War and wrote a general account on the hard living conditions of mountain populations on the eve of the Second World War: Krikos, *Meletes B*, pp. 7–53.

40 This so-called "restricted mobility" pastoralism dominated in many areas of central and southern Greece.

ously Greek mountain villagers could not see their children's future in agriculture, but out of it.[41]

This was not the case as far as the Austrian example is concerned.[42] True, cash was rare in Austrian peasant societies and subsistence farming was indispensable. There were smallholders in the Austrian Alps as well, and families who could hardly survive on agriculture alone. But in the eastern part of the Austrian Alps, where indivisible inheritance was the norm and the land passed to one (male) heir, there was also a strictly organized, and to a considerable extent, market-oriented agricultural economy. There were, so to speak, real peasants – some of them rich, others less prosperous – cultivating much larger landholdings (than the Greek ones) and keeping considerable numbers of cows.[43] Not all peasants lived in villages; many lived in relatively isolated settlements consisting of a few households or even in single farms, with the land surrounding the house and establishing an impressive whole. Animal husbandry was intensive and the most vital income source in the rural Alps. Therefore a permanent labour force was indispensable. Peasants would hire rural servants, men and women who would settle in the peasant households, becoming members of them, usually on the basis of annual contracts. Hired servants could be dispensed with when a farmer's children became old enough to replace them. However, in that case peasant children became in fact rural servants themselves, they were named after the work assigned to them and followed the strict rules governing a servant's daily life. Autobiographical evidence makes clear that family networks were important to finding the labour force, and indeed rural servants could be family members (brothers, sisters, cousins,

41 For more information on the economy and society in the village I studied, and generally on mountainous Central Greece see Papathanassiou, *Megalonontas ston oreino choro*, pp. 39–68.

42 For an analytical account of Austrian rural societies see Ortmayr, "Sozialhistorische Skizzen". For an account concentrating on Austrian mountain peasants and, consequently, for information on the economy and society of the eastern Austrian Alps see Papathanassiou, "Aspekte der bergbäuerlichen Lebenswelt", pp. 187–218.

43 To compare: In Tyrol one cow produced as much milk as four or five goats. With the exception of shepherds, other mountain village households in Greece had two or three goats each (though it remains unclear to me, whether some of them possessed a larger number of small milk animals, looked after by shepherds on the basis of contracts). A farmer with ten cows would count as a small peasant in Northeast Tyrol, where it was quite common for a peasant to have as many as fifty and up to a hundred cows: Wopfner, *Bergbauernbuch. Wirtschaftliches Leben*, pp. 205, 239, 422.

nephews, nieces, etc.), but also that the latter were principally designated according to their position within the group of rural servants.[44]

There functioned a rotation system, within the context of which the labour force moved from one peasant household to another, according to needs. Children of twelve, ten, eight years old, and sometimes younger, played a significant role in this "labour market". They were usually children of small peasants, children of cottagers depending on wealthy peasants and unable to feed their offspring. Or illegitimate children whose single mothers worked as rural servants and who usually spent their childhood in foster families, which were paid in return by the mother, both parents or the community.[45] In short, an elaborate agricultural economy and more or less wealthy peasants largely dominated the socio-economic landscape in these mountain regions of rural Austria. Rural populations saw their children's future within a given, strictly organized and in general smooth-functioning socio-economic and labour system.

It follows that various aspects of children's socialization had a different character and functioned in different ways from one society to the other. First of all, child labour was embedded within a broader agricultural economy, which in rural Austria was well-organized, productive and market-oriented (despite problems and the still great importance of subsistence farming), whereas in rural Greece it was part of separate co-existing household economies and much less connected with the children's future.

Maybe that is why Austrian autobiographical texts give the impression of intensive child labour, whereas Greek ones do not, although they too present child labour as a constituent of everyday life and as something taken for granted. But Greek informants do not recall child labour either in the self-evident way or in the detail that Austrian informants do (though the fact that Austrian autobiographical evidence consists mainly in written documents may partly account for this). In comparison with Austrian, Greek

44 In the 1960s the American anthropologists John Cole and Eric Wolf noted that status and kinship terminology in the German-speaking village of St. Felix in South Tyrol (Northern Italy) corresponded to hierarchical social relations formed on the basis of ownership, managerial rights and work obligations on the farms, see: Cole and Wolf, *Hidden Frontier*, pp. 239-242.

45 30 per cent to 90 per cent of the children born in the Alps region during the early 20th century were illegitimate. In 1934 50,000 foster children were counted in the Alps, that is almost one-third of all foster children in Austria: Ortmayr, "Sozialhistorische Skizzen", p. 348. On the rise of illegitimacy rates in rural areas since the 19th century, in association with economic developments, labour demands, marriage restrictions and increasing mobility see Mitterauer, *Ledige Mütter*, pp. 92-100.

autobiographical evidence lacks extensive descriptions of work, especially on the side of adults, as well as expressions referring to a relatively intensive working pace, although people interviewed were specifically asked about childhood experiences related to work. This may reflect a reality (Greek children may have worked less hard than Austrian children, because they did not work for the sake of a developed agricultural economy), but it may also be associated with the fact that in the collective consciousness of Greek mountain rural society, agriculture did not represent its future. Narratives of people who grew up in regions where commercial crops were cultivated or in fertile plains in Greece may have given an impression of work experience closer to that of the Austrian narratives.

Comparisons with Other Cases

Could we then reasonably assume that most Balkan peasants would be half-heartedly committed to agriculture and that child labour in the fields, animal husbandry, etc. served people's survival rather than the agricultural economy in the long term? This may have been generally true in the late nineteenth and the early twentieth century, at a time when the Balkan states were being shaped and reshaped, and land was being parcelled due to wars, political turmoil, various agrarian reforms, and overpopulation in the mountains, as well as the equal division of property among all (male) heirs. In the independent national states that were founded in this large part of Southeast Europe during the late nineteenth and the early twentieth century most of the land belonged to small landholders. In Bulgaria and Yugoslavia more than half of the agricultural land comprised holdings of less than ten hectares. In Greece, in the first half of the 1930s, the same was true for about 30 per cent of the land.[46] Furthermore, the agricultural economy in the Balkan states was based mainly on obsolete methods of cultivation and extensive animal husbandry. Ties to the market economy and the industrial sector were very loose, and agricultural production was very low by western, northern and central European standards. In the 1930s, the relevant index per person dependent on agriculture was estimated at fifty-eight for Austria against twenty for Bulgaria (which was the highest index of agricultural production in the Balkans).[47] Men in Balkan mountain villages, such as Bulgarian peasants in the Rhodopi Mountains[48] and Greek

46 Calculations based on data from a study conducted under the auspices of the League of Nations in the first half of the 1930s: Moore, *Economic Demography*, p. 82ff.

47 Sundhaussen, "Verpasste Agrarrevolution", p. 49.

48 Brunnbauer, *Gebirgsgesellschaften auf dem Balkan*, p. 179.

peasants on the mountains of Central Greece, were forced to look for jobs outside the local economy in order to survive. Households in the rural Balkans were principally built around blood relations on the male (the father's) side. However, household economies in the Balkans did not rely exclusively on a kinship-based labour force in all circumstances. Nor did all social formations in the Balkans lack the distinctive, all-encompassing economic character of the rural households of the Austrian Alps.

Although in autobiographical evidence from Bulgaria and Yugoslavia people generally describe the work assigned to them in their childhoods in a less informative and intensive way than their Austrian counterparts, experiences of hard and demanding work are to be found in autobiographical accounts by people who grew up in comparatively wealthy peasant families.[49] Moreover, scattered memories of undertaking work on behalf of other, wealthier peasants, point to rural labour markets taking shape particularly in periods of crisis and labour shortage. Angel Dshigrev, born in 1907 in the Bulgarian village of Kowatschewitza (in the southwest part of the Rhodopi Mountains) recalls:

> As the First World War came, it brought starvation and misery [...] Although we were only two children at home – me and my sister, who was older than me –, my mother took me to the village of Martschewo and put me there to work as cow herder; for a bushel of rye, I had to drive the family's five cows to pasture during the whole summer, from springtime up to Saint-Dimiter [Demetrios] day.[50]

According to the Bulgarian historian Kristina Popova, 10,336 agricultural labourers under fifteen years of age were counted in Bulgaria in 1920 – their number remained comparatively high in the following years.[51]

Furthermore, in particular socio-economic contexts in the Balkans, child work had a systemic function. Within the framework of enlarged, hierarchical social formations of semi-nomads (such as those in the northern Balkans and, indeed, the central-northern and northern parts of Greece), who kept large and even huge flocks of goats and sheep, child

49 See the cases of Safet N. and Milan M. from Bosnia-Herzegovina and Serbia respectively in Grandits and Kaser, *Birnbaum der Tränen*, pp. 56ff., 78ff.

50 Popova, *Ein roter und ein weißer Zwirn*, pp. 60, 61; for another example see *ibid*, p. 81. See also the case of Ivan A. from Bosnia-Herzegovina in Grandits and Kaser, *Birnbaum der Tränen*, p. 65ff.

51 Popova, *Ein roter und ein weißer Zwirn*, p. 37.

labour could not have served simply short-term needs. True, in the post-Ottoman period, due to wars, realignment of state borders and distribution of lands, winter pastures became less accessible than before and transhumant shepherd families less important in Balkan rural societies.[52] Still, in principle at least, child labour within groups of transhumant pastoralists must have had a systemic function, preparing (male) children to become transhumant shepherds themselves. In the Rhodopi Mountains transhumant pastoralists would send their sons to help adult herders and learn the job at their side.[53] And what the British anthropologist John Campbell observed in Northern Greece about the transhumant pastoralists (the so called Sarakatsani) he studied in the mid 1950s, is undoubtedly true for previous decades as well, when these semi-nomads represented a significant part of Balkan rural societies:

> Boys of five and six are given miniature shepherd crooks with which they solemnly help their fathers and uncles to control the sheep when they are mustered near the huts [...] At thirteen, when a boy leaves school, he generally begins his working life as a goatherd. He comes at once under the direction of his father who in his role of leader and co-ordinator of family labour group exerts a stronger authority over the boy than he has yet experienced...[54]

The same must have been true in regard to child labour within all those Southeast European rural patriarchal family formations that constituted particularly large economic and labour units and are usually referred to in the literature as "*zadrugas*", though such formations may have never been the dominant living pattern in the Balkans and were gradually disappearing as the new Balkan states succeeded the multiethnic empires.[55]

In their turn, the Austrian Alps included mountain regions, notably Western Tyrol and Vorarlberg, that bring the Balkans strongly to mind. Regions where people divided their landholdings equally among their children, land was parcelled, small peasantry and extreme poverty domi-

52 Arseniou, *Ta Tseligata*, pp. 38-41; Mazower, *The Balkans*, p. 40.

53 Brunnbauer, *Gebirgsgesellschaften auf dem Balkan*, pp. 250, 251.

54 Campbell, *Honour, Family and Patronage,* pp. 156, 157.

55 For the ongoing debate among historians on when and where such formations are to be found, and indeed on the usefulness of the term "*zadruga*" itself see *inter alii* Kaser, *Familie und Verwandtschaft*, pp. 37 ff.; Todorova, "Situating the Family", pp. 452-454. For a brief yet comprehensive discussion of the issue see Brunnbauer, *Gebirgsgesellschaften auf dem Balkan*, pp. 413-418.

nated. Peasants were at the same time hawkers, masons, domestic or factory workers, and men would spend months away from the villages at work of various kinds – much like their Balkan counterparts.

The main difference was probably that these Austrian small peasant families could find more regular economic outlets and occupations for children than Balkan peasants could. Children found work either in neighbouring and wealthy rural southern Germany, since the seventeenth century at least, or in industry, since the late eighteenth century. From early spring to late autumn, every year until the outbreak of the Second World War, children were sent to work on the farms of wealthy peasants in neighbouring southern Germany (Swabia) – though their number increased or decreased depending on food supply and appears to have reached a peak during the early nineteenth century.[56] At the time of the Habsburg Empire, Slovak and Hungarian children migrated from Czech- or Slovak-speaking southern Bohemia, Moravia and western Hungary to German-speaking northeastern and eastern Austria or to the southern parts of Lower Austria, in order to work as herders and learn German.[57] Furthermore, well-off German and Czech- or Slovak-speaking peasants and/or artisans would exchange their children, so that they would learn one another's language and get acquainted with different habits. Even if, as the Austrian ethnographer Helmut Fielhauer argues, child labour in the latter exchanges was of secondary importance, it was self-evident and turns up in people's memories.[58]

In general, it appears that there were far more organized, regular and extensive rural labour markets in Central Europe than in the Balkans. They crossed state and/or ethnic and linguistic borders, and child migrant workers played an important part in them. In Central Europe, direct rural child-labour markets gave peasants the chance to choose those children who would fit their labour needs. Children were taken by adults (sometimes by representatives of the local authorities, who wanted to control child migration and secure a minimum of school attendance) to particular venues, where negotiations regarding payment and conditions of labour took place. Hans Loacker, born in the community of Rankweil (district of Vorarlberg) in 1913, recounted how he was brought to such a "child market", to find work in one of the wealthy Swabian peasant households:

56 The case of the so-called *Schwabenkinder* is well researched in Austrian historiography. See for example Uhlig, *Schwabenkinder aus Tirol und Vorarlberg*.

57 See the study by Fielhauer, "Kinder-Wechsel".

58 Fielhauer, "Kinder-Wechsel", pp. 121, 122, 125, 126, 127, 129.

> My father was a worker and he had six children to feed. In early May 1926 Fathert Sittenthaler, who came from Feldkirch, led a group of about forty boys to Hergatz. There, peasant Buechele from Seibranz grasped me with the following words: "Boy, you belong to me". I was one of the last to be taken, which of course made me feel miserable. I had thought somewhat higher of myself.[59]

There is no evidence of similar labour markets providing the agricultural and pastoral economy with child workers in the Balkans at that time, although we know that in the early 1930s Bulgarian rural girls from twelve to eighteen years of age found jobs as domestic servants in urban centres at such markets:

> Indeed, on St Demetrios' Day (8 November) and St George's Day (6 May) there used to be a "servant bazaar" in Sofia. Village girls went to a certain place and stood in a row where housewives could look them over like heifers and choose a maid.[60]

It is tempting to think that political turmoil, fierce national conflicts and wars in the Balkans impeded the emergence of transnational rural labour markets. But then it is also true that child migrant workers crossing the borders between German- and Slovak-speaking populations disappeared after the Habsburg Empire was replaced by national states.

Gender

In both parts of Europe dealt with here, gender division of labour was crucial to organizing household economies and work processes. But perceptions of gender differed and this was reflected in the ways labour was divided by gender, giving work assigned to children a different meaning within the child-raising process.

Although all rural children worked, it seems that in the Balkans girls were overburdened in comparison to boys: they worked longer and undertook more tasks. This was clearly the case in the example from mountainous Central Greece. It came up in interviews with men, who would admit being exempted from work at the expense of their sisters. Boys appear to have enjoyed a sort of moral right to avoid or deny work – at least older boys and especially those who attended high school in winter and spent the

59 Märk, *Schwabenkinder aus Rankweil*, p. 17.
60 Sanders, *Balkan Village*, p. 120.

summer in the village.[61] The fact that school was primarily a boy's privilege confirms this. This was not a phenomenon restricted to Greece; in the Balkans girls attended school far more irregularly than boys did. This comes up very clearly in autobiographical evidence from Bulgaria and former Yugoslavia,[62] and is reflected in female illiteracy rates, which were far higher than male (around 1900 only 9 per cent of married women in Serbia were able to write their name).[63]

The childhood of girls was in a way shorter than that of boys, since they generally left school earlier and took a more active part in the adult world. All accounts point to young women (generally speaking after fifteen years of age) working in the fields and participating in agricultural tasks much more systematically than men. At peak seasons peasant households would mutually assist each other and cover one another's needs for additional labour. For the most part, mutual assistance was undertaken by female household members. Furthermore, at harvest or threshing time relatively wealthier peasants would employ groups of day-labourers, for the most part young women.[64] Consequently, when girls worked, they internalized their future tasks; they grew up to become, among other things, peasant workers.

In the eastern part of the Austrian Alps, both boys and girls internalized their future economic roles through work. In rural households there, labour was strictly divided by gender and autobiographical accounts reveal some discrimination in regard to women. (For example, female rural servants in Austria worked somewhat longer than male ones, since they would carry through various household tasks on Sundays and on festive days.)[65] However, labour was divided by gender in a much more balanced way than in the Balkans, because the cooperation of both sexes was indispensable for the functioning of this elaborated agricultural economy.

Moreover, in the Balkans girls grew up above all in order to get married and have children; in people's minds a girl's primary role in life was reproductive, despite the importance of work in her life. Normative dis-

61 Papathanassiou, *Megalonontas ston oreino choro*, pp. 197–204.

62 Popova, *Ein roter und ein weißer Zwirn*, pp. 112, 113; Grandits and Kaser, *Birnbaum der Tränen*, p. 87.

63 Sundhaussen, "Die verpasste Agrarrevolution", p. 57.

64 Popova, *Ein roter und ein weißer Zwirn*, p. 117; Sanders, *Balkan Village*, pp. 45, 46; Papathanassiou, *Megalonontas ston oreino choro*, pp. 102, 103. On labour assistance within the rural community in the Balkans see also Grandits and Kaser, *Birnbaum der Tränen*, p. 196.

65 See Schuster, *Auf der Schattseite*, p. 229.

course in contemporary Greek ethnographies reflects this way of thinking. It refers to the peasant, using the masculine noun for this word, and to *his* work, tasks, problems, etc., albeit together with information on working women that contradicts the discourse and reveals a reality confirmed by autobiographical accounts. In the words of one of my interviewees (notably a man), "most work would be a woman's work".[66]

In Greece the primacy of getting married and giving birth in girls' lives was clearly reflected in their play and games, which represented rites of passage (especially weddings).[67] It is hard to believe that this was not the case in the Balkans as a whole, although no such games are mentioned in the published autobiographical accounts from Bulgaria and the former Yugoslavia.[68]

Is it then by chance that Barbara Passrugger, who was born in 1910 and grew up in the mountainous region of Pinzgau (Salzburg), played "herder" in her early childhood? Could her play mean that girls in the Alps were raised first and foremost to become rural servants, agricultural labourers, peasants, in other words to have an active part in the rural economy?

> I played also with very simple things, for example with pinecones. The big ones were the cows, the smaller ones were the calves or the oxen. The pine-cones were tied with a string and I was walking holding them over the wooden planks and giving orders to the animals.[69]

And is it also by chance that I have not found any examples of girls in Austria representing rites of passage while playing?

School

As was and is the case with child work since the nineteenth century and the first attempts to make schooling compulsory – to various extents and in different ways – child labour in rural societies of Central and Southeast Europe conflicted with compulsory school attendance. But the different ways in which this conflict was handled and perceived by local societies were indicative of the significance of child labour in their social and economic structure.

66 Papathanassiou, *Megalonontas ston oreino choro*, p. 101.
67 Papathanassiou, *Megalonontas ston oreino choro,* pp. 280, 281.
68 See Popova, "Einleitung", pp. 37-39.
69 Passrugger, *Hartes Brot*, p. 28.

By the early twentieth century school had become an accepted institution in both Austria and the Balkans. In reality, school attendance in Austria did not become compulsory earlier than in the Balkan states, because – despite laws passed in the late eighteenth century – Austrian children were not actually obliged to attend school (for eight years) until 1869. By the late nineteenth century compulsory schooling had been introduced in the Balkans, shortly after the respective independent national states were proclaimed. Thus, compulsory school education was introduced in Greece (1834), Bulgaria (1879) and Serbia (1882).[70] In Greece, which was the first independent Balkan national state, children were legally obliged to attend school for four years. Around 1930 there were some reforms and compulsory attendance was extended to six years.

School affected not just the present, nor simply the short-term future, but the long-term prospects of rural societies as well, namely their children. Traditional and modern identities, religious and national ones would be forged or reinforced at school through lessons, celebrations and various activities. It was a most important mechanism for state penetration of rural societies and constituted a strictly organized space with specific rules that children had to comply with. It was essentially a disciplining mechanism that tended to substitute for the family, although in all cases the latter retained its primary position in regard to children's socialization.[71]

But laws introducing compulsory schooling and regarding school attendance were not observed regularly. Nowhere were they implemented fully, since school clashed with child labour in terms of time and available mental capacities. How did rural societies deal with this?

In comparison with the Balkan states, school holidays in Habsburg and interwar Austria appear to have been officially (at the local level) adapted in a much more attentive and specific way to the needs for rural child labour. Community and school councils – in which better-off peasants were very powerful – decided on the so-called *Schulbesucherleichterungen*: exemption from school attendance, which, according to the 1908 survey on child labour, "clearly aimed at enabling children to work" and affected above all children working in agriculture. Older children, between twelve and fourteen years of age, would in principle be exempted from school, since they were allowed to attend school once a week,[72] an experience that

70 Stojanović, "Children at School", p. 45; Sundhaussen, "Die verpasste Agrarrevolution", p. 57.

71 Papathanassiou, "Rural Childhood(s) in Mountain Regions", pp. 52, 53.

72 *Erhebung*, Issue 1, pp. 19, 3f. and Issue 2, p. 91.

recurs in many autobiographical documents. One woman, who entered rural service at the age of ten and grew up in interwar Austria, recalls:

> When I became thirteen, the peasant looked into it, that I be free from school attendance during the summer months [...] He just had to apply for it, when there was a lot of work to do, and there was more than enough work to do.[73]

The situation appears laxer in our evidence from the Balkans, despite information on school inspectors appointed by the central governments.[74] At least we do not find communities arranging schooling to fit peasants' labour needs (in any case, much less complicated than in Austria). In the Greek village I studied, personal arrangements were made between teachers and farmers. This certainly came up in Austria as well but there these were always together with or within the context of more formal arrangements. As one woman, drawing on her personal experience, put it:

> The parents would ask permission from the school (meaning the schoolteacher). (They would tell the schoolteacher): "Do not write down that she didn't come to school. I have work to do tomorrow. Maria or Giannoula, for example, is going to sow".[75]

Such arrangements must have been usual in other Balkan states as well. Until the Second World War, despite improvements, school attendance was anything but regular. This is certainly reflected in the high illiteracy rates, reaching at least 75 per cent of the population in the various Balkan states at the beginning of the twentieth century.[76] Illiteracy may have been due less to children not attending school because of work and more to children not attending school in the controlled (and indeed "regular") way that Austrian children did. Regulating "non attendance" corresponded to the needs of highly organized economies in Austrian rural districts. We should note, however, that according to school authorities and other contemporary reports, children of cottagers, landless peasants and particularly

73 Papathanassiou, *Zwischen Arbeit, Spiel und Schule*, p. 237 (also for other examples). "Summer months" included not only summer but also spring and autumn.

74 Sanders, *Balkan Village*, p. 132; Papathanassiou, *Megalonontas ston oreino choro*, p. 226.

75 Papathanassiou, *Megalonontas ston oreino choro*, pp. 214, 215.

76 Stojanović, "Children at School", p. 46. On Serbia see also Sundhaussen, "Die verpasste Agrarrevolution", p. 57.

children born out of wedlock were constantly discriminated against. Peasant employers would keep them, rather than their own sons and daughters, away from school in order to work. *Schulbesuchserleichterungen* put them in first place.[77]

It goes without saying that child labour went hand in hand with ambivalent, to say the least, attitudes towards school on the part of local populations. But in regions where people would not rely on agriculture for their future, school education was seen as a means of escaping the hardships of rural life.

At least this was the case in mountainous Central Greece, where people dreamt of their children finishing school, becoming civil servants[78] and substituting urban for rural life.[79] This was largely due to the particular way the civil service had developed in Greece since the first half of the nineteenth century, constituting a field where patron-client relations flourished and, generally speaking, jobs were offered in return for votes.

But we should note that this attitude applied to boys rather than girls, since the former were much higher-valued than the latter. In the Greek case, boys attended school more regularly and to a greater extent than girls did. School attendance was much less gender specific in Austria. But then, in Austria school would rather serve the functioning and development of the society in which children were already living; it was regarded much less as a means of escaping rural life. Parents in the Greek case would often try to let their boys finish school, that is attend a three-year secondary school (*scholarchio*) (until a reform changed school structure on the primary and the early secondary level in 1929) and high school. In the village I studied there was a *scholarchio* and consequently a significant number of boys (probably one-third of the primary-school boys around 1930) but just a few girls

77 Papathanassiou, *Zwischen Arbeit, Spiel und Schule*, pp. 239, 240.

78 According to a contemporary folklorist, who himself came from mountainous Central Greece, a villager's typical dream for his son, was to see him pass "from rural life to another life, a life lived on a salary": Loukopoulos, *Georgika tis Roumelis*, p. 2.

79 According to the Greek sociologist K. Tsoukalas, whose studies are based on aggregate data, an "excessive scholarization" of small peasants' sons, who then entered the Civil Service, building up a considerable part of the Greek petite bourgeoisie and middle class, took place in rural Greece since the late 19th century: Tsoukalas, *Koinoniki anaptyxi kai kratos*, p. 194; *Idem*, *Exartissi kai Anaparagogi*. Tsoukalas's view has been challenged lately: Bournazos, "I ekpaidefsi sto elliniko kratos", pp. 204, 205. In my research (Papathanassiou, *Megalonontas ston oreino choro*) I argued that this view corresponds to a dominant social will rather than to a dominant social practice; furthermore, that attitudes towards schooling differed, depending on fine but essential social differences which scholars tend to ignore.

attended it. It is most interesting that many boys who attended *scholarchio* came from neighbouring villages, which was a remarkable economic sacrifice on the part of their families.[80]

Furthermore, we should note that this attitude was more a social dream (albeit a very eloquent one) than a social reality. Not all boys who attended *scholarchio* or high school managed to graduate. Only a minority of comparatively better-off families could afford to send some of their sons and eventually their daughters (especially if they were promising pupils) to finish high school. This was before the Second World War successively located in two small towns several hours away on foot from the village – and later to the University in Athens.

Anyhow, the attitude of rural families in Greece was disproportionate to their actual economic situation. School education was highly valued by the village as a whole, irrespective of social practices. In people's eyes it was a symbolic way out of social and economic impasse, albeit an outlet that undermined links with traditional living patterns.

Entering the civil service appears to have been the main way in which school education could be utilized in the Balkans.[81] We need, however, more information on people's behaviour and perceptions in order to assess whether there was a "social dream" in regard to the education of the sons, similar to the Greek one. In the 1920s and 1930s, some Bulgarian peasants would send their sons to study at the University of Sofia or even abroad.[82]

Anyhow, even in places where there was not much to expect from agriculture, people realized the positive sides of school education without necessarily thinking that school would or should save their children from the hardships of rural life.

According to Sanders, in Dragalevtsy "the peasants, were, on the whole, favorable toward education" and "shrewd enough to see the economic advantages of formal schooling". But this is a general remark and Sanders also notes that, "most of the children had a great desire to study, but unfortunately many parents killed this enthusiasm. They [...] sent their children to tend the cattle...".[83] In his narrative, villagers appear to link their chil-

80 A few indicative numbers based on the sparse data of *scholarchio* archives kept in the high school of the small town of Lidoriki. In 1920 there were seven girls among the 78 schoolchildren; in the mid-1920s 76 of 97 schoolchildren came from neighbouring villages.

81 Sundhaussen, "Die verpasste Agrarrevolution", p. 57; Berend and Rànki, "Polen, Ungarn, Rumänien, Bulgarien und Albanien", p. 785.

82 Popova, "Einleitung", p. 34.

83 Sanders, *Balkan Village*, pp. 136, 134.

dren's (sons') future to the farm. The considerable size of the landholdings (on average about eighteen acres) and the generally flat ground may partly account for this, although the soil was of rather problematic quality.[84]

In the small peasant mountain regions of Western Tyrol school education is also reported to have been highly valued. The Austrian ethnographer Hermann Wopfner, who conducted fieldwork in the 1920s, directly linked such favourable attitudes towards school to poverty and the fact that people had to look for various jobs beyond agriculture in order to survive.[85] Concern to control school attendance was essential to the local authorities' decisions to organize children's migration to the farms of southern Germany since the late nineteenth century.[86] But there is no indication that in the eyes of the local authorities and of those child migrant workers from Western Tyrol and Vorarlberg, who were employed by German peasants each summer, as well as of their families, school education represented the main way to find an occupation – perhaps because people there could find a job in the textile industry. They could find an additional income working in proto-factories (from the last quarter of the eighteenth century) and later on (from the mid-nineteenth century) in modern factories and the railway, without necessarily having to abandon their village or the district they lived in.[87]

Concluding Remarks

To summarize, until at least the first decades of the twentieth century work constituted a fundamental experience for rural children, whether in Central or in Southeast Europe. (And probably for rural children in all parts of Europe where a distinction between urban and rural societies still existed, despite ongoing industrialization, commercialization and urbanization processes.) Furthermore, in both examples rural children carried out similar tasks (the most characteristic of which was animal herding). Child labour practices point to children and childhood being perceived in much the same way by all societies under consideration. Work was not incompatible with childhood. However, different social, economic and

84 Sanders, *Balkan Village*, pp. 42ff., 118–121.

85 Wopfner, *Bergbauernbuch. Bäuerliche Kultur und Gemeinwesen*, p. 320; Wopfner, *Bergbauernbuch. Siedlungs- und Bevölkerungsgeschichte*, p. 533.

86 Uhlig, *Schwabenkinder aus Tyrol und Vorarlberg*, pp. 195–218.

87 Wopfner, *Bergbauernbuch. Wirtschaftliches Leben*, p. 45.

cultural contexts gave children's work different economic, social and cultural meanings and functions. It served different purposes and affected growing up in different ways.

The extent to which rural societies saw their future, by which I mean their children's future, in the agricultural/pastoral economy gave children's work in rural areas its particular character and economic importance. In rural societies that did not see their future in agriculture – like the ones in mountainous Central Greece, in the western part of the Austrian Alps and probably in most of the Balkan mountainous regions – child work had a short-term economic character and did not prepare children for their future adult role within the rural economy. Where social roles were inextricably linked with the agricultural economy, as in parts of the Austrian Alps, child work was part of a well-organized division of labour, prepared children for their future social roles as adults and served the maintenance of economic and social structures. However, this by no means implies that some or even most Austrian rural societies were functioning as closed labour systems until well into the interwar period.

If rural societies saw their children's future in agriculture and attributed child work a crucial preparatory role, this does not necessarily mean that children would not turn their back on the rural economy and move to urban centres later, when they grew up. In the late nineteenth and the early twentieth century the rural population was constantly decreasing in Austria, and regions where indivisible inheritance dominated, were not exempted from migration to urban centres.[88] In fact, there was a deep concern on the part of state officials regarding the rural exodus (*Landflucht*) and the eventual collapse of the rural economy in Austria, in the aftermath of the First World War – though neither percentages nor absolute figures were extremely impressive.[89] Child labour was largely attributed to the lack of an adult labour force (*Leutenot*).[90] In the light of life stories and the self-evident character of child's work, such an explanation could mainly have functioned as an excuse for a very old practice, though rural exodus certainly influenced the ways in which labour was divided and more work was probably assigned to children than would be, had there been more rural servants available. In general, migration to urban centres was believed to have encouraged child labour in rural regions and vice versa.[91] Contem-

88 Papathanassiou, "Aspekte der bergbäuerlichen Lebenswelt", pp. 189-191.
89 Sandgruber, "Landwirtschaft in der Wirtschaft", pp. 262-265.
90 *Erhebung*, Issue 2, pp. 101, 102.
91 Hainisch, *Die Landflucht*, pp. 184-185.

porary scholars even assumed that hard work and exploitation in childhood (but not child work *per se*) discredited rural life in children's minds and souls, and made young men and women abandon it.[92] Should we then assume that in Austria abandonment of rural life concerned young adults rather than schoolchildren, individuals rather than family units? At least contemporaries appear to have thought so.

Does this in its turn imply that urbanization in the Balkans was less an individual and more a family matter? Balkan rural children grew up within societies where kinship was crucial to the formation of social relations and the institution of rural service did not exist. However, this does not mean that all of them, or even most of them, were protected from work outside their family and the village economy up to their early youth. As mentioned above, more than ten thousand agricultural labourers in Bulgaria were under fifteen years of age in 1920.[93] Although the urbanization process in the Balkans did not speed up until after the Second World War, even before then boys migrated to towns, got employed in odd jobs or worked in the building-trade at the side of the village men, and girls were sent to urban or semi-urban centres to work as domestic servants.[94]

In April 1883, as the debate on school laws was at its peak in the Austrian parliament, the representative of those deputies who opposed any reduction of compulsory schooling in favour of children's employment in agriculture, proclaimed that "with this voting, *the border line between western and eastern Europe* runs through the middle of this room". His words were followed by a "lively applause from the left side".[95] The Balkans were not explicitly mentioned, but it goes without saying that they were part of that "eastern Europe" to which the Habsburg Monarchy should not wish to belong.

In the light of regional comparative research such imagined border lines become less clear, branch off and cross each other. Central Europe and the

92 Simon, *Landwirtschaftliche Kinderarbeit*, pp. 353, 354.

93 Popova, "Einleitung", p. 37.

94 As mentioned above, in Bulgaria twelve-year-old girls are reported to have participated in servant labour markets in Sofia during the 1930s (Sanders, *Balkan Village*, p. 120); Papathanassiou, *Megalonontas ston oreino choro*, pp. 104-106; Popova, "Einleitung", pp. 36, 37. On children working as shepherds, shoe-cleaners, shop assistants, medical assistants, newsboys in the 1920s and 1930s see the paper by Miroslav Jovanović on Russian child refugees in the Balkans, see: Jovanović, "Accelerated Maturity", p. 206.

95 Stenographisches Protokoll. *Haus der Abgeordneten. IX. Session. 298 Sitzung, am 18. April 1883*, p. 10269.

Balkans appear at once close to and distant from one another. Comparing child labour in different countries or regions helps us to deconstruct stereotypes and avoid generalizations. The history of child labour may reveal as much about the children's part in the economy as about the ways in which adults deal with children's and, consequently, their societies' future. Thus shedding light on how macro-economic processes, such as industrialization or urbanization, interact with human experience.

CHAPTER 19

Understanding the Persistence of Child Labor in United States Crop Agriculture

Hugh D. Hindman

Agriculture has always been the largest child employing sector, even before child labor became a social and economic problem, and it remains the largest child employing sector in the world today. Further, it is a sector that is stubbornly resistant to reform. In many developed nations – nations that have effectively abolished most forms of industrial child labor – substantial problems remain in agriculture. Why is that?

This chapter examines the history of child labor in American commercial agriculture with an aim to understanding why it remains the least regulated child employing sector in the economy. The question can be asked broadly. Why was reform ultimately unsuccessful in agriculture (or, to what extent was it unsuccessful), and what are the consequences of leaving child labor in agriculture subject to forces of supply and demand? The question can also be asked somewhat more narrowly. Why was agriculture excluded from the original Fair Labor Standards Act (which is the principal source of U.S. child labor law), why did it remain excluded for so long, and why even today are provisions for child labor in agriculture much less stringent?

Whether the question is asked broadly or narrowly themes of agrarian romanticism and racism weigh heavily in the narrative of the answer. The former represents America's cultural love affair with all things rural. The latter, an equally culturally engrained hostility toward "other" people, represents America's "original sin".

The Rise of Commercial Agriculture in America

In early America, there were "two opposing blueprints for an agrarian economy: the New England-Midwestern model of small farms producing food crops and livestock for subsistence and local markets versus the Southern-Western model of plantations producing cash crops for distant markets. The former relied on freehold labor; the latter, on slave labor."[1]

The family farm has always occupied an important place in the political economy of American agriculture, and continues to do so today in spite of the near complete commercialization of agriculture. Further, the family farm has always been a "white" domain. Family farmers, past and present, have principally descended from Western and Northern European stock. Eastern and Southern European stock have come to be well represented on family farms, but typically only after two or three generations of assimilation into American culture. Further, the family farm is the social unit that fosters and sustains images of agrarian romanticism.

While many cultures share a romantic reverence for pre-industrial agrarian life, America's romance with agrarianism may be deeper than most, for at least three reasons: 1) absence of a feudal heritage; 2) ideals of Jeffersonian democracy; and 3) the role of the frontier. Without a feudal heritage and its adjunct, an institutionalized peasantry, American farm families emerged as a distinctive social and economic class – free, propertied, frugal, and hard-working – they were the kind of citizens that would make democracy possible. Jefferson himself went so far as to claim that "those who labour in the earth are the chosen people of God".[2] Agrarians asserted man's dominion over the earth while serving as stewards of the almighty's bounty. Finally, early America's status as a frontier nation reinforced the appeal of the yeoman ideal. "The steady westward march – from early colonial days up to the closing of the frontier in the 1890s – provided an outlet for independent-minded families dissatisfied with their current situation and sturdy enough to survive the rigors of frontier life."[3]

This reverence for all things rural produced an "agrarian fundamentalism" that pervaded American society. Economically, agricultural production was seen as the basis of all wealth and so, the well-being of agriculture was critical to the well-being of all society. Socially, farming is an occupation that was naturally seen as fostering a moral life. And politically, farming produced sturdy, self-sufficient, independent citizens making preservation of the family farm essential to democracy.[4]

But the commercial agricultural model, with its roots in the plantation South, ultimately won out. By the turn of the twentieth century, large

1 Chen, "Of Agriculture's First Disobedience", p. 1278.
2 Chen, "Of Agriculture's First Disobedience", p. 1295.
3 Hindman, *Child Labor*, p. 15.
4 Effland, "Agrarianism and Child Labor Policy", p. 285.

scale commercial farms had come to dominate, both in terms of agricultural output and especially in terms of agricultural employment.

At the time of the Civil War, America took four key steps in establishing a "developmental" agenda for agricultural policy.[5] First was the Homestead Act of 1862 that provided 160 acre grants to individuals willing to settle land west of the Mississippi River. The Homestead Act contributed greatly to the myth of agrarian romanticism.

> The idea of populating the plains with virtuous little homesteads, each owned in fee simple and purchased solely by the sweat of farmers' brows, touches something deep within the American sole [...] The image of farming in the American Heartland seems relentlessly romantic, bathed in far more sweetness and light than its morally dubious Southern and Western counterparts.[6]

Despite its intentions of vesting large numbers of individuals in small plots of land, the Homestead Act resulted in vast tracts of land accruing to moneyed interests.

Three other 1862 acts bolstered agriculture's developmental agenda. The Morrill Land Grant College Act created a nationwide network of public universities with a primary mission of teaching agricultural and mechanical arts. The Pacific Railway Act (1862) established a transcontinental railroad linking agrarian capitals of Omaha and Sacramento. Finally, in 1862 the US Department of Agriculture was created.[7]

These developments, along with technological advances in commercialized canning and development of the refrigerator car, stimulated the rise of commercial agriculture in America. "Bonanza Farms" emerged in the 1860s, for example, the Bonanza wheat farms in the Midwest and Plains. These were one crop farms that needed large amounts of seasonal labor, usually at harvest. Irrigation projects introduced in the 1880s encouraged a transition to fruits and vegetables on Western Bonanza farms, especially in California. Midwestern Bonanza farms, in turn, drove many Eastern farms out of wheat production and into truck farming of fruits and vegetables.[8] In the South, with its cotton mono-culture, the plantation system was not abolished with the abolition of slavery. Instead, large plantations

5 Hallberg, *Policy for American Agriculture*.
6 Chen, "Of Agriculture's First Disobedience", pp. 1316-1317.
7 Hallberg, *Policy for American Agriculture*.
8 Lyons-Barrett, "Child Labor in Commercialized Agriculture".

were divided into smaller plots and a system of sharecropping and tenant farming emerged, where families worked rented land in exchange for a share of the crop.

Demand for Child Labor in Commercial Agriculture

With the abolition of slavery and the rise of commercial agriculture following the Civil War, three broad groups of children could be found working in agriculture: 1) children of the New England-Midwestern family farms; 2) children, both black and white, of sharecroppers and tenant farmers in the Plantation South; and 3) children of landless migrant workers.

Children on the Family Farms

Agriculture is the economic sector most closely associated with pre-industrial economy, and the family farm bore the closest resemblance to the pre-industrial household. The yeoman household of rural pre-industrial America invokes images of sturdy self-sufficiency, family solidarity, and pure householding – household production for the household's own consumption, with perhaps some trade and barter with neighbors – and it became the rural version of the American Dream.

Children worked, often very hard and from a very young age, in the yeoman household, where the division of labor was based on sex and age. Work was hitched to circadian and seasonal rhythms that, while demanding, always permitted pauses for rest or instruction. The child's work and education were deeply inter-twined and embedded in household, kinship, and communal relationships. In this context, early work was considered entirely wholesome and the best preparation for life as a productive adult. Children on the family farms tended to grow up strong and hardy and, while having considerably less formal schooling than their urban counterparts, they acquired a diverse set of skills that would be highly valuable to productive adulthood. Rural labor was scarce and expensive.

> Only the most firmly established farming families could afford to hire hands. Instead of hiring workers, families trained their children from an early age to assume the work of the farm [...] Early rising, long hours of chores, and

high levels of responsibility from a young age were the rules, rather than the exception, for a child on a farm.[9]

These are the children whose images are evoked in agrarian romanticism.

Children of the Plantation South

In the post-Civil War South, the industrial plantation system was maintained, despite the loss of its slave labor supply, by shifting to a system of tenant farming and sharecropping. Owners sub-divided large plantations into smaller plots which were put to lease. Families were contracted to farm the smaller plots. In the early post-Civil War period, these were often the very same families that had worked on the plantation before the war, including both black former slave families and white "free" families that had served as overseers and in other roles. Lease arrangements varied, but generally the tenant received a fixed number of acres and housing in exchange for a share of the value of the crop produced. The portion of the value accruing to the tenant varied with assets supplied. Where the tenant provided only labor, the share was relatively small. Where the tenant supplied a team, tools, and farm implements, the share could be substantially larger. Acreage allotments, and thus earning potential, were also based on assets supplied by the tenant. Since most tenants, especially blacks, had little other than hand tools and their own labor, acreage allotments varied by family size. The more children available to work, the more acres.[10]

Children's work on the plantations bore a superficial similarity to work on the family farm in that it was carried out within the family. But there was an important difference. Tenant farmers, and especially sharecroppers who were disproportionately black, were almost invariably among the poorest of America's poor. White families, especially those that started with some assets beyond their labor, were often given the opportunity to purchase the acres they farmed. Few black families were permitted to attain land ownership. "Members of darker races, by and large, have never broken into the ranks of freehold farming, the rural embodiment of the American dream."[11] On the family farm, parental buffers could be placed around children to limit exploitation. That was not the case for the children of tenants and sharecroppers, whose parents lacked the capacity to prevent their own exploitation, let alone exploitation of their children.

9 Riney-Kehrberg, "The Limits of Policy", p. 53.
10 Hindman, *Child Labor*, pp. 274-275.
11 Chen, "Of Agriculture's First Disobedience", p. 1286.

It should be noted that, while there are numerous qualitative accounts of child labor among tenant and cropper children, the quantitative record is less clear. The Census Bureau, the Department of Labor, and the Department of Agriculture, counted the children of tenant farmers and sharecroppers as working on the family farm and, thus, they were not counted as farmworkers.

Children of the Landless Migrants

The third major child workforce in agriculture was comprised of the children of landless migrants. Among migrant workers, it is sometimes useful to distinguish two groups. There are "seasonal" workers working near their permanent residence. Seasonal work can be as light as going to the country for a couple weekends to harvest the local crop. Or it can be as intensive as moving to the country for an entire five to six months growing season. Then there are the true "migrants" who leave their permanent place of residence, often for extended periods, to follow the crops. Migrants, like sharecroppers, have always been among the poorest of the poor.

By the early 1900s, there were three major migratory streams in American agriculture: an East Coast stream, a mid-continental stream, and a West Coast stream.[12] The East Coast migratory stream served the truck farms of the mid-Atlantic and Northeast states. Every year thousands of Polish, Bohemian, Italian or other recent immigrant families, left cities like Baltimore and Philadelphia for an extended outing in the country. One prominent migration route began in May in the strawberry fields of Delaware and Maryland and ran through September, culminating in the cranberry bogs of New Jersey. Many of these same families, after their summer "vacation" in the country, opted for a winter "vacation" on the Gulf Coast working in shrimp and oyster canneries. Children who went out for the summer tour generally missed eight to twelve weeks of school each year. Children who went along for both the summer and winter tours rarely attended school.[13]

The mid-continental stream began in the Rio Grande Valley in Texas. It included a couple of sub-groups. First there was the Texas cotton group. "When cotton growing expanded into the Southwest in the 1920s and 1930s, growers generally followed the Western pattern of using migratory

12 Lyons-Barrett, "Child Labor in Commercialized Agriculture".

13 Hindman, *Child Labor*, ch. 9, esp. pp. 251-271 and 282-286.

labor instead of relying on long-term sharecroppers or tenants."[14] Next was the Great Lakes group that traveled as far as Michigan and Minnesota to work in sugar beets. Finally, there were branches that extended into the Rockies and Northern Pacific. Mexicans were always prominent in this stream and tended to undertake the longest migrations. Recent immigrants of a variety of Eastern and Southern European ethnicities worked seasonally as tenants and undertook shorter migrations.

The West Coast stream was dominated by single Chinese men until the 1900s. When the Chinese Exclusion Act of 1882 cut off this source of labor supply just as irrigation projects were dramatically expanding crop production, ethnic composition underwent a gradual shift. Around WW I, southern and eastern Europeans entered. Single male Filipinos came in the 1920s and 1930s. "Okies" formed a major proportion of this migratory scheme in the 1930s. Mexicans, who had always been a presence, filled in during wartime labor shortages, and form the core of migratory labor since WW II. Central Americans joined the stream after 1970.[15]

In all migratory streams, nearly all the workers were immigrants or children of immigrants; nearly all the growers, their employers, were white. In most cases, the migration was organized by padrones, coyotes, or other labor contractors. These were classic middle-men who extracted payments from both the growers and the farmworkers. The grower needed a large supply of labor for a short period of time that would, subsequently, be willing to move on. Labor contractors filled this need by contracting with heads of households for the labor of entire families in a classic family wage system. Since farmworkers were generally paid on some variation of a piece rate, the entire family was put to work. Children began helping at such young ages that the term "infant labor" was sometimes appropriate. To maximize family earnings, adults and older children concentrated on the main value-adding task while younger children helped out and performed ancillary tasks. Sometimes this ancillary work was relatively light, such as "tending the baby". Sometimes, however, ancillary work was some of the most physically demanding – carrying loaded containers to a central collection point.[16]

14 Lyons-Barrett, "Child Labor in Commercialized Agriculture", p. 8.
15 Lyons-Barrett, "Child Labor in Commercialized Agriculture", p. 8.
16 Hindman, *Child Labor*, ch. 9.

Myths and Realities

On the eve of America's child labor reform movement, all three groups of children in agriculture shared certain characteristics, but differed starkly in others. On the supply side, their time was allocated to labor in accordance with pre-industrial patterns of household labor. Family wage systems operate in their purest form in agriculture as the entire household, with a division of labor based on age and gender, pooled its production for a single payment.

One important difference was the relative poverty of the groups. While family farms ran the gamut from poor to wealthy, most were sturdy middle class. In contrast, most tenant families and nearly all sharecropper and migrant families were very poor. Thus, children's work contribution was more likely to provide the margin between subsistence and starvation. While children of family farms worked more and attended school less than their urban counterparts, they worked less and attended school more than sharecropper and migrant children.

Conditions of demand for labor provide, perhaps, the starkest contrast between the three groups of agricultural child workers. While elements of family farming had taken on commercial characteristics, crop diversity (often including animal husbandry) and concentration on serving local and regional markets provided buffers that permitted operation along pre-industrial patterns. Crucially, most family farms still produced much of the family's own subsistence, and youngest children were often concentrated in work directed to this goal. On the family farm, a pre-industrial household labor supply met an essentially pre-industrial pattern of demand.

The plantation South was, since its inception, organized on commercial principles, providing agricultural commodities to national and global markets. Product market demand fueled demand for a large, reliable labor force. First, slavery filled demand; after slavery, the share-cropping system prevailed. In both cases, market demand, mediated by large, powerful plantation owners, met an essentially captive labor force. After slavery, labor force composition shifted from the quasi-industrial cities of large plantations, to the household of the sharecropper. Under both systems, children were called upon to contribute early and substantially. Demand on children's time was moderated by the rhythm of the seasonal calendar. During peak periods, all hands were in the fields. During slower periods, time could be taken for instruction, learning, and, at least occasionally, leisure. The South remained the nation's dominant agricultural economy well into the twentieth century. Over half the farms, farm population, and farmworkers were in the South.

Children of the landless migrants confronted conditions of demand for their labor that were similar to those found in the plantation South in that the product market and production processes operated along commercial and industrial lines. But the call to migration adds a new dimension to conditions of demand. Migrants worked on crops – fruits, vegetables, nuts, and a range of others – that required little care for most of the crop cycle, and a large labor force for peak periods (typically the harvest). Perishable crops requiring an influx of labor that will be willing to move on when the work is done, coupled with the agricultural calendar, created demand for a migratory labor force. Wherever handwork or stoop labor was required, the children were asked to contribute.

In addition to the harvest, many perishable crops required immediate processing and canning. This provided additional work opportunities for migrant families and often comprised two stages. First came hulling and shucking. Then came canning. As agriculture became increasingly industrialized, the general pattern was that canning industrialized first, hulling and shucking second, and harvesting last. By the twentieth century, most canneries had become indistinguishable from factories. Industrial machinery and equipment, automated conveyor systems, large batch-processing methods, and integration with organized distribution channels, had re-organized canneries on industrial lines. Many hulling and shucking operations remained hand work. Wherever hand work was required, children were involved. But as hulling and shucking became increasingly automated and mechanized, opportunities for child work were circumscribed.

Demand for child labor was determined by a number of factors. Wherever light handwork was involved, most commonly in harvesting, but depending on the crop, often involved hulling or shucking, planting, or weeding, children worked. Children were especially adapted to stoop labor because of their "nearness to the ground".[17] The most common arrangement was for children to work alongside their parents, but in some seasonal or migratory streams older children might go to the country unaccompanied by an adult (the padrone would serve as "uncle"). Children did not work in all sectors of agriculture. Though many young children performed arduous work, where the labor required adult strength and endurance, as in threshing wheat, children were of little value except for the older boys.

17 Lyons-Barrett, "Child Labor in Commercialized Agriculture", p. 15.

Further as hand operations were successively mechanized, children were usually displaced, both because mechanization made apparent the factory-like, industrial quality of the work, and because young children lacked the skill to maintain productivity levels required by increased capitalization.

As America entered its child labor reform era, children of the family farms could be said to be living a life that approximated ideals of agrarian romanticism. Conditions for sharecropper and migrant children were so far removed from these romantic ideals, by virtue of their extreme poverty on the supply side, and the industrial markets they faced on the demand side, that it was pure myth. Thus, "the fraudulently romantic view of an agrarian utopia built solely by the labor of virtuous farmers blurs the very real atrocities committed in the name of bolstering agriculture".[18]

The Child Labor Reform Movement in Agriculture

Child labor reform was one of the principal aims of the Progressive Movement of early twentieth century America, and the National Child Labor Committee (NCLC), formed in 1904, led the charge. While there had been earlier calls for reform, especially from labor organizations such as the Knights of Labor, the American Federation of Labor, and the Industrial Workers of the World, and most states had adopted primitive law on child labor, it was not until the twentieth century that a true national movement emerged.

Abolition of child labor from the mines, mills, and factory stands as one of the greatest achievements of the Progressive Era and the NCLC. But progressives were less successful in attacking child labor in other sectors including street trades, industrial homework, and, most notably, agriculture. Most observers agree that the NCLC was ultimately unable to overcome some version of "agrarian romanticism". The resistance to regulation of child labor in agriculture, and limited scope of regulation, "seem most clearly explained by reference to popular acceptance of the ideas of agrarianism in American thought".[19] The general public could be aroused over images of children in mines, mills, and factories, but could not be moved to action against child labor in agriculture, even when presented with evidence of the conditions for children of sharecroppers and migrants. The countervailing image of children performing chores on the family farm

18 Chen, "Of Agriculture's First Disobedience", p. 1324.
19 Effland, "Agrarianism and Child Labor Policy", p. 285.

prevailed. Lewis Hine, the not yet famous social photographer, conducted the very first investigation for the NCLC in agriculture. He commented: "We have met everywhere the universal feeling that there is nothing harmful in outdoor work for children, no matter how young", cautioning his fellow progressives: "It will be well to keep this theory in mind".[20]

Some observers cite strategic and tactical errors by reformers. Anne Effland argues that reformers, themselves, embraced their own notions of agrarian romanticism.[21] Mary Lyons-Barrett points to "intellectual and ideological shortcomings" of the NCLC citing the "Committee's narrow focus on highly visible forms of child labor in factories, mines, and textile mills, to the neglect of child labor in agriculture, domestic service, and the street trades".[22] As a "striking illustration of romanticism," they note the orphan trains sponsored by Charles Loring Brace's Childrens' Aid Society that sought to place urban orphaned and unwanted children in the good country air and the inherent morality of the farmer's home. Over 200,000 orphans were sent westward from eastern urban slums. It was common practice for orphanages, reform schools, and other child-care institutions to place their charges out for agricultural labor.

While it is true that the NCLC "was unable to break down the aura of romantic charm that attended child labor in the fields",[23] it is difficult to criticize them for lack of effort. As early as 1905, the year after its founding, NCLC Trustees were calling for investigations in agriculture in Michigan and Maryland.[24] The first full scale investigation was conducted in 1909, only one year after the first major investigation in southern cotton textiles. Investigation reports in agriculture were published every year thereafter. In addition to publication in the NCLC's principal outlets, the *Child Labor Bulletin* and the *Annals of the American Academy of Political and Social Science*, numerous major articles appeared in *The Survey*, *Good Housekeeping*, *Arena*, and *The Outlook*. After 1921, when co-founder Felix Adler retired as Chair of the NCLC and was replaced by David F. Houston, who had been President Wilson's Secretary of Agriculture, nearly all of the NCLC's investigative resources were committed to agriculture.

From the beginning, the NCLC attacked child labor in agriculture as "factory work without the factory roof". In the end, however, "intensive

20 Hine, *National Child Labor Committee Investigation.*

21 Effland, "Agrarianism and Child Labor Policy", p. 286.

22 Lyons-Barrett, "Child Labor in Commercialized Agriculture", p. 34.

23 Trattner, *Crusade for the Children*, p. 153.

24 National Child Labor Committee Papers, *Minutes.*

field work failed to achieve anything more than confirmation of already known facts to which nobody listened".[25] Unable to successfully undermine agrarianism, reformers were forced to make tactical accommodations to it. They emphasized that all children, including farm children, need to be educated, and repeatedly pointed out the deleterious effects of farm-work on formal education. They successively chipped away at sectors of commercial agriculture that had become so industrialized they were safe to attack. In the process, however, "the agrarian ideal of the benefits of farm work remained intact", and further regulation of child labor in agriculture remained difficult.[26]

Legislative History

American System of Federalism

Before examining the legislative history of child labor law in agriculture, it is useful to consider three features of American Federalism that inhibited the development of child labor law in general, and agricultural child labor law in particular. First, remember that the US Constitution was adopted before the Industrial Revolution in America. So, while the Constitution extends great protection to property rights, it is silent on rights of wage earners.

Second, under the US Constitution, "farm interests enjoyed nearly two centuries of political dominion through disproportionately favorable representation" in the US Senate.[27] While the House of Representatives was apportioned roughly by population, each state was allocated two Senators. "More sparsely populated states – that is, relatively rural states – therefore enjoyed a lopsided advantage in the Senate."[28] This disproportionate balance favoring agricultural interests also carried over to the states where "farmers or their rural representatives held the balance of power in badly proportioned state legislatures; securing legislation to regulate agricultural child labor was thus extremely difficult".[29]

Third, under the American system of federalism, the federal government was long precluded from regulating employment relationships by the

25 Trattner, *Crusade for the Children*, p. 153.
26 Effland, "Agrarianism and Child Labor Policy", p. 282.
27 Chen, "Of Agriculture's First Disobedience", p. 1275.
28 Chen, "Of Agriculture's First Disobedience", p. 1276.
29 Trattner, *Crusade for the Children*, p. 139.

Tenth Amendment that reserved all rights not specifically elucidated to the otherwise sovereign states. There was an ongoing tension between the Commerce Clause that authorized Congress to regulate inter-state commerce and the Tenth Amendment. Until 1937, the US Supreme Court held consistently that Congress could only regulate commerce itself, and not conditions under which goods and services entered the channels of commerce. Thus, regulation of working conditions, generally, and child labor in particular, remained the province of state legislatures.

State Laws on Child Labor in Agriculture

By the time the NCLC was founded in 1904, most states had rudimentary child labor legislation. But it was a patchwork crazy quilt of legislation where laggard states often emulated more progressive states, but where progressive states were also held in check by the competitive advantage of laggard states.[30] Most state laws sought to limit the hours of children to encourage schooling. Some established minimum ages for certain categories of work, especially mining and manufacturing, and often night work. But most state child labor laws specifically exempted agriculture and none explicitly addressed agriculture.

Nebraska became the only state prior to WW I to explicitly address child labor in agriculture when it limited children under six to eight hours per day and forty-eight hours per week in sugar beets.[31] In 1913, New York amended its child labor law to classify canneries as factories.[32] Subsequently, a number of states followed suit. But, at a time when most states had set of fourteen year minimum for factory work, a sixteen year minimum for night work, and had hired factory inspectors, agriculture per se remained almost entirely unregulated.

To be sure, many state child labor laws restricted the work of children when required to be in school. But the practical effects of such restrictions were limited. Most compulsory schooling laws exempted children from school during peak periods of seasonal demand for farm labor. Local school authorities granted "beet vacations," "apple vacations," or "tobacco vacations" to assure that all hands would be available to harvest the dominant local crop. Further, migrant children, whose principal residence lay outside the local school district, were generally prohibited from attending the local schools.

30 Hindman, *Child Labor*, p. 58.
31 Lyons-Barrett, "Child Labor in Commercialized Agriculture".
32 Felt, *Hostages of Fortune*.

Even into the 1930s, when the federal government was finally poised to act on child labor, only four states (Nebraska, Wisconsin, Ohio, and California) explicitly regulated child labor in agriculture outside school hours. Obstacles to progress included the persistence of the agrarian "myth" of wholesome work in the good outdoors, the disproportionate representation of rural interests in state legislatures, and industry concern that elimination of child labor would impose undue costs.[33]

Early Attempts at Federal Child Labor Legislation

In 1906, shortly after the NCLC was organized, Senator Albert Beveridge introduced the first proposal for a federal child labor law. His Beveridge Bill, aimed squarely at child labor in mining and manufacturing, would not have covered agriculture. Indeed, Beveridge was one of those reformers who bought into agrarian romanticism, assuring agricultural interests that "I do not for a moment pretend that working children on the farm is bad for them".[34] Nevertheless, the Beveridge Bill never became law. The first child labor law enacted by Congress was the Keating-Owen Act of 1916. It barred goods from interstate commerce that were produced by children. Agriculture was exempted, but canneries were covered. Keating-Owen was found an unconstitutional breach of the Tenth Amendment and an overbroad assertion of the Commerce Clause. In response, Congress enacted the Child Labor Tax Act in 1919 imposing a ten per cent excise tax on goods produced with child labor, but this, too, was found unconstitutional as a thinly veiled attempt to skirt the limits of the Commerce Clause.

The Child Labor Amendment to the Constitution

After two successive federal laws were declared unconstitutional, the NCLC and their reform coalition saw no recourse but to seek a Constitutional Amendment explicitly authorizing Congress to regulate child labor. With surprisingly little debate, Congress passed the Child Labor Amendment in June 1924. The amendment was elegant simplicity. In two short sections, it authorized Congress to regulate the labor of persons under eighteen, and permitted states to adopt higher standards. If three-fourths of the states ratified the amendment, it would take effect and Congress would most certainly regulate child labor. Ratification of the Child Labor Amendment would have given Congress regulatory authority over child labor in agriculture. Whether Congress would have exercised these powers was an

33 Curtiss, "The Fair Labor Standards Act".

34 Abbott, *The Child and the State*, p. 474.

important part of the debate. Proponents tried to assure the nation that Congress would be reasonable, most likely adopting provisions along the lines of Keating-Owen. Opponents urged that Congress was likely to regulate to the limits of its authority.

The Child Labor Amendment had momentum coming out of Congress. But its bid for ratification in the states stalled. Proponents of the amendment had several problems convincing the nation of the merits of a constitutional amendment. By the 1920s, it was clear the industrial child labor was already on the way out. "Child labor in the mines, mills, and factories had, in fact, been reduced dramatically [...] The character of the child labor problem had changed."[35] By this time, the NCLC was devoting nearly all its resources to child labor in commercial agriculture (some also in street trades and tenement homework). This shift occurred just as the public was asked to consider the constitutional amendment. This put the NCLC in a public relations bind. If the debate was framed around children in mines, mills, and factories, they could generate public sympathy, but little support for a remedy that would no longer be needed. If the debate was framed around agriculture, they would almost certainly generate a backlash grounded in agrarian romanticism.

While agrarian themes played a prominent role in the public debate over the amendment, the record is not entirely clear just how aggressively farm interest groups opposed the measure. The two dominant interest groups were the Grange and the American Farm Bureau Federation (AFBF). The Grange did not oppose the amendment in Congress, and its Executive Committee actually voted to endorse the amendment, but the annual convention in November, 1924 voted overwhelmingly to oppose. The AFBF opposed the amendment fearing government might prohibit children from doing chores.[36] Nevertheless, as efforts to revive the amendment surfaced in the 1930s, the AFBF reversed its position and came out in favor.[37]

Active opposition in the farm community was organized, curiously, by the National Association of Manufacturers (NAM) and David Clark, publisher of the *Southern Textile Bulletin* – the same David Clark who, acting as self-appointed defender of both states' rights and the right to employ children, had orchestrated the constitutional challenges to the Keating-Owen

35 Hindman, *Child Labor*, p. 77.

36 Lyons-Barrett, "Child Labor in Commercialized Agriculture".

37 Trattner, *Crusade for the Children*.

Act and the Child Labor Tax Act.[38] NAM's opposition was not surprising in itself, even though there was, by now, relatively little child labor in most manufacturing. What was surprising was "its zealous effort to stimulate resistance from the farm community".[39] David Clark created an organization called the Farmers' States' Rights League in July 1924. Using funds raised from southern textile interests, it flooded western states with propaganda whenever and wherever the amendment came up for consideration. Still, Trattner concludes that NAM and Clark's efforts may not have been necessary as "agrarian hostility to the child labor amendment was already deep-seated and troublesome".[40]

Enactment of the Fair Labor Standards Act

In 1937, in what has become known as "the switch in time that saved nine," the US Supreme Court reversed its position on the Commerce Clause, and upheld several key New Deal laws thereby mooting the debate over Pres. Roosevelt's "court packing" scheme.[41] Congress was now authorized to regulate not just goods in commerce and the transportation of those goods, but also the conditions under which those good are produced. This paved the way for the Fair Labor Standards Act, enacted in 1938, and which contains, in addition to the nation's child labor laws, its minimum wage and hours and overtime laws.

There was remarkably little discussion about whether agriculture should be covered under the FLSA, it was simply excluded. The only provision that would have any effect on agriculture prohibited work while children were "legally required to be in school". But even this would have minimal effect. It did not apply to children on family farms, including tenant and sharecropper children, and it would not affect most migrant children since many were not legal residents of the state in which they worked, and so, were not subject to the compulsory schooling laws.

The casual exclusion of agriculture from the FLSA has caused most commentators to point to the overwhelming power and influence of agrarian romanticism. For example, Curtiss argues that provisions of the FLSA

38 Hindman, *Child Labor*, pp. 70-73 (Child Labor Tax Act), 66-69 (Keating-Owen Act), see also pp. 79-81.

39 Trattner, *Crusade for the Children*, p. 173.

40 Trattner, *Crusade for the Children*, p. 174.

41 Leuchtenburg, *The Supreme Court Reborn*.

were shaped by the debates over the Child Labor Amendment. "Given their temporal proximity, the adoption of the FLSA necessarily took into account many of the factors that defeated the ratification of the Child Labor Amendment in the states."[42] Two important factors included the myth of wholesome work coupled with a belief that parents have a right to raise their children as they see fit. Given the traditional reliance of farmers on family labor, "provisions of the FLSA vouchsafe for farmers the right to use their [own] children at any age for any employment on the farm".[43]

But while agrarian romanticism and agrarian interests undoubtedly played a role, there are other explanations for the agricultural exclusion. First, the FLSA "was very narrowly worded and exempted many workers simply to avoid prolonged legislative debate".[44] The reach of the Commerce Clause was still considered to be fairly narrow. In spite of the fact that its products would enter the stream of interstate commerce, "agriculture was characterized as a local activity, more properly regulated by local authorities".[45] At the time, it was estimated there were 850,000 working children under sixteen, seventy per cent of whom were in agriculture, but only three to six per cent (30,000 to 50,000) would be affected by the child labor provisions of the FLSA.[46] Thus, many sectors in addition to agriculture were excluded.

Linder offers an entirely different explanation for the exclusion, one that has little to do with the question of child labor and more to do with racism – pure and simple. He notes that, in addition to the FLSA, agriculture was excluded from every New Deal initiative aimed at the labor force. Franklin D. Roosevelt was elected in 1932 on a platform to end the depression. His running river of social legislation – New Deal – promised not only a new era of social and economic justice, but also a major new role for the federal government in regulating many aspects of economic activity that had previously been the domain of the states. An array of New Deal initiatives were aimed at labor. Some were considered temporary measures for the duration of the depression. The Civilian Conservation Corps (CCC – 1933) and the Work Projects Administration (WPA – 1935) sought to provide work relief for unemployed and the National Industrial Recovery Act (NIRA – 1933) sought to stabilize production, employment, hours, and wages in private

42 Curtiss, "The Fair Labor Standards Act", p. 316.
43 Curtiss, "The Fair Labor Standards Act", p. 319.
44 Lyons-Barrett, "Child Labor in Commercialized Agriculture", p. 201.
45 Johnson, "Did Old MacDonald Have a Farm?", p. 309.
46 Lyons-Barrett, "Child Labor in Commercialized Agriculture".

industry. Others were intended to be permanent. The National Labor Relations Act (1935), the Social Security Act (1935), and the Fair Labor Standards Act (1938) form three foundation pillars of today's US labor policy.

Roosevelt's difficulties with the Supreme Court are well documented and generally understood. Less well understood were Roosevelt's problems with Congress. Roosevelt was a Democrat. The American South – the states of the old confederacy – were also solid Democrat. In every New Deal congress, southerners controlled over half the chairmanships and leadership positions. Southern legislators were committed to maintaining the "plantation system" that kept blacks subjugated to a white aristocracy.

If he was to get his legislation enacted, "Roosevelt had no alternative but to cooperate with the Southerners who ran Congress".[47] By insisting that agriculture and domestic service – the other linchpin of the plantation system – be exempted from New Deal labor policy, Southern Democrats prevented three and a half million of the nation's five and a half million black workers from enjoying the benefits and protections of the Social Security Act, the National Labor Relations Act, and, most important for the present discussion, the Fair Labor Standards Act with its child labor provisions.

A Counter-Factual: Federal Regulation of Child Labor in Sugar Beets

There is evidence that, by the time the FLSA was enacted in 1938, "agrarianism" might have yielded its child labor force. The clearest evidence is the fact that federal regulation had restricted child labor in sugar beets since 1934.

Sugar beets required labor throughout the growing cycle. Beet companies contracted with families on the basis of the number of people who would work – more people, more acres. Russian-German families with permanent homes in nearby cities were transported to the beet fields by the beet companies. They typically spent five months in the beet fields and seven months back home. The NCLC estimated that one-third of children working in sugar beets were under eleven and most worked twelve hours per day.[48]

The 1934 Jones-Costigan Act incorporated sugar (both beets and cane) into the Agricultural Adjustment Act (AAA), making companies of the

47 Linder, "Farm Workers and the Fair Labor Standards Act", p. 1351.
48 Lyons-Barrett, "Child Labor in Commercialized Agriculture".

Sugar Trust eligible for federal subsidies. As a condition for accepting those subsidies, the act prohibited child labor under fourteen and restricted those fourteen to sixteen to eight hours per day. No other AAA support program included such restrictions. When the Supreme Court invalidated AAA in 1936, Congress re-established commodity supports in the 1937 Sugar Act which retained the child labor restrictions, with the result that many mothers and children remained in the cities, where the children could go to school, while fathers went out to the country for beets.[49]

Effland argues that sugar beets came to be regulated because they were so highly industrialized and simply came to be recognized as such.[50] This may be true, but this explains little, since many other agricultural commodities were just as heavily industrialized, and had been for many years. What other factors might explain why sugar beets, but not other agricultural commodities, came to be regulated? First, there was widespread populist disdain for the Sugar Trust. "Many people felt that since the sugar beet industry was heavily subsidized, more was to be expected of it in terms of wages and improved working conditions."[51] Second, sugar beets were really the only agricultural commodity grown in the Plains States, other than potatoes, that relied heavily on child labor, making it an especially salient example. Further, while they were children of recent immigrants, most of these children were white. Finally, the NCLC may have just gotten lucky when it found itself in a unique position to exercise leverage over the proposed legislation. When conditions of child workers in beets were brought to Roosevelt's attention, he authorized Secretary of Labor Frances Perkins to appoint an investigating committee, and she appointed Courtenay Dinwiddie, Executive Secretary for NCLC, as Chair.[52]

Subsequent Amendments to the flsa

The FLSA has been amended numerous times, but agriculture remains lightly regulated. In 1940, Congress appointed the House Select Committee to Investigate Migration of Destitute Citizens, better known as the Tolan Committee. It was estimated there were over 4 million migrant farmworkers at the time. In response to the Committee's investigations, the NCLC drafted a bill that incorporated "industrialized agriculture" into

49 Lyons-Barrett, "Child Labor in Commercialized Agriculture".

50 Effland, "Agrarianism", p. 288.

51 Lyons-Barrett, "Child Labor in Commercialized Agriculture", p. 193.

52 Lyons-Barrett, "Child Labor in Commercialized Agriculture", p. 193.

the FLSA. The bill was introduced with apparent widespread support in November 1941, but was forgotten after Pearl Harbor.

In 1949 the FLSA was amended to prohibit children under sixteen from working in agriculture "during school hours". The original prohibition – "while not legally required to be in school" – did not affect most migrant children; the new language did. In 1966, the FLSA was amended to prohibit children under sixteen from "hazardous" agricultural work and, significantly, to apply the minimum wage to most of agriculture. Finally, in 1974, minimum age standards were adopted in agriculture. Most child labor under twelve was prohibited (minimum age set at ten for small farms and certain specified crops). Children twelve and thirteen required parental consent. There were no hours restrictions imposed and the age limits did not apply to children on the family's own farm. These are the only restrictions on child labor in agriculture contained in the FLSA today, and they remain much weaker than the FLSA's restrictions on most child labor where eighteen is the minimum age for hazardous work, sixteen is the minimum for regular work, and, during a period of socialization from fourteen to sixteen, children may perform light work for light hours that does not interfere with schooling. Employment of children under fourteen is generally illegal.

Continued Demand for Child Labor in Agriculture

Given the minimalist nature of child labor regulation in agriculture, market forces continue to dominate supply and demand for working children. So, what changes has the market wrought? In particular, what has happened to the three main groups of working children seen at the birth of American commercial agriculture? What has happened to the children on the family-owned farms, the children of tenant farmers and sharecroppers, and, finally, the children of the landless migrants?

Children on the Family Farms

They are still there working. And they are still the embodiment of the agrarian romantic's ideal of wholesome work in the good outdoors, early lessons in responsibility under parental tutelage, and the molding of physically sturdy and morally upright future citizens. Today, nearly all of these children are white.

Today, most family farm children complete their primary and secondary education. But it has not always been so. A 1916 NCLC study showed that the top fifteen states in terms of children in agriculture was nearly identical to the top fifteen states with highest illiteracy rates. Progress on compulsory schooling made little headway until the 1920s, in part due the family's need for labor, in part due to accessibility problems of rural schools. Before WW II, while the average urban school term was 180 days, the average rural term was 140.[53] Family farm children continued to work long hours before and after school, on weekends, and sometimes instead of school. Attendance figures for rural children were low; rural children remained behind urban children in total years of education; and rural children made slower progress through the curriculum.[54]

Beyond compulsory schooling laws, child labor on the family farm remains completely unregulated. In other industries, parents can employ their own children at any age, except in mining and manufacturing and except in hazardous work. In agriculture, parents can employ their own children at any age and even for hazardous work. Ironically, children on the family farm face among the highest occupational fatality rates – substantially higher than that of seasonal and migrant children. Tractor rollovers are a leading cause of death.[55]

Children of Tenant Farmers and Sharecroppers

There has been a dramatic reduction in tenant farming and sharecropping, especially in the South, but also in other parts of the country, and with it, a dramatic decline in demand for child labor. From 1920-1930, the boll weevil resulted in the loss of over 100,000 southern farms and a 1.2 million decline in farm population. Next, the mechanical cotton picker that came into widespread use in the period between the World Wars reversed the work of the cotton gin. Where the cotton gin enabled large scale cotton plantations and slave labor to sweep the South, the mechanical picker dramatically reduced demand for manual labor.[56]

White tenant farmers, and second and third generation immigrant tenants, either ascended to farm ownership over time, or they eventually left farming. When they ascended to ownership, their children became the family farm children discussed above. When they left the farm, their children left with them and, as a generally rule, never returned to farm labor.

53 Lyons-Barrett, "Child Labor in Commercialized Agriculture".
54 Riney-Kehrberg, "The Limits of Policy".
55 US Department of Labor, *Report on the Youth Labor Force.*
56 Chen, "Of Agriculture's First Disobedience".

Confronting "virtually insurmountable barriers to widespread black ownership of farms," blacks, too, were leaving farming and the South in droves.[57] Over six decades, from 1910-1970, more than six and a half million blacks migrated South to North. By 1930, the exodus had been underway for some time, but its pace was about to accelerate dramatically. When blacks were exempted from New Deal labor legislation, thereby preserving a substantial agricultural to industrial wage differential, the opportunity cost of remaining in agriculture elevated to the industrial minimum wage. Finally, when wartime economic expansion created great demand for industrial labor, blacks showed up. "The jobs were there, the wages were better, and black America was ready to move."[58]

From 1900 through 1930, blacks represented a relatively constant fourteen per cent of farm operators (though a vast majority were tenant farmers and sharecroppers, not owners). By 1940 the per centage had declined to eleven. It continued to decline every decade after so that, by 1997, only 1 per cent (or 18,451) of farm operators were black. By the 1990s, the number of Hispanic farm operators had surpassed the number of blacks.[59] By the 1980s, when the Northern migration had run its course, ninety-eight per cent of farm operators – the managerial class in agriculture – were white, making it one of the most racially homogenous occupational groups in America.[60]

Children of Landless Migrants

Estimates of the numbers of children working as seasonal and migrant farmworkers in the US today vary widely.[61] In 1998, the General Accounting Office issued what they considered a conservative estimate of 300,000 youths from fifteen to seventeen.[62] The National Agricultural Workers Survey (NAWS) estimates six per cent of the seasonal and migrant workforce are fourteen to seventeen, a total of 125,000-130,000 youths.[63] The United Farm Workers union has estimated as many as 800,000 migrant children.[64] Finally,

57 Chen, "Of Agriculture's First Disobedience", p. 1304.
58 Chen, "Of Agriculture's First Disobedience", p. 1305.
59 US Department of Agriculture, *Black Farmers in America*.
60 Chen, "Of Agriculture's First Disobedience".
61 Hindman, "Unfinished Business".
62 US General Accounting Office, *Child Labor in Agriculture*.
63 US Department of Labor, *A Demographic and Employment Profile of United States Farm Workers*.
64 Tucker, *Fingers to the Boone*, p. 10.

the National Consumers League recently estimated 400,000 to 500,000 but did not distinguish between migrant children and family farm children.[65]

Today's migrant workforce is also ethnically homogeneous. It is almost entirely Hispanic and mostly Mexican. Among seasonal workers, Hispanics also comprise a majority, but substantial numbers of white children, often children of family farmers, hire themselves out as seasonal workers for short periods during peak local harvests. Mexicans began arriving in large numbers after the Mexican Revolution and especially during WW I when the US took on the role of chief food producer for its allies. High demand for agricultural production was the pull factor. Coupled with wartime restrictions on immigration from Europe, it created a high demand for Mexican labor. The Mexican Revolution in 1910 was the push factor. Before the revolution most Mexican migrants were long-term residents of the US, with homes in Texas and New Mexico. The revolution's political and economic unrest made it nearly impossible to make a living in agriculture, and so pushed agricultural workers north into the US.[66]

Mexican immigrants brought with them rural work customs of an extended family labor system to include orphaned grandchildren, nieces and nephews, and others into the work unit.[67] With increasing demand for agricultural labor during WW II, the Bracero Program was initiated to recruit Mexican labor. While the program was aimed at adult men, it also boosted both child labor and illegal immigration. Since WW II, the migrant agricultural workforce has been dominated by people of Mexican origin.

There were only two brief periods when non-immigrant Anglo-American children comprised a significant proportion of migrant child workers in agriculture. The exceptional quality of these episodes is instructive. First, during the Dust Bowl years ("when Oklahoma woke up in Kansas"), thousands of families migrated westward, especially to California, to join the migratory labor force. Between 1933 and 1938, 350,000 migrants, roughly half of them children, made their way to California.[68] "Okie" children became the most visible image of children in agriculture through the 1930s. The American public was shocked to see regular American children, children of sturdy agrarians no less, reduced to the level of migrant laborers (See John Steinbeck's *Grapes of Wrath*, 1936).

65 National Consumers League, *Child Labor in U.S. Commercial Agriculture.*
66 Lyons-Barrett, "Child Labor in Commercialized Agriculture".
67 Lyons-Barrett, "Child Labor in Commercialized Agriculture".
68 Lyons-Barrett, "Child Labor in Commercialized Agriculture".

The phenomenon of "Okie" children was, at least partly, responsible for revival of interest in the Child Labor Amendment in the 1930s. The Okies, fresh on the mind of Congress when the FLSA was debated, could have forced the question of child labor in agriculture. But, unlike immigrants, it was assumed that much Okie migration was temporary and would be solved when fathers found steady employment. This was an assumption shared by the Okies themselves, and, as it turned out, it was true. WW II ended the Okies' annual migration in agriculture, as they went off to munitions plants and shipyards, taking their children with them.[69]

The only other period when substantial numbers of white American children worked as migrant laborers was during WW II. During the war, many under eighteen – too young for military service, but old enough to want to aid the war effort – worked as temporary and emergency agricultural workers. Throughout the way years, one million to one and a half million youths came out to the farms each year. Most came out during summer months or for the harvest, thus working around school schedules; most were better characterized as seasonal workers as their migrations were usually confined to a local area; and most had no prior experience in agriculture, and never returned to agriculture after the war. But the marriage of agrarianism with war-time patriotism and sacrifice did much to repair the image of child labor in agriculture created by the Okies.

Today, very young children comprise a small and shrinking proportion of the migrant workforce. But Human Rights Watch has recently documented children as young as eight and nine working regularly.[70] Among fourteen to seventeen year-olds, while the majority were born in the US, increasing proportions have entered the country illegally. Astonishingly, eighty per cent are effectively emancipated minors, unaccompanied by a parent, and this proportion is growing.[71]

Given minimal child labor regulation, other regulatory interventions had the potential to influence child labor in agriculture. First and foremost was schooling. But schooling has always been problematic for migrant children. Early on it had been established that family farm children fared worse than non-farm children; that seasonal workers fared worse than family farm children; and that migrant workers fared worst of all. Migrants were less likely to attend school. When they did attend, they attended more irregularly, were more likely to be behind grade level, and less likely to

69 Lyons-Barrett, "Child Labor in Commercialized Agriculture".
70 Tucker, *Fingers to the Bone*, pp. 37-42.
71 US Department of Labor, *Report on the Youth Labor Force.*

finish. The more extended the migration, the greater the harm. And the effects compounded – the more years in migration, the greater the harm.[72] While there have been improvements in provision of schooling for migrant children, the basic pattern remains intact. In 1940, the Tolan Committee cited a study of 139 migratory cotton workers – seventy-nine did not attend school the previous year and thirty-eight had never attended school.[73] In 1960, Edward R. Murrow's *Harvest of Shame* – a film documentary depicting conditions of migrant farm workers asserted, with perhaps some hyperbole, that only one in five hundred children would finish grade school and only one in five thousand would finish high school. Today, among fourteen to seventeen year-old migrants, less than half, 47 per cent, attend school at grade level, and 37 per cent have dropped out of school.[74]

Minimum wage and hours and overtime provisions of the FLSA could have an effect on child labor independently of the child labor provisions. Application of the minimum wage to agriculture should, in theory, eliminate very young children and anyone else incapable of attaining average productivity equal to the value of the minimum wage. In practice, however, the effect of the minimum wage was muted by the prevalence of piece rate payment systems, by the pooling of family production for a single payment, and by common practices such as "shaving hours" to assure a minimum wage, at least on paper. An overtime premium might have limited the hours of child workers. But the absence of hours restrictions in agriculture mean that children as young as twelve may work unlimited hours, outside school hours. Given the perishable nature of many fruits and vegetables, on school days this might mean work for several hours before school, a six hour break for school, and then work until dark after school. On non-school days, the six hour break would be omitted.

Campaigns to unionize migrant farmworkers beginning in the 1960s have had some effects on conditions of migrant children. Early organizers such as Cesar Chavez and Dolores Huerta did not condemn child labor directly because too many parents were utterly dependent on the wages of their children. But they also understood that child labor depressed adult wages and that if parents belonged to the union they might see their wages rise and want their children in school.[75] While unionization remains spotty in commercial agriculture, unions have done much to ameliorate condi-

72 Folks, *Farm Labor vs. School Attendance.*

73 Lyons-Barrett, "Child Labor in Commercialized Agriculture".

74 US Department of Labor, *Report on the Youth Labor Force.*

75 Taylor, *Chavez and the Farm Workers.*

tions of children through bargaining over issues such as safety, housing, and hygiene.

In the post-WW II period, the pace of mechanization in agriculture accelerated and, where it did, child labor was progressively circumscribed. The mechanical cotton picker, which was coming into widespread use, eliminated much of the stoop labor. Likewise, sugar beets came to be almost entirely mechanized. Likewise, with many other crops. Many came to believe the worst evils of child labor in agriculture had been eliminated. But much hand harvesting remains in a wide variety of fruits, vegetables, nuts, flowers, and other crops. Wherever the work remains hand-labor intensive, the children are there. And, where the crop in question is perishable, the children will be working long hours.

US Agrarianism Today

Is America's romance with agrarianism dead yet? The National Consumers League recently commissioned a public opinion poll. While most Americans remain blissfully unaware of the nation's child labor problem, 88 per cent of respondents said that agricultural workers should enjoy the same benefits and labor protections that other workers enjoy. Eighty-nine per cent said that children who work in agriculture should be covered by the same laws as children who work in fast food restaurants. Based on responses like those, one might conclude that the romance is over and the time is ripe to bring agriculture in line with the rest of industry. On the other hand, nearly half the respondents (46 per cent) thought it was okay for children twelve and thirteen to work in agriculture, though only four per cent would put their own children to agricultural work at that age.[76] Americans continue to be quite tolerant of the idea of other people's young children working in the fields.

There are bills currently pending in Congress that would bring the FLSA's child labor standards in agriculture into line with standards for the rest of industry, but prospects for these bills are uncertain. It is too soon to tell whether America is ready to remove: "This inexcusable blot on the American economy and the nation's conscience."[77]

76 National Consumers League, *Child Labor in US Commercial Agriculture.*
77 Trattner, *Crusade for the Children.*

CHAPTER 20

Child Labour in Brazil: More than 500 Years of National Shame

Ana Lúcia Kassouf and Marcelo Justus dos Santos

Introduction

According to the International Labor Organization (ILO) there are more than two hundred million children working in the world with the majority engaged in the worst forms of child labour. Children are below fifteen years old, performing activities that may harm their physical and mental health, e.g. manipulating dangerous tools and machineries, working with chemicals and pesticides in agriculture, working in mines or stone crushing and working in construction. Many of these children do not attend school and probably never will, trapping them into a cycle of poverty.

Different forms of labour – whether light or heavy, visible or invisible, legal or illegal, poorly remunerated or non-remunerated, free or slave – have been part of the history of poor children in Brazil since the country was "discovered" in 1500. These child labourers have certainly helped to build the large economy that exists today. However, the cost of so many working children, although practically immeasurable, is unquestionably high.

The constitutional amendments of 1934, 1937 and 1946 set the minimum working age at fourteen years. However, the minimum age was lowered to twelve during the military dictatorship in 1967. The situation was only reviewed in 1988 when a constitutional amendment prohibited dangerous forms of labour for children under eighteen and any other form of labour for children under fourteen. Currently, due to an amendment passed in December 1998, the minimum working age is sixteen years old.[1] Notwithstanding the advances made in the regulation and aspired eradication

1 ILO, *Combatendo o trabalho infantil.*

of child labour in Brazil, studies show that there is still a high number of working children and adolescents.

Data from the 2005 Brazilian National Household Survey (PNAD) indicates that the number of working children and adolescents between the ages of five and fifteen exceeds 2.9 million. In spite of the sharp decrease that occurred mainly from the second half of the 1990s, this figure still represents 7.8 per cent of all children in the age group. In 1992, for example, the number of working children in the five to fifteen age bracket neared 5.5 million, or 14.6 per cent of the population in that age group. These statistics, however, do not include children and adolescents working in illegal activities such as prostitution and drug trafficking, nor those performing household tasks.

The first reports on child labour in Brazil appeared in indigenous societies during the country's colonization period and later on during the nearly four centuries of black slavery, when slaves' children engaged in tasks that extended far beyond their physical limits. The abolition of slavery led to an increase in the demand for child labour due to the industrialization process which started in the late nineteenth century and is very similar to other countries experiences with child labour. In 1890, 15 per cent of all people employed in industries in São Paulo were children and adolescents. In that same year, according to the Department of Statistics and Archives of São Paulo, child labour accounted for 25 per cent of the labour force in the textile industry. Twenty years later, that figure had increased to 30 per cent. In 1919, data from the State Labour Department showed that 37 per cent of all textile workers were children and adolescents. In the state capital the percentage was as high as 40.

The present situation emphasizes the importance of this study, as in 2005 nearly three million children aged from five to fifteen years old were still working in Brazil. As already mentioned, this excludes other unaccounted activities such as prostitution, drug trafficking and domestic labour. With 97 per cent of children in school, several laws prohibiting child labour, social programs transferring income to poor families, and society mobilizing to eradicate child labour, what causes children to work today? In the attempt to answer this question, we have recovered historical elements of child labour in Brazil, its origins, features and consequences, as well as its relation with the current exploitation of child labour.

The Origins of Child Labour in Brazil

Child and adolescent labour is not a new phenomenon in Brazil. In fact, its roots and features are bound up in the history of the country. Research on the history of child labour in Brazil has always concluded that the use of child and youth labour is associated with the development process of the country. However, there is almost no information on child labour in the past, for neither the colonial period or for the nineteenth century. According to Gutiérrez & Lewkowicz the lack of information is due to the fact that until at least the middle of nineteenth century there was no clear definition of a child or a youth.[2] The understanding of a phenomenon depends on the clear definition of the object of study and not having a clear definition of a child created difficulties in tracking information on child labour in the past. Only with the beginning of universal schooling and the concepts of labourers and children's rights child labour was seen as a problem, but was not seen as such throughout most of history.

Brazil was officially discovered in 1500 and populated since 1530. According to Ramos the first reports of children and adolescents working are from back in the days when men, women, boys and girls ventured towards the Land of Santa Cruz on sixteenth-century Portuguese vessels.[3] Back then, fifteen-year old girls were regarded as fit for marriage and nine-year old boys as suitable for work. The replacement of adult labour with child labour became indispensable for sea adventures. Evidence based on a list of payments to the crew of a Portuguese vessel allows one to conclude that approximately 22 per cent of the workers were minors, thus demonstrating the importance of children to transoceanic adventures.[4] Although the issue at the time was not the exploitation of *Brazilian* children, it illustrates an incentive to their subsequent exploitation as the use of poor children and adolescents as labour was regarded as normal by the Portuguese and subsequently by other Europeans who came to Brazil during the long immigration period that started in the nineteenth century and became more intense in the mid-twentieth century. Child labour in Brazil was first officially registered amongst indigenous children. According to Ferreira they helped adults extract *pau-brasil* (the native Brazilian tree) and

2 Gutiérrez and Lewkowicz, "Trabalho infantil em Minas Gerais".

3 Ramos, "A História trágico marítima".

4 *Ibid.* The author provides information taken from Barcellos, *Construções de Naus em Lisboa e Goa.*

build the first villages early in the twenty-first century.[5] In woodland areas they harvested honey, turtle eggs and other animal products, hunted birds, carried meat and weapons to the village and scared birds away from crops in the pre-harvest period. Despite the fact that these tasks were harmless for children, they marked the beginning of child labour in colonial Brazil. Although children already had responsibilities alongside the adults, according to ILO the arrival of Portuguese settlers led to a qualitative and quantitative change.[6]

In Brazil, the first organization to use child labour was most probably the Navy which, as pointed out by Venancio,[7] recruited children after the country's independence who were trained by the Apprentice Sailor Companies (*Companhias de Aprendizes Marinheiros*) and sent them without any combat training whatsoever to fight in the Paraguay War.[8] By investigating the Navy's medical files kept in the National Archives dating from the Paraguay War, the author concludes that many children between the ages of nine and twelve fought in the war and estimates that at least six hundred children in that age group were in the fields, rivers and seas where the battles took place. Data reported by Souza indicates that 1,470 minors were enlisted in the Brazilian Navy during 1868.[9] Venancio illustrates that sailor boys helped with the sails and loaded weapons with cartridges and gunpowder, serving as "cannon fodders" a task that must have exceeded their physical limits.[10] According to this author, although it was the admirals who were praised, those most exposed to mortal danger in the war against Paraguay were street boys or boys taken from their families to fight. Emídio Joaquim de Aguiar, Marcelino Ajala and Laurindo de Souza Albino are part of a list of children's names that can be found in the National Archives of the Paraguay War.

These registries document the first large scale exploitation of children in the armed forces in Brazil. More than a hundred years later the situation has not much improved with many children being used by drug dealers as watchers and drug sellers, carrying guns and being exposed to all sorts of risks in marginalized societies in the big cities of Brazil. These illicit activi-

5 Ferreira, *Trabalho infantil*.
6 ILO, *Boas práticas de combate ao trabalho infantil*.
7 Venancio, "Os aprendizes da guerra".
8 War that lasted from 1864 to 1870, between the Triple Alliance formed by Brazil, Argentina and Uruguay on one side, and Paraguay on the other.
9 Souza, *Escravidão ou morte*.
10 Venancio, "Os aprendizes da guerra".

ties are some of the most dangerous, involving physical and psychological threats to a child's life and have unfortunately been increasing at a fast rate in the country.

In chronological terms, child labour was also registered during the nearly four centuries of slavery in Brazil when the slaves' children were assigned tasks that far exceeded their physical capacity. According to ILO, several studies show that the children of slaves worked as hard as their parents did on the sugarcane plantations and for sugar production.[11] As for the slaveholders, slave children's work resulted in an increased worth of a slave as an adult, as they would have acquired certain skills that were valued in the slave market. Therefore, the explanation for child labour in that period lies in the system itself and in the speculative attitude of slaveholders.

Child labour in indigenous communities was not characterized as exploitation – at least until the arrival of the settlers – but rather reflected cultural aspects. And during slavery children and their parents were left with no option but to comply it. This was due to rising industry that, in view of the country's socioeconomic conditions, many children and adolescents were precociously pushed into the labour market. The causes and features of child labour should be investigated after 1888, when the abolition of slavery led to an increase in the demand for free labour, and child and adolescent labour began to be heavily used by capitalists. Despite specific legislation on the matter, child labour is still highly used in Brazil today. We therefore agree with the ILO's conclusion that the intensity of the problem nowadays suggests that capitalists still have a slavery-oriented mindset and, therefore, some of the historical roots that explain why the exploitation of child labour is accepted, somewhat naturally by society probably lie in slavery.

Child Labour and Brazil's Industrialization

The abolition of slavery in 1888 led to an increase in the demand for free labour to feed rising industry, which was in full expansion. Its development was very much similar to that of other countries in the world where the exploitation of children in factories also occurred on a grand scale. An example of that is the British textile industry in the seventeenth-century.[12] In fact, we can characterize Brazil's growing industrialization process in the beginning of the twentieth century as a period of great demand for

11 ILO, *Combatendo o trabalho infantile.*

12 Dulles, *Anarquistas e comunistas.*

child labour, mainly because the work of minors was not regulated and cost less than adult labour. As pointed out by Adorno, back then the discussion on the issue did not succeed due to the general understanding that child labour was a necessity.[13] For Rizzini the only reasons for regulating child labour were preventing excesses and better preparing children for work through professional institutes and schools.[14] According to Campos those institutions were established, among other reasons, because of the belief inherited from the British that idleness is the main source of evil and industry is the main virtue.[15]

It is common knowledge that the working class of São Paulo was formed mainly by immigrants, many of whom were children and adolescents. These were joined by waves of migrants encouraged by the large urbanization process triggered by industrialization, to make up the labour mass used in the cities' factories and streets. Moura emphasizes the fact that in the mid-1870s the number of ads published by industries recruiting children to work – mainly in the textile sector – already began to multiply in the São Paulo press.[16] According to Moura many of the workers were children,[17] such as Vicente Connuci and Angelina Rossi, Italian immigrants, or the son of José Miron, Núncio, Spanish, who in 1913, when he was ten years old, used to work in a paper factory on a famous street of Sao Paulo city called "25 de março".

According to this author, the presence of immigrant children and adolescents in the industrial labour force was probably the most striking proof that poverty had followed many immigrant families, which used to live in precarious conditions and therefore depended, in part, on the work of their own children.

As any child, the young workers liked to play. However, in doing so they would usually get into trouble in the factories and work places at that time. Moura described that in May 1905, Antonio Lombardo, fourteen years old, working in a shoe repair store, was beaten on his back with an iron chain, just because he was playing during work time.[18] In July 1907, André Francisco, twelve years old, accidentally hit his friend Marcellino

13 Adorno, "Criança".
14 Rizzini, "Principais temas abordados".
15 Campos, "Pobreza e trabalho infantil".
16 Moura, *Mulheres e menores no trabalho industrial.*
17 Moura, "Crianças operárias".
18 Moura, "Crianças operárias".

Villa Mizal, sixteen years old, with an iron bar that they were playing with at lunch time in "Penteado" factory.

Although child labour is concentrated in São Paulo due to industrialization, the employment of minors in (precarious) industries also took place in other states of Brazil. In Ribeirão Preto city, Fortunato Miningoti, fourteen years old, had his right hand smashed while operating a machine in "Oliveira" printer in May 1913. Maria Teixeira, thirteen years old, lost her hand when cleaning one of the machines in the textile factory "Tecidos Confiança Industrial" in Rio de Janeiro city.[19]

Using data from 1831, Gutiérrez & Lewkowicz show that in Minas Gerais State, at least 19 per cent of children between five and fourteen years old worked, reaching up to 60 per cent of children in some districts.[20] From eleven to twelve years old, the average percentage was 30 and between thirteen and fourteen years old 40 per cent of children were working. The tasks varied considerably from factories to agricultural activities. Only 16 per cent of non-slave children followed academic studies at the time. Botelho, after analyzing a list of inhabitants from Minas Gerais in 1830, concluded that the occupations of children followed those of adults and that the activity performed by children depended on the economic status of the locality.[21] The author shows that, in the nineteenth century, children of seven years old were considered to be ready to work and were seen as adults by fourteen years old.

There are reports that in the 1840s the rising industries already employed many children between the ages of five to twelve. The children came predominantly from charitable institutions and orphanages to work in the textile industry, where their working day lasted as long as twelve hours.[22] As an example of the heavy use of child and adolescent labour in the industries of those days, Foot and Leonardi report the case of a textile factory located in Parati, in the state of Rio de Janeiro, in which approximately 64 per cent of the labour force was made up of children during 1865.[23]

The importance of the child labour contribution to the family income is evident in the ads offering jobs in the early twentieth-century textile industries. Some of them only recruited families with children and/or adolescents willing to work, as they represented a reduction in the capitalist's

19 Moura, "Crianças operárias".
20 Gutiérrez and Lewkowicz,"Trabalho infantil em Minas Gerais".
21 Botelho, "O Trabalho de crianças e jovens".
22 Dulles, *Anarquistas e comunistas*; Foot and Leonardi, *História da indústria.*
23 Foot and Leonardi, *História da indústria.*

costs. Rizzini mentions, for example, the case of a factory located in Pernambuco, between 1930 and 1950, which offered housing to workers in a workers' village, depending on the family production and on the number of children to be used in the factory.[24] A recruitment prerequisite for was for the family to have children and adolescents that could be employed in the factory. These families were given a house in the village, the standard of which was subject to their production capacity. According to the author, to industrialists the work of children and adolescents represented a reduction in costs and a labour force trained from an early age. In the words of Moura, the work of children and adolescents in that period was a reflection of the low standard of living of working families which were subject to low salaries and to a significantly high cost of living.[25]

The growing use of child labour and the exposure of child workers to precarious working conditions can be seen in the records of industrial accidents in the city of São Paulo, which is one of the few sources of information on child labour in that period.

Moura, using articles from local newspapers, cites accidents involving children working in industries in São Paulo in the beginning of the twentieth century.[26] Armando Dias, for example, died in November 1913 whilst still very young, a victim of an electric shock when entering the textile industry where he worked. As indicated by the author, boys and girls were victims of industrial accidents on a daily basis. Hermínio, eight years old; Rosa, ten years old; Antonio, eleven years old; Gertudres, twelve years old; Guido, thirteen years old; are amongst many referred to, illustrating the damage that work inflicted on children and adolescents in São Paulo industry. Accidents involving children were very common, such as the case of Cesare Battiferri who was only fourteen years old when he suffered severe burns on his hands and face when reaching for a container full of boiling water in a textile factory of "Indústrias Reunidas Francisco Matarazzo". And Antonia Lima whose right arm was amputated when cutting tobacco in the "Arthur Pereira" factory when she was only twelve years old.

Physical violence was also common among young workers, as shown by Moura.[27] In October 1904, Vitto Lindolpho, ten years old, was brutally beaten by the owner of the shoe repair store where he was working because

24 Rizzini, "Pequenos trabalhadores do Brasil".

25 Moura, *Mulheres e menores no trabalho industrial.*

26 Moura, "Crianças operárias".

27 Moura, "Crianças operárias".

he thought the boy had stolen fifty thousand "réis". The teenager Francisco Augusto da Fonseca's face was severely beaten by the owner of a sandal factory in March 1902 for not fulfilling his tasks well enough.

As the author points out, many children and adolescents were left with irreversible physical injuries and sometimes suffered a premature death. In addition to the physical, damage of a mental and/or intellectual nature certainly affected thousands of children in those days. All existing reports indicate that minors worked in the worst possible conditions.

Moura also reports the case of a strike that broke out during 1917 in a textile and embroidery factory located in Lapa.[28] Adult workers demanded, amongst others, the dismissal of a forewoman who punished the girls by pulling their ears and even spanking them. As mentioned by Rizzini, the working conditions were dismal:[29] poor meals, unhealthy environment, authoritarianism in labour relations, long working hours and high incidence of diseases such as tuberculosis, which was incurable in those days.

Data from the Department of Statistics and Archives of the State of São Paulo shows that in 1890 in the state capital 25 per cent of the textile sector labour force consisted of children and adolescents. Nonetheless, the first regulation on child labour in the factories of São Paulo – which was actually a provision included in the Sanitary Code rather than a labour law itself – was only passed in 1894. The Code set the minimum age for the admission of children to employment in factories at ten and prohibited night work for children under eighteen. Sixteen years later the child labour contingent had increased to 30 per cent and according to data from the State Labour Department, it had increased further to 40 per cent in 1919.[30] In 1920, the census carried out by the General Directorate of Statistics for the State of São Paulo concluded that, in the state of São Paulo as a whole, 7 per cent of the labour force hired by the secondary sector was made up of children and adolescents.[31]

According to Moura, the growth of the industrial sector was one of the determining factors in the fate of many poor children and adolescents of São Paulo.[32] The situation was mirrored in other parts of the world where,

28 Moura, "Crianças operárias".

29 Rizzini, "Pequenos trabalhadores".

30 ILO, *Combatendo o trabalho infantile*. According to data from the Department presented by Rizzini, "Pequenos trabalhadores". In 1912 approximately 4 per cent of the labour force employed in the textile industry was made up of children under 12 years of age and 28 per cent of children and adolescents between the ages of 12 and 16 years.

31 Moura, *Mulheres e menores no trabalho industrial*; Faleiros, "Infância e processo político".

32 Moura, "Crianças operárias".

as in Brazil, child and adolescent labour gave legitimacy to workers' movements. Those leaders identified a precious cause that showed everyone the condition of the working class in its most miserable aspect: the exploitation of children and adolescents by businesspersons of that period.

New opportunities for using child and adolescent labour in cities emerged alongside the country's growing industrialization process, mainly as a result of the increasing rate of urbanization and expansion that boosted the process. The worst problem was probably not the increase in the number of working children but rather the emergence of new forms of child labour. Especially in informal activities such as peddling, shoe shining and selling or delivering newspapers on the streets, as well as those regarded as totally deplorable: prostitution and drug trafficking.

The emergence of new job opportunities for children certainly encouraged the migration of many families from rural to urban areas, where they saw opportunities for all members of the family. This rural exodus further aggravated certain social problems such as misery, poverty, violence and criminality.

It is interesting to see that, due to market forces, the recruiting of child and adolescent labour by entrepreneurs in that period pushed the wages of adult workers down. However, based on the discourse of famous capitalists of those days, Faleiros comments that the reason for employers to hire children and adolescents in their shops and factories was that their parents wanted them to work and that, in spite of the inconveniences, it was better to be working than to be exposed to the dangers of the streets.[33] We notice, however, that statements such as this reflect the mindset of the capitalists of that period, who exploited child and adolescent labour basically for two reasons: its' low relative cost and the opportunity to push the wages of adult workers down. The real interest of capitalists in the period was to keep wages down since, as reported by Faleiros, children were paid less than adults, even for equal jobs.[34] In the textile industry, for example, the average wage of a child worker was approximately one-third of that of an adult worker. It was only in 1908 that, as reported by Moura, the public became generally aware of the situation, as illustrated by newspaper articles of that period which reported that thousands of children were working in factories whereas thousands of young and strong men were unemployed.[35]

33 Faleiros, "Infância e processo político".
34 Faleiros, "Infância e processo político".
35 Moura, "Crianças operárias".

There are many reports of strikes during the country's intense industrialization period. The long lists of demands that were negotiated with the industrialists of those days often included the reduction of working hours for minors, an increase in their wages and, often attempts to eradicate child labour altogether. Therefore, the first laws regulating child and adolescent labour are probably due to the long battles fought by the adult workers, who sought to protect not the actual children but rather their own jobs and remuneration.

Child Labour in Brazil: Present Situation

It is nearly impossible to present and discuss a current picture of child labour without mentioning the advances made in the specific legislation and the several policies and programs aimed at eradicating child labour which were implemented in the country.

The history of Brazil shows that until a little over a century ago children had no rights to protect them from the exploitation of employers and, more often than not, from exploitation by their own families. The situation endured several centuries and only altered late in the nineteenth century. As emphasized by many authors, among them Pires,[36] it was only with the advancement of industry in Brazil that regulation and restriction of child labour was attempted. The topic only became publicly discussed with the advent of the Republic between defenders and opponents of child labour.

As reported by Campos, decree nr. 1,313 d.d. January 17th 1891 regulated the work of children employed in the factories of the Federal Capital.[37] Unfortunately the law was never complied with. According to the author, child labour was the subject of a conflict between entrepreneurs and workers that was actually a class struggle, the intensity of which can be seen in the constant demands of the movements organized by workers. In general, the demands were aimed at reducing the working hours of children under eighteen and to eradicate labour for children under fourteen. As reported by Dulles, 68 labour organizations met during the 4th Brazilian Workers' Congress held in Rio de Janeiro in 1912 to establish the Brazilian Labour Confederation,[38] an entity that fought for regulations limiting the working

36 Pires, "O Trabalho infantil".
37 Campos, "Pobreza e trabalho infantil".
38 Dulles, *Anarquistas e comunistas*.

hours of children under fourteen, as well as for other labour regulations. In 1917, the entire industrial sector came to a halt due to a strike by thousands of workers, who set up a Workers' Advocacy Committee to negotiate with the capitalists on behalf of workers. Their demands included the complete elimination of night work for women and children under the age of eighteen and of employment for children under fourteen in factories in the city of São Paulo. However, one can conclude from the outcome that the interests of the negotiating workers seem to have been similar to that of capitalists regarding child labour as no effective results were achieved in that area. In the same year, workers of the América Fabril textile company, located in Rio de Janeiro, went on strike to demand, among other things, schooling for working children. In 1919, the workers of São Paulo scored their first major victory by succeeding in passing a law that prohibited work for children under the age of fourteen.[39] Campos points out that, in spite of the advances made in the regulation of child labour, such as the Law on Industrial Accidents of 1919, the Minors Code was not published before 1927.[40] Among other things, the Code sought to organize different forms of labour, set the minimum age for work at fourteen, established the working day of six hours, and prohibited night work for minors.

The constitutional amendments of 1934, 1937 and 1946 set the minimum working age at fourteen. However, during the military dictatorship, the minimum age was lowered to twelve years old in 1980. This situation was only reviewed in 1988 when an amendment prohibited any form of night and hazardous work for children under eighteen years old and any other form of labour for children under the age of fourteen, with the exception of professional training and apprenticeship. An amendment passed in December 1998 and a law sanctioned in 2000 raised the minimum age to sixteen, except for apprentices, in which case the minimum age is fourteen.[41]

Nowadays, Brazilian laws establish eighteen as the minimum age for admission to employment or work which by its nature or the circumstances in which it is carried out is likely to jeopardize the health of young people and, more specifically, to any work or production involving pornographic material, entertainment (night clubs, pubs, casinos, circus, gambling) and street commerce. Furthermore, mining, stevedoring or any underground works are forbidden for those under twenty-one years of age.

39 Dulles, *Anarquistas e comunistas*.
40 Campos, "Pobreza e trabalho infantil".
41 ILO, *Combatendo o trabalho infantil*.

Despite the advances made, studies show that the number of working children and adolescents is still high. In fact, it was only in the late 1980s when the world noticed that approximately nine million children in Brazil were not enjoying their basic rights "guaranteed" by the Federal Constitution of Brazil – amongst others their right to attend school and play – that the country was shamed by a reality which, according to ILO, was cruel and inhuman.[42]

Nowadays, empirical analyses aimed at identifying the causes and consequences of, as well as the solutions for, child labour are facilitated by the availability of data and IT resources. This has resulted in a better understanding of the time distribution mechanisms in the household, their interactions with market forces and the effect of these interactions on child labour. In Brazil, the main instrument used to analyze child labour is the National Household Survey (PNAD).

Data from PNAD indicates that in 2005 the number of working children and adolescents between the ages of five and fifteen engaged mainly in agriculture and livestock activities, domestic work and peddling exceeded 2.9 million. This figure accounts for 7.8 per cent of all children of this age group, despite the sharp decrease during second half of the 1990s. In 1992 for example, the number of working children neared 5.5 million, or 14.6 per cent of the population in the age group of five to fifteen.

Most children do not receive any payment when working, mainly in rural areas, as they are engaged in household farm activities. However, when paid, their wages often represent a large portion of the families' income. In 2005, children's contribution to families' income was more than 20 per cent in 30 per cent of the families and in 8 per cent of the families it was even over 40 per cent of the family income.

The North-eastern, Northern and Southern regions embrace the largest percentage of children working in Brazil, in this order. They are engaged mainly in agriculture, commerce and service sectors of activity.

Data from 2005 show that children who go to school still work an average of 19.1 hours per week, while those not attending school on average work 32 hours per week. 44.1 per cent of the kids not attending school work more than forty hours per week, whilst only 9.7 per cent of those at school work more than forty hours/week. So, it seems that children that combine work and study tend to be employed in part-time jobs.

42 ILO, *Boas práticas de combate ao trabalho infantil.*

Figure 20.1 shows the percentages of children working and not working that are enrolled in school by age. The bars are always taller for children not working, mainly at older ages. However, in Brazil, a high proportion of students work while they attend school, showing that they are able to conciliate work with study, as indicated in figure 20.2. About 8.4 per cent of the population from seven to fifteen years old are working and studying and only 1 per cent is only working. This fact raises the concern about not only if child labour reduces school enrolment but also if working has a negative impact on the learning and school achievement of these students.

Figure 20.1. Proportion of Children 7 to 15 Years Old in School, when Working or Not

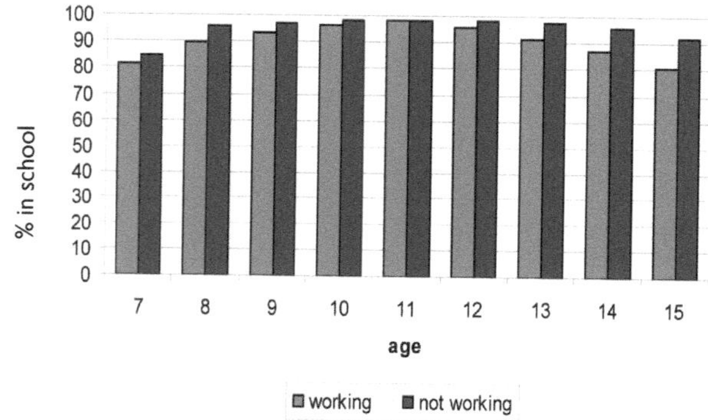

Source: data from Brazilian National Household Survey (PNAD 2005).

Figure 20.2. Proportion of Children 7 to 15 Years Old in School in Different Categories

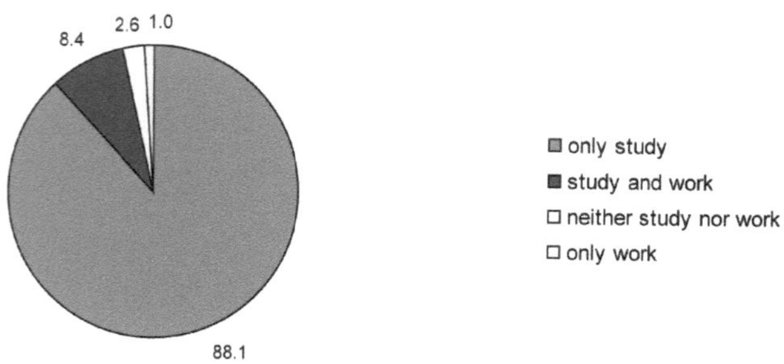

Source: data from Brazilian National Household Survey (PNAD 2005).

Although Brazil has stood out internationally for reducing by 40 per cent the number of children exploited in all of the so-called "legal" forms of labour, a tough reality presently faces thousands of children in the underground economy of sex and drug trafficking.[43]

Data presented by Ferreira shows that in the slums and shantytowns of Rio de Janeiro alone, more than three thousand children between the ages of nine and fifteen sell drugs and/or act as informants or "watch guards" in drug selling points (the so-called "*bocas de fumo*").[44] According to data from the Child and Juvenile Court of Rio de Janeiro, 4.6 per cent of all children brought before the Institution in 1991 were engaged in drug trafficking. The fact that in just seven years this figure increased to 38 per cent is strong evidence that Brazil is currently one of the major employers of child and adolescent labour. Although the money received by children and adolescents engaged in drug trafficking far exceeds salaries paid for legal activities, the damage done by illegal activities cannot be neglected. Rizzini reports the case of an eleven-year old boy who, in return for the gifts he received from drug dealers, informed them when the police arrived in the slum where he lived, in the West Side of Rio de Janeiro.[45] At the age of thirteen he was already selling marijuana, earning up to two hundred Reals a week. According to him, his dream was to buy a pair of brand name sneakers. But at fifteen he had been sent to an institution for juvenile offenders, from which, given the current situation of public security in Brazil, he will never recover. This pessimistic prospect shows the complexity of the subject owed to the many existing inter-relations.[46]

Several studies have investigated the causes of child labour in Brazil and there seems to be a consensus that although they are many, the most important ones are the poverty of families and the deficiencies of the educational system. Another factor that, although immeasurable, is relevant in explaining child labour, is the broadly disseminated belief that children should take on responsibilities in the household. According to Ferreira, an aspect that should be highlighted is the fact that Brazilian society has been historically tolerant towards the exploitation of children and adolescents.[47] This is mainly due to the myth that work contributes to education,

43 ILO, *Boas práticas de combate ao trabalho infantil.*
44 Ferreira, *Trabalho infantil.*
45 Based on the article entitled "Infância roubada" (Stolen Childhood) published in the *Folha de São Paulo* newspaper on May 1st, 1997.
46 Rizzini, "Pequenos trabalhadores do Brasil".
47 Ferreira, *Trabalho infantil.*

development and socialization, thus legitimating the exploiting intentions of unscrupulous employers whom, in our opinion, are interested solely in reducing their costs by employing cheaper labour.

Finally, regardless of the form of labour children and adolescents engage in, working at an early age implies underdeveloped potentials, as it impairs their education, physical health and frequently their mental health. As pointed out by Ferreira, these boys and girls age prematurely, are often exhausted and starving, face hardships of all sorts and are deprived of any type of assistance to their mental and intellectual development.[48]

Conclusions

Our first conclusion is that there is little data available to assess the exploitation of child and adolescent labour in the economic development of Brazil, a fact that was confirmed by the majority of the studies mentioned here. Most has been sourced from news published in those days and an appropriate assessment of the presence of child labour in the country's history is hampered by the limited number of official statistics available. Even today we do not have data that fairly reflects the total amount of child and adolescent labour used. In Brazil there are at least two activities that deserve to be singled out: child prostitution and the employment of children in the illegal drug industry (the so-called "narco-economy") which is flourishing in Brazil.

We have also concluded that despite the limited data, there is plausibility in the assumption that child labour is the result of submission to the rationale of capitalism in the same patterns as adult labour. However, even before capitalism struck root, children were already being exploited by slaveholders or Portuguese settlers.

Many studies have investigated the factors that cause children and adolescents to start working at an early age and in general have found the primary reason to be poverty. The roots of child labour in Brazil, however, seem to lie in the country's discovery, colonization, black slavery and finally, in the strong industrialization process started at the beginning of the twentieth century. Then there was enough space for its rapid growth due to the fast development of Brazilian industries, the lack of specific regulations and the greed of the capitalists of that period. They aimed to reduce their costs and

48 Ferreira, *Trabalho infantil*.

push the salaries of adult workers down due a resulting lower demand for adult labour. Several reports on strikes during the period indicate the presence of many children in the factories as, in addition to other objectives, those movements sought to limit the working hours for minors, increase their remuneration and sometimes even attempt to eliminate child labour. All these facts lead to an understanding that the fight against child labour in Brazil emerged as a secondary objective, as in fact the direct objective was to ensure adult workers more jobs and higher pay.

After recovering the long history of child workers in Brazil, we were almost seduced into attributing the present situation on its historical roots. That is as a consequence of the country's discovery and settling, of black slavery and of the strong industrialization process it experienced from the early to the mid-twentieth century – rather than on the country's socioeconomic conditions. But if this were true why, then, are there children still working in Brazil, considering the country has been discovered, settled and industrialized and that slaves were freed over a century ago? The answer lies in the fact that, on the one hand, contemporary capitalists seem to have inherited the slave-oriented mindset of slaveholders as well as the exploitation mindset of their predecessors. On the other hand, the socioeconomic conditions of the majority of the Brazilian population continue, as they did in the past, to push many children and adolescents into the labour market at an early age. We can therefore conclude that child labour today is closely related to the situation long ago as well as being strongly associated with the country's socioeconomic conditions. We cannot forget, much less deny, though that there have been significant advances in assistance to children over the years. For example, the recent implementation of policies that compensate poor families for enrolling their children in school and removing them from the workplace have been analyzed and praised for their efficacy in achieving the objective of reducing child labour and increasing school attendance. In Brazil, the School Grant (*Bolsa Escola*) or Family Grant (*Bolsa Família*) Program and the Program to Eradicate Child Labour (PETI) ensure income to poor families who would otherwise need to resort to child labour as a means of subsistence.

Nonetheless, in view of the current high number of children engaged in legal and/or illegal activities we must not forget and much less deny that there is a need for more action for the present and future well-being of Brazilian children. The fight against illegal activities should not focus only on the use of child labour, but also on the activities themselves, something that apparently is not being done efficiently, considering that the drug and sex markets are in full bloom.

CHAPTER 21

Child Labour in Medellín at the Beginning of the Twentieth Century

Carlos Edward García Londoño*

During the first thirty years of the twentieth century, the inhabitants of Medellín and of the neighbouring municipalities witnessed great transformations in their surroundings. The most notorious were related to the expansion of the coffee trade and to the start and the consolidation of the industrialization process experienced by the city.

These changes were even palpable for the sectors furthest from the city centre, also affected by the major growth in the built-up area of Medellín (which took place at a rate which has never been repeated)[1] and the disproportionate increase in the urban and rural population, due to the high level of immigration which arrived in the city. All were also able to observe that even customs and everyday life were gradually transformed.[2]

The major participation of children and teenagers in all sectors of the economy and society appeared to be less noteworthy at the time. But they were there, from the bean harvesting process on the coffee estates to work in the coffee processing factories and in the other factories located in the urban sector, and ranging from work in the home to work in the streets, in the informal sector of the increasingly agitated urban life of Medellín.

In this chapter we seek, precisely, to reconstruct this history of child labour, whether the children were artisans, wage-earners, prisoners or street traders. We will look at their everyday life, taking into account the difference of gender, the trade that they carried out and the social sector to which they belonged. Finally, we will deal with society's most generalized

* This article arises from the thesis "Niños trabajadores y vida cotidiana en Medellín, 1900-1930" presented to the Department of History of the National University (Medellín, 1995). Image editing: Patricia Londoño Vega.

1 Toro, "Medellín", p. 300.

2 Londoño, "La vida diaria", pp. 331-342.

attitude toward them and various significant behaviours which reveal the mentality of this period in relation to child labour.

But, who were the children at this time? In 1918, children under the age of fifteen represented a third of the city's population. Only half of those of school age had access to formal education, in official or private institutions.[3] The other half, belonging to the poor sectors of society, had to work to survive, whether in their homes, with their parents, or looking for work in the city's factories and workshops. There were also those who had to work in the street as street vendors or as beggars.

Artisan Children

Artisan families had traditionally added male and female adult labour to child labour in their workshops. Since the nineteenth century, drinks and food have been produced in their household facilities, such as maize liquor, beer, chocolate and maize flour.[4] There were many sugar mills, particularly in the Aburrá valley, where all the municipalities were major producers of sugar cane. Brown sugar loaf, brandy and, to a lesser extent, sugar were produced there.[5]

Nearly all artisan trades had activities carried out by children from a very early age. This was the case in homes which operated as cake shops, and in tile factories, brickworks, tailor's shops or casting and mechanical workshops. Children were moreover apprentices of their parents when these were builders, carpenters, shoemakers, saddlers, blacksmiths or locksmiths. They shared the vicissitudes of the world of work with them and the other adults. At home they prepared, for their everyday use, vegetable fibre cords, laces, and sacks; leather harnesses and whips; clay pots and dishes; and wooden articles, such as spoons and furniture.[6] Children participated greatly in the manufacture of all these articles, and in the domestic trades in estates and houses.

Many things changed in the city with the appearance of industry, including the former panorama of child labour. In addition to the artisan children who continued to work in the paternal workshop or in that of their protector, in these years it was possible to observe the emergence of

3 *Anuario Estadístico de Medellín, 1918*, pp. 20-21.
4 Brew, *Desarrollo económico de Antioquia*, p. 328.
5 Villegas, *Formación social del proletariado antioqueño*, p. 107.
6 Brew, *Desarrollo económico de Antioquia*, p. 329.

industrial child workers, who had to get up early and walk a long way to their jobs and share the exhausting days of work with the nascent proletariat to which they belonged.

Working Boys and Girls of Medellín, 1922-1927

One of the characteristics of the new workers of Medellín was that of having a very young, single, and mainly female workforce. Therefore, at that time, both children and women went out to work en masse outside the home. The latter worked alongside men. Girls were in the majority as regards children.

In 1916, 9 per cent of female workers in the city were under fifteen years old, some of them as young as five. At the same time, the percentage of male child workers of this age was 3.8 per cent.[7] These figures reflect the difference between sexes which, although real, was also due to the dispersion of the places of employment of male children, which prevented their statistical control.

Between 1916 and 1928, working girls "less than fifteen years old" made up six per cent of all the female working personnel. Despite the partial nature of the statistics, this percentage is representative of the high participation of children in the industrialization of the city.

We can, however, have a more approximate idea of the true presence of children in factories if we compare the outline in the following paragraph – prepared on the basis of the well-known statistical records, which only counted the female workers of Medellín – with fragmentary quantitative data compiled from the reports of the factory inspectors in the Aburrá valley industrial establishments.

It can be observed, for example, how in 1924, when the records registered 118 working girls, the factory inspector counted, from among all the working boys and girls, 579 *in an irregular situation,* not mentioning the rest. It can therefore be established, as other researchers of the problem had already sensed,[8] that the participation of both girls and boys in industry was much greater than that known only by means of the statistics for female workers.

7 *Anuario Estadístico de Medellín, 1916*, pp. 34, 42.

8 Botero Herrera, *Industrialización en Antioquia*, p. 137; Villegas, *Formación social del proletariado antioqueño*, p. 125.

The presence of children in all sectors of labour was of such a size that in a visit to the Medellín Telephone Company, at the time a specialized labour company, the inspector had to clarify that there "they do not give employment to children under the age of ten, or even accept them in the work rooms".[9]

Everyday Life in the Factories

The highest number of girl workers was found in the coffee processing factories. During the period 1916-1928 they made up 9.5 per cent, and in 1917 they reached 15 per cent of the whole group of female coffee factory workers. This was the most numerous sector of female workers, well above the textile weavers, the worst paid in the whole industry of Antioquia,[10] and the one which presented the greatest average overcrowding of its female workers.

When the girls and teenagers of the coffee processing factories began to handle the coffee, other children, assistants on the estates, had already participated in the process, which went from the sowing to the exporting. The depulped, fermented, washed and dried beans arrived in Medellín. In the coffee processing factories, moved by hydraulic or electric power, the coffee was stripped of its sheath and left in "almond" state. The work most carried out by girls was then performed: the separation and classification of the coffee, which was packed in bags and transported by rail toward the international markets.[11]

The second sector to which girl workers were linked was the textile factories. At the beginning of the century, the activities performed in these industries belonged to the only two sections which existed: spinning and weaving. The basic operations were guaranteeing the continuous flow of the yarn, connecting breakages, starting up the looms, replacing the empty yarn carriers and introducing the yarn into the auxiliary machines.[12]

9 Archivo Histórico de Antioquia (hereafter AHA), sg. 8933, *Acta del inspector de fábricas nr. 1110 (manuscrito)*, 27 August 1921, p. 111.

10 Botero Herrera, *Industrialización en Antioquia*, p. 140.

11 This description was made on the basis of information published in the article by Pérez, "Café Medellín", p. 223.

12 Mayor, *Ética, trabajo y productividad*, p. 254.

Many of these jobs were carried out by girls, above all those considered as "tasks adequate" for their age: threading the yarn carriers, handling the smaller machines or picking up the yarn on all fours under the machines.

The other industrial companies in which girls worked alongside women were the factories making cigarettes, fizzy drinks, beer and chocolates; in the printers', in the match factories and in different trades, corresponding to the workshops for dressmaking, shoemaking, ironing of clothes, button warehouses and hatmakers.

As for work in the match factories, extensive descriptions were published of the match manufacturing process and of their packing in cardboard boxes.[13] Less well known were the news of how risky the work was, given the possibility of the worker being burned on closing the boxes. For protection they only had a sponge soaked in water and, in the event of a fire, they had to throw the box far away.[14] The medical assistance and safety conditions in the event of accidents were minimal in almost all the industrial companies of the Aburrá valley.

Working Boys

There are only data differentiated by trades for the year 1916 on child labour. They highlight artisanal jobs (builders, carpenters, shoemakers, tailors) and industrial jobs in printers', mechanical and casting workshops, and some in textile industries.

It is moreover known that male workers were predominant in some food and in the beer factories, and were an absolute majority in the mosaic (tile) factories, glassworks, potteries and mechanical and casting workshops.[15] But there were men and boys in all sectors of industry, including the coffee processing factories and the match factories.

There were also cases in which there was a majority of boys in the company. In 1922, most of the workers of the Vidriería de Caldas glassworks were boys between the age of ten and fifteen. The same had occurred the previous year in the glassworks next to the Antioqueña Consolidada Brewery.[16]

13 *El Sol*, "En la fábrica de fósforos", Medellín, 28 August 1909.

14 Villegas, *Formación social del proletariado antioqueñ*, p. 199.

15 Villegas, *Formación social del proletariado antioqueñ*, p. 112.

16 AHA, sg. 8932, acta 364, 24 October 1921, p. 9; and *Ibid.*, acta 421, 28 March 1922, p. 66.

Figure 21.1. Coffee Harvesters Known in Antioquia as Chapoleras
Photograph by Melitón Rodríguez taken from: *Melitón Rodríguez fotografías*, El Áncora Editores, Bogotá 1985 and Germán Ferro, *A lomo de Mula*, Bancafé, Bogotá 1994.

Although they belonged to marginal sectors of society, these working boys also shared common customs and characteristics with other children and teenagers of that time. "All boys, in Medellín until the thirties, were *piernipeludo* (hairy legs) until they reached the age of fifteen, at that time", says the chronicler Rafael Ortiz.

On reaching that age, boys had to change their short trousers and pay for the *largada de pantalones*. This was a true ritual of initiation. At this time they acquired a "man's rights and as a symbol received the key to the house and the long trousers". Their new clothes moreover opened the door to the billiard rooms and freed them from street jibes and the "rigid and severe measures of control of minors".

As they had to take this step with their own resources, they often only had enough money for a simulated "*largada*": they then used long boots and black socks which reached the edge of the short trousers. But if they did not have enough money for boots or for socks, they went barefoot with their short trousers. Sometimes this lasted a long time and there were even boys who went around the street showing their hairy calves; this is where the name *piernipeludos* came from.[17]

17 Arango, *Estampas de Medellín antiguo*, p. 142.

Figure 21.2. Arriero, 1896
Photograph by Melitón Rodríguez taken from: Germán Ferro, *A Lomo de Mula*, Bancafé, Bogotá, 1994.

Among Adults

The everyday life of working girls was practically the same as that of working women in the incipient industries of Medellín, with some differences due to their age, which increased their not just physical but also psychological exploitation. Below is a description of the Bello Textile Factory, the company which had the most conflicts with the Factory Inspection Office for its irregularities and in which many girls worked:

> The building is clean and has sufficient light but completely lacks ventilation, as in addition to the factory being surrounded by a grove, the bars through which some air could come in despite the grove are blocked with windows; in such a way that the hygiene can be imagined that will exist in

> a factory in which over five hundred working women remain for more than ten hours breathing the same air at an extremely high temperature.[18]

The fact that men and women worked in the same space led to various relations between the bosses, the male and the female workers. For the women, in some cases this meant a situation different from the possibilities that they had enclosed in their home, but in others it meant that they were subject to violations, abuse and sexual blackmail, such as the case reported in 1920 by the strikers of the above-mentioned factory.[19] In the language of the time, this was reported as the problem of "morality in the factories".

It was not therefore unusual that in 1926 the factory inspector expressed to the government secretary: "I am pleased to declare that during the year in which this report is made, none of the female workers were dishonoured in the buildings of the companies, either by employers or male workers".[20]

The working day began very early. The workers who lived in the country had to get up at three or four in the morning to start at six. Due to the distance, they returned home late at night. In most factories the working day was of nine or ten hours, but they sometimes worked up to fourteen hours a day.[21]

In this description of the space in which children were mixed with adults, we will now refer to remuneration. At the beginning of the century, the majority of the establishments of Medellín determined their salaries in accordance with supply and demand of the labour that they needed.

Salaries were low, and there was no compulsory minimum wage. Moreover, there were great differences, in relation to remuneration, between men and women, even in the same trades. In general, women earned half or less than half of the salary of men, and children a great deal less. In 1920, the salaries of Coltejer fluctuated

> from forty cents to one peso a day for female workers, with the exception of some apprentices who only earned twenty cents. Male workers received a remuneration which went from the thirty cents which a boy earned to the two pesos a day which a male worker with good knowledge obtained.[22]

18 AHA, sg. 8930, acta 169, 28 September 1920, p. 89.
19 Velásquez, "Condición jurídica y social", IV, pp. 22, 36.
20 Vélez, "Informe del inspector de fábricas", p. 254.
21 Vélez, "Informe del inspector de fábricas", p. 19.
22 AHA, sg. 8929, acta 663, 21 May 1920, Coltejer, p. 162.

The low daily wages earned by workers were, however, reduced even more by the system of fines or wage reductions that the employers imposed on them as a sanction for any disciplinary failing or failing on performing their work. There was no minimum wage for adults, and there was certainly no legislation preventing the exploitation of child labour. In this respect, the factory inspectors confined themselves to demanding that not more than ten per cent of the day's wage should be charged from the workers as fines.

Finally, we will mention the religious activities in which both the girl workers and the other workers of Medellín participated. Organized by the company itself or by the Workers' Association (1912), the presence of the Catholic church in the factories could be clearly seen in the holding of spiritual retreats, some of them in the industrial facilities themselves, or in the ceremonies of exaltation of the image of the Sacred Heart of Jesus in the work rooms. Many female workers lived in the different associations that were subsequently created. There they were given religious and moral education, and they were advised on looking for work. Through them and other institutions, the church considerably influenced the working class of Medellín.

Conception of Childhood in the Legislation

At that time it was only forbidden to employ children under the age of ten. Those between ten and fifteen could be hired without any requirement concerning their education but with a working day no longer than eight hours. The 1918 labour legislation, known as the Factories Police, was ambiguous in this respect and included in a subsection the possibility of assigning "work adequate" for them to children of the above-mentioned ages.[23]

However, on observing the proceedings and the reports of the inspectors it can be seen that this requirement was not observed and that the inspectors tried to comply with the spirit of the law. The problem was their limited supervisory power and their inability to change the situation. In the event of finding children in an irregular situation, the inspectors could only demand the removal of those under the age of ten or a reduction of the working day for those between ten and fifteen years old. A typical sentence in the reports of the inspectors shows us the idea implicitly held

23 Departamento de Antioquia, "Ordenanza 25 de 1918. Policía de Fábrica", Ordenanzas de la Asamblea Departamental (Medellín, 1918), p. 46.

of children. Stating that "minors are not employed in this company" only meant that children under the age of ten were not found.

However, until the end of the twenties reports can be read which describe girls under the age of ten found separating coffee in the coffee processing factories. Or on cases of extended working days for the older ones who, according to the personal interpretation of an inspector, "were only obliged to work eight hours".[24] In any case, after 1918 the number of child workers continued to go down, now with the pressure of the legislation but also due to technical and administrative progress in the industries and, for the girls, due to the masculinization of the workforce which began starting from the thirties.[25]

However, as late as 1934, the Factory Inspection Office proposed a campaign which sought "to prevent night work for women and children, in accordance with the international conventions".[26] We only have figures on boy and girl workers from 1916, when the statistics office was set up. But the descriptions which exist for previous years show us a great presence of children in the factories, maybe greater than that which is known from the descending curve of 1916.

For example, the testimony of a former female textile worker from the Bello Factory (1905) maintains that "at the time of don Emilio girls started to work very young, to be able to afford the First Communion dress and they gave them stools to work".[27] Or the description, in 1909, of the Tamayo brewery, of which it was said that its workers, "some good lads [...] do the service like something natural [...] [as] almost all grew up next to the factory".[28] Likewise, if a regional comparison is made, we see that while in Bogotá the former workers declared that "many girls started at the age of fourteen" to work in textile industries, in Medellín they did so before reaching this age. This implies that the recruitment of boy and girl workers during industrialization was higher in Antioquia than in the rest of the country.[29]

24 A.H.A., sg. 8930, acta 195, 20 November 1920, *Vidriería de Caldas*, p. 124.
25 Mayor, *Ética, trabajo y productividad*, p. 284.
26 Vallejo, "Informe del inspector de fábricas", p. 80.
27 Cited by Arango, *Mujer, religión e industria*, p. 45.
28 *La Patria*, "Una empresa ejemplar", Medellín, 23 February 1909.
29 Archila, *Cultura e identidad obrera*, p. 119.

The Child Prisoners Also Work

Being deprived of their freedom did not save the children, teenagers and young adults from having to work, either as penance or as the only work possible in the institution. They shared various characteristics with the artisanal children and with the children working in the industries, in particular as regards the trades, discipline and religious practices in the place of work.

The Workshops of San Vicente stand out due to their early date, created by the Sociedad de San Vicente de Paúl (1882). Between 1889 and 1912, many poor and orphaned boys between six and fifteen years old were interned there, and they were offered food, religious education and instruction on technical work, especially the operation of looms, being expected to work in these occupations subsequently.

The interns were in charge of preparing wool, cotton, *cabuya* and *pita* fibre fabrics; they made blankets, cloths, towels, yarn ponchos and vests on the wooden looms available. There were also shoemaking, carpentry, tailoring, saddlery and printing workshops.[30]

The Workshops of San Vicente began with six orphans, but they subsequently had up to sixty pupils. Their industrial products received public distinctions and praise in the press. Their everyday life was marked by religious and labour duties, in a strict distribution of the hours of the day.[31]

Apart from the Workshops of San Vicente, there were also other institutions which included intense labour activity in their programmes of moral moulding of the behaviour of the children and teenagers interned in them. These were the first two prisons for minors which were founded in Medellín in 1914: the Casa de Menores and the Escuela Tutelar, male and female, respectively.

Between the years 1914 and 1920, the prison for male minors was known as the House of Correction and Work School. This first stage of the institution was characterized by a militaristic and authoritarian system. The harsh discipline imposed by the retired officials who ran it included frequent physical punishments, the prison cell and other humiliating forms of correction of the interns, who moreover had to carry out productive work as punishment or "penance for their conversion".

Starting from 1920, in accordance with the changes of orientation of the centre, it became known as the House of Minors and Work School. Its

30 Villegas, *Formación social del proletariado antioqueño*, p. 137.

31 *Ibid.*, pp.137-150; Castro, "Beneficencia en Medellín", pp. 30-37.

Figure 21.3. Industrial Printers
Photograph by Benjamín de la Calle, Centro de Memoria Visual, FAES.

new director, the educationalist Tomás Cadavid Restrepo, modified the punishments and sought to carry out an educational-psychological control of the interns, who were considered not as criminals but as "morally abnormal".[32]

The reforms included the expansion of the building and the carpentry, binding and locksmith's workshops. Hat weaving and tobacco growing began to be taught, and the loom workshops were inaugurated late. The first foundry was moreover assembled.[33] A master of the trade was at the head of each of the workshops, and was in charge of teaching the minors and of supervising their behaviour, as the educational reform formed part of their training for productive work, elementary instruction and religious education in this institution which had up to 240 minors interned in it.

The fundamental purpose of the Escuela Tutelar, run by a religious congregation not related to any modern educational trend, was the "moral regeneration and the modification of the conduct" of the criminal girls and young women, who until then were imprisoned together with adults in the women's prison. The means used were elementary instruction, religious education and work. However, according to recent studies with oral testi-

32 Villegas, *Formación social del proletariado antioqueño*, p. 156; Reyes, "Fueron los viejos tiempos tan maravillosos?", p. 598.

33 Marín, *Reconstrucción histórica*, p. 257; Saavedra, "Antioquia en los inicios del proceso de industrialización", pp. 120-121.

monies, the continuous domestic trades and religious practices were almost the only activities carried out there.[34]

The interns, both girls and young women, got up at four in the morning and worked and prayed all day until five in the afternoon, when they retired to attend the religious services. The domestic work, apart from that necessary to maintain the institution, consisted of washing and ironing the clothes of some religious communities resident in the city to order. In 1920, the School had 60 interns, from girls to women, "minors" who could be up to twenty-five years old. They all had to be virgins, in accordance with the requirements of the admission regulations.

The last institution that we will mention in this section is the Instituto Pedro Justo Berrío. In 1915, in view of the proliferation of young tramps and bootblacks who were multiplying in the capital of Antioquia, the bishop called upon the Salesians to look after them. Their specialization in care for the children emerging in industrial cities was well-known, giving them an elementary Christian education and training them in a manual trade. The Salesians were moreover in charge of continuing what remained of the traditional School of Workmanship and Trades, which had had its era of splendour in the last decades of the nineteenth century. The institution which they began to govern was the Instituto del Sufragio, which operated as a hospice and school for the city's tramps and bootblacks. It gradually became an industrial school, and in 1926 received the name Instituto Pedro Justo Berrío.[35]

The objective of all the institutions mentioned, apart from reformatory aims and the modification of the customs of the interns, was to train for work and to form a markedly moral character in those children from the poor sectors of the city so that they could subsequently work as artisans or labourers. This "pragmatic philanthropy"[36] was aimed at children and young people who could be productive, so that they would stop being a burden on society and reward it for the investment that it had made in their reeducation and training.

34 Reyes, "Fueron los viejos tiempos tan maravillosos", pp. 616-627.
35 Helg, *Educación en Colombia*, pp. 93-94.
36 Reyes, "Higiene y salud", p. 18.

Boys Walking around the Streets in Search of Clients

The street was the other work front where the children of Medellín could be found at the beginning of the century. The growth of the city, the new uses and customs and the accelerated rate that urban life was acquiring made street trade widespread. In the middle of this era it was possible to observe the small street sellers sharing the attempt to make a living with child beggars, scavengers, or simply tramps. The children walking around the city looking for clients included the bootblacks, frequently referred to as "*embetunadores*", who could be found in the city's parks; the *aguateros* (or *aguadores*), who transported large containers of water on their backs from the public ponds or from the streams to the different neighbourhoods; and the coal and wood merchants, who sold and delivered to homes the coal and the wood necessary for domestic consumption at the time.

Also walking around the city were fruit sellers, who set up outside schools, and flower sellers, who positioned themselves at the entry to temples and cemeteries; the newspaper sellers and the other working children of the time: child postmen and child coffee sellers. Many of these children's trades were also common in Bogotá, where other trades characteristic of this city were present: brick sellers and chimney sweeps.[37]

With the help of photographs, of the chroniclers, and of the studies on the everyday life of the time, it is possible to reconstruct the history of these marginal children of Medellín.

The Coffee-Selling Children

At the beginning of the twentieth century in Medellín, people preferred chocolate to coffee, as a non-alcoholic drink. This was curious in a city which was the centre of coffee exports. Drinking *tinto* (pure coffee) was however not very common. Despite the fact that the major fortunes had been accumulated exporting coffee beans, its consumption was very scarce, almost non-existent. Fizzy drinks had more success among the new public.

Businesses gradually began to sell ground coffee in boxes of a hundred small packets for eighty cents.[38] Its domestic consumption thus increased somewhat. Drinking *tinto* did, however, continue to be an upper class custom. "*Tinto* was considered to be an extravagant refinement and was only

37 Muñoz and Pachón, *Niñez en el siglo XX*, p. 38.
38 Ochoa, *Cosas Viejas de la Villa*, p. 87.

Figure 21.4. Children Working as Street Sellers During the Inauguration of Berrío Park, 1921

Photograph by Benjamín de la Calle, Centro de Memoria Visual, FAES.

taken after meals by important gentlemen, accompanied by a cigarette from Ambalema".[39]

At the beginning of the twenties, some sisters with the surname Melguizo had the idea of selling cups of *tinto* in the street. They hired boys to carry thermos flasks, china cups and saucers, sugar and teaspoons in a well-presented wooden box, which hung from their shoulders with a belt. "Selling coffee from office to office, from shop to shop, when coming out of the theatre, in Berrío Park and Bolívar Park, these boys had a tremendous success. Each boy sold an average of forty cups of coffee a day, at two or three cents the cup, being able to take a wage of fifty cents home".[40]

Very soon Medellín filled up with these street sellers, who carried up to six thermos flasks well supplied with hot coffee, in addition to a pot with clean water to wash the dirty dishes. Their distinctive clothing consisted of trousers half way down the leg, called "*cogepuerco*", generally light-coloured; a long coat and cap, both dark-coloured. There were all barefoot, with a white shirt.[41]

The business of coffee-selling children grew so much that, in the words of a witness, they became "an intolerable plague".[42] Competition had

39 Ochoa, *Cosas Viejas de la Villa*, p. 84.
40 Payne, "Crecimiento y cambio social".
41 Arango, *Estampas de Medellín antiguo*, pp. 27, 180.
42 Ochoa, *Cosas viejas*, p. 88.

grown considerably and was reflected in the different brands that the boxes contained: "Café Fénix", "Café Mundial", "Café Madrid", etc. But the quality of the coffee had gone down. The boys reduced their responsibility thanks to their anonymity in relation to their bosses and washed the crockery badly, prepared badly-tasting coffee to replace the one given to them in the establishments, which paid them for the distribution, and then the clients reduced their consumption.[43] In his chronicles, Lisandro Ochoa tells that he once saw a boy sitting on the steps of the vestibule of the Candelaria, spreading out on the ground the cups and saucers, which he rubbed with an even dirtier cloth. Once clean, according to him, he placed them in the box again, ready to continue the sale.[44]

By the forties, the coffee sellers had disappeared, because most bars and cafés began to serve *tinto* regularly and in a more hygienic manner, but they had established the custom of drinking coffee in all social classes.[45] Some of the young street sellers who stopped selling coffee found new employment in the streets of the city selling ice creams, made with scraped ice. They went around the streets calling out the name of their factory: "Polares", "Esquimales", or intoning advertising slogans: "Blackberry ice cream for the ladies", "Strawberry ice cream for the princess", "Pineapple ice cream for the girl", "Corncob ice cream for the good boy", etc.[46]

Child Postmen and Female Cheese Sellers

Another of the trades carried out by children at the beginning of the century in Medellín was that of postmen. The urban mail service was created and organized by the Sociedad de Mejoras Públicas in 1903, and by 1910, according to a photo taken in this year, its staff was essentially made up of children. They wore full uniform: light-coloured shirt, trousers to the ankles, long-sleeved jacket, both dark-coloured. On the left-hand side of the jacket, at chest height, the institution's badge. They also wore caps and black shoes.

The guild of "*vivanderos*" or street sellers of Medellín also included the fruit sellers, the ham and vegetable sellers, the sellers of milk, fresh from the nearby estates or houses, and the cheese sellers. The latter also had rep-

43 Arango, *Estampas de Medellín antiguo*, p. 27.
44 Ochoa, *Cosas viejas*, p. 88.
45 Payne, "Crecimiento y cambio social".
46 Arango, *Estampas de Medellín antiguo*, p. 28.

Figure 21.5. Correos Urbanos
Taken from: *Medellín el 20 de julio de 1910*,
album of the Society of Public Improvements of Medellín.

resentatives on the children's guild, who differentiated between the child cheese sellers and the female cheese sellers. The former brought "the best of Urrao, even if they were from elsewhere, because the cheeses from Urrao were reputable. They brought them in sacks and they were unwrapped, stuck together and gave off a strong acrid smell".[47]

Apart from home-made cheese, the female cheese sellers sold eggs, blackberries and figs. The latter were sold by the "*pucha*", measured by a wooden box of precise dimensions.

> The child cheese sellers only appeared on Mondays in the streets of the city and the other cheese sellers appeared every day in the morning with fresh produce which came from Santa Elena, Guarne, Rionegro, La Ceja, San Pedro, Girardota and other nearby towns with good dairies.[48]

Attitudes and Behaviour toward Working Children

A large part of public opinion chose not to see any problem with the generalized panorama of boys, girls and teenagers working in all sectors of society. According to this vision, children from the poor and marginalized

47 Arango, *Estampas de Medellín antiguo*, p. 109.
48 Arango, *Estampas de Medellín antiguo*, p. 109.

sectors were more likely to yield to vice, begging, crime and other misfortunes – such as prostitution for girls – and therefore it was a "blessing" that the industries and individuals found them employment or that they obtained it themselves.

Based on a traditional work ethics, which in Antioquia went back to many years before the era of industrialization,[49] articles were published in the press and many other writings spoke about the goodness of industrial employment. About the importance of technical and moral training that the factories provided for children and youths (the factory as school, inversion of the constant request to convert the school into a workshop).[50] And, in general, about the possibilities of social "redemption" offered by industry in the face of the acute situation of poverty and unemployment in Medellín.

The newspapers and magazines, in their frequent "visits to factories" (advertising features, in contemporary terms), described the industrialization of the city in a disproportionate manner and idealized the life of the workplaces. In relation to the working girls, the reporters talked about smiling girls happy with their work. In the Olano match factory, one of them said that there was "a spacious room where thirty happy and smiling girls worked, to the gentle murmur of the machines and in time to music with popular airs".[51]

The acceptance of child labour in the public mentality was such that not even on the occasion of the visit by president Rafael Reyes to the Bello Factory in 1908 was it considered necessary to hide the children. The chronicler who described the event indicates that there were 150 young ladies between eight and twenty years old, but what attracted the president's attention was that they were all barefoot.[52] Alejandro López did not have any qualms about employing children in his business descriptions made about the 1910 Industrial Exposition.[53] Nor did the young lawyer José Vásquez, twelve years later, on maintaining in his degree thesis that "in any case, a child who is not at school is better in a factory than in the street".[54]

49 Mayor, *Ética, trabajo y productividad*, pp. 270–272.

50 Saavedra, "Antioquia en los inicios del proceso de industrialización", p. 124.

51 *El Sol*, "En la fábrica de fósforos, Medellín", 28 August 1909. Cited by Botero Herrera, *Industrialización en Antioquia*, p. 151.

52 P.A., Pedraza, *Excursiones presidenciales, 1909*, p. 165. Cited by Payne, "Crecimiento y cambio social".

53 Alejandro López, "La Exposición Industrial", *La Organización*, Medellín, 29 July, 1 and 3 August 1910.

54 Vásquez, "Legislación obrera".

This class of labour ethics is even adopted by political opponents. A contributor to *El Luchador*, a working-class socialist newspaper of the time, said:

> Poor women, women from the country, those who work for a living, you are the arm of the mother country! Your duty is tough, but it is clear and to a certain extent easy to fulfil, you are obliged to work efficiently and happily. Do your job well and sing while you work. [...] And when you have children, let them receive a love of work and happiness with the milk from their mother's breast.[55]

But maybe the most permissive and indifferent behaviour expressed in Medellín toward child labour in industries was symbolized by a series of classified advertisements which appeared in one of the city's newspapers for three months. In them, an industrial company promoted the sale of plots for housing among its workers. Advertisements such as these, and particularly aimed at workers, proliferated at the time due to the scarcity of accommodation and to the construction boom in the city. What makes these advertisements stand out is that throughout the time they were published they always stressed that the prices of the weekly instalments to obtain the plot were so low that even "your little 12-year-old daughter can pay it working in the factory".[56]

The latest advertisement that we could find begins with the following question: "Do you believe that a 12-year-old girl can buy a plot of land? Nothing is easier. In Barrio Andalucía they will sell you a beautiful plot paying 50 cents each Saturday".[57] The advertisements included some which insinuated the possibility of linking all the children to work. All in the middle of praise for the company: "In the Bello Textile Factory you will find work, good treatment, morality and fair pay for your family. Why not buy a small plot in Barrio Andalucía which you can pay with the wages of just one of your daughters?"[58]

The fact that it was published on the first of May is ironic, because in actual fact child and family labour was so common that this possibility was

55 G. Martínez, "A las Mujeres pobres", *El Luchador*, Medellín, 31 January 1919.

56 *El Espectador*, Medellín, 10 April 1918. Cited by Botero Herrera, *Industrialización en Antioquia*, p. 144.

57 *El Espectador*, Medellín, 7 June 1918.

58 *El Espectador*, Medellín, 1 May 1918. Same advertisement appeared on 26 May and 1 June 1918.

a constant practice. In 1920, the chronicler of the Bello strike revealed that, in addition to the bad conditions of the rooms that the factory rented to the workers, the latter must have known that "to obtain one in rent it is necessary to have four female workers in the establishment: men do not count".[59]

With the publication of the classified advertisements it is shown that what the employers wanted was to bring young women, even girls, onto the labour market, and proletarianize the whole working family of Medellín, with the lure of acquiring accommodation.[60] Incidentally, this behaviour toward childhood also reflects the ideal model of family organization which the companies of Antioquia wished to promote in this first stage of industrialization. And we should not forget that there was also pressure from the heads of the households for them to give their children work as a way of supplementing family income.

Summary

The history of child labour is a long-lasting subject. It could almost be stated that it has been a constant in human history. However, at the beginning of the twentieth century a change in the type of child labour which came from the colony was witnessed in Medellín. Artisanal work was carried out at home, side by side with the parents and with very different labour and salary relations to those with the intervention of a boss, working hours and a wage. The emergence of industrial working children was the predominant example, together with the small street sellers, of child labour of the time. This was a very different occupation to the former kind of work, also very different to the work that children carry out today.

Nowadays children can be found working in the informal and in the construction sector, in urban areas; and in the working of coal mines and in farming activities, in rural areas.[61] Although there are cases of extreme abuse and exploitation, true social anachronisms which make us think that this first era has not yet finished, the differences are noted on comparing the current mentality toward children with that of before.

For the history of childhood the first three decades of the twentieth century in Medellín represent the worst period of child labour, that time when children were directly linked to the industrial sector as workers, mass

59 Salazar, *Niños y jóvenes trabajadores*.

60 El Curioso Impertinente, "La huelga de Bello", *El Espectador*, Medellín, 1 March 1920.

61 Botero Herrera, *Industrialización en Antioquia*, pp. 144–145.

abuse and exploitation of their labour force taking place. Working girls, on being more numerous and in view of what they represent, can be chosen as the symbol of this tough contribution of childhood to the city's socio-economic development. The generalization of child street sellers was also witnessed at this same time, as a demonstration of the process of urban growth.

The most generalized, although not the only, attitude in the face of child labour was one of acceptance, in a veiled or exalted manner. For employers child labour was a cheap and abundant resource. They therefore justified its industrial use as an option in the face of the unemployment and poverty of broad social sectors. They moreover argued that work for children was of a disciplinary nature and provided technical and moral training for the future adult workers.

Although the praises of the virtues of working from childhood were general throughout society, it should not be forgotten that those for whom it was the only option were those children from the poor sectors for whom school was not accessible and whose family context did not see it as a priority.

CHAPTER 22

Children's Work, Industrialism, and the Family Economy in Japan, 1872–1926

Osamu Saito*

Introduction

In the 1850s, Japan opened its ports to international commerce, thus ending two centuries of self-imposed isolation during which no Europeans except the Dutch had been allowed on Japanese soil. Visitors from abroad in the decades that followed were understandably eager to share their impressions of this newly accessible land. In the many books and travel journals written at the time, it is not unusual to find comments on how well the Japanese treated their children. Isabella Bird, for example, remarked in her book *Unbeaten Tracks in Japan,* published in 1880:

> I never saw people take so much delight in their offspring, carrying them about, or holding their hands in walking, watching and entering into their games, supplying them constantly with new toys, taking them to picnics and festivals, never being content to be without them, and treating other people's children also with a suitable measure of affection and attention. Both fathers and mothers take a pride in their children.[1]

Similar passages can be found in other publications. In *Japan Day by Day,* an American professor wrote:

> Again I must repeat that Japan is the paradise for children. There is no other country in the world where they are so kindly treated or where so much

* The research for this chapter was conducted as part of a Ministry of Education-funded joint project on industrial development and regional economies in pre-war Japan.

1 Bird, *Unbeaten Tracks in Japan*, p. 80.

> attention is devoted to them. ... However, this is all trite, as every book on Japan has said the same thing again and again.[2]

No doubt most Japanese mothers and fathers would agree with these authors, as suggested in the old Japanese saying: "Children are treasures".

Yet, this romantic view may well be misleading when discussing the problem of child labour. Industrialism, however alien it had been to Far Eastern soils, was undoubtedly the late nineteenth-century reality. During the 1880s and 1890s, a number of industrial enterprises sprang into existence in Japan. "When the present writer landed at Nagasaki in the spring of 1873, there existed in the whole country not a single "workman", using the term in its modern semi-political acception [sic]", wrote Basil Chamberlain, an Englishman who later became a professor of philology at the Imperial University of Tokyo. By the late 1890s, however, he noted:

> Not a month passes without seeing new manufactories of cement, carpets, soap, glass, umbrellas, hats, matches, watches, bicycles, smelting works, electrical works, steel foundries, silk, cotton, and woollen mills, machine-shops of every sort. Nor is everything left to private enterprise; the government steps in with liberal subsidies. The silk industry, once confined to certain narrow districts, is fast spreading over the entire centre and south. Formerly the Nakasendo was an old-world trail among the mountains. The last time we travelled along the new, finely graded carriage road, we were wakened every morning by the scream of the factory whistle. Journeying on and reaching the town of Kofu, we found its silk filatures to be now its most noteworthy sight, troops of girls coming in at five every morning and working straight on till eight at night – fifteen hours at a stretch![3]

Clearly, this British writer associated the coming of industrialism with the growth of child labour. Such a view seems to be shared by Japanese scholars. A recent article in the encyclopaedia of Japanese history, for example, states: "With the establishment of the mechanized large-scale industry in the industrial revolution, the substitution of children, youths and women for adult male workers took place".[4]

However, a cursory look at the literature reveals that surprisingly little has been written about industrial labour supplied by "children" as distin-

2 Morse, *Japan Day by Day*, pp. 351-352.

3 Chamberlain, *Things Japanese*, pp. 266-268.

4 "Jidō rōdō, nenshō rōdō", in *Nihonshi dai-jiten*, 1993, III, p. 924.

guished from "youths" and "women". Without established facts about child labour, therefore, it is difficult to assess the supposedly ill effects of advancing industrialism, and more specifically, to evaluate the view, which has recently gained support from specialists on the present-day Third World, that "compulsory primary education is the policy instrument by which the state effectively removes children from the labor force".[5] It is interesting to note in this connection what Clark Nardinelli has said about the case of Japan, where four years of schooling was made compulsory in 1879:

> Factory legislation came late in Japan. By the time the first Factory Act was passed in 1911, 98 per cent of the children between the ages of six and thirteen were in school, as were a high proportion of older children. The battle to get young children out of factories and into schools, then, was already over by the time factory legislation appeared in Japan.[6]

He too sees education as an important factor in removing children from the labour force, but seems to place more emphasis on family preferences than on government enforcement.

This chapter will examine the statistical evidence available on child labour in Japanese industry and children's involvement in paid employment in general in the late nineteenth and early twentieth centuries. Also examined are education statistics as well as case studies that help to illuminate the Japanese family's attitudes towards children and child work. Finally, an attempt will be made to place Japan's experience in a comparative context.

Table 22.1. Selected Chronology

1872	Promulgation of the Educational Ordinance by the new Meiji government, announcing the establishment of universal education.
1879	Education Law enacted, making four years of schooling compulsory.
1882	Investigation into working conditions in factories begun by the Industry Department of the Ministry of Agriculture and Commerce.
1887	Two bills for factory legislation drafted but not published. Subsequently various proposals discussed, but none formally presented to the Diet.
1900	School fees abolished for primary schooling.
1907	Compulsory schooling raised from four to six years.

5 Weiner, *The Child and the State in India*, p. 3.
6 Nardinelli, *Child Labour and the Industrial Revolution*, p. 147.

1911	First Factory Law passed through the Diet.
1916	Factory Law came into force. Employment of children under 12 prohibited.
1926	Other provisions in the 1911. Factory Law, the prohibition of night work and a 12-hour day for children under 15, came into force.

Note: Meiji designates the period from 1868 to 1912 during which Emperor Mutsuhito reigned.

Child Labour in Industry

Although factory legislation came late in Japan (see table 22.1), the debate on the factory question started as early as the 1880s with the first wave of "factory" industrialization. A majority of the newly built factories were modelled on Western mills and borrowed Western technology. What was borrowed, moreover, was not limited to tangible components of industrialism, but included ideas on how to combat the adverse by-products of the modern factory system. In 1882, backed by a small but enlightened group of bureaucrats and academics, research on factory legislation began within the Industry Department of the Ministry of Agriculture and Commerce. Various proposals were made and debated, but none of them was presented to the Diet. To make a further case for legislation, the Ministry thus conducted an investigation into working conditions of factories and workshops.[7] Thanks to this ministerial effort, therefore, the state of children in industry at the turn of the century is comparatively well documented.

Table 22.2 reports changes that occurred in the percentages of children in industrial employment during the period 1899-1914. The percentages are calculated from "factory censuses", which covered only factories with ten operatives or more in 1899, whereas in 1909 and 1914, they covered factories with five operatives or more. Caution must be exercised when comparing the absolute size of the workforce in these different periods. If allowance is made for this change in coverage, it is probable that the total industrial workforce doubled from 1899 to 1914. In proportional terms, only minor differences appear to exist in 1909 and 1914 between the cases with over five and with over ten operatives.

7 See Dore, "Modernizer as a Special Case"; and Taira, *Economic Development*, ch. 6.

As table 22.2 clearly shows, females outnumbered males in industry at this stage of development. Moreover, the female workforce was younger than the male. More than half of the female workers were under twenty years of age, a pattern that apparently did not change until the First World War. Among the female workers, the proportion of those under fourteen years of age was substantial in 1899 but declined during the next fifteen years. Most female workers were found in the textile industry, especially in cotton and silk: the textile industries altogether accounted for more than eighty per cent of the total female workforce surveyed in 1899.

Table 22.2. Children in Industrial Employment, by Age and Gender, 1899, 1909 and 1914

Year	*Proportion (%)*			*Total Workforce*
	Under 12	*Under 14*	*Under 20*	*(all ages)*
Males				
1899	–	6	–	138,119
1909	0.4	3	26	307,139
1914	0.3	3	27	383,957
Females				
1899	–	13	–	245,790
1909	1	7	58	493,498
1914	0.4	6	58	564,308

Sources: Ministry of Agriculture and Commerce (MAC), 32-nen *zenkoku kōjō tōkeihyō* (1902), *Meiji 42-nen kōjō tōkeihyō* (1910), and *Taisho 3-nen kōjō tōkeihyō* (1916).
Note: The 1899 survey covered factories (*kōjō*) with 10 operatives or more, while the 1909 and 1914 surveys also included those with 5–9 operatives.

The first Factory Law, passed in 1911, prohibited the employment of children under twelve years of age, though it was applied only to factories and workshops with fifteen operatives or more. However, even before the law came into force in 1916, the proportion of children under twelve, never very high to begin with, had fallen to less than 0.5 per cent of the total number of workers in industrial employment. It may not be a coincidence, therefore, that in the published report of the subsequent factory census, carried out in 1919, only one category was established for all ages under fifteen, suggesting that the number of children under this age was negligible.

A slightly different picture emerges from the same data if disaggregated by factory size (table 22.3). With regard to the male workforce, there is no evidence that more children were employed by larger factories. However, the pattern was different for females. In both the 1899 and 1909 censuses, the larger the factory, the higher the proportion of girls under fourteen. Since most factories of the 1000-plus category in earlier years were found in textiles, especially in cotton spinning, and since, as mentioned, their workforces were characteristically young and female, this pattern might be seen as evidence that, in Japan too, child labour was associated with the Industrial Revolution.

Table 22.3. Child Labour by Factory Size and Gender, 1899, 1909 and 1914

Factory size (operatives per establishment)	*Proportion under 14 (%)*					
	Male			*Female*		
	1899	*1909*	*1914*	*1899*	*1909*	*1914*
5-9	–	4	4	–	6	6
10-29	6	3	3	13	8	8
30-49	7	3	3	12	7	8
50-99	6	3	2	12	7	7
100-499	8	3	2	12	6	5
500-999	4	4	2	14	8	5
1000+	4	2	1	17	10	5

Sources: Ministry of Agriculture and Commerce (MAC), *32-nen zenkoku kōjō tōkeihyō* (1902), *Meiji 42-nen kōjō tōkeihyō* (1910), and *Taisho 3-nen kōjō tōkeihyō*(1916).
Note: The 1899 survey covered factories *(kōjō)* with 10 operatives or more, while the 1909 and 1914 surveys also included those with 5-9 operatives.

To verify this interpretation, we need to disaggregate the data by industry. Fortunately, a government survey for 1900 allows us to break down the national labour force into seventy industrial categories and, furthermore, provides us with additional information about the various characteristics of those industries. Only seven of the seventy industries will be considered here. Cotton spinning and silk reeling have been singled out because they are representative of the leading industries of the day, the former exemplifying industries transplanted from the West, and the latter being one of the few indigenous industries that underwent a successful transition to the factory. Also analysed are five industries in which under-fourteen workers made up more than twenty per cent of the total workforce. These are rug weaving, rope braiding (that is, the production of braided bands and belts used for kimono dress), matchmaking, glass-making and paper-products manufacturing.

The data presented in tables 22.4, 22.5 and 22.6 show that the numbers of child workers and their working conditions varied widely across these different industries. The cotton-spinning and silk-reeling industries, together accounting for as much as 46 per cent of the total workforce surveyed in 1900, employed female workers in large numbers. Although both were power-driven factory industries, some important differences existed between the two. Silk reeling was rural in location, which is reflected in a small factory size and a low number of days in operation. Working conditions were much harsher in the large, urban-based cotton spinning mills, which operated on a twelve-hour working day with a night shift. On the other hand, the other five were industries whose shares in the nation's labour force were small, and it seems that all were located in urban or suburban areas.

Several points can be made on the basis of tables 22.4–22.6. First, it is evident from table 22.4 that the proportion of workers under fourteen was substantially lower in the cotton and silk industries than in the case of the other five industries. Among the latter, particularly high percentages were to be found in the rug industry, where more than four in every ten male workers were under the age of fourteen years, and in the matchmaking industry, the largest of the five, where the proportion was more than one in three.

Secondly, as seen in tables 22.5 and 22.6, the five industries can be further grouped into two very different categories. Group II (rug weaving, rope braiding and matchmaking) had a 78 greater percentage of female workers, whereas Group III (glass-making and paper products) had more male workers, including a substantial number of apprentices. In fact, apprenticeship in glass-making factories accounted for much of its proportion of under-fourteen-year-olds (see table 22.5).

Thirdly, wages were low in Group II industries whereas workers in Group III were comparatively better paid. This is not because the former's workforce was predominantly female, whereas the latter employed more male labourers. Gender specific wage rates for children under fourteen in table 22.6 show, in fact, that although girls consistently earned less than boys, boys were also paid low wages in the three Group II industries. Both boys and girls in the matchmaking industry, for example, received 26 to 28 per cent less than their counterparts in glass-making and cotton spinning.

Table 22.4. Child Labour in Selected Industries, by Gender, 1900

Industry	*Proportion of workers under 14 (%)*			*Total no. of workers*
	Males	*Females*	*Total*	
Group I				
Cotton spinning	9	12	11	55,511
Silk reeling	4	10	10	124,241
Group II				
Rug weaving	42	13	20	1,031
Rope braiding	22	30	28	1,107
Matchmaking	38	35	36	12,804
Group III				
Glass-making	26	0	24	2,573
Paper products	15	24	20	1,085

Source: MAC, *Meiji 33-nen zenkoku kōjō tōkeihyō* (1993).
Notes: (1) Only factories (*kōjō*) with ten or more operatives were surveyed.
(2) "Workers" include not only *shokkō* (operatives) but also *totei* (apprentices).

It should be emphasized that the 1900 survey only covered workshops and factories with ten or more operatives. In these low-wage industries, therefore, it is very likely that those surveyed were the "tip of the iceberg". Its invisible part consisted of a number of small-scale workshops and an even greater number of out-workers. They were, in short, sweated trades, and it was in these trades that child labour was an especially difficult social problem. Contemporary journalists and government investigators were well aware of this. In fact, some of the evidence gathered by the government's Industry Department strongly indicates that child labour must have been more pervasive than the percentages in table 22.4 would suggest. In the rug industry, for example, the Osaka and Hyogo trade associations' data for 1901-1902 showed that exactly fifty per cent of the total employees (both sexes combined) were children under fourteen, of whom one in five was under the age of ten.[8] This difference in data undoubtedly arises because

8 Ministry of Agriculture and Commerce (MAC), *Kōjō tōkeihyō*, 1902, p. 92. The total number of employees was 9,378.

trade associations were umbrella organizations covering not just factories, but also small-scale family businesses and "putters-out" (that is, those who gave out work to be performed off the premises). The same may be said about the matchmaking industry. Indeed, in his classic account of working life in the lower classes of Meiji Japan, published in 1899, Gennosuke Yokoyama contrasted matchmaking with the cotton industry, noting that "in cotton mills the relationships between girls' work and working hours, between their work and health conditions, and the like, can be investigated, while in match-makers' workshops one can collect materials most suitable for an inquiry into child labour".[9]

Table 22.5. Characteristics of the Workforce in Selected Industries

Industry	*No. of workers per factory*	*Sex ratio*	*Proportion of apprentices to: Total workers (%)*	*Workers under 14 (%)*
Group I				
Cotton spinning	495	0.27	0.05	0.3
Silk reeling	49	0.07	4	18
Group II				
Rug weaving	16	0.29	0.04	0
Rope braiding	43	0.33	2	0.3
Matchmaking	70	0.35	1	1
Group III				
Glass-making	50	18.79	25	43
Paper products	32	1.02	7	16

Source: MAC, *Meiji 33-nen zenkoku kōjō tōkeihyō* (1903).
Note: Sex ratio (M/F) refers to workers including apprentices.

It is unlikely, therefore, that child labour increased with the advance of "industrialism" in modern Japan if the term refers to the emergence of the factory industry. The leading industrialists tended to employ more and more juvenile labour (that is, over the age of fourteen), but not necessarily more child labour. It is true that young mill girls had to work long hours and sometimes in unhealthy conditions, but not many school-age children

9 *Nihon no kasō shakai*, 1899; reprinted edn, 1949, p. 129.

were found among them.[10] It is also true that some of the cotton mills did employ children aged seven, eight or nine, but the overall proportion of those under ten years old never reached the one per cent mark. It is worth noting, furthermore, that the absolute size of the under-fourteen child population in those mills did not increase at all, even though, at the time, factory legislation had not yet been enacted.[11]

Table 22.6. Working Conditions in the Selected Industries, 1900

Industry	*Power-driven establishments (%)*	*Days in operation (per year)*	*Hours in operation (per day)*	*Daily wages for under-14*	
				Males (sen)	*Females (sen)*
Group I					
Cotton spinning	95	329	12 (21.8)	12.6	10.4
Silk reeling	83	186	10	11.7	9.6
Group II					
Rug weaving	0	289	9.5	7.0	6.7
Rope braiding	27	308	11	9.9	9.2
Matchmaking	3	31 3	10	9.2	7.7
Group III					
Glass-making	16	323	9.5	12.7	10.5
Paper products	3	300	10	11.7	9.7

Source: MAC, *Meiji 33-nen zenkoku kōjō tōkeihyō* (1903).
Note: The figure in parentheses in the column for hours in operation includes the night shift.

10 By 1905, primary schooling was nearly universal. Children were required to attend school for four years (roughly from the ages of 6 to 10 years). In 1907, the number of years of compulsory schooling was raised from four to six.

11 It should be stressed, however, that concern over child labour was not the sole motive of the government pressing for legislation. The public became increasingly worried about health conditions of juvenile workers as tuberculosis spread in both factories and in the countryside, from which mill workers were drawn. A government-commissioned survey conducted in 1909–1911 by a young medical researcher, Osamu Ishihara, revealed that the mortality rate was 6 per 1,000 for girls who died on factory premises, rising to 38 per 1,000 for mill girls who died at home, having, in all probability, been dismissed because they had tuberculosis. The results, the first of which appeared in 1910, became immediately known to the government and undoubtedly played a significant part in bringing the bill through the Diet in 1911. Some of Ishihara's findings are summarized in Hunter, "Textile Factories".

It was instead in some non-factory industries such as matchmaking and rug weaving that the real child labour problem seems to have existed. Most of these industries were not 'visible' in official statistics, but what is important to realize is that they were not slow-dying, traditional trades. A majority of them were new: matchmaking was introduced in Japan after the opening of the country, while rug weaving was an export industry which responded to the commencement of overseas trade. It was in pockets of such sweated trades that child labour was to be found.

Workforce Participation

To determine how many small children were actually employed in those sweated trades, and whether child labour there increased over time, we have to turn to other sources since none of the "factory" censuses covered all places of productive activity. Detailed tabulations of children's age-specific activity rates, ideally by single years, might do for this purpose, but readily available statistics do not exist for industrial districts, nor for the nation as a whole prior to the first national population census of 1920.

The only usable data for the pre-1920 period derive from a pilot census taken in 1879 in the Yamanashi Prefecture (formerly Province of Kai), whose results were published as the Kai Census Report in 1882. As Kai was a rural province, this census can hardly be considered as being representative of a country that had just embraced industrialism. Yet Kai was not entirely agricultural either. It was one of the areas where "proto-industrialization", particularly in the silk industry, was taking place. In fact, this was precisely the area in which Professor Chamberlain, during his journeys in the 1890s, noted troops of girls coming in and out of silk filatures. A substantial number of paid-employment opportunities for both women and children were therefore likely to have been available in this province, including jobs in the silk industry. Moreover, the Kai Census Report enables us to compute children's workforce participation rates by single years, an advantage not always found in later published census reports.

Age profiles of workforce participation calculated from this 1879 census are shown in figure 22.1, and are contrasted with a different profile derived from a survey of pauper children in 24 poor houses in 1902.

Figure 22.1. Age Profiles of Children's Workforce Participation: Children in Yamanashi Prefecture, 1879, and Pauper Children in 24 Poorhouses, 1902

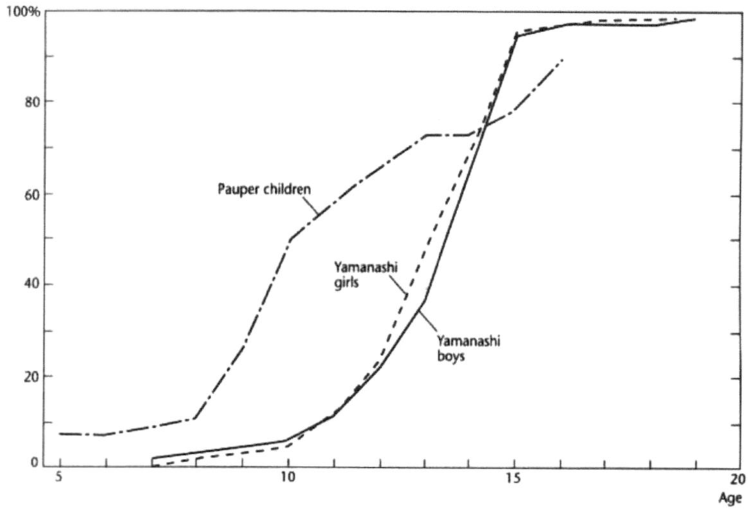

Source: Tōkeiin, Kai-no-kumi genzai ninbetsu shirabe (1882); and MAC, *Kōjō tōkeihyō* (1902), pp. 103-111.

There are no significant differences between the curves for Yamanashi boys and girls. Both show that few children entered the labour force before the age of eleven. The proportion working was slightly over ten per cent at age eleven for both sexes, but rose rapidly thereafter, reaching the 90 per cent mark by age fifteen. The quinquennial average for children aged ten to fourteen was 29 per cent for boys and 32 per cent for girls. Variations across the districts within the prefecture were not very large: the male percentage varied from 26 to 34 per cent while the female percentage varied from 22 to 46 per cent.

This pattern, which may be designated "late-starting", is in sharp contrast with the one for children in poor houses (most of which were actually orphanages and foundling hospitals). A majority of "pauper children" started working by age ten, and two thirds were in paid employment before age thirteen. Thereafter, the tempo of percentage increase is less rapid, probably because many of the children who stayed on in the poor houses were physically unfit or unable to work. If we calculate the mean age of entry into the workforce by applying a method used by demographers to calculate, on the basis of some reasonable assumptions, the "singulate mean age at marriage,"[12] then we have 13.4 years for both boys and girls in Yamanashi, and 10.8 years for pauper children. In other words, what figure 1 shows is a contrast between the early-starting and late-starting patterns of children's workforce participation, and it is probably safe to assume that the overall pattern for the nation was closer to the Yamanashi profile than to the one for pauper children.

As for a time trend over the period in question, we can compare the 1879 Yamanashi figures with those from the first national census in 1920 (when Yamanashi was still one of the major silk-producing prefectures). A close scrutiny of the definitions adopted by the census-takers on the two occasions reveal that part-time and occasional workers were included in the 1879 definition of those working but excluded in the 1920 one. By subtracting those in such a category from the 1879 figures, therefore, we can make the two cases comparable. The results show that the participation rate for boys in the age group five to fourteen decreased from 14 to 9 per cent over the four decades, while the rate for girls in the same age group changed little over the same period, from 14 to 13 per cent. If this can be a guide for a change that took place nationally, then it is unlikely that the rate of children's work-force participation increased during the early phases of industrialization.

The Role of Education

Much emphasis has been placed on the importance of primary education as a factor removing children from the labour force. Indeed, as early as 1872, the new Meiji government's Educational Ordinance declared that "every man shall, of his own accord, subordinate all other matters to the education of his children". At the primary level, age-old terakoya (temple schools) were replaced by Western-style formal education. Seven years later, a new, comprehensive law was enacted, making four years of schooling compulsory (although it was not free until 1900). Thereafter, primary school enrol-

12 The "singulate" mean age at marriage is an average age at first marriage calculated from census-type data on proportions left single in successive age groups. It is equivalent to the mean number of years spent in the single (never-married) state by those members of a given cohort who marry by age 50 (see Hajnal, "Age at Marriage"). Here the proportion not working is used instead of the proportion single (assuming that those who were not working had never been in the workforce before), and the end point is set at age 20 rather than 50.

ment showed an upward trend and, by 1905, reached nearly universal levels. In this respect, it is interesting to note that the educationalists' view has an affinity with one held by development economists working on long-term economic statistics in modern Japan. Basing their work on the assumption that school enrolment rates are the best guide for changing workforce participation rates of children, a group of economists attempted to estimate the number of gainfully employed child workers in the pre-1920 period. Their conclusion was that initial levels of workforce participation for children aged ten to fourteen were high, but that levels displayed an unmistakable downward trend as primary school enrolment rates increased.[13]

Table 22.7. Primary School Enrolment and Two Indicators of Educational Attainment, 1875-1925 (male children only)

Year	*Enrolment rate (%)*	*Proportion of those who could write (%)*	*Proportion of those who completed compulsory schooling (%)*
1875	51	–	–
1889	64	77	42
1895	77	89	66
1905	98	98	80
1915	99	99	89
1925	99	99	98

Sources: The first column is from the Ministry of Education's *Mombushō nenpō,* and the second and third from calculations made by Ikuko Kiyokawa, which are based on the Ministry of War's *Rikugunshō tōkei nenpō.* I am grateful to Mrs. Kiyokawa for allowing me to use her worksheets.

Notes: (1) The first column measures a male *gakurei* (school-age) population, defined as children between 6 and 14 years of age. However, it is likely that over-14-year-olds were included in that population. This was because not all children went to school at age 6: some were enrolled for the first time as late as age 10 or 11. In other cases, children who had dropped out earlier returned to school to finish the compulsory years. Unfortunately, it is not possible to know the exact mean age of each *gakurei* population.

(2) The second and third columns measure a population of males who were examined at age 20 for conscription 10 years later than the year shown in the table. Kiyokawa believes that this group of examinees corresponds roughly to the *gakurei* population on enrolment documents in the year specified.

13 Umemura et al., *Estimates of Long-term Economic Statistics.* To be fair, it should be noted that their intention was never to set out age-specific proportions of the gainfully employed. They were concerned with changing aggregates.

This estimation is not fully substantiated by the data relating to Yamanashi in 1879-1920, discussed earlier. While the rate of participation for boys showed a certain decline in Yamanashi, the magnitude of this decline was much less dramatic. Furthermore, the participation rate for girls remained virtually unchanged. The Yamanashi data, therefore, would seem to cast doubts on the assumption that any rise in the primary school enrolment rate must have resulted in a corresponding decrease in children's engagement in paid employment.

Thus, some other aspects of the "success story" often told on the basis of the Ministry of Education's primary school enrolment statistics need to be explored. Table 22.7 sets out the rate of primary school enrolment as well as two new indicators of educational attainment, both derived from conscription data.

On the basis of this information, it can be seen, first, that not all ever-enrolled children finished school. The difference between the enrolment and the completion rates was wide in early years – 22 percentage points in 1889. The difference narrowed in the 1890s, but widened again in 1900 after all fees were dropped for primary schooling, prompting substantial advances in enrolment rates. The gap stood at 18 points when the enrolment rate reached a saturation point in about 1905. It had again narrowed by the time factory legislation was enforced, although there was still a 10-point gap in 1915, partly because of the extension of years of compulsory schooling from four to six. In any case, if it was not the number of children who enrolled but rather the number who completed schooling that was really instrumental in removing children from the labour force, then Meiji Japan's records would look less impressive.

Since the data on completion are taken from conscription statistics, girls are not covered by this table, but several case studies suggest that their completion rates were substantially lower than those for boys. Indeed, the Ministry of Education issued in January 1894 instructions urging prefectural governments to make special arrangements for children who were unable to attend school. Thereafter a number of night classes, Sunday schools and the so-called childminders' classes appeared in clusters, especially at the turn of the century. Most were attached to state schools, but there are some examples where such arrangements were made in factories. According to a recent study of 318 known cases, a majority of students attending such classes were from eleven to fourteen years old, an age group in which most young girls were sent *away* from home to work as childminders.[14] Unfortunately, it is not possible to determine how widespread such half-time solutions were because no Ministry of Education data exist.

The second point to be noticed is that literacy, in the sense that boys could write their names, addresses and the like, was consistently higher than the rate of primary school enrolment. In 1889, when slightly less than 64 per cent of the nation's male children went to school, 77 per cent of them could write. Moreover, according to two prefectural surveys, conducted in 1910 and 1911, two out of every five boys who had never been to school or who had failed to complete compulsory schooling displayed basic literacy skills at the time of conscription.[15] This strongly suggests that school was not the only place where one could acquire literacy. Although it is difficult to know exactly where this ability was learned, these interesting findings might be taken to imply that "self-advancement" was an important virtue not only for elite ex-samurai but for common people as well.

Children in the Family Economy

The use of the term "self" in the preceding paragraph needs to be qualified. Self should not be taken to mean that anything individualistic emerged as an ideology among young Japanese. Rather, any virtue observed in Japanese society must be set in family values. Indeed, the profiles suggested earlier by figure 1 may well have reflected families' preferences for how children ought to be brought up, educated and trained as well as their attitudes about the appropriate age for children to join the labour force.

In this respect, it is interesting to consider nine of the 22 case studies assembled by the government's Industry Department for a chapter on the match industry in 1902.[16] All the cases concern families who lived in slums or poor neighbourhoods in Osaka and Kobe, two areas where child labour

14 These special arrangements are discussed in Osada, *Komori gakkō no jisshōteki kenkyū*, pp. 325–333.

15 Precisely, the proportion of those who attained some degree of literacy was 39 per cent for Kyoto (of the 1,398 conscripts considered) and 45 per cent for Osaka (of a total of 2,709). Calculated from *Sōtei kyōiku chōsa* for Kyoto Prefecture, 1910, and for Osaka Prefecture, 1911.

16 MAC, *Shōkkō jijō*, 1903, III, ch. 4. Of the 22 households surveyed, two are female-headed, one by a widow and the other by a single mother. The rest are families with both parents present. It appears that investigators deliberately excluded single-member households and most single-parent families.

appeared to be particularly concentrated. Most families surveyed had some members working in the match industry, and the nine chosen for in-depth analysis had at least one child between the ages of five and eleven years.

These nine cases reveal, first, that most children aged twelve or over and four out of five ten-and eleven-year-olds were working, but none of the children under ten was working away from home in paid employment. Secondly, if the husband earned fifty *sen* a day or over, the largest earnings in the sample, none of his family members was working. When, on the other hand, he earned only between 30 and 35 *sen* a day, usually either the wife or an adolescent child worked to supplement the family income. In one family, a fourteen-year-old girl was employed, whereas in another family, a thirteen-year-old girl stayed home to look after her younger brothers and sisters while her mother worked in the match factory (at twelve to thirteen *sen* a day). Thirdly, only when the wife could not make a living wage did children aged ten or eleven go to work. For example, in one family the husband was often unemployed and his wife was in poor health, so that the older children, aged twenty-two and seventeen, had to earn much of the household income. In other two cases, where the husband was sickly and even when he could work he only earned from 23 to 25 *sen* a day, it was the wife who worked as well as the children aged ten and eleven. Nevertheless, despite these extremely precarious circumstances, none of the *children* under ten in these three families was in paid employment. This does not necessarily mean that those young children were in school, although it is likely that most were as primary schooling was close to universal by 1905. In one case, a nine-year-old boy had been withdrawn from school, probably because he had to mind his younger siblings at home. Other cases have been recorded of working children who had an opportunity to learn at night schools that were provided by match-manufacturing companies.

The nine cases happened to be families with both parents present, but this should not be considered to have been the norm in the slums of Osaka and Kobe at the turn of the century. On the contrary, as officials in the welfare department of the Osaka Municipal Office found in a survey report in the 1920s, many slum-dwellers either lived alone or in families where the male breadwinner was absent or too ill to work.[17] There may have also been cases where children, having lost both parents, were admitted to orphanages. Under such conditions, one may predict that more children, say, under twelve were forced to work. Although no other data exist

17 Tamai, "Images of the Poor". For a useful overview of the poverty problem in modern Japan, see Chubachi and Taira, "Poverty in Modern Japan".

for urban slum areas, this is borne out by looking at 283 rural (or proto-industrial) families from four Yamanashi villages in the 1879 census (those with at least one child aged between five and eleven).[18]

A preliminary analysis of this proto-industrial sample reveals, first, that the proportion of families with children aged five to eleven working was not substantial (only 8 per cent). The probability of having a working child in that age group, however, varied considerably according to whether both parents were present or not. In the 221 families where both parents were present, the proportion of working children remained as low as 4 per cent; instead, in 62 households where one of the parents was absent, the proportion of working children soared to 22 per cent. Many of those 62 families were listed as not forming separate households. Other factors such as landholding and the mean size of the family workforce also had some discernible effects, but no factor had as much influence as the absence of one parent.

All this seems to suggest that the pattern of early starting in figure 1, presented earlier, corresponded to such cases, while the late-starting pattern was for "normal" families. In other words, the single most important factor was whether or not the family could stay on the normal course of the family life cycle.[19] When the head of a peasant family died, for example, the remaining members might have to sell most of the family assets. Then, in all likelihood, they would drift towards an urban slum, unless they were fortunate enough to be taken in by relatives. In either event, however, all members of what remained of the family would have to work, including small children. For poorer families, even the loss of the mother may well have resulted in small children's engagement in the labour market, since the mother was the "cornerstone" of such a family economy. Indeed, as a 1919 survey report on child labour in Osaka City put it, most labouring children were those suffering for want of parental "affection and attention", which actually meant that most of them had at least one parent who had either died or abandoned the family.[20]

18 The following analysis is based on the original returns for the four villages. For the nature of those village data, see Saito, "The Rural Economy", pp. 411-414.

19 In the Japanese context, it meant a stem-family life cycle pattern. It is interesting to note here that of the 22 poor households of Osaka and Kobe (see nt. 17 above), there is only one case where the husband's mother was co-resident, a characteristic stage of the stem-family life cycle.

20 Osaka Municipal Office, *Rōdō chōsa hōkōku,* 1919, III, p. 174.

However, there is no evidence that single-member and single-parent households increased in the underclass society during the late nineteenth and early twentieth centuries. On the contrary, a study carried out in Tokyo in the first two decades of this century shows that family formation increased in slums and slum-like communities of in-migrants despite an accelerating tempo of urban growth.[21] It is interesting to note that even in Osaka, the "Manchester of the East", the municipal office urged paupers to marry as part of its policy on poverty alleviation, the assumption being that, for the poor, family formation was the key to "getting by".[22] The overall pattern of children's entry into the labour force, therefore, must have remained that of late starting throughout the period in question.

Some Conclusions

By way of concluding this chapter, it may be useful to set the work experience of Japanese children in the industrialization process against that of British children in the Industrial Revolution. The first impression one probably has from the accounts in the previous sections is that Japan's industrialism did not lead to the extensive use of child labour. This inference is strengthened when the Japanese experience is compared, for instance, with the situation in the British cotton-spinning industry, the locus classicus for the exploitation of child labour in the Industrial Revolution. There, as many as 20 per cent of the workforce in 1816 were children under thirteen, and 7 per cent were under ten.[23] Another measure for such a comparison is age-specific participation rates of children in paid employment. On the face of it, more Japanese than British children joined the labour force. Take the ten to fourteen age group. Thirty-two per cent of the Yamanashi girls in this age group, for example, were working. The corresponding figure for England and Wales in 1851 was a little lower (20 per cent), but the regional variation was extremely wide, ranging from 8 to 51 per cent.[24] If Hugh Cunningham is correct in his interpretation that low activity rates

21 Nakagawa, "Family Formation and the Household Budget".

22 Tamai, "Images of the Poor".

23 Nardinelli, *Child Labor and the Industrial Revolution*, p. 109.

24 This is also confirmed by looking at two parish-level cases, where it is also shown that changes over time could take place in contrasting directions. See Saito, "Who Worked When". Some aspects of labour supply behaviour of the poor in this period are discussed in Saito, "Labour Supply Behaviour of the Poor".

for under-fourteen-year-olds in agricultural counties implies, not a lower supply, but instead a lower demand creating widespread rural unemployment among children in that age group,[25] then the contrast between the two cases should probably be reversed: the level of ten- to fourteen-year-old children's involvement in the labour market was higher in Britain than in Meiji Japan. Indeed, an influential work on British child labour, based on budget data, sets out more directly comparable figures. According to Sara Horrell and Jane Humphries, the mean age at first participation in the workforce in the period 1817-1839 was twelve years or lower – in sharp contrast with 13.4 years for the Yamanashi children of Japan. At the other end of the spectrum, children of British factory workers in 1787-1816 started on average to earn as early as 9.9 years of age, which declined to 8.3 years in the post-1816 period, whereas in Meiji Japan the average even for pauper boys was 10.8 years.[26]

Secondly, even in a proto-industrial setting, not many pre-adolescent children were in employment. This does not necessarily mean that children were kept at home as "treasures" of the family. Most under-twelve-year-olds were expected to help their parents in the fields as well as around the house. In comparative terms, however, they were generally "late starters" in supplying their labour to outside markets unless they lost a parent or familial support. This finding does not fit the image of the typical family in a proto-industrial economy, usually portrayed as a work group in which all members had to contribute to the family subsistence, including children, whose labour contribution was indeed regarded as a "vital necessity".[27] But the fact that in proto-industrializing Yamanashi few children under age eleven were found in the labour force suggests that their upbringing and education – whether or not in the form of formal schooling – were more valued than their meagre incomes, and that the deficit must have been made up for through the labour of their mothers as well as their elder brothers and sisters. In such a society, one may predict that married women and adolescent children were fully occupied, and this is exactly what the Yamanashi census and other case studies show. Moreover, what we have seen in the sample of poor families in the cities of Osaka and Kobe also fits in with this pattern. Virtually all the married rural women combined their domestic duties with productive activities. Even in the productive sphere, they were not confined to farming, but often took up jobs

25 Cunningham, "Employment and Unemployment of Children".

26 Horrell and Humphries, "Exploitation of Little Children".

27 Kriedte *et al.*, *Industrialization before Industrialization*, p. 55.

associated with the cottage industry as well. Grown-up children, too, were expected to contribute a substantial proportion of their wages to the family budget. Indeed, girls in spinning mills or silk filatures regularly sent as much as one third of what they earned back to their parental home.[28]

Finally, a few words are required about the role of state education. It is not incorrect to say that education was instrumental in removing Japanese children from the industrial workforce. But, at the same time, one should not overemphasize the role played by compulsory education. It is true that the Meiji government made every effort to enforce school attendance, which resulted in rising enrolment rates. However, families did sometimes withdraw their ten-, eleven- or twelve-year-old children from primary schools to send them to textile mills even after virtually universal enrolment was attained. This tendency was particularly marked for girls as the textile sector grew in the early decades of that century. Clearly, contrary to what today's experts on the Third World sometimes assume, compulsory education was not the only policy instrument for removing children from the labour force. On the other hand, literacy seems to have long occupied an important place in the Japanese family's priorities. As we have seen, the proportion of children who could read in the early years of industrialization was always higher than the rate of primary school enrolment. These children must have had access to some form of instruction outside school, or they may have taught themselves while working. All this suggests that a somewhat different family strategy was employed in peasant family economies, and this continued to be the principal strategy of the families during the early phases of industrialization in Japan. This strategy was different from the one observed in a number of Western European countries, and particularly Belgium, where married women tended to withdraw from the labour market when real wage levels started to rise, while children continued to work.[29]

28 For women's work and working hours in the peasant family economy, see Saito, "Gender, Workload and Agricultural Progress".

29 Cunningham, "Child Labour and Industrialization", p. 6.

CHAPTER 23

Labour in Childhood's Global Past: Child Work and Colonial Policies in Indonesia, 1800–1949

Ben White

Introduction: Labour in Childhood's Global Past

This paper explores changing patterns of children's employment in the (then) Netherlands East Indies, and changing colonial policies towards it. What kinds of work were part of Indonesian childhood's colonial past? How important was children's work in large- and small-scale production, in agriculture, crafts and industry, and in domestic work? How did colonial policies towards production, extraction, and labour affect childhood and child work? What, if any, policies attempted to shift the normative definition of childhood, in relation to work, education, marriage etc.? And how did children themselves respond to these changing constructions of, and interventions in, their lives?

The historical study of 'child labour' falls at the intersection of labour history and history of childhood. Three dimensions of the modern history and sociology of childhood are relevant here. First, we need to recognise childhood and youth – like other life-course stages – as social (and cultural, and political) constructions. This does not require us to become 'social constructivists', but it does require us to distinguish between the (changing and varied) lived experiences of *children* and the (changing and varied) dominant and contrapuntal ideas in society about actual, desirable or tolerable *childhoods*.[1] 'Child', 'childhood', and 'youth' are all understood and experienced in different ways in different societies, cultures and historical periods, and also – this aspect often less well recognised – in different social groups within societies. Second, we need to see children and young people as active agents influencing their own lives and the society around them, rather than (simply) as passive recipients of adult teaching and mores, and/

1 Cunningham, *Children and Childhood in Western Society*, p. 1.

or passive victims of adult exploitation and abuse.[2] Whether children are rightly perceived as (passive) victims 'or' (active) agents, is a non-question and a non-debate when posed in this limiting either/or form. Although a history of child labour inevitably becomes to a large extent "a history of what adults have done to children",[3] children, like adults, can be both victims (or beneficiaries) of structures, and individual or collective agents (of resistance and change). Finally, understanding children's changing place in family, community and society (and in work relations and labour markets) requires us to understand their changing relations with adults (age- or generation-based relationships): "writing the history of children, then, will involve confronting the politics of age relations".[4]

In Indonesia as in many other countries, the historical study of childhood (even on down-to-earth topics such as children's work), is plagued by the dearth of source materials, especially for the period of early colonial expansion. Printed and manuscript primary sources (such as government reports, publications of professional and philanthropic associations and societies, local archives) while not completely absent are relatively rare compared to the wealth of materials available to historians of European and North American childhood. Second, no matter which part of the world we are interested in, virtually all such materials are produced by professional middle classes (and in the colonial period, mainly European professionals) and by adults: children themselves leave few records. Voices of children are therefore largely absent, while adult voices may not even attempt to represent children's viewpoints, or may do this incorrectly; serious distortions may result, particularly in the denial of children's role as historical social actors and therefore of their historical identity.[5]

We will first examine children's lives and work in the early nineteenth century, and explore changes during the period of colonial forced cultivation (the so-called *cultuurstelsel,* roughly 1830-1870), and the subsequent opening up of large expanses of land to large-scale corporate plantation agriculture, in both Java and Sumatra, in the 'Liberal' period (ca. 1870 onwards). Throughout these periods, up to the beginning of the twentieth century, no serious official or social concerns about colonial 'child labour' were evident, nor any serious attempts to intervene in either the restric-

2 Heywood, *History of Childhood*, pp. 3-4.
3 Cunningham, *Invention of Childhood,* p. 16.
4 Hendrick, *Children, Childhood and English Society,* p. 4.
5 Hendrick, *Children, Childhood and English Society,* pp. 2-3; Hendrick, "Child as an Actor in Historical Sources", pp. 36-61.

tion of child work or the provision of education. Next, we look at the first major attempts to intervene in child employment patterns through child labour legislation (1925) and subsequent attempts to implement it in the twilight years of Dutch rule (to 1942) and the subsequent struggle for independence (1945-1949). Due to biases in available source materials and in the interests of colonial historians, our analysis leans heavily on material from the densely-populated island of Java (on which some two-thirds of Indonesia's population are found, on some seven percent of Indonesia's total land area), although we will also take some note of available reports on conditions in the main plantation regions outside Java.

This chapter draws on the author's earlier publications on the topic,[6] and like them is based mainly on published colonial reports and the recent work of other scholars. While aspects of Indonesian colonial childhood and child work are often mentioned in the work of social and economic historians (often alongside women's work), Indonesian childhood has not yet been the subject of a dedicated historical study based on primary sources. This makes comparison with other countries and regions difficult. Nevertheless, while child labour was present in Indonesian colonial export production, available evidence suggests that it did not play a crucial or indispensable role. This may have been the case more generally for the labour-abundant regions of South and Southeast Asia, in contrast to the much more sparsely populated countries of colonial Africa where historical studies show that child labour was considered essential for the success of colonial production.[7]

Childhood and Child Work in the Early Nineteenth Century

Although this chapter focuses mainly on the late colonial period and the early twentieth century it is useful to begin with the early nineteenth century, before the systematisation of colonial extractive policies from 1830 onwards. What kinds of work did children do, and how did the early

6 White, "Demand for Labour and Population Growth"; White, "Child Labour and Population Growth"; White, "'Agricultural Involution' and its Critics"; White, "Economic Diversification and Agrarian Change"; Lieten and White, "Children, Work and Education"; White, "Constructing Child Labour"; White and Tjandraningsih, *Child Workers in Indonesia*.

7 See for example Grier, *Invisible Hands;* Chirwa, "Child and Youth Labour on the Nyasaland Plantations"; Van Hear, "Child Labor"; Shivji, "Law and Conditions of Child Labour".

extractive policies of the Dutch East Indies Company (VOC), and those of local rulers, on which VOC policies were often based, affect their lives and work ?

In societies based on settled peasant agriculture, work is part of the core definition of childhood, in both agriculture, crafts and home-based manufacturing.[8] From the British interregnum (1811-1816) onwards, various reports provide scattered but useful information on aspects of children's lives in the early nineteenth century, including paid and unpaid work, as well as other dimensions such as education and age at marriage. Here is what Governor Raffles had to say about the role of children in Java's peasant economy, based on information collected by his team of field investigators:

> Both sexes arrive at maturity very early, and the customs of the country, as well as the nature of the climate, impel them to marry young; the males at sixteen, and the females at thirteen or fourteen years of age: though frequently the women form connexions at nine or ten [...]
> Children, which are for a very short period a burden to their parents, become early the means of assistance and a source of wealth. To the peasant who labours his field with his own hand [...] they grow up into a species of valuable property [...] As the labour of the women is almost equally productive with that of the men, female children become as much objects of solicitude of their parents as male: they are nursed with the same care and viewed with the same pride and tenderness. In no class of society are children of either sex considered an incumbrance, or the addition to a family as a misfortune.[9]

These observations are supported by the scattered references to children's work in various local officials' reports from the early nineteenth century. Summarising these, Elson concludes that children engaged in productive work (or at least released their elders for it) from an early age – often as young as five or six years – in such tasks as agricultural labour, guarding fields against birds and other pests, household chores and looking after cattle: "by the time they were in their early teens, they were fully engaged in the work cycles of the village".[10]

8 Stearns, *Childhood in World History*, p. 11.
9 Raffles, *History of Java*, pp. 69-71.
10 Elson, *Village Java*, p. 10.

Although European observers tended to exaggerate the homogeneity of Javanese "peasant society",[11] Raffles is correct in observing that during this period, in Java and other regions of settled peasant agriculture, children did indeed grow up in different "classes of society", clearly stratified rural communities in which differences in landholding were the primary determinant of local differentiation. Studies of different Javanese regions in the late eighteenth and early nineteenth century (on the eve of the *cultuurstelsel*) provide a fairly consistent picture in which three broad agrarian classes can be identified. In the middle was a large mass of peasants (often called *bumi* or *sikep*) with use-rights to land, and with heavy tribute or land-rent,[12] *corvée* (labour-tax)[13] and other obligations attached to those rights. Above them was a privileged, non-cultivator group of village officials who in addition to their own landholdings had control of a large portion (often one-fifth) of village land plus rights to the unpaid labour of the *sikep* to cultivate it; and below them was a substantial group of landless families and individuals attached as dependents to landed peasant households. Share-tenancy and wage-labour arrangements were common, and it is also clear that these dependent households, although not burdened themselves with tribute or *corvée* obligations, often bore the main burden of the obligations which formally devolved on their landed patron households.[14] This mode of extraction, already in place under pre-colonial indigenous rulers, allowed the VOC to employ "all the pre-existing machinery of despotism"[15] in securing the provision of export crops, by appropriating and adapting for themselves the rights of indigenous rulers to a share of peasant produce and/or labour.

The tax burden on peasants, therefore, placed heavy demands on the labour of both landed and landless households, and the work contributed by children was an important dimension of household survival. Elson cites a 1824 report from the Regency of Krawang (West Java) noting the difficulties which would accompany the provision of education for the children of the "lower classes": "their elders would have to go without the services

11 A distortion later perpetuated in Clifford Geertz, *Agricultural Involution*.

12 Often amounting to one-half of the crop on irrigated rice land.

13 Particularly in the upkeep of roads, bridges, irrigation works etc. but also working on land allocated to village and supra-village officials.

14 Breman, *The Village on Java;* Boomgaard, *Children of the Colonial State,* Ch. 5; Carey, "Waiting for the 'Just King'"; Elson, *Village Java,* Ch. 1; Knight, "Capitalism and Commodity Production"; White, "Agricultural Involution".

15 Raffles, *History of Java,* p. 151.

for which at present they can call upon them", and notes similar comments from Central Java.[16]

The Forced Cultivation System and Children's Work (1830s-1870s)

In 1830, following the collapse of the VOC in bankruptcy (1799), the British interregnum (1811-1816) and a long and heated debate about the best way to make the Indies profitable, Governor-General van den Bosch introduced a system of forced cultivation in which peasants – as a condition for access to land on which to grow their own crops – were required to provide part of their land and/or labour for the cultivation of export crops to be delivered against fixed prices, and European and indigenous officials were granted incentive payments *(cultuurprocenten)* based on the amount of commodities delivered. The system, which showed many local variations in its implementation, in effect systematized what the VOC had earlier attempted in various districts.

Like household-based contract farming everywhere, such arrangements leave the organization of labour to the contracted households and place great pressure on the labour of all household members. Did this make children's lives harder, and their work contributions heavier? Although no systematic reports on children's work are available from this period, scattered references in colonial reports and correspondence from many different parts of Java show that children, alongside women and men, were widely involved not only in household chores and subsistence production but also in the rapidly-expanding export crop sector, and in all the common export crops: indigo, cochineal, coffee, tea, cinnamon, tobacco and sugarcane. They also were frequently used to replace parents or patrons in forced-labour obligations. In Pasuruan, much of the construction work on sugar factories was done by young people between the ages of ten and fourteen.[17] The large landless groups who travelled as seasonal migrants throughout Java following the harvest seasons of the different crops often travelled as families, and both men, women, and children earned a wage; children's wages were generally on a par with women's wages (at about 60-80 per cent of the rate for adult men).

16 Elson, *Village Java,* p. 331.

17 Resident of Pasuruan, communication to the Governor General (1835), cited in Elson, *Village Java,* p. 383.

Some authors have suggested that the forced cultivation system promoted conditions of production similar to the "demographic hothouse" conditions of early industrialising Europe, favouring early marriage, early and intensive involvement of children in productive work, increased fertility and consequent population growth.[18] Various studies have documented the level of the forced labour demands of the export crop delivery system, to which were added the exactions of *corvée* labour and crops still levied by the local regents and lower officials for their own ends.[19] These examples – and other estimates from later in the nineteenth century on the burden of unpaid labour obligations in various parts of Java[20] – support the argument that the exaction of colonial 'rent' in its various and changing forms imposed labour demands which were not met simply by reductions in peasants' "spare time"[21] but required fundamental reorganization of the household's division of labour. During this period child-adult ratios do seem to have increased, and there is plausible, though not conclusive, evidence that average age at marriage may have declined.[22]

In the mid-nineteenth century, at the height of the forced cultivation regime, there were virtually no schools of any kind in Java, not even enough to fulfil the colonial demand for literate clerks, so that most regional government offices took in a number of young illiterate boys in a kind of apprenticeship:

> In almost all the Residents' and Assistant-residents' offices, these young boys, mainly relatives of local chiefs, learned to read, write and count with our [i.e. Roman] characters, up to the standard of editing official reports,

18 Alexander, "Labour Expropriation and Fertility"; Boomgaard, *Children of the Colonial State;* White, "Demand for Labour" and "Child Labour and Population Growth".

19 Alexander and Alexander, "Labour demands"; de Vries, *Landbouw en Welvaart;* Elson, *Village Java.*

20 *Eindresumé van het bij Besluit van den Gouverneur-Generaal van Nederlandsch-Indië van 24 Juli 1888 No. 8 bevolen Onderzoek naar de Verplichte Diensten der Inlandsche Bevolking op Java en Madoera (Gouvernementslanden),* 5 vols (Batavia, 1901-1903); Selosoemardjan, *Social Changes in Jogjakarta*, pp. 271-284; Arminius, "Het budget van een Javaanschen landbouwer". Arminius' remarkable time-allocation study in the Central Javanese district Bagelen documents the daily activities, incomes and expenditures of three peasants, every day for an entire year and shows clearly the large amounts of their working time (in one case, more than half) taken up by various kinds of unpaid labour-tax work.

21 As argued by Geertz, *Agricultural Involution*, p. 69.

22 Boomgaard, *Children of the Colonial State*, ch. 8.

> etc. It should be understood that this happened on an extremely limited scale.[23]

It was common for households with larger landholdings to take in the male children of landless and marginal-peasant households as live-in hired servants, receiving food and clothes for their labour (known in the Priangan region of West Java as *bujang anak*).[24]

How was "childhood" perceived and experienced during this period, and when was it considered to end, in an age before government interventions in the field of education or labour law began to influence the formal construction of childhood? As far as labour obligations to community and state were concerned, the boundary-line between "child" and "adult" seems to have been around fourteen years. In Cianjur (West Java) in the 1860s, only children below fourteen years (together with adult women) were exempted from the burden of *herendiensten* (corvée labour, which in this district mainly involved the forced cultivation of coffee) although in some tasks such as the coffee-harvest women and children often participated "voluntarily".[25] Many boys and girls below this age, however, were already married, and access to juvenile labour seems to have been at least one of the reasons for this (as we will see in the next section). There are indications, too, of an emerging transitional category of "youth"; by the late nineteenth century various reports mention the village-level institution of unmarried male adolescents (*sinoman* or *kanoman,* from Javanese *anom*, 'young') and in some districts a parallel female category (*byada*)who were called on for various services by the village administration. In one case (Indramayu, West Java) the *kanoman* were even allocated their own communal rice-fields.[26]

During this period, then, most children did not go to school, and were regarded as assets in directly productive work (both helping parents and earning wages), in taking part of the burden of forced-labour obligations, and in domestic work. We cannot tell how much this work interfered with (or possibly was combined with) children's other needs for rest and play. Work will have been the main medium of learning of life skills. There is no evidence that children's involvement in work, or their almost complete

23 *Algemene Onderwijsverslag* 1850-52, cited in Brugmans, *Geschiedenis van het Onderwijs*, p. 123.

24 Boomgaard, *Children of the Colonial State,* pp. 150-152.

25 Marle, "Beschrijving van een kaloerahan", pp. 11-12.

26 Boomgaard, *Children of the Colonial State*, pp. 66-67.

lack of access to formal schooling, were a matter for government or societal concern.

Child Work and Colonial Policies in the "Liberal" and "Ethical" Periods (Late Nineteenth and Early Twentieth Century)

The rapid expansion of large-scale, corporate plantations in the later nineteenth century was formally enabled by the new agrarian laws of 1870, which consolidated trends that in fact had been already emerging prior to 1870. The plantations brought new patterns of large-scale plantation wage employment in both Java and Sumatra, in which the labour force was drawn primarily from Java's landless and near-landless, recruited as coolie contract workers to Sumatra and generally on shorter-term arrangements in Java, and in which the labour inputs of children were a common, but not always an essential feature. The majority of Java's rural population, however, remained as a heavily-taxed peasantry and (near)-landless class. Of the six million persons recorded as having their main occupation in agriculture in 1905, about 40 per cent were wage-workers but only about 10 per cent of these were recorded as working in foreign estates.[27]

In rural crafts and small industries, children were commonly employed both as family helpers and for wages. The very low earnings in this sector – much less than prevailing agricultural wage rates – meant that all family members including children had to work in order to attain a survival income for the household, in conditions reminiscent of those which have been described for European "proto-industries" in the early industrial revolution. A good example is the pandanus hat weaving industry in Tangerang (West Java), which in 1908 produced about ten million handwoven "Panama" hats mainly for export to Europe and the USA, and was looked on by officials as a dynamic success story. It is an interesting case of an early "footloose" export industry, which relied for its competitive advantage (in relation to other production centres such as Manila) not so much on the availability of raw materials (the ubiquitous pandanus plant) as on its access to abundant cheap labour. Many local officials, responding to questions 390-391 of the so-called "Declining Welfare Enquiry" *("What kinds of industries deserve encouragement?"* and *"Which new industries could be generated? [give information on the prospects of success!]")* referred specifically to

27 White, "Economic Diversification and Agrarian Change", pp. 41-46.

Figure 23.1. Young Girls Weaving Panama Hats for Export in Mr. Petitjean's Factory, Tangerang ca. 1910

Photograph from C. Pleyte, *De Inlandsche nijverheid in West-Java als sociaal-ethnologisch verschijnsel* (Batavia, 1911).

the success story of Tangerang's hat industry and the possibilities of replicating it for other craft industries.[28] The pessimistic researcher Pleyte however, who visited many types of rural industry in West Java only a few years later to observe production and working conditions, saw the industry as a clear example of the impoverishment of workers that came with the emergence of a labour-intensive world-market product:

> The Tangerang hat industry provides an instructive and decisive answer about what kinds of benefits for the workers may be expected from other new industries, and one that deserves our attention all the more for the fact that it presently produces literally millions of hats, which in turn require the labour of thousands of hands to produce them. When one turns from this fine-looking achievement to the question: what value has this for the worker?, then one comes to the pitiful lesson: no more than the earning of a starvation wage. Even the most industrious men or women weavers can earn no more than 10 cents per day.[29] For this reason, in households with no

28 See for an example from West Java, *Samentrekking van de afdeelingsverslagen*, pp. 48–49.

29 This may be compared to adult male daily wages of 20–30 cents commonly reported in peasant and plantation agriculture in the same region.

> other income sources than hat weaving, all are compelled to help, including very young children, and one finds even the tiniest children, still dependent on mothers' care, already fellow-slaves in the struggle for their daily food.[30]

With only a few exceptions, there is no indication that the employment of children was considered a social issue in the Indies before the first World War. Work generally was considered a natural part of childhood, and children's wage-employment in particular seems to have been considered desirable. In the massive "Inquiry into the Declining Welfare of the Native Population of Java and Madura" of 1904-1905, officials in all of Java's 72 districts received a thick instruction manual containing 533 questions on economic and social conditions. These include quite detailed questions on access to education, literacy and other aspects of social welfare (such as child marriage, polygamy, prostitution, beggary and vagabondage, and poor relief) but only one question on children's employment, which rather surprisingly asks:

> 74. Is there generally *sufficient opportunity for wage-employment for men, women, and children*?, together with two follow-up questions,
> 75. Do many people take advantage of these opportunities? If not, why not?, and
> 76. How much can they earn per day, in cash (day- or piece-rates), working: a. for government (public) works, b. for Europeans, c. for natives, d. for foreign orientals?[31]

Many districts reported "sufficient employment for children" in a general way, and also gave concrete details of children's wage-rates and working hours. Not only native Javanese and "foreign Asiatic" enterprises, but also government and European enterprises (in nearly all cases, plantations) employed children on a large scale, as shown below.

In general, the working-day for children was reported as being the same as that of adults (most commonly between eight and ten hours), and children's wages were generally about one-half those of adult men, and 65-75 per cent of those of adult women.[32] In terms of both working hours and their relative wages compared to adults, Javanese child workers at this time

30 Pleyte, *Inlandsche nijverheid in West-Java,* p. 59.
31 *Leidraad voor het gewestelijke onderzoek naar de mindere welvaart der inlandsche bevolking op Java en Madoera* (Batavia, 1904), p. 4.
32 *Onderzoek* (1911), pp. 1-17; *Onderzoek* (1912), pp. 94-101.

seemed better off than their contemporaries in the farms and factories of Holland;[33] even in 1908 the Dutch trade unions were still campaigning for a maximum work-day of ten hours, and in many branches of both agriculture, industry, trade and services, work-hours for both adults and children were commonly twelve to fourteen hours.[34]

Table 23.1. Number of Districts Reporting Children's Wage-Employment in Various Types of Enterprise, Java 1904

Government works[a]	11
European enterprises[b]	31
"Foreign Orientals"[c]	15
Native agriculture[d]	18

Sources: for a, b and c: *Onderzoek* (1912, VIf), pp. 1-17;
for d: *Onderzoek* (1911, IXc), pp. 94-101.

The general view that employment was a natural and desirable element in Indonesian childhood is not surprising if we recall that at the beginning of the twentieth century only about one in two hundred native children attended formal school of any kind. In The Netherlands, by contrast, successive laws restricting various kinds of child employment had been introduced in 1874 and 1889, and 95 per cent of Dutch children were attending school even before the introduction of compulsory education in 1901. Colonial policies, in contrast to those of the mother country, placed no emphasis on popular education until the early twentieth century. It was not until the so-called "ethical policy" and the gradual establishment of village schools from 1907 onwards that villagers in most regions had any prospect of access to education. While various authors argued strongly, in the press and professional publications, that the introduction of the required ten thousand village schools should and could be done, not gradually but urgently and swiftly – even in one or two years, as argued by the former resident of Madura F. Fokkens[35] – the government chose the gradual option, with the result that even by the 1930s only about one-third of native children went to primary school. They attended these schools for only three years, and only two and a half hours each day, which therefore

33 White, *Children, Work and "Child Labour"*, pp. 10-11.

34 NVV/SDAP, *Arbeidersleven in Nederland*.

35 Fokkens, *Spoedige uitbreiding van volksonderwijs op Java*.

did not interfere greatly with their capacity to work, although it may have reduced their involvement in various kinds of full-time work away from home. Concerns about both employment and education of children were often linked (as in Europe)[36] to the need to "keep children out of mischief". Mr. Pott, the Director of Education, cynically reviewed an early experiment with village schools in Ambarawa (Central Java) in the 1890s:

> The intention was certainly a good one, namely to keep the young boys busy, who otherwise did nothing except tend the buffaloes [...] the schools indeed were of some use: the boys were kept out of mischief, such as setting things on fire (they had caused some serious fires in the past).[37]

Knowing from the Declining Welfare Enquiry reports that child employment was common in European plantation enterprises in Java, it is reasonable to assume that it was also common in the plantations of Sumatra and other islands. However, in its annual reports covering the years 1913 to 1925 the Labour Inspectorate (which prior to the establishment of the Labour Office in 1921 dealt only with the islands outside Java) made not a single mention of child workers. One reason for this may be that in the indentured labour régime prevailing until 1911, Sumatran plantations typically recruited adult male coolies (without families) and sufficient female coolies as "part of the bait that was supposed to allure male workers to Deli and part of the palliative that was supposed to keep them there".[38] Only after 1911 when company strategies shifted towards the establishment of a resident labour reserve through recruitment and formation of working families, would we expect to see growing numbers of resident children (and a large-scale potential child labour force) on the plantations.

The Labour Inspectorate Reports do note the half-hearted attempts of some plantation companies on Sumatra's East Coast to establish "company schools" for the children of their coolies. In 1913 the companies' flagging interest in providing schools was explained by the fact that

> The boys who had learned to read and write didn't stay on the estate, but tried above all to find clerical work [...] Moreover the coolies themselves

36 Cunningham, "Employment and Unemployment of Children", p. 121.
37 Brugmans, *Geschiedenis van het Onderwijs*, p. 307. Note the emphasis on the boy-child.
38 Stoler, *Capitalism and Confrontation*, p. 32.

have little interest; in many schools more children of the local population than of the coolies come to school.[39]

Similar reports were made in 1914 (when it was also reported that some recently opened plantation schools had since been closed) and 1917.[40] Only in 1919 could they report that the Inspector of Education and the Planters' Committee in Medan had generated some interest with the promise of limited government support for the establishment of plantation schools, and that it was expected that numbers of company schools would increase rapidly;[41] by the 1930s the proportions of *"schoolrijpe kinderen"* (those over six years of age) enrolled in plantation company schools had indeed risen to about 30 per cent.[42]

In summary then, colonial policies placed no emphasis on popular education until the early twentieth century; child employment was unregulated and its discussion not influenced by international developments, or by the emergence of social concern and legislation on these issues in the Netherlands itself. Concerns about both employment and education of children were often linked (as in Europe) to the need to "keep children out of mischief".

Regulating Childhood and Child Employment in the Late Colonial Period[43]

Late-colonial interventions in child employment (from the 1920s onwards) highlight the absurdities of introducing legislation regulating child work, based on European concerns about child labour in factories, in contexts where education is not compulsory, where most children do not go to school (and those who do, leave school by age ten), and where only a tiny fraction of child employment is factory labour.

39 Arbeidsinspectie, *Eerste verslag van den dienst der arbeidsinspectie en koeliewerving in Nederlandsch-Indië, deel I: Oostkust van Soematra* (Batavia, 1913), p. 85.

40 Arbeidsinspectie, *Derde verslag van den dienst der arbeidsinspectie en koeliewerving in Nederlandsch-Indië* (Weltevreden, 1914); Arbeidsinspectie, *Vierde verslag van den dienst der arbeidsinspectie en koeliewerving in Nederlandsch-Indië* (Batavia, 1917).

41 Arbeidsinspectie, *Vijfde verslag van den dienst der arbeidsinspectie en koeliewerving in Nederlandsch-Indië over der Jaren 1917 en 1918* (Weltevreden, 1919), pp. 39-40.

42 Kantoor van Arbeid, *Zestiende verslag*, pp. 156-157.

43 This section summarizes the more detailed account in White, "Constructing Child Labour", pp. 83-90.

As signatory to the Treaty of Versailles the Netherlands government was obliged to apply ILO convention no. 5 (1919) on "Minimal Age for Admission of Children to Industrial Employment" in its colonial possessions as well as at home. The Convention stipulated that

> Children under the age of fourteen years shall not be employed for work in any public or private industrial undertaking, or any branch thereof, other than an undertaking in which only members of the same family are employed.[44]

The Convention applied only to industry (thus excluding the agriculture, trade and service sectors), reflecting the tendency in Europe and North America to associate the 'child labour' problem with urban factory industries.

The recently-established colonial Labour Office circulated an Inquiry on the feasibility of applying the ILO Convention (with the minimum age reduced from fourteen to twelve years) to various departmental heads, regional and district authorities and a number of employers' organizations representing the main export crops. The sugarcane employers' association had already pre-empted the new ordinance by prohibiting the employment of children under twelve years in the sugar factories. In fact, the sugar industry did make extensive use of juvenile labour, not in its factories (which were covered by the Convention) but in the fields (which were not), in such tasks as fertilizing, planting, watering and weeding. One year after the ban, the sugar association's 138 factories reported using 14.4 million person-days of so-called "half-adult" *(halfwassen)* labour, as much as 23 per cent of all hired labour days in some districts.[45]

In the tobacco belt of Besuki (East Java) about five thousand children were at work, almost entirely girls. They worked from 6 am to 5 or 5.30 pm in both drying- and packing-sheds, particularly the latter, fetching and carrying bundles of tobacco leaf to the sorting- and stacking-women and bringing the sorted bundles to the weighing-scales and packing-chests. The tobacco industry's objections to the new Ordinance were overcome by formulating the definition of 'workplace' in such a way that the mainly open drying-sheds were not included,[46] with the consequence that some

44 International Labour Office, *Convention No. 5*, Article 2.
45 Levert, *Inheemsche arbeid in de Java-suikerindustrie*, p. 126.
46 *Volksraadstukken 1925*, p. 4.

of the largest concentrations of child employment in export production (in field work and in the drying-sheds) would be left undisturbed.

It had already been decided to re-define 'night-time' from the Convention's original "rest-period of eleven consecutive hours, which includes the hours between 10 pm and 5 am" to a period of only seven hours between 10 pm and 5 am; 'childhood' itself was also redefined by lowering the minimum age from fourteen to twelve years, although in the Netherlands itself the minimum age had just been raised to fourteen in the new Labour Law of 1919.[47] No attempt was made to shift the Convention's industrial focus to the conditions of the Indies' overwhelmingly agrarian economy; the new Ordinance was not intended to keep children away from the world of work, from agricultural production or even from earning money, and certainly not to push them into school – which is hardly mentioned in debates and discussions of this period – but only to exclude them from the world of 'industry' and large-scale, formal sector agro-processing in enclosed buildings.

In the 1920s then, we see the introduction of some rather unsuitable derivative legislation, aiming to restrict the employment of children but not touching the most important sectors of child employment, and not matched with any feeling of urgency about universalising access to primary education. We also see the emergence of a construction of the "child" as aged under twelve years, and of an intermediate transitional category of "half-adults" (*halfwassenen)* defined as beginning at age twelve and ending somewhere between fourteen and sixteen according to different definitions; and for both these categories, the need to alleviate concern that through restrictions on employment they might be prone to idleness and moral decay.

Enforcing Restrictions on Child Employment: The Late Colonial Years

In the 1930s the Labour Office was quite active in investigating and prosecuting violations of the new Ordinance. The most commonly-prosecuted enterprises were (in descending order of frequency): batik workshops, tobacco sorting and processing, kapok processing, textile-weaving, rice or maize milling, tea processing, ground-nut sorting, tapioca-making, coffee roasting, with smaller numbers in bakeries, leather tanneries, cotton siz-

47 *Volksraadstukken 1925*, p. 9.

ing, copper-beating, mosquito-coils, floor-tiles, fireworks, can factories, copra-drying, printing shops, glassworks, hat-weaving, kerupuk-making, cooking-oil, cigarette-papers, and tofu processing.[48]

In the plantation enterprises outside Java it was reported that child employment was limited to light garden- and fieldwork for a few hours only, such as picking caterpillars, collecting seeds and also – in tobacco farms – stringing up tobacco leaves in the drying sheds. In these regions monitoring of implementation of the 1925 Ordinance was mainly limited to the factories and work floors of the plantation companies which were subject to regular labour inspection:

> Only occasionally were visits made to smaller enterprises such as rice-mills, soap factories, bakeries, ice- and soft-drink factories, coffee roasters etc. [...] In the cases where children were found, or which gave rise to doubts whether the children had reached the age of 12, the employers were asked to consider replacing them with older workers, something which should present no difficulties in view of the abundant supply of adult workers.
> In some of the cases mentioned above, the court case led to acquittal, either because the children concerned had disappeared, or by decision of the judge – based on doctor's certificates provided by the employer – that they were older than 12 years. Regarding these certificates it should be noted that these were generally not provided with the children's fingerprints, so that it is not certain that the children appearing before the judge were indeed the same as those named in the charge slip.[49]

The inspectors also found children working in many other enterprises besides those prosecuted; generally, if only one or two children were involved, the employer was merely issued a warning. In some cases the children simply ran faster than the inspectors:

> In several Chinese cigar or cigarette-factories, batik workshops etc. we found that each time we visited, many children simply took to their heels through the many passages which such factory-complexes have [...] making it difficult if not impossible to establish a violation.[50]

48 White, "Constructing Child Labour", pp. 90-91
49 Kantoor van Arbeid, *Zestiende Verslag*, p. 131.
50 Kantoor van Arbeid, *Zeventiende Verslag*, p. 177.

We should not assume too easily that child labour was an important or necessary element in all labour-intensive agricultural or industrial enterprises producing for the market. In most districts of West Java for example, the Labour Office's detailed report on the hand-rolled cigarette industry found no child workers (of under twelve years) at all.[51] At least in some corners of the Labour Office, voices were raised in favour of extending child labour regulation to enterprises with less than ten workers. De Kat Angelino's extensive report on the batik industry noted that batik workshops where child workers were found were generally in the parental home and sometimes in "completely open spaces, under a roof on some poles in the parental compound, a shady spot in the yard", and therefore fell outside the 1925 regulations; nevertheless the workshops were

> very unhealthy places, where the labour of children under 12 years of age can no longer be permitted [...] Given the very unhealthy conditions in this industry, it seems desirable to prohibit the employment of children in even the smallest batik enterprises.[52]

Sometimes, the Labour Office went beyond the strict provisions of the Ordinance and persuaded employers' associations to enter voluntary agreements restricting the employment of juvenile workers even when these were not covered by the Ordinance. In the East Javanese tobacco regions of Besuki and Pasuruan, the tobacco companies agreed after long negotiations to limit work-hours of "half-adults" of twelve to sixteen years to eight hours per day during harvest and seven hours at other times, although these were not covered by any regulations, and it was found that the agreements had generally been adhered to. The Inspectors noted that persons of this age-group "were found in almost all kinds of enterprise, both inside and outside factories and workshops"; in some cases, where long working hours, hazardous work or unhealthy conditions suggested action, employers were urged to replace their young workers, even when these were working legally, with adults.[53]

In the Central Javanese principalities of Yogyakarta and Surakarta, where tobacco was also a major crop, the Principalities' Agricultural Association (VLV) agreed in 1927 to a temporary, voluntary measure: juvenile workers, "an absolute necessity in this industry" for timely processing of

51 Van der Reijden, *Rapport betreffende (...) industrie van strootjes.*
52 De Kat Angelino, *Rapport betreffende (...) batikkerijen*, p. 122.
53 Kantoor van Arbeid, *Zeventiende Verslag*, p. 178.

the harvested leaves, would either be divided into two part-time shifts, or replaced with adult workers, except in some tasks (particularly the sorting and smoothing out of the dried leaves) where the VLV insisted that restrictions would bring the enterprise into serious problems. To assess the VLV's claims, the Labour Office carried out a survey in 1928 covering both the enterprises and the villages where tobacco growers lived. The resulting report by Labour Inspector de Kat Angelino provides fascinating details of the labour process; while most of these are not of interest for our present purpose, some of the conclusions drawn by Labour Controller Raden Iskandar from his village-level interviews (and summarised in Chapter VII of the report) are quite revealing of prevailing views of the adults and children involved.

On the attitudes of the local population, Iskandar concluded:

> It can not be expected that people would understand that the prohibition of child labour is intended to promote the child's physical and mental development [...] If you ask [the villager] what he thinks about it, he will answer that he was ordered to keep the children at home, and that's why he does it. A woman overseer explained that the children were sent home because it was not good for them to be in the sorting-sheds [...] She had also noticed that small children in the sorting-sheds were often sick and vomited.[54]

On the attitudes of the children themselves, it was reported that some children came home in tears when turned away from the tobacco sheds. Children's interest in earning money, and their consciousness as workers, were also manifested in other not-so-childish ways, as experienced by a nursery foreman who had sent for some children to pick caterpillars off the young tobacco leaves. When the children appeared for payment, in what he thought to be too large numbers, their hands full of infested leaves, he tore them out of the children's hands and stamped on them, refusing to pay. Some of the disappointed children, whether in tears or not, then set a drying-shed on fire in protest.

As for the possible dangers of condemning children to idleness: there was no indication, Raden Iskandar reported, that children barred from the packing-sheds would be hanging around idle, at the mercy of the "demoralizing influences of the village":

54 De Kat Angelino, *Verslag betreffende (...) Vorstenlandsche tabaksondernemingen gehouden enquête*, pp. 143-144.

> Besides the fact that the child is an appreciable source of domestic help, there is always something to do in and around the village that brings in cash or saves on expenses [...] The young child can look after little brothers and sisters, whose working mother might otherwise have to hire help for this; the girls can cook rice and vegetables, clean the house and yard, bring meals to the parents [in the fields], gather firewood that otherwise would have to be bought, look for wild vegetables in the fields; the boys can graze the animals or ducks, cut fodder, help their fathers in all stages of rice and tobacco cultivation; many children earn money selling snacks, serving in food stalls, or running errands for neighbours.[55]

These remarks, besides offering a fine stereotype of gender divisions, underline the point that the child labour Ordinance and its enforcement apparatus were not intended to exclude children from the world of work, from agricultural production or even from earning money, and certainly not to push them into school – the latter, interestingly, is hardly mentioned in the entire report – but only to ban them from the world of 'industry' and large-scale, formal sector agro-processing in enclosed buildings.

Having never considered the age of their workers to be a matter of concern, and in the absence of any civil registration system, the administrators often reported problems in establishing the age of their younger workers. In Klaten, Raden Iskandar brought together a collection of children (from age eight and above) and young persons, male and female, and an adult man and woman for comparison, and invited a committee of five persons to estimate their ages (the local village head, schoolteacher, policeman, a foreman of the tobacco company and himself). Iskandar concluded: "considering their build, facial expression and general *habitus,* serious errors in estimating the age limits would be impossible". With the ages arrived at by this consensus pinned on placards to their shirts they were lined up in various combinations against a 1.60 metre measuring rod, with a *sapu lidi* on the ground in front of them,[56] and photographed. Three of these photos are reproduced in the report to provide a guideline for the administrators.[57]

55 De Kat Angelino, *Verslag betreffende (...) Vorstenlandsche tabaksondernemingen gehouden enquête*, p. 140.

56 The *sapu lidi*, a stiff broom made of the thin stems of dried coconut leaves, is found all over Indonesia and presumably functioned as a rough-and-ready measure for those not in possession of a measuring rod.

57 De Kat Angelino, *Vorstenlandsche tabaksenquête*, pp. 133-134.

Figure 23.2. Adult, Juvenile and Child Workers Lined up against a Measuring-Rod for Purposes of Determining Their Ages, on a Tobacco Plantation in Klaten, Central Java, Late 1920S

Photograph from P. de Kat Angelino, *Verslag betreffende eene door den inspecteur bij het Kantoor van Arbeid (...) op de Vorstenlandsche tabaksondernemingen gehouden enquête* (Weltevreden, 1929).

The 1925 Ordinance remained in force without changes for more than twenty years. In the late 1940s, on the eve of transfer of sovereignty to the Indonesian Republic, two parallel developments left the legal status of child workers in Indonesia in a state of some confusion. In 1948, in the heat of the revolution the provisional Republican government formulated a new Labour Act (re-enacted as Act no. 1 of 1951 shortly after the transfer of sovereignty) which included a (total) prohibition on employment of children under fourteen, defining "employment" for this purpose as work performed by a labourer with an industrial relation to an employer. The 1951 Act however included the provision that enactment of specific articles could be postponed; this provision was applied to the child labour clause, which was never subsequently brought into force by the establishment of implementation regulations and procedures. Meanwhile, in 1949 the beleaguered (Netherlands) Indies government had amended its 1925 Ordinance, raising the minimum age to fourteen years (but only, as explained above, applying to factories and enclosed industrial workplaces employing more than ten persons). Since the 1951 Act had no validity in the matter of child employment, most observers agree that, formally speaking, the amended 1925 Ordinance is the regulation that remained in force.[58]

The question is mainly academic however, since not a single case was prosecuted during the ensuing half-century until (and, so far as I know, since) passage of Indonesia's new Labour Law in 1997. Excepting a small minority of élite children, the "prolongation of childhood" which the majority of Indonesia's children experience today through more general and longer schooling, increasing age at marriage and later entry into labour markets, is a post-colonial phenomenon, and has resulted from the rapid expansion of education opportunities rather than from Indonesia's ineffective child labour laws.[59] But that is another story.

58 ILO, *Child Labour in Indonesia;* Bessell, "The Politics of Child Labour in Indonesia".

59 Post-independence developments in Indonesian child labour conditions and policies are discussed in Bessell, "The Politics of Child Labour in Indonesia"; White and Tjandraningsih, *Child Workers in Indonesia*; and White, "Constructing Child Labour".

CHAPTER 24

A History of Child Labor in China*

Joshua H. Howard

Revelations of abusive child labor practices at four Pearl Delta factories manufacturing sportswear for the 2008 Beijing Olympics, followed by an exposé that several hundred children had been abducted from Henan province and sold into forced servitude to work in the brick kilns of Shanxi provoked moral outrage and a massive state crackdown. Some 35,000 police officers were mobilized in Henan alone to free more than five hundred mentally handicapped adults and children who "had been forced to labour for up to eighteen hours a day, beaten and burnt by foremen and imprisoned by guards and savage dogs".[1] Despite the arrest of some 168 people, the case raised anew questions regarding the party-state's ability to resolve glaring contradictions between China's self-styled socialism and its immersion in the global capitalist market, and the widening regional and class disparities resulting from market reforms. For older generations who had experienced or witnessed the misery and brutality of child labor prior to the 1949 revolution, the cases reopened old scars in the national psyche.

To be sure, children had long played an important role in China's economy. Children traditionally participated in agricultural and household work and, by the Tang dynasty (618-907 CE), they assumed apprenticeships outside the home in such crafts as bricklaying or weaving. By the fifteenth century, the commercialization of sericulture in the lower Yangzi region led children to help family members pick mulberry leaves, raise silk worms and work in the silk cottage industries. Yet a consciousness of child labor and its manifestation in language are of much more recent origins, dating to the late nineteenth century when China began to industrialize. The term for child labor, *"tong gong"* seems to have been first coined by West-

* The author would like to express his gratitude to Giancarlo Falco for his careful reading of the manuscript and his useful comments.

1 Young, "Brick Kiln 'Slavery' Exposé".

erners during the 1880s as evident in an 1882 British Consulate's commercial report documenting numerous women and children employed by the Shanghai No.3 British-American Silk Factory. One of, if not the earliest Chinese acknowledgments of and restriction of child labor, appears in regulations prohibiting women and boys under thirteen from any work in the coal pits of the Kaiping colliery founded in 1878. "Although it is permitted to employ thirteen to eighteen year old children, they must be supervised separately [based on their age]."[2]

Recognition of child labor in both foreign and Chinese sources reflected the development of industrial capitalism in the context of semi-colonialism. After 1895 the rapid growth of British and Japanese textile mills in Shanghai and China's other treaty ports opened to the West after the Opium Wars intensified the use of child labor. The legal privileges and tax advantages accorded to foreign enterprises, coupled with their higher capitalization and greater technical and management experience, allowed foreign firms to dominate the textile and tobacco industries, two of the three industries along with match and matchbox production that exploited child labor in mass. One can suggest that Chinese capitalists by the mid 1920s turned somewhat belatedly to large-scale employment of children, so that they could gain a competitive advantage. Child labor reached its peak by the late 1920s, present in both modern large-scale factories, where factory discipline systematically reinforced the exploitation of children, and in the handicraft industries and workshops transitioning to factories where traditional effective ties between apprentices and masters were unraveling and being displaced by labor-capitalist ties.

Child labor at this time became a target of Marxist intellectuals and Christian reformers intent on achieving social justice and strengthening China by exposing its societal evils. The moralistic undertones are conveyed in a mid 1930s description of child labor:

> In rural districts ten and twelve year old boys can be seen coming up out of the mouths of primitive mines, straining at loads of coal attached by rope to their shoulders, providing cheaper labor than animals or machinery. Hundreds of pasty-faced young girls trudge home in the gray dawn of the Shanghai morning after twelve or fourteen hours on the night shift in the cotton mills. Little children, fortunately not so many in recent years, may be seen in the silk filatures, hardly tall enough to reach the basins at which they

2 Sun, *Zhongguo jindai gongyeshi ziliao*, pp. 1232-1233.

> stand dipping the silk cocoons in boiling water, their fingers a horrid sight, the atmosphere in the room so humid and the odor so fetid that fainting is not uncommon.[3]

Just as child labor served critics of capitalism, its gradual abolition and the promotion of childhood development was linked to the rising tide of Chinese nationalism. As one reformer argued, "only by having the growth of sound children can we have a healthy citizenry and only with a healthy citizenry can we have a healthy nation. If we desire to advance our society, a strong and wealthy nation, and a revitalized people, we must protect children's welfare".[4]

As in the experience of Western industrial capitalism, the advent of machinery in China provided an opening to hire children as unskilled and cheap labor. The textile industry, which played the dominant role in most countries industrial revolutions, placed children at center stage. The cotton mills' demand for intensive labor and nimble fingers rather than strength put a premium on child labor. Writing *Capital* during the heyday of child labor, Marx observed that mechanization increased demand for employing "labourers of slight muscular strength, and those whose bodily development is incomplete, but whose limbs are all the more supple. The labor of women and children was, therefore, the first thing sought by capitalists who used machinery." Marx would also explain how machinery diminished the need for labor and thus depressed wages; consequently, "[i]n order that the family may live, four people must now, not only labour, but expend surplus-labour for the capitalist. Thus we see, that machinery, while augmenting the human material that forms the principal object of capital's exploiting power, at the same time raises the degree of exploitation".[5]

The double yoke of capitalism and imperialism heightened the exploitation of children during China's early industrialization. Children from six to fifteen years of age worked the same or even longer working hours than adults, since they were expected to arrive fifteen to twenty minutes early to do preparatory work and then sweep up the workshop after production. The average workday lasted from twelve to fourteen hours, but with night shifts in large-scale plants increasingly common after 1912, the founding of the Republic, twelve hours became the norm until 1946 when ten hours became standard. Most laborers had one day of rest every two weeks. A

3 Wagner, *Labor Legislation in China*, p. 29.
4 Liu, "Xiandai Zhongguo tonggong wenti", p. 10.
5 Marx, *Capital*, pp. 372-373.

1925 survey of the cotton mills in Shanghai, the chief employer of children, found that workers labored in the mills between 300–350 days of the year.[6] The dramatist Xia Yan's 1935 piece of reportage, "Contract Labor," vividly describes the three scourges – noise, dust and humidity – suffered by young girls employed in the cotton mills. "The bellow of motors, the slapping of the belts, the whirr of spindles and the clacking of wheels...every hideous noise in the world seems to have converged in this building." In the blowing and card rooms, girls opened up bales of raw cotton to then loosen and clean the cotton. "Cotton fluff flies about as if some devil were in it, getting into your eyes, nose, mouth, ears and every pore of your body, sticking to your hair and eyebrows." "In textile mills run in the colonialists' own country, the work in the card room and blowing room is usually done by men. But in Shanghai, where they do not have to fear public opinion or state inspection, work too heavy for women is given to these girls who receive less than one third of a man's pay."[7] To no surprise, children disproportionately fell victim to industrial accidents. Of the 374 textile workers treated at the Shanghai Industrial Hospital between its founding in 1919 and 1923, some hundred were children. A quarter of all patients suffered permanent disabilities and two percent died from their injuries.[8]

Children suffered from physical and verbal abuse in both domestic and foreign owned workshops, but the Japanese factories held particular notoriety. In the Qingdao cotton mills managed by Japanese, thirteen to fourteen year olds had to stand at work for thirteen to fourteen hours on the night shifts.

> During the winter, if they dozed off, the Japanese [supervisor] would spray the child's head with a waterspout so that their clothes and flesh became icy cold. The child was not allowed to stop work, let alone cry, and would still be beaten, cursed and fined. In the summer time, they would tie up the child and hang them from a bobbin. After 30 minutes they would let the child loose, give the child another beating and deduct two days of wages. [...] The beating of workers by Japanese was common, and no distinction was made between boys or girls. The slightest disobedience would lead them to use vicious means and beat the child mercilessly.

6 Sun, *Zhongguo gongren yundongshi*, p. 19.

7 Hsia, "Contract Labour and Postscript", pp. 53, 55.

8 'Shanghai gongyun zhi' bianzuan weiyuanhui (ed.), *Shanghai gongyun zhi*, p.123.

In some cases, children were killed in the mills, like the twelve year old in the Qingdao cotton mill whose "brains were dashed".[9] The abuse inflicted by foreign supervisors, whether Japanese or Western (White Russians were favorite hires in British-owned factories), may explain the terrified reaction of children to Mrs. McGilliway, a member of the Child Labor Commission set up in 1923. "She felt certain that most of them were no more than ten years old, and perhaps less. They all struck her as being physically underdeveloped, and almost all were in a wretched state of health, some having running sores on their legs or scabs covering their heads. All the children seemed exhausted; many were terrified when spoken to, and some even ran away."[10]

Although global capitalism did not create child labor in China, it did foster its growth judging from the higher proportion of child labor employed by Western owned textile firms relative to Asian owned mills in Shanghai. Jean Chesneaux's data from 1923-1924 indicates that roughly the same percentage of children labored in foreign and Chinese cotton mills, but that the proportion of girls employed in Western silk filatures, particularly those owned by French and Italians, was more than twice the rate in Chinese firms.

Other sources, however, indicate that the cotton mills shared this disparity in child employment. Gannett found only 5.5 per cent of the workers in the Japanese-owned mills were children under twelve, and in the Chinese mills some 13 per cent. But nearly 18 per cent of all workers toiling in the British mills were children, and in the French and Italian cotton mills 46 per cent of the workforce were children.[11] The lower rate of child labor in Chinese owned firms was linked to the provenance of Chinese capitalists who hailed from the Yangzi delta region and were well connected to local labor networks. Without access to these networks and impeded by language barriers, foreign firms became dependent on labor contractors who recruited children from the more impoverished northern Jiangsu region. Generally speaking, Chinese owned textile plants retained a large proportion of adult males in the workforce until 1927, when they took advantage of changes in production processes and began to shift to a more feminized and younger workforce in the hope of avoiding a reoccurrence of the strike waves that had facilitated the ascension of the Nationalist government.

9 Lu and Liu, "Minguo chunian de tonggong yanjiu", p. 53.

10 Chesneaux, *Chinese Labor Movement*, p. 74.

11 Gannett, *Young China*, p. 19.

Table 24.1. Workers Employed in Shanghai's Foreign and Chinese-Owned Textile Firms (1923-24)

Number	*Ownership*	*Men*	*Women*	*Boys* < *12*	*Girls* < *12*
Cotton mills					
18	China	8,682 (27%)	19,822 (62%)	1,005 (3%)	2,610 (8%)
24	Japan/UK	15,048 (26%)	38,157 (66%)	1,615 (3%)	2,690 (5%)
Silk filatures					
39	China	2,274 (9.5%)	17,895(75%)	105 (0.5%)	3,461 (15%)
6	Italy	203 (3%)	3,160 (49%)	440 (7%)	2,620 (41%)
5	France	219 (4%)	2,650 (48%)	372 (7%)	2,227 (41%)
9	UK	235 (3%)	3,618 (53%)	552 (8%)	2,469 (36%)
7	USA	140 (3%)	3,050 (69%)	–	1,250 (28%)

Source: Jean Chesneaux, *The Chinese Labor Movement, 1919-1927*, p. 74.

Foreign firms were quicker to perceive children as more "manageable" than adult workers. A Japanese cotton mill in Shanghai, for instance,

> employed large numbers of children and women, who were more easily tyrannized than the resistant adult male workers. Thus the factory resorted to a wily scheme—training a group of boys and girls, known as *'yangchenggong,'* and teaching them to be as obedient as slaves. As they grow older, they will replace the adult male workers. The 'troublesome elements' will be fired, making the factory hands entirely women and children, who will be freely abused and exploited without offering any resistance.[12]

Seeking to economize and profit, foreign capital naturally looked to child labor as the cheapest source of labor. In almost all industries, children occupied the lowest tier of the wage scale. According to the Department of Social Affairs, child workers in the Shanghai cotton mills earned from one half to two thirds the wage income received by adult workers. (See table 24.2.) Table 24.3, based on the same government source, demonstrates that

12 "Shanghai Xiaoshadu Riben shachang zhi da bagong", in: Liu Mingkui, *Zhongguo gongren jieji lishi zhuangkuang*, 1, pt. 1, p. 581.

children's wages across industries generally ranged between one third to one half that of adult males and between 50 to 90 per cent of women's wages.

Table 24.2. Average Daily Wage of Shanghai Cotton Mill Workers (1929)

	Number	*Wage (yuan)*
Spinning		
Men	7,558	0.55
Women	27,574	0.45
Children	1,161	0.30
Weaving		
Men	2,558	0.72
Women	7,128	0.54
Children	394	0.35

Source: Zhu Bangxin and Hu Lin'ge, *Shanghai chanye yu Shanghai zhigong*, pp. 54–55.

These wage figures are incomplete, however, since thousands of children were employed as apprentices or contract laborers and received little or no wages for up to three years. The description of contract laborers by the Shanghai Child Labor Commission matches the ILO's recent definition of "unconditional worst forms of child labor," which includes debt bondage and slavery.

> This Commission member has heard that certain contractors obtain young children from the countryside through fraudulent means by giving their parents only 2 yuan per month as pay for their child's labor. After the young child has worked in the factory, the labor contractor can earn a profit of 4 yuan each month per child. The food and lodging of the children are atrocious. They do not receive a cent. Their living situation is no different than that of a slave.[13]

13 Shanghai shehui kexueyuan lishi yanjiusuo bian, *Wusa yundong shiliao*, 2 vols., 1, p. 258.

Table 24.3. Average Daily Wage Rates (Yuan) in Shanghai Industries (1928)

Industry	*Men*	*Women*	*Children*
Cotton spinning	1.04	0.69	0.33
Cotton weaving	0.67	0.53	0.27
Silk reeling	0.44	0.55	0.34
Silk weaving	1.11	0.77	0.40
Glass	1.03	0.32	0.28
Matches	0.74	0.35	0.29
Paint	0.79	0.40	0.40
Paper making	1.14	0.39	0.35
Printing	0.66	0.39	0.20
Machinery	0.73	0.40	0.29
Electric machinery	0.63	0.46	0.26
Canned goods	0.51	0.29	0.12
Condiments	0.74	0.49	0.09
Hardware tools	0.54	0.30	0.18
String	0.32	0.24	0.29
Boxes	0.52	0.40	0.25

Source: Xing Bixin *et al.* (eds), *Di er ci Zhongguo laodong nianjian* (Beiping: Shehui diaochasuo, 1932), pp. 39-42.

Poverty aggravated the use of child labor during China's Republican era (1911-1949). The large majority of first generation workers in the textile industry, for instance, were migrants from the countryside who had been forced off the land. Between 1916-1922 some 70 per cent of workers who joined the Shanghai cotton mills owned by the Rong family, were either tenant farmers or had hired out their labor. After arriving in Shanghai, mothers would find work in the cotton mills and bring one or two of their children to work alongside them.[14] Education might have provided one alternative to laboring in the mills, but public schooling was lacking for the more than forty million children of school age in the early 1930s. "There

14 Shanghai shehui kexueyuan jingji yanjiusuo jingjishi zu bian, *Rongjia qiye shiliao shangce,* 2 vols. 1, pp. 118-121.

are fewer than 1,500 middle schools in the entire country, which means that there is only one middle school for every 300,000 Chinese."[15] Thus child labor became a product of economic survival. Moreover, low wages earned by adults relative to household expenditures forced parents to push their children into employment to earn supplemental income. According to data collected in a 1918-1920 survey of Beijing families holding four to five people, the minimum annual expenditures for food was 132.4 yuan, but the average income for 80 per cent of all workers was only between 66-93 yuan. Even families with both parents and children working had a hard time making ends meet. A 1927 survey of 48 working-class families in Beijing found that over a six-month period, the average monthly family income was 93.45 yuan, 8 yuan less than their average monthly expenditure.[16] Given that almost the entirety of a family's income was spent on food, lodging and clothing, even if schools had been more widespread, parents had no money to invest in their child's education. Parents, too, viewed the factory as a safer haven for the child than if left to roam the streets. For these reasons, workers may have shared the employers' attitude that child employment was an act of charity. "It added to the family income and removed the anxiety of the parents for the safety of their children, who from the parents' point of view were safer and more comfortable in the mills than they would be if left to roam the streets."[17] This perspective contributed to a vicious cycle, since workers did not correlate child labor with depressed adult wages, which in turn encouraged child labor. During the teens and 1920s the following scenario in Shanghai was the norm for urban working class families. Both parents would join a factory workforce or, if only the husband worked in a factory, the wife would be hired out as a maid or servant. Children sought work in factories or collected trash and begged in the streets.

The cultural practices that migrant workers brought with them to the city sustained child labor and rendered workers acquiescent in its practice. Although women as they entered the workforce began to have more say determining when and whom they married, marriage transactions prevailed through the 1930s. Poor first-generation workers from the countryside regarded the purchase of a child bride *(tongyangxi)* for their sons as a good investment to increase their labor force and to perpetuate the family line.

15 Lowe, *Facing Labor Issues in China*, p. 105.

16 Li, *Qingmo Minchu Zhongguo chengshi shehui jieceng yanjiu*, pp. 496-497.

17 Lowe, *Facing Labor Issues in China*, p. 8.

> When the son was about ten years old, the parents would return to their native village, spend 20 to 30 yuan and buy a 7–8 or 13–14 year old daughter from a poor family and bring her back to Shanghai where they would raise her. They would wait until the child bride was 12 or 13 to ask someone's help to introduce her as a child laborer into a cotton mill, where she would learn the job and then stay on as a mill hand. Once the boy and girl were both 17–18 years old they could formally marry.[18]

Similarly, new in-laws would send child brides to work in the silk filatures where they would remain for many years, moving up the ranks from cauldron girl to silk reeler and perhaps foreman.

Quantifying Child Labor

It remains difficult to pinpoint the extent of child labor in China owing to the relatively late development of statistical surveys, widespread only by the 1920s, and the different standards used to tabulate the number of child laborers. Industrial surveys usually underrepresented the extent of child labor by restricting themselves to factories employing more than thirty workers, thereby ignoring the numerous children employed in small-scale factories, sweatshops, home factories, and shops. Some surveys even omitted the category for child labor as the Nationalist government sought to make a good impression on international organizations, such as the ILO. Most surveys of child labor were also limited to a regional and temporal basis because of endemic warfare. The outbreak of the Sino-Japanese War in 1937 and the subsequent formation of Wang Jingwei's collaborationist regime in Nanjing, the relocation of Chiang Kai-shek's Nationalist government to Sichuan, and the development of Communist base areas in northern China, precluded a strong centralized state from addressing child labor on a national scale. Thus, although qualitative sources suggest a decline in the proportion and extent of child labor after 1937, this impression is difficult to confirm given the relative lack of quantitative sources.

As China's industrial and financial capital, Shanghai became the focus of various industrial studies that suggest the proportion and magnitude of child labor. In 1899, some seven thousand children and twenty thousand women formed the majority of Shanghai's total factory workforce of

18 Li, *Qingmo Minchu Zhongguo chengshi shehui jieceng yanjiu*, p. 507.

34,500.[19] Shanghai's early industrialization was geared towards light industry, especially textiles, which employed predominantly women and children. By 1924 the Shanghai Municipal Council's Child Labor Commission found 173,272 children employed by the 275 factories surveyed: 105,921 girls and 44,741 boys between twelve and sixteen years of age; 18,135 girls and 4,475 boys under the age of twelve.[20] Communist critics of the practice claimed that as many as a fourth of Shanghai's light industrial workforce were children between seven to fourteen years of age.[21] Nationwide, the 1930 Ministry of Industry survey of 799,912 workers employed in 28 cities and 9 provinces showed that roughly 7 per cent were children. These figures, however, should be treated as low estimates. The textile industry, for instance, employed 41,794 children or 8.4 per cent of 497,420 workers; the furniture industry employed 2,185 children or 8.1 per cent of 26,970 workers; and the clothing industry employed 2,250 children or 7.6 per cent of 29,374 workers.[22] A survey of 222,000 factory workers in Shanghai and published in 1930 found as much as 21 per cent of the 52,463 silk reelers were children. In Shanghai's machine industries, which relied heavily on apprentices, 24 per cent of the total 7,635 employees were children.[23]

In contrast to the industrial experience of Great Britain, children played a relatively minor role in the mining industries of China. Boys in their early teens worked in China's small native mines, but most large-scale modern collieries reported no child employment. Protective legislation of 1925, which banned employment of males under twelve by mining companies and limited females and males between twelve and seventeen to surface work, contributed to the relative absence of child labor. The practice of foot binding in North China and the abundance of cheap male adult labor also explain the low level of female child employment. Moreover, whereas children in England engaged in mining because their family and the broader community was dependent on mining, Chinese practiced mining as a subsidiary occupation and thus most children opted for agricultural labor.[24]

19 Smith, *Like Cattle and Horses*, p. 18.

20 Li, "Shanghai de tonggong wenti", p. 516.

21 "Zhongguo Gongchan Qingniantuan de guoqu yu xianzai" (Dec.31, 1928) in: Zhongguo Xinminzhu zhuyi Qingniantuan Zhongyang Weiyuanhui Bangongting ed., *Zhongguo qingnian yundong lishi ziliao* IV, p. 503.

22 Wagner, *Labor Legislation in China*, p. 7.

23 Stuart and Fang, "A Statistical Study of Labor and Industry", p. 1099.

24 Wright, *Coal Mining in China*, p. 162.

Regional Distribution of Child Labor

More children were employed in southern provinces, such as Guangdong, Jiangsu and Zhejiang, where light industries were dominant. Women and girls were concentrated in silk reeling and weaving, cotton spinning and weaving, embroidery, hosiery, knitting, pottery, and furniture making.[25] One important exception to this regional distribution was the northern seaport city of Tianjin, where numerous boy laborers wove silk and cotton, spun cotton and wove carpets. Up to a fifth of the workforce in Tianjin industries were children, more than double the rate in Shanghai.[26] Unlike Shanghai industrialists, who consciously replaced male with allegedly more docile female employees in the wake of the nationalist class-inflected labor movement of the mid 1920s, Tianjin textile owners continued to employ boys and adult males until the Japanese occupation of the late 1930s. Women in North China were more constrained to the home so most rural migrants to Tianjin were male, further skewing the city's population imbalance.

A division of labor based on sex largely shaped the basic types of child labor. Boys occupied most apprentices and resided in the shops, small workshops, laundries, or factories where they learned their trade or skill. Girls either lived at home and worked with their mothers in home industries, were sold and employed as domestic workers, slave girls *(yatou),* and sex workers, or accompanied their mothers or went alone to do simple tasks as piece workers or factory hands. The contracting out of jobs to hundreds of thousands of women and their children developed on the periphery of China's treaty port cities where foreign capital and export firms were concentrated. Production of embroidery, lace work, hair nets and match boxes depended on contractors, who distributed materials to farm houses and then paid extremely low wages by the piece. Mother and child, for instance, made two thousand match boxes per day during the non-farming season, earning enough to pay for the workers' food. By the turn of the century, women and girls also sought employment in workshops as casual piece workers, filling match boxes, winding yarn, sewing soldiers' uniforms, and so forth.[27]

Women employed in manufacturing plants often preferred their children's presence to leaving them home alone, thus children entered the fac-

25 "Child and Woman Labor in China, 1930" in *Nankai weekly statistical service* Vol. 4, No. 9 (March 2, 1931), pp. 49-54.

26 Stuart and Fang, "A Statistical Study of Labor and Industry", p. 1101.

27 Orchard, "Man-power in China", pp. 571-572.

tories as babies and began assisting their mothers when they reached the age of five. Writing in *The Nation* in 1927, Lewis Gannett noted conditions during the night shifts resembling makeshift dormitories.

> Walking through these dimly lit mill-rooms one sees baskets containing children, sleeping or awake, between the whirring, clacking machines. Sometimes a tot of two or three sits cheerfully playing with cotton waste in the aisles through which the foreman guides the visitor. Girls a little older help their mothers tend the rows of spindles, and the deftness of five-year-old fingers is amazing.[28]

Conditions in Shanghai's silk filatures were much the same.

> Here are mothers working with nursing babies lying on the floor beside them or strapped to their backs. The children learn to work as soon as they are able to walk. Here they toil in the hot steam with their hands deftly manipulating the cocoons in the boiling hot water. The employers say the agile hands of little children are best adapted to this rapid work.[29]

Both workers and employers viewed the presence of young children in the factory as an opportunity for informal on-the-job training. As one former mill hand recalled: "When I was ten years old, the workshop buildings were being erected. I often went with people to the compound in order to play there, and by playing around I just learned [the job]. At the age of thirteen I entered the factory to work in the spinning room."[30] Interviews with two hundred former mill hands indicate that approximately two-thirds entered the workforce as a child under the age of thirteen.[31] Children learned a variety of tasks. At the age of five, children wound yarn, pasted or filled match boxes. In the cotton mills, most children worked in spinning departments, where ten year olds helped with doffing and spinning. Hand reeling rooms in modern cotton mills employed children almost exclusively, to the extent that they "have more the appearance of over crowded elementary school rooms than of factories".[32] In the silk filatures, children as young as six years of age stood for five to six hours at a stretch over basins

28 Gannett, *Young China*, p. 19.
29 Finch, "Battle against Child Labor in China", p. 761.
30 Köll, *From Cotton Mill to Business Empire*, p. 113.
31 Mu Xuan and Xuexi Yan, *Dasheng shachang gongren shenghuo de diaocha*, p. 183.
32 Orchard, "Man-power in China", p. 577.

of near boiling water, where they beat and brushed cocoons to free the silk filament for reeling. As one factory inspector described a Shanghai filature: "Tiny children stood for an eleven-hour day, soaked to the skin in a steamy atmosphere, their fingers blanched to the knuckles and their bodies swaying from one tired foot to the other, kept at their task by a stern overseer who did not hesitate to beat those whose attention wandered."[33]

Conditions for children employed in the cigarette and tobacco factories were generally better than the textile industries with shorter work hours (eight to ten hours per day) and less frequent night work. By the mid 1930s in Shanghai this industry employed over eleven thousand women and close to eight hundred children.[34] Despite somewhat better conditions of work, the experience could be just as traumatic if one was abused by foremen as revealed by the oral history of a woman who began working for the Nanyang Brothers Tobacco Company in Shanghai when only eight years old.

> At the time my hand was not big enough to divide the operation into two stages and place five cigarettes at a time into the copper boxes. On my third day at work, one of the foremen, Ah Hsin, came over to watch me quite a few times. I was so scared that I made the mistake of putting only nine cigarettes in one of the 50 foil-wrappings. Since at that time we were all new at our work, what we had done would have to be checked by the foremen before we could take it to the accounts section to receive our wages. (At the time the South Seas Tobacco Company was paying out cash for wages, and the pay for doing 50 packets was 2 *tongban*.) The sharp eyes of the foremen scrutinized every one of the packets that I had done, and when she discovered that there were only 9 cigarettes in one of the packets, she pulled at my pigtail and demanded that I should go with her to the accounts section. I was trembling, speechless; and I was especially afraid of going to the accounts section. I begged her not to take me there, but she kept pulling at my pigtail and insisted that I had to go. The scene at that moment was like that of a policeman dragging a rickshaw-man off to the police station because the rickshaw-man had gone the wrong way. Then I burst into tears and I was dragged to the accounts section, where I was ordered to pay a cash penalty of 200 *wen*. On that day, I had done only 80 *wen's* worth of work, and the matter was only settled after I had gone home during the lunch period and brought back 12 *tongban*. On returning home that evening, I went into a fever, and I

33 Cited in Perry, *Shanghai on Strike*, p. 170.

34 Wang, *Travail industriel des femmes et des enfants en Chine*, p. 66.

> remained in bed with a coma for half a month. I can never forget that particular sickness [...].[35]

Contract Labor System

Adolescent girls were typically employed in the silk filatures and cotton mills after being bought and sold through the contract labor system, a transaction referred to as "plucking mulberry leaves." According to one observer:

> Often the children are brought in from the country by a contractor, who follows disaster like vultures and pays starving parents about a dollar a month for a contract which amounts to slavery; the girls live for years in his compound, eating his food, or in the factories, eating factory rice, working sometimes fifteen or sixteen hours a day, and often sleeping on the floor beneath their machines.[36]

In its broad contours the description is accurate. Japanese managers first adopted this recruiting system to avoid linguistic barriers and the challenges of recruiting workers directly although the practice quickly became widespread. By the late 1920s, members of Shanghai's criminal underworld, especially the notorious Green Gang, had cornered the cotton mill labor market with the encouragement of mill owners seeking to render the workforce more pliant after the heated labor battles of the mid 1920s. Agents recruited girls from impoverished rural families to the north of the Yangzi River, paying in allotments ten to thirty dollars to the parents in return for at least three years of their child's labor. Contractors would often hire out the child to cotton mill foremen who would guarantee a post in the cotton mill and take twenty to thirty per cent of the child's wages. The remainder would go to the contractor. Contract workers shared the same arduous twelve-hour shifts as other mill hands, but their isolation and total dependence on the contractor for room and board made them vulnerable to physical and sexual abuse.[37] Xia Yan describes the contract girls as a "'tinned labour force' whom the capitalists sealed off tightly from any

35 Andors, *Workers and Workplaces*, pp. 177-178.

36 Gannett, *Young China*, p. 19.

37 See "Contract Child Labor" in *The China Critic,* vol. 5, no. 20 (May 19, 1931), p. 1, 1, and Honig, *Sisters and Strangers*, pp. 94-131.

contact with the outer air," as the loft-houses where the girls slept were guarded by sentries and thugs hired by the labor contractors.[38] Until the outbreak of the Anti-Japanese War in 1937, the contract labor system flourished in Shanghai. The war's ravages on society, which included the selling of orphans, perpetuated the contract labor system. Although the contract labor system persisted until 1949, with a growth in the number of state-owned mills, managers in Shanghai and throughout China increasingly turned to mill agents to recruit teenage girls and adopted training programs to wield direct control over the workforce. Under this system, fourteen to eighteen year old girls were tested for height, literacy and dexterity before assuming an apprenticeship of up to two years. The girls would then be hired as a full time wage-earning worker.

Apprenticeships

Apprenticeships had traditionally been the preserve of boys and male adolescents, functioning to disseminate trade education and provide poor children a livelihood. Of all industrial sectors, the machinists trade in Shanghai employed the greatest proportion of apprentices, but most children hired were at the cut-off age of fifteen or sixteen. Facing less stringent demands on physical endurance and fewer age restrictions (most machine shops stipulated that apprentices be between fifteen to twenty years old), children opted to work in provision shops, the handicraft sector and partially mechanized industries, such as tailoring, carpet making, dye-works, printing, leather manufacturing, and soap making. Under contract for periods of three years or more, the apprentice was taught a skill that, in theory, would guarantee employment in the particular trade. Masters would also provide apprentices a nominal payment to cover room and board. Conditions were onerous with working hours lasting up to fourteen hours per day and restricted mobility. One could leave the workshop only in the event of a death or marriage in the family. Apprentices were frequently called upon to render services to the master's family in addition to their duties in the shop.

By the 1920s, the customary guild apprenticeship system designed to protect entrance to a craft had devolved into a disguised form of cheap child labor. The traditional saying, "a full three years [of service], one out

38 Hsia, "Contract Labour and Postscript", p. 61.

and one in," reflecting the restrictions habitually placed on the number of apprentices accepted, no longer applied.[39] Employers continued to exploit apprentices in terms of long contracts and abysmal work conditions, but no longer guaranteed future employment after the completion of the contract. In Tianjin and Beijing, the number of apprentices working as handloom weavers, hosiery knitters, glass makers, mat weavers and carpet makers far exceeded that of regular workers, making it difficult to receive the necessary training to become a journeyman.[40] Observers of the Beijing carpet factories concluded that this form of apprenticeship "does not educate them, it fails to give them proper moral standards, it does not give them a trade which they can ply, nor does it make them in any way independent. It is a 'blind alley' job in every way. At present it can certainly be called nothing less than indentured child labor".[41]

Starting in the 1930s, the use of apprentices in modern capitalist enterprises declined. The proportion of apprentices working in Shanghai's machinery industry, for instance, was cut in half from the estimated seventy to eighty per cent prior to 1927. Economic downturns and war caused owners to opt for hiring temporary workers.[42] Moreover, the development of capitalist enterprises, which emphasized a division of labor and skills that required less time to acquire, rendered obsolete the traditional master-apprentice relationship based on affective ties. Consequently, managers replaced such relationships with more impersonal training classes where they could exercise direct control over the labor force. Nonetheless, as the following table indicates, apprentices continued to play an important role in industries transitioning from workshop to factory, as well as handicraft industries and the commercial sector.

By the early 1940s, China employed an estimated twenty to thirty million apprentices. "In the interior cities, almost every third person you meet on the street is an apprentice, or some one who has gone through the system."[43] Although over nineteen million children were enrolled in schools during 1942 according to the Ministry of Education, the remaining eighty million youth either looked to farming or employment in com-

39 'Shanghai gongyun zhi' bianzuan weiyuanhui, *Shanghai gongyun zhi*, p. 108.

40 Chesneaux, *Chinese Labor Movement*, pp. 54-55.

41 Lowe, *Facing Labor Issues in China*, p. 25.

42 For the apprentice system in the machinist trade, see Zhongguo kexueyuan jingji yanjiusuo, Zhongyang gongshang xingzheng guanliju jiqi gongye shiliaozu, eds., *Shanghai minzu jiqi gongye* 2 vols (Beijing: Zhonghua shuju, 1966), II, pp. 807-828.

43 Liao, "Apprentices in Chengtu".

merce, handicrafts or industry. Apprenticeships continued to offer the hope of technical training given the continued inadequacy of the education system, particularly for rural-based children.

Table 24.4. Proportion of Apprentices Employed in Shanghai (1930s)

Industry or commercial sector	*Percentage of apprentices in workforce*
Handicrafts	42
Daily goods	14
Furniture	42
Smeltery	57
Metal works	54
Textiles	30
Timber	40
Papermaking	39
Imitation leather	46
Chemical	12
Machinery	40-50
Cloth stores	20
Hardware stores	30-40

Source: Shanghai gongyun zhi bianzuan weiyuanhui, ed., *Shanghai gongyun zhi* (Shanghai: Shanghai shehui kexueyuan chubanshe, 1997), p. 109.

Protective legislation

Impetus for legislation derived from the introduction of the modern factory system as well as the intensification of the older industrial regime. Foreign influence also played an important role in the movement to eliminate child labor. A proposal offering legal protection to children under the age of fifteen in the form of a mandated eight hour work day was brought to the attention of Chinese authorities in 1919 at the International Labor Conference in Washington.[44] Under pressure from the International Labor Organization and the student movement decrying a brutal crackdown on railroad strikers, the Peking government followed suit in 1923 with China's

44 "Labor Conditions and Labor Regulations", p. 4.

first legislation. A provisional Factory Law called for prohibiting employment of girls under twelve and boys under ten and enacted an eight hour day for adolescent workers (boys under seventeen, girls under eighteen) in all factories with at least one hundred employees. But, the law remained a dead letter without provisions for enforcement.

In Shanghai, recognition that child labor was a problem came to the fore in May 1922 during a National Christian Conference, which adopted a program inspired by the 1919 Washington Conference. At the prodding of the YWCA and the Federation of Women's Boards of Foreign Missions, the Municipal Council of the International Settlement of Shanghai established a Child Labor Commission, whose 1924 report recommended prohibiting the employment of children under ten years of age, rising to twelve years within four years from the implementation of such regulations. The Commission also recommended that the Council seek to prohibit children under fourteen years of age from working longer than twelve hours in any 24 hour period and to have one hour of compulsory rest during these twelve hours. Children under fourteen years of age should have 24 hours of continuous rest at least every fourteen days. The Council should seek power to prohibit employment of children under fourteen years of age in hazardous working conditions and to close any dangerous or hazardous premises where such children are employed until they are made to do so. The Commission also recommended that punishments for violators consist of fines as well as imprisonment.[45] With the exception of the last two clauses, the recommendations were moderate in substance. Nevertheless, when the Municipal Council attempted to submit a bylaw regulating child labor at a meeting of ratepayers of the International Settlement for their vote, the bylaw failed to generate a sufficient quorum to pass the legislation.[46] Soon after, mass labor and student demonstrations known as the May 30th movement erupted across the nation. Subsequent efforts by the Shanghai Municipal Council to pass regulations on Chinese children, however well intentioned, were perceived as an attempt to extend foreign power and jurisdiction over Chinese lives, and were duly rejected.

Despite these first abortive attempts, the development of trade unions and the labor movement pushed for industrial legislation to curb child labor. Children often actively participated in these labor struggles. The Chinese Communist Youth League reported that,

45 Wagner, *Labor Legislation in China*, p. 85.
46 Chesneaux, *Chinese Labor Movement*, p. 229.

> Guangdong, Shanghai and Zhenjiang all had child workers or students take the initiative in the struggle. During September [1928], several thousand child workers and women workers at the Zhenlun and Huaishen silk filatures of Zhenjiang demanded improvement in their treatment and went on strike. Among the 60,000 workers in Shanghai who struck in March and June, the majority were children and youth.[47]

Appealing to class and national unity, the Guomindang at its Second National Congress in 1926 responded to the labor movement by calling for the prohibition of child labor for children under the age of fourteen, the regulation of the apprentice system, and the abolition of the contract-labor system.[48] Once in power, the Nationalist government promulgated the 1929 Factory Law (revised in 1932), the first industrial legislation with national scope. The law prohibited children under the age of fourteen to be employed in any factory, although children between the ages of twelve to fourteen who were already employed before the Law was promulgated could have the age limit extended. In a departure from previous legislation, the Factory Law redefined child laborers to those between fourteen and sixteen years of age and permitted them to be employed only for light work. Night work would be abolished for children and the work day limited to eight hours. The Factory Law also regulated apprenticeships, mandating that no more than a third of the factory's regular workforce be apprentices, restricted apprenticeships to those thirteen and older, restricted the work day to eight hours, and stipulated that apprentices be supplied with room, board and medical care, and an allowance for incidentals.[49]

These laws were more easily promulgated than enforced. The Nationalist government postponed key provisions, for instance, waiting until 1936 to enforce the prohibition of night work for women and children. The absence of a factory inspection system, and birth or health certificates needed to register the ages of children, made enforcement all the more difficult. Employers through the 1940s continued to resort to height measurements rather than use age as criteria for employment. Moreover, the law did not apply to factories with fewer than thirty employees, thus providing no protective measures where it was most needed. Finally, in contrast to protective legislation of most other countries during their early stages of industrialization, the Factory Law neglected to address the issue

47 Lu and Liu, "Minguo chunian de tonggong yanjiu", p. 54.
48 Lowe, *Facing Labor Issues in China,* p. 75.
49 See original Factory Law in Wagner, *Labor Legislation in China,* pp. 268-269.

of compulsory schooling, which would have removed children from the labor force.

Both employers and workers voiced opposition to the Factory Law. Some employers argued that they would be forced to dismiss thousands of workers in order to enforce the law. Others maintained that the legislation unfairly targeted Chinese businesses because extraterritoriality meant the regulations would not be enforced among foreign concerns.[50] If schooling was not mandatory, free or widespread, it was inevitable that workers would bemoan the loss of their children's jobs and income. In turn, the Communist Youth League criticized the Nationalist government for failing to provide tuition-free nurseries and elementary schools or to ensure adequate wages so that parents would no longer have to depend on their children's income.[51]

The Chinese Communist Party had pressed for labor legislation protecting children since 1922, but not until 1930 after it had established the Jiangxi Soviet, did it promulgate a labor code. Like the Nationalist Factory Law, the Communist labor law prohibited the employment of children under the age of fourteen. Night work, too, was abolished for all workers under the age of eighteen. In other respects, the Communist law proved more progressive with regard to adolescents between sixteen and eighteen year of age. Their working day, for instance, would not exceed six hours. For children between fourteen and sixteen, who would only be allowed to work if labor inspection bodies had granted permission, the working day would not exceed four hours. Finally, the old system of apprenticeship and of "training workers" was to be strictly prohibited.[52] The scarcity of industry in the Communist's rural and remote base areas and their frequent mobility meant that the Party had little chance to implement the laws.

Protective legislation promulgated by both political parties marked an important shift in how leaders conceived of child labor. The very definition of the child became more expansive by raising the benchmark from twelve to sixteen years of age. Increased awareness of the child coincided with Nationalist government efforts to popularize education, thus providing an alternative to child labor. By the early 1940s, close to twenty million chil-

50 Lowe, *Facing Labor Issues*, pp. 90–96.

51 "Zhongguo de tonggong wenti" (Jan. 30, 1929) in: Zhongguo xinminzhu zhuyi qingniantuan and Zhongyang weiyuanhui bangongting, eds., *Zhongguo qingnian yundong lishi ziliao 1929*, 1958), v, p. 48.

52 *Fundamental Laws of the Chinese Soviet Republic with an introduction by Bela Kun* (London, 1934), pp. 54–58.

dren were enrolled in schools throughout the country. The relative paucity of documentation decrying child labor as a moral evil during the war years of 1937-1949 suggest that employment of children was on the decline compared to its frequency during the 1920s. *Shanghai chanye yu Shanghai zhigong*, the most comprehensive and critical analysis of each industrial sector's working conditions and labor movement, cites 1937 statistics revealing that only 15 per cent of the 40,000 workers in the silk industry were between the ages of twelve and eighteen and "very few" were under eleven to twelve years of age.[53] Although the proportion of child labor to the total factory workforce in Nationalist wartime China remained steady at about eight per cent, the roughly 20,000 children employed (according to a 1943 Ministry of Economics survey) mark a sharp reduction from fifteen years earlier.[54] Similar trends are apparent in Shanghai's postwar industrial surveys. Children comprised 3.6 per cent of the roughly 150,000 workers surveyed in 1946, and a 1948 survey of various industries found only 418 children employed in the cotton mills.[55] Only Tianjin witnessed a resurgence of child labor during the war. By 1946 close to 100,000 children were employed, as employers during the Japanese Occupation looked to children as an abundant and docile labor supply.[56]

Child labor on the wane

The reduced demand for child labor was partly a consequence of the growing importance of the state-owned heavy industrial sector, which increased demand for skilled male labor and forced managers to adhere more closely to industrial legislation. Moreover, modern factories' demand for skilled labor stemming from technological advances, such as the introduction of central boiler systems in silk filatures, may have rendered child labor uneconomical and contributed to its decline during the 1930s. Production processes in the textile industry were also reorganized, thereby increasing the intensity of work throughout the 1940s. At the Yufeng cotton mill, the largest textile mill in wartime Nationalist China, the work load per individual worker increased two to three times between 1939 and 1947. Regulations in 1939 stipulated that workers would oversee 64 spindles on eight wooden rods. By 1947, intensity had increased to handling 36 rods and 288 spindles. At the same time, the speed of the rollers on the spinners doubled

53 Zhu Bangxin and Lin-ge Hu, *Shanghai chanye yu Shanghai zhigong* p. 187.
54 Epstein, *Notes on Labor Problems in Nationalist China*, p. 37.
55 Liu and Tang, *Zhongguo jindai gongren jieji he gongren yundong*, pp. 47, 61.
56 *Ibid.*, p. 51; Hershatter, *Workers of Tianjin*, p. 53.

from 80 to 160 rotations per minute with a portion of machines reaching up to 210 rotations per minute.[57] This increase in the intensity of work put a premium on youth. Approximately seventy per cent of cotton mill workers in the Nationalist wartime capital of Chongqing were girls and young women, most between the ages of fourteen and eighteen.[58]

A shift in public attitudes spearheaded by intellectuals may have also accelerated the decline in the use of child labor. The early 1920s witnessed the appearance of children movies in which children, typically presented as orphans or street urchins, serving as a metaphor for China's social ills. More concerned with the need to stabilize the family than about child labor per se, Zheng Zhengqiu's 1926 film, "Yi ge xiao gongren" [A child laborer] sought to inculcate proper values and reform society. Zheng posited that society could only be mended with a strong family. "Only children can save the family; only the family can save the group, which is the salvation for the country and society."[59] By the early 1930s, reformist visions had become radicalized. Inspired by proletarian artists and proponents of the Socialist Realism movement, such as Maxim Gorky and Aleksandr Davidenko, Chinese revolutionaries created film, literature and music depicting child labor as a social problem. Shen Xiling's 1933 film, "Nuxing de nahan" [The Outcry of the Women], for instance, addressed the plight of contract laborers although government censorship blunted its social criticism. In the field of music, Nie Er, whose song, "March of the Volunteers" was later chosen as the Chinese national anthem, composed three songs during the early 1930s which addressed child labor in its broadest dimensions: "Xiao gongren" [Little worker], "Maibao zhi sheng" [Voice of the newsboy], and "Maibaoge" [Song of the Newspaper Seller]. The latter song would become one of the most popular children songs of the twentieth century with its lively rhythm and facile melody. Nie captures the newspaper girl's innocence and bright optimism, but also injects a social commentary to galvanize public sympathy for the girl's struggle.

La, la, la! La, la, la!
I am a young hawker of newspapers,
Enduring the hunger, enduring the cold I run through the streets,

57 Chongqing di yi mianfangzhi chang gongyu shi bian xie zu (eds), *Chongqing Yufeng shachang gongyunshi yanjiu ziliao huibian*, p. 21.

58 Zhonghua quanguo zonggonghui ziliaoshi fanyin (ed.), "Zhanhou Yu shi fangzhi gongren yu gongren yundong", p. 3.

59 Zhang, *Zhongguo shaonian ertong dianying shilun*, p. 22.

Not eating my full, not sleeping well,
Who can I relate my bitter life?
There will come a day when the light dawns.

Despite progressive laws on paper, a weakened central government embattled in the Anti-Japanese War from 1937–1945 and then a civil war against the Communists thwarted enforcement of protective legislation across the country. Moreover, the public outcry that had contributed to these laws dissipated during the War of Resistance against Japan. The issue of child labor became subsumed under a broader patriotic discourse that muted public criticism of child labor as a social ill while encouraging children to work as a form of participation in China's resistance to foreign invasion. Rather than offer a social commentary or evoke sympathy for the tribulations of children, children songs were now composed to mobilize the people on a patriotic footing against the Japanese invasion. Lu Luo's "Ertong xianfeng" [Children vanguard], for instance, presents children as heroes saving the nation and building a new society. Children's work has assumed a new meaning outside the context of factory labor. "We are modern child workers, wanting to construct a new society and new world; clench your fist, raise your head, bravely advance, defy death and never retreat. Struggle for our people's survival, liberate the people from their fetters, little friends unite and struggle!"[60]

In trying to make ends meet in a war torn country with an economy in shambles, workers unavoidably sought employment rather than social justice and the protection of children. This sentiment is illustrated by a 1949 case at the Nationalist government owned Shanghai No.2 Cotton mill involving former apprentices *(yangchenggong)* who opposed management plans to hire thirteen to fourteen year old girls to replace them. In an effort to block the move, the former apprentices (now in their 30s) demanded that no apprentice be hired unless the former apprentices were retained; that recruitment of *yangchenggong* be limited to Shanghai locals, that is, the children of the former *yangchenggong*; and that *yangchenggong* should be given a wage increase.[61] One can hardly fault the former apprentices for their inclination to protect their own immediate interests, but their lack of opposition to child labor – a reflection of their precarious economic sta-

60 Originally from *Shenghuo zhishi,* Vol. 2 no. 12 republished in *Dajia chang* vol 1 (Beijing: Shidai chubanshe, n.d.).

61 Zhonggong Shanghai shiwei dangshi yanjiushi, Shanghaishi zonggonghui bian (eds), *Shanghai di er mian fangzhichang gongren yundongshi,* pp. 129–130.

tus – prolonged its practice. Not until after the 1949 Revolution when a reunified China under Communist control began to address the structural reasons underlying child labor and popularized education in both rural and urban areas, did the numbers of child laborers significantly recede.

CHAPTER 25

The Globalization of Child Labor in Colonial Zimbabwe

Beverly Grier

In the last decades of the nineteenth century, as child labor was beginning to wane in most sectors of the economies of Western Europe and North America, it was about to gain momentum in the newly colonized territories of sub-Saharan Africa. The cheap raw materials that would be exported from the colonies to metropolitan countries and other global markets would be produced with considerable amounts of child labor. However, to date, very little research has been done on child labor in colonial African economies, to the detriment of a fuller understanding of a range of issues, including: how raw materials were produced so cheaply for European and North American industries and consumers during a period of intense competition between established and emerging industrial powers; the nature of the transformations African societies underwent in order to produce raw materials for global markets; and, the role colonial states played assisting local and metropolitan capitalists to gain access to children's labor for use in the export sector.[1] The purpose of this chapter is to examine the use of children's labor in the economy of one such African colony – Zimbabwe (Southern Rhodesia) – where *picaninnies* were an integral part of the labor force that produced raw materials for export to global markets. The state played a critical role in making children's labor available to European or settler capital in the agricultural and mining sectors and in disciplining child workers while they were away from home and on the job. Though child wage labor was widely accepted within official, settler, missionary,

1 The literature is small but growing. See for e.g. Grier, *Invisible Hands*; Grier, "Child Labor in Africa"; Grier, "Pawns, Porters, and Petty Traders"; Anti-Slavery Society, *Child Labour in South Africa*; Beinart, "Transkeian Migrant Workers and Youth Labor"; Chirwa, "Child and Youth Labour on the Nyasaland Plantations"; Kayongo-Male and Walji, *Children at Work in Kenya*; Neves, "Economy, Society and Labour Migration in Central Mozambique".

and even African communities in the colony, it was not without conflict or controversy in some segments of the local and metropolitan societies. The debates, which came to a head in the 1920s, with the passage of the Native Juveniles Employment Act of 1926, underscored just how critical child labor was to colonial Zimbabwe's linkages to the global economy.

Child Labor in Peasant and Settler Colonial Africa: An Overview

Before looking at the specific case of colonial Zimbabwe, it is important to point out that the forms child labor took in colonial Africa varied greatly, depending in large part upon the presence or absence of European settlers. In colonies such as the Gold Coast (Ghana), Nigeria, Senegal, Cote d'Ivoire, and Uganda, where the production of cocoa, coffee, cotton, groundnuts, and other raw materials for export was based on African peasant holdings, child labor took the form primarily of family-based labor, though in West Africa there was a considerable amount of non-kin servile child labor in the form of "pawns" (debt servants).[2] In the gold-, diamond-, coal-, and tin-mining industries and in the urban formal and informal sectors of peasant-dominated colonial Africa, some children worked for wages in cash or in kind. However, family-based labor, rather than wage labor, was the predominant form of child labor in these colonies. By contrast, in colonies such as Zimbabwe, Kenya, Nyasaland (Malawi), Namibia, and South Africa – where large numbers of Europeans settled and dominated the local economy and where the penetration of capitalist relations of production was broad and deep – substantial numbers of children worked as wage laborers on settler- and corporate-owned farms and estates and in the mining economy, producing tea, sugar, sisal, tobacco, wine, wheat, gold, diamonds, coal, and copper for export to metropolitan and other global markets. Very often, they worked hundreds of miles away from home. Large numbers also produced for the export sector as part of family units on labor tenant (or squatter) farms. On these farms, African male family heads signed contracts with landowners, agreeing to make the labor of their families (wives and unmarried children) available in exchange for access to some cultivation and grazing land. Finally, in settler Africa, many children continued to work as part of family units on peasant holdings in the reserves. In most settle-dominated colonies, peasant families on the

2 On pawns or debt servitude, typically involving children and women, see Grier, "Pawns, Porters, and Petty Traders"; Falola and Lovejoy, *Pawnship in Africa*.

reserves responded to new market opportunities for foodstuffs in the early days of colonial rule (or, in the case of South Africa, in response to the discovery of diamonds and gold in the last quarter of the nineteenth century), only to be deliberately "squeezed" out of the market by land, agricultural, and labor laws and policies that favored settler producers over peasants.[3] In large numbers, members of these families, beginning with men and boys, found themselves fleeing rural poverty and landlessness to search for wage labor in the settler- and corporate-controlled agricultural and mining sectors.

South Africa stands out as a settler colony because of the early date of its colonization and incorporation into the global economy (1652). However, in many ways it became the template for the settler colonies that followed during the age of European imperialism in the late nineteenth century. From the 1650s to the 1830s, Afrikaner (Dutch) settlers drew upon two sources of child labor to produce wheat, wine, meat, vegetables, and other goods to provision Dutch and other European trade ships rounding the Cape of Good Hope and for sale in Europe itself. The first source was slave labor imported from the Dutch East Indies and elsewhere in Africa. Slave children were also "produced" locally, from coerced sexual relationships between Dutch masters and imported enslaved women. The second source was African children who had been "orphaned" by Afrikaner raids on neighboring African groups and then "apprenticed" and sold to farmers and other settler employers at the Cape.[4] Over the centuries, tens of thousands of child workers from both sources were in great demand and formed an important factor in the domestic and export economies of the Cape Colony. As Afrikaner settlers moved deeper into the interior of present-day South Africa in the nineteenth centuries (to escape the British who took control of the Cape in 1806), they took over more African land, capturing and apprenticing additional children. They also enclosed defeated indigenous peoples as labor tenants onto their newly-claimed farms, a pattern that would be repeated by British settlers in Zimbabwe and Kenya in the 1890s and 1900s. After the discovery of diamonds and gold in South Africa

3 On the process of "squeezing out" the African peasantry, see Palmer, *Land and Racial Domination in Rhodesia*, pp. 80-103. See also Palmer and Parsons, *The Roots of Rural Poverty in Central and Southern Africa*; Berman and Lonsdale, *Unhappy Valley*, 1.

4 For an overview of child slavery in South Africa, see Anti-Slavery Society, *Child Labour in South Africa*. For detailed studies of child slavery, child captivity, and apprenticeship (known as *Inboekstelsel,* in Afrikaans), see Eldredge and Morton, *Slavery in South Africa*.

in 1860s and 1880, respectively, the British conquest of African groups that had remained independent of Afrikaner control, the confiscation of their land, and their removal to segregated and increasingly overcrowded reserves generated a cheap migrant labor force, consisting of both children and adults, for wage work in capitalist farming and mining, domestic service and commerce. This pattern of conquest, land confiscation, and displacement of Africans into overcrowded reserves was also replicated by settlers in Zimbabwe and Kenya, beginning in the 1890s, with the same results for children's labor.

The distinct economic structures and social relationships of peasant- and settler-dominated colonial Africa had a number of critical implications for children's labor. First, the loss of land to settlers and the removal of Africans to reserves set in motion a process of land shortage, proletarianization for many, and rural impoverishment for most. This led, in turn, to generalized rural flight, first of males (young and old) and then of females, in search of wage labor. A process such as this never got underway in peasant-dominated Africa where the land remained in African hands and children did not enter the migrant wage labor force in large numbers. Second, because of settlers' needs for abundant and cheap labor to meet metropolitan demands for cheap commodities, the state in these colonies was intimately involved in helping settlers to gain access to cheap male labor, including child labor. In the early years, before land shortages and rural poverty began to expel large numbers of Africans from the reserves, the state used extra-economic means, such as forced labor and taxation, to push men and boys out. Moreover, the state in settler colonies rigidly controlled the movements of African men, male youths, and boys once they left the reserves to work. Laws requiring migrants to carry passes and sign labor contracts were backed by penal sanctions for violators, particularly deserters. By contrast, in peasant Africa, the demand for labor was met largely by peasants' families.[5] Africans were not required to carry passes and labor contracts were the exception. Third, education for African children was more readily available in peasant Africa than in settler Africa, as educated Africans were needed to fill the lower ranks of white collar jobs in the state and private sectors. The missionary presence was larger, there

5 This not to minimize the considerable numbers of male migrants (mostly adults, but also women and children) from the French colonies in the dry and resource-poor Sahel who, through share-cropping and other arrangements, formed a considerable proportion of the labor force growing cocoa and other crops in Cote d'Ivoire, Ghana, and Nigeria.

were more government schools, and parents could pay school fees using their cash crop earnings. By contrast, in settler Africa, education policy revolved around the needs of the settler community: schooling for African children threatened settler access to child labor and jeopardized continuing settler domination of skilled and white-collar jobs.

Producing for Global Markets: Child Labor in Mining, Agriculture and Related Sectors

Picanannies, as settlers and officials called prepubescent and pubescent African children, were employed in every sector of colonial Zimbabwe's economy, growing tobacco, tea, cotton, maize, and other crops on settler farms and corporate estates, mining asbestos, mica, gold, coal, and other minerals on small and large mines, and doing domestic work in the mining compounds and in settler homes.[6] "The younger a boy leaves home the better labourer he becomes", wrote the Charter District Native Commissioner (NC) in 1904, reflecting the widely held European view that early wage work taught African children discipline and the "love of labor" which would benefit them and the colony for years to come.[7] In the growing and handling of certain crops, such as tobacco, tea, and cotton, children's "tiny fingers" were said to have been preferred by employers to the large and clumsy fingers of adult workers. As important as "tiny fingers" might have been, they were only a bonus to the employers. Child workers, as children, were attractive primarily because they were cheaper, easier to control, and more expendable in times of economic downturn than were adult workers.

From the beginning, a number of forces came together to ensure that child labor would be integral and critical to the capitalist economy of colonial Zimbabwe. First, most of the settlers came up from South Africa where, as was pointed out earlier, child labor had been an integral feature of the labor economy for almost 250 years. South African child labor patterns in agriculture and in mining were transferred whole cloth to colonial Zimbabwe. Second, for most of the colonial period, but in the early decades in particular, the majority of Zimbabwe's settlers suffered from a

6 What follows is based on Grier, *Invisible Hands*.

7 Comments of J.W. Posselt, Native Commissioner, Charter District, Southern Rhodesia. See his full written comments on labor conditions in colonial Zimbabwe in South Africa, *South Africa Native Affairs Commission, 1903-5*, 5, *Minutes of Evidence*, App. D, *Written Replies to Circular Questions*, Cd. 2399 (Cape Town, 1905), p. 352.

lack of capital.[8] They kept production costs low by using, whenever possible, the cheapest of all labor – child labor. Third, and related to this, settler farmers and mine owners were under pressure to produce cheaply for metropolitan industries and consumers, as access to protected sources of cheap raw materials was one of the primary reasons for the colonization of Africa at the end of the nineteenth century, a time when Britain faced growing competition from newly industrializing France, Germany, and the United States. Finally, when the settlers arrived in the territory, they found African children, like their adult counterparts, fully engaged in every aspect of the precapitalist economy: farming, herding, hunting, fishing, mining, cooking, child care, and craft making. Moreover, in the early days of colonial rule, they found that large numbers of relatively young boys (eight to ten years of age) left their rural homes to search for wage work on the mines and in towns. The reasons for this "voluntary" labor are explored below. Suffice it to say here that the appearance of young boys eager to work, along with African children's considerable work in the precolonial indigenous economy, made it easier for employers and British colonial officials to justify using African child labor in an era when child labor in Britain and most other parts of Western Europe and North America had fallen into disfavor and was being progressively eliminated from the economy.

In 1890 diamond-mining magnate Cecil Rhodes and the Pioneer Column of his privately-owned British South Africa Company (BSAC), marched into present-day Zimbabwe to claim the territory for the British Crown. They believed that they were capturing a territory whose wealth in gold would rival the gold mines of South Africa's Rand.[9] However, when, within a decade and a half, it became clear that Zimbabwe was not going to be the "Second Rand", the Company's directors gave instructions to diversify the colony's economy through settler-based export agriculture.

8 On the problems faced by poorly-capitalized settlers in mining and agriculture and on the colonial state's role in helping them to address these problems, see for example van Onselen, *Chibaro*; Phimister, *An Economic and Social History of Zimbabwe*.

9 From 1890 to 1923, the colony of Southern Rhodesia was governed by Rhodes's British South Africa Company, though after the African rebellion of 1896-1897, officials on the ground were appointed by the British Government in London. In 1923, the settlers voted for a "Responsible Government", rather than to join the Union of South Africa. From 1923 until 1965, when the white minority declared its independence from Britain, domestic policy was controlled by settler-elected governments, in a dominant partnership with the Foreign Office in London. For details, see Murray, *The Governmental System of Rhodesia*; Palley, *The Constitutional History of Southern Rhodesia*.

Though mining was eventually overtaken by export agriculture in terms of its contributions to the economy, it continued to play an important role[10]

The colony had workable deposits of gold, coal, asbestos, mica, and manganese, the mining and related economic activities of which, from the outset, involved child labor. As early as 1898, mining companies and colonial officials were routinely posting wage rates for only two categories of workers: adult male Africans and *picaninnies*, with wages being paid in each category "according to age and ability".[11] Boys under fourteen worked in below- and above-ground mining in gold and coal mines, though they were banned from underground mining in 1911. The jobs that younger boys could be found doing most often around most mining complexes was domestic work in the single-sex compounds that mining companies built to house their African workers. Boys cooked and cleaned for older mine workers whose numbers on large mines could run to six- and seven-hundred workers. In many cases, they serviced older mine workers sexually in the all-male compounds.[12] Whether children's work involved non-mining domestic tasks such as cooking and cleaning or providing sex and other domestic services for some miners, it was not insignificant for the profits of mine owners. Employing cheap child labor for mining-related work directly and indirectly lowered mine owners' overall costs of production. Allowing sexual relations between single migrant miner workers and boys cost mine owners less than providing family housing and paying a family wage.

In the base metals industries of asbestos and mica, boys and adolescent males formed a considerable proportion, if not the majority, of the work force in the above-ground operations. They were cheaper to employ, a critical factor for the base metals industry where, according to Charles van Onselen, lower profit margins "made it impossible for the base metal mines to compete even with the meager wages that were paid to black workers in the voracious gold mining industry".[13] Asbestos and mica mine owners, therefore, turned to younger male workers to stay afloat and earn a

10 For details, see Phimister, *Economic and Social History of Zimbabwe*.

11 Southern Rhodesia, Native Department, 1. Matabeleland, *Report of the Chief Native Commissioner for the Year Ending 31st March 1898* (Salisbury, 1898), p. 216; *Report of the Chief Native Commissioner, Matabeleland, for the Year Ended 31st March, 1901* (Salisbury, 1901), p. 6. Hereafter CNC *Annual Report*.

12 For details on sodomy of boys and on relationships with so-called male "mine wives" on the mines in southern Africa, see for e.g., van Onselen, *Chibaro*, p. 124-125; Harries, "Symbols and Sexuality"; Moody, "Migrancy and Male Sexuality".

13 Van Onselen, *Chibaro*, p. 125.

profit. On asbestos mines, boys were put to work separating asbestos fibers from the rock matrix. A settler member of the Legislative Council told his colleagues in 1910 that one asbestos mine "confined itself entirely to piccaninnies: that mine was in an exceptionally fortunate position in getting piccaninnies to do the work as well and at a cheaper rate than the ordinary mines had to pay".[14] At one mica mine, the government Compound Inspector reported in 1926, three hundred of the eight hundred workers were boys and adolescent males. The Chief Native Commissioner (CNC) wrote somewhat defensively of that mine:

> Native juveniles who are voluntary employees are engaged on a monthly basis. They are paid four shillings per month and upwards, according to their age, together with free food and quarters. Their ages range from 10 to 15 years. No juveniles are employed in underground work or on work involving heavy manual labour. Their work consists of cutting, splitting and sorting mica, a task which is of the lightest nature and is eminently suited to juveniles.[15]

Though some of the boys who worked on the mines came from nearby African reserves, most did not. They traveled considerable distances to the mining centers, where, like their adult counterparts, they were provided with food and living accommodations as wages in kind. Migrant boys (and men) came not only from inside the colony but from the neighboring colonies of Nyasaland (Malawi), Northern Rhodesia (Zambia), and Portuguese Mozambique. Traveling by foot, many local and foreign boys often went to the mines in the company of older male relatives. Others, particularly local boys, left home on their own. Professional recruiters were also used to channel child and adult labor to the mines. In 1899, the BSAC and the mining companies jointly formed two Labour Boards, one for each province (Matabeleland and Mashonaland) to recruit local labor. Again, posted wage rates fell into two categories only: "wages of able-bodied men" (25s. to 60s. per month, with rations) and "wages of piccaninnies" (5s. to 15s. per month, with rations). A total of 10,787 workers were recruited by the

14 Southern Rhodesia, *Legislative Council Debates*, June 2, 1910 (Salisbury, 1911), p. 73. Hereafter, *SRLCD*.

15 Cited in Telegram from the Governor of Southern Rhodesia to the Secretary of State for Dominion Affairs, November 24, 1927, No. 18 in Southern Rhodesia, *Papers Relative to the Southern Rhodesia Native Juveniles Employment Act, 1926, and the Southern Rhodesia Native Affairs Act, 1927*, Cmd. 3076 (London, 1928), p. 28. Hereafter *NJEA Papers*.

Matabeleland Board alone between January 1899 and March 1900, a significant number, it is safe to say, being under the age of fourteen. In 1905, the provincial boards were replaced by one quasi-state recruiting organization, the Rhodesia Native Labour Bureau (RNLB) which operated until 1933. The RNLB recruited primarily in the neighboring colonies, contracting child and adult workers for very low wages. Referred to by local workers as *chibaro* or "slave" labor, these contract workers were the cheapest of all workers, with the child recruits being the cheapest of them all.

Though many boys were leaving home to find wage work in the mines and towns and on the few early productive settler-owned farms, during the first three decades of colonial rule, most boys like most men remained in the peasant sector, growing subsistence crops and expanding farm production to meet the food needs of the mines and emerging towns. As most of the early settlers were interested in mining rather than farming, their BSAC-backed claims to 15.8 million acres of land (one-sixth of the colony's total acreage) by 1896 had little impact on the African peasantry's access to its ancestral farmland. African families were allowed to remain on the land, in exchange for rent in cash or in kind, paid to the new landowner. They met these charges by growing large quantities of grains and vegetables and producing beer and beef for the new markets. This expansion in farm production was achieved largely through an intensification of the labor of African women and girls whose responsibilities it had always been to plant, weed, harvest, process, and store food crops, and of boys who were responsible for herding animals and scaring off crop pests.[16] New tasks, such as transporting crops to market by headloading and brewing large quantities of beer for sale in mining towns were added. These also fell to women and children, girls in particular. Though this cheaply-produced food did not enter global markets, by feeding mine workers at low cost, it subsidized the cheap production of gold, coal, and other minerals that did enter global markets.

In 1908, the BSAC embarked upon a plan to diversify the colony's economy by encouraging white settlement and farming.[17] Within a few years, the plan began to show results, in terms of the number of new immigrants and farmers on the land and their farm output. In 1912, for the first time, settlers overtook African farmers as suppliers of food to the mines. African markets continued to expand, but peaked around 1916 and began to decline shortly thereafter. At long last, white farmers were taking up their land claims and putting the land under crops. They were aided by access

16 See Grier, *Invisible Hands*, pp. 95–101; and Schmidt, *Peasants, Traders, and Wives*.

17 For details, see Palmer, *Land and Racial Domination*, pp. 80–103.

to cheap land and credit, agricultural extension services, and negative policies toward African producers such as increased poll taxes, the introduction of new taxes, increased rents, and forced cattle dipping. A law passed in 1908 initiated the process of eliminating "kaffir farming" (the renting land by settlers to Africans in exchange for cash). African families were given the choice of remaining on their ancestral land, as labor tenants, or moving into the reserves. Most chose the reserves though land and water were insufficient to produce marketable surpluses there. As land shortages and rural poverty set in during the early 1920s, large numbers of African males began to pour out of the reserves in search of wage labor on settler farms, in the mines, and in town. Women and younger children as well searched for work on nearby settler farms. Elsewhere, I show that boys and adolescent males formed the leading edge of this mass rural exodus of male workers, serving as the proverbial "canary in the coal mine", signaling the proletarianizing forces at work.[18]

Between 1925 and 1928, about two thousand new settlers arrived in the colony under a British government post-war settlement scheme. As more settlers took up farming, they focused not only on maize and beef to supply the mines, but on an array of crops such as tobacco, cotton, tea, coffee, sugar, and rice destined for global markets. The mid-1920s saw a boom in cotton and tobacco production and export, encouraged by high prices and cheap labor. Cotton output increased from 1.7 million pounds in 1923-1924 to 8.2 million pounds in 1925-1926, before dropping back to 735,000 pounds in 1926-1927, due to pests. Tobacco output increased from 3.4 million pounds in 1923-1924 to 24.5 million pounds in 1927-1928. Settlers accomplished this expansion of export production in large measure by utilizing the labor of boys and adolescent males, often in the labor force on their own, and women accompanied by younger children from the increasingly impoverished reserves. The NC for the Makoni District wrote in his report for 1924 that "the women and children will turn out freely for the cleaning of lands and picking of cotton, and will work well if properly treated". The NC for Lomagundi noted that "in many instances women and children assisted to reap the cotton crop [... this emphasized] the importance of exploiting this source of labour to cotton and tobacco, work which calls for quick-fingered workers". Many of the children were "young children between the ages of 6, 7 or 8 years". What was not being given was the reason even young children accompanied their mothers: low wages paid to

18 Grier, *Invisible Hands*, pp. 101-109.

adult workers for piece and task work on settler farms obliged parents to bring along children to assist them make a decent wage. Though children were paid less than the adults per task and piece, they did not always earn less, one grower-legislator pointed out, noting, "in regard to this casual labour, such as cotton picking, it involved a period of about two months during which you want the labour. The picannins come in very handy in this work. I find that in working rice they earn higher wages on piece work than do adults".[19]

It was in tea growing where the greatest concentration of child labor could be found. Commercial production was begun in the early 1930s by two British tea planters from Assam, India. Tea production in India relied upon family labor, with a division of labor by gender and age, from planting to plucking and processing. These relations of production were difficult to replicate in colonial Zimbabwe, without providing valuable farm land to labor tenants. Desirous of the small "nimble fingers" for tea plucking to which they had been accustomed in Assam, the tea planters established "farm schools" to attract large numbers of child workers. African boys and girls and adolescents from eight to sixteen years of age worked on the tea estate for part of the day and attended classes for the remainder. By the early 1950s, the Rhodesia Tea Estates had four farms, growing coffee as well as tea and employing and schooling more than 1,600 children and adolescents. These part-timer student-workers made up between seventy to eighty per cent of the regular workforce. Adult males and older adolescent males were hired for full-time and heavier work, while women and additional children were hired on a casual basis during the busiest seasons. The education and books of part-timers were "free", students having to pay only for their uniforms. They were paid a small amount on the task work basis, with bonuses for plucking additional tea leaves or coffee beans. They were housed in dormitories and fed in cafeterias. The work was year-round, an unusual pattern for farming in the colony. The farm school system using child and adolescent labor made tea growing for export economically feasible. It also made it fairly profitable for the owners, the government Labour Officer writing in 1949:

> … without the attraction of free education and school books, plus pay, I doubt whether the tea company could operate successfully. How far the

19 CNC *Annual Report 1924* (Salisbury: Government Printer, 1925), p. 6, 5; Southern Rhodesia, *Legislative Assembly Debates*, November 9, 1926 (Salisbury, 1926), pp. 262, 267. Hereafter *SRLAD*.

> employment of child labour for profit at sub-economic wages (plus free education and board) can be defended on ethical grounds is a matter for consideration. [...] under these conditions tea can be produced cheaper in S. Rhodesia than Assam.[20]

Though the tea estate schools were not the earliest farm schools in colonial Zimbabwe, with state encouragement, they helped to set off an explosion of such schools in the 1940s and 1950s on maize, tobacco, cotton, and other farms. By the early 1960s, there were officially almost seven hundred such schools in the agricultural districts, employing and purporting to educate thousands of children and adolescents. Hundreds of other farm schools were believed to operate unofficially, that is, without a government permit and inspection. Some were established to attract family labor and stabilize the farm labor force, as labor tenancies gave way to wage labor. African parents were eager to educate their children and children were less likely to desert a farm with a school, even if they were required to work. Many other farm schools were established in this period along the lines of the tea estate schools in that they were designed to attract a labor force consisting primarily of children and adolescents. Some farm schools provided a quality education, while others did not. Of the latter, a government report noted:

> The purpose of this type of recruitment is not to provide school children with an education, but to provide the farm-owner with an inexpensive labour force. [...] The child is clearly an employee on the farm. [...] There may be scores of such 'farm schools' some of them housing two hundred or more children.[21]

The Colonial State and Child Labor

As we have seen, one of the arguments officials used to justify child labor was that the children entered the labor force voluntarily. A closer examination of how and why boys, in particular, but also girls, entered the labor

20 Southern Rhodesia, *Report of the Labour Office, Eastern Districts, September 1949* (Salisbury, 1950), p. 3. For further details on the part-time system, see Grier, *Invisible Hands*, pp. 161–95.

21 Southern Rhodesia, *Report of the Southern Rhodesia Education Commission, 1962*. A.V. Judges, Chairman (Salisbury, 1963), pp. 56–57.

force reveals the critical role of the state. It is true that many boys fled parental control and the intensification of their labor in commercialized peasant farming for the independence of migrant labor and the "bright lights" of the towns. As the CNC put it in 1926:

> The towns and mines and other industrial centres have, ever since the occupation of Southern Rhodesia, attracted a large number of native lads of ages ranging from about 10 years to 14 years. European employers have readily taken them into service at low rates of pay. Some have left their homes with the consent of their parents; others again have run away to see the world, leaving the family flocks and herds unattended.[22]

However, many boys were "encouraged" to leave home in the early years by tax and pass laws. Many more would be expelled from the rural areas by the state's policies on African land ownership and settler agriculture, in short, by the development of export-oriented capitalist agriculture.

As long as peasant families retained sufficient land to grow their own food and to meet their cash needs through marketed produce, men and boys entered and remained in the colonial wage labor force on their own terms. Mine owners and settler farmers constantly complained about labor shortages and desertions and pressured the state to act on their behalf. The state's response was to increase taxes, tighten pass and labor contract laws, and recruit labor domestically and from the neighboring colonies. Provisions dealing with expanding the number of child workers were integral to each of these strategies for increasing the size of the labor force. It is important to note, however, that many boys, eager to escape the patriarchal controls of fathers and other senior male kin, used new tax and pass laws as tools for redefining childhood and junior status. Migrant labor for boys and adolescent males quickly became a *rite de passage* for African male youth. This would work to the benefit of settlers and the export economy until the mass rural exodus of boys, after the First World War.

In 1894, the BSAC imposed a 10s. tax on every African hut in the colony, as a way of stimulating labor. This tax was viewed by Africans as a collective tax, the responsibility for which fell on all family members, young and old. The habit of fathers sending out their unmarried sons (both young and older) to earn their fathers' tax money began at this time. This tax did not

22 Memorandum explanatory of the Bill to provide for the employment of Native Juveniles, by the Chief Native Commissioner, Southern Rhodesia, to the Governor, April 12, 1926, 2 in *NJEA Papers*, p. 10.

generate sufficient labor, for reasons stated earlier. Forced labor of men, women, and children was also used, but when it provoked a widespread African revolt in 1896 and 1897 it had to be abandoned. In 1901, the hut tax was transformed into an individual or head tax, payable by every African male "of the age of 18 years and upwards". The CNC wrote in 1902 that the new head tax

> has been paid up exceedingly well, and far beyond my expectations. The young men have come forward and paid their tax cheerfully, and it is with pleasure that I have to report that in various districts some young boys, under the age of eighteen, were very dissatisfied when their money was handed back to them, and informed that they were too young to pay.[23]

As settlers still complained of shortages, the head tax was doubled in 1904. The increased tax was to be paid by all "adult male natives", but the new tax law omitted a definition of "adult". Officials relied on a new pass law enacted at the same that lowered the age of male registration from eighteen to the "apparent age of fourteen". From this date onward, "adult native" was interpreted to mean the "age of puberty" or fourteen for tax and pass registration purposes. The message was that this was the age that African males were expected to enter the wage labor force. These measures went some way toward stimulating not only pubescent boys to turn out to work but younger boys as well, one Native Commissioner reporting in 1904 that

> Owing to the New Tax Ordinance, many natives have already proceeded to the mines to earn the necessary money to meet the payment of the new tax in August next. [...] A fairly large number of youths, from 12 to 17 years of age, proceeded with the men to the mines, to work for white men as house and horse boys.[24]

It was probably around this time when officials also began to issue what they called "underage" passes and to register "underage" labor contracts for boys who clearly had not yet reached puberty or fourteen. They did this to accommodate the large number of such boys who were entering the labor market and the large number of settlers who wanted to employ them. As labor contracts could only be signed by Africans sixteen years of age and older, these underage documents did not have the force of law. It

23 CNC *Matabeleland Annual Report 1902*, p. 6.
24 "Gutu-Chilimanzi District", in CNC *Matabeleland Annual Report 1904*, p. 13.

is unclear how children who deserted or otherwise violated their underage labor contracts were dealt with under the law. Nonetheless, by 1920, officials were routinely issuing underage passes and registering underage labor contracts and employers were routinely paying the contract registration fee for each child worker. In that year, the Superintendent of Natives in Bulawayo, the second largest city in the colony, wrote that, in the month of November alone, he had issued 392 contracts to "youths too young to be registered with certificates [i.e., passes]".[25]

It was also in 1920 that officials began to receive complaints from settler employers, particularly farmers, that underage passes and contracts were being flagrantly violated by young workers, the Superintendent at Bulawayo reporting:

> Should one of these lads find his work uncongenial, he leaves without ceremony. He has found that no action will be taken against him because of his legal incapacity to contract himself. [...] the effect on the juveniles seems to call for serious consideration. Such an initiation to the field of labour is unfortunate, as at the outset of their careers they conceive of a contempt for a labour contract which must be demoralising.[26]

The Superintendent pointed to another problem that bode ill for controlling child workers and socializing young boys into their adult roles as compliant workers: the large numbers of boys under fourteen who were leaving the reserves, making their way to the towns and mining centers of the colony, and living not by wage employment but "by their wits". Several years later, in 1926, when the problem had grown even more serious, the CNC wrote:

> Hundreds of young boys may be found in any of our larger centres. Many are idle and many are in nominal or questionable employ by natives of most undesirable habits of life; all alike are open to evil temptations, and fall an easy prey to degrading associations. They form a community from which

25 Superintendent of Natives, Bulawayo, to CNC, November 8, 1920, 2 in *NJEA Papers*, p. 10.

26 Superintendent of Natives, Bulawayo, to CNC, November 8, 1920, 2 in *NJEA Papers*, p. 11.

> ultimately the habitual loafer and the offender and hardened criminal are largely recruited.[27]

What officials were witnessing after the war and in the 1920s was a mass rural exodus of boys and adolescent males in search of wage labor. Underage passes and labor contracts were not sufficient to discipline and control such large volumes of boys who were desperately escaping growing land shortages and poverty in the reserves. A potential boon to settler employers because their labor was cheap, child workers and unemployed child urban migrants (so-called "vagrants") had to be brought under a stricter form of discipline. Otherwise, they would threaten the settler project and the export economy upon which it was based.

In the midst of labor shortages associated with the cotton and tobacco booms, settler farmers put forward their own solution to these problems in 1925: three-to-five-year forced apprenticeships or indentures for African boys in the colony under the age of fourteen. Colonial officials rejected this, for the most part, proposing instead to legalize passes and contracts for African boys and girls under the apparent age of fourteen. In other words, the state proposed to give children's passes and contracts the force and sanction of law, making it possible to prosecute and punish them for pass and contract violations. The Native Juveniles Employment Act (NJEA) of 1926 was designed to do just this. It contained five main provisions. First, it required all children, male and female, to obtain a pass or registration certificate before leaving the reserves. It also required that all foreign-born children entering the colony from neighboring territories obtain a pass at the NC office closest to the border. The pass would entitle the bearer to sign a legal labor contract, without parental permission. Like adults, children with passes could be tracked and prosecuted for desertion, as the pass document contained information such as the signature of all employer with whom the child worker had completed a contract. The absence of this signature was sufficient proof for authorities to arrest a child (or adult) worker for desertion. Second, NCs were given the power to terminate or cancel contracts that were not in the interest of child workers, inspect places where children were employed, and, upon application of a parent or guardian or if the NC deemed it advisable, order the child to return home. Third, the NJEA empowered NCs to hear the complaint of an employer against child workers and punish children for violating of their contracts with a fine or

27 CNC to Secretary, Department of Administrator, November 16, 1926, 2 in *NJEA Papers*, p. 12.

a whipping with a light cane. Fourth, employers who hired children who did not possess passes could be fined or imprisoned. Finally, in a nod to the farmers' demand for binding children to apprenticeships, the NJEA empowered NCs to detain a vagrant child, that is, any child found unemployed and without parent or guardian, and "contract him for a period of service not exceeding six months to any fit and proper person willing to engage him".[28]

The Controversy: "A Peculiarly Odious Form of Child Slavery or Serfdom"

Though child labor for African children was widely accepted by most officials, settlers, missionaries, and Africans, and though its use in the colonies escaped notice back in the metropole, opposition to several provisions of the NJEA did emerge in some circles in the colony and in Britain. The most outspoken local opponent was Anglican Church missionary Arthur Shearly Cripps, followed by Wesleyan Methodist Church missionary John White. Francis Hadfield, a member of the colony's Legislative Assembly, was the only settler-legislator to speak publicly in opposition to any aspect of the bill. Due in part to Cripps's efforts, the NJEA received widespread attention in Britain where opponents included leaders of the Aborigines Protection Society (APS) and the Society of Friends, several Labour Party Members of Parliament (MPS), and editors of a number of liberal newspapers, most notably the *Manchester Guardian*, the *New Statesman*, and the APS-affiliated *Westminster Gazette*. It is important to point out that most of these critics did not oppose child labor as such, but instead objected to several of the NJEA's provisions. Specifically: the law's failure to set a minimum age at which children could obtain passes and sign labor contracts without parental permission; the use of whipping to enforce the pass law and labor contracts; and, the involuntary nature of labor contracts for child vagrants. The defense of the NJEA, particularly by officials, and the fact that child labor itself was not really questioned by most NJEA opponents, underscored broad agreement on the importance (and the legitimacy) of child labor to the colony's linkages with the global economy.

Taking their cues from the nineteenth-century British anti-child labor campaign that equated child labor with slavery, critics such as the editors of the *Westminster Gazette* dramatized the failure of the NJEA to set a minimum

28 Native Juveniles Employment Act, 1926, Clause 6, reprinted as 1 in *NJEA Papers*, p. 7.

age for children's passes and labor contracts, calling up images of "child slaves" in colonial Zimbabwe. The headlines of an October 1927 article read: "Africa's Child Slaves", "Appeal to British M.P.'s", "New Slave Laws by Rhodesia", "Boy and Girl Babies in the Mines", and "Whip for Piccanins". The article asserted:

> Extraordinary measures, which can only be described as a Government sanction of child slavery, have been introduced into recent legislation in Southern Rhodesia. An Act, which has just been passed, sanctions: The indenture of children, both boys and girls, to work in the mines and elsewhere. As there is no minimum age-limit, children can be taken into the mines as soon as they can walk.[29]

Several days of questions in the British Parliament picked up on this theme, with Labour MPs accusing the Conservative Party Prime Minister of signing off on a law that allowed the slavery of "little children" within the British Empire, the running of mica mines wholly with child labor of both sexes, and the indenturing of "little children" as "little slaves".[30] In their publicized condemnations, the secretaries of the APS argued that "the NJEA permitted 'quite young native children' to sign labor contracts without the 'advice, explanation, or consent of any parent, or person *in loco parentis*'".[31] And Hadfield expressed the fear that without an age minimum and without a limit on the number of times a vagrant child could be involuntarily contracted, a young child of eight or nine might be bound to one or more employers until he or she reached the age of fourteen.[32]

The defense mounted by colonial officials demonstrated their view that early wage work for African children was essential to the colony's economy. In debate on the bill, the Attorney General said that he "did not anticipate that children younger than eight or nine years of age would be engaged to perform a contract of any sort".[33] As noted earlier, children of this age had been found to be cheap and very useful picking cotton, tying hands of tobacco, and harvesting rice. Equally revealing was the response

29 *Westminster Gazette,* October 26, 1927.

30 Great Britain, House of Commons, *Extract from Official Report*, December 5, 1927, 19 in NJEA *Papers*, pp. 29, 30.

31 Travers Buxton and John H. Harris to Secretary of State for Dominion Affairs, February 4, 1927, 3 in NJEA *Papers*, p. 16.

32 SRLAD November 2, 1926, 14.

33 House of Commons, *Extract*, December 12, 1927, 21 in NJEA *Papers*, p. 31.

of local officials to an order from the Secretary of State for Dominion Affairs (who was under pressure to act, in response to criticisms of the NJEA in Britain) to set a minimum age for contracting children in the colony. Officials chose the age of ten, based on a census of juvenile pass registrations that showed that 63 per cent of the boys who were issued with passes in 1928 were twelve years of age and younger, while 36 per cent were eleven and under. Thus, to set the minimum age of children's labor contracts at eleven and twelve would result in an unacceptable "diminution of juveniles allowed to enter the labour market".[34] Moreover, rather than incorporating this age limit into an amendment to the NJEA, local officials took the politically safer but less effective route of issuing a circular letter to all district officials informing them that "'the Government does not approve of children under 10 years of age entering contracts of service' or leaving home without their parents' permission".[35]

Cripps, who a few years earlier had voiced his objection to children working in town but not on farms, referred to the use of whipping children (or adults) to enforce pass laws and labor contracts as "a parasitic adjunct of various forms of slavery".[36] Officials countered that whipping had long been the accepted form of punishment for children, black or white, in the colony. It traced its origins to Cape legislation dating from 1869. Whipping, they noted, was used for boys (though not girls) who violated criminal law or the law governing children apprenticed by their parents. Its objective was to keep children out of jail and away from contact with adult criminals. However, another objective of this provision of the NJEA was to discipline children for the purposes of extracting compliant labor in the workplace. This was made clear by the Attorney General who, in the Legislative Assembly debate on the bill, admitted:

> Even whipping might appear to be a drastic method of treating a juvenile who is merely guilty of breach of contract; but I think it is justifiable. After all, these juveniles are quite young, and one of the objects of this Bill is to

34 Dispatch from the Governor of Southern Rhodesia to the Secretary of State for Dominion Affairs, January 18, 1927, 25 in *NJEA Papers*, p. 35; CNC to the Secretary to the Premier (Native Affairs), "Native Juveniles in Employment", January 12, 1928, 2, National Archives of Zimbabwe S138/255. Hereafter, NAZ.

35 H.J. Taylor, CNC, Circular Letter No. 0.356/28, January 19, 1928, NAZ S138/255.

36 Arthur Shearly Cripps to Governor, August 29, 1926, NAZ S138/255.

inculcate in them the observance of their word. They must be taught that they have to obey.[37]

It was the six-months involuntary labor contracts for vagrant boys (though not girls) that generated the most criticism and the most vigorous defense by officials. In some respects, this was due to timing. The British government had just thrown its support behind the International Labour Organization's (ILO) 1926 Draft Convention Against Forced Labor. Opponents of the NJEA, such as the APS secretaries, argued that the threat of whipping to enforce voluntary or involuntary contracts placed the NJEA squarely within the category of "forced labor", as defined by the ILO Draft Convention. As John White put it: "If you arrest a loitering juvenile, engage him to a master at whose choice he has no say, and compel him to work for wages and for a period you alone determine, then it is forced labour".[38] Cripps compared involuntary contracts for vagrant children to the South African frontier practice of kidnapping and bonding African children (so-called apprenticeships). In his letter to the Governor, he stated: "I submit that in this Bill, as at present drafted, the familiar features of an old menace to Native Rights and Liberties out here are easily discernible. I should myself define this menace as the 'pseudo-apprenticeship of young Natives to approved employers.' This menace has made periodical reappearances". The NJEA would create "a peculiarly odious form of child slavery or serfdom" in the colony, by "binding down comparatively helpless juvenile Native employes [sic] to serve European employers under stringent conditions in such a Colony as our own".[39] Significantly, the NJEA did not require officials to search for the parents of vagrant children or return the children to their rural homes, leading some to suspect that the state intended to round up unattached children en mass and contract them out to private employers.

Stunned by this criticism and fearful of more adverse publicity in Britain that might lead to pressure for greater control or even the elimination of child labor in the colony, officials in both London and Salisbury emphasized the protective aspects of the NJEA: the provisions for inspecting places where children worked, canceling contracts, and returning children to their homes. The Secretary of State assured the British Parliament

37 *SRLAD* November 2, 1926, 12.

38 *Rhodesia Herald*, November 5, 1926, quoted in Chaduka, "Britain and Southern Rhodesia", p. 78.

39 Cripps to Governor.

that the NJEA did not add a single child to the labor force in the colony. In some instances, he asserted, it resulted in the replacement of children by adults. Charles Coghlan, who held the post of Minister of Native Affairs as well as that of Premier, argued that the law was passed for the well-being of the children rather than in the interests of employers. The law would ensure that both employers and child workers would be held to the labor contracts they signed. It sought to keep children from drifting into town, loafing about, and coming under bad influences. The discipline the NJEA would instill would redound to the children as well as to employers and the colony. African chiefs and parents, district officials reported, favored the law because it facilitated the tracing and return of their runaway children.[40]

Though opposition to the NJEA did not result in the law's amendment or repeal, it did prevent officials from implementing the provision for involuntary six-month contracts for child vagrants. Within a few months of the passage of the NJEA, officials in London and in the colony showed signs of backing away from one of the concerns that prompted them to write the law in the first place: the "hundreds of boys" who drifted to the towns and lived a life of idleness and crime. Thus, the Secretary of State for Dominion Affairs could write the APS in 1928 that officials never intended mass round-ups and indentures for large numbers of unemployed and unattached boys: "It is not anticipated that many juveniles will be dealt with under this Section – at the most a Native Commissioner will exercise his powers of 'contracting' juveniles one [sic] or twice a year". After one year of the NJEA's operation, the CNC reassured Premier Coghlan that "No instance has yet occurred of a contract, indenture, or apprenticeship under section 6, and it is not anticipated that the application of the section referred to will be exceedingly rare. Cases of the kind will be scrutinised closely".[41] It would seem that officials concluded that it was not worth jeopardizing the access of the larger body of employers (mine owners, better-capitalized farmers and estate-owners) to "voluntary" child labor just to make available relatively small numbers of involuntary child labor to a small section of poorly-capitalized farmers. Pursuing the latter course would only open the door to more scrutiny and criticism and might ultimately lead to intervention in the flow of "voluntary" child labor itself.

40 For details, see Grier, *Invisible Hands*, pp. 134–144.

41 Letter from the Dominions Office to the Secretaries, the Anti-Slavery and Aborigines Protection Society, May 13, 1927, 12 in *NJEA Papers*, p. 23; CNC to Secretary to the Premier, 26 in *NJEA Papers*, p. 40.

Put into the even larger context of the needs of settler export-based economy as a whole, involuntary child labor contracts were not the true aim of the NJEA. They were inserted into the bill to satisfy the farmers' lobby. The NJEA's core objective was to "regularize"[42] child labor by transforming its status from extra-legal to legal so that child workers could be systematically (rather than haphazardly) disciplined and controlled. Thus, the long-term objective of the NJEA was to entrench child labor, to embed it more deeply into the fabric of the colony's labor regime. Critics seemed to have missed this point altogether, perhaps because they did not see child labor per se as a problem, at least, for African children.

The data collected by officials on passes issued to children under the age of fourteen give some indication of the extent to which boys were involved in migrant labor. In the first ten years of the NJEA's operation, more than 100,000 local or Zimbabwean boys and more than 100,000 foreign-born boys were issued with "juvenile passes". Passes issued to Zimbabwean boys under fourteen ranged from 34 per cent to 44 per cent of passes issued to all Zimbabwean African males in the years 1927 to 1936. Perhaps because of the distances they had to travel, foreign-born boys who were issued with passes made up smaller percentages of all foreign-born males issued with passes: on average, 21 per cent of passes issued to males from Northern Rhodesia (Zambia); 15 per cent of males from Nyasaland (Malawi); and, 24 per cent of males from Mozambique. As noted earlier, a 1928 census showed that more than one-third (35 per cent) of boys issued with passes were ten years of age and younger. More than one-quarter (27 per cent) of the juvenile passes went to boys who were eleven years old and another one-quarter (27 per cent) went to boys who were twelve years of age.

As revealing as this data is, it underestimates the number of boys and adolescent males who were in the wage labor force. Officials reported that while many boys signed up for passes, many did not. Neither did most employers ask children for their passes before hiring them. Officials lacked the staff to enforce the NJEA which came into operation just before the onset of the global Depression (with its local bankruptcies of farmers and mine owners), drought, and movement of more Africans onto the reserves. Throughout much of the decade of the 1930s, the labor market was characterized by a surplus of men and boys searching for work and wage cuts for those fortunate enough to get jobs. Increasingly, boys and adolescent males went to the urban areas to search for work in the informal sector, causing

42 This term is also used by Chaduka, "Britain and Southern Rhodesia", p. 78.

considerable alarm among officials by the post-war period. Rates of "social crimes" (theft, housebreaking, and assault) soared, as children attempted to survive on their own in town.[43]

The Post-War Years

Like the economies of most African colonies in the years following the Second World War, that of colonial Zimbabwe experienced a large increase in the global demand for its raw materials. To meet this demand and to take advantage of higher world prices, farmers and mine owners stepped up the production of tobacco, tea, cotton, sugar, coal, manganese, chromium, and other commodities. The settler-dominated government had another incentive to increase the production of raw materials for export: in pursuit of its policy of import substitution industrialization, it used the foreign exchange earned by raw materials exports to pay for the importation of capital goods. As over the previous half-century, child labor was an important factor in keeping costs down, particularly in agriculture, where most child labor was now concentrated. Two developments further increased the demand for child labor in export agriculture: the near-completion of the transition from labor tenancies to permanent resident wage labor on farms and, ironically, mechanization.[44]

Laws passed during the 1930s and 1940s forced settlers to bring an end to the labor tenancy system and convert labor tenants into full-time resident laborers on their farms. Extra-legal tenancies continued, but most settlers complied. It was in their interests to do so during these boom years, as the land previously used by tenants for subsistence crops could be put to productive use under export crops. As noted earlier, farmers set up schools on their farms to attract and retain (i.e., stabilize) a resident wage labor force that consisted of entire families. The men and older teenage unmarried sons worked full-time on the farm, while the women, girls and younger boys were called out to work during planting and harvesting seasons. In 1962, it was estimated that more than 800,000 Africans lived on settler farms as resident wage laborers. A considerable proportion of these were children under sixteen, the new age of majority after the NJEA was amended in 1947 to make it conform with other laws in the colony covering children and adolescents. As noted earlier, more than 100,000 farm children

43 For details, see Grier, *Invisible Hands*, pp. 197–215.

44 What follows draws upon Clarke, *Agricultural and Plantation Workers*.

were enrolled in "farm schools" However, these schools opened and closed according to the labor needs of the farmer. Children were also pulled from school by their parents because of the low wages paid to adults: children's "extra hands" went a long way toward making a living family wage in piece and task work. As few farm schools provided an education beyond the first two or three years of schooling, most older children (twelve years of age and older) ended up working more regularly in the fields, on a full- or part-time basis.

As the farm labor force became more permanent and global demand for crops increased, most settlers invested in farm equipment that required training to operate and maintain. Thus, numerous service jobs emerged on settler farms, accompanied by a "stratification" of the labor force. Moreover, according to D.G. Clarke, from the 1960s onward, farm ownership came to be concentrated into the hands of smaller numbers of large-scale and corporate owners with the capital to invest in mechanization.[45] The end result was a greater reliance upon women and children for seasonal (casual) work over time. Many of the female and child workers came from the farmers' own compound, the wives and children of male resident workers. Others were hired on a daily basis from nearby reserves. Clarke estimates that in the 1960s, "juveniles" comprised fourteen per cent of the total farm labor force (permanent and casual), though he notes that girls were substantially undercounted.

Farm work was the lowest paid of all wage work in colonial Zimbabwe. If they could, Africans, both children and adult, avoided it, preferring work in the mines and in urban areas. Not only was farm work poorly paid, but the living and working conditions were degrading. Though the situation improved over time, as settlers began to use carrots as well sticks, farmers continued to be a law unto themselves on their own farms, meeting out "rough justice" to employees with impunity. It was for these reasons (among others, such as underemployment, lack of money, and lack of access to education) that children increasingly fled the rural areas for the towns, even if their only hope of employment was the informal sector or survival through petty crime. When Rhodesia became the independent state of Zimbabwe in 1979, hundreds of thousands of children still resided on settler farms, as full- and part-time workers producing crops destined for global markets.

45 Clarke, *Agricultural and Plantation Workers,* p. 19.

Though most post-war formal sector jobs in the urban areas went to adults, there is evidence that some urban-based industrial employers were eager to reap the competitive advantages that came with employing cheap children and adolescent male labor. A government committee of enquiry in the early 1950s found that boys as young as seven and eight years old were working in large tobacco-processing factories. The owner of one such factory told the committee that he was "willing to pay as well as anyone", but insisted that "the employment of piccannins and juveniles (large piccannins) was essential and 'there was no other alternative'". A toy factory in Salisbury that produced for local and perhaps regional markets was said to be "cluttered up with machines and natives falling over each other, mostly of the juvenile type".[46] In both cases, in line with the law in other British colonies since the 1930s, the employment of children under sixteen for "industrial work" was illegal.

Conclusion

This chapter on child labor in colonial Zimbabwe ends in the 1960s, the eve of the 1965 declaration of independence from Britain by the white minority regime of Ian Smith and the start-up of war between this regime and African nationalist guerrillas. Using Zimbabwe as a case, I have attempted to show that with the expansion of a European empire into this part of sub-Saharan Africa came major changes to and increases in child labor. In the precolonial economy, African children's labor had contributed to the reproduction of the household economy. With colonization, their labor was incorporated into a global system of production of cheap raw materials for consumption in metropolitan markets. Without their parents, children traveled or were transported great distances to work in mines and on farms and estates. Their labor was pervasive and a critical element that employers calculated upon. For most employers, child labor was an important factor keeping their costs down. For some, such as asbestos and mica mine owners, the tea estates, and farmers who operated farm schools, child labor was the primary factor that kept costs down and made their products competitive.

Child labor use during the colonial period set the stage for child labor use in the post-colonial period, in spite of the expansion of primary and

46 Quoted in Gray, *The Two Nations*, pp. 209-210.

secondary schooling for Africans. The tea estates continued to operate with an overwhelmingly child and adolescent labor force in tea and coffee growing. Children's "tiny fingers" were still valued in cotton picking. The school year was organized around the agricultural season, with large numbers of children and adolescents being trucked from their homes to settler farms to harvest crops. Structural adjustment policies imposed on Zimbabwe in the 1980s led to cutbacks in education spending, the imposition of school fees, and the consequent increase in drop-out rates, making these children available for employment. The HIV/AIDS crisis presents perhaps the most serious challenge yet, as it simultaneously decreases the number of able-bodied adults in the work face and swells the number of orphans without parents to support them.

CHAPTER 26

Child Labour and the Development of Capitalist Agriculture in Ghana

Nick Van Hear

As in most of Africa, Ghanaian children are widely engaged in agriculture. Participation in household production is almost universal, but children are also increasingly employed as hired agricultural labourers: this paper is concerned chiefly with the latter. The first section examines the incorporation of children into the cocoa economy during the colonial period. The paper then briefly touches on pawning and fostering as institutions for the recruitment of child labour. The third section considers the employment of children in capitalist agriculture that developed in the North of Ghana from the late 1960s, and indicates some of the ways in which children have resisted exploitation.

Child Labour in the Colonial Period

The first three decades of this century saw immense changes in the Gold Coast. In this period after the consolidation of formal British rule a typical colonial economy was established. Export production, concentrated mainly in the south, was increasingly brought under European control and an infrastructure was developed to facilitate export. Gold mining expanded and a few plantations were set up. Railways and a deep water harbour were built, and roads developed. The most spectacular development, however, was in cocoa production which was in the hands of African entrepreneurs who sold the crop to European trading companies. Introduced in 1879, exports of cocoa rose from 536 tons in 1900 to 22,600 tons by 1910, and reached 176,000 tons in 1920.[1]

1 Hill, *The Gold Coast Cocoa Farmer.*

The North became the chief source of labour for all of these developments. Despite some dissenting voices, the region was administered as a labour reserve, and the roots of the North's underdevelopment may be traced to this period. Forced labour, initially recruited for the mines, was outmoded as seasonal migration developed, a concomitant of the region's underdevelopment. There was a heavy demand for carriers by the mining industry, for the construction of public works, and not least for headloading cocoa, and children figured largely in the latter.

As the cocoa industry boomed, so the number of children employed in carrying increased, and by 1914 it was observed that,

> a large number of the children in this colony are engaged daily in heavy weight carrying. It is in fact their daily occupation [...] A great deal of this cocoa carriage is in the hands of the Wangaras [a tribe from the north] and it is not unusual to see immature children amongst them.[2]

Suggestions that the Masters and Servants Ordinance be invoked to curb the employment of children were rejected as "impracticable", and it was hoped that head carriage would die out with the development of road transport. But vast numbers of carriers continued to be employed. There were warnings about the deleterious effects of the work on children's health,

> I was forcibly struck with the number of young adults, principally girls, who were carrying loads of cocoa that were evidently quite beyond their physical strength ... there is little doubt that such continued physical strain in early adult life would certainly have a very harmful effect on the future of the race.[3]

But no action was taken by the colonial authorities.

The cocoa boom of 1919-1920 was the peak of employment of cocoa carriers. Under the more energetic governorship of Guggisberg, roads were rapidly developed and large numbers of labourers were released from carrying, causing widespread unemployment which was exacerbated by the slump of 1930-1931. Headloading of cocoa to the transport depots continued, however, and in the major towns.

As well as for carriage, the expanding cocoa industry required labour for the cultivation of the crop. Initially family labour was sufficient, but after

2 (Public Record Office) PRO CO 96/546/26081: "Child Cocoa Carriers" (1.7.1914).
3 Gold Coast: *Annual Report of the Medical Department* (1920).

about 1910 cocoa farmers began to hire labour, principally migrants from the Northern Territories (NTs), the French Territories and from Togoland, to clear new lands and to farm them.

Labour migration was at first seasonal and of young unmarried men, but communities of settled immigrants, known as *Zongos,* rapidly developed in the major towns of the cocoa districts. In 1935, with a revival of the cocoa industry after the slump, it was observed that more and more women and children were coming down with the labourers. The seasonal migration of young men employed on annual contracts (i.e. hired for a year and paid at the end of it), piece work or daily paid work continued, but settled labourers demanded more secure sharecropping arrangements.

Children worked on cocoa farms as members of sharecroppers' families, and were thus not directly employed by farm-owners, who nevertheless benefitted from their labour. Children also cultivated sharecroppers' food farms, thus freeing them for cocoa work, and helped to head-load harvested cocoa to the marketing points. The latter work was unpaid or paid by the load according to the form of the sharecropping agreement. As members and workers of sharecroppers' families, children were affected by the vagaries of the cocoa buying price, and some sharecroppers were often extremely badly off.

Despite the explosion in the hiring of labour, including children for the carrying and cultivation of cocoa and the abuses that were coming to light, the colonial administration made little attempt to investigate the conditions of child employment. The only interventions occurred when labour supply to expatriate concerns, principally mining, was threatened by the demands of African cocoa entrepreneurs. The only existing legislation was the Masters and Servants Ordinance which bore the heavy imprint of the post-Abolition era. Several of the conventions passed at the League of Nations International Labour Conference in 1921 concerned the employment of children; for agricultural work a minimum age was set except for work outside school hours, while work was not to interfere with schooling. But the opinion of the colonial administration was that the implementation of this and other conventions was impracticable, and the response was a prevaricating "steps will be taken [...] as local conditions may decide".[4]

In the late 1930s, however, consideration of the conditions of recruitment and employment of children was forced on the colonial administration. The demand for labour had increased as the economy picked up

4 Ghana National Archives Adm. 8/1/885: "Convention concerning the rights of Association and Combination of Agricultural Workers" (n.d.).

from the slump of the early 1930s, and for the first time there were reports of direct recruitment of children from the North under annual and other forms of labour contract. The Chief Commissioner of the NTs described the practice to the Colonial Secretary:

> These labourers are frequently youths of 14 or 15 with no previous experience of work or conditions in the south who leave their homes without the knowledge or consent of their parents. In some cases written agreements are made but in most cases it is only verbal. Labourers go of their own free will but in many cases they are deceived as to their destination and the nature of the work. The system is open to grave abuse and there is already evidence of an undesirable type of recruiter in some of the larger towns. There is little doubt that the terms of whatever contract are frequently not observed by the employers who take advantage of the ingenuousness of the labourers.[5]

The paternalistic conscience of British imperialism was at last stirred: "[...] it is our humane duty to protect the interests of these primitive people".[6]

Most of the children were from the extreme North of the country – the present Upper Region – and in particular from the over-populated Northeast. The headmen of their tribes living in the major towns on the north-south route – Tamale, Salaga, Ejura and Kumasi – were involved in the traffic. In one case a Frafra headman in Tamale recruited a gang of seven labourers for a road contractor. A District Commissioner who intercepted them noted that

> [...] they were half starved and in a filthy condition. I found the whole thing was rotten. The boys were to pay their transport from Tamale and by working very hard they might possibly have earned their lorry fare, chop money and a shilling or so over. Three of the gang were children of thirteen or so, who could not possibly earn their fare and even a reasonable amount of chop money.[7]

Other children, without being told where they were going, were recruited to work on cocoa farms. An example was given of a Kusasi boy of around fourteen who had been promised a ride to Tamale from Bawku in the Northeast. He managed to escape from the lorry at Krachi, more than

5 Ghana National Archives, Tamale Adm. 1/164: "Native Labour".
6 Ghana National Archives, Tamale Adm. 1/164: "Native Labour".
7 Ghana National Archives, Tamale Adm. 1/164: "Native Labour".

a hundred miles further South en route to an unknown destination. On reaching Kumasi the children were distributed to farmers or agents in return for a commission.

Soon after these reports the NTs were declared prohibited to unlicensed recruiters but the practice continued illegally. Many labourers found that contracts were broken on arrival in the South, and in many more cases workers were not paid after completing their contracts, and had to return home destitute.

Few child workers were taken from their home communities at this time, but were runaways picked up as they made their way South. By the early 1940s such "truants", often ten or twelve-year-olds, were very common. They stole livestock or cash for the journey South. All attempts to stem this "voluntary" flow of children failed, despite repatriation of the "urchins" by the Labour Department.

What then were the forces behind this migration of children and young men? The explanation of the colonial administration was that they wanted to "see the world", and there is some truth in this. But a fuller explanation has to be sought in the underdevelopment of the North. Despite some unacknowledged voices of protest from its DCs, the region continued to be administered as a labour reserve, and little effort was put into developing agriculture. The degeneration of peasant agriculture in some areas made migration for the young the only alternative and, by removing the fittest labour, furthered the degeneration. In the worst years famine, a result of the underdevelopment of agriculture, drove whole families to migrate. At the same time, the introduction and spread of coinage and the penetration of European goods, particularly cloth, had created the need for cash, and since there were few cash earning opportunities in the North, and those existing were low paid, migration south was again the only means of earning it. Taxation was not instrumental in forcing migration as in other parts of Africa, although this and other harsh measures in French territories further North drove out many migrants. Migration was then motivated by the underdevelopment of the North, and "seeing the world" was the cultural concomitant of underdevelopment.

Children continued to run away from the North in the 1940s and 1950s and were prey to the touts, agents, "collectors", lorry drivers and headmen of the flourishing illegal recruitment system that had grown up to supply the cocoa farmers with labour. The mines also secretly benefitted from this "blackbirding", as it was known. Such recruiting thrived well into the 1950s and recruiters penetrated nearer to the places of origin of the labourers. In 1958, after independence, the Northern Region's Labour Officer reported,

> [...] the position is disturbing in Kusasi area where children are being kidnapped from their homes and taken to Ashanti. At the time of my visit to Tumu two such boys had disappeared the day before, taken by Ashanti women traders. The Tumu-koro expressed concern.[8]

A recruiter was arrested in a Brong-Ahafo cocoa town with a group of seven labourers recruited in Bawku. Two were adults and the rest twelve or thirteen years old, all recruited without the consent of their parents. The commission was £4 for two workers to cover "transport expenses".

The Labour Department gave up trying to police illegal recruiting in 1958, admitting that it was "rampant", and there are no records of the practice after this. Labourers interviewed in Tamale, Bolgatanga and Bawku, however, recently confirmed that the practice still went on, particularly in the aftermath of the Aliens Compliance Order of 1969 which resulted in the exodus of most foreign labourers and created a labour shortage. As recently as 1980 a cocoa farmer was jailed for seven years for the "theft" of two boys aged nine and ten.[9]

Labour legislation has remained a dead letter. International conventions, including one on the employment of women and children of 1937, were incorporated into existing labour law, and a number of Labour Ordinances were consolidated into the Labour Code of 1948. But these, like further international declarations of the 1950s, had little effect in the Gold Coast as it moved into independence. On labour conditions it was held that, "the relationship between the farmer and his labourer is so intimate that outside interference [...] will tend to dislodge this intimacy which will not be in the interest of the labourer." And again in 1956, "the time is not yet ripe for progressive legislation to rationalize conditions of service on cocoa farms".[10] Legislation since independence in 1957 – principally the Labour Decree of 1967 – has confirmed colonial law on the employment of children and has remained similarly ineffective, as will be shown below.

8 Ghana Labour Department, File KI 80.
9 Ghana, *Daily Graphic* (7.1.1980).
10 Ghana Labour Department, File KM 17.

The Pawning and Fostering of Children

As well as waylaying runaway children, recruiters took advantage of another practice that was widespread: pawning. The abolition of slavery in 1874 did not end it. Open slave raiding continued in the North until the British consolidated their rule just after the turn of the century, and slavery persisted clandestinely afterwards. Some of the early migrant workers may then have been slaves or pawns sent by chiefs or private masters to bring back cash or trade goods. According to peasant farmers interviewed recently in Bolgatanga, the pawning of children to Ashanti recruiters in exchange for food during times of famine was very common, and local songs in the 1950s accused fathers of selling their sons' labour to pay taxes. Pawning was officially noted in 1948:

> In the NTs too, children are usually pawned in exchange for food rather than in payment of debts, and generally speaking in those areas along the northern frontier where famine or semi famine conditions have been known to occur at certain times of the year.[11]

The line is very thin between this pawning and some forms of fostering which are widespread in Ghana and have been reported among the Ewe, Dagomba, Gonja and the immigrant Mossi and Hausa. Children are commonly fostered by kin, often siblings, and the practice is used to assert ties of kinship – often fictional – and to show amity and respect, etc. It also has important economic functions. Like all children, fostered children are expected to perform time-consuming but necessary household tasks: households without child labour are rarely economically viable. The foster parents in exchange are responsible for the welfare, keep and discipline of the child.[12]

Fostering is not limited to real or fictional kin, however. Children are sometimes adopted by their masters to learn a trade, and while some of these relationships are on the familial model, others are unequivocally those of employer and employee. The employment of children from different ethnic communities by Kumasi women is very common. In the 1960s the parents were paid between six pennies and two shillings a day, and the employers were responsible for feeding and clothing the children. Signifi-

11 Ghana National Archives, Tamale Adm. 1/301: "Slave Dealing".
12 On fostering, see Schildkrout, *People of the Zongo*; Oppong, *Growing Up in Dagbon*; Goody, "Kinship Fostering in Gonja".

cantly, it was often Kotokoli and other Togolese migrant farm labourers who hired out their children while at work. Although Schildkrout insists that these child servants were required to do less domestic service than the employers' own children, there is a definite class dimension to this practice. This dimension is even clearer in a case reported in the Eastern Province in the 1950s when Akim farmers demanded maid-servants from immigrant Ewe labourers wanting sharecropping contracts.

> [The maidservant] got nothing back for her services and was usually given unfair treatment. In some cases they were the victims of premature cohabitation.[13]

The labourers protested to the local chief about "the semi-slave treatment meted out to these maids" and there was a threat of unrest in the area as the farmers sacked the Ewes and took on Northerners instead in reprisal. By 1955 the practice had evidently faded out in this area, but the institution of fostering and the potential – for abuse remain, as the Ghana Government acknowledged in a reply to a UN questionnaire in 1970.[14]

Child Labour and the Development of Capitalist Agriculture in the North[15]

Since the 1950s farming has grown more commercialized outside the cocoa areas, and young migrants from the North have travelled to food farms in the Brong-Ahafo region rather than to the cocoa farms further south. More recently, the North itself has experienced capitalist agricultural development. With the help of large state subsidies, lenient credit terms and cheap tractors, large-scale private rice farming took off in the late 1960s in the Dagomba district around Tamale and in the Fumbisi valley further north.[16]

These developments much increased the use of hired labour in the North, particularly that of children. In the rice areas large-scale farmers hire two kinds of labour: permanent workers as general labourers and tractor and combine operators, and, despite mechanization, a large amount of casual labour at peak periods such as weeding and harvesting. Children

13 Ghana Labour Department, File KM 17: "Cocoa Farm Labour".
14 According to Patrick Montgomery of the Anti-Slavery Society.
15 This section is based on fieldwork carried out by the writer in northern Ghana in 1978 and 1979, under the sponsorship of the Social Science Research Council.
16 See Shepherd, "The Development of Capitalist Rice Farming".

were rarely employed as permanent workers, although as the rice industry boomed, young men, some scarcely in their teens, flocked to attach themselves as apprentices or mates to tractor drivers employed by private farmers or state companies. This influx, coupled with unemployment as farmers reduced their acreages after three years of drought, enabled farmers to increase the already rampant exploitation of tractor drivers and their mates. Meagre wages were cut or not paid at all, and since mates were not paid by farmers but received only "chop money" from their masters, the poor condition of the tractor drivers was passed on to them. Faced with unemployment, however, young workers were prepared to accept these poor conditions just to keep their jobs; the status of "apprentice", such that it was, disappeared as young workers remained mates for five, six, or seven years.

Children were more important as casual workers and they formed the bulk of the casual labour force in the rice industry. Traditionally, young Dagomba boys farmed and tended livestock for their fathers from an early age but apart from harvesting corn and groundnut farms for richer peasants, work paid in kind but sometimes in cash, there was very little hired labour. Girls had little to do with cultivation but helped older women to carry and process harvested crops. The advent of the rice industry changed all this, introducing hired labour on a scale never seen before in the North, and drew large numbers of boys and girls into the casual labour market.

Casual labour is always in short supply. The large-scale rice farmers originally took labour from the villages immediately surrounding their farms, but as village men became conscious of their exploitation they withdrew to expand their own farms, leaving rice labouring to women and children. Workers from Tamale, many of whom were small boys, had to be transported long distances to supplement the village workers, an importation which increased as village women, unable to secure higher wages, insisted on shorter hours and put less effort into their work.

By the mid-1970s, then, there were two sources of casual labour, and children figured largely in both. Women, girls and some boys were drawn from the villages surrounding the farms and, as labour grew scarce, from villages further afield. Secondly, at the "labour markets" or "by day centres" that had developed on the major roads out of Tamale and in some of the larger villages, casual workers waited to be collected and transported to farms by trailer or truck. The majority of these workers were small boys of primary school age. They were thought to be unskilled, incapable and weak by employing farmers, who preferred the young unmarried men, Middle Form Four leavers and secondary school students who also gathered at the labour markets. These youths had a special relationship with the small children, and had indeed worked as "by days" when younger. The urban casual workers also included numbers of orphans and boy thieves: "the homeless ones" and "those with no mother and no father" who had run away from the surrounding villages to Tamale and slept around the filling stations and market areas. Some of them eked out a dubious living as "queue contractors", waiting in line at the supermarkets and stores to buy scarce goods to resell to market women, and occasionally came for rice labouring.

The urban labour force was predominantly male, but women and girls did gather at the "by day centres" to be collected by the trucks of the Ministry of Agriculture and the Food Production Corporation. They were employed on a semi-permanent basis. Finally there were some adults, mostly unemployed artisans and laid-off tractor drivers, who occasionally worked as casual labourers.

The continuing labour shortage strengthened the bargaining power of casual workers and they were able to resist exploitation more successfully than their older friends employed as tractor drivers' mates. The struggle between employers and workers intensified as farmers tried by various means to extract more labour for less pay. This struggle could be seen every morning as one or two youths bargained on behalf of the rest of the labourers with farmers or their managers over whether the work was to be on a by day basis or piece work basis, over the time of finishing work, the amount of piece work which was measured in paces, and over the rate of pay.[17] Farmers were singled out as *dariga* ("cheat") or *allaha* ("wanting cheap"). Dariga men would renege on agreements reached during bargaining, while allaha men offered very low rates of pay. They could be recognized, it was said, because they always hired young boys who could be paid low wages and easily cheated:

17 In 1978 youths were paid C4 or C5 for daily rated work, and up to C8 for piece work. Small children were paid C2 to C3, while the statutory minimum wage was C4. By 1980 youths had pushed their wages up to Clo following an increase in the statutory minimum wage. In 1978 the official exchange rate was C2 to £1, and after devaluation £1 exchanged for approximately C5. However, rampant inflation and black marketeering meant that the real value of the wage was much lower: in 1978 a loaf of bread cost C2 to C3 and a tuber of yam C2 to C4. (C = Ghanian Cedi).

> if you see a trailer full of small boys it means the farmer is a cheat. He will cheat the small boys and pay them small, or he will pace out 20 by 20 instead of 15 by 15.[18]

The bargaining process seemed incomprehensibly disorderly, but behind the chaos there was an informal but forceful organization among the labourers based on an acute sense of their bargaining power and solidarity. This was most obvious in the youths' protective role towards the children: they bargained on their behalf and prevented the children from joining dariga farmers and being cheated. Often tractors would draw up which would be approached by only a few small boys who were immediately called back by their seniors. This boycotting of dariga farmers was effective and was accompanied by the jeering of the assembled workers as empty trailers left the by day centres.

For their part the small boys confirmed that they "followed the grown-ups" so that they were not cheated. They were not as gullible as their seniors made out, however, and were quite capable of independent action. They often decided for themselves whether an offer was worthwhile and snubbed farmers who tried to cheat them. The humiliation of being ridiculed by young children was deeply felt by dariga and allaha farmers.

The struggle against exploitation was also much in evidence at the workplace itself. Once en route to the farm in a farmer's trailer the labourers were a captive workforce simply because they had no means of returning home. To come home independently they would have to pay the fare themselves, and transport was in any case scarce. The farmers were well aware of this, and it was a potent means of labour control for them. Once at the farm they could reduce the rate agreed on, or resort to such ludicrous ruses as widening their strides when pacing out piece work plots to increase the area to be worked. Labourers might also find their working day was extended beyond the agreed time, or that far more work was involved than they had bargained for.

Labourers responded in a number of ways. Some grudgingly accepted the revised terms of work, or left to try to make their own way home. More commonly in the late 1970s, however, workers resorted to collective action; they refused to work, sat down, and demanded to be taken home. Threats of violence were thrown in to intimidate intransigent farmers or managers. It was frequently the youths who took the lead in these actions,

18 This and the following quotations are from young agricultural workers interviewed in Tamale, Northern Ghana, in 1978.

but small boys also acted independently. A group of them commented: "Once a farmer cut 30 by 30 instead of 15 by 15. We refused to work and told him to bring us home or we use knife to threaten him." The eruption of actual violence was not uncommon. Violence also broke out if farmers refused to pay after the work was completed, if they disputed its quality, or attempted to delay payment.

Thus, while the farmers as employers were dominant, gross exploitation was rarely possible. Having given up any illusions in constitutional means of settling disputes – the police were invariably on the side of the freely bribing farmers – labourers increasingly took direct and often violent action. These actions included small children acting both with the young men and independently. If the labourers did not feel confident enough to resist the farmers at the workplace, they used the boycott. They spread word about bad treatment to other workers at the by day centres, and discouraged small children from joining dariga men. The effectiveness of this collective action was realized:

> If the farmer is bad, the group won't go again and it affects him. It is something like a strike. And he will beg us to come. It affects him if one says he won't come, and it affects him more if a group won't go.

Village workers faced the same forms of exploitation, in particular the reneging of agreements over pay. Their tactics of resistance were much the same, and the boycott was especially effective since it meant that farmers were forced to import labour at great cost from outside. But villagers rarely resorted to violence and were more fatalistic; children followed the women workers and seemed rarely to take collective action themselves. Villagers' resistance more usually took covert forms, as did that of Tamale labourers if they could not confront the farmers directly. They worked slowly or carelessly, hid in the bush, and deliberately wasted time while working. Dariga would make them intensify this by trampling, cutting or uprooting rice while weeding. Arson was another means of getting back at dariga farmers. It was frequently threatened in order to coerce farmers who had gone back on agreements or refused to pay after the work was done. While most of the very frequent fires on northern rice farms were accidental, labourers readily admitted that they were responsible for some of them: "If the farmer is a dariga man, as the by days are leaving the last one will drop a match in the field". Both village and town labourers resorted to arson, and although there is no means of knowing if child workers started fires, there is certainly no reason to exclude them. Finally, children were involved in another form of covert resistance – theft.

During the late 1970s, then, farmers were faced with an increasingly militant casual labour force that was ready to contest exploitation. Despite their apparent disorganization, the labourers, including children, used a number of potent weapons. They could go slow or work badly, go on sit-down strikes, boycott dariga farmers and, if these tactics were ineffective, they could resort to physical attacks on their employers, sabotage and threats of arson. The farmers' response was to increase labour control. Supervision was intensified and piecework extended to women and children. The divisions between youths and the children were played upon by appealing to pride in workmanship. Lists of "good" workers were introduced by some farmers, and workers disciplined by the threat of being struck off. These treasures had little effect, but of greater significance was the downturn in rice farming in 1978 and 1979. Fewer farmers came to collect labour from the by day centres and those that did could dictate their own terms. Small children were left behind in favour of the youths. This underlines the fact that the labourers were only able to take action when they were in great demand, at peak periods in the farming calendar. During slack periods, workers needing cash had to accept the farmers' terms, and they were able to cut wage rates, increase piece work, or extend the working day with impunity.

The development of the rice industry has incorporated children in northern Ghana into cash earning as never before. Children are also employed in other occupations stimulated by the rice expansion: in rice milling and marketing, and in construction, often of houses for prosperous rice farmers, for which they are paid a daily wage (4 Ghananian Cedi, GHC to 5 GHC in 1978). Further north, in Upper Region, children are not only employed on rainfed rice farms like those of the Dagomba district, but are also widely hired by commercial farmers on the Vea Irrigation Project near Bolgatanga to sow, weed and harvest rice on the irrigated plots. They suffer the same kinds of exploitation as elsewhere in the North – a long working day, refusal by farmers to pay proper wages, and extremely low pay (1 GHC to 2 GHC in 1978) – and they resort to similar kinds of resistance – go-slows, sabotage, stealing rice, arson, blocking irrigation channels, etc.

The children on the Vea scheme often cut out school attendance in order to work on the rice fields. Schooling has rapidly expanded in Ghana since the 1950s when Nkrumah's government inaugurated a campaign of mass education. Attendance grew in the 1950s and 1960s and this undoubtedly affected the supply of labour to agriculture. Nevertheless, although it might be expected that universal schooling might make child labour "illegitimate" in popular consciousness (as well as in law), children are still widely employed in agriculture, particularly in the North, as has been shown. In Dagomba the incorporation of children into agricultural wage labour appears to have had little effect on school attendance. Despite compulsory schooling, both state and Koranic schools have always found it difficult to enrol pupils, and parents are generally unwilling to send their children to school. Work on the father's farm takes preference over school, and for large numbers of small boys it was "no school, always farming". Very few girls go to school in this strongly Islamic society.

Nor do popular ideas about child labour in Dagomba appear to have changed as a result of the exploitation of children by large-scale rice farmers. There is no evidence, for example, that parents were exerting pressure on their children to withdraw from rice labour, as adult labourers had themselves done in the early 1970s. The only articulated consciousness of their exploitation comes, not surprisingly, from the children themselves, and from their older co-workers. This apparent lack of parental concern might be attributed to several factors. First, children are relatively autonomous. They were rarely sent out to work by their fathers, although in many cases the earnings were handed over to the parents. Children were adamant that they decided when to work, and they disposed of at least part of the money as they wanted. Secondly, no notion had developed of what constituted acceptable child employment and unacceptable exploitation: the assumption was simply that all children should work. Lastly, peasant farmers were themselves involved in the commercial expansion of food farming and increasingly utilized both paid and unpaid child labour themselves.

Some Conclusions

The development of capitalist agriculture in Ghana has increasingly drawn children into wage employment, and this paper has described some of the forms of exploitation and resistance accompanying this incorporation. In contrast to the partial success of such resistance in combatting this exploitation, legislation has signally failed to improve the lot of children at work. Legislation in the late 1950s and the Labour Code of 1967 confirmed colonial labour law on children but, as in the colonial period, it has had no effect – not least perhaps because of the involvement of civil servants and members of government in capitalist farming, particularly in the North.

Nor does the introduction of universal schooling since the 1950s appear to have stopped the employment of children in the North, although it may have diminished such employment in the South.

The universal participation of children in domestic labour, and the assumption that all children work, has sanctioned their incorporation into wage work outside the domestic sphere. At the same time, the fact that they are supported by the domestic economy and are easily reabsorbed into it, means that they may be paid low wages and are easily disposed of when no longer needed. This flexibility is perhaps the chief advantage of child labour to farmer-employers, particularly suiting the seasonal nature of agricultural work. Children can also be called upon when other sources are exhausted, or when other labourers will not accept the conditions of employment and, as in the domestic sphere, they can be allotted the most monotonous and time-consuming jobs. Finally, children are thought by employers to be easily cheated and less likely to resist than other workers. But, as the account of the rice industry has shown, they are not nearly so compliant as popularly supposed, and have shown a capacity for effective resistance – such resistance constrains their utilization and exploitation.

CHAPTER 27

Landlords, the State, and Child Labor in Colonial Swaziland, 1914-1947

Hamilton Sipho Simelane

Studies of colonial labor relations in Swaziland have concentrated on themes ranging from mobilization to gender distinctions, but with a primary focus on the recruitment of adult males for South African mines.[1] Studies concentrating on the involvement of women in labor migration have only recently emerged,[2] while a few scholars have emphasized local capitalist dynamics in shaping Swazi labor relations.[3] Yet the analysis of Swazi labor history still fails to involve all the participants in the labor process. One of the critical missing elements is the involvement of children in both paid and unpaid labor in colonial Swaziland.[4] Swazi children have remained "invisible" because their role in the colonial labor process was scantily recorded.[5] In comparable regions, some scholars have argued that children remain invisible in African labor studies because they have been viewed as appendages of their parents, particularly their mothers.[6] This notion has persisted in Swaziland and studies of Swazi labor history have thus failed to acknowledge that children's labor was the object of distinct

1 Such researchers include Crush, *The Struggle for Swazi Labour*; Booth, "The Development of the Swazi Labour Market"; and Simelane, "Labour Migration and Rural Transformation".

2 Miles, "Missing Women".

3 For more detail, see Crush, *The Struggle for Swazi Labour*; Booth, "Capitalism and the Competition"; and Simelane, "Capitalism and the Development of the Swazi Working Class".

4 For purposes of this study a child is either a boy or girl who has not reached puberty. In terms of chronological age, we will limit the term "child" to persons of 16 years and below. It is estimated that the puberty stage among Swazi children at that time began at 17 years.

5 The same observation is made in Grier, "Invisible Hands".

6 See Hansen, "Labour Migration and Urban Child Labour"; and Chirwa, "Child and Youth Labour on the Nyasaland Plantations".

forms of domination and control in the emerging capitalist practice of the colonial period.

This chapter concentrates on integrating children's experiences into Swazi labor history for a better understanding of the complex process of capitalist transformation. Between 1914 and 1947, settler farmers in Swaziland looked to child labor to solve the problem of labor shortages caused by the persistent desertion of adult male workers.[7] Child labor was deployed in a range of situations in colonial Swaziland,[8] but this paper will focus on the use of child labor on the farms of white settler landlords whose ascendency accompanied the consolidation of colonial capitalist relations of production. The period from 1914 to the early 1930s was dominated by unpaid child labor mobilized through relations of labor tenancy, while the period after 1932 shows an increase in paid child labor. This is a preliminary study whose main objective is to encourage research in an otherwise neglected aspect of Swazi colonial history.

The focus here on male child labor is due in part to the difficulty of accessing information on female child labor through colonial records. One of the factors behind this is that female labor was the object of excessive patriarchal control in Swaziland. As will be demonstrated below, parents were reluctant to release young girls onto farm or other forms of employment because they believed that girls beyond the daily control of parents would adopt bad habits. The same attitude was shared by the traditional ruling elite. Patriarchal control made it difficult to articulate female child labor into the colonial division of labor. Female child labor was nonetheless a constant feature of the colonial labor process, and with more authoritative research (beyond the scope of this chapter), its nature and intensity can be revealed.

7 The dates that form the perimeter of issues covered here coincide with important events in the political economy of colonial Swaziland. The year 1914 is the date from which tenancy arrangements assumed a legal status in that those Swazi who were not in a position to evacuate concession land were required to enter labour tenancy agreements with their landlords. The end of World War II saw the beginning of intensive capitalization of the Swazi economy, which resulted in the establishment of agro industrial businesses with a much stronger demand for labor. This development produced a decline in the power of landlords as major local employers.

8 The scope of the deployment of child labor in colonial Swaziland was very wide. Child labor could be analyzed at the level of homestead production for the purposes of family reproduction. At another level children were employed in most industries, especially mining, despite legislation prohibiting the employment of children under twelve in such enterprises. These levels of child labor deployment do not form part of this chapter for considerations of length.

The Foundations of Child Labor in Colonial Swaziland

For a better understanding of the operations of child labor in colonial Swaziland, we need to understand those material conditions that made it essential and operative. This section of the chapter analyzes the conditions that made it possible for landlords to mobilize paid or unpaid child labor for farm operations.

To a large extent child labor in colonial Swaziland was founded on the nature of the colonial political economy. The most crucial element of the colonial political economy was the transfer of most land into the hands of European settlers.[9] The British government was convinced at the beginning of the colonial period that the development of Swaziland would best be achieved if European settlers had easy access to land. Through the Crown Lands Order and the Concession Partition Proclamation of 1907, about two-thirds of the total land area of the country was alienated to European settlers.[10] Jonathan Crush has interpreted this proclamation as a piece of "social engineering" deliberately put into place for the purpose of labor mobilization.[11] While this remains a controversial assertion, the proclamation certainly played a crucial role in assisting settler farmers and South African mines to mobilize labor in Swaziland. George Grey was appointed as special commissioner to demarcate the land into different zones for purposes of ownership. The land was divided among the Swazi, the British Crown, and private landowners (concessionaires).[12] Over thirty reserves were created for Swazi occupation, forming patches all over the country. Peasants were given a five-year grace period at the expiration of which they were required to evacuate private concessions and move into areas designated for Swazi occupation.[13] Researchers have shown that when the five-year grace period elapsed in 1914, approximately twenty

9 Crush, "The Colonial Division of Space".

10 The issues leading to this proclamation have been the subject of several studies. See Boyce, "The Swaziland Concessions"; Mashasha, "The Road to Colonialism"; Kings, *Commoners and Concessionaires*; and Simelane, "Landlessness and Imperial Response in Swaziland".

11 Crush, "The Colonial Division of Space".

12 For more details, see Public Record Office [hereafter, PRO], DO, 119/816/4416, Swaziland Partition Scheme.

13 Parsons, "Thoughts on the Social and Economic History of Swaziland", p. 4.

thousand Swazi peasants remained on private land as squatters,[14] after concluding agreements with land owners to regulate their tenancy.[15]

The developments summarized above produced one of the important elements of social differentiation in colonial Swaziland, creating a class of landlords on the one hand and landless squatters on the other. The relationship between the two was essentially a labor relation, highlighted by the tenancy arrangements concluded between them.[16]

Three forms of tenancy arrangements emerged. In some cases landlords required rents of £1 or £2 from their tenants. This was especially the case with absentee landlords or those who were not engaged in agricultural production. The majority of such landlords were found in the Highveld and Lubombo Escarpment. Failure to pay rent normally resulted in eviction. For instance, in 1942 the Swaziland Corporation evicted fifteen families from its property because they had failed to pay the required rent.[17] In 1943 the same company requested the district commissioner of Central District to remove thirteen families from Peebles North Farm.[18]

A second form of tenancy was more labor oriented, as landlords demanded unpaid labor service in exchange for rent-free occupation of the estate by tenants. Describing this form of tenancy the high commissioner explained:

> Most of the labour is of the labour tenant class, which, as in the Union, is permitted to occupy a portion of the European owner's land on condition that the Native occupant performs a specific number of month's labour on the European land. The European proprietor in most cases has no responsibility whatsoever towards these occupants in respect of the condition under which they live.[19]

In the third form of tenancy arrangement, the landlord agreed to employ tenants on his farm at prevailing wage rates. The main condition here was

14 For more details, see Crush, "Landlords, Tenants and Colonial Social Engineers".

15 PRO, DO35/935/Y569/30, Swaziland Affairs: Land for Natives.

16 For further details on tenancy in colonial Swaziland see Crush, "Landlords, Tenants and Colonial Social Engineers".

17 Swaziland National Archives (hereafter SNA), File 452, Ejection of Natives from European-owned land.

18 SNA, File 452, Allister Miller, Director of Swaziland Corporation LTD, to District Commissioner, Central District, 21 July 1943.

19 SNA, RCS 101/36, Letter from W.H. Clark, High Commissioner to South Africa, to Malcolm MacDonald, Dominions Office, 25 November 1938.

that the landlord enjoyed the right of first call on the tenants' labor services. Liberal though this arrangement appeared, the tenants were forced to forego better job offers if called upon by their landlords at the same time. Furthermore, there was no guarantee that the tenants would receive current wage rates. For instance, towards the end of World War I, the ordinary farm wage for adult males was between fifteen and twenty shillings per month.[20] In the same period, tenants on European-owned farms received wages of between ten and twelve shillings per month. This form of tenancy became a crucial material condition for the mobilization of labor, including that of children. Labor tenancy became a framework within which landlords attempted to meet their labor requirements. For the whole system to operate satisfactorily, all that was left was for the colonial state to regulate such arrangements, which it did in part through the Masters and Servants Law.

Landlords and other employers were also able to integrate pre-colonial forms of labor mobilization into the new labor environment of the colonial period. Traditional practices of labor utilization became useful in providing landlords with some of the required labor as the mobilization and deployment of child labor at homestead level neatly articulated with the need for the mobilization and deployment of child labor on settler farms. While colonialism infused capitalist relations of production, traditional forms of labor mobilization continued to operate in the reserves.

One of the most important dynamics in traditional Swazi society was the creation, acquisition, control, and appropriation of the labor power of family members by family heads.[21] The labor power of women and children in particular was recognized as a resource to be deployed by family heads for purposes of family reproduction. "Children as they grow older are expected to participate in family tasks, particularly fieldwork. Girls take over certain domestic responsibilities, and boys tend and herd cattle."[22] Through participation in work activities children were integrated into community life, a process through which they acquired skills and attitudes to work.[23] Until they were married, boys and girls remained dependents

20 Crush, "Landlords, Tenants and Colonial Social Engineers", p. 247.

21 Such a scenario has been widely observed in other African regions. See Terray, "Long Distance Exchange and the Formation of the State"; Meillassoux, *Maidens, Meal and Money*; and Stichter and Parpart, *Patriarchy and Class*.

22 Booth, *Swaziland*, p. 52.

23 The same observation has been made in the case of Malawi; see Chirwa, "Child and Youth Labour on the Nyasaland Plantations".

of their fathers who exercised authority and control over them in many ways.[24] Landlords' mobilization of child labor, therefore, was largely built upon such traditional practices of labor mobilization.

In colonial times, especially under the various tenancy arrangements, it was correctly assumed that the landlords' control of the labor of male family heads meant, by extension, the control of the labor of all family members, especially women and children. It should be noted, however, that landlords were able to mobilize child labor by concluding arrangements with the fathers of the children involved. Once such arrangements were concluded, family heads instructed their children to work in the fields of the landlords.[25]

The underdevelopment of African production in the reserves assisted landlords in the mobilization of child labor. Beginning in the 1930s, in the wake of the Depression, peasant production of foodstuffs was insufficient to satisfy the needs of the reserves.[26] It was in the 1940s, however, that the crisis of low food production in the reserves became so acute that malnutrition increased.[27] Between 1941 and 1942 the country experienced a general decline in maize production of approximately 20 per cent.[28] In early 1943, colonial officials estimated that the country's maize harvest would be 45 per cent of normal, sorghum 80 per cent, and groundnuts 110 per cent.[29] Famine conditions were reported in most parts of the country. An editorial in *The Times of Swaziland* blamed producers for the outbreak of famine:

> In this territory partly owing to an erratic season in certain districts, partly due to the lethargy of European farmers and neglected methods which natives are allowed to indulge in when cultivating their lands, the shortage

24 According to Swazi law and custom the dominance of fathers over their sons ends when the sons get married; from that time they are recognized as men capable of making independent family decisions and can discuss national issues with other men. The dominance of fathers over unmarried sons remained effective irrespective of chronological age. The labor of unmarried sons remained subject to regimentation and appropriation by their fathers.

25 The power of family heads in this direction was at times checked by wives who refused to release their children if they felt that the work involved was too strenuous. See, for e.g., Kuper, *An African Aristocracy*, p. 140.

26 Palmer and Parsons, *The Roots of Rural Poverty*.

27 For more details see Jones, *A Study of Swazi Nutrition*.

28 *Times of Swaziland*, 6 January 1941. See also Booth, "Homestead, State and Migrant Labour".

29 PRO, DO35/1190/Y1207/2, Food Supply in Basutoland, Bechuanaland Protectorate, and Swaziland.

> of their staple food implies a period of acute starvation during the period before the reaping of the 1943–44 crop. At present the almost unprecedented incidence of Swazies [sic] purchasing mealies in June has been recorded.[30]

The most important end result of declining production in the reserves was to change the deployment of homestead labor. More women and children were released from homestead production activities to work on settler farms as wage laborers for purposes of putting bread in the family basket.[31] Landlords took advantage of declining agricultural production in the reserves to mobilize children for work in the farms. They sent recruits to the reserves to mobilize children with the message that they should take up jobs on the farms to earn money to buy food for their families. Recruitment directed toward children was more pronounced when landlords found it difficult to mobilize adult labor.

The above discussion shows that the use of child labor in settler farms in colonial Swaziland grew out of material realities. It survived because the country was undergoing transformation whereby precolonial and colonial practices were intermixed. What propelled the use of child labor even further was the gradual disintegration of traditional practices and the ascendancy of capitalist labor relations of the colonial period. For instance, by the 1930s some Swazi children voluntarily left their homes to seek wage employment. Parental control was under stress and traditional forms of child control were no longer sufficient to keep children under family control.

Landlords and Unpaid Child Labor

The period from 1914 to the early 1930s was broadly characterized by landlords' mobilization of child labor through tenancy arrangements. Labor tenancy was not a strategy devised specifically to mobilize child labor, but employers were always willing to utilize it for that purpose. In the majority of cases child labor mobilized through labor tenancy was unpaid, because most landlords were reluctant to employ tenants at prevailing wage rates.

30 *Times of Swaziland*, "Politics vs. Self-Help", 24 June 1943.

31 For more details on the stress families were subjected to as a result of low agricultural production, see Great Britain, *Financial and Economic Situation of Swaziland: Report of the Commission Appointed by the Secretary of State for Dominions Affairs (The Pim Report)*, Cmd. 4114, HMSO, 1932.

Under labor tenancy children were employed in agricultural tasks at the request or command of the landlord. Landlords enjoyed the right to call upon the offspring of tenants to provide unpaid labor even at the tender age of seven years. This was especially the case with young boys, who were integrated into the farm labor force at an early age. It appears that from the inception of British colonialism to the beginning of the Depression, labor tenancy was the main means of supplying farms with both adult and child labor.

The landlord determined the amount of time children were required to work on the farm per year. In the majority of cases, especially in southern Swaziland, landlords demanded as much as six months' unpaid labor service. The tenants' children would work for the landlord continuously for six months and then devote the rest of the year to family labor or to personal engagements.[32] The landlords always made sure that the children were not all out of the farm at the same time. This was done through drawing up a timetable that ensured that the call-up periods were different for various tenants, and also for different members of each tenant household. The operation of time allocation by the landlord was well explained by Mpisini Nyawo who said:

> I think I started working in the landlord's farm when I was seven years. According to the arrangement I worked for the landlord for a period of six months continuously and for the other six months I was at home. We somehow alternated with my brother because after completing my six months he would then take over. This was not done by us alone but all the boys whose families resided in the farm or even in neighbouring farms.[33]

In this type of arrangement children were always present in the farm labor force. The time schedule that governed child labor was the same as that which governed adult labor. Boys formed the majority of children employed on the farms. They were typically deployed in cattle herding, as most farmers were not able to fence their farms. This arose from the fact that landlords in colonial Swaziland, like their counterparts in neighboring

32 For most of the colonial period farm labor relations in Swaziland were highly influenced by what was happening in South Africa. The tenancy arrangements in Swaziland described in this paper were similar to what was happening in South African farms. This was strengthened by the fact that most landlords in colonial Swaziland were looking forward to the possible incorporation of Swaziland into South Africa.

33 Mpisini Nyawo, Interview, Mafutseni, 29 May 1996.

South Africa, were active pastoralists. In the case of Swaziland, concentration on cattle keeping was also an indication of the low level of capitalization of farming activities. Farm cattle herding came in two stages. The first stage was calf herding, usually done by boys between the ages of seven and nine. These youngsters were required to look after the calves within the vicinity of the main house. They were not allowed to venture to distant parts of the farm because they were not able to defend the calves against lions or other predators. Calf herding usually went up to mid-day, when milking was conducted. After that, the calves were allowed to graze with the cows and the young boys were released to go home. The participation of young boys in this type of activity was very common in the southern parts of the country where landlords were almost at the same level with neighboring Swazi peasants as far as economic fortunes were concerned.[34]

The second stage of cattle herding was conducted by boys from age ten and above. This articulated well with cattle herding in Swazi reserves where cattle herding had generally been entrusted to boys of sixteen and under. Because emergent capitalist agriculture, as symbolized by farm production, incorporated elements of the established traditional division of labor, landlords seem to have followed traditional practices of child labor deployment. Some scholars have noted that "herding was work which demanded considerable skills, entailed responsibility, and could involve hardship".[35] Even on settler farms, cattle sometimes had to be taken long distances to suitable pasture and water. It was the responsibility of the cattle herder to keep the animals off the fields during the growing season. Throughout the farms in colonial Swaziland, especially in the southern parts of the country, letting the cattle stray was usually punished severely at the hands of the landlord. The use of violence against young cattle herders in the farms is well portrayed by Fanaza Shongwe, who remembered:

> My family used to reside on a farm that was owned by a Boer farmer around Nhlangano. When I was eleven years old, I was called upon by the landlord to herd his cattle. This was after I had herded his calves for four years. The landlord had about eighty-three cattle which I was to make sure did not stray away from the farm. One day one of the bulls became uncontrollable and strayed into the neighbouring Swazi reserve where it mated with some

34 For more detail, see Great Britain, *The Pim Report*.

35 Beinart, "Transkeian Migrant Workers and Youth Labour", p. 56.

> Swazi cattle. When the landlord heard of the incident, he kicked me twice with his boot and proceeded to give me ten strokes on my buttocks.[36]

This kind of treatment was partially premised on traditional practices. Such incidents became more common as the number of cattle increased on settler farms and the quality of the pastures declined. Herders were forced to take the animals further into the farm each day for grazing. The cattle had to be returned to their kraals by nightfall. Day-to-day cattle herding on settler farms, during the period under review, resembled what was happening in Swazi homesteads. Despite such similarities, child labor in Swaziland was being moulded in a more capitalist context in the sense that even activities such as cattle keeping were now governed by employer-employee relations as against family relations.

In both stages of cattle herding, the youngsters were not paid wages. Their labor service was viewed as a contribution to their families' usufruct privileges in the farm. Some of the people who participated in such labor relations still vividly remember their contribution to farm labor. Fenisi Mazibuko worked for Mr. F. Swanapoel, a Boer farmer in the southern part of the country:

> Before the coming of the Great War (meaning the Second World War) my family was occupying a portion of Mr. Swanapoel's farm. In return, all family members were required to offer their labour services to our landlord. I started off by herding his calves and later it was cattle. Even young members of the family were required to work for Mr. Swanapoel. For all the work we did in his farm we received no pay. We were all working for the family's occupation of a portion of the farm.[37]

Cattle herding was not the only activity that needed child labor in the farms. Youngsters, both boys and girls, were sometimes called upon to assist in domestic chores. Although figures are not available, it appears that boys featured prominently in domestic activities. It seems that Swazi landlords found it difficult to acquire the labor of girls, even under the highly regimented labor tenancy system, due to resistance from parents. The traditional Swazi social structure emphasized control over young girls, and women in general. The prevailing attitude was that young girls working away from home would be difficult to control. The tendency among ten-

36 Fanaza Shongwe, Interview, Manzini, 3 June 1996.
37 Fenisi Mazibuko, Interview, Nhlangano, 5 June 1996.

ant families and neighboring peasant families was to release boys more easily than girls for most labor engagements outside the homestead. Normally, this presented no problem to landlords because their main aim was to get the needed labor irrespective of gender distinctions. Despite parental resistance girls were at times found in main houses as nannies. Boys dominated the scrubbing and polishing of floors, and washing dishes.

Agricultural work on the farms occupied the energies of both children and their parents. The type of work performed by children in the fields depended on the time of the year. Weeding was the dominant activity at the beginning of the ploughing season. Among the poorer farmers in the southern part of the country, weeding the landlord's field was done through the labor of the tenant's family. This was especially the case because the southern farmers had limited financial resources to mechanize their production. Oral evidence suggests that the children who were utilized in weeding fields were brought by their mothers. Tengetile Zwane explained:

> During the time when whites owned farms in the country, women did most of the weeding. This was the case because the owners of the farms demanded that we should work in their fields for nothing. Faced with huge fields to weed, our mothers had to mobilize whatever labour was available to make sure that they finished as quick as possible. I think at that time I was ten years old. I had to go to the landlord's fields to weed.[38]

The main reason why mothers took their children with them is that they were serving two masters at the same time. While they were obliged through tenancy arrangements to weed the landlord's fields, they were also responsible for producing their own crops for domestic consumption. The weeding season, therefore, put a lot of pressure on family labor such that children were increasingly incorporated into farm activities as laborers. The same kind of arrangement extended to harvesting activities, where parents enlisted their children's labor. The fact that children worked alongside their parents in these farm activities has probably influenced analysts not to recognize them as integral part of the farm labor force. It is clear, however, that children were a part of farm labor either because they were called upon by their landlords or by their parents, who needed assistance.

The seasonality of the labor process created a conflict between tenants and landlords, as both required intensive labor during the same periods.

38 Tengetile Zwane, Interview, Manzini, 3 June 1996.

This conflict was intensified by broad landlord demand for tenant labor. Tenants attempted to resolve this conflict in two ways. In some instances they used those children who were not on call by the landlord so as to quickly finish the job on the farm and then shifted their labor resources to family fields. This approach tended to increase child labor on the farms at some periods. The second approach was for the children who were not on call to perform some of the fieldwork in the homestead in the parents' absence. Whatever approach was adopted, domestic agricultural production suffered.

Some of the participants in this system have argued that although they were required to work at a tender age and for no pay, the system had some positive elements. Ndabikhona Khoza pointed out:

> I worked for my landlord for several years for no pay except allowing our family to stay in his farm. Like all other farmers of the time, he was harsh. In spite of his harshness, he provided me with food and some clothing for the duration of my stay. In some instances he even assisted me with some basic home requirements. He treated me almost the same way as my parents. I learned a lot from him and it was under his guidance that I grew to value the importance of hard work.[39]

In spite of this positive comment, the ability of the landlords to access child labor under the coercive labor tenancy system raises some concerns. For instance, although research into this area is still underdeveloped, some evidence indicates that it deprived some children of the opportunity to attend school because they were required to work in the landlord's farm for half the year. This was revealed through the testimony of Dabula Mamba who said:

> There were several disadvantages to labour tenancy, especially for children. Landlords usually pressed that the offspring of labour tenants should start working for them at an early age. In most instances children were out working in farms as early as at the age of seven. This was unfortunate because this was the age at which the children were supposed to be beginning school. The need to work in the landlord's farm made it impossible for the children of labour tenants to attend school except in those very few cases where the landlords were understanding. In my family my elder brother never went to

39 Ndabikhona Dlamini, Interview, Ezulwini, 12 June 1996.

> school because of this reason. I was able to go as far as Standard 6 because I stayed with my uncle in a Swazi reserve.[40]

The present lack of research on child labor in colonial Swaziland makes it difficult to estimate the number of children who were in the same situation as Dabula. Recognizing the fact that the value of education among the Swazi at this time was not highly perceived, the number must have been small.

Under tenancy arrangements landlords enjoyed the power to define work relationships. This was the case because under colonial laws landlords had the power to enforce summary eviction as long as they were operating within the context of the arrangements. The landlords had no power over the labor of Swazi children and adults outside their farms.

Children and Wage Employment, 1932-1947

While labor tenancy was crucial in giving landlords access to child labor in the period from 1914 to about 1932, farm labor relations in Swaziland underwent some transformation after 1932. During this period there was a shift towards engaging children and adults in farm labor as paid hands. Several developments made this shift possible. First, evidence suggests that settler production in Swaziland took a more commercial line as a result of the capitalization of production between 1921 and 1929. The process began when between 1922 and 1927 the Union Bank offered white settlers a loan fund of £696,753 for general agricultural improvement and £689,715 for stock purchases.[41] In 1929 the British government established what was called the Land and Agricultural Loan Fund for the benefit of white settlers.[42] By the end of 1930 loans amounting to about £24,000 had been given to individual white settlers under this fund.[43]

The capitalization of settler production adversely affected labor tenancy, which for some time had assured the landlords of a steady labor supply. Growing commercialization of production was accompanied by landlords'

40 Dabula Mamba, Interview, Ezulwini, 17 June 1996.

41 Great Britain, *Swaziland Colonial Reports*, 1922-1927.

42 Great Britain, *Swaziland Colonial Annual Report*, 1930.

43 For more detail on the capitalization of settler agricultural production after the First World War, see Simelane, "The Colonial State and the Entrenchment of Settler Economic Power".

restriction of usufruct rights. This came in the form of tenant eviction to open up the land to commercial agriculture or ranching. Colonial officials pointed out that "the trend was that if a European purchased a farm which he intended to occupy and farm commercially, he would evict the peasant farmers residing there".[44] The period from the 1930s onwards was characterized by several evictions, much to the discomfort of the colonial government, which was pressed to find land for the victims.[45] For instance, in 1935 fifteen homesteads were under notice of eviction from the farm of H.J. Carrol; in 1941 twenty homesteads were evicted from a farm in Hlathikhulu; in 1942 another fifteen homesteads were evicted from Farm Nine; in 1943 thirteen homesteads were evicted from Peebles North; and in the same year thirty homesteads were evicted from a farm belonging to J.J.C. Roberts and H. Muller. These evictions led to the dissolution of tenancy as a labor mobilizing mechanism. Landlords could no longer rely on the system to satisfy their labor demands. It became important for landlords to shift to wage labor, a device that also proved unreliable as far as adult male labor was concerned.

As labor tenancy was disintegrating and wage labor was growing on the farms, the landlords found themselves unable to attract sufficient numbers of farm workers to keep their operations at profitable production levels and they began to complain about what they called the "labor problem". In the mid-1930s most landlords were complaining that they were unable to obtain sufficient laborers or to keep those already employed. One farmer pointed out:

> So far as labour is concerned, it is getting scarce, there is no doubt about it. We can not keep our complement of natives. As a matter of fact, I was reproached the other day for having raised wages. Well, I had to raise wages in order to keep my natives from going elsewhere. Today I have not my full complement; I am about 30 to 40 boys short. The young Swazi today, immediately he has paid his taxes, is proceeding to Johannesburg for adventure like a white man going to another country. He is not keen on working in his own territory.[46]

44 PRO, D035/1181/Y962/2/1, Grants from Colonial and Welfare Fund.

45 For further detail on how the colonial government responded see Simelane, "Landlessness and Imperial Response".

46 PRO, D093/3, Minutes of the Fifth Session of the Sixth Advisory Council of the Swaziland Territory, 15 April, 1938.

The problem of labor shortage increased during the Second World War as Swazi men were recruited for military service. It is estimated that by 1942 approximately 23 per cent of the Swazi adult male population was out of the country either in the war or working in South Africa.[47] This impinged upon the capacity of landlords to recruit adult male labor, and they blamed the government for the shortage. In 1942 D.R.K. Keith, a landlord in the Central District, complained, "Farmers were definitely promised that the administration would see that the necessary labour would be forthcoming, but like many other of the government's promises, it has never been implemented".[48] Another farmer complained:

> More than half my gardens are lying idle today. Why? Just because I can not get the labour to carry on. When Messrs Elder and Thornton came around here asking us to produce, I readily agreed. They told me they had made all arrangements and all I had to do was to apply to the A.D.C. and I would get labour. I did so, but today have not even got a reply to my letter.[49]

Most landlords suffered as a result of workers deserting to take up employment in South African mines.[50] As one landlord from the southern part of the country commented: "The position in the south is that these natives are deserting wholesale."[51] Yet another landlord pointed out: "We have had a lot of trouble about this in the past. Hundreds of pounds were spent by some of us on natives and some of them gave us a lot of trouble by clearing off to the labor agents and getting to Johannesburg."[52] Some landlords complained that in the process of deserting, "the native just clears off and you find your machine running without a native, because he knows perfectly well that he can leave at a moment's notice".[53] The majority of workers involved in desertion were those residing outside the landlord's farm. Some were tenants who had decided to relocate into the Swazi reserves. Desertion left the white landlords with few hands to work in the fields.

47 Simelane, "War, Economy, and Society in Swaziland", p. 142.

48 *Times of Swaziland*, 19 March 1942.

49 *Times of Swaziland*, 26 March 1942.

50 For the purposes of this chapter the term desertion means the act of abandoning work, usually without notice and with no intention of returning. In most instances it was undertaken in protest against unsatisfactory working conditions.

51 PRO, DO93/2, Minutes of the Second Session of the Sixth Advisory Council of the Swaziland Territory, 3 December, 1936.

52 *Ibid.*

53 *Ibid.*

The intensity of the problem was expressed during the course of the war by a farmer from the southern part of the country who said,

> A month ago I had eight natives working, of these one has left, two have given notice to leave, and two have indicated a desire to do the same. Perhaps, now probably, the three will want to go. The result is that I can not plough all my fields. I have been forced to again offer my land to the government for food production.[54]

Swazi landlords faced a problem with adult male workers because they continued to offer low wages in a regional environment offering options. By the 1930s the Swazi labor market had grown very competitive as South African mines continued to wage a vigorous recruiting campaign in the country. Swazi landlords and employers in general were failing to compete with South African mines in terms of wages. As one employer said, "a great many natives on the farms have got to a stage where they are useful, then on account of wages they go to the mines".[55] During the war wages in the Witwatersrand rose by 24 per cent,[56] while on Swazi farms they remained stagnant between five and forty shillings per month with accommodation and food.[57] As a result, Swazi workers tended to prefer wage employment on the South African mines. It became essential for employers in general to find a solution to the problem. Some landlords attempted to employ labor from neighboring Mozambique, but these workers came in insufficient numbers.[58]

Faced with the shortage of adult male labor, landlords began to focus on paid child labor as a compromise. Landlords and other employers posted wage rates for young boys, who were generally referred to as "piccaninnies" (or "pikininis"), in an attempt to attract them to farm labor. Evidence suggests that they were successful in attracting a number of young boys. There were three main circumstances under which children took up wage employment on the farms. In some instances children "ran away" from their homes onto settler farms in search of wage employment, perhaps to

54 *Times of Swaziland*, 30 September 1943.

55 SNA, RCS 613/21, Minutes of the First Advisory Council of the Swaziland Territory, 18 October 1921.

56 Booth, "The Development of the Swazi Labour Market", p. 45.

57 PRO, DO67/15, Swaziland Blue Books of Statistics, 1940.

58 SNA, File 1467, Recruitment into Swaziland of Natives from Portuguese East Africa.

escape the work of herding their fathers' cattle.[59] In Swaziland this might not have been the case because some of the boys who "ran away" onto settler farms performed the same duty of cattle herding in their new places of employment. It is possible, however, that some of the boys left their homes to escape excessive parental control under the traditional social structure. In colonial terminology, these children were referred to as "independent" or "unaccompanied" children.

A second circumstance that pushed some children onto settler farms as laborers was destitution. Some children found themselves starving in the reserves and had to fend for themselves to survive. The condition of destitution appears to have been prominent in Swaziland during the war period and after.[60] The increase in the number of destitute was indicated by a colonial official who observed that "a definite class of destitute natives is coming into existence and paupers from this class of persons are increasing in number".[61] The escape of destitute children onto settler farms was an indication of a crack within the Swazi indigenous social structure, in which the security of the individual was supposed to be guaranteed by society at large.[62] Traditionally, at the end of each harvest members of a chieftaincy were required to pay tribute in the form of maize and other crops. The main purpose of the tribute was insurance against want for members of society. It was expected that if any member became destitute, he/she would take refuge in the chiefs kraal and be supported through tribute from society. It appeared, however, that by 1945 Swazi chiefs were failing to support destitute members of society, for any one of a number of reasons. Perhaps families were no longer able to pay tribute because of the underdevelopment of the reserves, or destitution had become too widespread for chiefs to cope with, or chiefs were using the tribute for their personal purposes. The end result was that destitute children were forced to drift to areas where they could sell their labor power for survival.

A third circumstance involved children who entered the farm labor system as wage earners under the direction of their parents or guardians, especially fathers.[63] Such trafficking of children by parents was made possible

59 In the case of Zimbabwe this point has been raised by Grier, "Invisible Hands", p. 44.

60 For details, Packard, "Maize, Cattle and Mosquitoes".

61 SNA, File 1155, Mbabane District Annual Report, 1946.

62 Such a social system was not peculiar to Swaziland but seems to have formed the basic structure of peasant societies. For a more detailed discussion, see Scott, *The Moral Economy of the Peasant*.

63 PRO, DO93/3, Minutes of the Third Session of the Sixth European Advisory Council of the Swaziland Territory 1937.

by the Masters and Servants Act of 1899, which provided for the signing of contracts of service between employers and the parents or guardians of children under the age of sixteen. The act did not specify any minimum age for such children. The Masters and Servants Act also made it possible for a father, mother, or guardian to apprentice his or her child under the age of sixteen. The decision by parents to contract their children to farm labor seems to have coincided with the deterioration of living conditions in Swazi reserves. Although figures are not available, it appears that during the Second World War an increasing number parents contracted their children to farm labor, especially boys. The deterioration in the standard of living was indicated by an increase in health disorders and declining levels of food production in the reserves.

For instance, by 1944 malnutrition disorders were reported to have reached high levels in most of the country's medical centers.[64] In June 1945 Dr. Selby from the non-European Hospital in Johannesburg visited the country and in November of the same year Dr. Squires also made a brief visit. Both observers blamed the shortage of food for the spread of malnutrition.[65] Medical officers also pointed out that the deterioration in the standard of living that resulted in malnutrition was driving children and women into wage employment.[66] Child labor, therefore, also became a means of getting money to support peasant families under stress. In most agricultural activities the children worked alongside their parents. This was an advantage to the landlords because the children were disciplined and controlled by their parents in the work place. The parent was responsible for the behavior of the dependents whose labor he/she supplied. In the majority of cases, landlords did not sign contracts with the parents but made verbal agreements.

Employer focus on paid child labor happened at a time when the British government was calling upon colonial governments to stop the employment of children under the age of twelve.[67] The British government was responding to pressure from the International Labor Organization (ILO), which attempted to discourage the employment of children, especially those under the age of twelve. When the Dominions Office proposed that the employment of children under the age of twelve should be stopped

64 PRO, DO35/1182/Y1032/13, Swaziland Medical and Sanitary Report, 1944.

65 PRO, DO35/1182/Y1032/1/4, Swaziland Medical and Sanitary Reports, 1945.

66 PRO, DO10/14/1082, Swaziland Nutrition Council Proclamation, No. 11 of 1945.

67 PRO, D035/926/Y473/15, Despatch from the High Commissioner to the Dominions Office, 26 July 1939.

in the High Commission Territories (Bechuanaland Protectorate, Basutoland, and Swaziland), the Swaziland European Advisory Council, a body dominated by employers, protested. Landlords and other employers made numerous arguments in favor of employing children of all ages. At one instance the use of child labor was expressed as a measure of relief for children of destitute Swazi families during times of food shortage because in such periods, "very often you find little boys walking about looking for work because they have no food to eat at their kraals".[68] Another member of the Council justified the employment of Swazi children in terms of biological adaption and social upbringing. He argued: "The native child develops very much more rapidly physically and I would even say mentally, to a certain age than the European child. He is thrown more upon his own resources, and nature helps him to develop more rapidly."[69] Some extended the argument to argue that a Swazi child of ten was as strong as a European child of thirteen.[70] All these were simply justifications for continued access to the labor power of children. Swazi children were a cheap source of labor and could be assigned numerous adult tasks. The cheap labor of children was critical to the profit margins of white farmers and to supplying farming operations with the required work force.

Swazi employers convinced the high commissioner that the employment of children below the age of twelve should be allowed to continue. In his response to the Dominions Office he argued that it would not be wise to effect a change in Swaziland because it was common practice for children under twelve to obtain employment in the farms and other areas.[71] The high commissioner also argued that "while it was true that a great deal of native child labor was engaged in domestic service in both urban and rural areas, it was generally to the benefit of the child to be employed as it is fed, given a good home, and taught to do something useful".[72] He suggested that if the children were not employed in the farms they would be "lying in idleness in their kraals",[73] and pointed out that the employment of Swazi children should be viewed as part of their training because there was no compulsory schooling. He assured the Dominions Office that, "as

68 SNA, Minutes of the Third Session of the Sixth Advisory Council of the Swaziland Territory, 30 April 1937.

69 *Ibid.*

70 *Ibid.*

71 PRO, DO35/926/Y473/15, Despatch from the High Commissioner (South Africa) to the Dominions Office, 26 July 1939.

72 PRO, DO35/926/Y473/15, Minimum Age for Employment of Children in Swaziland.

73 *Ibid.*

regards domestic service with Europeans, children so employed suffer no hardships and they are properly fed and housed and taught a great deal that is useful to them in after life".[74] The high commissioner also informed the Dominions Office that "in view of the malnutrition that undoubtedly exists in the Territory the fact that a considerable number of children are getting regular and adequate meals is of considerable importance in their early stage".[75]

Despite some reservations that, "the prohibition of the employment of children in non-industrial and industrial occupation is such a desirable advance in social legislation that we should not like to feel it was being ruled out without the fullest consideration",[76] the Dominions Office did not force the Swaziland colonial government to stop the employment of children under twelve. The politically volatile war period and racial tensions in Southern Africa made the Dominions Office reluctant to put pressure on the colonial government. One official from the Dominions Office admitted, "to try to put through legislation on the lines proposed without at least the acquiescence of the European inhabitants would be to encourage them to demand transfer to the Union".[77] This meant victory for the landlords and the only disadvantage they suffered was that children in their employment could not be legally penalized for such actions as refusal to perform services, neglect of duty or lack of diligence, absence without permission or valid excuse, and desertion.[78]

The landlords looked to the colonial state for help in mobilizing child labor. They called upon the state to enact legislation making it compulsory for children to be attached to an employer and to amend the Masters and Servants Law so that they could tie workers under sixteen to contractual agreements.[79] Through this demand landlords wanted to eliminate parents who played the role of middleman in the employment of their children. The problem with this arrangement was that the children could desert

74 *Ibid.*

75 PRO, DO35/926/Y473/15, Memorandum from High Commissioner to South Africa to Sir Thomas Inskip, Dominions Secretary.

76 PRO, DO35/926/Y473/15, Memorandum from Dominions Office to the High Commissioner, South Africa.

77 *Ibid.*

78 PRO, DO10/13/1099, South Africa High Commission Territories Authenticated Proclamations, 1942–43: Swaziland Native Labour (written contracts) Proclamation No.6 of 1943.

79 PRO, DO93/2, Minutes of the Second Session of the Sixth Advisory Council of the Swaziland Territory, 3 December, 1936.

and the employer had no legal recourse for punishing the uncontracted workers. Such pressure on the state became even more pronounced during World War II as landlords argued that the state was obliged to assist them because it had sanctioned recruitment for the war effort.[80] The colonial government did little to assist the settlers as it had to juggle the interests of the settlers and those of the Swazi in the reserves.[81]

In terms of the type of work involved, children working as paid labor performed the same duties as the children of labor tenants. As indicated above, these duties included planting, weeding, reaping, herding livestock, and putting up grain stores. Individually, landlords did not employ large numbers of children, but child wage earners were a permanent feature of the farm labor force. Their wages on the farms were calculated on a monthly basis and the landlords supplied food and in some instances lodging. In most farms children were paid three to five shillings per month. The working conditions on the farms were generally poor, as Zakhele Mhlongo confirmed:

> I left home when I was about ten years to work in Mr. Snayman's farm. There were four of us working for him and we were accommodated in a small room away from the main house. There was no place for cooking in the house, so we had to make a fire outside. Another problem was that we had to sleep on the floor as we were not provided with beds. Sleeping on the floor was better in summer, but in winter we had a lot of problems. Another problem with working for Mr. Snayman was that he used to flog us even for minor mistakes.[82]

Children continued to work under poor conditions because the colonial state failed to provide a mechanism for supervising working conditions on farms. This lack of supervision was pointed out by the acting government secretary:

> I am not fully satisfied that existing arrangements in Swaziland for the supervision of conditions under which farm labourers work are adequate, and I am inviting the attention of the Resident Commissioner to the impor-

80 For more detail, see Simelane, "Labour Mobilization for the War Effort".

81 For more detail on this position of the colonial state, see Lonsdale and Berman, "Coping with the Contradictions".

82 Zakhele Mhlongo, Interview, Maliyaduma, 28 May 1996.

tance of arranging for this to form one of the normal duties of administrative, medical and other officers.[83]

He was concerned that such supervision should take place, especially on the issue of workers' accommodation on the farms. He continued:

> I appreciate that no law exists whereby a master can be required to provide accommodation for his servants up to a certain standard, but as the Deputy Resident Commissioner suggests, should officers discover unsatisfactory living conditions they should bring them to the notice of the employer, and it is hoped that in the employers' own interest, steps be taken by him to ameliorate the position.[84]

The children responded in different ways to hardships on the landlords' farms. One of the common responses was desertion, especially among unaccompanied boys, because under existing labor laws they could not be prosecuted for desertion, insubordination, failure to perform work, using insulting or abusive language toward the employer, and other actions deemed in breach of contract for adults under the Masters and Servants Act. The boys consciously used desertion as a form of resistance against exploitation and abuse. As Ndzingeko Dlamini explained:

> Towards the end of the war I left home on my own to work on a farm next to Hlathikulu. The landlord was giving us a lot of trouble. The money he paid was two shillings per month and this was lower than what other farmers were paying. In addition we had to sleep in a room whose floor was just dust. To avoid these bad conditions I left his farm and fortunately I found work in a tin mine next to Mbabane.[85]

Some of the boys deserted because landlords used violence against them. Evidence suggests that acts of violence were committed against the boys for what seem to have been minor offenses. One such act was mentioned by Sozabile Myeni, who worked for a Boer farmer next to Mhlosheni.

83 SNA, RCS 101/36, Letter from L.T. Puttick, Acting Government Secretary, to all District Commissioners, Assistant District Commissioners, Principal Agricultural Officer, Principal Medical Officer, and Chief of Police.

84 *Ibid.*

85 Ndzingeko Dlamini, Interview, Mafutseni, 23 May 1996.

> I worked in my employer's farm for about three months. I liked working for him because his farm was close to my reserve. The problem was that he seemed to enjoy flogging me. In a week I think he flogged me three times. His son was about my age and he enjoyed discussing things with me. One day I was standing with his son behind my hut. When my master arrived he called me and gave me fifteen strokes, saying I called his son to my house, and this was not true because the boy came on his own. The following day I left his farm.[86]

Desertion disrupted the labor supply and increased the cost of employing such children. Even the colonial state was concerned about the fact that unaccompanied children who "find work uncongenial, leave without ceremony".[87] In spite of the difficulties faced by children in their work places, the number involved in child labor tended to increase from year to year after the beginning of the Second World War. This development was not unique to children as the number of Swazi taking up wage employment during this time showed an upward surge commensurate with an increase in employment opportunities, especially in agricultural enterprises.[88]

The increasing number of children who independently took up wage employment became a source of concern to the indigenous elite and to parents in general. Parents were content as long as children were contracted by them to the different landlords and other employers. When children began to leave home and take up wage employment independently, many parents began to fear that their authority was declining. The same concern was shared by the indigenous ruling class, which saw the new development as a threat to the base of their political power. They believed that parental, chiefly, and monarchical control should be enforced at all levels of the indigenous social structure. They blamed colonialism and its new economic order for the emergence of independent working children. This was expressed by a member of the Swazi National Council who said: "It is the European that has done us some harm. The economic conditions of today are such that it has become necessary for many of our children and women to work for money."[89] In an attempt to stop the increase in the number of

86 Sozabile Myeni, Interview, Manzini, 25 May 1996.
87 PRO, DO35/914/Y180/1/A, Native Labour: Registration of Contracts of Employment of Indigenous Workers.
88 For more detail see Simelane, "Capitalism and the Development".
89 SNA, File 1444, Meeting of the Decline of Tribal and Parental Control Committee, Lozitha, 16 June 1944.

children taking up wage employment, the indigenous ruling class formed what was called the Decline of Tribal and Parental Control Committee. S.T.M. Sukati and Prince Makhosini, both members of the committee, argued that children should first seek the permission of their parents before becoming wage earners.[90] Such sentiments were shared by King Sobhuza II who issued the following instruction to all indigenous Swazi:

> No Swazi male under the first payment of tax (18 years) and no female child shall undertake employment with any person unless such youth/female child had first obtained a written permission from the chief under whom he or she lives. If any person disobeys this order they may be punished if taken before a native court.[91]

The Swazi National Council also demanded that the colonial government legislate against the employment of children. Colonial officials were urged to forbid local employers from engaging the services of children unless they had a permit issued by a chief responsible for the child or children concerned. Such demands were not, however, accepted by the colonial government which continued to assist landlords in the process of labor mobilization.

The protest of the indigenous ruling class was not based on concern for the interests of the children themselves. According to the traditionalists, child wage employment outside parental control was a threat to the traditional social structure. As more children were independently taking up wage employment, it was clear that both chiefs and homestead heads were losing control of young people, especially their capacity to exploit the labor of their dependents. This labor was important for the process of accumulation at homestead level and beyond. Furthermore, engagement in wage labor threatened fathers' loss of control over bridewealth in the form of cattle. Thus members of the Decline in Tribal and Parental Control Committee emphasized the need to control the movement of girls to the different areas of employment. The increase in children's employment certainly constituted a major transformation in Swazi society. These developments broke traditional barriers and practices; hence the resistance of homestead heads who were also members of the indigenous ruling class. There was no way, however, in which the traditionalists could stop the process of change,

90 SNA, File 1444, Meeting of the Resident Commissioner with the Swazi National Council at Lobamba, 28 June 1945.

91 *Ibid.*

as children were by the end of the 1940s well integrated into the colonial labor culture.

Conclusion

This chapter has shown that child labor was an important element of colonial labor relations in Swaziland. This was especially the case in farming activities where landlords put into place strategies for channelling labor onto their farms. These strategies included involving the labor of children in tenancy labor arrangements and later attracting children through wages. In this manner, the same strategies used to mobilize adult labor were used to harness the labor of children. In analyzing these issues the author has argued that child labor was an integral part of the labor process in colonial Swaziland. The fact that recruiting strategies were mainly designed for adult workers should not cloud the significant role played by children in assisting employers to solve the problem of labor shortage.

The mobilization of child labor in colonial Swaziland was premised on traditional practices of labor mobilization. Traditional acceptance of male dominance and the ability of male homestead heads to control the labor of family members enabled landlords to mobilize the labor services of children. Under labor tenancy arrangements, agreements were concluded with male heads but were binding on all homestead members. It was largely the responsibility of the homestead head to make sure that even the labor of children was available to the landlord on demand. Even under conditions of wage labor, traditional parental roles played an important role in the mobilization of child labor. Parents, notably fathers, contracted their children, especially boys, to work for landlords and other employers. This shows that the use of the labor of children was not a product of colonialism. What happened in the colonial period was the articulation of labor mobilization practices of traditional Swazi society with the new and developing capitalist culture of production, in which money and its accumulation played an important role.

The use of child labor on settler farms developed in stages, although some overlap was always discernible. It appears that unpaid child labor dominated on settler farms up to the early 1930s. Such labor was acquired through the system of labor tenancy into which children were incorporated. However, from about 1932 on, evidence suggests that more and more landlords relied on remunerated child labor to conduct their farming operations. This change was induced by the shortage of adult male labor, as

Swazi men were increasingly showing preference for mine labor in South Africa, where wages were higher, and were later recruited for military service in World War II. The intensification of the process of underdevelopment in Swazi reserves, reflecting population congestion and overgrazing, tended to push more parents to send their children out for wage employment. Such a development took place much to the discomfort of the traditional ruling class, which felt that the engagement of children in wage labor was a threat to traditional forms of authority.

It is evident, therefore, that child labor became fully integrated into the labor relations of the colonial period. The emerging capitalist farmers were always eager to employ children because their labor was cheap. Also, in most instances, the landlords did not have to concern themselves with issues of control because that was largely left to the children's parents. In making children "visible" within the context of the colonial labor process, the Swazi experience provides an opportunity to better understand the processes of proletarianization and socialization in colonial Africa.

CHAPTER 28

Labor Migration and Urban Child Labor During the Colonial Period in Zambia*

Karen Tranberg Hansen

My questions are not, strictly speaking, demographic; for age was an elusive variable hardly considered by colonial census takers. Detailed information about urban children and their activities thus slipped between the established categories used in census enumerations. If age was a troublesome variable for census takers, so (in the view of colonial administrators) were the children who kept appearing in the cities fresh from the bush. Lengthy debates about the problems presented by their presence in the towns and the enactment of formal rules and regulations to repatriate them to their villages give ample evidence of their presence in towns.

Much like women, children were among the missing migrants;[1] and their activities – just like women's often uncounted and non-enumerated work – were not taken account of in employment statistics. I shall piece together a sketch of children's migration and the nature of their work in the towns based on colonial archival materials, comments on children drawn indirectly from the authorities' discussions about the problems women's urban migration entailed, and a variety of other sources. My argument is not with demography but rather with anthropology, particularly with those who continue to use the idiom of *kinship* when accounting for children's work, masking it as training or helping under the aegis of fostering.

* This is a revised version of a paper entitled "'Members of the Family': Paid Servants and Kept Relatives in Urban Zambian Households", presented at the annual meeting of the American Anthropological Association, Denver, 1984. In the present version, the discussion of the colonial period has been expanded and the sections on postcolonial developments have been almost eliminated. The information on which the paper is based is a by-product of my research on domestic service in Zambia, particularly of my sifting through files upon files in the National Archives of Zambia pertaining to women's migration. The research was funded by a grant from the U.S. National Science Foundation, no. BNS-8303507.

1 Fetter, "The Missing Migrants".

Such accounts need to be spelled out in their historical specificity, which I seek to do for the case of the colonial towns in Northern Rhodesia by asking questions about what role to attribute to children's work activities.

Children and Domestic Labor in the Colonial Situation

Substantive evidence about children in Zambia's towns during the colonial period hardly exists, as only men in gainful employment were enumerated in the majority of that era's urban census records. The researcher has great problems finding more than scattered, isolated, and impressionistic comments on urban children's activities for most of the colonial period. More helpful for my subsequent discussion is a series of social surveys undertaken in the towns in the early 1950s under the auspices of the Rhodes-Livingstone Institute.

Till the mid-1940s it was colonial labor policy to recruit a migrant male labor force that returned to the rural areas after completing work contracts. Women and children were to reside in the villages, maintaining households and fields. But the reality was somewhat different, as most of the mining companies already since the 1930s had encouraged men to bring wives and children to town so as to increase labor productivity. Women and children also migrated on their own. In the official view of the time, such women were assumed to make their living by immorality, since there was no wage employment for them.[2] And the children were held to be unruly and without parental control. Colonial authorities cooperated with the rural native authorities in making a system of rulings to prevent unattached women and unaccompanied children from migrating to towns. Yet by the mid-1930s, the number of women and children in towns was increasing. By this time more than half of the able-bodied male population was working for wages away from home – as many outside the territory as within it.[3]

The fragmentary information I have collected from colonial records and culled from the literature on that era suggests that private householders and industry benefited from children's work, while children were considered a problem by colonial authorities, rural native authorities, and parents alike – but not for the same reasons. I shall address these issues in turn.

Women's and children's presence in towns was noted with much concern in the report commissioned after the first African strike on the Copperbelt

2 See Hansen, "Negotiating Sex and Gender in Urban Zambia".
3 Roberts, *A History of Zambia*, p. 191.

in 1935: miners and other workers lay down their tools when tax increases were suddenly announced. To supplement the substandard food rations issued to husbands, many wives cultivated gardens on plots made available by the mines. Authorities sometimes regarded this practice as costly since some women "employ a boy to do the housework while they are on the plots".[4] "Children", wrote the compound manager at Roan Antelope mine in Luanshya in 1937, "are useful to parents in tilling the gardens, or in many cases obtaining additional revenue for the family by working for other natives or Europeans in the residential quarter".[5] *Piccaninnies* (piccannins), as they then were called, worked for "single natives … to wash their clothes, clean their huts, and generally fag for them".[6] They also worked for African women, among whom the wives of clerks, according to the manager, "consider they are higher up on the social scale by the fact that they are able to employ a servant".[7]

Children worked in other towns as well. A 1937 report from Broken Hill Industrial Area noted that boys of about ten years of age and up migrated from other districts in search of work and adventure. Some arrived alone, others were brought by elder brothers

> who subsequently move to some other centre, leaving the youngster behind. […] They can rarely obtain regular employment, and what employment they do obtain is so poorly paid [..] that they cannot live without assistance […] They are not [usually] without relatives or friends to assist them, but when they are, they have to make up by dishonest means.[8]

Some of these boys had been brought to towns by relatives other than parents for the purpose of cooking for them en route and attending to their wants in the compounds. In 1938 children were employed in this way in the Broken Hill mine compound. Some of them worked for single men; but in Lusaka that same year more children were employed as servants by married African couples than by bachelors. In the official view such employment by Africans was considered an unnecessary luxury, either because cooked

4 United Kingdom, *Report of the Commission Appointed to Inquire into the Disturbances on the Copperbelt, Northern Rhodesia, July-September 1935* (Lusaka, 1935), p. 505.
5 Spearpoint, "The African Native", p. 49.
6 Spearpoint, "The African Native", p. 46.
7 Spearpoint, "The African Native", p. 18.
8 National Archives of Zambia (NAZ) SEC 1/1312: Administration of Native Labour, Investigations of Labour Conditions in Northern Rhodesia (1936-37). Central Province, 1937, pp. 15-16.

food rations were issued to workers in many industries or because workers had wives who ought to do the cooking.[9]

Children's employment was governed by the 1933 Ordinance on Employment of Women, Young Persons, and Children, which was framed in accordance with the International Labour Convention. The prescribed minimum age for employment of children in industry was fourteen years. The question of the age at which children were to be allowed to work brought about controversy in the Legislative Council.[10] In the Northern Rhodesian ordinance the minimum age was placed at twelve, with the stipulation that children under fourteen could be employed in industrial undertakings if the governor issued a license.[11]

Both mines and private householders benefited from this arrangement. While they did not do underground work, several boys were employed in the mining compounds to sweep, gather firewood, cut grass, and so on. There were 95 of them in the Broken Hill mine compound in 1938 and 166 in 1940.[12] The hiring of miners' children as *piccaninnies,* sweepers, and so forth on the Roan Antelope mine is also reported to have been widespread.[13] Because there were few schools, such activity was hardly considered work at all. The few schools available in the mining towns catered to a tiny proportion of the school-age youth. Thus, in Broken Hill only 750 out of 1,500 African children of school age went to school in around 1940.[14] Children were thought not to have any rival claims on their time, so work was held to be better than idleness and perhaps likely to inculcate habits of industry.[15] For work would keep children "out of mischief and under control" at the same time as it would subject them to "a certain amount of discipline".[16]

Time and again suggestions were made that children over ten years of age who did not reside with parents should be repatriated to their vil-

9 NAZ/SEC/1349, Children in Industrial Areas. Repatriation (1938-1945). May 1938; September 1938; January 1938.

10 Northern Rhodesia, *Legislative Council Debates,* vol. 2 (1933), cols. 107-130, NAZ/SEC 1/1316: Labour. Employment of Children (1938-1945).

11 Large numbers of children below the minimum working age labored in the tobacco industry, and in subsequent years calls for the recruitment of children as farmhands were made when farm labor was short. Women were also recruited for such work.

12 NAZ/SEC 1/1316.

13 Chauncey, "The Locus of Reproduction", p. 142.

14 Wilson, *An Essay on the Economics of Detribalization*, pt. 1, p. 32.

15 Orde-Browne, *The African Labourer*, p. 109.

16 NAZ/SEC 1/1316: August 1938, April 1940.

lages. Another suggestion discriminated between children in terms of their fathers' occupations: children of government servants, clerks, messengers, police, and those who had been born in towns might be allowed to stay, whereas children of unemployed fathers were to be repatriated.[17] Added concern about children's presence in towns was raised in the 1938 report on labor conditions in Northern Rhodesia, whose author stressed the likely rise of juvenile delinquency.[18] Another report from the same year put this squarely, pointing to "the serious danger of the production of a demoralised class of young hooligans who will become very dangerous elements later on".[19] Monies were appropriated for the repatriation of children, and the authority for moving them was found in the Juvenile Offenders Ordinance.[20] The perception of danger implicit in children's presence in towns was influenced by the assumption that "parental authority has largely disappeared in [the] unfamiliar surroundings and the trouble is accentuated by the large proportion of temporary marriages".[21] Although the extent to which urban children were "uncontrolled" (that is, not under parental authority) is not known, it is certain that Africans viewed the concept of *parental authority* far less exclusively than did colonial authorities. Parental authority extended beyond the biological parents to classificatory mothers' brothers (in the region's matrilineal societies) and fathers' brothers (in the patrilineal groups) and revolved in general around seniority regardless of the specifics of descent. Rather than concerning parental authority per se, the assumption that children were uncontrolled highlighted another, more crucial issue. For the presence of both women and children in towns accentuated both the colonial authorities' fear of the rise of a proletarianized urban population in need of basic services and the rural native authorities' concern about the loss of tribal allegiance and the undermining of their own authority.

Officials expressed their fear about the growing numbers of children in the towns in terms of *detribalization*. Their concerns are summed up in the following annual report:

> More and more women are accompanying or joining their husbands in the urban areas, and while these women still visit the rural areas more frequently

17 NAZ/SEC 1/1348: "Native Education on the Mines", May 1938.
18 Orde-Browne, *Labour Conditions*, pp. 67–68.
19 *Report of the Commission to Inquire*, p. 47.
20 Heisler, *Urbanization and the Government*, pp. 99–100.
21 *Report of the Commission to Inquire*, p. 47.

> than the men and so keep a connection with tribal life, this state of affairs cannot be expected to last forever. A new generation born in the towns is growing up and presents an increasing problem. These children would under native custom be cared for and disciplined in most clacs by grandparents and the maternal uncle, but these people have themselves often left the village to seek work and a livelihood in the towns, so the mother in the town has to look after her children entirely by herself and this she has in many cases still to learn to do. It is because in so many cases the customary guardians of children are not in the villages that schemes for repatriating children from the urban areas to their villages often break down. Children not under parental control may be sent home or fetched home by the native authorities but soon run away again to the towns because there is no longer anyone at home who is by custom primarily responsible for their care and upbringing.[22]

The question of how to control the migration of women and children was frequently on the agenda at meetings of the rural native authorities. If children grew up in town, new allegiances might arise and customary authority no longer be observed. To maintain the vestiges of such authority by controlling the young generation one chief suggested: "Our children should be well looked after and taught by ourselves in the villages. Then when they are of full age, they can go to town to seek work."[23] Among other suggestions were that "not more than two small children live in town with parents" (older children living "with grandparents according to custom") and that "schools be in rural and not urban areas".[24]

If the colonial and rural native authorities viewed children's presence in towns as problematic (though for different reasons), so did parents and guardians. Low wages, the rationing system, and lack of space made children in the compounds a heavy economic burden for their caretakers. Many parents found it expensive to support children in town, most had little room, and some felt that a rural upbringing was better for them. Until the mid-1940s family housing was not generally available to urban African workers. The previously mentioned policy of treating Africans as short-term urban workers who would return to their villages was built into the wage scales, the physical layout of compounds, and the regulations govern-

22 Northern Rhodesia, *Annual Report,* p. 7.

23 NAZ: Extracts from the third meeting of the Southern Province African Provincial Council, Livingstone, June 1946. Statement by Chief Musokotwane.

24 NAZ: Points raised by Chiefs attending Course at Chalimbana, 26 October 1946.

ing visitation practices. Wages hardly increased during the 1930s and many households had a hard time making ends meet. Most couples shared rooms with other couples. Where family housing was available, space was too scant to allow the customary separation of sleeping arrangements by age and sex. Godfrey Wilson has described how young children and visitors were present in all the compounds in Broken Hill around 1940 and how they slept either in the same room as their parents and hosts or in the open air. "The African dislike this necessity intensely, but cannot avoid it", he reported.[25] The arrangements for older children were that boys slept with adult friends in bachelor quarters, and girls in the homes of women whose husbands worked at night.[26] While the size of food rations depended on whether men workers were married, they were not influenced by the number of children and dependents. Since neither food nor room was directly provided for children, many urban parents allowed their sons to work for others in order to lessen the pressure on both household budget and space. This practice, according to Wilson, was "exceedingly common". Groups of single male workers sharing huts included young boys "who were not yet wage earners and who [did] the cooking".[27] Such young boys might be related to one of the men, having accompanied him to town or been sent to him by parents or relatives already in town: "A boy over six, who is with his parents, joins a group of single men in this way, whenever possible."[28] In addition, several youngsters worked as "young kitchen- or nurse-boys" in the European residential areas.[29]

During the last half of the 1940s the governing authorities finally recognized that large numbers of urban Africans were in the towns to stay. Copper prices had risen sharply in the world market in the postwar economic boom, and labor shortages were felt in all sectors of the economy. A more stabilized labor force was needed; and mines, local authorities, and private employers were charged with providing more housing for married Africans in addition to the usual bachelor quarters. Yet construction of houses for urban African workers was slow and could not accommodate the continuous rural influx, many of whom found shelter in squatter settlements.[30] The African population in wage employment in the country's main towns

25 Wilson, *An Essay on the Economics of Detribalization*, pt. 1, p. 25.
26 Wilson, *An Essay on the Economics of Detribalization*, pt. 1, p. 25.
27 Wilson, *An Essay on the Economics of Detribalization*, pt. 2, p. 75.
28 Wilson, *An Essay on the Economics of Detribalization*, pt. 2, p. 75.
29 Wilson, *An Essay on the Economics of Detribalization*, pt. 2, p. 75.
30 For the growth of squatting, see Hansen, "Lusaka's Squatters".

had grown from 37,527 to 68,214 between 1931 and 1946 and stood at 128,224 in 1956.[31] At a district commissioners' conference at the end of the war the compounds were described as "filling with youth, sixteen years and under, attracted by the chance of a little money and freedom from village discipline. Indians, African clerks and messengers", the report continued, "employed them as servants and had them sleep in their kitchens". This practice, incidentally, was singled out for "its moral[ly] bad effects as wives of clerks, etc. were able to get cheap domestic servants".[32]

The migration from the rural areas had by then profoundly and adversely altered local productive systems so that most village societies had become dependent on urban wage labor. Children and youth had become more attracted to towns than ever before; for a system of compulsory primary education for children between the ages of twelve and sixteen had been introduced in the early 1940s, first in the Copperbelt towns and later in Broken Hill and Livingstone. It never included Lusaka, where the provision of school facilities was sorely lacking.[33] To make children attend school, the Employment of Women, Young Persons, and Children Ordinance was amended in 1949 to prevent the employment of young persons between twelve and sixteen in industrial enterprises without the permission of a district or labor officer.[34] Because of the urban school bias, more young siblings, nephews, and nieces came to town to live with uncles and elder brothers, hoping to get into school. But the number of school places was not sufficient, and young boys continued to find their way into jobs in private households. From Livingstone in 1944[35] and from Broken Hill in 1948 came complaints that the compulsory education scheme was being hampered by Europeans who hired African boys to work in their gardens and kitchens.[36]

Some of these children contributed to strained household budgets; for the cost of living for Africans had risen one hundred per cent between 1939 and 1946, far surpassing wage increases.[37] Other boys worked to get by on their own. According to a 1945 report, many schoolboys lived with friends and relatives, staying only three months on average and moving on when

31 Northern Rhodesia, *Report of the Census*, p. 69.
32 NAZ/SEC 1/1316, August 1945.
33 NAZ/SEC 2/28: Annual Reports, African Affairs (1948). Central Province.
34 Northern Rhodesia, *Legislative Council Debates*, vol. 66 (1949), col. 460.
35 *Livingstone Mail*, 22 September 1944, p. 5.
36 NAZ/SEC 2/82.
37 Colonial Reports, *Annual Report, Northern Rhodesia* (London, 1947), p. 7.

people got tired of them. None got sufficient food from the people with whom they lived, and they had partly to fend for themselves. This they did by begging at the mine feeding store or the markets, earning money as golf caddies, and theft. Many lived in the mine bachelor quarters. They were allowed to sleep in the houses occupied by single men and were given the scraps left over after the men were fed. In return they were expected to keep the housing clean and sometimes to do the washing. They were seldom paid any wages, although they were sometimes promised five shillings or seven shillings sixpence per month. They were usually told they had lost their pay because of bad behavior. Teachers felt that such boys should be sent home unless they had a parent or guardian approved by the headmaster of their school.[38]

Thus, some boys found school places but no relations. An article reporting on the compulsory education scheme commented that in the late 1940s at least half of the children in the Copperbelt schools were not living with their parents or any recognized guardian. "When the parents are present", the article continued, "their influence is too often weak or negative, due to inadequate housing – or indifference".[39] Some of these boys were taken into the country to camps in order to learn about the rural way of life. Others were brought there by force. Between 1941 and 1943 a total of 515 children had been repatriated from the Copperbelt towns. With a control agency – the school – now present in some towns, child repatriations initially declined and were reported to be negligible in 1943.[40] Yet the practice regained currency in the early 1950s when authorities, perhaps fearing the political mobilization that was sweeping the towns, once again became concerned about the "unfortunate increase in the number of young boys coming to the line of rail from the rural areas without guardians". In 1951 some were repatriated to their home districts.[41] In 1952 the government ordered the return of all "solitary" children from Broken Hill to their parents' villages,[42] and in that same year twenty-five Lozi children were repatriated from Livingstone.[43]

38 NAZ/SEC 1/1338: Monthly Reports. Labour Department (1945). Western Province, Nkana.

39 Holmes, "Urban Schoolboys", p. 31.

40 NAZ/SEC 1/1349, September 1943.

41 NAZ/NR 3/199, Annual Reports. Senior Labour Officer. Lusaka District (1950-1960), Midland and Southern area, 1951.

42 Swanzy, "Quarterly Notes", p. 20.

43 Swanzy, "Quarterly Notes".

The repatriation of children was not particularly effective. Urban children not under parental control might well be returned to villages by urban authorities or fetched by rural native authorities. But they soon went to town again because their customary guardians in many cases themselves were residing in towns. People who remained in the villages were in many cases unable to produce sufficient food, and research carried out from the 1930s on has shown that villagers had less to eat than townspeople.[44] Bruce Fetter's argument that women who migrated were responding to the growing disparity between rural and urban conditions may easily be extended to their children.[45] Once back in town, African boys continued to seek work. According to a 1954 report, some European mothers were even content to entrust their children and babies to the care of youngsters (i.e., young boys). Other African boys worked as golf caddies, while grass cutting was popular with schoolboys during their holidays. The attraction to employers, the report ends, "is that their wages are relatively low".[46] Employers could hire juvenile workers from a growing labor supply because of the lack of school facilities.[47]

Judging from the records, it appears that girls rarely worked away from home and that they were not farmed out to relatives to the same extent as boys. In the earlier years parents found it difficult to socialize girls in the urban setting, which was held to provide many temptations.[48] J. Clyde Mitchell's 1951 Copperbelt studies reveal a definite inequality of numbers in the ten-to-fourteen-year age group, indicating perhaps that parents sent puberty-age daughters back to the villages. Some boys and girls lived elsewhere in towns, separate from their parents. More boys than girls did so, most of them attending schools but some working as domestic servants.[49] Merran McCulloch's 1952 survey of Livingstone also shows a disproportion

44 Richards, *Land, Labour, and Diet in Northern Rhodesia*; Thompson, "Two Studies of African Nutrition"; Fetter, "Relocating Central Africa's Biological Reproduction", pp. 473-474.

45 Fetter, "Relocating Central Africa's Biological Reproduction", p. 475.

46 NAZ/NR 3/199: Southern Area, 1945.

47 In a 1956 report the African Education Department pointed to the lack of school facilities for forty-five thousand African urban children; see *Central African Post*, 29 July 1957, p. 7.

48 See Lehmann, "Marriage, Divorce, and Prostitution"; and Lehmann, "Lives of African Adolescent Girls".

49 Mitchell, "African Urbanization", pp. 4, 6.

between marriageable men disappeared to towns and the young women.[50] D. Bettison's 1954 survey of Lusaka's African townships shows an even proportion of young men and women residing with parents and the rest scattered across other parts of town, other towns, and rural areas.[51] Between 1954 and 1957 the proportion of children resident with parents in Lusaka had grown from 76 per cent to 90 per cent for both sexes.[52] In addition to resident children – and compensating, at least in terms of numbers, for those who had left – many urban households hosted live-in relatives. On the Copperbelt in 1951 Mitchell found co-residents in 3.5 per-cent of the households; McCulloch found them in one-fifth of Livingstone's married households and several others in the single quarters.[53] Approximately one-third of Lusaka's African households in 1957 hosted live-in relatives who were going to school, working elsewhere, looking for work or housing, doing the household work, or any combination of these.[54] Arnold Epstein's work on Ndola in 1950-1956 and Hortense Powdermaker's work on Luanshya in 1953-1954 offer rich details on the texture of African life in the rapidly growing Copperbelt towns, the new options confronting parents and children, and their problems and challenges in pursuing them.[55]

The information presented so far certainly shows that children were present in towns from the earliest colonial years and that many young boys worked, especially in private households, with or without pay. According to the 1956 census, three times as many juvenile boys as adult women were employed in all economic sectors in Northern Rhodesia's towns.[56]

But what do we make of this and the other bits of evidence about children's work? Did the role children's work played in the rural societies from which they came carry over, unaltered, into the urban situation? The ethnographic record provides evidence of the training and socialization function of rural children's work.[57] Young girls were first encouraged to imitate

50 McCulloch, "A Social Survey", p. 16. For a discussion of the problem of underreporting girls in their early adolescence, see van de Walle, "Note on the Effect of Age Misreporting".

51 Bettison, "Numerical Data on African Dwellers", p. 29.

52 Bettison, "Numerical Data on African Dwellers", p. 32.

53 Mitchell, "African Urbanization", p. 7; McCulloch, "A Social Survey", p. 22.

54 Bettison, "Numerical Data on African Dwellers", p. 50.

55 Powdermaker, *CopperTown*; Epstein, *Urbanization and Kinship*.

56 There were a total of 4,616 male juveniles compared to 1,594 adult females in wage employment in the towns of Northern Rhodesia in 1956. These numbers are abstracted from Federation of Rhodesia and Nyasaland, *Census of the Population, 1956*, table 80.

57 Among the ample studies of rural societies are two with special focus on childhood: Read, *Children of Their Fathers*; and Mbikusita-Lewanika, "Zambian Society".

– and later expected to perform – much of adult women's work in and around the household, thus receiving education for adulthood in the homes of parents, guardians, or other relatives; they were rarely restricted to their individual family. Small boys would learn to do household tasks in similar contexts: sweeping huts, fetching water, keeping fires going, and cooking; at the time of puberty they were removed from the women's circle.

The functions of such activities tended to become transformed in the towns because of the growing dependence on the cash nexus. Due to the vagaries of urban living, strained household budgets, and lack of family housing, many such "helping" services were performed in return for support in the form of food, shelter, or money. Urban children's struggles for livelihoods in the Northern Rhodesian towns may have had much in common with those Suzanne Comhaire-Sylvain described at Kinshasa (then an African ward) in Leopoldville in the early 1940s. Reporting a "frightening [...] proportion of undernourished children",[58] she noted avenues children pursued to get more food: finding someone willing to support them or share with them, stealing, or working. Some children would find a protector among relatives and in return for upkeep be obliged to work in the home or away from it. Groups of boys would get together, pooling whatever resources they had laid their hands on. Better still, they would find paid work. She found a good percentage of working children, almost all of them boys. Many schoolboys worked as part-time servants for Europeans, some sold newspapers, some carried shopping parcels, some hawked flowers and fruit, and some made handicrafts: paper flowers, string belts, baskets, and reed models of boats, trucks, or aircrafts. Some of the modelmakers formed an association of their own, trying to keep up a regular supply to satisfy their customers. Many of these boys had left school because they wanted to make a living on their own, and some were unable to go to school because they were orphans or their parents did not live in Leopoldville. Some of the boys without relatives would pool their resources and use a rotational system for dividing up their individual shares.

Children in Northern Rhodesia's towns are likely to have undertaken many more activities directed at economic survival than those mentioned in the scattered evidence from the colonial records. The pieces of evidence from those records may only form the tip of an iceberg, concealing a children's work culture and social organization of its own that to some extent provided the props that were missing in the cities: economic support and

58 Comhaire-Sylvain, *Food and Leisure*.

shelter. The information I have provided here suggests that although children in the Northern Rhodesian towns often provided services to kin, such work was not the result of the customary obligations that placed them at the beck and call of relatives. Young boys worked to lessen the pressures on their urban families' substandard household budgets and housing space, to provide alternatives to the lack of rural earning opportunities, or to eke out a living on their own. Although not all of them were paid, they all were units of labor. They worked cheaply and did the dirty work that – in ways so far largely unaccounted for – helped relieve the colonial administration of paying living wages and providing acceptable housing. They continued to do so on the eve of, and in the wake of, independence in 1964. The time slice 1963-1968 is the only one I have located that has employment statistics for domestic service categorized by sex *and* age.[59] Table 28.1 shows that juveniles (i.e., those under eighteen) were employed as domestic servants in larger numbers than adult women from 1963 through 1966. Their total number in this sector is likely to have been much larger, as the table includes only enumerated servants. After 1966 the number of enumerated juvenile servants dwindles, probably due to the expansion of the primary school sector after independence.

Table 28.1. Africans Employed in Domestic Service and Total Wage Employment

Type of Work	*1963*	*1964*	*1965*	*1966*	*1967*	*1968*
Domestic Service						
Men	27,240	26,800	31,500	31,231	31,508	36,491
Women	708	700	815	1,498	1,549	1,758
Juveniles[a]	1,090	1,037	1,839	663	60	80
Total Wage Employment						
Men	149,959	159,250	179,800	127,100	145,180	157,717
Women	3,125	3,303	4,389	3,803	3,742	3,911
Juveniles	3,437	2,736	10,313	11,312	4,017	1,069

Sources: Northern Rhodesia and Republic of Zambia: Annual Reports, *Labour Department*, 1963-1968.
Note: Excluding government employees; excluding North-Western Province.
a Young persons under 18 years of age.

59 Labour Department, *Annual Report*.

Children and Domestic Work after Independence

At independence, the rules and regulations that had structured rural-urban migration and access to work and to housing were done away with. More people went to towns, especially women, anticipating new employment opportunities.[60] By the early 1980s half of Zambia's population lived in towns. The population had grown by more than three per cent per year, and children below age fifteen now composed half of the country's total population. The educational system expanded rapidly in the immediate wake of independence; and more little children, particularly girls, were sent to school than ever before.

But not all children get school places. Of those who do, few qualify for entry into secondary schools. A new segment of children has entered the private household market. Today young girls can be seen in the sort of domestic work that tended to be done by boys in a previous era: some girls do service work at substandard wages, and others do household work in the homes of relatives in return for their upkeep. In Zambia *keeping relatives* means providing them with shelter, food, and occasional clothing. Some of the kept girls are town-born-and-bred, and others continue to arrive from the rural areas. "Children", says Elizabeth Colson for the Gwembe Tonga, "are exchanged freely between rural areas and city for a variety of purposes".[61] This must be explained against the background of the postcolonial economic decline, during which new pressures have been placed on rural and urban economies, housing stock, and private household budgets. In this situation everyone works at making a living, but fewer and fewer do so by being wage-employed.[62]

60 Jackman, "Recent Population Movements in Zambia". Regarding Zambian demography and the 1963 and 1969 population censuses; see also Ohadike and Tesfaghiorghis, *The Population of Zambia*; and Ohadike, "Demographic Perspectives in Zambia".

61 Colson, "The Reordering of Experience", p. 10.

62 This situation is by no means unique to Zambia, yet few studies have been undertaken about childrens work elsewhere in Africa. For some examples, see the work of Schildcrout, e.g., "Age and Gender in Hausa Society"; Schildcrout, "Women's Work and Children's Work". In the aftermath of the 1979 International Year of the Child, more studies of children's work in developing countries began to appear. Among examples from this wave of studies are Mendelievich, *Children and Work*; Rodgers and Standing, *Child Work, Poverty, and Underdevelopment*; White and Tjandraningsih, *Child Workers in Indonesia*; and Jolly and Cornia, "The Impact of World Recession". Without discussing children's work at all, Mwanamwambwe and Zenebeworke describe shortfalls in education, health, and basic amenities: Mwanamwambwe and Zenebeworke, *Children in Zambia*.

Among the many who do not pursue an occupation but still work, are young Zambian women below the age of eighteen who mind children and do household work in the homes of relatives. Other young women do the same kinds of work in the homes of nonrelated Zambians, in return for which they receive puny wages and are said to be members of the family. Most parents dislike to farm out their school-level girls in this way. Yet some will still do so, rationalizing their step by reckoning that domestic service will prepare their daughters for their future roles as mothers. In contrast, parents say that young boys must be able to fend for themselves. They need skills different from those acquired in domestic service in order to be able to take care of future wives and children, as well as of parents in old age. If they can at all afford to, parents struggle to send young boys to special schools to retake failed classes, have them join formal or nonformal training workshops, or sign them up as apprentices with informal sector artisans.[63] Such opportunities are limited for young girls. Many young boys roam the streets, selling *michanga* (cigarettes) by the stick, checking passengers into minibuses, washing cars, guarding parked cars, doing any casual work they can find, and generally living by their wits. If boys can at all avoid domestic service, they do so.

Conclusions

Colonial authorities, alarmed at the prospect of a town-born generation growing up, considered children's presence in the towns to be a problem. Control over children's movements between villages and towns was a key to the administrations' attempt to delay the urban proletarianization process. Only by disciplining and training children at an early age in "tribal custom" in the villages could they ensure the reproduction of such customs. Children in towns without parents or guardians would never learn where they really belonged but would turn into hooligans and delinquents and grow up with no respect for tribal authority. By not improving the prospects for rural livelihoods and by for a long time retaining the illusion that African townspeople were temporary urban residents who did not need family wages and family housing, the colonial administration created the very problem it most feared: urban proletarianization. Increasing numbers of men and women – adults, young people, and children – migrated to

63 Extensive research on youth training has been undertaken by Hoppers, "Youth, Apprenticeship, and Petty Production in Lusaka".

the towns, where they all, in many different ways, contributed to the making of an African urban working-class culture and a social-organizational setup aimed at confronting the color bar restrictions of their day: substandard wages and substandard housing. Children's migration and urban work must be explained against that background.

To do this we must flesh out Elizabeth Colson's statement: certainly, children *are* exchanged freely between rural areas and towns in Zambia for a variety of purposes. But while such exchanges have been noted, they have neither been consistently described nor subjected to analysis. Writing about such practices generally, Ester Goody notes that because many ethnographers "do not enquire about the residence of children and [the use] of classificatory kinship terminology means that such information is likely to come to light only accidentally".[64]

As I have shown, rural-urban exchanges of children in Zambia have been noted from the early colonial days through the present. They were and are influenced by the different income opportunities in rural, as compared to urban, areas; the differential availability of schools; patterns of housing and lack of space; and crisis within families. The underlying assumption – and perhaps the reason why these practices have not been accounted for – has been that such arrangements reflected customary, shared rights in children within descent groups and that the placing of children with others therefore composed some sort of traditional responsibility system along the lines of fosterage.

While that might have been so in the distant past, it was not always the case in the towns during the colonial era; nor is it the case for all the children who today are kept in the households of others. The placing of children with kin, according to Goody, can only be effective within a system in which *claims* on kin have meaning.[65] The relationship gives rise to *reciprocal claims,* which have to be honored. When the claims are no longer reciprocal, the system ceases to be effective. She further suggests that

> where differentiation and hierarchy are well advanced, there is little that poor relatives can do to reciprocate. At this point transactions become subject to calculations of equity. Masters take apprentices in exchange for a fee and the right to their labour for a fixed period. Mistresses pay housemaids; school boys pay boarding fees.[66]

64 Goody, *Parenthood and Social Reproduction*, p. 331.
65 Goody, *Parenthood and Social Reproduction*, p. 278.
66 Goody, *Parenthood and Social Reproduction*, p. 280.

The Zambian situation I have described is approaching this point.

Although children placed with urban kin to do unpaid household work or with urbanites known to parents and guardians to work as servants for a pittance are recruited and controlled by personal relationships of kinship or quasi-parental authority, their work does not represent some lingering survival of primordial relationships belonging to a distant past. Such work, during the colonial period and at the present time, represents an *extraction of labor in a relationship merely cast in the familial idiom*. Whether exchanges of children between kin and nonkin were prevalent among Zambian ethnic groups prior to the rise of capitalist production or not is largely irrelevant to the question of what economic role the household labor of such children performs in the economy.

In the short term, children's work helps poor parents make a living, at least temporarily, by freeing them from the responsibility of support; and support in cases where a child worker's pay is remitted directly to parents, adults come in part to depend on their children's earnings. In the long term, children's work in private homes – like women's unpaid household labor and adult domestic servants' labor – helps produce labor power at little cost to the state. While all household members do this to some extent, children do it optimally for the state; for though *in* these households, they are not *of* them (since work, not familial affection or loyalty, is the reason for their presence) and can make no claim on them. Their role may continue to be spoken of in the language of kinship, but its functions have altered. Such children are units of labor whose work is consumed with little or no remuneration. Compared to adults, child workers have restricted control over the conditions of their labor and are more vulnerable to the whims of adults. And because they are more subordinated than adults in the labor process, they are subject to more invidious forms of exploitative relations than exist within the household.

CHAPTER 29

No Place for Children: The Peculiar Case of Australia, 1850-1919

Bradley Bowden

Introduction

One of the most dramatic consequences of industrialization and modernization was the movement of child and adolescent workers out of the household economy and into the waged labour market. So common was the young's entry into the workforce during initial periods of industrialization that Hugh Hindman has concluded: "We know no major advanced nation that did not go through a stage of pervasive child labor on the path to advancement".[1] Is this supposition true? This chapter will suggest that, at least in Australia, it is not.

The late nineteenth century in Australia was a period of economic and demographic transformation. The population and workforce expanded rapidly, the former increasing from 1,156,000 in 1861 to 3,690,000 in 1901. An extraordinarily high birth rate meant that the young made up a growing percentage of the potential labor force. By 1881 the Australian population's median age was only 20.08.[2] The number of youngsters capable of entering the Australian labor market grew, both absolutely and relatively, during the 1890s. Yet, it will be argued, despite these circumstances the young made only a modest contribution to the labor force. In the relatively populous Australian colonies of Victoria and Queensland those aged nineteen years or under made up barely seventeen per cent of the workforce (prior the establishment of the Australian Commonwealth in 1901 its states remained self-governing British colonies). Unlike the situation applying in the industrial districts of Britain and the United States, there was virtually no demand for workers aged fourteen years or less.

1 Hindman, *Child Labor*, pp. 4-5.
2 *Australian Commonwealth Census of 1911* (Melbourne, 1912), p. 101.

Why, when demographic changes meant that those aged nineteen years or younger made up such a large percentage of the population, were children and youths so underrepresented in the Australian workforce? The explanation is found in the peculiar structure of the Australian economy. As Queensland's Agent-General advised a House of Commons Committee in 1890, those who found most difficulty in obtaining work were those who "cannot do manual labour; it is manual labour that we want".[3] Pastoral activities, mining, building and transportation were the principal drivers of economic growth and employment. In these occupations employers continued to place a premium on the adult male able to "roll up his shirt-sleeves and work with his hands".[4]

While Australia's peculiar economic structure meant that most work required adult labor this did not totally preclude the exploitation of children and adolescent employees. The limited demand for young workers meant that there were always more young job seekers than there were jobs available. When the young did find work it was normally in the more backward and unproductive sectors of the economy. In these areas – the most prominent of which were domestic service, textile and clothing manufacture, and boot and shoe making – exploitation was commonplace. But, unlike the situation that prevailed in the Northern Hemisphere, the manufacturing sector in Australia was of limited importance. The agricultural sector made an even more modest contribution to the national economy. These factors curtailed the demand for child and adolescent labor.

A Peculiar Immigrant Society

In all market economies the participation of children and adolescent youths in the paid workforce is determined by two factors: the supply of children and employer demand for this form of labor. In Europe, the eighteenth and nineteenth centuries witnessed a marked increase in supply, whether measured in absolute or proportional terms. In England in 1671 there were 657 children aged under fourteen years for every 1000 adults aged between twenty-five and sixty. By 1826 there were 1120 children per 1000 adults.[5] Many nineteenth century economists assumed that demand created its own supply. John Stuart Mill concluded that the cotton industry's demand

3 Ashe, "Testimony", p. 1552.
4 Ashe, "Testimony", p. 1552.
5 Cunningham, "Employment and Unemployment of Children", p. 147.

for "infant labour" caused families to act in ways that favoured an "increase of population".[6] The assumption that there is a close correlation between the number of youngsters seeking work and those obtaining it is, however, a dubious one. As Hugh Cunningham has noted in his studies of nineteenth century England, "the supply of children is no indicator of the level of demand for child labour". Cunningham believes that in industrializing England the demand for child labor was restricted to particular districts and economic sectors. In most areas "under- and unemployment were the norm".[7]

If we need to be wary of making correlations between the supply of children and the demand for child labor in industrializing Europe, even more caution needs to be applied when extrapolating such concepts to immigrant societies such as Australia. Australia's demographic and economic patterns did not mirror those of the Old World. The Gold Rushes of the 1850s resulted in a population dominated by adult males. There were abnormally small numbers of five to nineteen year olds.[8] While Europe's population began to age during the latter half of the nineteenth century Australia's grew younger. Natural increase overtook immigration as the main driver of Australian population growth as the young immigrants who arrived after the Gold Rushes started families. These immigrant families were typically large. By 1891 the average completed family comprised seven children.[9] Reflecting this demographic transition 48.5 per cent of Australian males and 55.8 per cent of Australian females were recorded as infants, children or adolescents in 1881.[10]

After 1891 the number of Australian youngsters capable of entering the workforce grew markedly as those born in the preceding decade approached their teens. At the century's end, in all four eastern mainland colonies (South Australia, Victoria, New South Wales and Queensland), the largest quinquennial cohort was that aged between ten and fourteen years, followed by those aged between fifteen and nineteen years.[11] There

6 Mill, *Principles of Political Economy*, I, p. 344.
7 Cunningham, "Employment and Unemployment of Children", pp. 147–148.
8 Hall, "Some Long Period Effects", p. 44.
9 Hicks, *"This Sin and Scandal"*, p. xiv.
10 *Australian Commonwealth Census of 1911*, p. 104.
11 *Australian Commonwealth Census of 1911*, p. 101; Caldwell, "Population". Prior to the publication of the Commonwealth census of 1911 each colony (later state) conducted their own censes. In compiling historical statistics, economic historians have tended to focus only on the more populous, eastern mainland colonies, ignoring Tasmania and Western Australia.

were comparatively few prime age adults to be had. In the large northern colony of Queensland those aged between twenty and thirty years accounted for 24.6 per cent of all Queensland males in 1886. But by 1901 only 17.6 per cent of males were in this age cohort.[12]

While Australia's demographic profile was characterized by its youth the nation's peculiar economic structure limited the young's employment opportunities. Australia's "comparative advantage" lay in highly productive rural pursuits (notably wool production) and metalliferous mining rather than manufacturing. Both the pastoral and mining sectors were located in the interior. Work in these sectors was highly productive and physically demanding, unsuited to child labor.

Pastoral work involved, in addition to shearing, laborious tasks such as dam construction and fence-building. The work was seasonal, requiring pastoral workers to travel vast distances across the Australian "outback". Pastoral properties were frequently hundreds of kilometres apart, requiring workers to camp overnight along creeks and billabongs (seasonal lakes formed along river courses as water levels rose and fell) as they walked between jobs. In 1891, at the peak of the pastoral boom, Queensland gave work to 8,748 shearers and pastoral laborers. Of these, only 237 were under fifteen years of age. Mining, by the late nineteenth century, involved highly-mechanized work carried out deep underground. By 1901 one-eighth of Australia's adult male workforce was employed in towns where the principal source of employment was mining and/or smelting.[13] But mining also employed relatively few youngsters. In Queensland, where mining was particularly important, there were 16,375 miners in 1901. Virtually all were twenty years of age or older. Only 0.7 per cent of all miners were aged fourteen years or younger.[14]

In northern Australia job opportunities for the children of immigrant families were also restricted due to the presence of substantial unfree or semi-free workforces. Along the fertile coastal lowlands of Queensland sugar was the main agricultural crop. It was grown and processed by "bonded" laborers, imported from the South Pacific Islands. They were engaged under conditions that were, in many circumstances, little removed from slavery. Even here, however, children were conspicuous by their absence. Of the 11,678 workers recorded employed in the Queensland

12 *Queensland Census of 1901*, p. 65, Tbl. XLI.

13 Blainey, *The Rush that Never Ended*, p. 245.

14 *Queensland Censes of 1891*, pp. 244-245, 272; *Queensland Census of 1901*, p. 276.

sugar industry in 1901 only forty-eight were under fifteen years of age.[15] The pearling and beche-de-mer industries along Australia's northern coast were also dominated by bonded Asian labor (most pearlers were Japanese adult males).

White settlement in the pastoral interior depended heavily on aboriginal labor. This aboriginal contribution went largely unrecorded due to non-inclusion of Aboriginals in Australian census figures prior to 1967. While their fathers and older brothers worked as stockmen, aboriginal children were employed on most of the larger pastoral stations to assist with household duties. Their presence at the household hearth reflected the aberrant circumstances that prevailed on the Australian frontier. Few pastoralists and shearers brought their own young children with them to face the perils of the "bush". In 1886 almost half of the "sons and daughters" recorded on Queensland pastoral properties were over twenty years of age.[16] For the pastoral aristocracy, aboriginal children also proved a useful accompaniment to any cross-country trip. The sister of one such pastoralist wrote in March 1864:

> People who are going for a long journey almost always take a blackboy with them. They are the most useful servants in the bush, get up the horses in the morning, light fires at night, and know by a sort of instinct if there are any wild blacks lurking in the neighbourhood of their camp.[17]

Despite their utility, the total number of aboriginal children employed as servants could probably have been measured in hundreds, rather than thousands, given that the pastoral industry was dominated by a handful of huge properties.

The harsh Australian landscape also limited opportunities for European-style agriculture during the nineteenth century. The interior was better suited to the raising of sheep and cattle. In 1886-1890 agriculture's share of Gross Domestic Product (GDP) was a mere 5.8 per cent. By contrast the pastoral sector was responsible for one-eighth of Australia's economic output.[18] This made unpaid work on the family farm, and the performance of paid chores on neighboring properties, much less important in Australia than it was in Europe or North America.

15 *Queensland Census of 1901*, pp. 248-249.
16 *Queensland Census of 1886*, p. 171.
17 Adams, *Letters of Rachael Henning*, p. 161.
18 Butlin, *Investment in Australian Economic Development*, p. 22.

Climate and geography worked against the employment of children from European families in the interior. But even the cities, where most of the population lived, provided the young with limited work opportunities. As urban historians have noted, Australia's nineteenth century cities were very different from the "industrial" cities of Western Europe. They were "commercial" cities whose *raison d'etre* was to provide a transport and financial link between the export-oriented economy in the interior and the world's markets.[19] While manufacturing's share of Australian GDP more than doubled between 1861 and 1900 it remained a modest contributor to national wealth. In the boom years of 1886-1890 manufacturing's share of GDP was 11.8 per cent. This was less than construction (16.5 per cent) or transport and distribution (16.3 per cent).[20] Most jobs in the housing and civil construction sectors required physical strength and skill. Employment in road and rail transport was highly seasonal. The flow of work was tied to the annual movement of wool bales from the interior to the coast. When work was available it was typically arduous. As one Melbourne newspaper recorded in 1886 in describing a carter's job: "He is out in all weather, and, except in very few cases, he has very heavy lifting to do loading and unloading his cart".[21]

Although most Australian jobs required adult workers, a growth in manufacturing employment during the final decades of the century was nevertheless associated with the emergence of significant (by Australian standards) pockets of child and adolescent labor. The small-scale, unproductive nature of Australian manufacturing meant that its share of total employment, while modest, was greater than its contribution to national wealth. Manufacturing employment also varied significantly from colony to colony. It was most important in Victoria. Twenty per cent of Victorians were factory workers in 1891. By contrast, only fifteen to sixteen per cent of the South Australian, Queensland and New South Wales workforce was engaged in manufacturing. There were relatively few factory workers in the outlying colonies of Western Australia and Tasmania, both of which were heavily geared towards mining and rural pursuits. In all colonies, including Victoria, manufacturing was carried out under primitive, small-scale conditions, bearing little resemblance to the large mechanized

19 McCarthy, "Australian Capital Cities"; Lawson, *Brisbane in the 1890s*. For discussion of the social structure of "commercial" cities in the New World see, Scobie, *Argentina*; and Ward, *Cities and Immigrants*.

20 Butlin, *Investment in Australian Economic Development*, p. 22.

21 *Age*, 22 January 1886, p. 6.

establishments of industrializing Europe and North America. Productivity and wages were both low. Capital investment was minimal.[22] Fit and robust adults were generally far better remunerated by mining or building work. From the early 1880s such "backwater" enterprises diverged from the Australian norm as they began hiring large numbers of juvenile workers. The peculiar structure of the national economy ensured, however, that child and adolescent labor was confined to a relatively small number of trades.

"Sweated Trades" and Child and Adolescent Participation Rates

While most jobs in late nineteenth century Australia were unsuited to children the issue of child labor nevertheless caused growing concern. It had been thought that such evils had been totally left behind in the Old World. Royal Commissions, parliamentary enquiries and official reports constantly investigated child employment practices.[23] This concern largely reflected the growth of what were popularly referred to as "sweated trades", a term which denoted the fact that employment in these sectors was carried on under "sweatshop" conditions.

The largest of the "sweated trades" were clothing and textile manufacture, and boot and shoe making. Printing, baking, biscuit making, and tobacco manufacture were also regarded as "sweated." The rapid growth of juvenile employment in these trades is attributable to two factors. First, Australia's population expansion created a demand for cheap, locally-produced manufactured goods. In Victoria and Queensland the imposition of tariffs encouraged this trend. Secondly, certain occupations witnessed a process of technological innovation that allowed for the displacement of skilled male labor. Clothing manufacture was revolutionized by the "Singer" sewing machine, invented in the United States in the 1850s. In boot-making the Blake-McKay sole-stitching machine could be operated with minimal training. By the late 1870s such machines were readily available at low cost in Australia. Lithographic machines, which utilized photographic plates, transformed the printing trade. Printing had previously required the hand-setting of type.[24] All these machines were capable of being operated by non-apprenticed juveniles and women. Raelene Fran-

22 Butlin, *Investment in Australian Economic Development*, pp. 201, 206.

23 "Report on the Employment of Children", VI.

24 Bowden and Bowden, "Women do the Machinery"; Hagan, *Printers in Politics*, pp. 38–39.

ces has observed that, in the clothing trade, mechanization "was accompanied by the increasing employment of non-indentured juveniles in place of trained adult workers".[25] In printing, Jim Hagan records that "the unlimited employment of boys in country and suburban offices" had a "depressing effect on printers' wages".[26]

The conditions under which women, children, and adolescents were employed in the "sweated trades" were certainly due cause for national embarrassment. In 1891 a visiting delegation of Royal Commissioners toured a tobacco factory adjacent to the main street of one of the nation's largest capital cities. They discovered ten "girls" at work in a tiny room "ingrained with filthy greasy matter, from which smells of the most offensive character exude". Room temperatures were in excess of 40°.[27] Horrific injuries were all too common across the "sweated trades". While none of the Australian colonies maintained reliable health and safety statistics, the Victorian factory inspectors' reports from 1899 to 1905 revealed the systematic neglect of the young's safety. Young workers suffered burns from molten metal; broken, cut or amputated fingers, hands, arms or legs from saws, presses, guillotines or machinery; loss of hair and scalp from machinery accidents; loss of vision from foreign objects; and a variety of injuries from workplace falls.[28]

While the sub-standard employment practices within the "sweated trades" attracted public scrutiny we need to be careful in extrapolating trends from these industries to the wider Australian economy. A number of studies based on the analysis of Australia's colonial census reports suggest that these "sweated trades", and domestic service, were the only ones where children and adolescents were recorded as comprising a significant part of the workforce. Ann Larson's detailed study of late nineteenth century employment patterns in Melbourne, Australia's most industrialized capital city, found that only seventeen per cent of the city's total male workforce was aged nineteen years or under. Even among females, where marriage tended to curtail workforce participation, seventy-five per cent of those in the labor force were aged twenty years or more. There was notably little demand for the labor of those aged fourteen years or under. Only three per cent of the male and female workforce was found in this age category. More than two-thirds of children attended school on a regular basis. Where children did work they were most commonly involved

25 Frances, *Politics of Work*, p. 17.
26 Hagan, *Printers and Politics*, p. 62.
27 *Royal Commission with Minutes of Evidence*, (1892), IV, p. 1300.
28 Bowden and Penrose, "Origins of Child Labour in Australia", p. 132.

in doing "small jobs" for neighbouring householders and local shopkeepers and tradespeople. Larson's work suggests that child labor on a significant scale was restricted to a handful of industries, most notably clothing manufacture, boot and shoe making, and printing. Among female Victorian clothing workers, forty-one per cent were aged nineteen years or less. Among males, thirty-six per cent of printers and twenty-one per cent of bootmakers were also aged nineteen years or younger.[29]

Statistics from New South Wales, Australia's largest colony, reveal a similar story. In 1901 there were only 1,473 metropolitan industrial workers aged fifteen years or under. Fifty-eight per cent of these worked in just three industries – clothing and textiles, food and drink, and metal working. The industrial employment of young females was even more concentrated. Most worked in a single sector – clothing and textile manufacture. In New South Wales, from 1901 to 1905, this sector provided between seventy-eight and eighty per cent of all recorded industrial jobs for females aged less than sixteen years.[30]

Table 29.1. Child and Adolescent Participation in Key Industries: Queensland 1891, 1901

	1891	*1901*
Mining – Total workforce	11,627	16,375
Mining – Aged 19 years or less	474 (4.1%)	1,231 (7.5%)
Mining – Aged 14 years or less	71 (0.6%)	113 (0.7%)
Building – Total workforce	10,767	9,883
Building – Aged 19 years or less	896 (8.3%)	891 (9.0%)
Building – Aged 14 years or less	121 (1.1%)	95 (1.0%)
Pastoral – Total workforce	8,748	11,199
Pastoral – Aged 19 years or less	1,382 (15.8%)	1,824 (16.3%)
Pastoral – Aged 14 years or less	237 (2.7%)	435 (3.9%)

Figures in parentheses represent percentages of the total occupational workforce.
Source: *Queensland Census of 1891* and *1901*.

29 Larson, *Growing Up in Melbourne*, pp. 116, 125, 114-115.
30 Bowden and Penrose, "Origins of Child Labour in Australia", p. 130.

My analysis of census statistics in Queensland, Australia's third largest colony, has found an almost identical pattern. Those aged nineteen years or under made up 17.1 per cent of the workforce in 1891, despite the fact that this youthful cohort made up 46.2 per cent of Queensland's total population. Ten years later not much had changed. In 1901 those aged nineteen or under comprised 18.1 per cent of the workforce.[31] As table 29.1 indicates, the key sectors of the colonial economy – pastoralism, mining and building – employed few adolescents and even fewer children (those aged fourteen or under). Significantly, changed economic conditions – the 1890s was a period of economic depression after the boom years of the 1880s – had virtually no impact on where children and adolescents were employed. Sectors that did not employ youngsters in 1891 still avoided employing them a decade later.

In Queensland, as in Victoria, there was only a small number of occupations where children and adolescents made up a significant percentage of the workforce. By far the most significant was domestic service – an employment area that always seemed to escape the attention of Royal Commissioners and other public investigators. In the late nineteenth century there were more than twice as many Queensland youngsters engaged as domestics as were employed in textile manufacture (including clothing and boot and shoe manufacture). The Queensland censes of 1891 and 1901 indicate that there were only six occupations where child and adolescent workers comprised twenty per cent or more of the total occupational workforce in both census years – domestic service, pupil teaching, textile manufacture, grocery retail, drapery retail, and printing (see table 29.2). In 1891 these six occupations provided jobs for forty-nine per cent of the 19,839 Queenslanders aged nineteen years or less who were active participants in the non-rural workforce. Ten years later these trades still employed 36.8 per cent of non-rural child and adolescent workers.[32] Even in these occupations, however, most jobs were held by those aged between fifteen and nineteen years. Printing consistently employed more children aged less than fifteen years than any other, although this industry employed relatively few people.

31 Bowden, "An Economy Ill-suited to Younger Workers", p. 118.
32 *Queensland Census of 1891*; *Queensland Census of 1901*.

Table 29.2. Occupations with High Child and Adolescent Participation: Queensland 1891, 1901

	1891	*1901*
Domestics – Aged 19 years or less	5,633 (27.6%)	7,167 (28.4%)
Domestics – Aged 14 years or less	1,111 (5.4%)	1,419 (5.6%)
Textile Manufacture – Aged 19 years or less	2,743 (37.0%)	3,386 (34.7%)
Textile Manufacture – Aged 14 years or less	425 (5.7%)	325 (3.3%)
Pupil Teaching – Aged 19 years or less	553 (22.6%)	1,003 (30.8%)
Pupil Teaching – Aged 14 years or less	23 (0.9%)	72 (2.2%)
Printing – Aged 19 years or less	254 (49.1%)	312 (46.7%)
Printing – Aged 14 years or less	41 (7.9%)	64 (9.6%)
Drapery Retail – Aged 19 years or less	286 (27.1%)	785 (31.6%)
Drapery Retail – Aged 14 years or less	34 (3.2%)	86 (3.5%)
Grocery Retail – Aged 19 years or less	288 (27.6%)	710 (26.6%)
Grocery Retail – Aged 14 years or less	51 (4.9%)	109 (4.1%)

Figures in parentheses represent percentages of the total occupational workforce.
Source: Queensland Census of 1891 and *1901*.

If we turn our attention from the young's share of the workforce to the overall participation rates of children and adolescents the census figures once again indicate a limited demand for younger workers. In Queensland, as in Victoria, the great majority of children and adolescents were not members of the paid workforce. In 1891 there were 28,408 youngsters aged nineteen years or under in paid employment, in both the rural and urban sectors. The total number in this age cohort was 286,307, giving a labour force participation rate of 9.9 per cent. Excluding those under ten years of age from calculations, the workforce participation rate rises to thirty-eight per cent. In the ensuing decade the participation rate for those in the ten to nineteen years age group fell marginally to 36.4 per cent. This was despite the relative decline in the number of prime age adult males. For these younger Queenslanders the prospect of obtaining employment rose with age. Only 2.5 per cent of the colony's 47,184 "industrial" workers were under fourteen years of age in 1891.[33] In short, while there was a large supply of youthful labor potentially available to employers this source was poorly utilised. Most Australian employers preferred to pay a financial premium and secure an adult worker.

Regulation and its Impact

The most obvious explanation for the continued existence of the "sweated trades" (where women and children were subject to poor wages, long hours and substandard working conditions) was the absence of any effective regulatory framework prior to the 1890s. Unlike their British counterparts, Australian trade unions had shown scant interest in factories acts and child labor protection. Relatively few workers had been employed in factories. The Gold Rushes had, in the 1860s and early 1870s, skewed the demographic structure, creating an adult dominated workforce. Victoria did not pass Australia's first factories and shops act until 1873. Other colonies were still without factories and shops acts twenty years later. Tasmania, where there was little manufacturing, was still devoid of such legislation in 1900.

During the early 1890s a broad liberal-labor alliance emerged, intent on regulating the industrial employment of women and children. No powerful vested interests were opposed. Miners, pastoralists, builders and the larger factory owners employed very few children. As a result, factories and shops acts were enacted in South Australia in 1894, in Queensland and New South Wales in 1896, and in Western Australia in 1897. These acts, and their subsequent amending bills, broadly followed in the footsteps of earlier British factories and shops legislation. They prohibited the employment of children less than fourteen years, except in special, approved circumstances. The hours of work for "young persons" (initially defined as those between fourteen and sixteen years) were restricted. Victoria went a step further. In 1896 it established "wages boards" to fix working conditions in the "sweated trades", including clothing manufacture, and shoe and boot manufacture.[34]

33 *Queensland Census of 1891*; *Queensland Census of 1901*.
34 Fry, "Condition of the Urban Wage-Earning Class", pp. 142-202.

As was the case elsewhere in the world the passage of protective legislation in Australia had limited impact. In 1901 Queensland's participation rate for those aged sixteen years or under was virtually unchanged from a decade earlier. In New South Wales, there was also little change. In 1897 boys aged less than sixteen years represented 5.1 per cent of all male industrial workers in the Sydney metropolitan area. In 1907 they accounted for 5.7 per cent. During the same period females aged under sixteen years even increased their share of the female industrial workforce in the metropolitan districts from 8.3 per to 10.9 per cent.[35]

Some industries, such as baking, witnessed a marked growth in the number of child and juvenile workers. In this sector new industrial oven technologies allowed for the displacement of more expensive adult labor. In New South Wales boys aged less than sixteen years accounted for fourteen per cent of the bakery workforce in 1901. Four years later they represented twenty-two per cent of all bakers. One Royal Commissioner was "struck by the number of very young and undersized boys" who carried trays of biscuits to the mouths of ten metre long ovens. The Commissioner reported that the heat was "very severe" and that the boys "were lean and pale to a degree that left no doubt as to the effect on them". He quoted one observer who referred to the bakehouse as "a kindergarten in an inferno".[36]

The limited impact of protective legislation partly reflected inadequacies in the factories and shops laws. Small factories, employing less than four workers, were often exempt. This had the perverse effect of forcing young workers to leave larger employers and obtain employment with their smaller and less reputable competitors.[37] Colonial education acts also did little to restrict children from seeking work. Children were usually only required to attend school until their twelfth birthday. In South Australia, where compulsory education was introduced in 1873, children needed to attend school for 105 days per year. Things were even worse in Queensland. In this colony compulsory education was, in theory, introduced in 1875. But the act's compulsory attendance clauses were not brought into force until 1900. Before that, attendance was effectively voluntary.[38]

Household economics also helps explain the young's continuing presence in the nineteenth century Australian labor market, albeit at relatively low levels. As a number of labor economists suggest, the participation of

35 Bowden and Penrose, "Origins of Child Labour in Australia", p. 131.

36 Bowden and Penrose, "Origins of Child Labour in Australia", p. 131.

37 *Queensland Parliamentary Debates, 1900*, p. 1951.

38 Bowden and Penrose, "Origins of Child Labour in Australia", p. 130.

children is largely a parental decision.[39] While adult male wages in Australia were amongst the highest in the world there were many who suffered from economic disadvantage. Work was often highly seasonal, leaving families with frequent lean periods.[40] Strenuous toil left a trail of dead and injured male breadwinners. Widows, and abandoned wives, were often the sole family support. The early 1890s was a particularly hard time. Economic depression left up to thirty per cent of breadwinners without a job. In all these circumstances the income from the family's younger members, no mater how small, was an important supplement to the household budget. As one young female shop assistant informed a group of inquiring royal commissioners in 1891, "we all do our duty in supporting the family".[41] Most Australian families would also have concurred with David Montgomery's assessment that the quickest and safest path to a successful career "passed through apprenticeship and experience, not class-rooms".[42] This dictum was particularly applicable to the Australian situation where most jobs required brawn rather than book learning.

Although there are a number of factors that usefully explain the persistence of exploitative child labor practices in Australia during the nineteenth century the peculiar structural characteristics of the nation's labor market were the most important. There were many children and adolescents but relatively few jobs where they could be gainfully employed. There is no evidence that employers found any problem in replacing a child or adolescent worker no matter how little he or she paid. One Queensland employer informed a Royal Commission during 1891 there were always "more applying" for work than there were jobs available.[43] At more prestigious establishments, employers were able to demand the payment of a 'premium' from parents or guardians, ranging from £50 to £100, for taking on an apprentice. Such payments, however, did not necessarily guarantee proper training. One cynic in the clothing trades remarked: "it is a rule of the firms to take a premium, but not to teach the boys the trade [...] the boys sweep out the place, and never get taught the trade".[44]

39 Basu and Van, "Economics of Child Labour"; Basu, "Child Labor".
40 Lee and Fahey, "A Boom for Whom?".
41 "Report of Queensland Royal Commission into Factories", II, p. 813.
42 Montgomery, *Fall of the House of Labor*, p. 131.
43 "Report of Queensland Royal Commission into Factories", II, p. 849.
44 "Report of Queensland Royal Commission into Factories", II, p. 1111.

Workplace Ageing and Primacy of the Adult Male

During the late nineteenth century the supply of children and adolescents far exceeded the labor force demand. By 1900, however, the supply was drying up. Relatively few Australians were born during the depression years of the 1890s. Whereas a woman whose peak childbearing years were in the 1870s would have had at least seven children, by the early 1900s women were only having on average 3.6 children.[45] In consequence, the Australian workforce began a long ageing process. The first census report for the new Commonwealth of Australia, published in 1911, noted that, in comparison with 1881, there was "a heavy proportionate reduction" in the "number of infants, children and adolescents".[46]

The most immediate effect of workforce ageing was felt in trades such as clothing, which had given work to a disproportionate number of youngsters. In 1886 those aged nineteen years or under comprised 45.3 per cent of Queensland's clothing workforce. Fifteen years later this age group comprised only 34.7 per cent of Queensland's clothing workers.[47] The large cohort who entered the labor market during the 1880s was staying on, limiting opportunities for those born after them. This trend was most pronounced among female workers. During the 1890s Depression many women chose the workbench over wedlock. In 1891 more than sixty per cent of Australian women aged between fifteen and forty-four years were married. By 1901 only forty-six per cent were bound by matrimony.[48]

As those born in the 1880s came of age, and the supply of young jobseekers diminished, Australia's adult males reasserted their position of workplace primacy. In 1907 the concept of adult male primary was given *de facto* legislative force when Justice Higgins, President of the newly created Commonwealth Conciliation and Arbitration Court, handed down his famous "Harvester Judgement". Under the terms of the Australian constitution – which in 1901 provided for the federation of the former colonies (new states) to form an independant nation – the Court existed for the arbitrated settlement of "interstate industrial disputes"; a task achieved through the determination of "awards" that established legally-enforceable working conditions. Higgins, in his 1907 judgement, stipulated principles that would underpin all commonwealth awards. He ruled that each adult

45 Hicks, *This Sin and Scandal*, pp. xv, 3.
46 *Australian Commonwealth Census of 1911*, p. 104.
47 *Queensland Census of 1891*; *Queensland Census of 1901*, pp. 244–245.
48 Forster, "Aspects of Australian Fertility", pp. 110–111.

male should receive an income capable of supporting "the normal needs" of a family under conditions appropriate to "a civilized community".[49] Work was perceived to be properly the domain of adult males rather than women and children.

The principles enunciated by Justice Higgins soon bound a majority of Australian workplaces. Federal awards grew in number and scope. Western Australia, New South Wales and Queensland also legislated for compulsory arbitration. The other states (South Australia, Victoria and Tasmania) adopted a system of "wages boards". This gave Australia, along with New Zealand (which also developed a compulsory arbitration system), the world's most highly regulated industrial relations framework. Awards and wages board determinations reinforced the status of the adult male worker. Limitations were imposed on the employment of juveniles. The apprenticeship system was given new force.

The new regulated industrial relations system had a noticeable effect on the clothing and boot trades – the principal employers of younger workers and women outside domestic service. In November 1909, Justice Higgins made the first federal award for the boot trade. In his judgement Higgins made it clear that he intended to stamp out the use of "boy labour" (most youngsters in the boot trade were male). Condemning the use of non-apprenticed youngsters as "a perpetual menace to the peace of the community", he observed:

> A boy is taken into the factory at 13, 14, or 15. He is put on to any work that suits the employer and the employer is under no obligation to teach him anything [...] to get any work at all he struggles to be taken on at less than the minimum wage. If he is taken on, he probably deprives a competent journeyman.[50]

To end such practices, Higgins's award stipulated that: "No lad not apprenticed shall be employed or retained in employment after he had attained the age of sixteen, or for a longer period than twelve months".[51] This provision effectively ended the boot trade's use of non-apprenticed youth labour. In reflecting upon this award, Frances has observed that "it is impossible to overestimate the gain which Higgins award represented to male workers".[52]

49 *Commonwealth Arbitration Reports, 1907-1908* (Melbourne, 1908), p. 3.
50 *Commonwealth Arbitration Reports, 1910* (Melbourne, 1910), p. 16.
51 *Commonwealth Arbitration Reports, 1910* (Melbourne, 1910), p. 29.
52 Frances, *Politics of Work*, p. 155.

Nine years later Higgins finally arbitrated an award for the clothing trade. Once again he sought, as Ellem has noted, "to protect men's employment".[53] For skilled work such as cutting and pressing, Higgins awarded "the same pay for women as for men". This curtailed female employment in these areas by adding to its cost. Higgins also tightly regulated the use of young, non-apprenticed "improvers". In general, no more than one "improver" or apprentice could be engaged for every male or female tradesperson. These provisions severely restricted the employers' capacity to engage younger workers in lieu of adults.[54] Such judgements ensured that, even in the clothing trade, the more skilled and well-paid work would remain the preserve of the adult male. The job roles of younger males were carefully defined and regulated. Opportunities for young females were restricted.

The workplace principles enforced by Australia's system of compulsory awards were peculiar. But the tight restrictions that it imposed on the use of children and adolescents had a limited impact outside a small range of urban trades. Australia was a peculiar country. There was never much demand for child labor.

Conclusion

Australia's population in the late nineteenth century was a youthful one. Half of all Australians were under twenty years of age. But the young were under-represented in the workforce. Unlike the industrialized nations of the Northern Hemisphere, child labor was neither widespread nor economically significant. Census reports and other statistical evidence indicate that, at any given time, almost two-thirds of those aged between ten and nineteen years remained outside the paid labor force. Very few children under the age of fourteen years were employed. The low participation rates of children and adolescents in the colonial workforce reflected the peculiar demands of the Australian labor market. Pastoral activities, mining, building and transportation remained the principal drivers of economic growth and employment. In the interior employers complained constantly about the shortage of available labor. Echoing this lament, one parliamentarian observed during 1882 that:

53 Ellem, *In Women's Hands*, p. 110.

54 *Commonwealth Arbitration Reports, 1919* (Melbourne, 1919), p. 705.

> The price of labour, owing to its great scarcity, had gone up to an almost prohibitory extent [...] In the interior men could not be obtained to shepherd sheep, erect fences, and to do the ordinary work on stations. A similar stagnation prevailed on the tinfields, the sugar lands, and the gold-fields.[55]

Employers confronting such labor shortages would, however, have received little benefit from the arrival of wagon loads of children and adolescents at their gates. On the pastoral properties few youngsters would have been strong enough to even restrain one of the large Merino sheep that were the backbone of the industry. Gold miners would have gained little from sending children deep underground to operate rock drills and pack dynamite.

Unsuited to work in the highly productive and highly paid sectors that were the mainstay of Australia's economy the young found themselves on the under-valued margins of the colonial labor force. The largest concentrations of juvenile workers were found in domestic service and in the so-called "sweated trades" that flourished in the quarter century after 1880. In these trades – clothing manufacture, boot making, printing – technological innovation allowed for the displacement of adult males. But these sectors were too small to absorb the large supply of younger Australians who were capable of work. By 1910 child and adolescent labor was declining in even those trades where it had been most entrenched, such as clothing and boot making. The supply of young workers diminished as the population aged. More significantly, these trades – like all other Australian industries – came within the ambit of the new Commonwealth's highly regulated industrial relations system, which enshrined the view that work was properly the function of adult males. The workforce was no place for children.

55 *Queensland Parliamentary Debates, 1882*, p. 113.

Collective Bibliography

Abbott, Grace (ed.), *The Child and the State*, 2 vols (Chicago, IL, 1938).

Adams, David (ed.), *The Letters of Rachael Henning* (Ringwood, 1969).

Adman, Marie Elisabeth, *Via kai Poniria. Andres kai Gynaikes s' ena elliniko chorio* (Athens, 1987).

Adorno, Sérgio, "Criança: A lei e a cidadania", in: Irene Rizzini (ed.), *A criança no Brasil hoje: Desafio para o terceiro milênio* (Rio de Janeiro, 1993), pp. 101-112.

Afonso, Óscar and Álvaro Aguiar, "A internacionalização da economia", in: Pedro Lains and Álvaro Ferreira Silva (eds), *História económica de Portugal 1700-2000*. 3 vols. Vol. 3 (Lisbon, 2005), séc XX, pp. 305-341.

Aguiar, Álvaro and Manuel M.F. Martins, "A indústria", in: Pedro Lains and Álvaro Ferreira Silva (eds), *História económica de Portugal 1700-2000*. 3 vols. Vol. 3 (Lisbon, 2005), séc XX, pp. 185-226.

Alexander, Jennifer and Paul Alexander, "Labour Demands and the 'Involution' of Javanese Agriculture", *Social Analysis*, 3 (1979), pp. 22-44.

Alexander, Paul, "Labour Expropriation and Fertility: Population Growth in Nineteenth-Century Java", in: W. Penn Handwerker (ed.), *Culture and Reproduction* (New York, 1986), pp. 259-262.

Alfred, Samuel Kydd, *The History of the Factory Movement* (London, 1857).

Altmeyer, J.J., *Quelques mots sur l'enseignement primaire obligatoire. Mémoire des loges belges sur l'instruction obligatoire et projet de loi* (Brussels, 1859).

Amar, M., "Sullo stato attuale delle leggi europee sul lavoro delle donne e dei fanciulli", *Giornale degli economisti*, 2 (1875).

Américi, Laurence, "La Caisse d'épargne des Bouches-du-Rhône au XIXe siècle: un outil financier au service de l'intervention sociale" (PhD thesis, Université de Provence, 2000).

Anderson, Michael, *Family Structure in Nineteenth-Century Lancashire* (Cambridge, 1971).

Anderson, Michael, "Households, Families and Individuals: Some Preliminary Results from the National Sample from the 1851 Census of Great Britain", *Continuity and Change*, 3 (1988), pp. 421-438.

Anderson, Michael, "The Social Implications of Demographic Change", in: F.M.L. Thompson (ed.), *Cambridge Social History of Britain, 1750-1950*. 3 vols. Vol. 2 (Cambridge, 1990), pp. 1-70.

Andors, Stephen, *Workers and Workplaces in Revolutionary China* (White Plains, NY, 1974).

Andreev, E.N., *Rabota maloletnikh v Possii i zapadnoi Evrcpe*, vol. 1 (St. Petersburg, 1884).

Angelova, Milena, "The Student Summer Camps in Bulgaria between the Two World Wars", in: Slobodan Naumović and Miroslav Jovanović (eds), *Childhood in South East Europe: Historical Perspectives on Growing Up in the 19th and 20th Century* (Belgrade, 2001), pp. 163-175.

Anker, Richard, "The Economics of Child Labour: A Framework for Measurement", *International Labour Review*, 139 (3) (2000), pp. 257-280.

Anti-Slavery Society, *Child Labour in South Africa: A General Review*, Child Labour Series, 7 (London, 1983).

Aquilonius, Klas, *Svenska folkskolans historia*. 5 vols. Vol. 2 (Stockholm, 1942).

Arango, Luz Gabriela, *Mujer, religión e industria. Fabricato 1923-1982* (Medellín, 1991).

Arango, Rafael Ortiz, *Estampas de Medellín antiguo* (Medellín, 1983).

Archila, Mauricio, *Cultura e identidad obrera* (Bogotá, 1991).

Ariès, Philippe, *Centuries of Childhood: A Social History of Family Life* (New York, 1962).

Arminius, "Het budget van een Javaanschen landbouwer", *De Indische Gids*, 11 (1889), I, pp. 1685-1720; II, pp. 1885-1917; III, pp. 2149-2186.

Arseniou, Lazaros, *Ta Tseligata* (Athens, 1972).

Ashagrie, Kebebew, "Statistics on Child Labour: A Brief Report", *ILO Bulletin of Labour Statistics* (1992-1993), pp. xi-xxii.

Ashe, Thomas, "Testimony before the House of Commons Select Committee on Emigration", in: *Queensland Votes & Proceedings, 1891*. 4 vols. Vol. 2 (Brisbane, 1892), pp. 1551-1554.

Ashton, T.S., *The Industrial Revolution 1760-1830* (New York, 1964).

Asselain, Jean-Claude, *Histoire économique de la France du XVIIIe siecle à nos jours*, 2 vols (Paris, 1984).

Bacon, David, *The Children of NAFTA: Labor Wars on the U.S./Mexican Border* (Berkeley, CA, 2004).

Badinter, Elisabeth, *The Myth of Motherhood: An Historical View of the Maternal 'Instinct'* (London, 1981).

Bakker, Nelleke, Jan Noordman, Marjoke Rietveld-van Wingerden (eds), *Vijf eeuwen opvoeden in Nederland: Idee en praktijk, 1500-2000* (Assen, 2006).

Balabanov, M., *Ocherki po istorii rabochego klassa v Rossii* (Kiev, 1924).

Ballestrero, M.V., "Tre proposte ottocentesche per la disciplina del lavoro dei fanciulli", in: G. Tarello (ed.), *Materiali per una storia della cultura giuridica*. Vol. 8:2 (Bologna, 1978), pp. 217ff.

Balthazar, H., "Groei tot een industriële grootstad", in: J. Decavele *et al.* (eds), *Gent. Apologie van een rebelse stad* (Antwerp, 1989), pp. 155-183.

Barbagli, Marzio, *Educating for Unemployment: Politics, Labor Markets, and the School System – Italy, 1859-1973* (New York, 1982).

Barcellos, C., *Construções de Naus em Lisboa e Goa para a Carreira da Índia no Começo do Século XVII* (Lisbon, 1989).

Bardini, C., *Senza carbone nell'età del vapore. Gli inizi dell'industrializzazione italiana* (Milan, 1998).

Barroso, José Luís, "O papel dos parceiros sociais e da sociedade civil no combate à exploração do trabalho infantil, em Portugal", in: Conferência Internacional sobre Políticas de Combate à Exploração do Trabalho Infantil na Europa (ed.), *Actas da Conferência Internacional Políticas de Combate à Exploração do Trabalho Infantil na Europa*. Vol. 1 (Lisbon, 2001), pp. 237-242.

Basu, Kaushik, "Child Labor: Cause, Consequence, and Cure, with Remarks on International Labor Standards", *Journal of Economic Literature*, 37 (1999), pp. 1083-1119.

Basu, Kaushik and Pham Huong Van, "The Economics of Child Labour", *American Economic Review*, 88 (1998), pp. 412-427.

Becchi, Egle, "L'Ottocento", in: Egle Becchi and Dominique Julia (eds), *Storia dell'infanzia, Dal Settecento a oggi*, vol. 2 (Bari, 1996), pp. 160ff.

Becker, Gary S., *Human Capital. A Theoretical and Empirical Analysis with Special Reference to Education* (New York, 1964).

Becker, Gary, "A Theory of the Allocation of Time", *Economic Journal*, 75 (1965), pp. 493-517.

Beinart, William, "Transkeian Migrant Workers and Youth Labour on the Natal Sugar Estates 1918-1948", *Journal of African History*, 32 (1991), pp. 41-63.

Beinart, William, "Transkeian Migrant Workers and Youth Labor on the Natal Sugar Estates, 1918-1948", in: Alan H. Jeeves and Jonathan Crush (eds), *White Farms, Black Labor: The State and Agrarian Change in Southern Africa* (Portsmouth, NH, 1997), pp. 147-171.

Belfanti, Carlo Marco, "Rural Manufactures and Rural Proto-Industries in the 'Italy of the Cities' from the Sixteenth through the Eighteenth Century", *Continuity and Change*, 8 (1993), pp. 253-280.

Benoit, Martine, "Les Couvents ateliers au XIXe siècle", *Le Peuple Français*, 22 (1976), pp. 22-26.

Berend, Iván T. and György Rànki, "Polen, Ungarn, Rumänien, Bulgarien und Albanien, 1914-1980", in: Wolfram Fischer (ed.), *Handbuch der europäischen Wirtschafts- und Sozialgeschichte*. Vol. 5 (Stuttgart, 1987), pp. 769-840.

Berg, Maxine and Pat Hudson, "Rehabilitating the Industrial Revolution", *Economic History Review*, 45 (1992), pp. 24-50.

Berman, Bruce and John Lonsdale, *Unhappy Valley: Conflict in Kenya and Africa*. Bk. 1: *State and Class* (London, 1992).

Bessell, Sharon, "The Politics of Child Labour in Indonesia: Global Trends and Domestic Policy", *Pacific Affairs*, 72 (1999), pp. 353-371.

Bettison, David G., "Numerical Data on African Dwellers in Lusaka, Northern Rhodesia", *Rhodes-Livingstone Communication*, 16 (Lusaka, 1959).

Bird, I.L., *Unbeaten Tracks in Japan* (London, 1880).

Bjurling, Oscar, *Stadens fattiga. Malmö Stads fattigvårds 150-åriga historia* (Malmö, 1956).

Bjurman, Eva Lis and Lars Olsson, *Barnarbete och arbetarbarn* (Stockholm, 1979).

Blainey, Geoffrey, *The Rush that Never Ended: A History of Australian Mining* (Melbourne, 2003[5]).

Boli, John, *New Citizens for a New Society: The Institutional Origins of Mass Schooling in Sweden* (Oxford, 1989).

Bolin-Hort, Per, *Work, Family and the State: Child Labour and the Organization of Production in the British Cotton Industry, 1780-1920* (Lund, 1989).

Bonomi, S., "Sul lavoro dei fanciulli negli opifici", *Annali universali di medicina*, 221 (1872), pp. 3ff.

Boomgaard, Peter, *Children of the Colonial State* (Amsterdam, 1989).

Booth, Alan R., "The Development of the Swazi Labour Market, 1900-1968", *South African Labour Bulletin*, 7 (1982), pp. 34-57.

Booth, Alan R., *Swaziland: Tradition and Change in a Southern African Kingdom* (Boulder, CO, 1983).

Booth, Alan R., "Capitalism and the Competition for Swazi Labour, 1945-1960", *Journal of Southern African Studies*, 13 (1986), pp. 125-150.

Booth, Alan R., "Homestead, State and Migrant Labour in Colonial Swaziland", in: J. Daniel and M.F. Stephen (eds), *Historical Perspectives on the Political Economy of Swaziland: Selected Articles* (Kwaluseni, 1986), pp. 17-50.

Booth, Charles, "On Occupations of the People of the United Kingdom, 1801-1881", *Journal of the Royal Statistical Society*, 49 (1886), pp. 314-435.

Borderías, Cristina. "Suponiendo que este trabajo lo hace la mujer. Organización y valoración de los tiempos de trabajo en la Barcelona de mediados del siglo XIX", in: Cristina Carrasco (ed.), *Tiempos trabajo y genero* (Barcelona, 2001), pp. 103-131.

Borderias, Cristina. "La transición de la actividad femenina en el mercado de trabajo Barcelonés (1856-1930): Teoría social y realidad historica en el sistema estadístico moderno", in: L. Galvez and C. Sarasua (eds), *Eficiencia o privilegios? Mujeres y hombres en el mercado de trabajo* (Alicante, 2003), pp. 241-276.

Borras Llop, José Maria, "El trabajo infantil en la industria barcelonesa segun el censo obrero de 1905", *Historia Social*, 33 (1999), pp. 25-48.

Borrás Llop, José María, "El trabajo infantil en el mundo rural español, Género, edades y ocupaciones", in: José Miguel and Martinez Carrion (eds), *El nivel de vida en la España Rural* (Alicante, 2002), pp. 497-548.

Borrás Llop, José María, "Mercado laboral, escolarización y empleo infantil en una comarca agrícola e industrial (el Vallès Occidental, 1881-1910)", *Cuadernos de Historia Contemporánea*, 24 (2002), pp. 233-262.

Botelho, Tarcísio Rodrigues, "O Trabalho de crianças e jovens no Brasil imperial: Minas Gerais, 1831-1832", *História: Questões & Debates*, 39 (2003), pp. 191-220.

Botero Herrera, Fernando, *La industrialización en Antioquia: génesis y consolidación, 1900-1930* (Medellín, 1985).

Boulay, J. Du, *see* Du Boulay, J.

Bourcart, Jean-Jacques, "Proposition sur la nécessité de fixer l'âge et de réduire les heures de travail des ouvriers des filatures", *Bulletin de la Société Industrielle de Mulhouse*. Vol. 1 (1828), pp. 325-328.

Bourguignon, François and Pierre-Andre Chiappori, "Collective Models of Household Behavior: An Introduction", *European Economic Review*, 36 (1992), pp. 355-365.

Bournazos, Stratis, "I ekpaidefsi sto elliniko kratos", in: Christos Hatziiossif (ed.), *Istoria tis Elladas tou 20ou aiona, 1900-1922. Oi aparches*. Vol. 1, part 2 (Athens, 2000), pp. 189-281.

Bowden, Bradley, "An Economy Ill-suited to Younger Workers: Child and Youth Workforce Participation in Colonial Queensland, 1886-1901", *Australian Economic History Review*, 46 (2006), pp. 111-129.

Bowden, Bradley and Toni Bowden, "'The Women do the Machinery': Craft, Gender and Work Transformation in the Brisbane Boot Trade", *Labour History*, 86 (2004), pp. 75-92.

Bowden, Bradley and Beris Penrose, "The Origins of Child Labour in Australia 1880-1907: a Health and Safety Perspective", *Journal of Occupational Health and Safety: Australia and New Zealand*, 22 (2006), pp. 127-135.

Boyce, A.N., "The Swaziland Concessions and their Political Consequences 1876-1908" (M.A. thesis, University of South Africa, 1947).

Brabander, G.L. de, J. Gadisseur, R. Robyn and J. Liébin (eds), *De industrie in België. Twee eeuwen ontwikkeling, 1780-1980* (Brussels, 1981).

Brace, Charles L., *The Norse-Folk, or a visit to the homes of Norway and Sweden* (London, 1857).

Braun, Hélène and Michel Valentin, *Villermé et le travail des enfants: Hier et aujourd'hui* (Paris, 1989).
Braverman, Harry, *Labor and Monopoly Capital: The Degradation of Work in the Twentieth Century* (New York, 1974).
Breman, Jan, *The Village on Java and the Early Colonial State* (Rotterdam, 1980).
Bretoni Jovine, D., *L'alienazione dell'infanzia. Il lavoro minorile nella società moderna* (Rome, 1963).
Brew, Roger, *El desarrollo económico de Antioquia desde la independencia hasta 1920* (Bogotá, 1977).
Bruckmüller, Ernst, *Sozialgeschichte Österreichs* (Vienna, 2001).
Brugmans, I.J., *Geschiedenis van het Onderwijs in Nederlandsch-Indië* (Groningen, 1938).
Brugmans, I.J., *De arbeidende klasse in Nederland in de 19de eeuw, 1813-1870* (Amsterdam, 1971).
Brunnbauer, Ulf, *Gebirgsgesellschaften auf dem Balkan. Wirtschaft und Familienstrukturen im Rhodopengebirge (19./20. Jahrhundert)* (Vienna, 2005).
Bull, Edvard, "Barnarbeid i norsk industri", *Nordisk Tidskrift för vetenskap, konst och industri*, 29 (1953), pp. 97-111.
Buret, Eugène, *De la misère des classes laborieuses, en Angleterre et en France* (Paris 1840).
Burggraeve, A. De, *see* De Burggraeve, A.
Burke, Peter, *Popular Culture in Early Modern Europe* (Aldershot, 1994).
Burr-Litchfield, Robert, "The Family and the Mill: Cotton Mill Work, Family Work Patterns, and Fertility in Mid-Victorian Stockport", in: A.S. Wohl (ed.), *The Victorian Family: Structure and Stresses* (New York, 1978), pp. 180-196.
Butlin, N.G., *Investment in Australian Economic Development 1861-1900* (Canberra, 1976).

Cabré, Anna, *El sistema català de reproducció* (Barcelona, 1999).
Cabrini, A., *La legislazione sociale (1859-1913)* (Rome, 1913).
Caizzi, Bruno, *Storia dell' industria italiana dal xviii secolo ai giorni nostri* (Torino, 1965).
Caldwell, J.C., "Population", in: Wray Vamplew (ed.), *Australians: Historical Statistics* (Sydney, 1987), pp. 23-41.
Cammarosano, Somonnetta Ortaggi, "Labouring Women in Northern and Central Italy in the Nineteenth Century", in: John A. Davis and Paul Ginsborg (eds), *Society and Politics in the Age of the Risorgimento* (Cambridge, 1991), pp. 152-183.
Campbell, John K., *Honour, Family and Patronage. A Study of Institutions and Moral Values in a Greek Mountain Community* (New York, 1974).
Campinho, Alberto, *Regime jurídico do contrato de trabalho de menores* (Braga, 1995).
Campos, Herculano Ricardo, "Pobreza e Trabalho Infantil sob o Capitalismo" (Ph.D. thesis, Universidade Federal do Rio Grande do Norte, 2001).
Camps, Enriqueta, *La formación del mercado de trabajo industrial en la Cataluña del siglo XIX* (Madrid, 1995).
Camps, Enriqueta, "Family Strategies and Children's Work Patterns: Some Insights from Industrializing Catalonia, 1850-1920", in: Hugh Cunningham and Pier Paolo Viazzo (eds), *Child Labour in Historical Perspective, 1800-1985* (Florence, 1995), pp. 57-72.
Camps, Enriqueta, "Transitions in Women's and Children's Work Patterns and Implications for the Study of the Family Income and the Household Structure: A Case Study from the Catalan Textile Sector, 1850-1925", *The History of the Family. An International Quaterly*, 3 (1998), pp. 137-154.
Camps, Enriqueta, "Trabajo infantil y estrategias familiares durante los primeros estadios de la industrialización catalana (1850-1925). Esbozos a partir del estudio de un caso", *Cuadrenos de historia contemporánea*, 24 (2002), pp. 263-280.

Camps, Enriqueta, "Wage Structures and Family Economies in the Catalan Textile Industry in an Age of Nascent Capitalism", *Continuity and Change*, 19 (2004), pp. 265-281.
Camps, Enriqueta, "Poverty and Children's Work in Spain and Latin America: Some Preliminary Remarks", *Barcelona Economics Working Paper Series*, nr. 225 (2006).
Candeias, António *et al.*, *Alfabetização e escola em Portugal nos séculos XIX e XX: Os censos e as estatísticas* (Lisbon, 2004).
Cardoso, Manuel Pereira, "O Caso Português: Quantificação, Caracterização do Trabalho Infantil e Medidas Adoptadas no Combate à sua Exploração", in: *Actas da Conferência Internacional Políticas de Combate à Exploração do Trabalho Infantil na Europa*. Vol. 1 (Lisbon, 2001), pp. 171-176.
Carey, Peter, "Waiting for the 'Just King': the Agrarian World of South-Central Java from Giyanti (1755) to the Java War (1825-1830)", *Modern Asian Studies*, 20 (1986), pp. 59-137.
Carles, Émilie, *see* Émilie Carles
Carreras, A., "Un ritratto quantitativo dell'industria italiana", in: F. Amatori (ed.), *Storia d'Italia, L'industria*. Annali 15 (Turin, 1999), pp. 179-272.
Carvalho, Rómulo de, *História do ensino em Portugal: Desde a fundação da nacionalidade até ao fim do regime de Salazar-Caetano* (Lisbon, 2001).
Castro, María Patricia, "Beneficencia en Medellín, 1880-1930" (MA thesis, Universidad de Antioquia, 1994).
Caty, Roland and Éliane Richard, "Un négociant dans la ville: activité, fortune, pouvoirs. Victor Régis à Marseille (1830-1881)", in: M. Collin (ed.), *Ville et port, XVIIIe-XXe siècles* (Paris, 1994), pp. 153-164.
Caty, Roland, Éliane Richard and Pierre Échinard, *Les Patrons du Second Empire Marseille*. Vol. 5 (Paris, 1999).
Caty, Roland, "Le Travail des enfants dans l'industrie et l'artisanat en Provence au XIXe siècle", *Les Amis du Vieil Istres*, 22 (2000), pp. 131-141.
Caty, Roland (ed.), *Enfants au travail: Attitude des elites en Europe occidentale et méditerranéenne aux XIXe et XXe siècles* (Aix-en-Provence, 2002).
Cerdà, Ildefons, "Monografía estadística de la clase obrera de Barcelona en 1856", in: Instituto de Estudios Fiscales (ed.), *Teoría general de la urbanización y aplicación de sus principios y doctrinas a la reforma y ensanche de Barcelona* (Barcelona, 1971), pp. 182-212.
Chaduka, N.K., "Britain and Southern Rhodesia, 1923-1939: British Opinion and The Politics of 'African Affairs'" (M.A., University of Liverpool, 1970).
Chagas Lopes, Margarida and Pedro Goulart, *Educação e trabalho infantil em Portugal* (Lisbon, 2005).
Chamberlain, B.H., *Things Japanese* (3rd edn: London, 1898, complete edn Tokyo, 1885).
Chandavarkar, R., *The Origins of Industrial Capitalism in India: Business Strategies and the Working Classes in Bombay, 1900-1940* (Cambridge, 1994).
Chang, Ha-Joon, *Kicking away the Ladder: Development Strategy in Historical Perspective* (London, 2002).
Chassagne, Serge, "La naissance de l'industrie cotonnière en France, 1760-1840" (Ph.D. diss., École des Hautes Etudes en Sciences Sociales, Paris, 1986).
Chassagne, Serge, *Le coton et ses patrons, France 1770-1840* (Paris, 1991).
Chassagne, Serge, "Le Travail des enfants aux XVIIIe et XIXe siècles", in: Egle Becchi and Dominique Julia (eds), *Du XVIIIe siècle à nos jours. Histoire de l'enfance en Occident*. Vol. 2 (Paris, 1996), pp. 224-272.
Chauncey, George Jr., "The Locus of Reproduction: Women's Labour in the Zambian Copperbelt, 1927-1953", *Journal of Southern African Studies*, 7 (1981), pp. 135-164.

Chen, Jim, "Of Agriculture's First Disobedience and Its Fruit", *Vanderbilt Law Review*, 48 (1995), pp. 1261-1332.
Chesneaux, Jean, *The Chinese Labor Movement, 1919-1927* (Stanford, CA, 1968).
"Child and Woman Labor in China, 1930", *Nankai weekly statistical service*, vol. 4 (March 2, 1931), pp. 49-54.
Childs, Michael J., *Labour's Apprentices: Working Class Lads in Late Victorian and Edwardian England* (Montreal, 1992).
Chirwa, Wiseman Chijere, "Child and Youth Labour on the Nyasaland Plantations, 1890-1953", *Journal of Southern African Studies*, 19 (1993), pp. 662-680.
Chlepner, B., *Cent ans d'histoire sociale en Belgique* (Brussels, 1956).
Chongqing di yi mianfangzhi chang gongyu shi bian xie zu (eds), *Chongqing Yufeng shachang gongyunshi yanjiu ziliao huibian* [Selected research materials on the history of the labor movement at Chongqing's Yufeng cotton mill] (Chongqing, 1985).
Christensen, Jørgen Peter, "Rationalisering og arbejderne – dansk industri i mellemkrigs-tiden", in: Flemming Mikkelsen (ed.), *Produktion & arbetskraft i Danmark gennem 200 år* (Copenhagen, 1990), pp. 123-157.
Chubachi, M. and K. Taira, "Poverty in Modern Japan: Perceptions and Realities", in: H. Patrick (ed.), *Japanese Industrialization and Its Social Consequences* (Berkeley, CA, 1976), pp. 391-437.
Church, Roy, *The History of the British Coal Industry* (Oxford, 1986).
Cipolla, C.M., *Storia economica dell'Europa pre-industriale* (Bologna, 1980).
Claparède, E., *Psychologie de l'enfant: Pédagogie experimentale* (Geneva, 1926, first ed. 1909).
Clapham, J.H., *An Economic History of Modern Britain: The Early Railway Age* (Cambridge, 1964).
Clarke, D.G., *Agricultural and Plantation Workers: A Report on Conditions of Labour and Subsistence* (Gwelo, 1977).
Clarkson, L.A., *Proto-Industrialization: The First Phase of Industrialization?* (Basingstoke, 1985).
Clerck, K. De, *see* De Clerck, K.
Cole, John W. and Eric R. Wolf, *The Hidden Frontier. Ecology and Ethnicity in an Alpine Valley* (New York, 1974).
Coleman, Donald C., "Labour in the English Economy of the Seventeenth Century", *Economic History Review*, 8 (1955-1956), pp. 280-295.
Colón, A.R. and P.A. Colón, *A History of Children: A Socio-Cultural Survey across Millennia* (Westport, CT, 2001).
Colson, Elizabeth, "The Reordering of Experience: Anthropological Involvement with Time", *Journal of Anthropological Research*, 40 (1984), pp. 1-134.
Comhaire-Sylvain, Suzanne, *Food and Leisure Among the Urban African Youth of Leopoldville* (Cape Town, 1950).
Confraria, João, "Política económica", in: Pedro Lains and Álvaro Ferreira Silva (eds), *História económica de Portugal 1700-2000*. 3 vols. Vol. 3 (Lisbon, 2005), séc XX, pp. 397-421.
Coninck-Smith, Ning de, Bengt Sandin and Ellen Schrumpf (eds), *Industrious Children: Work and Childhood in the Nordic Countries, 1850-1990* (Odense, 1997).
Consonni, G. and G. Tonon, "Alle origini della metropoli contemporanea", *Lombardia. Il territorio, l'ambiente, il paesaggio. L'età delle manifatture e della rivoluzione industriale*. Vol. IV (Milan, 1984), pp. 89-164 and 286-290.
Cookson, J. E., *The British Armed Nation, 1793-1815* (Oxford, 1997).

Coombs, Simone and Deborah Radburn, "Children and Young People on the Land", in: Michael Winstanley (ed.), *Working Children in Nineteenth-Century Lancashire* (Preston, 1995), pp. 72-92.

Coppejans-Desmedt, H. and G. van Schoenbeek, "Van passiviteit tot sociale beweging", in: Guido L. De Brabander *et al.* (eds), *De Industrie in België: Twee eeuwen ontwikkeling, 1780-1980* (Brussels, 1981), pp. 127-142.

Corner, P.R., *Contadini e industrializzazione: Società rurale e impresa in Italia dal 1840 al 1940* (Rome-Bari, 1993).

Cornia, G.A., R. Jolly and F. Stewart (eds), *Adjustment with a Human Face*. 2 vols (Oxford, 1987-1988).

Coronel Sr., S., "De Leidsche wolfabrieken en haar invloed op de gezondheid der arbeiders", *Nederlandsch Tijdschrift voor Geneeskunde*, 8 (1864), pp. 225-239.

Cottereau, Alain, "The Distinctiveness of Working-Class Cultures in France, 1848-1900", in: Ira Katznelson and Aristide R. Zolberg (eds), *Working-Class Formation: Nineteenth-Century Patterns in Western Europe and the United States* (Princeton, NJ, 1986), pp. 111-154.

Cova, A. "Tradizione e innovazione nel mutato contesto politico e territoriale dell'età francese", in: S. Zaninelli (ed.), *Storia dell'industria lombarda*. Vol. 1: *Dal Stettecento all'Unita: Un sistema manifetturiero aperto al mercato* (Milan, 1988), pp. 103-197.

Crafts, N.F.R., *British Economic Growth during the Industrial Revolution* (Oxford, 1985).

Creighton, Colin, "The Rise of the Male Breadwinner Family: A Reappraisal", *Comparative Studies in Society and History*, 38 (1996), pp. 310-337.

Creighton, Colin, "The Rise and Decline of the 'Male Breadwinner Family' in Britain", *Cambridge Journal of Economics*, 23 (1999), pp. 519-541.

Cristofoli, M.C. and M. Pozzobon, *I tessili milanesi. Le fabbriche, gli industriali, i lavoratori, il sindacato dall'Ottocento agli anni '30* (Milan, 1981).

Cross, Gary, *A Quest for Time: The Reduction of Work in Britain and France, 1840-1940* (Berkeley, 1989).

Crubellier, Maurice, *L'Enfance et la jeunesse dans la société française, 1800-1950* (Paris, 1979).

Crush, Jonathan S., "The Colonial Division of Space: The Significance of the Swaziland Land Partition", *The International Journal of African Historical Studies*, 3 (1980), pp. 71-86.

Crush, Jonathan S., "Landlords, Tenants and Colonial Social Engineers: The Farm Labour Question in Early Colonial Swaziland", *Journal of Southern African Studies*, 2 (1985), pp. 235-257.

Crush, Jonathan S., *The Struggle for Swazi Labour, 1890-1920* (London, 1987).

Cunningham, Hugh, "The Employment and Unemployment of Children in England c. 1680-1851", *Past & Present*, 126 (1990), pp. 115-150.

Cunningham, Hugh, *The Children of the Poor: Representations of Childhood since the Seventeenth Century* (Oxford, 1991).

Cunningham, Hugh, "Child Labour", *Labour History Review*, 56 (3) (1991), pp. 48-51.

Cunningham, Hugh, *Children and Childhood in Western Society since 1500* (London, 1995).

Cunningham, Hugh, "Child Labour and Industrialization", *Working paper for the International Labour Office* (Geneva, 1995).

Cunningham, Hugh, "Combating Child Labour: The British Experience", in: Hugh Cunningham and Pier Paolo Viazzo, *Child Labour in Historical Perspective, 1800-1985: Case Studies from Europe, Japan and Colombia* (Florence, 1996), pp. 41-55.

Cunningham, Hugh, "The Decline of Child Labour: Labour Markets and Family Economics in Europe and North America since 1830", *Economic History Review*, 52 (2000), pp. 409-428.

Cunningham, Hugh, "How Many Children were 'Unemployed'?: Reply", *Past and Present*, 187 (2005), pp. 203-215.
Cunningham, Hugh, *The Invention of Childhood* (London, 2006).
Cunningham, Hugh and Pier Paolo Viazzo (eds), *Child Labour in Historical Perspective, 1800-1985: Case Studies from Europe, Japan and Colombia* (Florence, 1996).
Cunningham, Hugh and Shelton Stromquist, "Child Labor and the Rights of Children: Historical Patterns of Decline and Persistence", in: Burns H. Weston (ed.), *Child Labor and Human Rights: Making Children Matter* (Boulder, CO, 2005), pp. 55-83.
Curtiss, Davin C., "The Fair Labor Standards Act and Child Labor in Agriculture", *University of Iowa Journal of Corporation Law*, 20 (1995), pp. 303-329.

Dahlén, Marianne, *The Negotiable Child: The ILO Child Labour Campaign 1919-1973* (Uppsala, 2007).
Damsma, Dirk, *Familieband: Geschiedenis van het gezin in Nederland* (Utrecht, 1999).
Davin, Anna, "Working or Helping? London Working-Class Children in the Domestic Economy" in: J. Smith, I. Wallerstein and H. Evers (eds), *Households in the World Economy* (Beverly Hills, CA, 1984), pp. 215-232.
Davin, Anna, *Growing up Poor: Home, School and Street in London, 1870-1914* (Londen, 1996).
De Burggraeve, A., "Rapport sur l'état physique et moral des enfants employés dans les manufactures, usines et mines de Belgique", *Bulletin de l'Académie Royale de Médecine* (1840-1841).
De Clerck, K., B. De Graeve and F. Simon, *Dag meester, goedemorgen zuster, goedemiddag juffrouw. Facetten van het volksonderwijs in Vlaanderen, 1830-1940* (Tielt-Weesp, 1984).
De Groux, *Congrès de l'Association pour le Progrès des sciences sociales, 1862* (Brussels, 1863).
De Herdt, René, "Child Labour in Belgium, 1800-1914", in: Hugh Cunningham and Pier Paolo Viazzo (eds), *Child Labour in Historical Perspective, 1800-1985: Case Studies from Europe, Japan and Colombia* (Florence, 1996), pp. 23-39, also reprinted in this volume as Chapter 9.
De Herdt, René and Bie De Graeve, *Kinderarbeid van omstreeks 1800 tot 1914: Catalogus van een Tentoonstelling Centrum voor kunst en cultuur, Gent 8 december 1979 - 27 januari 1980* (Ghent, 1979).
De Herdt, René and Bie De Graeve, *Kinderarbeid 1800-1914* (Ghent, 1992).
De Jong, *see* Jong, de
De Kat Angelino, *see* Kat Angelino, de
De Mause, Lloyd B. (ed.), *The History of Childhood: The Untold Story of Child Abuse* (London, 1974).
De Nauw, P., "De Geraardsbergse kantnijverheid", *Tijdschrift voor Geschiedenis van Techniek en Industriële Cultuur*, 5 (1987), pp. 3-14.
De Neve, M., "Kinderarbeid te Gent van 1830 tot 1914", *Tijdschrift voor Industriële Cultuur*, 10 (1992), pp. 4-43.
De Regt, *see* Regt, de
De Vries, *see* Vries, de
De Vroede, Maurits, "Onderwijs 1840-1870", in: *Algemene Geschiedenis der Nederlanden. Nieuwste Tijd*. Vol. 13 (Bussum, 1978), pp. 328-351.
De Vroede, Maurits, "Van oud naar nieuw 1792-1842", in: Philippe Annaert and F. Ollevier (eds), *De lagere school in België: Van de middeleeuwen tot nu* (Brussels, 1986).
De Weerdt, D., *De Gentse textielbewerkers en arbeidersbeweging tussen 1866 en 1881. Bijdrage tot de sociale geschiedenis van Gent* (Louvain, 1959).

De Weerdt, D., "De arbeiderstoestanden van 1876 tot 1914", in: *Geschiedenis van de Socialistische Arbeidersbeweging in België* (Antwerp, 1960), pp. 395-412.
De Weerdt, D., *En de vrouwen? Vrouwen, vrouwenbeweging en feminisme in België, 1830-1960* (Ghent, 1980).
De Weerdt, D., "Zwetende arbeidsters en zuchtende dames", *Tijdschrift voor Geschiedenis van Techniek en Industriële Cultuur*, 4 (1986).
De Winne, Auguste, "A travers les Flandres", in: A. De Winne, *Door Arm Vlaanderen* (Louvain, 1909).
Depaepe, M., "Kwantitatieve analyse van de Belgisch lagere school, 1830-1911", *Tijdschrift voor nieuwste geschiedenis. Revue Belge d'Histoire contemporaine*, 5 (1979), pp. 21-81.
Déguignet, Jean-Marie, *Mémoires d'un paysan Bas-Breton* (Ar Releg-Kerhuon, 1998).
Desmed, R. "À propos du mémoire de la Loge des 'Amis Philanthropes' sur l'enseignement primaire obligatoire et laïque", *Revue belge de philologie et d'histoire*, 53 (1975) pp. 375-401.
Desmed, R., "La franc-maçonnerie belge et la laïcisation de l'enseignement 1830-1914", in: J. Préaux (ed.), Église et Enseignement Actes du colloque du Xe anniversiare de l'institut d'Histoire du Christianisme de l'Université Libre de Bruxelles. 22-23 avril 1976 (Brussels, 1977), pp. 197-222.
Destanque, Robert *see* Émilie Carles
Destriveaux, P.J., *Discours sur l'instruction publique* (Liège, 1824), in: J. Bartier, "Les milieux laïques et la liberté de l'enseignement en Belgique au XIXe siècle", in: J. Préaux (ed.), *Eglise et enseignement Actes du colloque du Xe anniversiare de l'institut d'Histoire du Christianisme de l'Université Libre de Bruxelles. 22-23 avril 1976* (Brussels, 1977), pp. 181-196.
Deu, Esteve, *La indústria tèxtil llanera de Sabadell, 1896-1925* (Sabadell, 1987).
Devinat, Paul, *Scientific Management in Europe* (Geneva, 1927).
Devleeshouwer, R., "Logique sociale et legislation du travail en Belgique au cours de la première moitié du XIXe siècle", *Revue de l'Institut de Sociologie de l'Université de Bruxelles* (1962), pp. 449-519.
Dewerpe, A., *L'Industrie aux champs: essai sur la proto-industrialisation en Italie du Nord (1800-1880)* (Rome, 1985).
Dhondt, J., "De opkomst van de burgerij als politieke macht en de groei van de arbeidersstand (1786-1856)", in: J. Dhondt, *Geschiedenis van de Socialistische Arbeidersbeweging in België* (Antwerp, 1960), pp. 33-50.
Dhondt, J., *Machten en Mensen. Hommes et Pouvoirs* (Ghent, 1976).
Dokka, Hans-Jørgen, *Fra almueskole til folkeskole: Studier i den norske folkeskolens historie i det 19. hundreåret* (Bergen, 1967).
Dolléans, Edouard and Georges Dehove, *Histoire du travail en France: Mouvement ouvrier et législation sociale* (Paris, 1953).
Dore, R.P., "The Modernizer as a Special Case: Japanese Factory Legislation 1882-1911", *Comparative Studies in Society and History*, 11 (1969), pp. 433-450.
Dormois, Jean-Pierre, *The French Economy in the Twentieth Century* (Cambridge, 2004).
Douailler, S. and P. Vermeren, "Les enfants du capital", *Les Révoltes logiques*, 3 (1976), pp. 8-43.
Drufy, Horace Bookwalter, *Scientific Management: A History and Criticism* (New York, 1915).
Du Boulay, Juliette, *Portrait of a Greek Mountain Village* (Oxford, 1979).
Ducpétiaux, Édouard, *Quelques mots sur l'état actuel de l'instruction primaire en Belgique et sur la nécessité de l'améliorer* (Brussels, 1839).
Ducpetiaux, Édouard, *Memoire sur le pauperisme dans Ies Flandres* (Brussels, 1850).
Dulles, John W. Foster, *Anarquistas e comunistas no Brasil, 1900-1935* (Rio de Janeiro, 1977).

Dunlop, O. J. and Richard D. Denman, *English Apprenticeship and Child Labour: A History* (London, 1912).
Dupin, Charles, *Du travail des enfants qu'emploient les ateliers, les usines et les manufactures* (Paris 1840).
Dupont-Bouchat, Marie-Sylvie, "Le travail des enfants dans les pénitenciers", *Cahiers de la Fonderie*, 7 (1989), pp. 19-23.
Dupont-Bouchat, Marie-Sylvie, "L'ère Ducpétiaux. L'enfance coupable et la prison (1830-1880)", in: Id., *De la prison à l'école*, pp. 27-48.
Dupont-Bouchat, Marie-Sylvie, *De la prison à l'école. Les pénitenciers pour enfants en Belgique au XIXe siècle (1840-1914)*, Standen en Landen series (Heule-Courtrai, 1996).
Dupree, Marguerite, *Family Structure in the Staffordshire Potteries, 1840-1880* (Oxford, 1995).
Düsterhaus, Gerhard, *Das ländische Schulwesen im Herzogtum Preussen im 16. und 17. Jahrhundert* (Bonn, 1975).

Eaton, Martin, "Child Labor in Portuguese Textiles", in: Hugh Hindman (ed.), *The World of Child Labor. An Historical and Regional Survey* (New York, 2009), pp. 649-651.
Eaton, Martin and Carlos Pereira da Silva. "Portuguese Child Labour: Manufacturing for Change or Continuing Exploitation in the Textiles Industry", *Childhood*, 5 (1998), pp. 325-343.
Edgren, Lars, *Lärling – Gesäll – Mästare hantverk och hantverkare i Malmö 1750-1847* (Lund, 1987).
Eeckhout, van den, *see* Van den Eeckhout
Effland, Anne B.W., "Agrarianism and Child Labor Policy for Agriculture", *Agricultural History*, 79 (2005), pp. 281-297.
Eklof, Ben, *Russian Peasant Schools: Officialdom, Village Culture, and Popular Pedagogy, 1861-1914* (Berkeley, 1986).
Eldredge, Elizabeth A. and Fred Morton (eds), *Slavery in South Africa: Captive Labor on the South African Frontier* (Boulder, CO, 1994).
Ellem, Bradon, *In Women's Hands: A History of Clothing Trades Unionism in Australia* (Sydney, 1987).
Ellena, Vittorio, "La statistica di alcune industrie italiane", *Annali di statistica*, s. II, v. 13 (1880), pp. 1-141.
Elson, Robert, *Village Java under the Cultivation System* (Sydney, 1994).
Émilie Carles, as told to Robert Destanque, *A Wild Herb Soup: The Life of a French Countrywoman*. Transl. by Avriel H. Goldberger (London, 1992).
Engberg, Elisabeth, "Boarded Out by Auction: Poor Children and their Families in Nineteenth-Century Northern Sweden", *Continuity and Change* 19 (2004), pp. 431-457.
Engberg, Elisabeth, *I fattiga omständigheter: Fattigvårdens former och understödstagare i skellefteå socken under 1800-talet* (Umeå, 2005).
Engerman, Stanley, "The History and Political Economy of International Labour Standards", in: Kaushik Basu, Henrik Horn, Judith Shapiro and Lisa Roman (eds), *International Labor Standards: History, Theory and Policy Options* (Oxford, 2003).
Ennew, Judith, William E. Myers and Dominique Pierre Plateau, "Defining Child Labour as if Human Rights Really Matter", in: Burns H. Weston, *Child Labor and Human Rights*, (Boulder, 2005), pp. 27-54.
Epstein, Arnold. L., *Urbanization and Kinship: The Domestic Domain on the Copperbelt of Zambia 1950-1956* (London, 1981).
Epstein, Israel, *Notes on Labor Problems in Nationalist China* (New York, 1949).

Erisman, Friedr., *Untersuchungen über die körperliche Entwicklung der Fabrikarbeiter in Zentralrussland* (Tübingen, 1889).

Faleiros, Vicente de Paula, "Infância e processo político no Brasil", in: Francisco Pilotti and Irene Rizzini (eds), *A Arte de governar crianças: A história das políticas sociais, da legislação e da assistência à infância no Brasil* (Rio de Janeiro, 1995), pp. 47-98.

Falola, Toyin and Paul E. Lovejoy (eds), *Pawnship in Africa: Debt Bondage in Historical Perspective* (Boulder, CO, 1994).

Farnie, D.A., *The English Cotton Industry and the World Market 1815-1896* (Oxford, 1979).

Federation of Rhodesia and Nyasaland, *Census of the Population, 1956* (Salisbury, 1960).

Federico, G., "Per una storia dell'industria serica italiana", *Annali di Storia dell'impresa,* IV (1988), pp. 112-130.

Federico, G., *Il filo d'oro. L'industria mondiale della seta dalla restaurazione alla grande crisi* (Venice, 1994).

Feinstein, Charles H., "Pessimism Perpetuated: Real Wages and the Standard of Living in Britain During and After the Industrial Revolution", *Journal of Economic History,* 58 (1998), pp. 625-658.

Fellman, Susanna, "The Professionalisation of management in Finland: The Case of the manufacturing Sector, 1900-1975", *Scandinavian Economic History Review,* 49 (2001), pp. 5-27.

Felt, Jeremy P., *Hostages of Fortune: Child Labor Reform in New York State* (Syracuse, NY, 1965).

Fernández-Kelly, Maria Patricia, *For We Are Sold, I am My People: Women and Industry in Mexico's Frontier* (Albany, NY, 1983).

Ferreira, Eleanor Stange, *Trabalho infantil: História e situação atual* (Canoas, 2001), pp. 61-114.

Fetter, Bruce S., "The Missing Migrants: African Seeds in the Demographers Field", *History in Africa,* 11 (1984), pp. 99-111.

Fetter, Bruce S., "Relocating Central Africa's Biological Reproduction, 1923-1963", *International Journal of African Historical Studies,* 19 (1986), pp. 463-475.

Fielhauer, Helmut Paul, "'Kinder-Wechsel' und 'Böhmisch-Lernen'. Sitte, Wirtschaft und Kulturvermittlung im früheren niederösterreichisch-tschechoslowakischen Grenzbereich", *Österreichische Zeitschrift für Volkskunde,* 81 (1978), pp. 115-148.

Finch, Percival, "Battle against Child Labor in China", *Current History Magazine* (August 1925), pp. 759-765.

Fischer, E.J., *Fabriquers en fabrikanten: De Twentse katoennijverheid en de onderneming S.J. Spanjaard te Borne tussen circa 1800 en 1930* (Utrecht, 1983).

Flora, P., *State, Economy and Society in Western Europe 1815-1975: A Data Handbook.* 2 vols. Vol. I, *The Growth of Mass Democracies and Welfare States* (London/Frankfurt, 1983).

Florence, Philip Sargant, *Use of Industrial Statistics in the Investigation of Industrial Fatigue: A Manual for Field Research* (New York, 1918).

Florence, Philip Sargant, *Economics of Fatigue and Unrest and the Efficiency of Labour in English and American Industry* (London, 1924).

Floud, R., K. Wachter and A. Gregory, *Height, Health and History: Nutritional Status in the United Kingdom, 1750-1980* (Cambridge, 1990).

Fokkens, F., *Spoedige uitbreiding van volksonderwijs op Java dringend noodzakelijk* (The Hague, 1909).

Folks, Gertrude, *Farm Labor vs. School Attendance,* National Child Labor Committee Publication nr. 300 (New York, 1920).

Follows, John W., *Antecedents of the International Labour Organisation* (Oxford, 1951).

Foot, Francisco Hardman and Victor Leonardi, *História da indústria e do trabalho no Brasil: Das origens aos anos vinte* (São Paulo, 1982).
Forster, Colin, "Aspects of Australian Fertility, 1861-1901", *Australian Economic History Review*, 14 (1974), pp. 105-122.
Foundanopoulos, Kostas, "Misthoti Ergassia", in: Christos Hatziiossif, *Istoria tis Elladas tou 20ou aiona, 1900-1922, Oi aparches*. Vol. 1, Part 1 (Athens, 2000), pp. 87-121.
Frances, Raelene, *Politics of Work: Gender and Labour in Victoria 1880-1939* (Melbourne, 1993).
Franklin, Stephen, "Child Labor on Decline Globally. Improvements since 2000", *Chicago Tribune*, mai 5, 2006.
Fry, Eric, "The Condition of the Urban Wage-Earning Class in Australia in the 1880s" (Ph.D. thesis, Australian National University, 1956).
Funck, J.M., *De l'Enseignement primaire obligatoire en Belgique* (Brussels, 1858).
Füssel, Hans-Peter and Peter M. Roeder, "Recht – Erziehung – Staat", *Zeitschrift für Pädagogik* 49 (2003), *47. Beiheft*, pp. 7-25.
Fyfe, Alec, *Child Labour* (Cambridge, 1989).

Gaillard, Lucien, "La vie ouvrière et les mouvements ouvriers à Marseille de 1848 à 1879" (PhD thesis, Université de Provence, 1972).
Galbi, Douglas, "Child Labour and the Division of Labour in the Early English Cotton Mills", *Journal of Population Economics*, 10 (1997), pp. 357-375.
Galvez-Muñoz, Lina, *Compañía Arrendataria de Tabacos, 1887-1945* (Madrid, 2000).
Gannett, Lewis S., *Young China* (New York, 1927).
Gårdlund, Torsten, *Industrialismens samhälle* (Stockholm, 1942).
Gardner, Phil, *The Lost Elementary Schools of Victorian England: The People's Education* (London, 1984).
Garoupa, Nuno and Leonor Rossi, "Instituições e quadro legal", in: Pedro Lains and Álvaro Ferreira Silva (eds), *História económica de Portugal 1700-2000*. 3 vols. Vol. 3 (Lisbon, 2005), séc XX, pp. 423-450.
Garth, Thomas Russel, *Mental Fatigue during Continuous Exercise of a Single Function* (New York, 1918).
Gaunt, David, *Familjeliv i Norden* (Stockholm, 1996).
Gaus, H., *Politieke en sociale evolutie van België* (Louvain, 1992).
Geertz, Clifford, *Agricultural Involution: The Processes of Ecological Change in Indonesia* (Berkeley, 1963).
Geijer, Erik Gustaf, *Samlade skrifter*. Vol. III (Stockholm, 1874).
Geijerstam, Gustaf af, *Arbetareförhållanden i Stockholm* (Stockholm, 1894).
Genovesi, Giovanni, *Storia della scuola in Italia dal Settecento a oggi* (Rome-Bari, 1998).
Ge Rondi, Carla, "La dinamica demografica delle province lombarde", *Bollettino Società italiana di Demografia storica*, 28 (1998), pp. 63-88.
Gessen, V.I., *Trud detei i podrostkov v Rossii. Ot XVII veka go Oktiabr'skoi Revoliutsii* (Moscow, 1927).
Gide, Charles and Charles Rist, *A History of Economic Thought*. Transl. by R. Richards (London, 1915).
Gilbert, D., *Les filatures de lin, étude d'hygiène professionnelle* (Brussels, 1902).
Glickman, Rose L., *Russian Factory Women: Workplace and Society, 1880-1914* (Berkeley, 1986).
Goetz-Girey, Robert, *Croissance et progress à l'origine des sociétés industrielles* (Paris, 1966).
Goldberg, Ellis, *Trade, Reputation, and Child Labor in Twentieth-Century Egypt* (New York, 2004).
Goldin, Claudia, *Understanding the Gender Gap* (Oxford, 1990).

Goldin, Claudia and Kenneth Sokoloff, "Women, Children, and Industrialization in the Early Republic: Evidence from the Manufacturing Censuses", *Journal of Economic History*, 42 (1982), pp. 741-774.

Goldin, Claudia and Donald O. Parsons, "Parental Altruism and Self-Interest: Child Labor among American Families", *Economic Inquiry*, 27 (1989), pp. 637-659.

Gomes, Soeiro Pereira, *Esteiros* (Lisbon, 1979).

Goody, Ester, "Kinship Fostering in Gonja", in: Philip Mayer (ed.), *Socialization: The Approach from Social Anthropology* (London, 1970), pp. 51-74.

Goody, Esther, *Parenthood and Social Reproduction* (Cambridge, 1982).

Göransson, Anita, *Från familj till fabrik. Teknik, arbetsdelning och skiktning i svenska fabriker 1830-1877* (Lund, 1988).

Göransson, Anita, "Gender and property rights; capital, kin and owner influence in nineteenth and twentieth century Sweden", *Business history*, 35 (1993), pp. 11-32.

Gorp, P.J.M. van, *Tilburg: Eens de wolstad van Nederland. Bloei en ondergang van de Tilburgse wollenstoffenindustrie* (Tilburg, 1987).

Gorshkov, Boris B., "Factory Children: An Overview of Child Industrial Labor and Laws in Imperial Russia, 1840-1914", in: Michael Melancon and Alice K. Pate (eds), *New Labor History: Worker Experiences and Identity in Russia, 1840-1918* (Bloomington, IN, 2002), pp. 9-33.

Gorshkov, Boris B., "Toward a Comprehensive Law: Tsarist Factory Labor Legislation in European Context, 1830-1914", in: Susan P. McCaffray, Michael S. Melancon (eds), *Russians Envision their Place in Europe, 1789-1914: A Member of the Family* (New York, 2005), pp. 49-70.

Gorshkov, Boris B., *Russia's Factory Children: State, Society, and Law 1800-1917* (Pittsburgh, PA, 2009).

Goulart, Pedro and Arjun S. Bedi, "Child Labour and Educational Success in Portugal", *Economics of Education Review*, 27:5 (2007), pp. 575-587.

Grandits, Hannes and Karl Kaser (eds), *Birnbaum der Tränen. Lebensgeschichtliche Erzählungen aus dem alten Jugoslawien* (Vienna, 2006).

Gray, Richard, *The Two Nations: Aspects of the Development of Race and Relations in the Rhodesias and Nyasaland* (London, 1960).

Great Britain, *Swaziland Colonial Annual Report*, 1930.

Great Britain, *Swaziland Colonial Reports*, 1922-1927.

Green, David R., *From Artisans to Paupers: Economic Change and Poverty in London, 1790-1870* (Aldershot, 1995).

Greene, J.W. et al., *From Forge to Fast Food: A History of Child Labor in New York State*. Vol. I: *Colonial Times Through the Civil War* (Troy, NY, 1995).

Greenwood, James, *The Seven Curses of London* (Oxford, 1981, 1st ed.1869).

Grenadou, Ephraïm and Alain Prévost, *Grenadou: paysan français* (Paris, 1966).

Grenholm, Carl-Henric, *Arbetets mening: En analys av sex teorier om arbetets syfte och värde* (Uppsala, 1988).

Grier, Beverly, "Invisible Hands: The Political Economy of Child Labour in Colonial Zimbabwe, 1890-1930", *Journal of Southern African Studies*, 20:1 (1994), pp. 27-52.

Grier, Beverly, "Pawns, Porters, and Petty Traders: Women in the Transition to Cash Crop Agriculture in Colonial Ghana", *Signs*, 20 (1994), pp. 27-52.

Grier, Beverly, "Child Labor in Africa: A Critical Overview", *African Studies Review*, 47 (2004), pp. 1-25.

Grier, Beverly C., *Invisible Hands: Child Labor and the State in Colonial Zimbabwe* (Portsmouth, NH, 2006).

Grootaert, Christian and Ravi Kanbar, "Child Labour: An Economic Perspective", *International Labour Review*, 134 (1995), pp. 187-203.
Gubin, É. and P. Lefevre, "Obligation scolaire et société en Belgique au XIXe siècle. Réflexions à propos du premier projet de loi sur l'enseignement obligatoire (1883)", *Revue belge de philologie et d'histoire*, 63 (1985), pp. 324-376.
Gubin, Éliane, "Femmes, travail, protection: le débat en Belgique au XIXe siècle", *Cahiers Marxistes*, 172 (1990), pp. 41-49.
Gubin, Éliane, "Postface", in: Roland Caty, *Enfants au travail: Attitude des elites en Europe occidentale et méditerranéenne aux XIXe et XXe siècles* (Aix-en-Provence, 2002), pp. 267-276.
Guérard, B. (ed.), *1892-1913. L'inspection du travail française et le travail des enfants* (Paris, 1999).
Guereña, Jean Louis, "Infancia y escolarización", in: José María Borrás Llop and Josette Borderies Guereña (eds), *Historia de la infancia en la España contemporánea 1834-1936* (Madrid, 1996), pp. 349-418.
Guillaume, Pierre, "Le travail des enfants trouvés à Bordeaux dans la première moitié du XIX siècle", in: Roland Caty (ed.), *Enfants au travail: Attitudes des élites en Europe occidentale et méditerranéene aux XIX et XX siècles* (Aix-en-Provence, 2002), pp. 109-122.
Guillon, Jean-Marie, "Enfance assistée, enfance exploitée? La colonie agricole de Porquerolles", in: Roland Caty (ed.), *Enfants au travail: Attitudes des élites en Europe occidentale et méditerranéene aux XIX et XX siècles* (Aix-en-Provence, 2002), pp. 137-152.
Guiral, P., "Brèves observations sur le travail des enfants dans les Bouches-du-Rhône au milieu du XIXe siècle", *8e Colloque d'histoire sur l'artisanat et l'apprentissage* (Aix-en-Provence, 1965), pp. 57-68.
Guiral, P. and F. Reynaud (eds), *Les Marseillais dans l'histoire* (Toulouse, 1988).
Gullickson, Gay L., *Spinners and Weavers of Auffay: Rural Industry and the Sexual Division of Labour in a French Village, 1750-1850* (Cambridge, 1986).
Gunnlaugsson, Gísli Ágúst, *Ómagar og utangarðsfolk. Fátækramál Reykjavíkur, 1786-1907* (Reykjavík, 1982).
Gunnlaugsson, Gísli Ágúst, "'Everyone's Been Good to Me, Especially the Dogs'. Foster-Children and Young Paupers in Nineteenth-Century Southern-Iceland", *Journal of Social History*, 27 (1993), pp. 341-358.
Gutiérrez, Horácio and Ida Lewkowicz, "Trabalho infantil em Minas Gerais na primeira metade do século XIX", *Locus: revista de história*, 5 (1999), pp. 9-21.
Guttormsson, Loftur, *Bernska, ungdómur og uppeldi á einveldisöld: Tilraun til félagslegrar og lýðfræðilegrar greiningar* (Reykjavík, 1983).

Haer, van, *see* Van Haer
Hagan, J., *Printers in Politics: A History of the Australian Printing Unions 1850-1950* (Canberra, 1966).
Hainisch, Michael, *Vorschläge zur Regelung der Kinderarbeit vom wirtschaftlichen und sozialpolitischen Standpunkte.* Gutachten, Berichte und Materialien zu den Verhandlungsgegenständen des Zweiten Österreichischen Kinderschutzkongresses in Salzburg 1913. Schriften des Zweiten Österreichischen Kinderschutzkongresses. Vol II (Vienna, 1913).
Hainisch, Michael, *Die Landflucht* (Jena, 1924).
Hair, Paul E.H., "The Social History of the British Coalminers" (Ph.D. thesis, Oxford 1955).
Hair, Paul E.H., "Children in Society, 1850-1980", in: T. Barker and M. Drake (eds), *Population and Society in Britain, 1850-1980* (London, 1982), pp. 34-61.

Hajnal, J., "Age at Marriage and Proportions Marrying", *Population Studies*, 7 (1953), pp. 111-136.

Hall, A.R., "Some Long Period Effects of the Kinked Age Distribution of the Population in Australia", *Economic Record*, 39 (1963) pp. 43-55.

Hallberg, Milton C., *Policy for American Agriculture: Choices and Consequences* (Ames, IA, 1992).

Hammond, John L. and Barbara Hammond, *The Skilled Labourer, 1760-1832* (London, 1920).

Hammond, John, L. and Barbara B. Hammond, *The Town Labourer, 1760-1832: The New Civilisation* (London, 1966, first ed. 1917).

Hansen, Karen Tranberg, "Lusaka's Squatters: Past and Present", *African Studies Review*, 25 (1982), pp. 117-136.

Hansen, Karen Tranberg, "Negotiating Sex and Gender in Urban Zambia", *Journal of Southern African Studies*, 10 (1984), pp. 219-238.

Hansen, Karen Tranberg, "Labour Migration and Urban Child Labour During the Colonial Period in Zambia", in: Bruce Fetter (ed.), *Demography from Scanty Evidence: Central Africa in the Colonial Era* (Boulder, CO, 1990), pp. 219-234.

Hareven, Tamara K., *Family Time and Industrial Time* (Cambridge, 1982).

Harnetty, Peter, *Imperialism and Free Trade: Lancashire and India in the Mid-Nineteenth Century* (Manchester, 1972).

Harries, Patrick, "Symbols and Sexuality: Culture and Identity on the Early Witwatersrand Gold Mines", *Gender and History*, 2 (1990), pp. 218-236.

Harries, Patrick, *Work, Culture, and Identity: Migrant Laborers in Mozambique and South Africa, c. 1860-1910* (Portsmouth, NH, 1994).

Hawes, Joseph M., *Children in Urban Society: Juvenile Delinquency in Nineteenth-Century America* (New York, 1971).

Hawes, Joseph M. and N. Ray Hiner (eds), *Children in Historical and Comparative Perspective: An International Handbook and Research Guide* (New York, 1991).

Hear, van *see* Van Hear

Hedenborg, Susanna, *Det gåtfulla folket: Barns villkor och uppfattningar av barnet i 1700-talets Stockholm* (Stockholm, 1997).

Hedmo, Tina, Kerstin Sahlin-Andersson and Linda Wedlin, "Fields of Imitation: The Global Expandion of Management Education", in: Barbara Czarniawska and Guje Sevón (eds), *Global Ideas: How Ideas, Objects and Practices Travel in the Global Economy* (Malmö, 2005), pp. 190-212.

Hedvall, Barbro, "Debatten om barnarbete i industri och hantverk 1850-1883", in: Ingrid Hammarström (ed.), *Ideologi och socialpolitik i 1800-talets Sverige* (Uppsala, 1978), pp. 127-219.

Heisler, Helmuth, *Urbanisation and the Government of Migration* (London, 1974).

Helg, Aline, *La educación en Colombia, 1918-1957. Una historia social, económica y política* (Bogotá, 1987).

Hendrick, Harry, "Constructions and Reconstructions of British Childhood: An Interpretative Survey, 1800 to the Present", in: Allison James and Allan Prout (eds), *Constructing and Reconstructing Childhood* (London, 1990), pp. 35-59.

Hendrick, Harry, *Children, Childhood and English Society, 1880-1990* (Cambridge, 1997).

Hendrick, Harry, "The Child as an Actor in Historical Sources: Problems of Identification and Interpretation", in: Pia Christensen and Allison James (eds), *Research with Children* (London, 2001), pp. 36-61.

Henriques Carneiro, A., *Evolução e controlo do ensino em Portugal* (Lisbon, 2003).

Heppe, H., *Geschichte des deutschen Volkschulwesens*. 5 vols. Vols 1, 2, 3 (Gotha, 1858).

Herdt, R. De, *see* De Herdt, R.

Hershatter, Gail, *Workers of Tianjin, 1900-1949* (Stanford, CA, 1986).

Hetherington, E. Mavis, Richard M. Lerner and Marion Perlmutter (eds), *Child Development in Life-span Perspective* (Hillsdale, NJ, 1988).

Hetherington, Penelope, "Child Labour in Swan River Colony, 1829-1850", *Australian Historical Studies*, 25 (98) (1992), pp. 34-52.

Heywood, Colin, *Childhood in Nineteenth-Century France: Work, Health and Education among the "Classes Populaires"* (Cambridge, 1988).

Heywood, Colin, "The Catholic Church and the Formation of the Industrial Labour Force in Nineteenth-Century France: An Interpretative Essay", *European History Quarterly*, 19 (1989), pp. 509-533.

Heywood, Colin, *A History of Childhood: Children and Childhood in the West from Medieval to Modern Times* (Cambridge, 2001).

Heywood, Colin, *Growing Up in France: From the Ancien Régime to the Third Republic* (Cambridge, 2007).

Hicks, Neville, *"This Sin and Scandal": Australia's Population Debate 1891-1911* (Canberra, 1978).

Higgs, Edward, "Women, Occupations and Work in the Nineteenth-Century Censuses", *History Workshop*, 23 (1987), pp. 59-80.

Higgs, Edward, *Making Sense of the Census* (London, 1989).

Hilden, Patricia, *Women, Work, and Politics: Belgium, 1830-1914* (Oxford, 1993).

Hill, Christopher, *Reformation to Industrial Revolution* (Harmondsworth, 1971).

Hill, Polly, *The Gold Coast Cocoa Farmer: a Preliminary Survey* (London, 1956).

Hindman, Hugh D., *Child Labor: An American History* (Armonk, NY, 2002).

Hindman, Hugh D., "Unfinished Business: The Persistence of Child Labor in the US", *Employee Rights and Responsibilities Journal*, 18 (2006), pp. 125-131.

Hine, Lewis W., *National Child Labor Committee Investigation Report nr. 216. Delaware Agriculture* (New York, 1910).

Hobbs, Sandy, Jim McKechnie and Michael Lavalette, *Child Labor: A World History Companion* (Santa Barbara, CA, 1999).

Hobsbawm, Eric, "Custom, Wages and Work-Load in Nineteenth-Century Industry", in: E.J. Hobsbawm, *Labouring Men: Studies in the History of Labour* (London, 1964), pp. 344-370.

Hobsbawm, Eric, *Labouring Men: Studies in the History of Labour* (London, 1974).

Hogan, D. J., *Class and Reform: School and Society in Chicago, 1880-1930* (Philadelphia, PA, 1985).

Holmes, H., "Urban Schoolboys Go to the Country", *Rhodes-Livingstone Journal*, 9 (1950), pp. 31-36.

Homburg, Heidrun, "Anfänge des Taylorsystems in Deutschland vor dem Ersten Weltkrieg", *Geschichte und Gesellschaft*, 4 (1978), pp. 170-194.

Honeyman, Katrina, *Child Workers in England, 1780-1820: Parish Apprentices and the Making of the Early Industrial Labour Force* (Aldershot, 2007).

Honig, Emily, *Sisters and Strangers: Women in the Shanghai Cotton Mills, 1919-1949* (Stanford, CA, 1986).

Hopkins, E., *Childhood Transformed. Working-Class Children in Nineteenth-Century England* (Manchester, 1993).

Hoppers, Wim, "Youth, Apprenticeship, and Petty Production in Lusaka", *International Journal of Educational Development*, 3 (1984), pp. 113-128.

Horn, Pamela, "Pillow Lace-Making in Victorian England: The Experience of Oxfordshire", *Textile History*, 3 (1972), pp. 100-115.
Horn, Pamela, "The Agricultural Children Act of 1873", *History of Education*, 3:2 (1974), pp. 27-39.
Horn, Pamela, "Child Workers in the Pillow Lace and Straw Plait Trades of Victorian Buckinghamshire and Bedfordshire", *Historical Journal*, 17 (1974), pp. 779-796.
Horn, Pamela, *Children's Work and Welfare, 1780-1890* (Cambridge, 1994).
Horrell, Sara, "Home Demand and British Industrialization", *Journal of Economic History*, 56 (1996), pp. 561-604.
Horrell, Sara and Jane Humphries, "'The Exploitation of Little Children': Child Labour and the Family Economy in the Industrial Revolution", *Explorations in Economic History*, 32 (1995), pp. 485-516.
Horrell, Sara and Jane Humphries, "Child Labour and British Industrialization", in: Michael Lavalette (ed.), *A Thing of the Past? Child Labour in Britain in the Nineteenth and Twentieth Centuries* (Liverpool, 1999), pp. 76-100.
Horrell, Sara, Jane Humphries and Hans-Joachim Voth, "Destined for Deprivation: Human Capital Formation and Intergenerational Poverty in Nineteenth-Century England", *Explorations in Economic History*, 38 (2001), pp. 339-365.
Houston, Robert Allan, *Literacy in Early Modern Europe* (Harlow, 2002).
Hsia, Yen, "Contract Labour and Postscript" (Originally published in 1936), trans. Gladys Yang, *Chinese Literature*, 8 (1960), pp. 47-63.
Huart, F., "La Société protectrice des Enfants martyrs de Bruxelles, 1892-1912" (MA thesis, Université catholique de Louvain-la-Neuve, 2 vols, 1994).
Humphries, Jane, "Protective Legislation, the Capitalist State and Working Class Men: The Case of the 1842 Mines Regulation Act", *Feminist Review*, 7 (1981), pp. 1-35.
Humphries, Jane, "Short Stature among Coalmining Children: A Comment", *Economic History Review*, 50 (1997), pp. 531-537.
Humphries, Jane, "Female-Headed Households in Early Industrial Britain: The Vanguard of the Proletariat?", *Labor History Review*, 63 (1998), pp. 31-65.
Humphries, Jane, "At what cost was pre-eminence purchased? Child Labor in the Industrial Revolution", in: Peter Scholliers and Leonard Schwarz (eds), *Experiencing Wages: Social and Cultural Aspects of Wage Forms in Europe since 1500* (Oxford, 2003), pp. 251-268.
Humphries, Jane, "Child Labor in the Industrial Revolution: The Evidence from Working Class Autobiographies", *Oxford University Economic and Social History Working Papers* (2003).
Humphries, Jane, "Child Labor: Lessons from the Historical Experience of Today's Industrial Economies", *World Bank Economic Review*, 17 (2003), pp. 175-196, also reprinted in this volume as Chapter 2.
Humphries, Jane, "The Parallels between Past and Present", in: Kaushik Basu, Henrik Horn, Judith Shapiro and Lisa Roman (eds), *International Labour Standards: History, Theory and Policy Options* (Oxford, 2003), pp. 84-98.
Humphries, Jane, "Household Economy", in: Roderick Flood and Paul Johnson (eds), *Industrialization, 1700-1860.* Cambridge Economic History of Britain, Vol. 1 (Cambridge, 2004), pp 238-267.
Humphries, Jane, *Childhood and Child Labour in the British Industrial Revolution* (Cambridge, 2010).
Hunter, Janet, "Textile Factories, Tuberculosis and the Quality of Life in Industrializing Japan", in: Janet Hunter (ed.), *Japanese Women Working* (London, 1993), pp. 75-84.

Hutchins, Elizabeth, L. and Amy Harrison, *A History of Factory Legislation* (London, 1926, first ed. 1903).

Hutt, William, H., "The Factory System of the Early Nineteenth Century", in: F.A. Hayek (ed.), *Capitalism and the Historians* (London, 1954), pp. 160-188.

IAC/CNASTI, *O Trabalho infantil em Portugal* (Lisbon, 1996).

IEFP, "Regulamento de 1891 sobre o trabalho das mulheres e menores", *Dirigir* 3:23 (1992), pp. 36-40.

IGT, "Centenário de uma lei histórica", *Boletim da IGT*, 17 (1991).

ILO/International Labour Organization, *Boas práticas de combate ao trabalho infantil*, Os 10 anos do IPEC no Brasil, IPEC – Brasil (Brasília, 2003).

ILO/International Labour Organization. *Combatendo o trabalho infantil: Guia para educadores*, IPEC – Brasil (Brasília, 2001).

ILO/International Labour Organization, *The End of Child Labour: Within Reach. Global Report Under the Follow-up to the ILO Declaration on Fundamental Principles and Rights at Work* (Geneva, 2006).

ILO/International Labour Office, *Child Labour in Indonesia* (Jakarta, 1994).

ILO/International Labour Office, *Child Labour: Targeting the Intolerable* (Geneva, 1996).

ILO/International Labour Office, *Convention No. 5 on Minimal Age for Admission of Children to Industrial Employment* (Geneva, 1919).

International Arbeitsrecht gestaltet durch die Internationale Arbeitskonferenz. Übereinkommen und Empfehlungen von dreiundzwanzig Tagungen der Internationalen Arbeitskonferenz in den Jahren 1919-1937 (Geneva, 1938).

Ipsen, Carl, *Italy in the Age of Pinocchio: Children and Danger in the Liberal Era* (New York, 2006).

Ireland, Tom, *Child Labor as a Relic of the Dark Ages* (New York, 1937).

Isberg, A.I., *Malmö Stads 600-årsjubileum* (Malmö, 1919).

Jablonka, Ivan, "Paths Towards Autonomy: The Living Conditions of Fostered Children in Western France in the Early 20th Century", *The History of the Family*, 6 (2001), pp. 401-421.

Jackman, Mary Elizabeth, "Recent Population Movements in Zambia: Some Aspects of the 1969 Census", *Zambian Papers*, 8 (Lusaka, 1973).

Johansson, Alf, *Den effektiva arbetstiden: Verkstäderna och arbetsintensitetens problem 1900-1920* (Uppsala, 1977).

Johansson, Alf, *Arbetarrörelsen och taylorismen: Olofström 1895-1925* (Lund, 1990).

Johansson, Ulla, "Fattigvård i Sverige under 1700-talet", in: Karl-Gustaf Andersson, Ulla Johansson and Ståle Dyrvik (eds), *Oppdaginga av fattigdomen: Sosial lovgivning i Norden på 1700-talet* (Oslo, 1983), pp. 217-357.

Johnson, Victoria V., "Did Old MacDonald Have a Farm? Holly Farms Corp. v. National Labor Relations Board", *University of Colorado Law Review*, 69 (1998), pp. 295-330.

Jolly, Richard and Giovanni Andrea Cornia (eds), "The Impact of World Recession on Children", special issue of *World Development*, 12 (1984).

Jones, Sonya M., *A Study of Swazi Nutrition: Report of the Swaziland Nutrition Survey 1961-1962 for the Swaziland Administration* (Durban, 1963).

Jong, G.F.A. de, "Enige sociale aspecten van de arbeid in de textielindustrie gedurende de 19e eeuw", in: H.F.J.M. van den Eerenbeemt and H.J.A.M. Schurink (eds), *De opkomst van Tilburg als industriestad: Anderhalve eeuw economische en sociale ontwikkeling* (Nijmegen, 1959), pp. 167-199.

Jonge, J.A. de, *De industrialisatie in Nederland tussen 1850 en 1914* (Nijmegen, 1976).
Jørgensen, Harald, *Studier over det offentlige fattigvæsens historiske udvikling i Danmark i det 19. Aarhundrede* (Copenhagen, 1940).
Jovanović, Miroslav , "Accelerated Maturity: Childhood in Emigration (Russian Children on the Balkans 1920-1940)", in: Slobodan Naumović and Miroslav Jovanović (eds), *Childhood in South East Europe: Historical Perspectives on Growing Up in the 19th and 20th Century* (Belgrade, 2001), pp. 199-214.

Kallivretakis, Leonidas, *I dinamiki tou agrotikou eksynchronismou stin Ellada tou 19ou aiona* (Athens, 1990).
Kantoor van Arbeid, *Zestiende verslag van de Arbeidsinspectie (1933, 1934, 1935 en 1936)* (Batavia, 1937).
Kantoor van Arbeid, *Zeventiende verslag van de Arbeidsinspectie (1937 en 1938)* (Batavia, 1939).
Kaser, Karl, *Familie und Verwandtschaft auf dem Balkan. Analyse einer untergehenden Kultur* (Vienna, 1995).
Kat Angelino, P. de, *Verslag betreffende eene door den inspecteur bij het Kantoor van Arbeid (...) op de Vorstenlandsche tabaksondernemingen gehouden enquête* (Weltevreden, 1929).
Kat Angelino, P. de, *Rapport betreffende eene gehouden enquête naar de arbeidstoestanden in de batikkerijen op Java en Madoera,* (Batikrapport) 3 vols (Batavia, 1930-1931).
Kaufhold, Karl Heinrich, "Die Diskussion um die Neugestaltung des Arbeitsrechts im Deutschen Reich 1890 und die Novelle zur Reichsgewerbeordnung", *Zeitschrift für Arbeitsrecht*, 22 (1991), pp. 277-322.
Kayongo-Male, Diane and P. Walji, *Children at Work in Kenya* (Nairobi, 1984).
Kettunen, Pauli, "Taylorismin tulo Suomeen", in: Matti Peltonen (ed.), *Arki ja murros* (Helsinki, 1990), pp. 361-397.
Keune, A.W.M., "De industriële ontwikkeling gedurende de 19e eeuw", in: H.F.J.M. van den Eerenbeemt and H.J.A.M. Schurink (eds), *De opkomst van Tilburg als industriestad. Anderhalve eeuw economische en sociale ontwikkeling* (Nijmegen, 1959), pp. 11-60.
Key, Ellen, *Barnets århundrade.* 2 vols, vol. 1 (Stockholm, 1900).
Kharaba, Ivan, "Élites économiques et administratives du Var et des Bouches-du-Rhône face à l'élaboration des lois sur le travail des enfants au XIXe siècle", in: Caty, R. (ed.), *Enfants au travail. Attitudes des élites en Europe occidentale et méditerranéenne aux XIXe et XXe siècles* (Aix-en-Provence, 2002), pp. 11-21.
Kings, Philip Bonner, *Commoners and Concessionaires: The Evolution and Dissolution of the Nineteenth Century Swazi State* (Johannesburg, 1983).
Kirby, Peter, "Aspects of the Employment of Children in the British Coalmining Industry, 1800-1872" (Ph.D. thesis, Sheffield, 1995).
Kirby, Peter, "Causes of Short Stature among Coalmining Children, 1823-1850", *Economic History Review*, 48 (1995), pp. 687-699.
Kirby, Peter, "Short Stature among Coalmining Children: A Rejoinder", *Economic History Review*, 50 (1997), pp. 538-542.
Kirby, Peter, "The Historic Viability of Child Labour and the Mines Act of 1842", in: Michael Lavalette (ed.), *A Thing of the Past? Child Labour in Britain in the Nineteenth and Twentieth Centuries* (Liverpool, 1999), pp. 101-117.
Kirby, Peter, *Child Labour in Britain, 1750-1870* (London, 2003).
Kirby, Peter, "A Short Statistical Sketch of the Child Labour Market in Mid-Nineteenth Century London", *Continuity and Change,* 20 (2005), pp. 229-245.
Kirby, Peter, "How Many Children were 'Unemployed' in Eighteenth- and Nineteenth-Century England?", *Past & Present*, 187(1) (2005), pp. 187-202.

Kirov, A., *Na zare iunosheskogo dvizheniia v Rossii* (Kharkov, 1926).

Kirschner, S., *Ideological Themes in Movements for Child Labor Reform and in Images of Children in Literature in 19th Century England and America* (Cambridge, 1983).

Kitteringham, Jennie, "Country Work Girls in Nineteenth-Century England", in: Raphael Samuel (ed.), *Village Life and Labour* (London, 1975), pp. 75-138.

Kloek, Els, *Wie hij zij, man of wijf: Vrouwengeschiedenis en de vroegmoderne tijd* (Hilversum, 1990).

Knight, Roger, "Capitalism and Commodity Production in Java", in: Hamza Alavi *et al.*, *Capitalism and Colonial Production* (London, 1982), pp. 119-159.

Knox, William, "British Apprenticeship, 1800-1914" (Ph.D. thesis, Edinburgh 1980).

Kocka, Jürgen, "The Rise of the Modern Industrial Enterprise in Germany", in: Alfred D. Chandler Jr. and Herman Daems (eds), *Managerial Hierarchies: Comparative Perspectives on the Rise of the Modern Industrial Enterprise* (Cambridge, 1980), pp. 77-116.

Köll, Elisabeth, *From Cotton Mill to Business Empire: The Emergence of Regional Enterprises in Modern China* (Cambridge, MA, 2003).

Konttinen, Esa, "Central Bureaucracy and the Restriction of Education in Early Nineteenth-century Finland", *Scandinavian Journal of History*, 21 (1996), pp. 201-220.

Kowler, Eileen and Albert Martins, "Eye Movements of Preschool Children", *Science New Series*, 215 (1982), pp. 997-999.

Kriedte, Peter, Hans Medick and Jürgen Schlumbohm, *Industrialization before Industrialization* (Cambridge, 1981).

Krikos, Alexandros, *Meletes B* (Athens, 1991).

Krueger, Alan, "International Labor Standards and Trade", in: Michael Bruno and Boris Pleskovic (eds), *Proceedings of the Annual World Bank Conference on Development Economics, 1996* (Washington, DC, 1997).

Kruithof, J., "De grootte van het Belgisch proletariaat tijdens de eerste helft van de negentiende eeuw", in: J. Dhondt, *Geschiedenis van de Socialistische Arbeidersbeweging in België* (Antwerp, 1960), pp. 193-210.

Krumbholz, Joachim, *Die Elementarbildung in Russland bis zum Jahre 1864: Ein Beitrag zur Entstehung des Volkschulstatuts vom 14. Juli 1864* (Wiesbaden, 1982).

Kuczynski, Jürgen, *Die Geschichte der Kinderarbeit in Deutschland 1750-1939*. Vol. 1 (Berlin 1958).

Kunze, Peter, *Sorbisches Schulwesen: Dokumentation zum sorbischen Elementarschulwesen in der sächsischen Oberlausitz des 18./19. Jahrhunderts* (Bautzen, 2002).

Kuper, Hilda, *An African Aristocracy: Rank Among the Swazi* (New York, 1947).

Kussmaul, Ann, *Servants in Husbandry in Early Modern England* (Cambridge, 1981).

Kussmaul, Ann, "The Ambiguous Mobility of Farm Servants", *Economic History Review*, 34 (1981), pp. 202-235.

Kuypers, J., *Bergop!* (Antwerp, 1957).

"Labor Conditions and Labor Regulations in China", *International Labor Review*, 10 (Dec. 1924), p. 4.

Lains, Pedro and Álvaro Ferreira Silva (eds), *História económica de Portugal 1700-2000*. 3 vols (Lisbon, 2005).

Lains, Pedro, "Catching-up to the European core. Portuguese economic growth, 1910-1990", *Explorations in Economic History* 40 (2003), pp. 369-386.

Larson, Ann, *Growing Up in Melbourne: Family Life in the Late Nineteenth Century* (Canberra, 1974).

Läsning i blandade ämnen (H.A. Nordström, Stockholm, 1797-1801).

Lavalette, Michael, *Child Employment in the Capitalist Labour Market* (Aldershot, 1994).
Lavalette, Michael, *A Thing of the Past? Child Labour in Britain in the Nineteenth and Twentieth Centuries* (Liverpool, 1999).
Law, Christopher M., "The Growth of Urban Population in England and Wales, 1801-1911", *Transactions of the Institute of British Geographers*, 41 (1967), pp. 125-143.
Lawson, Ronald, *Brisbane in the 1890s: A Study of an Australian Urban Society* (St Lucia, 1973).
Lazonick, William, "Industrial Organization and Technological Change: The Decline of the British Cotton Industry", *Business History Review*, 57 (1983), pp. 195-326.
Le Roy Ladurie, Emmanuel, "Preface" to Emile Zola, *La Terre* (Paris, 1980), pp. 7-23.
Lebrun, Pierre *et al.*, "Essai sur la revolution industrielle en Belgique, 1770-1847". *Histoire quantitative et developpement de la Belgique*. Vol. 2 (Brussels, 1979).
Lee, Jenny and Charles Fahey, "A Boom for Whom? Some Developments in the Australian Labour Market 1870-1891", *Labour History*, 50 (1987), pp. 1-27.
Lehmann, Dorothea, "Marriage, Divorce, and Prostitution of African Women in a Changing Society", in: Northern Rhodesia Council of Social Services, *Report of the Annual Conference, 1961, on Marriage and the Family* (Lusaka, 1961), pp. 27-35.
Lehmann, Dorothea, "Lives of African Adolescent Girls in a Copperbelt Township", in: George J. Snowball (ed.), *Science and Medicine in Central Africa* (Oxford, 1965), pp. 645-653.
Leidraad voor het Gewestelijke Onderzoek naar de Oorzaken der Mindere Welvaart van de Inlandsche Bevolking op Java en Madoera (Batavia, 1904).
Leuchtenburg, William E., *The Supreme Court Reborn: The Constitutional Revolution in the Age of Roosevelt* (Oxford, 1995).
Levert, P., *Inheemsche arbeid in de Java-suikerindustrie* (Wageningen, 1934).
Levine, Marvin, *Children for Hire: The Perils of Child Labor in the United States* (Westport, CT, 2003).
Levine, Susan, "'Picannin' Wages and Child Labor in the South African Agriculture, Mining, and Domestic Service Industries: 1658 to the Present", *Anthropology of Work Review*, XVII (1-2) (1996), pp. 42-50.
Lewin, Heinrich, *Geschichte der Entwicklung der preußischen Volkschule und der Förderung der Volksbildung durch die Hohenzollern* (Leipzig, 1910).
Li, Dazhao, "Shanghai de tonggong wenti" [Shanghai's child labor problem] *Zhongguo gongren* [The Chinese worker], 4 (1925), pp. 516-521.
Li, Mingwei, *Qingmo Minchu Zhongguo chengshi shehui jieceng yanjiu, 1897-1927* [Research on China's urban social strata during the late Qing and early Republic, 1897-1927] (Beijing, 2005).
Liao, T'ai-ch'u, "The Apprentices in Chengtu During and After the War", *The Yenching Journal of Social Studies*, 4 (1948), pp. 1103-1120.
Lieten, Kristoffel, "Child Labour: Questions on Magnitude", in: Kristoffel Lieten and Ben White (eds), *Child Labour: Policy Options* (Amsterdam, 2001), pp. 49-66.
Lieten, Kristoffel and Ben White, "Children, Work and Education: Perspectives on Policy", in: Kristoffel Lieten and Ben White (eds), *Child Labour: Policy Options* (Amsterdam, 2001), pp. 1-11.
Lieten, G.K., "Child Labour in South Asia: An Account of Numbers", in: G.K. Lieten, Ravi Srivastava and Sukhadeo Thorat (eds), *Small Hands in South Asia: Child Labour in Perspective* (New Delhi, 2004), pp. 37-60.
Lieten, G.K., *Child Labour: Burning Questions* (Amsterdam, 2005).
Liliequist, Marianne, *Nybyggarbarn: Barnuppfostran bland nybyggare i frostviken, Vilhelmina och tärna socknar 1850-1920* (Umeå, 1991).

Liljevall, Britt, "Minnen av barnarbete runt sekelskiftet 1800", in: Mats Sjöberg (ed.), *Jordbrukets barn: Barns och ungdomars fostran i agrara miljöer* (Stockholm, 2004), pp. 60–91.

Linder, Marc, "Farm Workers and the Fair Labor Standards Act: Racial Discrimination in the New Deal", *Texas Law Review*, 65 (1987), pp. 1335–1393.

Linné, Carl von, *Den öländska och gotländska resan in 1745* (Stockholm, 1977).

Lis, Catharina and Hugo Soly, *Poverty and Capitalism in Pre-Industrial Europe* (Hassocks, 1979).

Liu, Mingda and Yuliang Tang, *Zhongguo jindai gongren jieji he gongren yundong* [China's modern working class and labor movement]. Vol. 13 (Beijing, 2002).

Liu, Shuncheng, "Xiandai Zhongguo tonggong wenti" [Child labor in modern China], *Laogong yuekan* [Labor monthly], 5 (1936), p. 10ff.

Liu, Tessie, *The Weaver's Knot: The Contradictions of Class Struggle and Family Solidarity in Western France, 1750-1914* (Ithaca, NY, 1994).

Lleras-Muney, Adriana, "Were Compulsory Attendance and Child Labor Laws Effective? An Analysis from 1915 to 1939", *Journal of Law and Economics*, 45 (2002), pp. 401–436.

Llonch, Montserrat, "La feminització del treball textil a Catalunya (1891–1959)", in: M. Llonch (ed.), *Treball textil a la Catalunya contemporania* (Lleida, 2004), pp. 77–93.

Lloyd, Rosemary, *The Land of Lost Content: Children and Childhood in Nineteenth-Century French Literature* (Oxford, 1992).

Londoño, Carlos Edward García, "Niños trabajadores y vida cotidiana en Medellín, 1900–1930" (thesis presented to the Department of History of the National University (Medellín section), 1995).

Londoño, Patricia, "La vida diaria: usos y costumbres", in: Jorge Orlando Melo (ed.), *Historia de Antioquia* (Bogotá, 1988), pp. 306–342.

Lönnroth, Louise, "Översikt över fattigvårdens utveckling i Sverige med speciell inriktning på omsorg om fattiga barn från 1600-talet till 1847", in: Anne Banér (ed.), *Ur barndomens historia* (Stockholm, 1995), pp. 89–104.

Lonsdale, John and Bruce Berman, "Coping with the Contradictions: The Development of the Colonial State in Kenya, 1895–1914", *Journal of African History*, 20 (1979), pp. 487–506.

Lorimer, Frank, "The Economics of Family Formation under Different Conditions", *World Population Conference*. Vol. 2 (Belgrad, 1965), pp. 92–95.

Lory, J. "L'enseignement libre vu par les libéraux dans l'enquête scolaire parlementaire de 1880–1884", in: *Église et Enseignement*. Actes du Colloque du xe anniversaire de l'Institut d'histoire du christianisme du l'Université libre de Bruxelles, 22–23 avril 1976 (Brussels, 1977), pp. 223–239.

Lory, J., *Libéralisme et instruction primaire, 1842-1879: Introduction à l'étude de la lutte scolaire en Belgique*. Vol. 1 (Louvain, 1979).

Loukopoulos, Dimitris, *Georgika tis Roumelis* (Athens, 1983, first edn 1938).

Lowe, C.H., *Facing Labor Issues in China* (1934; reprint, Washington, DC, 1977).

Lu, Luo, "Ertong xianfeng" [Children vanguard], *Dajia chang*, 1 (Beijing, n.d.).

Lu, Yungeng and Changfei Liu, "Minguo chunian de tonggong yanjiu" [Research on child labor during the early Republic], *Minguo dang'an* [Republican archives] (Feb. 2002), pp. 49–55.

Lundberg, Sofia, "Child Auctions in Nineteenth Century Sweden: An Analysis of Price Differences", *Journal of Human Resources*, 35 (2000), pp. 279–298.

Lundberg, Sofia, *"Going Once, Going Twice, Sold!": The Economics of Past and Present Public Procurement in Sweden* (Umeå, 2001).

Lundh, Christer, *Life Cycle Servants in Nineteenth Century Sweden: Norms and Practice*, Lund papers in Economic History, 84 (Lund, 2003).
Lundström, C.F., *Tändsticksindustrien, dess uppkomst och närvarande ståndpunkt* (Stockholm, 1899).
Lungonelli, M., "Tra industria e burocrazia: gli esordi della statistica industriale in Italia", *Studi storici,* 28 (1987), pp. 277-295.
Luykx, T., *Politieke geschiedenis in België van 1789 tot heden* (Brussels, 1964).
Lyons, John. S., "Family Response to Economic Decline: Handloom Weavers in Early Nineteenth-Century Lancashire", *Research in Economic History,* 12 (1989), pp. 45-91.
Lyons-Barrett, Mary, "Child Labor in Commercialized Agriculture, 1890-1966" (Ph.D., University of Nebraska, 2002).

MacIntosh, R., *Boys in the Pits: Child Labour in Coal Mines* (Montreal, 2000).
MacLeod, Christine, *Inventing the Industrial Revolution: The English Patent System* (Cambridge, 1988).
Macmillan Puissant, J., "Un lent et difficile processus de democratisation", in: Hervé Hasquin (ed.), *La Wallonie. Le pays et les hommes. histoire-economies-societe,* II: *De 1830 en nos jours* (Brussels, 1976).
Maddison, Angus, *The World Economy: Historical Statistics* (Paris, 2003).
Magraw, Roger, "'Not Backward but Different': The Debate on French 'Economic Retardation'", in: Robert S. Alexander (ed.), *French History since Napoleon* (London, 1999), pp. 336-363.
Mantoux, Paul, *The Industrial Revolution in the Eighteenth Century* (London, 1928).
Mareska, J. and J. Heyman, *Enquête sur le travail et la condition physique et morale des ouvriers employés clans les manufactures de coton à Gand, Extrait des Annales de la Société de Médecine de Gand* (Ghent, 1845).
Marín, Antonio, *Reconstrucción histórica de la Escuela de Trabajo San José, 1914-1991* (Medellín, 1992).
Märk, Josef (ed.), *Schwabenkinder aus Rankweil. Sonderdruck aus dem Jahresbericht 1981 der Bürgergemeinschaft Rankweil* (Feldkirch, 1981).
Markusen, Ingrid, "The Development of Writing Ability in the Nordic Countries in the Eighteenth and Nineteenth Centuries", *Scandinavian Journal of History,* 15 (1990), pp. 37-63.
Marle, H. W. van, "Beschrijving van een kaloerahan in de noorder-afdeeling van het regentschap Tjiandjoer, residentie Preanger-regentschappen, 1860", *Bijdragen tot de Taal-, Land- en Volkenkunde,* 8 (1861), pp. 1-15.
Martinez, Oscar, *Border People: Life and Society in the U.S. – Mexico Borderlands* (Tucson, AZ, 1994).
Martinson, Floyd M., *Growing Up in Norway, 800 to 1900* (Carbondale, 1992).
Marucco, D., *L'amministrazione della statistica nell'Italia unita* (Rome-Bari, 1996).
Marvel, Howard P., "Factory Regulation: A Reinterpretation of Early English Experience", *Journal of Law and Economics* 20 (1977), pp. 379-402.
Marx, Karl, *Capital: A Critique of Political Economy,* 2 vols. (Moscow, 1965).
Mashasha, Francis J., "The Road to Colonialism: Concessions and Collapse of Swazi Independence, 1875-1926" (Ph.D. thesis, Oxford University, 1977).
Masjoan, Eduard, *Neomalthusianismo y anarquismo ibérico* (Icaria, 1997).
Mateus, Abel, "Tecnologia", in: Pedro Lains and Álvaro Ferreira Silva (eds), *História económica de Portugal 1700-2000.* 3 vols. Vol. 3 (Lisbon, 2005), séc XX, pp. 125-156.

Mattsson, Viking, "Ammor och barnafödande i Malmö 1750-1850", *Scandia,* 46 (1980), pp. 173-198.

Mause, L.B. de, *see* De Mause, L.B.

Maynes, Mary Jo, *Taking the Hard Road: Life Course in French and German Workers' Autobiographies in the Era of Industrialization* (Chapel Hill, NC, 1995).

Mayor, Alberto, *Ética, trabajo y productividad en Antioquia* (Bogotá, 1989).

Mazower, Mark, *The Balkans* (London, 2001).

Mbikusita-Lewanika, Inonge M., "Zambian Society: An Oral History of an Unwritten Culture" (Ph.D., New York University, 1979).

McCaffray, Susan P., "Origins of Labor Policy in the Russian Coal and Steel Industry, 1874-1900", *Journal of Economic History,* 47 (1987), pp. 951-996.

McCarthy, J.W., "Australian Capital Cities in the Nineteenth Century", *Australian Economic History Review,* 10 (1974), pp. 107-137.

McCulloch, Merran, "A Social Survey of the African Population of Livingstone", *Rhodes-Livingstone Paper,* 26 (Lusaka, 1956).

McKendrick, Neil, "Home Demand and Economic Growth: A New View of the Role of Women and Children in the Industrial Revolution", in: Neil McKendrick (ed.), *Historical Perspectives: Studies in English Thought and Society* (London, 1974), pp. 152-210.

McNeill, J.R., *The Mountains of the Mediterranean World. An Environmental History* (Cambridge, 1992).

Medick, Hans, "The Proto-Industrial Family Economy: The Structural Function of Family during the Transition from Family to Industrial Capitalism", *Social History,* 3 (1976), pp. 291-315.

Meersch, Vander, *see* Vander Meersch

Meillassoux, Claude, *Maidens, Meal and Money: Capitalism and Domestic Community* (Cambridge, 1981).

Melancon, Michael S., *The Lena Goldfields Massacre and the Crisis of the Late Tsarist State* (College Station, TX, 2006).

Melton, James Van Horn, *Absolutism and the Eighteenth-Century Origins of Compulsory Schooling in Prussia and Austria* (Cambridge, 1988).

Mendelievich, C. (ed.), *Children and Work* (Geneva, 1979).

Mensbrugghe, vander, *see* Vander Mensbrugghe

Merli, S., *Proletariato di fabbrica e capitalismo industriale. Il caso italiano 1880-1900* (Florence, 1972).

Merzario, R., "Città-campagna: vicende della 'gens comacina' tra Settecento e Ottocento", in: G. Rumi, V. Vercelloni and A. Cova (eds), *Como e il suo territorio* (Milan, 1995).

Midré, Georges, *Bot, bedring eller brød: Om bedømming og behandling av sosial nød fra reformasjonen til folketrygden* (Oslo, 1990).

Miles, Miranda C., "Missing Women: A Study of Swazi Female Migration to the Witwatersrand, 1920-1970" (M.A. thesis, Queen's University, 1991).

Mill, John Stuart, *Principles of Political Economy.* 2 vols (Toronto, 1964 [1848]).

Milogolova, I.N., "Semeinye razdely v russkoi poreformennoi derevne (na materialakh tsentral'nykh gubernii)", *Vestnik Moskovskogo universiteta,* series 8: History, 6 (1987), pp. 37-46.

Minge-Kalman, Wanda, "The Industrial Revolution and the European Family: The institutionalization of 'Childhood' as a Market for Family Labor", *Comparative Studies in Society and History,* 20 (1978), pp. 456-463.

Ministère de l'emploi et de la solidarité, "Les Enfants et les jeunes au travail. Études et documents pour l'histoire de l'administration du travail" (Cahier du comité d'histoire, supplément avril 2001).

Ministère de l'Interieur, *Enquête sur la condition des classes ouvrières et sur le travail des enfants*. 3 vols (Brussels, 1848).

Ministère de l'Intérieur, *L'Enseignement populaire en Belgique au XIXe siècle* (Gand, 1979).

Ministère du Commerce, *Rapports sur l'application pendant l'anneé 1894 des lois règlementant le travail* (Paris, 1895).

Mitch, David F., *The Rise of Popular Literacy in Victorian England: The Influence of Private Choice and Public Policy* (Philadelphia, PA, 1992).

Mitch, David F., "The Role of Human Capital in the First Industrial Revolution", in: Joel Mokyr (ed.), *The British Industrial Revolution: an Economic Perspective* (Boulder, CO, 1993).

Mitchell, Brian R., *European Historical Statistics 1750-1975*, 2nd revised edition (London, 1981).

Mitchell, Brian R., *British Historical Statistics* (Cambridge, 1988).

Mitchell, J. Clyde, "African Urbanization in Ndola and Luanshya", *Rhodes-Livingstone Communication*, 6 (Lusaka, 1954).

Mitterauer, Michael, *Ledige Mütter. Zur Geschichte illegitimer Geburten in Europa* (München, 1983).

Moehling, Carolyn M., "State Child Labor Laws and the Decline of Child Labor", *Explorations in Economic History*, 3 (1999), pp. 72-106.

Mofford, Juliet, *Child Labor in America* (Carlisle, MA, 1997).

Moioli, A., "Assetti manifatturieri nella Lombardia politicamente divisa della seconda metà del Settecento", in: S. Zaninelli (ed.), *Storia dell'industria lombarda*, v. 1 (Milan, 1988), pp. 10-24.

Mokyr, Joel, *The Lever of Riches. Technological Creativity and Economic Progress* (New York, 1990).

Mónica, Maria Filomena, *Educação e sociedade no Portugal de Salazar. A escola Salazarista de 1926-1939* (Lisbon, 1978).

Monlau, Felipe and Joaquim Salarich, "Higiene pública", in: José María Lopez Piñeiros (ed.), *El testimonio de los médicos españoles del siglo XIX acerca la sociedad de su tiempo. El proletariado industrial* (Madrid, 1960), pp. 57-65.

Monnier, Frédéric, *De l'organisation du travail manuel des jeunes filles. Les internats industriels.* (n.p., Chaix & Cie, 1869).

Monteleone, G. "La legislazione sociale al Parlamento italiano. La legge del 1886 sul lavoro dei fanciulli", *Movimento operaio e socialista*, XX,4 (1974), pp. 229-284.

Montgomery, Arthur, *Industrialismens genombrott i Sverige* (Stockholm, 1947).

Montgomery, David, *The Fall of the House of Labor: The Workplace, the State and American Labor Activism, 1865-1925* (New York, 1987).

Moody, T. Dunbar, "Migrancy and Male Sexuality on the South African Gold Mines", *Journal of Southern African Studies* 14 (1988), pp. 228-255.

Moore, Wilbert E., *Economic Demography of Eastern and Southern Europe* (Geneva, 1945).

Morelli, A., "Les médecins parlementaires belges aux XIXe-XXe siècles", *L'engagement social et politique des médecins. Belgique-Canada, Socialisme*, 2 (hors-série, 1993), pp. 9-18.

Morse, E.S., *Japan Day by Day, 1877, 1878-79, 1882-83* (Boston, MA, 1917).

Moura, Esmeralda Blanco B. de, *Mulheres e menores no trabalho industrial: Os fatores sexo e idade na dinâmica do capital* (Petrópolis, 1982).

Moura, Esmeralda Blanco B. de, "Crianças operárias na recém-industrializada São Paulo", in: Mary Del Priore (ed.), *História das crianças no Brasil* (São Paulo, 2004), pp. 231-258.

Mu Xuan and Xuexi Yan, *Dasheng shachang gongren shenghuo de diaocha (1899-1949)* [Investigation of the life of workers in the Dasheng spinning mills, 1899-1949] (Nanjing, 1994).

Mueller, Eva, "The Economic Value of Children in Peasant Agriculture", in: Ronald Ridker (ed.), *Population and Development: the Search for Selective Interventions* (Baltimore, MD, 1976), pp. 98-153.

Muñoz, Cecilia and Ximena Pachón, *La niñez en el siglo XX* (Bogotá, 1991).

Muñoz-Abeledo, M. Luisa, "Hombre, mujeres y latas: la segmentación laboral en la industria de conservas de pescado", in: L. Galvez and C. Sarasúa (eds), *Privilegios o eficiencia? Mujeres y hombres en el mercado de trabajo* (Alicante, 2003), pp. 279-306.

Murat, Daniel, "Le Travail des enfants abandonnés du Gard dans les filatures de soie", in: Roland Caty, *Enfants au travail: Attitude des elites en Europe occidentale et méditerranéenne aux XIXe et XXe siècles* (Aix-en-Provence, 2002), pp. 153-167.

Murray, J.D., *The Governmental System of Rhodesia* (Oxford, 1970).

Murray, John E. and Ruth Wallis Herndon, "Markets for Children in Early America: A Political Economy of Pauper Apprenticeship", *Journal of Economic History*, 62 (2002), pp. 356-382.

Murray, M., "Children's Work in Rural New South Wales in the 1870s", *Journal of the Royal Australian Historical Society*, 79 (1993), pp. 226-244.

Mwanamwambwa, Catherine and Zenebeworke Tadesse, *Children in Zambia* (Stockholm, 1979).

Myllyntaus, Timo, "Education in the Making of Modern Finland", in: Gabriel Tortella (ed.), *Education and Economic Development since the Industrial Revolution* (Valencia, 1990), pp. 153-171.

Nakagawa, K., "Family Formation and the Household Budget in Early Twentieth-Century Tokyo", *Continuity and Change*, 15 (2000), pp. 77-98.

Nandrin, J.P., "La genèse du droit du travail en Belgique. Plaidoyer pour une chronologie", *Juris Scripta Historica*, Koninklijke Akademie, vol. XIII (Brussels, 1997), pp. 256-288.

Nardinelli, Clark, "Child Labor and the Factory Acts", *Journal of Economic History*, 40 (1980), pp. 739-755.

Nardinelli, Clark, "Corporal Punishment and Children's Wages in Nineteenth Century Britain", *Explorations in Economic History*, 3 (1982), pp. 238-295.

Nardinelli, Clark, *Child Labor and the Industrial Revolution* (Bloomington, IN, 1990).

Nauw, P. de, *see* De Nauw, P.

Nederveen Meerkerk, Elise van, *De draad in eigen handen: Vrouwen en loonarbeid in de Nederlandse textielnijverheid, 1581-1810* (Amsterdam, 2007).

Nederveen Meerkerk, Elise van, "Child Labor in the Netherlands during Proto- and Early Industrialization", in: H. Hindman (ed.), *The World of Child Labor: An Historical and Regional Survey* (New York, 2009), pp. 625-628.

Nederveen Meerkerk, Elise van and Ariadne Schmidt, "Tussen arbeid en beroep. Jongens en meisjes in de stedelijke nijverheid, ca. 1600-1800", *Tijdschrift voor Sociale en Economische Geschiedenis*, 3 (2006), pp. 24-50.

Nederveen Meerkerk, Elise van and Ariadne Schmidt, "Between Wage Labor and Vocation. Child Labor in Dutch Urban Industry", *Journal of Social History*, 41 (2008), pp. 717-736.

Nejrotti, Mariella, "Aspetti della condizione femminile nel comasco alle origini dell'industrializzazione", in: I. Granata and A. Scalpelli (eds), *Setaioli e contadini. L'industrializzazione a Como dall'unità al fascismo* (Milan, 1992).

Nestor, Ulla, "Varför minskade barnarbetet?", *Arbetarhistoria*, 21 (1997), pp. 35-44.

Neve, M. de, *see* De Neve, M.

Neves, Joel Mauricio Das, "Economy, Society and Labour Migration in Central Mozambique, 1930-c.1965: A Case Study of Manica Province" (Ph.D., School of Oriental and African Studies, University of London, 1998).

Newcomer, Mabel, "The Professionalisation of Management", *Business History Review*, 22 (1955), pp. 54-63.

Nicolau, Roser, "Trajectoires regionales dans la transition demographique espagnole" (unpublished Ph.D Thesis, CNRS, Paris, 1990).

Nieuwenhuys, Olga, *Children's Lifeworlds: Gender, Welfare and Labour in the Developing World* (London, 1994).

Nuñes, Ana Bela, "Government Expenditure on Education, Economic Growth and Long Waves: The Case of Portugal", *Paedagogica Historica*, 39 (2003), pp. 559-581.

Nuñez, Clara E., *La fuente de la riqueza: Educacion y desarrollo económico en la España contemporanea* (Madrid, 1992).

NVV/SDAP, Nederlandsch Verbond van Vakvereenigingen, *Arbeidersleven in Nederland. Resultaten der enquête, ingesteld door het NVV in het najaar van 1907 naar de wenschelijkheid en mogelijkheid van beperking van den arbeidsduur voor volwassenen tot 10 uren per etmaal en afschaffing, respectievelijk beperking van nacht- en kinderarbeid* (Amsterdam 1908).

Nygren, Rolf, "Barnarbete och arbetsavtalets frihet: en studie kring vår första samlade lagstiftning om skydd av minderårig arbetskraft i industriellt yrke", in: Jan Sundin (ed.), *Kontroll och kontrollerade* (Umeå, 1982), pp. 197-266.

Nyström, Per, *Stadsindustriens arbetare före 1800* (Stockholm, 1955).

Ochoa, Lisandro, *Cosas viejas de la Villa de la Candelaria* (Second edn, with prologue by Roberto Luis Jaramillo, Medellín, 1984).

Ohadike, Patrick, "Demographic Perspectives in Zambia", *Zambian Papers*, 15 (Lusaka, 1981).

Ohadike, Patrick and Habtemariam Tesfaghiorghis, *The Population of Zambia* (Paris, 1975).

Olsson, Lars, *Då barn var lönsamma. Om arbetsdelning, barnarbete och teknologiska förändringar i några svenska industrier under 1800-talet och början av 1900-talet* (Stockholm, 1980).

Olsson, Lars, "Den vita piskan", in: Alf Johansson, Susanne Lundin and Lars Olsson, *Dagsverken. 13 essäer i arbetets historia* (Lund, 1994), pp. 46-76.

Olsson, Lars, "'We Stand Here as Sellers and Buyers in Relation to each Other'. On Work, Culture, and Consciousness Among Swedish Typographers in the Late 19th and Early 20th Centuries", *Scandinavian Journal of History*, 19 (1994), pp. 201-221.

Olsson, Lars, *Då barn var lönsamma: Om arbetsdelning, barnarbete och teknologiska förändringar I några Svenska industrier under 1800- och början av 1900-talet* (Lund, 1999).

Onderzoek naar de mindere welvaart van de inlandsche bevolking op Java en Madoera. IXC: *Overzicht van de uitkomsten der gewestelijke onderzoekingen naar de economie van de Desa,* deel III: *Bijlagen* (Batavia, 1911).

Onderzoek naar de mindere welvaart van de inlandsche bevolking op Java en Madoera. VI: *Overzicht van de uitkomsten der gewestelijke onderzoekingen naar den inlandsche handel en nijverheid,* deel IV: *Overzicht,* VI: *Bijlagen* (Batavia, 1912).

Onselen, van, *see* Van Onselen

Oppong, Christine, *Growing up in Dagbon* (Accra, 1973).

Orchard, Dorothy J., "Man-power in China: Part One", *Political Science Quarterly*, 50 (1935), pp. 561-583.

Orde-Browne, Granville St. John, *The African Labourer* (London, 1933).

Orde-Browne, Granville St. John, *Labour Conditions in East Africa* (London, 1946).

Osada, Mitsuo, *Komori gakkō no jisshōteki kenkyū* [Empirical Studies on Childminders' Schools], (Tokyo 1995), pp. 325-333.

Ortmayr, Norbert, "Sozialhistorische Skizzen zur Geschichte des ländliches Gesindes in Österreich", in: Norbert Ortmayr (ed.), *Knechte* (Vienna, 1992), pp. 297-376.

Owen, E.R.J., *Cotton and the Egyptian Economy 1820-1914: A Study in Trade and Development* (Oxford, 1969).

Packard, Randall, "Maize, Cattle and Mosquitoes: The Political Economy of Malaria Epidemics in Swaziland", *Journal of African History*, 24 (1984), pp. 189-212.

Palley, Claire, *The Constitutional History of Southern Rhodesia, 1888-1965, With Special Reference to Imperial Control* (Oxford, 1966).

Palmer, Robin and Neil Parsons (eds), *The Roots of Rural Poverty in Central and Southern Africa* (Berkeley, 1977).

Palmer, Robin, *Land and Racial Domination in Rhodesia* (Berkeley, 1977).

Papathanassiou, Maria, *Zwischen Arbeit, Spiel und Schule. Die ökonomische Funktion der Kinder ärmerer Schichten in Österreich 1880-1939* (Vienna, 1999).

Papathanassiou, Maria, "Aspekte der bergbäuerlichen Lebenswelt in Österreich – vom späten 19. Jahrhundert bis in die Zwischenkriegszeit", in: Maria Schuster, *Arbeit gab's das ganze Jahr. Vom Leben auf einem Lungauer Bauernhof* (Vienna, 2001), pp. 187-243.

Papathanassiou, Maria, "Rural Childhood(s) in Mountain Regions of Austria and Greece: A Comparative Approach (c. 1900-1940)", in: Slobodan Naumović and Miroslav Jovanović (eds), *Childhood in South East Europe: Historical Perspectives on Growing Up in the 19th and 20th Century* (Belgrade, 2001), pp. 45-65.

Papathanassiou, Maria, *Megalonontas ston oreino choro. Paidia kai paidiki ilikia sto Krokylio Doridas tis protes dekaeties tou 20ou aiona* (Athens, 2003).

Papathanassiou, Maria, "Protected from Work? Children in discourse and children's experiences in Central Europe", *La Revue de GRAAT (Groupe de Recherches Anglo-Americaines de Tours)*, 36 (2007), pp. 141-167.

Parr, Joy, *Labouring Children: British Immigrant Apprentices to Canada, 1869-1924* (London, 1980).

Parsons, Neil, "Thoughts on the Social and Economic History of Swaziland", *Ngadla! A History Society Journal of ubs (ucs)*, 1 (1976), pp. 3-9.

Passrugger, Barbara, *Hartes Brot. Aus dem Leben einer Bergbäuerin* (Vienna, 1989).

Paterson, Sarah V. *et al.*, "Development of Structure and Function in the Infant Brain: Implications for Cognition, Language, and Social Behaviour", *Neuroscience & Biobehavioral Reviews*, 30 (2006), pp. 1087-1105.

Payne, A., "Crecimiento y cambio social en Medellín", *Estudios Sociales*, 1 (1986), pp. 1-94.

Peeters, Harry, Lène Dresen-Coenders and Ton Brandenbarg (eds), *Vijf eeuwen gezinsleven. Liefde, huwelijk en opvoeding in Nederland* (Nijmegen, 1988).

Pereira, P.T. and P.S. Martins, "Portugal", in: C. Harmon, I. Walker and N. Westergaard-Nielsen (eds), *Education and Earnings in Europe* (Cheltenham, 2001).

Pérez, Luis F. and Enríque Restrepo Jaramillo (eds), *Medellín en 1932* (ed. Completa Medellín, 2004 [1932]).

Perrot, M., *Enquêtes sur la condition ouvrière en France au 19e siècle* (Microéditions Hachette, Paris, 1972).

Perry, Elizabeth J., *Shanghai on Strike: The Politics of Chinese Labor* (Stanford, CA, 1993).

Petmezas, Sokratis, "Agrotiki Oikonomia", in: Christos Hatziiossif (ed.), *Istoria tis Elladas tou 20ou aiona, 1900-1922. Oi aparches.* Vol. 1, 1st Part (Athens, 2000), pp. 53-85.

Petterson, Lars, *Frihet, jämlighet, egendom och Bentham: Utvecklingslinjer i svensk folkundervisning mellan feodalismen och kapitalismen, 1809-1860* (Stockholm, 1992).

Phimister, Ian, *An Economic and Social History of Zimbabwe, 1890-1948* (London, 1988).

Pierrard, Pierre, *Enfants et jeunes ouvriers en France, XIXe-XXe siècles* (Paris, 1986).

Pinchbeck, Ivy and Margaret Hewitt, *Children in English Society.* 2 vols. Vol. 2 (London, 1973).

Pinto, Fábio Machado, "A universidade e o trabalho infantil: A produção docente sobre o trabalho infantil na universidade federal de Santa Catarina e na Universidade Técnica de Lisboa" (Master Thesis, ISEG-UTL, 1997).

Pio, G., *Mines et mineurs de Provence* (Aix-en-Provence, 1984).

Pires, Júlio Manuel. "O Trabalho infantil na legislação Brasileira." in: *IV encontro nacional de estudos do trabalho*, Anais da associação Brasileira de estudos do trabalho (ABET) (São Paulo, 1995), pp. 241-251.

Pitaud, Henri, *Le pain de la terre. Mémoires d'un paysan vendéen du début du siècle* (Paris, 1982).

Pleyte, C., *De Inlandsche nijverheid in West-Java als sociaal-ethnologisch verschijnsel* (Batavia, 1911).

Pollard, Sidney, *European Economic Integration 1815-1970* (London, 1974).

Pollock, Linda, *Forgotten Children: Parent-Child Relations from 1500 to 1900* (Cambridge, 1983).

Popova, Kristina (ed.), *"Ein roter und ein weißer Zwirn". Jugend auf dem Balkan* (Vienna, 1996).

Popova, Kristina, "Einleitung", in: Kristina Popova (ed.), *"Ein roter und ein weißer Zwirn". Jugend auf dem Balkan* (Vienna, 1996), pp. 15-51.

Popova, Kristina, "'Impure Person has No Success in Life and That is Why the One Starves': The Ideology of the Union for Child Protection in Bulgaria and the Appearance of Health-educating Rhetoric About Children in Bulgaria (1930s-1940s)", in: Slobodan Naumović and Miroslav Jovanović (eds), *Childhood in South East Europe: Historical Perspectives on Growing Up in the 19th and 20th Century* (Belgrade, 2001), pp. 149-162.

Postma, A., *De mislukte pogingen tussen 1874 en 1889 tot verbetering en uitbreiding van de kinderwet-Van Houten* (Deventer, 1977).

Pot, G.P.M., *Arm Leiden. Levensstandaard, bedeling en bedeelden, 1750-1854* (Hilversum, 1994).

Pott-Buter, Hettie, *Facts and Fairy Tales about Female Labor, Family and Fertility* (Amsterdam, 1993).

Powdermaker, Hortense, *Copper Town. Changing Africa: The Human Condition on the Rhodesian Copperbelt* (New York, 1962).

Prieto, Norma Iglesias, *Beautiful Flowers of the Maquiladora* (Austin, TX, 1997).

Puissant, Jean, "Un lent et difficile processus de démocratisation", in: Hervé Hasquin (ed.), *La Wallonie. Le pays et les homes. Histoire – Economies – Sociétés.* II: *De 1830 à nos jours* (Brussels, 1980), pp. 159-190.

Quetelet. L.A.J., *Sur l'homme et le developpement de ses facultees ou essai de statistique sociale* (Paris, 1835). (Revised and reissued in 1869 under the title *Physique sociale*).

Raffles, Stanford, *The History of Java.* 2 vols (London, 1817).

Rahikainen, Marjatta, "Miesten maailma: Ariman lasitehdas muistitiedon ja historiankirjoituksen valossa", in: Marjatta Rahikainen (ed.), *Matkoja moderniin* (Helsinki, 1996), pp. 139-165.

Rahikainen, Marjatta, "'Ingen mat utan arbete': Arbetshusen för fattiga skolbarn i Helsingfors 1883-1945", *Historisk Tidskrift för Finland*, 83 (1998) pp. 289-307.

Rahikainen, Marjatta, "Children and 'the Right to Factory Work': Child Labour Legislation in Nineteenth-Century Finland", *Scandinavian Economic History Review*, 49 (2001), pp. 41-62.

Rahikainen, Marjatta, "Historical and Present-Day Child Labour: Is there a Gap or a Bridge between them?", *Continuity and Change* 16 (2001), pp. 137-156.

Rahikainen, Marjatta, "Compulsory Child Labour: Parish Paupers as Indentured Servants in Finland, c.1810-1920", *Rural History*, 13 (2002), pp. 163-178.

Rahikainen, Marjatta, "First-Generation Factory Children: Child Labour in Textile Manufacturing in Nineteenth-Century Finland", *Scandinavian Economic History Review*, 50 (2002), pp. 71-95.

Rahikainen, Marjatta, *Centuries of Child Labour: European Experiences from the Seventeenth to the Twentieth Century* (Aldershot, 2004).

Rahikainen, Marjatta, "At What Cost was Economic Modernization Purchased? Comparing Child Labor in Asia and Europe", in: Takehito Onishi and Benny Teh Cheng Guan (eds), *The Shape of the East Asian Economy to Come* (Cambridge, 2007), pp. 199-211.

Rammohan, Anu, "The Interaction of Child-Labour and Schooling in Developing Countries: A Theoretical Perspective", *Journal of Economic Development*, 2 (1998), pp. 85-99.

Ramos, Fábio Pestana, "A História trágico-marítima das crianças nas embarcações portuguesas do século XVI", in: Mary Del Priore (ed.), *História das crianças no Brasil* (São Paulo, 2004), pp. 19-54.

Rashin, A. G., *Formirovanie rabochego klassa Rossii* (Moscow, 1958).

Raßmann, J., *Geschichte der preußischen Volkschule* (Goslar, 1914).

Read, Margaret, *Children of Their Fathers: Growing up Among the Ngoni of Nyasaland* (London, 1959).

Reeder, Linda, "Women in the Classroom: Mass Migration, Literacy and the Nationalization of Sicilian Women at the Turn of the Century", *Journal of Social History*, 32 (1998), pp. 101-124.

Regt, Ali de, "Children in the Twentieth Century Family Income: From Co-providers to Consumers", *The History of the Family*, 9 (2004), pp. 371-384.

Reher, David S and Enriqueta Camps, "Las economías familiares dentro de un contexto histórico comparado", *Reis*, 55 (1991), pp. 65-92.

Reijden, B. van der, *Rapport betreffende eene gehouden enquête naar de arbeidstoestanden in de industrie van strootjes en inheemsche sigaretten op Java.* Deel 1: *West Java* (Bandung, 1934).

Reis, Jaime, "O analfabetismo em Portugal no século XIX: Uma interpretação", in: Jaime Reis, *O atraso económico Português, 1850-1930* (Lisboa, 1993), pp. 227-253.

Reis, Jaime, "Economic Growth, Human Capital Formation and Consumption in Western Europe Before 1800", in: Robert C. Allen, Tommy Bengtsson and Martin Dribe (eds), *Living Standards in the Past: New Perspectives on Well-Being in Asia and Europe* (Oxford, 2005), pp. 195-225.

Reybaud, Louis, *Etudes sur le régime des manufactures* (Paris, 1859).

Reyes, Catalina, "Fueron los viejos tiempos tan maravillosos? Aspectos de la vida social y cotidiana de Medellín, 1890-1930" (M.A. dissertation, Universidad Nacional, 1993).

Reyes, Catalina, "Higiene y salud en Medellín, 1900-1930", *Revista de Estudios Sociales*, 7 (1994), pp. 13-43.

Richard, Éliane, "Protection et utilisation des enfants dans les orphelinats et pénitenciers de l'abbé Fissiaux, en Provence au XIX siècle", in: Roland Caty (ed.), *Enfants au travail: Attitudes des élites en Europe occidentale et méditerranéene aux XIX et XX siècles* (Aix-en-Provence, 2002), pp. 123-135.

Richards, Audrey I., *Land, Labour, and Diet in Northern Rhodesia: An Economic Study of the Bemba Tribe* (London, 1939).

Riginos, Michalis, *Morfes Paidikis Ergassias sti Viomichania kai ti Viotechnia 1870-1940* (Athens, 1995).

Riginos, Michalis, "Formes du travail des enfants dans l'industrie et l'artisanat en Grèce (XIXe-XXe siècles)", in: Roland Caty (ed.), *Enfants au travail. Attitudes des elites en Europe occidentale et méditerranéenne aux XIX et XX siècles* (Aix-en-Provence, 2002), pp. 59-70.

Riis, Jacob, *How the Other Half Dies: Studies among the Tenements of New York* (New York, 1957).

Riney-Kehrberg, P., "The Limits of Policy: Rural Children and Work in the United States and New Zealand, 1870-1920", *History of the Family*, 6 (2001), pp. 51-67.

Ristović, Milan, "Children and Work", in: Milan Ristović and Dubravka Stojanović (eds), *Childhood in the Past. 19th and 20th Century. Additional Teaching Materials* (Belgrade, 2001), pp. 77-79.

Rizzini, Irma, "Principais temas abordados pela literatura especializada sobre infância e adolescência: Séculos XIX e XX", in: Irene Rizzini (ed.), *Olhares sobre a criança no Brasil: Séculos XIX e XX* (Rio de Janeiro, 1997), pp. 39-77.

Rizzini, Irma, "Pequenos trabalhadores do Brasil", in: Mary Del Priore (ed.), *História das crianças no Brasil* (São Paulo, 2004), pp. 377-406.

Rizzo, T.L., *La legislazione sociale della nuova Italia (1876-1900)* (Naples, 1988).

Roberts, Andrew, *A History of Zambia* (New York, 1976).

Rodgers, Gerry and Guy Standing, *The Economic Roles of Children, in Low-Income Countries: A Framework for Analysis* [Population and Labour Policies Programme, Working Paper No. 81] (Geneva, 1979).

Rodgers, Gerry and Guy Standing (eds), *Child Work, Poverty, and Underdevelopment* (Geneva, 1981).

Rodhe, Edvard, "Den svenska folkskolans förhistoria särskilt under medeltiden", in: Edvard Rodhe and Victor Fredriksson (eds), *Svenska folkskolans historia: Första delen* (Stockholm, 1940).

Rodolico N. (ed.), *Storia del Parlamento italiano*. Vol. 17 (Palermo, 1969).

Rollet, Catherine, *Les Enfants au XIXe siècle* (Paris, 2001).

Romano, R., *La Modernizzazione Periferica. L'alto Milanese e la Formazione di una Società Industriale (1750-1914)* (Milan, 1990).

Romano, R., *L'industria cotoniera lombarda dall'Unità al 1914* (Milan, 1992).

Roque Antunes, António, *Algumas características da população jovem* (Lisboa, 1996).

Rosés, Joan R., "The Early Phase of Catalan Industrialization, 1830-1861" (Unpublished Ph.D. Thesis, European University Institute, Florence, 1998).

Roussel, Théophile, *Rapport sur les resultats de l'enquête concernant les orphelinats et autres établissements de charité, consacrés à l'enfance, présenté à la Commission du Sénat* (1882).

Royal Commission with Minutes of Evidence into Queensland's Shops, Factories and Workshops, Queensland Parliamentary Votes & Proceedings 1891. 4 vols. Vol. IV (Brisbane, 1892), pp. 756-1141.

Roy Ladurie, le, *see* Le Roy Ladurie

Runeby, Nils, "Americanism, Taylorism and Social Integration: Action Programmes for Swedish Industry at the Beginning of the Twentieth Century", *Scandinavian Journal of History*, 3 (1978), pp. 21-46.

Saavedra, María Claudia, "Antioquia en los inicios del proceso de industrialización: algunos aspectos relativos a la capacitación técnica", *Lecturas de Economía*, 37 (1992), pp. 105-126.

Saito, Osamu, "Who Worked When: Life-time Profiles of Labour Force Participation in Cardington and Corfe Castle in the Late Eighteenth and Early Nineteenth Centuries", *Local Population Studies*, 22 (1979), pp. 14-29.

Saito, Osamu, "Labour Supply Behaviour of the Poor in the English Industrial Revolution", *Journal of European Economic History*, 10 (1981), pp. 633-652.

Saito, Osamu, "The Rural Economy, Commercial Agriculture, By-employment and Wage Work", in: M.B. Jansen and G. Rozman (eds), *Japan in Transition: From Tohngawa to Meiji* (Princeton, 1986), pp. 400-420.

Saito, Osamu, "Children's Work, Industrialism and the Family Economy in Japan, 1872-1926", in: Hugh Cunningham and Per Paolo Viazzo (eds), *Child Labor in Historical Perspective, 1800-1985: Case Studies from Europe, Japan and Colombia* (Florence, 1996), pp. 73-90, also reprinted in this volume as Chapter 22.

Saito, Osamu, "Gender, Workload and Agricultural Progress: Japan's Historical Experience in Perspective", in: R. Leboutte (ed.), *Proto-industrialization: Recent Research and New Perspectives. In Memory of Franklin Mendels* (Geneva, 1996), pp. 129-151.

Salazar, María Cristina, *Niños y jóvenes trabajadores. Buscando un futuro mejor* (Bogotá, 1990).

Sallee, S., *The Whiteness of Child Labor Reform in the New South* (Athens, GA, 2004).

Samyn, Jan. *Uit het martelaarsleven van de kinderen der vlasfabriek. Onderzoeken op de Buiten door Jan Samyn* (1914), Ghent: Volksdrukkerij, pp. 8-24.
See http://www.cageweb.be/cageweb-view?q=Jan+Samyn&start=5&filter=&sort (last accessed 28 March 2010).

Sanders, Irwin T., *Balkan Village* (Lexington, 1949).

Sanderval, Georges Olivier de, *Mémoires d'Aimé Olivier comte de Sanderval* (Rennes, 1961).

Sandgruber, Roman, *Ökonomie und Politik. Österreichische Wirtschaftsgeschichte vom Mittelalter bis zur Gegenwart* (Vienna, 1995).

Sandgruber, Roman, "Die Landwirtschaft in der Wirtschaft – Menschen, Maschinen, Märkte", in: Franz Ledermüller (ed.), *Geschichte der österreichischen Land-und Forstwirtschaft im 20. Jahrhundert. Politik, Gesellschaft, Wirtschaft* (Vienna, 2002), pp. 191-408.

Sandin, Bengt, *Hemmet, gatan, fabriken eller skolan. Folkundervisning och barnuppfostran i svenska städer 1600-1850* (Lund, 1986).

Sandin, Bengt, "Education, Popular Culture and the Surveillance of the Population in Stockholm between 1600 and the 1840s", *Continuity and Change*, 3 (1988), pp. 357-390.

Sandin, Bengt, "In the Large Factory Towns: Child Labour Legislation, Child Labour and School Compulsion", in: Ning de Coninck-Smith, Bengt Sandin and Ellen Schrumpf (eds), *Industrious Children: Work and Childhood in the Nordic Countries 1850-1990* (Odense, 1997), pp. 17-46.

Sandrin, Jean, *Enfants trouvés, enfants ouvriers, XVIIe-XIXe siècles* (Paris, 1982).

Santos, M.C., "Education and Earnings Differentials in Portugal" (Ph.D. Thesis, Universidade do Porto, 1995).

Sarasúa, Carmen, "Understanding Intra-Family Inequalities: The Montes de Pas, Spain, 1700-1900", *The History of the Family: An International Quaterly*, 3 (1998), pp. 173-198.

Sarmento, Manuel, A. Bandeira and R. Dores, *Trabalho domiciliário infantil: um estudo de caso no vale do ave* (Lisbon, 2005).

Schenkeveld, Willemien, *Het Kinderwetje van Van Houten* (Hilversum, 2003).

Schenkeveld, Willemien, "Maastricht: de fabrieken van Petrus Regout: Kinderarbeid en de wet-Van Houten", in: Jan Bank, Marita Mathijsen, *Plaatsen van herinnering. Nederland in de negentiende eeuw* (Amsterdam, 2006), pp. 312-325.

Schildkrout, Enid, *People of the Zongo: the transformation of ethnic identities in Ghana* (Cambridge, 1978).

Schildkrout, Enid, "Age and Gender in Hausa Society: Socio-Economic Roles of Children in Urban Kano", in: Jean S. La Fontaine (ed.), *Sex and Age as Principles of Social Stratification* (London, 1979), pp. 109-137.

Schildkrout, Enid, "Women's Work and Children's Work: Variations among Muslims in Kano", in: Sandra Wallman (ed.), *Social Anthropology of Work* (London, 1979), pp. 69-86.

Schmidt, Elizabeth, *Peasants, Traders, and Wives. Shona women in the history of Zimbabwe, 1870-1939* (Portsmouth, 1992).

Schmitz, Cathryne, Elizabeth KimJin Traver and Desi Larson, *Child Labor: A Global View* (Westport, CT, 2004).

Scholliers, Peter, "Grown-ups, boys and girls in the Ghent cotton industry: the Voortman Mills, 1835-1914", *Social History*, 20 (1995), pp. 201-218.

Scholliers, Peter, *Wages, Manufacturers and Workers in the Nineteenth-Century Factory: The Voortman Cotton Mill in Ghent* (Oxford, 1996).

Schrumpf, Ellen, "From Full-Time to Part-Time: Working Children in Norway from the Nineteenth Century to the Twentieth Century", in: Ning de Coninck-Smith, Bengt Sandin and Ellen Schrumpf (eds), *Industrious Children: Work and Childhood in the Nordic Countries, 1850-1990* (Odense, 1997), pp. 47-73.

Schuster, Maria, *Auf der Schattseite* (Vienna, 1997).

Schwarz, Leonard D., *London in the Age of Industrialisation: Entrepreneurs, Labour Force and Living Conditions, 1700-1850* (Cambridge, 1992).

Schwarz, Leonard D., "English Servants and their Employers during the Eighteenth and Nineteenth Centuries", *Economic History Review*, 52 (1999), pp. 236-256.

Scobie, James, *Argentina: A City and a Nation* (New York, 1964).

Scott, James C., *The Moral Economy of the Peasant: Rebellion and Subsistence in South East Asia* (New Haven, CT, 1976).

Scott, Peter, "Women, Other 'Fresh' Workers, and the New Manufacturing Workforce in Interwar Britain", *International Review of Social History*, 45 (2000), pp. 449-474.

Sellberg, Hjalmar, *Staten och arbetarskyddet 1850-1919. En studie i svensk socialpolitik* (Uppsala, 1950).

Selosoemardjan, *Social Changes in Jogjakarta* (Ithaca, NY, 1962).

'Shanghai gongyun zhi' bianzuan weiyuanhui (ed.) [Editorial committee of the Chronicle of the Shanghai labour movement], *Shanghai gongyun zhi* [Chronicle of the Shanghai labor movement] (Shanghai, 1997).

Shanghai shehui kexueyuan jingji yanjiusuo jingjishi zu bian (ed.), *Rongjia qiye shiliao shangce* [Historical materials of the Rong family enterprises] 2 vols. (Shanghai, 1962).

Shanghai shehui kexueyuan lishi yanjiusuo (ed.), *Wusa yundong shiliao* [Historical materials on The May Thirtieth Movement] 2 (Shanghai, 1981).

"Shanghai Xiaoshadu Riben shachang zhi da bagong" [The big strike in the Japanese cotton mill at Xiaoshadu], *Xiangdao* [The Guide], No. 102 (Feb.14, 1925) in: Liu Mingkui (ed.), *Zhongguo gongren jieji lishi zhuangkuang* [Historical conditions of the Chinese working class]. Vol. 2 (Beijing, 1985).

Shepherd, A.W., "The Development of Capitalist Rice Farming in Northern Ghana" (Ph.D. dissertation, Cambridge, 1919).

Shivji, Issac, "Law and Conditions of Child Labour in Colonial Tangyanika, 1920-1940", *International Journal of the Sociology of Law*, 13 (1985), pp. 221-235.

Shorter, Edward, *The Making of the Modern Family* (London, 1977).

Silva, Manuela, *A pobreza infantil em Portugal* (Lisbon, 1991).

Silver, Arthur W., *Manchester Men and Indian Cotton 1847-1872* (Manchester, 1966).

Silver, Harold, "Ideology and the Factory Child: Attitudes to Half-Time Education", in: Phillip McCann (ed.), *Popular Education and Socialization in the Nineteenth Century* (London, 1977), pp. 141-166.

Simelane, Hamilton S., "The Colonial State and the Entrenchment of Settler Economic Power in Swaziland 1907-1938", *Uniswa Journal of Research*, 1 (1988), pp. 571-593.

Simelane, Hamilton S., "Landlessness and Imperial Response in Swaziland, 1938-1950", *Journal of Southern African Studies*, 17 (1991), pp. 714-741.

Simelane, Hamilton S., "War, Economy, and Society in Swaziland, 1939-1945" (Ph.D. thesis, University of Toronto, 1991).

Simelane, Hamilton S., "Labour Mobilization for the War Effort in Swaziland, 1940-1942", *International Journal of African Historical Studies*, 26 (1993), pp. 541-575.

Simelane, Hamilton S., "Capitalism and the Development of the Swazi Working Class, 1947-1962", in: Nomthetho Simelane (ed.), *Social Transformation: The Swaziland Case* (Dakar, 1995).

Simelane, Hamilton S., "Labour Migration and Rural Transformation in Post-Colonial Swaziland", *Journal of Contemporary African Studies*, 13 (1995), pp. 207-227.

Simon, Helene, *Landwirtschaftliche Kinderarbeit. Ergebnisse einer Umfrage des Deutschen Kinderschutzverbandes über Kinderlandarbeit* (Berlin, 1925).

Simon, Jules, *L'ouvrier de huit ans* (2me ed. Paris 1867).

Simonde de Sismondi, J.C.L., *Nouveau principes d'économie politique ou de la richesse dans ses rapports avec la population* (Paris/Genève 1951 [1819]).

Sjöberg, Mats, *Att säkra framtidens skördar: Barndom, skola och arbete i agrar miljö: Bolstad pastorat 1860-1930* (Linköping, 1996).

Sjöberg, Mats, "Working Rural Children: Herding, Child Labour and Childhood in the Swedish Rural Environment 1850-1950", in: Ning de Coninck-Smith, Bengt Sandin and Ellen Schrumpf (eds), *Industrious Children: Work and Childhood in the Nordic Countries 1850-1950* (Odense, 1997), pp. 106-128.

Sjöberg, Mats, "'En källa till välmåga och framgång': Barn och jordbruksarbete i tid och rum", in: Mats Sjöberg (ed.), *Jordbrukets barn: Barns och ungdomars fostran i agrara miljöer* (Stockholm, 2004), pp. 18-59.

Sköld, Johanna, *Fosterbarnsindustri eller människokärlek: Barn, familjer och utackorderingsbyrån i Stockholm 1890-1925* (Stockholm, 2006).

Smit, Cor, "De asem van Beëlzebub: De modernisering van de Leidse textielindustrie 1800-1865", in: J.K.S. Moes and B.M.A. de Vries (eds), *Stof uit het Leidse verleden: Zeven eeuwen textielnijverheid* (Utrecht, 1991), pp. 125-144.

Smit, Cor, "Actie of onderzoek? De activiteiten van de Maatschappij ter bevordering van de Nijverheid en de Hervormde Diaconie tegen kinderarbeid", *Jaarboek der sociale en economische geschiedenis van Leiden en omstreken 1994* (Leiden, 1994), pp. 48-97.

Smit, Cor, "Fabriekskinderen. Kinderarbeid in de Leidse textielindustrie in de negentiende eeuw", *Textielhistorische bijdragen*, 36 (1996), pp. 61-96.

Smit, Cor, *Ondernemers en geleerden: Leiden 1778-2003* (Leiden, 2003).

Smit, Cor, "Arbeidersvrouwen tussen fabriek en huisgezin. Deel I: Arbeid van Leidse vrouwen in fabrieken en werkplaatsen, 1800-1910", *Jaarboek voor de sociale en economische geschiedenis van Leiden en omstreken 2004* (Leiden, 2005), pp. 91-141.

Smit, Cor, "Leidse kinderen tussen fabriek en school, 1840-1914", in: *Leidschrift*, jrg 20, nr. 2, *Van kind tot burger. Onderwijs en volksopvoeding in Nederland 1780-1920* (2005), pp. 73-91.

Smit, Cor, "Work, Education, and Discipline: Attitudes towards Child Labor in The Netherlands, 1500 to 1875", in: Hugh Hindman (ed.), *The World of Child Labor: An Historical and Regional Survey* (New York, 2009).

Smith, Michael Stephen, *The Emergence of Modern Business Enterprise in France, 1800-1930* (Cambridge, MA, 2006).

Smith, S.A., *Like Cattle and Horses: Nationalism and Labor in Shanghai, 1895-1927* (Durham, NC, 2002).

Smits, Jan Pieter, "Economische ontwikkeling, 1800-1995", in: R. van der Bie and P. Dehing (eds), *Nationaal goed. Feiten en cijfers over onze samenleving, ca. 1800-1999* (Voorburg, 1999), pp. 15-36.

Snell, Keith D.M., *Annals of the Labouring Poor: Social Change and Agrarian England, 1660-1900* (Cambridge, 1985).

Snell, Keith D. M. and Jane Millar, "Lone Parent Families and the Welfare State: Past and Present", *Continuity and Change*, 2 (1987), pp. 387-422.

Snell, Keith D. M., "The Sunday School Movement in England and Wales: Child Labour, Denominational Control and Working Class Culture", *Past and Present*, 164 (1999), pp. 122-168.

Soares, Fernando Brito, "A agricultura", in: Pedro Lains and Álvaro Ferreira Silva (eds), *História económica de Portugal 1700-2000*. 3 vols. Vol. 3 (Lisbon, 2005), séc XX, pp. 157-183.

Socialdepartementet, *Rationaliseringsutredningen, Del I & II: SOU 1939:13 & 1939:4* (Stockholm 1939).

Solberg, Anne, "Seeing Children's Work", in: Ning de Coninck-Smith, Bengt Sandin and Ellen Schrumpf (eds), *Industrious Children: Work and Childhood in the Nordic Countries, 1850-1990* (Odense, 1997), pp. 186-209.

Sörensen, Anna, *Svenska folkskolans historia*. 5 vols. Vol. 3 (Stockholm, 1942).

Soresina, M., "Le fonti per la storia della Lombardia nelle grandi inchieste nazionali e nei censimenti. Saggio di una bibliografia 1861-1961", *Storia in Lombardia*, 1 (1991), pp. 189-196.

Souza, Jorge Prata de, *Escravidão ou morte: Os escravos Brasileiros na guerra do Paraguai* (Rio de Janeiro, 1996).

Spearpoint, Frank, "The African Native and the Rhodesian Copper Mines", *Supplement to the Journal of the Royal African Society*, 36 (1937).

Springer, Jane, *Listen to Us: The World's Working Children* (Toronto, 1997).

Stearns, Peter N., *Childhood in World History* (New York, 2006).

Steels, M., *Geschiedenis van het stedelijk onderwijs te Gent, 1828-1914* (Ghent, 1978).

Stewart, J., "The Political Economy of Agrarian Education: England in the late Nineteenth Century", *Agricultural History Review*, 42 (1994), pp. 126-139.

Stichter, Sharon and Jane L. Parpart (eds), *Patriarchy and Class: African Women in the Home and Workforce* (Boulder, CO, 1988).

Stojanović, Dubravka, "Children at School", in: Milan Ristović and Dubravka Stojanović (eds), *Childhood in the Past. 19th and 20th Century. Additional Teaching Materials* (Belgrade, 2001), pp. 45-48.

Stojanović, Dubravka, "Children in Villages and in Towns", in: Milan Ristović and Dubravka Stojanović (eds), *Childhood in the Past. 19th and 20th Century. Additional Teaching Materials* (Belgrade, 2001), pp. 9-12.

Stoler, Ann, *Capitalism and Confrontation in Sumatra's Plantation Belt, 1870-1979* (Second edn, Ann Arbor, 1995).

Stone, Lawrence, *The Family, Sex and Marriage in England, 1500-1800* (London, 1997).

Strindberg, Axel, *Arbetare och radikaler i 1700-talets Sverige* (Stockholm, 1935).

Stuart, Maxwell and Fu-an Fang, "A Statistical Study of Labor and Industry in China", *Chinese Economic Journal*, 7 (October 1930), pp. 1081-1121.

Sugarman, Susan, *Piaget's Construction of the Child's Reality* (Cambridge, 1986).

Sun, Maosheng, *Zhongguo gongren yundongshi* [History of the Chinese labor movement] (Shenyang, 1987).

Sun, Yutang, *Zhongguo jindai gongyeshi ziliao, 1840-1895* [Documentary materials regarding China's modern industrial history]. Vol. 2 (Beijing, 1957).

Sundhaussen, Holm, "Die verpasste Agrarrevolution. Aspekte der Entwicklungsblockade in den Balkanländern vor 1945", in: Roland Schönfeld (ed.), *Industrialisierung und gesellschaftlicher Wandel in Südosteuropa* (Munich, 1989), pp. 45-60.

Swaan, Abram de, *In care of the state: health care, education and welfare in Europe and the USA in the modern era* (Cambridge, 1988).

Swanzy, Henry. "Quarterly Notes: Central Africa", *African Affairs. Journal of the Royal African Society*, 51 (1952), pp. 18-21.

Sylvère, Antoine, *Toinou: Le cri d'un enfant auvergnat* (Paris, 1980).

Taira, K., *Economic Development and the Labor Market in Japan* (New York, 1970).

Tamai, K., "Images of the Poor in an Official Survey of Osaka, 1923-26", *Continuity and Change*, 15 (2000), pp. 99-116.

Taylor, Frederick Winslow, *The Principles of Scientific Management* (New York, 1911).

Taylor, Ronald B., *Sweatshops in the Sun: Child Labor on the Farm* (Boston, 1973).

Taylor, Ronald B., *Chavez and the Farm Workers* (Boston, MA, 1975).

Terray, Emmanual, "Long Distance Exchange and the Formation of the State: The Case of the Abron Kingdom of Gyaman", *Economy and Society*, 3 (1973), pp. 315-345.

Thane, Pat, 'Childhood in History', in: M. King (ed.), *Childhood, Welfare and Justice: A Critical Examination of Children in the Legal and Childcare Systems* (London, 1981).

Themse, van, *see* Van Themse

Thépot, A., *Les Ingénieurs des mines au XIXe siècle. Histoire d'un corps technique d'État, 1810-1914*, vol. 1 (Paris, 1998).

Thijs, A., "De Overleveringen", in: R. Baetens, *Industriele Archeologie in Vlaanderen. Theorie en Praktijk* (Antwerp, 1986).

Thompson, Betty Preston, "Two Studies of African Nutrition", *Rhodes-Livingstone Paper*, 24 (Manchester, 1954).

Thompsom, Edward P., "Time, Work-discipline and Industrial Capitalism", *Past & Present*, 38 (1967), pp. 56-97.

Thompson, Edward P., *The Making of the English Working Class* (Harmondsworth, 1968, 1980, first edn 1963).

Thompson, Edward P. and Eileen Yeo (eds), *The Unknown Mayhew* (Harmondsworth, 1973).

Tiano, Susan, *Patriarchy on the Line: Labor, Gender and Ideology in the Mexican Maquila Industry* (Philadelphia, PA, 1994).

Tiukavkin, V.G., *Velikorusskoe krest'ianstvo i Stolypinskaia agrarnaia reforma* (Moscow, 2001).

Todorova, Maria, "Situating the Family of Ottoman Bulgaria within the European Pattern", *The History of the Family*, 4 (1996), pp. 443-459.

Toro, Constanza, "Medellín: desarrollo urbano, 1880-1950", in: Jorge Orlando Melo (ed.), *Historia de Antioquia* (Medellín, 1988), pp. 299-306.

Toutain, J.C., *La population de la France de 1700 à 1959* (Paris, 1963).

Trattner, Walter I., *Crusade for the Children: A History of the National Child Labor Committee and Child Labor Reform in America* (Chicago, IL, 1970).

Truquin, Norbert, *Mémoires et aventures d'un proletaire à travers la revolution* (Paris, 1977).

Tsoukalas, Konstantinos, *Koinoniki anaptyxi kai kratos. I syngrotissi tou dimossiou chorou stin Ellada* (Athens, 1986).

Tsoukalas, Konstantinos, *Exartissi kai Anaparagogi. O koinonikos rolos ton ekpaideftikon michanismon stin Ellada (1830-1922)* (Athens, 1992).

Tucker, Lee, *Fingers to the Boone: United States Failure to Protect Child Farmworkers* (Washington, DC, 2000).

Tugan-Baranovsky, Mikhail I., *The Russian Factory in the 19th Century* (Homewood, 1970, first Russian ed. 1898).

Tunander, Gunnar, *Fattigskola – Medborgarskola* (Malmö, 1946).

Tuttle, Carolyn, "A Revival of the Pessimist View: Child Labor and the Industrial Revolution", *Research in Economic History*, 18 (1998), pp. 53-82.

Tuttle, Carolyn, *Hard at Work in Factories and Mines: The Economics of Child Labor During the British Industrial Revolution* (Boulder, CO, 1999).

Tyl, Yves, "L'enfant rebelle ou le patronat dépassé? Le cas d'Alsace au XIXe siecle", in: Roland Caty, *Enfants au travail: Attitude des elites en Europe occidentale et méditerranéenne aux XIXe et XXe siècles* (Aix-en-Provence, 2002), pp. 189-199.

Uhlig, Otto, *Die Schwabenkinder aus Tirol und Vorarlberg* (Innsbruck, 1986).

Umemura, M. *et al.*, *Estimates of Long-term Economic Statistics of Japan since 1868*, II: *Manpower* (Tokyo, 1988).

Ure, Andrew, *The Philosophy of Manufactures* (London, 1835).

Valério, Nuno (ed.), *Estatísticas históricas Portuguesas*, vols 1-2 (Lisbon, 2001).

Vallejo, Juan, "Informe del inspector de fábricas", in: *Informe del Secretario de Gobierno* (Medellín, 1934).

Vallstrand, Lennart, "Glasarbetarminnen från Surte", *Arbetarrörelsens Årsbok* (Stockholm, 1974), pp. 9-50.

Van de Velde, M. and A. Vinck, *Geschiedenis van de Socialistische Arbeidersbeweging te Boom* (Boom, 1978).

Van de Walle, *see* Walle, van de

Van den Eeckhout, P. and I. Hannes, "Sociale verhoudingen en structuren in de Zuidelijke Nederlanden, 1770-1840", in: *Algemene Geschiedenis der Nederlanden*, Nieuwste Tijd, vol. 10 (Bussum, 1981), pp. 467-475.

Van der Reijden, *see* Reijden, van der

Van Hear, Nick, "Child Labor and the Development of Capitalist Agriculture in Ghana", *Development and Change*, 13 (1982), pp. 499-514, also reprinted in this volume as chapter 26.

Van Nederveen Meerkerk, *see* Nederveen Meerkerk, van

Van Onselen, Charles, *Chibaro: Migrant Mine Labour in Southern Rhodesia, 1900-1933* (London, 1976).

Van Themsche, Guy, *Les Paradoxes de l'État.* L'Etat *face à l'économie de marché. XIXème et XXème siècles* (Brussels, edn Labor, 1997).

Van Zanden, *see* Zanden, van

Vandenbroeke, Chris, *Sociale geschiedenis van het Vlaamse volk* (Beveren, 1981).

Vander Meersch, P.C., *De l'etat de la mendicite at de la bienfaisance dans la province de la Flandre Orientale, depuis le regne de Marie-Therese, jusqu'a nos jours, 1740-1850* (Brussels, 1852).

Vander Mensbrugghe, G., "Quetelet", in: *Biographie Nationale* (Brussels, 1905), pp. 468-477.

Varlez. L., *Les salaires dans l'industrie Gantoise*, Vol. I., *Industrie cotonniere*, and Vol. II, *Industrie de la filature du lin.* (Brussels: Ministere de I'Industrie et de Travail, Office de Travail, 1901-1904).

Vásquez, José R., "Legislación obrera" (law thesis, Universidad de Antioquia, 1922).

Veiga, Teresa Rodrigues, "A transição demográfica", in: Pedro Lains and Álvaro Ferreira Silva (eds), *História económica de Portugal 1700-2000.* 3 vols. Vol. 3 (Lisbon, 2005), séc XX, pp. 37-63.

Velásquez, Magdala, "Condición jurídica y social de la mujer", in: Gloria Zea, Enrique González Villa and Camilo Calderón Schrader (eds), *Nueva Historia de Colombia.* 6 vols. Vol. IV (Bogotá, 1989).

Veld, Theo, "Volksonderwijs en leerplicht: Een historisch sociologisch onderzoek naar het ontstaan van de Nederlandse leerplicht, 1860-1900" (Ph.D. thesis, Universiteit Leiden, 1987).

Velde, van de *see* Van de Velde

Vélez, Daniel, "Informe del inspector de fábricas", in: *Memoria del Secretario de Gobierno de Antioquia* (Medellín, 1921).

Vélez, Daniel, "Informe del inspector de fábricas", in: *Memoria del Secretario de Gobierno de Antioquia* (Medellín, 1926).

Venancio, Renato Pinto, "Os aprendizes da guerra", in: Mary Del Priore (ed.), *História das crianças no Brasil* (São Paulo, 2004), pp. 192-210.

Veraghtert, Karel, "Ambacht en nijverheid in de Zuidelijke Nederlanden, 1790-1840", in: D.P. Blok *et al.* (eds), *Algemene Geschiedenis der Nederlanden*, 10. Nieuwste Tijd (Bussum, 1981), pp. 253-288.

Verdon, N., "The Rural Labour Market in the Early Nineteenth Century: Women's and Children's Employment, Family Income, and the 1834 Poor Law Report", *Economic History Review*, 55 (2002), pp. 299-323.

Vernon, H.M., *Industrial Fatigue and Efficiency* (London, 1921).

Viet, V., *Les Voltigeurs de la République. L'inspection du travail en France jusqu'en 1914* (Paris, 1994).

Vila, Cecilia Muñoz, "The Working Child in Colombia since 1800", in: Hugh Cunningham and Pierre Paolo Viazzo (eds), *Child Labour in Historical Perspective, 1800-1985.* pp. 97ff.

Villegas, Hernán Darío, *La formación social del proletariado antioqueño* (Medellín, 1990).

Villeneuve-Bargemont, Jean-Paul-Alban, *Économie politique chrétienne* (Brussels, 1837).

Villermé, Louis René, *Discours sur la durée trop longue du travail des enfants dans beaucoup de manufactures* (Paris, 1837).

Villermé, Louis René, *Tableau de l'état physique et moral des ouvriers employés dans les manufactures de coton, de laine et de soie.* 2 vols. (Paris 1840).

Villot, Ernest, "Étude sur le bassin de Fuveau et sur un grand travail à y exécuter", *Annales des Mines*, 8e série, t. IV (1883), pp. 5-66.

Vleggeert, J.C., *Kinderarbeid in Nederland, 1500-1874: Van berusting tot beperking* (Assen, 1964).
Vleggeert, J.C., *Kinderarbeid in de negentiende eeuw* (Bussum, 1967).
Von Linné, see Linné, von
Vries, Egbert de, *Landbouw en welvaart in het regentschap Pasoeroean*, 2 vols (Wageningen, 1931).
Vries, Jan de, 'The Industrial Revolution and the Industrious Revolution', *Journal of Economic History*, 54 (1994), pp. 249-270.
Vroede, M. De, *see* De Vroede, M.

Wackling, Sara, *Hundrade minnen från Österbotten* (Helsingfors 1974, first ed. 1844-1845).
Wagner, Augusta, *Labor Legislation in China* (1938; reprint, New York, 1980).
Wall, Richard, "The Age at Leaving Home", *Journal of Family History*, 3 (1978), pp. 181-202.
Wall, Richard, "Work, Welfare and the Family: An Illustration of the Adaptive Family Economy", in: Lloyd Blonfield, Richard Smith and K. Wrightson (eds), *The World we Have Gained* (Oxford, 1986), pp. 251-294.
Wall, Richard, "La contribución de las mujeres casadas a la economía familiar bajo distintos sistemas familiares: algunos ejemplos de mediados del siglo XIX a partir del trabajo de Fredreik Le Play", in: Enriqueta Camps and Pilar Pérez-Fuentes (eds), *Revista de demografía histórica*, XII:3/2 (1994), pp. 183-198.
Walle, Etienne van de, "Note on the Effect of Age Misreporting", in: William Brass et al. (eds), *The Demography of Tropical Africa* (Princeton 1968), pp. 143-150.
Walvin, James, *A Child's World: A Social History of English Childhood 1800-1914* (Harmondsworth, 1982).
Wang, Simine, *Le travail industriel des femmes et des enfants en Chine* (Paris, 1933).
Ward, David, *Cities and Immigrants: A Geography and Change in Nineteenth-Century America* (New York, 1971).
Waß, Barbara, *"Für sie gab es immer nur die Alm..." Aus dem Leben einer Sennerin* (Vienna, 1994).
Weber, Therese (ed.), *Häuslerkindheit. Autobiographische Erzählungen* (Vienna, 1992).
Weerdt, D. De, *see* De Weerdt, D.
Weiner, Myron, *The Child and the State in India: Child Labor and Education Policy in Comparative Perspective* (Delhi, 1990).
Weissbach, L.S., *Child Labor Reform in Nineteenth-Century France: Assuring the Future Harvest* (Baton Rouge, LA, 1989).
Weston, Burns H. (ed.), *Child Labor and Human Rights: Making Children Matter* (Boulder, CO, 2005).
White, Ben, "Demand for Labour and Population Growth in Colonial Java", *Human Ecology*, 1 (1973), pp. 217-236.
White, Ben, "Child Labour and Population Growth in Rural Asia", *Development and Change*, 13 (1981), pp. 587-610.
White, Ben, "'Agricultural Involution' and its Critics: Twenty Years After", *Bulletin of Concerned Asian Scholars*, 15 (1983), pp. 18-31.
White, Ben, "Economic Diversification and Agrarian Change in Rural Java, 1900-1990", in: Paul Alexander, Peter Boomgaard and Ben White (eds), *In the Shadow of Agriculture* (Amsterdam, 1991), pp. 41-69.
White, Ben, *Children, Work and "Child Labour": Changing Responses to the Employment of Children* (The Hague, 1994).

White, Ben, "Constructing Child Labour. Attitudes to juvenile work in Indonesia, 1900-2000", in: R. Elmhirst and R. Saptari (eds), *Labour in Southeast Asia. Local Processes in a globalised world* (London, 2004), pp. 77-105.

White, Ben and Indrasari Tjandraningsih, *Child Workers in Indonesia* (Bandung, 1998).

Williams, Suzanne, *Child Workers in Portugal* (London, 1992).

Williamson, Jeffrey G., *Coping with city growth* (Oxford, 1990).

Wilson, Godfrey, "An Essay on the Economics of Detribalization in Northern Rhodesia", *Rhodes-Livingstone Paper*, 5, pt. 1,2 (1941 and 1942).

Wilson, John E., *British Business History, 1720-1994* (Manchester, 1995).

Winberg, Christer, *Folkökning och proletarisering. Kring den sociala strukturomvandlingen på Sveriges landsbygd under den agrara revolutionen* (Göteburg, 1975).

Winberg, Christer, *Fabriksfolket: Textilindustrin i Mark och arbetarrörelsens genombrott* (Göteborg, 1989).

Winne, A. De, *see* De Winne, A.

Winqvist, Andreas, "Andreas Winqvists Minnen och Anteckningar", edited with comments by Leif Ljunggren, in: Leif Ljunggren (ed.), *Malmö Fornminnesförenings Årsbok* (Malmö, 1948).

Winstanley, Michael (ed.), *Working Children in Nineteenth-Century Lancashire* (Preston, 1995).

Wirilander, Kaarlo, *Herrskapsfolk: Ståndspersoner i Finland 1721-1870* (Stockholm, 1982).

Wopfner, Hermann, *Bergbauernbuch. Siedlungs- und Bevölkerungsgeschichte* (Innsbruck, 1995).

Wopfner, Hermann, *Bergbauernbuch. Bäuerliche Kultur und Gemeinwesen* (Innsbruck, 1995).

Wopfner, Hermann, *Bergbauernbuch. Wirtschaftliches Leben* (Innsbruck, 1997).

Wormser, R., *American Childhoods: Three Centuries of Youth at Risk* (New York, 1996).

Wright, Tim, *Coal Mining in China's Economy and Society, 1895-1937* (Cambridge, 1984).

Wrigley, Edward A., "Men on the Land and Men in the Countryside: Employment in Agriculture in Early Nineteenth-Century England", in: Lloyd Bonfield, Richard M. Smith and Keith Wrightson (eds), *The World we have Gained* (Oxford, 1986), pp. 295-336.

Wrigley, E. Anthony and R.S. Schofield, *The Population History of England, 1541-1871* (Cambridge, 1981).

Wylie, Laurence, *Village in the Vaucluse* (Cambridge, MA, 1964).

Young, Nick, "Brick kiln 'slavery' exposé follows Olympic child labour report" (June 17, 2007) in: http://www.chinadevelopmentbrief.com/node/1152.

Yves, Tyl, "L'enfant rebelle ou le patronat dépassé? Le cas d'Alsace au XIXe siecle", in: Roland Caty, *Enfants au travail: Attitude des elites en Europe occidentale et méditerranéenne aux XIXe et XXe siècles* (Aix-en-Provence, 2002), pp. 189-199.

Zamagni, V., *Dalla periferia al centro. La seconda rinascita economica dell'Italia (1861-1990)* (Bologna 1990).

Zanden, Jan Luiten van, *De economische ontwikkeling van de Nederlandse landbouw in de negentiende eeuw, 1800-1914* (Ph.D. thesis, Universiteit Wageningen, 1985).

Zanden, Jan Luiten van and Arthur van Riel, *Nederland 1780-1914. Staat, instituties en economische ontwikkeling* (Amsterdam, 2000).

Zaninelli, S., "Il lavoro dei fanciulli nell'industria lombarda alla metà del secolo XIX", *Annuario del Centro studi cisl*, II (1962-1963), pp. 1-20.

Zaninelli, S., "Aspetti economico-produttivi, di mercato e tecnologici", in: S. Zaninelli (ed.), *Storia dell'industria lombarda*, v. II, t. 2 (Milan, 1992), pp. 1-155.

Zelizer, Viviana A., *Pricing the Priceless Child: The Changing Social Value of Children* (New York, 1985).

Zelnik, Reginald E., *Labor and Society in Tsarist Russia: The Factory Workers of St. Petersburg* (Stanford, CA, 1971).

Zelnik, Reginald E., *Law and Disorder on the Narova River: The Kreenholm Strike of 1872* (Berkeley, CA, 1995).

Zhang, Zhilu, *Zhongguo shaonian ertong dianying shilun* [Historical essay on China's youth and children films] (Beijing, 2005).

Zhonggong Shanghai shiwei dangshi yanjiushi, Shanghaishi zonggonghui bian (eds), *Shanghai di er mian fangzhichang gongren yundongshi* [History of the Shanghai No.2 Cotton Mill labor movement] (Beijing, 1995).

"Zhongguo de tonggong wenti" [China's child labor problem] "Hongqi" [Red Flag] No.11 (Jan. 30, 1929) in: Zhongguo xinminzhu zhuyi qingniantuan and Zhongyang weiyuanhui bangongting (eds), *Zhongguo qingnian yundong lishi ziliao 1929 (1 yue-6 yue)* [Historical materials of the Chinese youth movement, Jan.-June 1929] 5 (Beijing, 1958).

"Zhongguo Gongchan Qingniantuan de guoqu yu xianzai" (Dec. 31, 1928) [The past and present of the Chinese Communist Youth League] in: Zhongguo Xinminzhu zhuyi Qingniantuan Zhongyang Weiyuanhui Bangongting (ed.), *Zhongguo qingnian yundong lishi ziliao* [Historical materials of the Chinese youth movement] vol. 4 (Beijing, 1957).

Zhongguo kexueyuan jingji yanjiusuo, Zhongyang gongshang xingzheng guanliju jiqi gongye shiliaozu (ed.), *Shanghai minzu jiqi gongye* [Shanghai's Chinese-owned machine industry] 2 vols. (Beijing, 1966).

Zhonghua quanguo zonggonghui ziliaoshi fanyin (ed.), "Zhanhou Yu shi fangzhi gongren yu gongren yundong" [Textile workers and the labor movement in postwar Chongqing] (Beijing, 1955).

Zhu, Bangxin and Lin-ge Hu, *Shanghai chanye yu Shanghai zhigong* [Shanghai industry and workers] (1939; reprint, Shanghai, 1984).

Zucchi, J.E., *The Little Slaves of the Harp: Italian Child Street Musicians in Nineteenth-Century Paris, London, and New York* (Montreal, 1992).

List of Tables and Figures

List of Abbreviations

AAA Agricultural Adjustment Act
ABdR Archives départementales des Bouches-du-Rhône (Marseille)
ABET Anais da associação Brasileira de Estudos do Trabalho (São Paulo)
AD Archives Départementales
AFBF American Farm Bureau Federation
AHA Archivo Histórico de Antioquia (Colombia)
AIDS Aquired Immune Deficiency Syndrome
AN Archives Nationales (Paris)
APS Aborigines Protection Society
AV Archives départementales du Var (Draguignan)
BSAC British South Africa Company
CAP Common Agriculture Policy
CBS Centraal Bureau voor de Statistiek (Statistics Netherlands)
CCC Civilian Conservation Corps
CISL Confederazione Italiana Sindicati dei Lavoratori (Italian Trade Unions Confederation)
CNASTI Confederação Nacional de Acção Sobre Trabalho Infantil (National Confederation of Action on Child Labour, Portugal)
CNC Chief Native Commissioner (Matabeleland)
CNRS Centre National de la Recherche Scientifique (Paris)
DDB Demographic Data Base (Sweden)
EEC European Economic Community
ESALQ Escola Superior de Agricultura "Luiz de Queiroz" (São Paulo)
ESSHC European Social Science History Conference (6TH: march 22-25, 2006, IISH Amsterdam)
EU European Union
FAES Fundación Antioqueña de Estudios Sociales (Colombia)
FLSA Fair Labor Standards Act

GDP	Gross Domestic Product
GIASE	Gabinete de Informação e Avaliação do Sistema Educativo (Bureau for Information and Evaluation of the Education System; Portugal)
GRAAT	Groupe de Recherches Anglo-Americaines de Tours
HIV	Human Immunodeficiency Virus
HRA	Härnösand Regional Archives (Sweden)
IAC	Instituto de Apoio à Criança (Institute of Support for Children, Portugal)
IEFP	Instituto do Emprego e Formaçao Profissional (Portuguese Public Employment Service/PES)
IGT	Inspecção-General do Trabalho (Inspector-General of Labour, Portugal)
IISH	International Institute of Social History (Amsterdam)
ILO	International Labour Organization/Office
IMF	International Monetary Fund
INE	Instituto Nacional de Estatística (National Statistics Institute, Portugal)
IREWOC	International Research on Working Children
ISEG/UTL	Instituto Superior de Economia e Gestão/Universidade Técnica de Lisboa
IT	Information Technology
JTAB	Jönköpings Tändsticksfabriks AB
KAPOW	Kids and the power of work
kk	kaiserlich-königlich (imperial-royal)
LABPROJ	ILO database
MAC	Ministry of Agriculture and Commerce (Japan)
MAIC	Ministry of Agriculture, Industry and Commerce (Italy)
MP	Member of Parliament
MSA	Malmö Stadsarkiv (Malmö town archives, Sweden)
MURST	Ministero per l'Università et per la Ricerca Scientifica e Technologica (Ministry of University and Scientific and Technological Research, Italy)
NAFTA	North American Free Trade Agreement
NAM	National Association of Manufacturers
NAWS	National Agricultural Workers Survey
NAZ	National Archives of Zambia/National Archives of Zimbabwe
NC	(Charter District) Native Commissioner
NCLC	National Child Labor Committee

NGO	Non Gouvernemental Organization
NHM	Nederlandsche Handel-Maatschappij (Dutch Trading Company)
NIRA	National Industrial Recovery Act
NIWI	Nederlands Instituut voor Wetenschappelijke Informatiediensten (Netherlands Institute for Scientific Information services)
NJEA	Native Juveniles Employment Act (Rhodesia)
NMN	Nederlandsche Maatschappij ter bevordering van de Nijverheid (Dutch Society for the Advancement of Industry)
NTS	Northern Territories
NVV	Nederlandsch Verbond van Vakvereenigingen (Dutch League of Trade Unions)
PETI	Program to Eradicate Child Labour (Brazil)
PNAD	Pesquisa Nacional por Amostra de Domicílios (Brazilian National Household Survey)
PRO	Public Record Office
RAL	Regional Archives of Leiden (Holland)
RNCB	Rhodesia Native Labour Bureau
SCB	Statistiska centralbyrån (statistics Sweden)
SDAP	Sociaal-Democratische ArbeidersPartij (Social Democratic Labour Party, Holland)
SFS	Svensk Författningssamling (Swedish legislation)
SMA	Skellefteå Municipal Archive (Sweden)
SNA	Swaziland National Archives
SOS	Sweden's Official Statistics
SRLAD	Southern Rhodesia, Legislative Assembly Debates
SRLCD	Southern Rhodesia, Legislative Council Debates
UBS(UCS)	University of Botswana (University Colleges of Swaziland)
UNICEF	United Nations International Children's Emergency Fund
VFHN	Vereeniging voor Fabrieks- en Handwerk Nijverheid (Association for Factory and Handicraft Industry)
VLV	Vorstelandsche Landbouw Vereeniging (Principalities' Agricultural Association, Indonesia)
VOC	Verenigde Oost-Indische Compagnie (Dutch East India Company)
WPA	Work Projects Administration
WW I	World War I
WW II	World War II
YWCA	Young Women's Christian Association

Subject Index

Name Index

Geographical Index

Notes on Contributors

ARJUN SINGH BEDI is a Professor in the Economics of Development at the Institute of Social Studies, Erasmus University Rotterdam, the Netherlands. He studied at Delhi University and at Tulane University, New Orleans, and has held positions at the University of Bonn and Columbia University. His research focuses on labour and human resource economics in developing countries. His work has been published in several international economics and development journals including *Journal of Development Economics*, *Economic Development and Cultural Change*, *Journal of Development Studies*, *World Development*.

BRADLEY BOWDEN is a labour and economic historian currently employed as an Associate Professor at the Griffith Business School, Australia. He has published extensively on working life in late nineteenth and early twentieth century Australia. In 2009, his work entitled *Re-Considering the Use of Child Labor: Why Nineteenth Century Australia was Different to Other Industrializing Nations* received the prestigious John F. Mee Award for the best contribution in the field of management history. Bowden has also acted as the lead editor of *Work and Strike in Paradise: One Hundred and Fifty Years of Labour Relations in Queensland 1859-2009* (2009).

ENRIQUETA CAMPS is Associate Professor at the Department of Economics and Business Administration, Universitat Pompeu Fabra, Barcelona, Spain. Her research focuses on labour and gender, population dynamics and human capital formation. Her publications include "Transitions in Women's and Children's Work Patterns" in *The History of the Family. An International Quarterly* (1998) and "Wage Structures and Family Economies in the Catalan Textile Industry in an Age of Nascent Capitalism", in *Continuity and Change* (2004).

ROLAND CATY is a historian working at the Université de Provence, France, who has specialized in economic and social history of the Provence, and published widely on the harbour of Marseille. Much of his work has been on the social and religious attitudes of the elites in Southern France in the nineteenth and twentieth century. He also edited *Enfants au travail, Attitudes de élites en Europe occidentale et méditerranéenne au XIXe et XXe siècles* (2002).

HUGH CUNNINGHAM is Emeritus Professor of Social History at the University of Kent, UK. He is the author of various articles on child labour: "The Employment and Unemployment of Children in England, c. 1680-1851", *Past & Present* (1990), "The Decline of Child Labour: Labour Markets and family Economies in Europe and North America since 1830", *Economic History Review* (2000), and, with Shelton Stromquist, "Child Labor and the Rights of Children: Historical Patterns of Decline and Persistence", in Burns H. Weston (ed.), *Child Labor and Human Rights* (2005). His books include: *The Children of the Poor: Representations of Childhood since the Seventeenth Century* (1991); *Children and Childhood in Western Society since 1500* (2005), and *The Invention of Childhood* (2006).

RENE DE HERDT has been the driving force behind the Museum for Industrial Archaeology and Textiles (MIAT) in Ghent, Belgium, since 1976 and has published extensively on industrial archaeology, the educational function of museums and the history of Ghent. Among his recent books are *The 20th Century, from Consumption towards Globalisation* (2007) and *Gentse Floraliën 1808-2008. History in Flowers – Flowers in history* (2009). A *liber amicorum* was published in 2010 by Ann van Nieuwenhuyse and Sofie de Schampheleire, *Geschiedenis: Zijn Leven, Zijn Werk. Huldeboek Rene De Herdt.*

ELISABETH ENGBERG is a researcher at the Centre for Population Studies, Umeå University, Sweden. On the history of child labour, she recently published "Boarded out by Auction: Poor Children and Their Families in Nineteenth-Century Northern Sweden", *Continuity and Change* (2004) and *I fattiga omständigheter: Fattigvårdens former och understödstagare i 1800-talets Skellefteå* (2005).

BORIS GORSHKOV teaches World, European and Russian history at Auburn University, Alabama, USA. He is the author of "Factory Children: An Overview of Child Industrial Labor and Laws in Imperial Russia, 1840-1914", in Michael Melancon and Alice K. Pate, *New Labor History* (2002), and "History of Child Labor in Imperial Russia", in Hugh D. Hindman (ed.), *The World of Child Labor: A Historical and Regional Survey* (2009). He published the following books: *A Life under Russian Serfdom: The Memoirs of Savva Dmitrievich Purlevskii, 1800-68* (2005) and *Russia's Factory Children, Society, and the State: Childhood, Apprenticeship and the Law, 1800-1917* (2009)

PEDRO GOULART is a PhD student at the International Institute of Social Studies, Erasmus University of Rotterdam, the Netherlands. Previously, he has worked at the Portuguese Ministry of Labour. His research interests range from labour and economics of education to economic history and development economics. He has published in peer reviewed journals (*Economics of Education Review*, 2008; *European Urban and Regional Studies*, 2009) and published several (edited) books and book chapters.

BEVERLY GRIER is Professor and Chair of the Department of Liberal Studies, North Carolina Agricultural and Technical State University, Greensboro, NC, USA. She has published many articles and books on Africa. These include the seminal article "Pawns, Porters, and Petty Traders: Women in Transition to Cash Crop Agriculture in Colonial Ghana", *Signs* (1992) and "Child Labor in Colonial Africa", in Hugh D. Hindman (ed.), *The World of Child Labor: A Historical and Regional Survey* (2009). Her book *Invisible Hands: Child Labor and the State in Colonial Zimbabwe, 1890-1965* (2005) has been widely acclaimed.

ELIANE GUBIN is Professor of History at the Université Libre de Bruxelles, Belgium, and the joint president of the Archive of Women's History (Carhif-AVG). She has published numerous historical studies on immigration, social exclusion, labour and education policies, and recently also various studies on gender issues, such as *Choisir l'histoire des femmes* (2007), *Dictionnaire d'histoire des femmes* (2005) and *Women Changing the World: A History of the International Council of Women* (2005).

KAREN TRANBERG HANSEN is Professor of Anthropology at Northwestern University, USA. She is an economic anthropologist and has conducted most of her research on urban livelihoods in Lusaka, Zambia. Her books include: *Distant Companions: Servants and Employers in Zambia, 1900-1985* (1998) and *Keeping House in Lusaka* (1997). She co-edited *Reconsidering Informality: Perspectives from Urban Africa* (2004), and is chief author of Karen Tranberg Hansen *et al.*, *Youth and the City in the Global South* (2008).

COLIN HEYWOOD is Professor of Modern French History at the University of Nottingham, UK. His historical research on childhood began in the late 1970s with a study of child labour, apprenticeship and education: *Childhood in Nineteenth-Century France* (1988). Later on, he published *A History of Childhood* (2001), *Growing Up in Modern France: From the Ancien Régime to the Third Republic* (2007) and edited *A Cultural History of Childhood and Family in the Age of Empire* (2010). Heywood also has pursued researches into the economic, social, cultural and political life of the French town of Troyes during the nineteenth century, and he is currently working on A History of Childhood and Youth in Modern Europe.

HUGH D. HINDMAN is Professor of Labor & Human Resources at Appalachian State University, Boone, NC, USA. He has published numerous articles on child labour along with two books: *Child Labor: An American History* (2002) and, as editor, *The World of Child Labor: An Historical and Regional Survey* (2009).

JOSHUA H. HOWARD is the Croft Associate Professor of History and International Studies at the University of Mississippi, USA. He is the author of *Workers at War: Labor in China's Arsenals, 1937-1953* (2004).

JANE HUMPHRIES is Professor of Economic History at the University of Oxford and a Fellow of All Souls College, Oxford, UK. Jane Humphries has worked on many issues to do with growth and development and also has a longstanding interest in labour markets. She has published extensively on gender, the family and the history of women's work. Her most recent book is *Childhood and Child Labour in the British Industrial Revolution* (2010). She is currently President of the Economic History Society.

ANA L. KASSOUF is a full Professor in the Department of Economics at University of Sao Paulo, Brazil. She has published extensively in English and in Portuguese on education, child labour and social programs in Brazil, including articles in *Economic Development and Cultural Change*, *Applied Economics*, and the *Brazilian Review of Econometrics*.

PETER KIRBY is Lecturer in Economic History in the University of Manchester, UK. He is the author of *Child Labour in Britain, 1750-1870* (2003). His articles on child labour have been published in *Past and Present*, *Economic History Review* and *Continuity and Change*. His forthcoming book *Child Labour and Industrial Health, 1780-1850* (2012) explores the history of industrial health amongst children in cotton manufacture.

KRISTOFFEL LIETEN is Professor of Child Labour Studies at the University of Amsterdam and at the International Institute of Social History in Amsterdam, the Netherlands. He is also the Director of the Institute for Research on Working Children (IREWOC) in Leiden, Netherlands. He has worked extensively on social and political developments in South Asia and presently conducts research on child labour, street children and deprived children in general. His recent books include *Children, School and Work. Glimpses from India* (2005), *Children, Structure and Agency: Realities across the World* (2008), *Child Rights and Child Labour* (2009), *Working Boys and Girls at Risk: Child Labour in Urban Bangladesh* (2011) and *Hazardous Child Labour in Latin America* (2011).

CARLOS EDWARD GARCÍA LONDOÑO is an historian working at the department of history in the Universidad Nacional de Colombia in Medellin, Colombia, where he did his Ph.D. in 1995 on *Child Labourers and their Daily Life in Medellin, 1900-1930*.

ELISE VAN NEDERVEEN MEERKERK studied social and economic history in Utrecht. She is currently working as a postdoctoral researcher at the International Institute of Social History, Amsterdam, the Netherlands. Her publications include "Child Labour in Proto-Industrial and Industrializing Netherlands", in: Hugh D. Hindman (ed.), *The World of Child Labor: A Historical and Regional Survey* (2009); "Between Wage Labor and Vocation: Child Labor in Dutch Urban Industry, 1600-1800", *Journal of Social History* (2008) and "Market Wage or Discrimination? The Remuneration of Male and Female Wool Spinners in the Seventeenth-Century Dutch Republic", *Economic History Review* (2010).

LARS OLSSON is Professor of History at the Linnaeus University, Växjö, Sweden. His research involves the relationships between politics, technology and economics in capitalist society from the late 18th century to the present. His doctoral dissertation (1980, reprinted 1995 and 1999) concerns the rise, function and abolishment of child labour in Swedish factories. His many studies, in Swedish, German, English, Italian, Danish and Russian, describe the struggle between labour and capital within the context of changing production processes and politics. Migration, as well as gender and ethnic relations, are discussed in continued research on immigration into Sweden and in a textile factory in Minneapolis.

MARIA PAPATHANASSIOU studied history in Athens, London and Vienna. She currently teaches European History at the Hellenic Open University in Greece. Her main interests lie in the history of children, history of work, rural history and historical anthropology. Her publications on child labour in Europe include a book in German, *Zwischen Arbeit, Spiel und Schule, Die* ökonomische *Funktion der Kinder* ärmerer *Schichten in* Österreich *1880-1938* (1999), as well as various articles – among others "Approaches to the history of Child Labour in Europe", *Jahrbuch für Wirtschaftsgeschichte/Economic History Yearbook* (2007). She is also the author of a book in Greek on the history of children in rural Greece.

ANTONIA PASI, who did her doctorate in Economic History, has worked throughout her career at the University of Pavia, Italy, on issues related to economic and social history and historical demography and has been a member of various national councils focusing on studying the development of the Italian population. After her retirement, Pasi has pursued her particular interests in childhood, foundlings and welfare. Her recent publications include: "Milan entre le XIXe et le XXe siècle: industrialisation, travail des mères et assistence à la petite enfance", in E. Sonnino, *Living in the City* (2004) and, with G. Panella, *La misura del 'merito scolastico' ed i suoi effetti sulle politiche di sostegno del sistema educativo di istruzione e istruzione* (2008).

MARJATTA RAHIKAINEN is Associate Professor at the Department of Political and Economic Studies, University of Helsinki, Finland. Her recent publications on child labour history include *Centuries of Child Labour: European Experiences from the Seventeenth to the Twentieth Century* (2004) and "At What Cost Was Economic Modernization Purchased? Comparing child labor in Asia and Europe", in T. Onishi & B. Teh Cheng Guan (eds.), *The Shape of East Asian Economy to Come: Lonely Rhetoric or Global Reality* (2007).

OSAMU SAITO is Visiting Leverhulme Professor at the University of Cambridge and Professor Emeritus, Hitotsubashi University, Japan. His publications include: "Who worked when: life-time profiles of labour force participation in the late eighteenth and mid-nineteenth centuries", *Local Population Studies* (1979), reprinted in N. Goose (ed.), *Women's Work in Industrial England: Regional and Local Perspectives* (2007), and "Labour Supply Behaviour of the Poor in the English Industrial Revolution", *Journal of European Economic History*, (1981).

MARCELO JUSTUS DOS SANTOS is Professor in the Department of Economics at Ponta Grossa State University, Brazil. He has published articles on criminality, health and child labour.

HAMILTON SIPHO SIMELANE, earlier in the department of history at the University of Swaziland, presently works at the University of Kwazulu-Natal, South Africa. He has published various articles on the political economy of labour mobilisation and on economic relations in Rwanda and Swaziland. He is also the author of *Colonialism and Economic Change in Swaziland, 1940-1960* (2003).

COR SMIT (1954) is an independent researcher and PhD-student. His publications on the history of child labour include: "Fabriekskinderen. Kinderarbeid in de Leidse textielindustrie in de negentiende eeuw", *Textielhistorische bijdragen* (1996); *Kinderarbeid. J.J. Cremer en de Leidse fabriekskinderen* (2008); "Work, Education, and Discipline: Attitudes towards Child Labor in The Netherlands, 1500 to 1875" in: Hugh D. Hindman (ed.), *The World of Child Labor: A Historical and Regional Survey* (2009).

CAROLYN TUTTLE is Full Professor and Betty Jane Schultz Hollender Chair at Lake Forest College, Illinois, USA. Her research interests includes: Child Labor During the British Industrial Revolution, Child Labor in Latin American Countries, and Women in the Workforce and sweatshop labour on the Mexican-American border. She published *Hard at Work in Factories and Mines: The Economics of Child Labor During the British Industrial Revolution* (1999) and a number of articles in Hugh D. Hindman (ed.), *The World of Child Labor: A Historical and Regional Survey* (2009) and in the *Oxford Encyclopaedia of Economic History* (2003).

NICHOLAS VAN HEAR is the Deputy Director at the Centre on Migration, Policy and Society (COMPAS), University of Oxford, UK. With a background in development studies, he works on forced migration, conflict, diaspora, transnationalism and related issues, and has field experience in Africa, the Middle East, South Asia and Europe. His books include *The Migration-Development Nexus* (2003), and *Catching Fire: Containing forced migration in a volatile world* (2006). Early, he wrote on child labour in Ghana and published in *Development and Change* (1982) and *Review of African Political Economy* (1984).

BEN WHITE is Professor of Rural Sociology at the International Institute of Social Studies, Erasmus University Rotterdam and Professor of Social Sciences at the University of Amsterdam. His main research interests are on agrarian problems and the anthropology and history of childhood and youth, especially in Indonesia. Books and edited volumes include *Child Workers in Indonesia* (with Indrasari Tjandraningsih, 1998) and *Rights and Wrongs of Children's Work* (with Michael Bourdillon, Deborah Levison and William E. Myers, 2010).

INTERNATIONAL AND COMPARATIVE SOCIAL HISTORY

1. *Racism and the Labour Market: Historical Studies.* Edited by Marcel van der Linden and Jan Lucassen in collaboration with Dik van Arkel, Els Deslé, Fred Goedbloed, Robert Kloosterman and Kenneth Lunn. 1995.
2. *Social Security Mutualism: The Comparative History of Mutual Benefit Societies.* Edited by Marcel van der Linden in collaboration with Michel Dreyfus, Bernard Gibaud and Jan Lucassen. 1996.
3. *The International Confederation of Free Trade Unions.* Edited by Marcel van der Linden. 2000.
4. *Migration, Migration History, History: Old Paradigms and New Perspectives.* Edited by Jan Lucassen and Leo Lucassen. 1997, 1999, 2005.
5. *Free and Unfree Labour: The Debate Continues.* Edited by Tom Brass and Marcel van der Linden. 1997.
6. *The Rise and Development of Collective Labour Law.* Edited by Marcel van der Linden and Richard Price. 2000.
7. *Urban Radicals, Rural Allies: Social Democracy and the Agrarian Issue,* 1870–1914. Edited by Aad Blok, Keith Hitchins, Raymond Markey and Birger Simonson. 2002.
8. *Between Cross and Class: Comparative Histories of Christian Labour in Europe* 1840–2000. Edited by Lex Heerma van Voss, Patrick Pasture and Jan De Maeyer. 2005.
9. *Global Labour History: A State of the Art.* Edited by Jan Lucassen. 2006, 2008.
10. *Wages and Currency: Global Comparisons from Antiquity to the Twentieth Century.* Edited by Jan Lucassen. 2007.
11. *A Dream Deferred: New Studies in Russian and Soviet Labour History.* Edited by Donald Filtzer, Wendy Z. Goldman, Gijs Kessler and Simon Pirani. 2008.
12. *ILO Histories: Essays on the International Labour Organization and Its Impact on the World During the Twentieth Century.* Edited by Jasmien Van Daele, Magaly Rodríguez García, Geert Van Goethem and Marcel van der Linden. 2010.
13. *Child Labour's Global Past,* 1650-2000. Edited by Kristoffel Lieten and Elise van Nederveen Meerkerk. 2011.

Kolibri 360 GmbH
Ferdinand-Jühlke-Straße 7
99095 Erfurt, Deutschland
produktsicherheit@kolibri360.de